Business Torts and Unfair Competition Handbook

Second Edition

ABA
SECTION OF
ANTITRUST
LAW

ABA
Defending Liberty
Pursuing Justice

This volume should be officially cited as:

ABA SECTION OF ANTITRUST LAW,
BUSINESS TORTS AND UNFAIR COMPETITION
HANDBOOK, 2D EDITION (2006)

Library of Congress Control Number: 2006921299
ISBN: 1-59031-653-3
ISBN-13: 978-1-59031-653-5

Discounts are available for books ordered in bulk. Special consideration is given to state bars, CLE programs, and other bar-related organizations. Inquire at ABA Publishing, 321 N. Clark St, Chicago, Illinois 60610.

10 09 08 07 06   5 4 3 2 1

www.ababooks.org

Contents

FOREWORD

The Section of Antitrust Law of the American Bar Association is pleased to present *Business Torts and Unfair Competition Handbook, Second Edition*, a practical guide to the substantive and procedural issues that frequently arise in business tort and unfair competition litigation. The goal of this handbook is to make this developing area of the law more accessible to antitrust and non-antitrust practitioners alike.

We are deeply indebted to many attorneys who contributed their time and talents to the creation of this practice guide. Special thanks go to Jay Bogan and Mike Ferrill, who drafted sections of the practice guide and who are responsible for editing this volume and coordinating the drafting of its many contributors, as well as to their Assistant Editors, Leslie S. Hyman and Scott S. Thomas.

Donald C. Klawiter
Chair, Section of Antitrust Law
American Bar Association
January 2006

PREFACE

This handbook traces its origins to a presentation at the American Bar Association's 1990 annual Meeting in Chicago by Harvey I. Saferstein, the first chairman of the Business Torts and Unfair Competition Committee of the Section of Antitrust law.[1]   That presentation, and its accompanying surveys both of antitrust practitioners from around the country and of judicial decisions over the past thirty years, validated a perceived trend toward the increased use of business tort claims in addition to, and often in lieu of, "traditional" antitrust claims.

In 1992, members of the Business Torts and Unfair Competition Committee prepared a Working paper, entitled *Tortious Interference and Competition: A Survey of the Law in Selected States*, which examined the various interference torts, and highlighted the diverse ways in which courts around the country grapple with, and ultimately resolve, the role of competition policy in the field of business torts. This working paper was followed up that year by a Spring Meeting program put on by the Business Torts and Unfair Competition Committee, entitled "The Emerging Role of State Court Claims in Antitrust litigation." The panel for that program was composed of a distinguished group of participants, including Professor Thomas E. Kauper of the University of Michigan Law School and a number of private practitioners with substantial expertise in antitrust and business tort litigation. That program explored the practical and procedural "tricks" and "traps" in litigation involving the interplay of antitrust and business tort claims.

The first edition of this handbook, published in 1996 by the Business Torts and Unfair Competition Committee, built upon the Section's prior work in this area. This second edition is a substantive update of that prior work and is being published nearly ten years later by the Business Torts and Civil RICO Committee, a new committee formed as the result of the merger of the Business Torts and Unfair Competition and Civil RICO Committees. Like the first edition, this second edition is intended as a practical litigator's guide for the handling of the

---

1.   *See* Harvey I. Saferstein, *The Ascendancy of Business Tort Claims in Antitrust Practice*, 59 Antitrust L.J. 379 (1991).

substantive and procedural issues that abound at the increasingly busy intersection of antitrust and business tort law.

Acknowledgement of those whose efforts have made this handbook possible must begin with those responsible for the publication of the first edition, notably, Harvey Saferstein, who laid the groundwork for the first edition, Allan Van Fleet, the chair of the former Business Torts and Unfair Competition Committee during the time much of the first edition was being prepared, vice chair Mike Ferrill (the editor of the first edition), as well as Thomas J. Collin and Pamela Hobbs, co-vice chairs at the time who offered invaluable suggestions and assistance. Special thanks are also due the authors of the original chapters: Monty Gray and Robert Homchick (Chapter 1 – The Evolving Role of Business Torts in Antitrust Litigation), Pamela Hobbs (Chapter 2 – Application of Antitrust Principles to Business Tort Claims, Chapter 6 – Fraud and Misrepresentation, and Chapter 8 – Limitations on Punitive Damages), Mike Ferrill (Chapter 3 – Federal Law of Unfair Competition), Timothy J. Burke (Chapter 4 – Commercial Disparagement and Defamation), Derek G. Howard and Mary B. Cranston (Chapter 5 – The Interference Torts), Erika S. Carter (Chapter 7 – Misappropriation of Trade Secrets), David Wicklund (Chapter 9 – Subject Matter Jurisdiction in Antitrust and Business Tort Litigation, and Chapter 13 – Issues Relating to Parallel Litigation), Barrie L. Brejcha (Chapter 10 – Personal Jurisdiction, Process and Venue in Antitrust and Business Tort Litigation), Michael M. Conway and Paul K. Vickrey (Chapter 11 – Forum Selection in Antitrust and Business Tort Litigation), Barbara Friedman Yaksic and Josh M. Friedman (Chapter 12 – Removal and Remand), and Charles L. Stern, Jr. (Chapter 14 – Preemption and Commerce Clause Issues).

The authors of this second edition were able to build on the exceptional work of the original authors. The second edition authors are: James F. Bogan III and Scott S. Thomas (Chapter 1), Scott Martin (Chapter 2), Mike Ferrill and M. Elizabeth Nagy (Chapter 3), the Honorable Edward C. LaRose (Chapter 4), Ellen S. Moore and the Honorable Mike Urbanski (Chapter 5), Kathleen M. Beasley (Chapter 6), Todd S. Parkhurst and Mike Cooper (Chapter 7), Bradley Kenneth Reynolds and Rhona E.F. Reynolds (Chapter 8), K. Todd Wallace (Chapter 9), David J. Lenci (Chapter 10), Steven L. Merouse (Chapter 11), David A. Westrup (Chapter 12), John E. Floyd and Benjamin E. Fox (Chapter 13), and James W. Boswell III and Emily J. Culpepper (Chapter

14). We note with great sadness that Ellen S. Moore, who with the Honorable Mike Urbanski updated Chapter 5 of this handbook, passed away in March 2005 after a courageous bout with cancer.

We are greatly indebted to our Assistant Editors, Leslie S. Hyman and Scott S. Thomas, who were of invaluable assistance in the editorial process and the preparation of the manuscript. Additional thanks are due Andrew J. Yoder and Meagan M. Gillette for their research assistance, and a personal debt of gratitude extends to Carol Martin, who provided tremendous help in the preparation of the manuscript.

We are pleased to present *Business Torts and Unfair Competition Handbook, Second Edition*, and trust that it proves useful to practitioners in this challenging area of business litigation.

James F. Bogan III, Editor
A. Michael Ferrill, Editor

INTRODUCTION

The relationship between antitrust and business tort laws is a familiar and uneasy one. Both trace their antecedents to the common law of England, and generally address competitive conduct. Yet in this country antitrust and business torts have developed as separate branches of the law, largely in different judicial systems. Moreover, they are commonly perceived to be grounded in different policy objectives: often it is said that where antitrust seeks to promote competition, business torts seek to prevent competition that is deemed wrongful.[1] As an historical consequence, much competitive conduct is subject to varying, and often contradictory, legal rules.

There are further complications. Although antitrust law has primarily developed within a single judicial system (i.e., the federal courts), business torts are creatures of state law, and thus vary to greater or lesser degrees from state to state. Furthermore, antitrust law today is not all of a piece: as evolving rules governing standing and competitive effects have generally narrowed the range of private civil liability under the federal antitrust laws, legislatures and courts have expanded the scope of antitrust liability at the state level. Concurrently, state legislatures have enacted legislation supplementing the common law of unfair competition, and state courts have greatly expanded common law business torts and the civil liabilities arising from them. As a result, competitors face a greatly expanded range of legal rules and potential liabilities under state law.

This shift in the relative prominence of federal antitrust law and state statutory and common law has produced another, more subtle, effect. In years past plaintiffs often sought to bolster their antitrust claims with proof of business torts or other acts of unfair competition, and defendants resisted such efforts on the theory that antitrust and business tort doctrines reflected different policy concerns. Today the roles often are reversed. Encouraged by their recent successes in

---

1. *See* Nw. Power Prods., Inc. v. Omark Indus., Inc., 576 F.2d 83, 88 (5th Cir. 1978) ("the purposes of antitrust law and unfair competition law generally conflict"); *see generally* H.B. THORELLI, THE FEDERAL ANTITRUST POLICY 4-5, 12 (1955).

narrowing the scope of antitrust liability through the use of standing doctrines, competitive injury requirements and other arguments grounded in economic theory, defendants increasingly seek to transport those defenses into business tort litigation. Defendants often argue that "mere competition" cannot be tortious, and that conduct that is lawful, indeed encouraged, under the antitrust laws should not be punished. Further movement toward the goal of harmonizing antitrust and business tort law is reflected in the American Law Institute's Restatement (Third) of Unfair Competition, which eschews the rationale that competition is a mere "privilege" in favor of recognizing an affirmative "freedom to compete" in the marketplace.[2] In these and like ways the very nature of the relationship between antitrust, business tort and unfair competition law is being reconsidered.

The interplay of federal and state laws regulating competitive conduct frequently gives rise to an abundance of opportunities and potential pitfalls. Choices among available statutory and common law causes of action, as well as between state and federal courts and the courts of different states, may determine important issues relating to subject matter and personal jurisdiction, service of process and venue, removal and remand, choice-of-law and choice-of-forum, transfer and stays of litigation, forum non conveniens, abstention doctrines, issue and claim preclusion, preemption and Commerce Clause questions, and a host of other issues. Appreciation of the "tricks and traps" presented by such procedural and evidentiary considerations should inform choices among available claims and fora. By grouping these issues into topics that correspond to practical problems business litigators commonly face, this book seeks to serve as a useful tool for the practitioner. Of course, given the breadth of the substantive and procedural issues addressed, this handbook is not intended to be an exhaustive treatment of the legal issues involved. Where appropriate, citations to scholarly treatises, in addition to caselaw and other primary sources, are provided.

Because the relationship between antitrust and business tort law impacts many of the issues to follow, *Chapters One* and *Two* address that topic first. *Chapter One* traces the evolving role of business torts in antitrust litigation, beginning with early caselaw equating unfair competition with a per se violation of the antitrust laws, to modern

---

2.   RESTATEMENT (THIRD) OF UNFAIR COMPETITION § 1 cmt. a (1993).

authority recognizing that acts of unfair competition, although often relevant to an antitrust claim, are not alone sufficient to establish such a claim.

Chapter Two explores the extent to which antitrust concepts have been invoked in business tort litigation. It focuses on two of the most hotly-contested areas, the "competitive privilege" and the so-called "*Noerr-Pennington*" defense, and also addresses the relevance of the intracorporate conspiracy doctrine and various evidentiary and procedural principles developed in antitrust cases to tort claims involving competitive behavior.

Chapter Three surveys the field of unfair competition, tracing this concept from the original proscription against the "palming off" of one's goods as those of another, to its current generic description as "all statutory and nonstatutory causes of action arising out of business conduct which is contrary to honest practice in industrial or commercial matters."[3] This chapter then focuses on the federal law of unfair competition, including section 43(a) of the Lanham Act[4] and briefly examines section 5 of the Federal Trade Commission Act and so-called "Little FTC Acts."[5]

Chapter Four addresses the business torts of commercial disparagement and defamation, which are analytically similar yet different in important respects. This chapter also briefly examines First Amendment limitations upon such claims.

Chapter Five offers a general overview of the interference torts, including tortious interference with contract and tortious interference with prospective advantage. Survey evidence suggests that these are the most popular business torts from the plaintiff's standpoint.[6] This chapter

3. Am. Heritage Life Ins. Co. v. Heritage Life Ins. Co., 494 F.2d 3, 14 (5th Cir. 1974) (citing 3 R. CALLMANN, THE LAW OF UNFAIR COMPETITION § 4.1, at 120 (3d ed. 1969)).
4. 15 U.S.C. § 1125(a).
5. 15 U.S.C. § 45.
6. *See* Harvey I. Saferstein, *The Ascendancy of Business Tort Claims in Antitrust Practice*, 59 ANTITRUST L.J. 379, 383-85, 392, 403 (1991) (tortious interference claims appear in antitrust cases twice as frequently as the next most popular business tort claim).

outlines the elements of these claims and available defenses, and highlights the principal differences among jurisdictions.

Chapter Six addresses the common law and statutory torts of fraud and negligent misrepresentation, including section 12(2) of the Securities Act of 1933, section 10(b) of the Securities Exchange Act of 1934 and SEC Rule 10b-5, and the RICO statute. *Chapter Seven* examines the field of misappropriation of trade secrets, which has received a new treatment in the Restatement (Third) of Unfair Competition.

Chapter Eight addresses recent developments in the area of punitive damages. It examines recent decisions of the United States Supreme Court, as well as decisions of the state and lower federal courts.

Chapters Nine and *Ten* open the procedural discussion, addressing the threshold issues of subject matter jurisdiction, personal jurisdiction and venue. They examine general principles governing federal and state court jurisdiction over antitrust and business tort claims, supplemental jurisdiction, service of process, venue and other practical considerations.

Chapter Eleven addresses additional practical issues that may impact the choice of forum, including choice-of-law, pleading and discovery differences, summary judgment procedure and other practical considerations such as differences in jury voir dire, numerosity and unanimity, and time-to-trial.

Chapter Twelve involves the frequently-contested matter of removal and remand, and addresses such topics as removal jurisdiction, fraudulent joinder, the well-pleaded and artfully-pleaded complaint doctrines and strategies for facilitating and defeating remand.

Chapter Thirteen addresses the increasingly-complex area of parallel and successive suits. It examines such topics as stays of litigation, abstention, anti-suit injunctions, venue contents and issue and claim preclusion.

Chapter Fourteen examines issues that frequently arise in business tort cases under the Supremacy and Commerce Clauses of the United States Constitution. It focuses on efforts by defendants to challenge the specific application of business tort laws to their conduct on the grounds that enforcement is contrary to federal law or would unduly burden interstate commerce.

PART I

Business Tort Law

The Evolving Role of Business Torts in Antitrust Litigation

Application of Antitrust Principles to Business Tort Claims

Federal Law of Unfair Competition

Commercial Disparagement and Defamation

The Interference Torts

Fraud and Misrepresentation

Misappropriation of Trade Secrets

Limitations on Punitive Damages

CHAPTER I

THE EVOLVING ROLE OF BUSINESS TORTS IN ANTITRUST LITIGATION

Many violations of the antitrust laws do not involve attempts to injure competitors; indeed, so-called "hard core" antitrust violations – such as price-fixing and customer allocation – benefit competitors at the expense of consumers. Attempts to injure competitors, however, also may result in antitrust injury. This chapter traces the role of business torts and unfair competition in private civil litigation under the antitrust laws. Chapter 2 reverses the lens, examining the application of antitrust principles to business tort claims. – Eds.

A. Introduction

Antitrust and business tort claims and defenses frequently converge in the same litigation. Although these two areas of the law cover common ground, they have developed separately and reflect different policy concerns.

The U.S. Supreme Court has stressed that the antitrust laws were enacted for "the protection of competition, not competitors."[1] A federal appellate court similarly has remarked:

---

1. Brown Shoe Co. v. United States, 370 U.S. 294, 320 (1962); Brunswick Corp. v. Pueblo Bowl-O-Mat, Inc., 429 U.S. 477, 488 (1977) (quoting *Brown Shoe*); *see also* Hunt v. Crumboch, 325 U.S. 821, 826 (1945) (Sherman Act "does not purport to afford remedies for all torts committed by or against persons engaged in interstate commerce"); Brooke Group Ltd. v. Brown & Williamson Tobacco Corp., 509 U.S. 209, 225 (1993) ("Even an act of pure malice by one business competitor against another does not, without more, state a claim under the federal antitrust laws[.]"); *see generally* 1 LOUIS ALTMAN, CALLMANN ON UNFAIR COMPETITION, TRADEMARKS & MONOPOLIES § 4:3 (4th ed. 2004) ("Unfair competition and obstruction of free competition are both included in the definition of 'unfair methods of competition' contained in section 5 of the Federal

[T]he purposes of antitrust law and unfair competition law generally conflict. The thrust of antitrust law is to prevent restraints on competition. Unfair competition is still competition and the purpose of the law of unfair competition is to impose restraints on that competition. The law of unfair competition tends to protect a business in the monopoly over the loyalty of its employees and its customer lists, while the general purpose of the antitrust laws is to promote competition by freeing from monopoly a firm's sources of labor and markets for its products.[2]

This distinction was not always clear. Antitrust plaintiffs once argued forcefully, and with some success, for the application of business tort principles into antitrust law. Today business tort defendants frequently argue for the reverse.

B.   The Antiquated Pick-Barth Doctrine

In 1932, antitrust law and the business tort of unfair competition came together in *Albert Pick-Barth Co. v. Mitchell Woodbury Corp.*[3] In that case, the plaintiff alleged a scheme by the defendants to appropriate the plaintiff's business by hiring away the plaintiff's employees and inducing them to take the plaintiff's customer lists, business plans, and other records.[4] The First Circuit affirmed the district court's antitrust judgment for the plaintiff, announcing the rule that, "[i]f a conspiracy is proven, the purpose or intent of which is by unfair means to eliminate a competitor in interstate trade and thereby suppress competition, such a conspiracy . . . is a violation of section 1 of the Sherman Act" as a matter of law.[5] Thus, in *Pick-Barth*, the business tort of unfair competition was elevated to the status of a per se antitrust violation when conducted in the context of an agreement among competitors, joining the list of "practices which because of their pernicious effect on competition and lack of any redeeming virtue are conclusively presumed to be unreasonable and

---

Trade Commission Act. These two types of anti-competitive conduct nevertheless differ in nature.").

2.   Nw. Power Prods., Inc. v. Omark Indus., Inc., 576 F.2d 83, 88 (5th Cir. 1978).

3.   57 F.2d 96 (1st Cir. 1932).

4.   *Id.* at 97-98.

5.   *Id.* at 102.

therefore illegal without elaborate inquiry as to the precise harm they have caused or the business excuse for their use."[6]

Unlike other rules of per se illegality under the antitrust laws, *Pick-Barth*'s focus was on "fairness" to competitors, rather than on the anticipated effect of the defendant's actions on the market. Nonetheless, when the First Circuit revisited *Pick-Barth* almost thirty years later in *Atlantic Heel Co. v. Allied Heel Co.*,[7] it again concluded that "the purpose of destroying a competitor by means that are not within the area of fair and honest competition is a purpose that clearly subverts the goal of the Sherman Act."[8] Presented with misdeeds factually similar to those alleged in *Pick-Barth*,[9] and relying upon the Supreme Court's intervening decision in *Klor's, Inc. v. Broadway-Hale Stores, Inc.*,[10] which involved a conspiracy to eliminate a competitor through a "group boycott" or "concerted refusals . . . to deal,"[11] the *Atlantic Heel* court reaffirmed that a conspiracy to destroy a rival constituted a per se violation of Section 1 of the Sherman Act.[12]

Very few other cases have followed the First Circuit's *Pick-Barth* rationale; those that have done so similarly have addressed egregious practices.[13] In *C. Albert Sauter Co. v. Richard S. Sauter Co.*,[14] for

---

6. N. Pac. Ry. v. United States, 356 U.S. 1, 5 (1958).
7. 284 F.2d 879 (1st Cir. 1960).
8. *Id.* at 884.
9. *Id.* at 879-80.
10. 359 U.S. 207 (1959).
11. *Id.* at 210, 213, *cited and quoted in Atl. Heel Co.*, 284 F.2d at 882-83.
12. 284 F.2d at 881, 884 (quoting and reaffirming *Pick-Barth*). The majority concluded that, like *Pick-Barth*, "the complaint in the instant case alleges a conspiracy to destroy a competitor by means so inimical 'to free and full flow of interstate trade' as to constitute a per se violation of Section 1 of the Sherman Act." *Id.* at 884 (citation omitted). However, in a concurring opinion, Chief Judge Woodbury along with Judge Aldrich concluded that they saw "no occasion at this stage of the case to express wholehearted endorsement of the rule laid down" in *Pick-Barth* as it was "unique on its facts in 1932" and perhaps stood alone thirty years later, *id.* at 884-85 (Woodbury, C.J., concurring).
13. In *Perryton Wholesale, Inc. v. Pioneer Distrib. Co. of Kan.*, 353 F.2d 618 (10th Cir. 1965), the Tenth Circuit concluded in that case that "the intent of the conspiracy was to eliminate the competitor predominant in the area by the subversion of its employees"; accordingly, "[s]uch elimination

example, the Eastern District of Pennsylvania held that the defendants' tortious acts, which included hiring away the plaintiff's key employees, misappropriating the plaintiff's confidential business information, intentionally confusing customers by using a deceptively similar trade name, and disparaging the plaintiff's business, amounted to a per se violation of section 1 because they "'unreasonably' restrain[ed] competition"; the defendants' conspiracies were "accompanied with a specific intent to accomplish a forbidden result."[15]

C.   The Decline of Pick-Barth and the Requirement of Competitive Injury

Subsequent decisions, however, have questioned the *Pick-Barth* doctrine's rationale, or else have limited those decisions to their facts.[16] In *George R. Whitten, Jr., Inc. v. Paddock Pool Builders, Inc.,*[17] the First Circuit revisited the proposition that unfair competitive practices accompanied by an intent to hurt a competitor constitute a per se violation of the antitrust laws. After considering the "aggregation of dirty tricks, played by those with little market power," allegedly committed by the defendants on their smaller competitor, the court

---

destroys rather than maintains competition, is an unreasonable restraint of trade, and violates [section 1]." 353 F.2d at 622.

14.   368 F. Supp. 501 (E.D. Pa. 1973).

15.   *Id.* at 512-14 ("in our opinion, *Perryton, Pick-Barth* and *Atl. Heel* should be followed in this Circuit"). After the *Sauter* case was decided, the Tenth Circuit, revisiting its decision in *Perryton*, decided that *Perryton* did not embrace *Pick-Barth*'s per se rule and that a conspiracy to eliminate a competitor by unfair means is to be evaluated under "the rule of reason." Midwest Underground Storage, Inc. v. Porter, 717 F.2d 493, 496 (10th Cir. 1983); *see also* Craig v. Sun Oil Co. of Pa., 515 F.2d 221, 224 (10th Cir. 1975) (*Perryton* "is not necessarily a per se case").

16.   *See, e.g.,* Metal Lubricants Co. v. Engineered Lubricants Co., 411 F.2d 426, 430-31 (8th Cir. 1969) (limiting *Atl. Heel* to its facts); duPont Walston, Inc. v. E.F. Hutton & Co., 368 F. Supp. 306, 308-09 (S.D. Fla. 1973); Frederick Chusid & Co. v. Marshall Leeman & Co., 326 F. Supp. 1043, 1063 (S.D.N.Y. 1971).

17.   508 F.2d 547 (1st Cir. 1974).

concluded that, while the actions were unfair and reprehensible, they did not constitute a per se antitrust violation.[18]

The *Whitten* court offered several reasons for refusing to apply the per se rule. On a practical level, the court noted that *Pick-Barth* and *Atlantic Heel* involved condemned anticompetitive practices that were not so uncommon as to encompass only the very few cases affirming them. Therefore, the *Whitten* court reasoned that *Pick-Barth* and *Atlantic Heel* provided no clear basis upon which to distinguish the "unfair" practices that would amount to an antitrust violation from those that would not.[19] Additionally, the court observed that tort law is available to deal with "garden variety" unfair competitive business practices and that extending the per se classification to competitive torts would tend to create a federal common law of unfair competition, a task the federal courts have long resisted.[20]

Instead, the court analyzed the defendants' conduct under "the rule of reason," which inquires into the effect of the unfair practices on the relevant market.[21] While the plaintiff may have lost some contracts as a result of the defendants' actions, the *Whitten* court observed that there

---

18. *Id.* at 559, 561-62 (defendant must be "a significant factor in the market" and there must be "an effort . . . to eliminate a competitor" or "crippl[e] the organization of a competitor," and it is insufficient that defendant "has subordinated business morality").

19. *Id.* at 561 ("We acknowledge, forty-two and fourteen years [after *Pick-Barth* and *Atl. Heel*, respectively], that we have some doubts about our pronouncements. It is . . . clear that we have only two lineal descendants in all these years [i.e., citing *Perryton* and *Sauter*,] and we cannot believe that sharp practice [of such extreme conduct] has been so rare.").

20. *Id.* at 560-61 ("[E]xtending a per se classification to the kinds of competitive torts confronted here would go far to yielding to a long resisted temptation to create a federal common law of unfair competition.").

21. *Id.* at 559 ("Most generalized anti-compe[ti]tive conduct is subjected to a 'rule of reason' analysis, involving among other factors, a study of the consequences of the conduct on the affected market.") (citing Bd. of Trade of Chicago v. United States, 246 U.S. 231 (1918); United States v. Topco Assocs., Inc., 405 U.S. 596 (1972)). For a detailed exposition and critical examination of the courts' application of the rule of reason, see Michael A. Carrier, *The Real Rule of Reason: Bridging the Disconnect*, 1999 BYU L. REV. 1265 (1999).

was no evidence of harm to competition. The number of competitors was not affected, and the market was neither fixed nor manipulated. The defendants' behavior, regardless of how offensive it may have been, therefore did not amount to an antitrust violation.[22] The court, however, stopped short of formally overruling *Pick-Barth*. Noting that the pirating of key employees and theft of trade secrets involved in *Pick-Barth* and *Atlantic Heel* – efforts "to eliminate a competitor" – were going for the "jugular," the court concluded that the defendants' conduct in *Whitten* affected only "lesser arteries" – "concentrating on winning customers" – and thus rendered use of the per se rule inappropriate.[23]

Later cases widened the analytical breach between antitrust and business torts. In *Northwest Power Products, Inc. v. Omark Industries, Inc.*,[24] the Fifth Circuit in 1978 considered "unfair conduct" similar to that alleged in *Pick-Barth*: solicitation of the plaintiff's employees, misappropriation of customer lists, and circulation of false and disparaging comments to the plaintiff's customers about its alleged financial difficulties. The effect of the defendants' actions was to diminish the plaintiff's market share while increasing that of one defendant.[25] Upon the plaintiff's invoking *Pick-Barth*, the court discussed it at length and forcefully rejected it.[26] Rather than condemn

---

22. *George R. Whitten, Jr., Inc.*, 508 F.2d at 559-62.

23. *Id.* at 561-62 (concluding that "[i]nsofar as *Pick-Barth* and *Atl. Heel* may be said to stand for the broad proposition that unfair competitive practices accompanied by an intent to hurt a competitor constitute per se violations of the antitrust laws, we do not now accept their teaching," nevertheless, "[w]e do not feel it necessary to criticize their results on the fact situations there present"); *see also* Tower Tire & Auto Ctr. v. Atl. Richfield Co., 392 F. Supp. 1098, 1101-07 (S.D. Tex. 1975) (discussing decisions extending from *Pick-Barth* to *Whitten* that defined the requisite intent for a per se violation).

24. 576 F.2d 83 (5th Cir. 1978).

25. *Id.* at 85-86.

26. *Id.* at 86-90. The court took pains to demonstrate that "[t]he decisions applying the *Pick-Barth* rule as a per se offense have not closely analyzed the question of whether a conspiracy to eliminate a competitor by unfair means is the kind of conduct so contrary to the purposes of the Sherman Act that it deserves per se treatment." *Id.* at 87. Recognizing that "[s]cholarly analysis has also found little merit in the *Pick-Barth* doctrine," *id.* at 88 (citing several authors), the court summarized its critics' "telling

the defendants' conduct as a per se violation of Section 1, the court concluded that the defendants' tortious acts actually had a positive effect on competition. By replacing the plaintiff, which had a 20 percent share of the market, with one of the defendants, which achieved an 11.5 percent share, the alleged conspiracy actually enhanced rivalry and created greater competitive possibilities.[27]

The *Northwest Power* court gave two reasons why a defendant's market power is critical in determining whether unfair competition amounts to an antitrust violation. First, absent some market impact comparable to that prohibited by the law of mergers, antitrust interests are not implicated. Second, only when the defendant gains an increment of monopoly power through unfair competition are treble antitrust damages appropriate, as "[s]ingle damages or equivalent injunctive relief is thought sufficient to compensate a firm for unfair competition."[28]

---

points," noting, for example, that the First Circuit's definition of "unfair means" failed to draw a bright line of illegality essential to a per se rule that is necessary to guide business planning. In addition, because antitrust law is designed to prevent restraints on competition by safeguarding against monopoly a firm's markets and sources of labor, while the law of unfair competition imposes restraints on competition by protecting a business in its customer lists and employee loyalty, the purposes of antitrust law and unfair competition law generally conflict. *Id.* The court also stressed that "Congress has repeatedly declined to create a federal law of unfair competition and "the Federal Trade Commission has the power to correct 'unfair or deceptive acts or practices.'" *Id.* at 90 (quoting 15 U.S.C. § 45(a)(1)). However, because "the Sherman Act does not give that power to private plaintiffs," "[c]ourts should be circumspect in adopting doctrines that have even the appearance of disturbing a congressional balance of remedies." *Id.* Concluding that "the line drawn by the *Pick-Barth* doctrine is so vague, and the circumstances in which its application manifests any injury to competition so dependent on individual facts that it does not merit the per se characterization some of the early cases give it," the *Northwest Power* court rejected *Pick-Barth*'s per se rule and "adopt[ed] a rule of reason to be applied on a case-by-case basis in situations where competitive forces protected by the Sherman Act suffer some palpable injury." *Id.*

27. *Id.* at 91.
28. *Id.* at 89.

The *Northwest Power* court determined that the defendant conspicuously lacked the kind of market power necessary to raise antitrust concerns and affirmed summary judgment to the defendants. The court concluded that the plaintiff made no showing that substitution of one distributor for another affected consumers in the relevant market.[29]

Several other courts likewise have rejected *Pick-Barth*'s application of the per se rule on the ground that no harm to consumers was shown. These courts have concluded that the elimination of a competitor through unfair means must be evaluated under the rule of reason:

> The line of cases of which *Pick-Barth* . . . was the progenitor is now regarded by some as an aberration in antitrust law. The courts now often substitute for the per se approach an in-depth analysis of the nature of the antitrust charge on a case-by-case basis, measuring the harm to general competition in the market under the rule of reason. Thus, it must now be shown that there was an actual conspiracy to induce the aggrieved party's employees to switch their allegiance, and that its purpose and effect was not just to establish a new competitor by unfair means (which only serves to increase competition), and not just to injure a competitor's operation, but *solely* to eliminate the plaintiff as a competitor from the market.[30]

---

29. *Id.* at 90.
30. 1A ALTMAN, *supra* note 1, § 9:19. For a compilation of other cases addressing the relationship between business torts and antitrust law in light of *Pick-Barth*, see UXB Sand & Gravel, Inc. v. Rosenfeld Concrete Corp., 599 A.2d 1033, 1036-37 (R.I. 1991); *see also, e.g.*, Military Servs. Realty, Inc. v. Realty Consultants of Va., Ltd., 823 F.2d 829, 831 (4th Cir. 1987); Seaboard Supply Co. v. Congoleum Corp., 770 F.2d 367 (3d Cir. 1985) ("diversion of customers does not amount to per se violation[,] and no rule of reason claim has been established"); L.A. Draper & Son v. Wheelabrator-Frye, Inc., 735 F.2d 414, 421 & n.11 (11th Cir. 1984) (court evaluating under a rule of reason analysis because, while "[u]nfair competitive means can be actionable under other legal theories," "to avail itself of treble damages under § 1 of the Sherman Act, [the plaintiff] must show harm to competition in general, as well as its own injury as a competitor"; A.H. Cox & Co. v. Star Mach. Co., 653 F.2d 1302, 1308 n.7 (9th Cir. 1981); Havoco of Am., Ltd. v. Shell Oil Co., 626 F.2d 549, 555-56 (7th Cir. 1980); Juneau Square Corp. v. First Wis. Nat'l Bank of Milwaukee, 624 F.2d 798, 812-13 (7th Cir. 1980) ("The definition of

D. The Additional Requirement of "Antitrust Injury"

As noted above, a plaintiff cannot establish an antitrust claim by alleging its business was harmed by a competitor's inequitable and unfair practices; the plaintiff must go farther and establish an actual restraint upon competition in the marketplace. In addition, to prevail on an antitrust claim, the plaintiff must show "antitrust injury." This requirement was first articulated by the Supreme Court in 1977 in *Brunswick Corp. v. Pueblo Bowl-O-Mat, Inc.*[31] There, the plaintiffs alleged that the defendant, one of the nation's largest bowling equipment manufacturers and bowling center operators, violated section 7 of the Clayton Act by acquiring bowling centers that had defaulted in their payments for equipment. The plaintiffs, competing bowling center operators, sought treble damages for the anticipated increase in profits the plaintiffs would have reaped had the bowling centers instead gone out of business.[32] Rejecting this claim, the Court emphasized that the antitrust laws are designed to protect competition, not individual competitors, and that it would be inimical to the purpose of the antitrust laws to award the plaintiffs damages for profits they would have realized had competition been *reduced* by the defendant's staying out of the market.[33]

To recover antitrust damages, the Court explained, a plaintiff must prove more than that its injury was causally linked to an illegal presence in the market; rather, plaintiffs must prove "antitrust injury . . . of the type the antitrust laws were intended to prevent."[34] Such "injury should

---

'unfair methods' is simply too amorphous a basis upon which to predicate a departure from the rule of reason."); Stifel, Nicolaus & Co. v. Dain, Kalman & Quail, Inc., 578 F.2d 1256, 1260-62 (8th Cir. 1978); Universal Analytics, Inc. v. MacNeal-Schwendler Corp., 707 F. Supp. 1170, 1181 n.14 (C.D. Cal. 1989), *aff'd*, 914 F.2d 1256 (9th Cir. 1990); Am. Standard Life & Accident Ins. Co. v. U.R.L., Inc., 701 F. Supp. 527, 534-35 (M.D. Pa. 1988); Merkle Press, Inc. v. Merkle, 519 F. Supp. 50, 52-53 (D. Md. 1981) ("It is obvious that the per se aspects of the *Pick-Barth* doctrine have lost their vitality.").

31. 429 U.S. 477.
32. *Id.* at 479-80.
33. *Id.* at 488; *see also Brown Shoe Co.*, 370 U.S. at 329-30.
34. *Brunswick Corp.*, 429 U.S. at 489; *see also Topco Assocs., Inc.*, 405 U.S. at 608 ("Antitrust laws in general, and the Sherman Act in particular, are

reflect the anticompetitive effect either of the violation or of anticompetitive acts made possible by the violation.[35]

The antitrust injury requirement stands as an additional barrier to competitor plaintiffs seeking to recover antitrust damages.[36] As the Seventh Circuit observed:

> "[T]here is a sense in which eliminating even a single competitor reduces competition. But it is not the sense that is relevant in deciding whether the antitrust laws have been violated." Competition means that some may be forced out of business. The antitrust laws

---

the Magna Carta of free enterprise. They are as important to the preservation of economic freedom and our free-enterprise systems as the Bill of Rights is to the protection of our fundamental personal freedoms.").

35. *Brunswick Corp.*, 429 U.S. at 489; Blue Shield of Va. v. McCready, 457 U.S. 465, 482-84 (1982) ("'[C]ompetitors may be able to prove antitrust injury before they actually are driven from the market and competition is thereby lessened.'") (quoting *Brunswick Corp.*, 429 U.S. at 489 n.14); *see also, e.g.*, Glen Holly Entm't Inc. v. Tektronix Inc., 352 F.3d 367, 379 (9th Cir. 2003) ("Given that customers are the intended beneficiaries of competition, and that customers are presumptively those injured by its unlawful elimination, for pleading purposes we conclude that [the plaintiff] has satisfied the requirement that it adequately allege antitrust injury to its business."); *In re* Cardizem CD Antitrust Litig., 332 F.3d 896, 909-11 & n.15 (6th Cir. 2003) ("Our conclusion that the Agreement was a per se illegal restraint of trade does not obviate the need to decide whether the plaintiffs adequately alleged antitrust injury") (applying *Brunswick* and finding antitrust injury); Midwest Gas Servs., Inc. v. Ind. Gas. Co., 317 F.3d 703, 710-13 (7th Cir. 2003) (applying *Brunswick* in assessing whether plaintiffs suffered antitrust injury under sections 1 and 2).

36. *See* Ronald W. Davis, *Standing on Shaky Ground: The Strangely Elusive Doctrine of Antitrust Injury*, 70 ANTITRUST L.J. 697, 701-05 (2003) (discussing *Brunswick* and other key cases of Supreme Court antitrust jurisprudence); *see also* Edward A. Snyder & Thomas E. Kauper, *Misuse of the Antitrust Laws: The Competitor Plaintiff*, 90 MICH. L. REV. 551, 576-81 (1991) (empirical study suggests that, while it may have been the Court's intent to deter antitrust actions by competitors, *Brunswick* has had little effect on the frequency and disposition of competitor plaintiff antitrust suits).

are not designed to guarantee every competitor tenure in the marketplace.[37]

---

37. Great Escape, Inc. v. Union City Body Co., 791 F.2d 532, 540 (7th Cir. 1986) (quoting Prods. Liab. Ins. Agency, Inc. v. Crum & Forster Ins. Cos., 682 F.2d 660, 663 (7th Cir. 1982)); *see also* Colo. Interstate Gas Co. v. Natural Gas Pipe Co. of Am., 885 F.2d 683, 697 (10th Cir. 1989) (treble damages "too harsh a remedy for unfair methods of competition that only threaten to have a transitory impact on the marketplace").

CHAPTER II

APPLICATION OF ANTITRUST
PRINCIPLES TO BUSINESS TORT CLAIMS

> *As the role of business torts in establishing antitrust violations has diminished, business tort claims have enjoyed increasing prominence in their own right. This chapter examines how business tort defendants have attempted to use some of the concepts successfully invoked in defense of antitrust claims when defending against tort claims based upon competitive conduct. – Eds.*

A. Introduction

As defensive theories have proliferated in private antitrust litigation and business tort claims have grown in popularity,[1] business tort defendants have come to rely upon principles that have been used successfully to defend against antitrust claims. This chapter focuses upon two of the most popular – the so-called "competitive privilege" and the Noerr-Pennington doctrine – and briefly examines several others that have been used with varying degrees of success in litigation involving claims of anticompetitive conduct.

B. The Competitive Privilege

As noted in Chapter 1, antitrust plaintiffs in years past attempted with some success to import business tort principles into antitrust cases. Today the situation is reversed. As business torts have gained prominence and antitrust defenses have strengthened, business tort defendants increasingly have sought to import antitrust concepts into business tort cases. Foremost among these is the so-called "competitive privilege."

---

1.   *See* Chapter 1.

Business tort doctrine long has recognized a privilege for conduct that is legitimately competitive.[2] This privilege is embodied in the formulation of standards concerning tortious interference with business relations set forth in the Restatement (Second) of Torts,[3] and in the more recent Restatement (Third) of Unfair Competition, which recognizes a broader "freedom to compete."[4] This more recent Restatement rejects the view that competition is a "privilege" as to which the defendant has the burden of proof; instead, it places the burden upon the plaintiff to allege and prove something other than that the defendant engaged in mere competition.[5]

1. *General Principles*

"One of the most firmly established principles of the common law is that competition is not a tort."[6] Although competition literally is an intentional interference with a competitor's prospective contractual relations, to conclude that it is therefore tortious would disrupt the system of free enterprise and thus makes no sense from a legal or economic standpoint.[7]

The law of contract exists to provide a means of enforcing business expectations; however, when a business relation affords the parties no enforceable expectations, but only the hope of continued benefits, it must allow for the rights of others,[8] since no business has a proprietary interest

---

2. *See, e.g.*, The Schoolmaster's Case, Y.B. 11, Hen. IV, f.47 pl. 21 (C.P. Hil. Term 1410); *see also* Pac. Express, Inc. v. United Airlines, Inc., 959 F.2d 814, 818-20 (9th Cir. 1992).

3. RESTATEMENT (SECOND) OF TORTS § 768 (1977).

4. RESTATEMENT (THIRD) OF UNFAIR COMPETITION § 1 (1993).

5. *Id.* at cmt. a.

6. Speakers of Sport, Inc. v. ProServ, Inc., 178 F.3d 862, 865 (7th Cir. 1999) (citing Keeble v. Hickeringill, 103 Eng. Rep. 1127 (K.B. 1706-07)); *see also* Frandsen v. Jensen-Sundquist Agency, Inc., 802 F.2d 941, 947 (7th Cir. 1986)); Grempler v. Multiple Listing Bureau, 266 A.2d 1 (Md. App. 1970).

7. *ProServ*, 178 F.3d at 865; *Frandsen*, 802 F.2d at 947; *see also* Macklin v. Robert Logan Assocs., 639 A.2d 112, 119 (Md. App. 1994).

8. *See* Bed, Bath & Beyond of La Jolla, Inc. v. La Jolla Vill. Square Venture Partners, 60 Cal. Rptr. 2d 830, 837-38 (Cal. App. 1997); Belden Corp. v. InterNorth, 413 N.E.2d 98, 101 (Ill. App. 1980); *Macklin*, 639 A.2d at 119.

in its customers.[9] Thus, while a company is not justified in inducing a breach of contract simply because it is in competition with one of the parties to the contract and seeks to further the company's own economic interests, competitive freedom is of sufficient importance to justify inducement of a third party to abandon his relationship with another in the absence of an existing contractual relationship.[10]

Applying this reasoning, courts generally have held that, while competition is not a defense to a claim of interference with an existing contract not terminable at will, it is a valid defense to a claim of interference with a contract that *is* terminable at will, or to a claim of interference with prospective advantage.[11] Many of these decisions have relied upon section 768 of the Restatement (Second) of Torts, which provides:

> (1) One who intentionally causes a third person not to enter into a prospective contractual relation with another who is his competitor or not to continue an existing contract terminable at will does not interfere improperly with the other's relation if

---

9. *See* Prudential Ins. Co. of Am. v. Sipula, 776 F.2d 157, 163 (7th Cir. 1985).
10. *See Macklin*, 639 A.2d at 120; Imperial Ice Co. v. Rossier, 112 P.2d 631, 633 (Cal. 1941); Republic Tobacco, L.P. v. N. Atl. Trading Col., 254 F. Supp. 2d 1007, 1011-12 (N.D. Ill. 2003).
11. *See* Navellier v. Sletten, 262 F.3d 923, 937-38 (9th Cir. 2001); Int'l Sales & Serv. v. Austral Insulated Prods., 262 F.3d 1152, 1159 (11th Cir. 2001); Nobody in Particular Presents, Inc. v. Clear Channel Commc'ns, Inc., No. 01N1523, 2004 U.S. Dist. LEXIS 5665 (D. Colo. April 2, 2004); Cacique, Inc. v. Gonzalez, No. 03C5430, 2004 U.S. Dist. LEXIS 4966 (N.D. Ill. March 26, 2004); *ProServ*, 178 F.3d at 865; Fred Siegel Co. v. Arter & Hadden, 85 Ohio St. 3d 171, 180 (1999); Automated Solutions Enters. v. Clearview Software, Inc., 567 S.E.2d 335 (Ga. App. 2002); Volt Servs. Group v. Adecco Empl. Servs., Inc., 35 P.3d 329 (Or. App. 2001); Edwards v. Anaconda Co., 565 P.2d 190 (Ariz. App. 1977); Heavener, Ogier Servs. v. R.W. Fla. Region, 418 So. 2d 1074 (Fla. App. 1982); *Belden*, 413 N.E.2d at 101-02; *Macklin*, 639 A.2d at 120; N. Plumbing & Htg. v. Henderson Bros., 268 N.W.2d 296 (Mich. App. 1978); United Wild Rice v. Nelson, 313 Nw.2d 628 (Minn. 1982); Martin v. Phillips Petroleum Co., 455 S.W.2d 429, 435 (Tex. App. 1970); Wilder v. Cody Country Chamber of Commerce, 868 P.2d 211, 225 (Wyo. 1994).

1. the relation concerns a matter involved in the competition between the actor and the other and

2. the actor does not employ wrongful means and

3. his action does not create or continue an unlawful restraint of trade and

4. his purpose is at least in part to advance his interest in competing with the other.

(2) The fact that one is a competitor of another for the business of a third person does not prevent his causing a breach of an existing contract with the other from being an improper interference if the contract is not terminable at will.

The rule stated in this section is a special application of the principle that actionable interference must be "improper,"[12] and rests upon the notion that an individual's privilege to engage in business and to compete with others implies a privilege to induce third persons to do business with the individual rather than with competitors.[13] Accordingly, it is generally accepted that no tort is committed by a competitor who causes a third person not to enter into a prospective contractual relation, or to discontinue an existing contract terminable at will, so long as the competitor does not employ improper means and his purpose is at least in part to advance an interest in competing.[14] Under the Restatement, however, the competitive privilege does not apply to a claim of interference with an existing contract not terminable at will.[15]

---

12. RESTATEMENT (SECOND) OF TORTS § 768(1) cmt. b (1977).

13. *See* Bailey v. Allgas, Inc., 284 F.3d 1237, 1256-57 (11th Cir. 2002); Reazin v. Blue Cross/Blue Shield, 663 F. Supp. 1360, 1492 (D. Kan. 1987), *aff'd*, 899 F.2d 951 (10th Cir. 1990).

14. *See Bailey*, 284 F.3d at 1257; Int'l Sales & Serv. v. Austral Insulated Prods., 262 F.3d 1152, 1159 (11th Cir. 2001); *Navellier*, 262 F.3d at 937-38; Waldrep Bros. Beauty Supply v. Wynn Beauty Supply Co., 992 F.2d 59, 63 (4th Cir. 1993); Altrutech, Inc. v. Hooper Holmes, Inc., 992 F. Supp. 1264, 1268 (D. Kan. 1998); *Reazin*, 663 F. Supp. at 1492; Pino v. Prudential Ins. Co. of Am., 689 F. Supp. 1358, 1363 (E.D. Pa. 1988); W. Oliver Tripp Co. v. Am. Hoechst Corp., 616 N.E.2d 118, 125 (Mass. App. 1993); Killian Constr. Co. v. Jack D. Ball & Assocs., 865 S.W.2d 889 (Mo. App. 1993).

15. RESTATEMENT (SECOND) OF TORTS § 768(2) cmt. h (1977); *see also Macklin*, 639 A.2d at 119; Omedelena v. Denver Options, Inc. 60 P.3d

It is generally recognized that where the interference is intended at least in part to advance the competing interest of the party causing the interference, it will not give rise to liability unless the means employed are "improper" or "wrongful."[16] "Wrongful means," as that term is used in Restatement section 768, refers to means that are intrinsically wrongful, that is, conduct that is itself capable of forming the basis for liability of the actor.[17] Conduct found to fall within this definition includes physical violence,[18] coercion,[19] fraud and misrepresentation,[20]

717, 725 (Colo. App. 2002) (holding that a contract is not terminable at will when it can be dissolved but at a penalty). For other cases applying RESTATEMENT § 768, *see* Int'l Data Payment Sys. v. Meridian Bank, 212 F.3d 849, 856-58 (3d Cir. 2000); Brokerage Concepts v. U.S. Healthcare, Inc., 140 F.3d 494, 529-34 (3d Cir. 1998); DP-TEK, Inc. v. AT&T Global Info. Solutions Co., 100 F.3d 828 (10th Cir. 1996); SuperTurf, Inc. v. Monsanto Co., 660 F.2d 1275, 1286 (8th Cir. 1981) (regarding tort claim); Morton Bldgs. of Neb., Inc. v. Morton Bldgs., Inc., 531 F.2d 910, 916 n.5, 917 (8th Cir. 1976) (no antitrust claim because actions were justified by "valid business reasons"); Machine Maint. & Equip. Co. v. Cooper Indus., 661 F. Supp. 1112, 1115-16 (E.D. Mo. 1987) (regarding tort claim); C.R. Bard, Inc. v. Wordtronics Corp., 561 A.2d 694, 696-97 (N.J. 1989) (tort case); Avtec Indus. v. Sony Corp., 100 A.2d 712, 715 (N.J. 1985) (tort case); Guard-Life Corp. v. S. Parker Hardware Mfg. Corp., 406 Ne.2d 445, 448-49 (N.Y. 1980) (tort case); Walter v. Murphy, 573 Ne.2d 678, 680 (Ohio 1988) (tort case); Ron Tonkin Gran Turismo, Inc. v. Wakehouse Motors, Inc., 611 P.2d 658, 664 (Or. 1980) (tort claim).

16. *Navellier*, 262 F.3d at 937-38; *Int'l Sales & Serv.*, 262 F.3d at 1159; *Waldrep*, 992 F.2d at 63; Strapex Corp. v. Metaverpa NV, 607 F. Supp. 1047, 1050 (S.D.N.Y. 1985).

17. *See* Amerinet, Inc. v. Xerox Corp., 972 F.2d 1483, 1507 (8th Cir. 1992); Energex Enters. v. Anthony Doors, Inc., 250 F. Supp. 2d 1278, 1285-86 (D. Colo. 2003); Parsells v. Manhattan Radiology Group, L.L.P., 225 F. Supp. 2d 1217, 1237-38 (D. Kan. 2003); *Macklin*, 334 Md. at 301-06.

18. *See Energex Enters.*, 250 F. Supp. 2d at 1285-86; Am. Bldgs. Co., v. Pascoe Bldg. Sys., Inc., 392 S.E.2d 860, 863 (Ga. 1990); Guard-Life Corp. v. S. Parker Hardware Mfg. Corp., 428 N.Y.S.2d 628, 632 (N.Y. 1980).

19. *See Reazin*, 663 F. Supp. at 1492.

20. *See Automated Solutions Enters.*, 567 S.E.2d at 339; *Energex Enters.*, 250 F. Supp. 2d at 1285-86; *Am. Bldgs.*, 392 S.E.2d at 863; *Reazin*, 663 F. Supp. at 1492; *Guard-Life*, 428 N.Y.S.2d at 632.

breach of fiduciary duty,[21] defamation,[22] antitrust violations,[23] wrongful use of confidential information,[24] and civil suits and criminal prosecutions.[25] Bringing civil litigation ordinarily is wrongful, however, only if the defendant has no belief in the merit of the litigation, or if, although having some belief in its merit, he nevertheless institutes the litigation in bad faith, and for purposes of harassment.[26] Generally, requirements for improper conduct also have been framed in the case law in terms of an improper state of mind.[27]

Mere persuasion alone, even though knowingly directed at interfering with a prospective contract, will not constitute "wrongful

---

21. *See* CGB Occupational Therapy v. RHA Health Servs., 357 F.3d 375, 388-89 (3d. Cir. 2004); Occusafe, Inc. v. EG&G Rocky Flats, 54 F.3d 618, 623 (10th Cir. 1995); *see also* United Int'l Holdings, Inc. v. Wharf (Holdings) Ltd., 210 F.3d 1207, 1227 (10th Cir. 2000).

22. *See* Zimmerman v. DCA at Welleby, Inc., 505 So. 2d 1371, 1374-75 (Fla. App. 1987); *Am. Bldgs.*, 392 S.E.2d at 863.

23. *See* HJ, Inc. v. ITT Corp., 867 F.2d 1531, 1548 (8th Cir. 1989); Fishman v. Estate of Wirtz, 807 F.2d 520, 546-47 (7th Cir. 1986); *Am. Bldgs.*, 392 S.E.2d at 863.

24. *See Am. Bldgs.*, 392 S.E.2d at 863; Island Air, Inc. v. LaBar, 566 P.2d 972 (Wash. App. 1977).

25. *See Energex Enters.*, 250 F. Supp. 2d at 1285-86; *Am. Bldgs.*, 392 S.E.2d at 863; *Guard-Life*, 428 N.Y.S.2d at 632.

26. *See* Erlandson v. Pullen, 608 P.2d 1169 (Or. App. 1980); *see* Mantia v. Hanson, 79 P.3d 404, 409-411 (Or. App. 2003) (explaining Oregon cases including *Erlandson*); *cf.* Int'l Shortstop, Inc. v. Rally's, Inc., 939 F.2d 1257, 1268-71 (5th Cir. 1991). Regarding the availability of the *Noerr-Pennington* doctrine to defend tort claims based upon litigation activities, *see infra* Part C.

27 . *See* Int'l Mktg., Ltd. v. Archer-Daniels-Midland Co., 192 F.3d 724, 731 (7th Cir. 1999) (defendant "ineligible for the competition defense only if its conduct is motivated solely by spite or ill will; citing Stolgberg v. Brauvin Realty Servs., Inc., 691 Ne.2d 834, 846 n.2 (Ill. App. 1998)); L&M Enters. v. BEI Sensors & Sys. Co., 231 F.3d 1284, 1288 (10th Cir. 2000) ("malice is a predicate for tortious interference and is not limited to cases involving allegations of defamatory conduct"); *see* Nobody in Particular Presents, Inc. v. Clear Channel Commc'ns, Inc., No. 01N1523, 2004 U.S. Dist. LEXIS 5665, at 205-7 ("improper conduct has to be intentional").

means" for purposes of section 768.[28] However, if the defendant acts with the intent to cause financial injury to the plaintiff, even if he acts at least in part to advance his own interest in competing with the plaintiff, his conduct may not be privileged.[29] An erroneous belief that a contract is unenforceable may not be a defense either.[30]

As the Restatement (Third) of Unfair Competition recognizes, "[t]here is as yet no consensus with respect to the allocation of the burdens of pleading and proof under the general tort of intentional interference with prospective economic relations."[31] Some courts have held that the plaintiff bears the burden of proving that the interference was "improper," or that the defendant's conduct exceeded the scope of the competitive privilege.[32] Other courts have held that the privilege is a defense to be proven by the defendant.[33] Where the privilege is raised as a defense, it sometimes is held that the burden lies with the plaintiff to demonstrate malice sufficient to overcome the privilege.[34]

---

28. *See* Apollo Tech. v. Centrosphere Indus., 805 F. Supp. 1157, 1205 (D.N.J. 1992) (citing cases); *Reazin*, 663 F. Supp. at 1492.

29. *See* Yoakum v. Hartford Fire Ins. Co., 923 P.2d 416, 424 (Idaho 1996) (proof can result from showing either improper motive *or* wrongful means); Ramirez v. Selles, 784 P.2d 433, 436 (Or. 1989); *see also Int'l Sales & Serv.*, 262 F.3d at 1159 (citing other standards to determine whether conduct is privileged).

30. *See* Ancora Capital & Mgmt. Group, L.L.C. v. Corporate Mailing Servs., 214 F. Supp. 2d 493, 499 (D. Md. 2002), *rev'd on other grounds*, No. 02-1245, 2003 U.S. App. LEXIS 56 (4th Cir. 2003).

31. RESTATEMENT (THIRD) OF UNFAIR COMPETITION § 1 cmt. a (1993) (citing RESTATEMENT (SECOND) OF TORTS § 767 cmt. k (1977) ("there is little consensus on who has the burden of raising the issue of whether the interference was improper or not and subsequently of proving that issue")); *see also Republic Tobacco*, 254 Supp. 2d at 1011-12.

32. *See, e.g., Amerinet*, 972 F.2d at 1506-07; Gemini Aluminum Corp. v. Cal. Custom Shapes, Inc., 95 Cal. App. 4th 1249, 1256-57 (Cal. App. 2002); Wagenseller v. Scottsdale Mem'l Hosp., 710 P.2d 1025, 1043 (Ariz. 1985).

33. *See Int'l Mktg.*, 192 F.3d at 731; Greenberg v. Mount Sinai Med. Ctr., 629 So. 2d 252, 255 (Fla. App. 1993); *Ramirez*, 784 P.2d at 435.

34. Cacique, Inc. v. Gonzalez, No. 03C5430, 2004 U.S. Dist. LEXIS 4966 at 5-8 (N.D. Ill. March 26, 2004; Ray Dancer, Inc. v. DMC Corp., 594 Ne.2d 1344, 1350 (Ill. App. 1992).

The Restatement (Third) of Unfair Competition rejects the notion that competition is a defense, justification, or privilege, in favor of "a general principle of non-liability."[35] Some state courts have indicated a preference for the Restatement view. Specifically, Kansas has predicted an adoption of the Restatement,[36] Arizona has adopted the Restatement when there is no applicable Arizona law,[37] and Pennsylvania has recognized a common law unfair competition claim from the Restatement as well.[38] Many courts limit an unfair competition claim to what is explicitly actionable under the Restatement: deceptive marketing, infringement of trademarks, and appropriation of trade secrets.[39] Pennsylvania has shown a willingness to adopt a broader approach to what is subject to liability for unfair competition under the Restatement, which provides for "other acts or practices of the actor determined to be actionable as an unfair method of competition, taking into account the nature of the conduct and its likely effect."[40]

2. *The Role of the "Competitive Privilege" in Business Tort Litigation*

Applying the foregoing principles, several courts have rejected business tort claims based on conduct amounting to nothing more than legitimate, albeit fierce, competition. For example, in *Speakers of Sport, Inc. v. ProServ, Inc.*,[41] the Seventh Circuit affirmed a summary judgment in favor of a defendant sports agency that had raised the competitive privilege. The plaintiff agency had a prior business relationship with

---

35. RESTATEMENT (THIRD) OF UNFAIR COMPETITION § 1 cmt. a (1993).
36. *See* Airport Sys. Int'l, Inc. v. AIRSYS ATM, Inc., 144 F. Supp. 2d 1268, 1270 (D. Kan. 2001).
37. Brooks Fiber Commc'ns v. GST Tucson Lightwave, 992 F. Supp. 1124, 1131 (D. Ariz. 1997).
38. Fresh Made, Inc. v. Lifeway Foods, Inc., No. 01-4254, 2002 U.S. Dist. LEXIS 15098 (E.D. Pa. 2002).
39. *See* RESTATEMENT (THIRD) OF UNFAIR COMPETITION § 1(a)(1)-(3) (1993); *see also* Auto Channel, Inc. v. Speedvision Network, L.L.C., 144 F. Supp. 2d 784, 789-90 (W.D. Ky. 2001); Accessible Techs., Inc. v. Paxton Auto. Corp., 2002 U.S. Dist. LEXIS 19278 (D. Kan. 2002).
40. RESTATEMENT (THIRD) OF UNFAIR COMPETITION § 1(a)(3) (1993); *see* Air Prods. & Chem. v. Inter-Chemical Ltd., No. 03-CV-6140, 2003 Dist. LEXIS 23985, 34-35 (E.D. Pa. 2003).
41. 178 F.3d 862 (7th Cir. 1999).

baseball player Ivan Rodriguez. The plaintiff claimed that the defendant engaged in tortious interference by making promises of endorsement deals to lure Rodriguez's business. Those endorsement deals were never attained.[42] Writing for the Seventh Circuit, Judge Posner noted that

> There is in general nothing wrong with one sports agent trying to take a client from another if this can be done without precipitating a breach of contract. That is the process known as competition, which though painful, fierce, frequently ruthless, sometimes Darwinian in its pitilessness, is the cornerstone of our highly successful economic system.[43]

The contract between the plaintiff and Rodriguez was terminable at will, and the court recognized that, under Illinois law, interference with an at-will contract can still form the basis of a claim for tortious interference. The court, however, invoked section 768 of the Restatement (Second) of Torts for the proposition that the competitive privilege provides a defense to a claim of interference based on the inducement of the lawful termination of a contract that is terminable at will.[44]

While the right to compete by fraud is not included in the competitive privilege, the court concluded that to make it a tort for a competitor to make a promise that he knows he cannot fulfill would practically attach grave legal risks to anyone making a promise to lure a customer away.[45] The court then held that the Illinois principle that promissory fraud is not actionable unless it is part of a scheme to defraud, that is, unless it is one element of a pattern of fraudulent acts, prevented the recognition of such a tort.[46] The court further held that the promise made by the defendant was a valid sales pitch that the promisee would understand as "aspirational rather than enforceable."[47]

The court noted that there was some support for competitive behavior being tortious, even when otherwise lawful, when a competitor

---

42. *Id.* at 864.
43. *Id.* at 865.
44. *Id.*
45. *Id.* at 865-66.
46. *Id.* at 866. The court noted, however, that this Illinois formulation of fraud has been criticized and rejected in most states. *Id.*
47. *Id.*

uses "unfair" tactics determined by "an established standard of a trade or profession" or "recognized ethical rules or established customs or practices in the business community."[48] However, the court rejected this standard:

> Illinois courts have not yet embraced the doctrine, and we are not alone in thinking it pernicious. . . . [T]he established standards of a trade or profession in regard to competition, and its ideas of unethical competitive conduct, are likely to reflect a desire to limit competition for reasons related to the self-interest of the trade or profession rather than to the welfare of its customers or clients. . . . [T]he tort of interference with business relationships should be confined to cases in which the defendant employed unlawful means to stiff a competitor.[49]

Thus, applying the competitive privilege, the court affirmed the district court's summary judgment in favor of the defendant.[50]

Applying similar reasoning, other courts have rejected business tort claims based upon lawful price-cutting[51] and the targeting of the plaintiff's customers for special deals,[52] concluding that such conduct does not transgress the "rules of the game."[53] For example, the court in *Energex Lighting Industries v. North American Phillips Lighting Corp.*[54] refused to impose tort liability on a competitor for reducing his prices,

---

48. *Id.* at 867 (quoting Yoakum v. Hartford Fire Ins. Co., 923 P.2d 416, 423-24 (Idaho 1996) and RTL Distrib., Inc. v. Double S Batteries, Inc. 545 Nw.2d 587, 591 (Iowa App. 1996)).

49. *Id.*

50. *See id.* at 868 (also noting that the plaintiffs could not establish entitlement to damages).

51. *See* Energex Lighting Indus. v. N. Am. Phillips Lighting Corp., 765 F. Supp. 93 (S.D.N.Y. 1991); *cf.* C.E. Servs., Inc. v. Control Data Corp., 759 F.2d 1241, 1249 (5th Cir. 1985).

52. *See Energex*, 765 F. Supp. at 109; Caller-Times Pub. Co. v. Triad Comm., Inc., 855 S.W.2d 18 (Tex. App. 1993); *cf. C.E. Servs.*, 759 F.2d at 1249.

53. *Energex*, 765 F. Supp. at 109; *see generally* Int'l Sales & Serv. v. Austral Insulated Prods., 262 F.3d 1152, 1159 (11th Cir. 2001) (noting the standards to determine whether conduct is privileged, including abiding by "rules of combat").

54. 765 F. Supp. 93 (S.D.N.Y. 1991).

emphasizing that "stiff competition and price-cutting go on every day in the business world."[55]

Just as antitrust principles may be invoked in the defense of business tort claims, such principles may be used offensively. For example, proof of predatory pricing may support not only a claim under section 2 of the Sherman Act,[56] but a tortious interference claim as well.[57] In addition, proof of an anticompetitive motive may supply the "malice" necessary to support a claim of tortious interference, even where an accompanying antitrust claim fails for lack of proof that competition was harmed.[58]

C. The *Noerr-Pennington* Doctrine

1. *General Principles*

The *Noerr-Pennington* doctrine takes its name from decisions of the United States Supreme Court in *Eastern Railroad Presidents Conference v. Noerr Motor Freight*,[59] and *United Mine Workers of America v. Pennington*.[60] In *Noerr*, a group of truckers alleged that a publicity and lobbying campaign conducted by the defendant railroads through deceptive means, urging the passage of laws regulating the trucking industry, was designed to restrain trade in the long distance freight hauling business in violation of the Sherman Act.

---

55. *Id.* at 109.
56. 15 U.S.C. § 2.
57. *See, e.g., C.E. Servs.*, 759 F.2d at 1249; *accord* H.J. Inc. v. Int'l Tel. & Tel. Corp., 867 F.2d 1531, 1548 (8th Cir. 1989) (attempted monopolization established improper interference under section 768 of the RESTATEMENT (SECOND) OF TORTS); Key Enter. of Del. v. Venice Hosp., 919 F.2d 1550, 1568 (11th Cir. 1990), *vacated and reh'g granted*, 979 F.2d 806 (11th Cir. 1992) (antitrust violations negated justification defense).
58. *See* Kiepfer v. Beller, 944 F.2d 1213 (5th Cir. 1991); Deauville Corp. v. Federated Dep't Stores, 756 F.2d 1183, 1195 (5th Cir. 1985) (anticompetitive intent); Sun Dun, Inc. v. Coca-Cola Co., 740 F. Supp. 381, 397-98 (D. Md. 1990) (alleged antitrust violation satisfied one requirement of malice necessary to state a claim of tortious interference with business relations).
59. 365 U.S. 127 (1961).
60. 381 U.S. 657 (1965).

After a judgment in favor of the plaintiffs was affirmed on appeal, the Supreme Court reversed in a unanimous opinion, holding that the Sherman Act is inapplicable to a mere attempt to influence the passage or enforcement of legislation, even when the sole purpose of such an attempt is to restrain competition.[61]

The Court offered two reasons for its holding in *Noerr*. First, the Court perceived an "essential dissimilarity" between agreements to petition for legislation that would restrain trade and private agreements to directly restrain trade through price-fixing, boycotts and the like.[62] To condemn the former "would impute to the Sherman Act a purpose . . . which would have no basis whatever in the legislative history of that Act."[63] Second, the Court noted that to condemn petitioning conduct "would raise important constitutional questions" under the First Amendment.[64]

While acknowledging in dicta that application of the Sherman Act might be justified where a publicity campaign ostensibly directed towards influencing government action was actually nothing more than an attempt to interfere directly with the business relationships of a competitor,[65] the Court declined to apply this "sham exception" to the facts before it, noting that it was uncontroverted that the defendants "were making a genuine effort to influence legislation and law enforcement practices."[66]

In *Pennington*, the Court reiterated the principle that joint efforts to influence public officials do not violate the antitrust laws even when they are intended to eliminate competition, and held that such conduct is not illegal either standing alone or as part of a broader scheme that itself is violative of the Sherman Act.[67]

Subsequently, in *California Motor Transport Co. v. Trucking Unlimited*,[68] the Court applied *Noerr* to protect attempts to influence

---

61. *See* 365 U.S. at 136-38.
62. *See id.* at 136.
63. *Id.* at 137.
64. *Id.* at 137-38.
65. *See id.* at 144.
66. *Id.*
67. *See* 381 U.S. at 670.
68. 404 U.S. 508 (1972).

judicial and other adjudicatory proceedings. The lower courts have since extended the reach of *Noerr* to attempts to influence actions of law enforcement agencies as well.[69]

In *Allied Tube & Conduit Corp. v. Indian Head, Inc.*,[70] however, the Supreme Court refused to extend *Noerr* to an attempt by a group of manufacturers of steel conduit to influence a private fire protection association's revisions of its electrical code, which was routinely adopted into law by a substantial number of state and local governments. The Court held that when "an economically interested party exercises decision making authority in formulating a product standard for a private association that comprises market participants, that party enjoys no *Noerr* immunity from any antitrust liability flowing from the effect the standard has of its own force in the marketplace."[71]

Noerr protection also was denied in *FTC v. Superior Court Trial Lawyers Association*,[72] which involved a refusal by a group of attorneys to accept assignments to represent indigent criminal defendants until the city government increased the fees for such work. The Supreme Court held that the group's conduct constituted an illegal boycott and that *Noerr* did not immunize that conduct, since the boycott was the *means* by which the group sought to obtain the favorable legislation.[73] The Court also rejected the contention that First Amendment concerns raised by the "expressive content" of the boycott warranted the application of *Noerr*, noting that all boycotts require communication among participants.[74]

The Supreme Court has addressed the parameters of *Noerr*'s so-called "sham exception"[75] in several opinions. In *City of Columbia v. Omni Outdoor Advertising*,[76] the Court held that the "sham exception"

---

69. *See, e.g.*, King v. Idaho Funeral Serv. Ass'n, 862 F.2d 744 (9th Cir. 1988) (trade association effort to influence state licensing agency); Ottensmeyer v. Chesapeake & Potomac Tel. Co., 756 F.2d 986, 993-94 (4th Cir. 1985) (cooperation with police).
70. 486 U.S. 492 (1988).
71. *Id.* at 509-10.
72. 493 U.S. 411 (1990).
73. *See id.* at 424-25.
74. *Id.* at 429-32.
75. *See* 365 U.S. at 144.
76. 499 U.S. 365 (1991).

was inapplicable to a corporation that successfully lobbied a city to enact billboard zoning ordinances to protect the corporation's control of the local billboard market, as the corporation did nothing more than lobby for the ordinance.[77] The Court also declined to recognize a separate "conspiracy exception" to *Noerr*.[78]

Though the "sham" exception was first articulated in *Noerr*, the Supreme Court introduced the modern test to determine whether a litigation is a sham in *Professional Real Estate Investors v. Columbia Pictures Industries ("PRE")*.[79] Under the *PRE* two-prong test, it must be shown that: (1) the allegedly tortious litigation is "objectively baseless in the sense that no reasonable litigant could realistically expect success on the merits," and (2) the alleged tortfeasor has a subjective intent "to interfere directly with the business relationships of a competitor."[80]

2.   *The Applicability of* Noerr *to Business Tort Claims*

The lower courts have applied *Noerr* to immunize from antitrust liability a wide variety of activities involving attempts to influence public officials or obtain government action.[81] A number of courts also have applied *Noerr* to protect First Amendment petitioning of the government from non-antitrust claims brought under state and federal law, including civil rights claims under 42 U.S.C. §§ 1983 and 1985.[82] In the context of

---

77. *Id.* at 380-82. The city was held to be immune under Parker v. Brown, 317 U.S. 341 (1943).

78. 499 U.S. at 382-84.

79. 508 U.S. 49 (1993).

80. *Id.* at 60.

81. *See* Oberndorf v. Denver, 900 F.2d 1434 (10th Cir. 1990) (challenge to condemnation plan); Indep. Taxicab Drivers' Employees v. Greater Houston Transp. Co., 760 F.2d 607 (5th Cir. 1985) (obtaining exclusive concession at municipal airport); Metro Cable Co. v. CATV of Rockford, Inc., 516 F.2d 220 (7th Cir. 1975) (opposition to exclusive cable franchise); Sherman College of Straight Chiropractic v. Am. Chiropractic Ass'n, 654 F. Supp. 716 (N.D. Ga. 1986), *aff'd*, 813 F.2d 349 (11th Cir. 1987) (lobbying state boards to exclude graduates).

82. *See* Video Int'l Prod. v. Warner-Amex Cable Commc'ns, 858 F.2d 1075 (5th Cir. 1988); Gorman Towers v. Bogoslavsky, 626 F.2d 607, 614-15 (8th Cir. 1980); Stern v. U.S. Gypsum, Inc., 547 F.2d 1329, 1343 (7th Cir. 1977); Manistee Town Ctr. v. City of Glendale, 227 F.3d 1090 (9th Cir. 2000); Mariana v. Fisher, 338 F.3d 189 (3d Cir. 2004); Hirschfeld v.

business torts, the doctrine has been applied with some regularity to bar claims of interference with contractual or business relations.

One of the earliest and most often cited of such cases is *Sierra Club v. Butz*,[83] in which the Sierra Club sought declaratory and injunctive relief against a lumber company and others to prohibit logging activities in an area sought to be congressionally designated as a "wilderness area." The defendants filed a counterclaim alleging interference with business relations, and the Sierra Club moved to dismiss the counterclaim on the grounds that its actions constituted protected petitioning activities. The district court granted the motion, relying on *Noerr* and holding that when a party's "interference" consists of petitioning a governmental body to alter policy, the First Amendment shields it from liability.[84]

Sierra Club has been followed by a number of courts holding that the *Noerr-Pennington* doctrine is not limited to antitrust claims. For example, in *Video International Production v. Warner-Amex Cable Communications*,[85] a nonfranchised cable television company sued the City of Dallas and the sole local franchised cable television company, alleging that the defendants had attempted to use the city's zoning ordinances to drive the plaintiff out of business. The jury found in favor of the plaintiff on its antitrust, civil rights and tortious interference claims.[86] Affirming the district court's determination that the *Noerr-Pennington* doctrine shielded the defendant television company from liability, the Fifth Circuit held that *Noerr* is applicable to claims of tortious interference: "There is simply no reason that a common-law tort doctrine can any more permissibly abridge or chill the constitutional right of petition than can a statutory claim such as antitrust."[87]

Similarly, in *South Dakota v. Kansas City Southern Industries*,[88] the Eighth Circuit applied *Noerr* to reverse a jury verdict in an action

---

Spanakos, 104 F.3d 16 (2d Cir. 1997); Chantilly Farms, Inc. v. W. Pikeland Township, No. 00-3903, 2001 U.S. Dist. LEXIS 3328 (E.D. Pa. 2001); Forces Action Project v. Cal., No. C 99-0607 MJJ, 2000 WL 20977 (N.D. Cal. 2000).

83. 349 F. Supp. 934 (N.D. Cal. 1972).
84. *Id.* at 938.
85. 858 F.2d 1075 (5th Cir. 1988).
86. *Id.* at 1080.
87. *Id.* at 1084.
88. 880 F.2d 40 (8th Cir. 1989).

brought by the state of South Dakota alleging Sherman Act violations and interference with contractual relations based on a railroad's opposition to a pipeline project. Noting that section 767(e) of the Restatement (Second) of Torts provides that one of the factors to be considered when determining whether interference with contractual relations is "improper" is the social interest in protecting the defendant's freedom of action, the court held that section 767(e) creates a zone of privileged activities, one of which involves the First Amendment right to petition the government.[89]

Also following *Sierra Club*, the California Supreme Court, in *Pacific Gas & Electric Co. v. Bear Stearns & Co.*,[90] held that *Noerr* may shield those who do not bring a judicial proceeding but induce others to do so. In that case, an investment bank induced a water agency to initiate judicial proceedings to terminate a contract it had with an electricity provider. The electricity provider responded by suing the investment bank for intentional interference with contractual relations and intentional interference with prospective economic advantage. The court relied on *Sierra Club* (as well on its own line of decisions on malicious prosecution) to conclude that a person need not be a litigant to be afforded *Noerr* protection.[91]

Other courts have applied *Noerr* analysis to tort and non-antitrust statutory claims without reference to *Sierra Club*. For example, in *Wright v. DeArmond*,[92] the Seventh Circuit held that the position taken by city commissioners in negotiating a consent decree in an action under the federal Voting Rights Act was analogous to "sham" litigation unprotected by the First Amendment. The court observed that the consent decree benefited the commissioners personally, and thus declined to apply *Noerr* to immunize the commissioners from liability under state conflict of interest laws. The court found that the city had no possibility of prevailing in the action, and that the commissioners had used their leverage in settlement negotiations to obtain personal benefits

---

89. *Id.* at 50-51.
90. 791 P.2d 587 (Cal. 1990).
91. *See id.* at 595-98. *But see* Dr. Reddy's Labs., Ltd. v. aaiPharma, Inc., No. 01 Civ. 10102 (LAP), 2002 U.S. Dist. LEXIS 17287 (S.D.N.Y. 2002) (denying *Noerr* immunity to a party other than the one who petitioned the government).
92. 977 F.2d 339 (7th Cir. 1992).

such as job placement, the opportunity to set their own salaries, and insulation from political fallout.

In *Eaton v. Newport Board of Education*,[93] the Sixth Circuit applied *Noerr* to an action arising out of public lobbying by a teachers' union, during which a school principal was labeled a "racist." The principal ultimately was dismissed, and thereafter brought suit under the civil rights laws. Vacating a judgment in favor of the principal, the court held that, under *Noerr*, "liability may not be assessed under [42 U.S.C.] § 1983 or the antitrust laws except in very limited circumstances, for actions taken when petitioning authorities to take official action, regardless of the motives of the petitioners, even where the petitioning activity has the intent or effect of depriving another of property interests."[94]

In *Oregon Natural Resources Council v. Mohla*,[95] the Ninth Circuit applied *Noerr* to an alleged abuse of judicial proceedings. A contractor sued the United States and a competing contractor to enjoin logging activities on a tract of land located in a national forest. The defendant contractor counterclaimed, alleging abuse of administrative and judicial process and interference with business relations arising out of the plaintiff's attempts to enjoin its business activities. The Ninth Circuit held that *Noerr* barred the counterclaim, and that the mere allegation that the plaintiff had knowingly made misrepresentations to the court was insufficient to invoke the "sham" exception.[96]

The doctrine of res judicata has barred business tort claims arising out of the same facts as antitrust claims previously rejected under the *Noerr* doctrine. In *Hufsmith v. Weaver*,[97] a lawsuit arising out of the defendants' opposition to the issuance of certain tax-exempt industrial revenue bonds, the Eighth Circuit held that its judgment in a prior interlocutory appeal that *Noerr* barred the plaintiff's Sherman Act claim

---

93. 975 F.2d 293 (6th Cir. 1992).
94. *Id.* at 298.
95. 944 F.2d 531 (9th Cir. 1991).
96. *Id.* at 536; *see also* Village Supermarket v. Mayfair Supermarkets, 634 A.2d 1381 (N.J. Super. 1993) (*Noerr* immunized a competitor from liability for interference with contractual and prospective economic advantage in an action arising out of the competitor's opposition to a store owner's request for a zoning variance).
97. 817 F.2d 455 (8th Cir. 1987).

also barred the plaintiff's tortious interference claim under the doctrine of res judicata.[98] The court noted that it had "long indicated" that *Noerr* may be extended beyond the area of antitrust.[99]

Noerr also has been invoked to immunize a party from claims arising from the filing of an administrative complaint against a competitor.[100] In *Cheminor Drugs, Ltd. v. Ethyl Corp.*,[101] an American manufacturer of bulk ibuprofen successfully brought an antidumping action in the Department of Commerce and U.S. Court of International Trade (ITC) against an Indian competitor. The competitor responded by filing suit against the American manufacturer with claims that included tortious interference with contract, tortious interference with prospective economic advantage, and unfair competition. In its motion for summary judgment, the Indian manufacturer asserted that its competitor had made false statements to the ITC and had brought the administrative action solely for anticompetitive purposes. The Third Circuit held that "the same First Amendment principles on which *Noerr-Pennington* immunity is based apply to the [state] tort claims."[102]

It remains uncertain to what extent activities related to litigation – though not actually a part of the litigation – are immunized by *Noerr*. There is some controversy, for example, over whether threats of

---

98. *See id.* at 460-61.
99. *Id.* at 458.
100. *See* Bayou Fleet, Inc. v. Alexander, 234 F.3d 852, 861-63 (5th Cir. 2000) (lobbying of local councilmember and agency deemed protected); Eurotech, Inc. v. Cosmos European Travels Aktiengesellschaft, 189 F. Supp. 2d 385, 391-95 (E.D. Va. 2002) (applying *Noerr* protection to institution of a WIPO infringement proceeding).
101. 168 F.3d 119 (3d Cir. 1999).
102. *Id.* at 128; *see also* Bristol-Myers Squibb Co. v. IVAX Corp., 77 F. Supp. 2d 606, 608-09 (D. N.J. 2000) In that case a drug manufacturer sued its competitors for patent infringement, who in turn counterclaimed for, inter alia, unfair competition for the manner in which the plaintiff had obtained its patents from the government. Although the New Jersey Supreme Court had not addressed the issue of whether *Noerr* applied to the state law tort claim of unfair competition, the court relied on the Third Circuit's decision in *Cheminor* to hold that "state law tort claims must be dismissed when they are grounded upon allegations of injury that arise from government action." *Id.* at 616.

litigation between private parties are within *Noerr*'s ambit.[103] As to non-judicial acts related to litigation, some courts have adopted the standard articulated in *Coral States Marketing, Inv. v. Hunt*[104] that *Noerr* shields acts that are "reasonably and normally attendant upon protected litigation."[105] In *Alexander Binzel Corp. v. Nu-Tecsys Corp.*,[106] for example, a district court held that non-judicial acts attendant to a lawsuit, such as the issuing of public statements, are immunized by the *Noerr* doctrine only to the extent they constitute assertions within "the legal and factual bases of the lawsuit."[107] In that case, a manufacturer of welding equipment brought suit against a corporation in the same industry asserting multiple claims, including trademark infringement, unfair competition and violations of the Lanham Act. The defendant counterclaimed, asserting that the plaintiff had engaged in unfair competition when it distributed a letter at a trade show stating that the defendant's products were "counterfeit." The plaintiff argued that the *Noerr* doctrine immunized it from any liability arising from distribution of the letter because "it was issued as publicity incidental to the lawsuit."[108] The court concluded that because "a jury could reasonably conclude that the counterfeit statement was literally false" and the counterfeit issue was not raised at trial, the statement was beyond the scope of "the legal and factual bases of the suit" and thus unprotected by *Noerr*.[109]

The courts have been less willing to apply *Noerr* in other contexts. In *IBP Confidential Business Documents Litigation*,[110] the Eight Circuit

---

103. *Compare* Globetrotter Software, Inc. v. Elan Computer Group, Inc., 362 F.3d 1367 (Fed. Cir. 2004) (threat of litigation conferred *Noerr* immunity); *with* Republic Tobacco v. N. Atl. Trading Co., No. 98 C 4011, 1999 WL 1270681 *2 n.2 (N.D. Ill. 1999) (threats of litigation deemed unprotected by *Noerr* as such threats are between private parties, and not a governmental agency). *see also* Cardtoons v. Major League Baseball Players Assoc., 208 F.3d 885 (10th Cir. 2000) (prelitigation threats unprotected by the First Amendment).
104. 694 F.2d 1358 (5th Cir. 1983).
105. *Id.* at 1367.
106. No. 91 C 2092, 2000 WL 310304 (N.D. Ill. 2000).
107. *Id.* at *3-*4.
108. *Id.*
109. *Id.* at *5.
110. 755 F.2d 1300 (8th Cir. 1985).

addressed the argument that *Noerr* should be available to shield a former employer accused of sending a letter to a congressional subcommittee in which the defendant in essence called the plaintiff a liar and a thief.[111] Noting that the First Amendment does not afford absolute immunity from liability for defamatory speech, the court held that *Noerr* is inapplicable to tort actions alleging defamation.[112] Expressing the view that the "actual malice" standard articulated in *New York Times v. Sullivan*[113] provides the "necessary insulation" for the First Amendment interests at stake,[114] the court declined to follow *Webb v. Fury*.[115] In that case, the Supreme Court of Appeals of West Virginia, relying on *Noerr*, extended absolute immunity from defamation liability to all communications made in the course of petitioning the government, irrespective of whether such communication occurred in the confines of an actual proceeding. While conceding that the courts had extended *Noerr* beyond the antitrust context to a limited extent, the Eighth Circuit concluded that *Webb* overstated the reach of the doctrine.[116]

The *IBP* court explained that while *Noerr* prohibits courts from awarding compensation for the consequences of protected activity, it carves out exceptions. One such exception is for activities which, although ostensibly directed toward influencing government action, actually are no more than attempts to harm another (the so-called "sham exception"). Another exception is for those activities that are not immune even if undertaken in a genuine attempt to influence government action, such as violence and other illegal acts.[117] The court then concluded that, because the First Amendment does not afford absolute protection for defamatory speech under the *New York Times* rule, *Noerr* does not preclude liability for damages resulting from defamatory statements made in the course of petitioning the government.[118] The court based its conclusion on the policy of accommodating the state's legitimate interest in redressing wrongful injury to reputation, "even

---

111. *Id.* at 1310-14.
112. *Id.* at 1313-14.
113. 376 U.S. 254 (1964).
114. *IBP Confidential Business Documents Litig.*, 755 F.2d at 1315.
115. 282 S.E.2d 28 (W. Va. 1981).
116. *IBP Confidential Business Documents Litig.*, 755 F.2d at 1312.
117. *Id.* at 1313.
118. *Id.* at 1313-14.

when that injury is inflicted during the course of genuine petitioning activity."[119]

Similarly, in *Florida Fern Growers Association, Inc. v. Concerned Citizens of Putnam County*,[120] a Florida court declined to apply *Noerr* to claims of interference with business relations arising out of the filing of petitions with a water management district challenging the issuance of water use permits to fern growers. The court noted that the Florida Supreme Court had rejected *Sierra Club's* application of *Noerr* to tort claims,[121] finding that Florida law already provides protection for the First Amendment right to petition the government.[122] Acknowledging that Florida law recognizes a conditional privilege for statements of a citizen to a government authority, and that this qualified privilege "carries with it the 'obligation to employ means that are not improper,'" the court held that factual questions remained as to whether *Noerr* had been exceeded.[123]

There also is authority for the proposition that *Noerr* does not extend immunity to alleged in fraud or misrepresentation. In *In re American Continental Corp./Lincoln Savings & Loan Securities Litigation*,[124] in which the defendant was charged with knowingly making misrepresentations to federal regulators, the district court held that *Noerr* is unavailable to immunize defendants against claims of fraud.[125] The court reasoned that a rule excusing misrepresentations in the area of banking and securities, in which the truth of the information conveyed is fundamentally at issue, would undermine the fabric of those systems.[126]

Courts have continued to apply the "sham" exception to the *Noerr* doctrine in the business tort context. Courts hearing business tort claims consistently apply the *PRE* test,[127] and continue to emphasize that the

---

119. *Id.* at 1314.
120. 616 So. 2d 562 (Fla. App. 1993).
121. *See* Londono v. Turkey Creek, 609 So. 2d 14 (Fla. 1992).
122. 616 So. 2d at 565.
123. *Id.* at 569.
124. 794 F. Supp. 1424 (D. Ariz. 1992).
125. *Id.* at 1448.
126. *Id.*
127. *See* Bayou Fleet, Inc. v. Alexander, 234 F.3d 852 (5th Cir. 2000); Eurotech, Inc. v. Cosmos European Travels Aktiengesellschaft, 189 F.

"objectively baseless" standard must be satisfied before subjective intent is properly considered.[128] Some courts have insisted that "objectively baseless" is a high standard to meet.[129]

At least one circuit has been unwilling to extend the *Noerr* doctrine beyond Sherman Act claims on the grounds that such immunity can only be derived from the First Amendment. In *Cardtoons v. Major League Baseball Players Ass'n*,[130] the Tenth Circuit explained that *Noerr* immunity is premised on the two independent rationales: the Supreme Court's interpretation of the Sherman Act and the First Amendment right to petition.[131] Application of *Noerr* defenses to claims not brought under the Sherman Act necessarily lacks the first prong which may be inappropriate,[132] and can lead to adjudicative inconsistencies.[133] Therefore, under the Tenth Circuit's reasoning, non-Sherman Act

---

Supp. 2d 385 (E.D. Va. 2002); Agfa Corp. v. United Mktg. Group, Inc., No. 02 Civ. 8468 (LAP), 2003 U.S. Dist. LEXIS 11760 (S.D.N.Y. 2003). *But see* Wawa, Inc. v. Alexander J. Litwornia & Assocs., 817 A.2d 543, 548 (Pa. Super. 2003) (concluding that the proliferation of "false information aimed at interfering directly with the business relations of a competitor" is the type of conduct that "translates into a 'sham' of inaccurate information communicated to incite the public").

128. IGEN Int'l, Inc. v. Roche Diagnostics GMBH, 335 F.3d 303, 312 (4th Cir. 2003) ("[E]ven litigation that is deceitful, underhanded, or morally wrong will not defeat immunity unless it satisfies the objective baseless requirement.").

129. Matsushita Elecs. Corp. v. Loral Corp., 974 F. Supp. 345, 355-56 (S.D.N.Y. 1997) (Even though the plaintiff was granted summary judgment in the complained-of judicial proceeding, that does not translate into proof that "no reasonable litigant could reasonably expect success on the merits" under the circumstances at bar.).

130. 208 F.3d 885 (10th Cir. 2000).

131. *See id.* at 888-89 (The court also noted that the Supreme Court has only applied the *Noerr* doctrine to antitrust claims.).

132. *See id.* at 809 ("Antitrust cases that grant *Noerr* immunity do so based upon *both* the Sherman Act and the right to petition. These precedents, founded in part upon a construction of the Sherman Act, are not completely interchangeable with cases based solely upon the right to petition.").

133. *See id.* at 889 n.4 (distinguishing *PRE* from Bill Johnson's Restaurants Inc. v. NLRB, 461 U.S. 731 (1983), on the grounds that the former is an antitrust case while the latter is not.).

defenses based on petitioning activity are to be evaluated solely on the basis of First Amendment protection.[134] Several lower courts have been persuaded by this reasoning.[135]

D. The Intracorporate Conspiracy Rule

In *Copperweld Corp. v. Independence Tube Corp.*,[136] the Supreme Court held, as a matter of law, that the coordinated activities of a corporation and its parent, subsidiary, or affiliate, or their respective officers, employees and agents, do not constitute an unlawful conspiracy within the meaning of section 1 of the Sherman Act.[137] The theory underlying the so-called "*Copperweld* rule" is that, by virtue of their relationship, corporations under common control, as well as their

---

134. *See id.* at 889 ("To the extent that Supreme Court precedent can be read to extend *Noerr* outside of the antitrust context, it does so solely on the basis of the right to petition."); *see also* We, Inc. v. City of Philadelphia, 174 F.3d 322, 327 (3d Cir. 1999) ("[T]he purpose of *Noerr-Pennington* as applied in areas outside the antitrust field is the right to petition.").

135. *See* Porsche Cars No. Am., Inc. v. Lloyd Design Corp., No. 1:99-CV-1560A-JEC, 2002 U.S. Dist LEXIS 9612 *129-*131 (N.D. Ga. 2002) (In light of the absence of Eleventh Circuit authority on whether *Noerr* applies to pre-litigation communication between private parties, the court is persuade by the Tenth Circuit's reasoning.); DIRECTV, Inc. v. Cavanaugh, No. 03-60001, 2003 U.S. Dist. LEXIS 24561 *32-*36 (E.D. Mich. 2003) (Declining to apply *Noerr* outside of the antitrust context, in light of *Cardtoons*, and employing instead a First Amendment inquiry); *see also* Unique Coupons, Inc. v. Northfield Corp., 2000 WL 631324 *2-*3 (N.D. Ill. 2000) (noting the confusion within the case law, in light of *Cardtoons*, of whether the *Noerr* doctrine extends to pre-litigation publicity in the non-antitrust context); A Fisherman's Best, Inc. v. Recreational Fishing Alliance, 310 F.3d 183 (4th Cir. 2002) (declining to determine whether *Noerr* extends to non-antitrust claims and instead affirming the lower court's determination on First Amendment grounds). *But see* Suburban Restoration Co. v. ACMAT Corp., 700 F.2d 98, 101 (2d Cir. 1983) (noting that in the past *Noerr* has been described as a First Amendment doctrine, and thus potentially applicable to statutory and state law claims).

136. 467 U.S. 752 (1984); *see also* Guzowski v. Hartman, 969 F.2d 211 (6th Cir. 1992); Century Oil Tool v. Prod. Specialties, 737 F.2d 1316 (5th Cir. 1984).

137. 15 U.S.C. § 1.

representatives, have a unity of interest that negates the plurality of actors required for a section 1 conspiracy.[138]	Stated another way, because such coordinated action does not involve the "sudden joining of economic resources that had previously served different interests,"[139] the concerted action necessary for section 1 liability is lacking.

Business tort defendants have invoked the *Copperweld* rule with varying degrees of success. For example, in *Metropolitan Life Insurance Co. v. La Mansion Hotels & Resorts, Ltd.*,[140] a Texas appellate court held:

> Since we are not here dealing with an alleged violation of the Sherman Act, the holding [in *Copperweld*] concerning the meaning of that statute is irrelevant. We are here concerned with an alleged conspiracy under common law theories. Under the common law, a parent corporation and its subsidiary are separate legal entities.[141]

Applying similar reasoning to RICO claims, the Seventh Circuit in *Ashland Oil, Inc. v. Arnett*[142] observed:

> Since a subsidiary and its parent theoretically have a community of interest, a conspiracy "in restraint of trade" between them poses no threat to the goals of antitrust law – protecting competition. In contrast, intracorporate conspiracies do threaten RICO's goals of preventing the infiltration of legitimate businesses by racketeers and separating racketeers from their profits.[143]

---

138. *Copperweld*, 467 U.S. at 769. The courts recognize an exception when the corporate officer, employee or agent is shown to have an "independent personal stake" in the subject matter of the alleged conspiracy. St. Joseph's Hosp. v. Hosp. Corp. of Am., 795 F.2d 948, 956 (11th Cir. 1986).
139. *Copperweld*, 467 U.S. at 771.
140. 762 S.W.2d 646 (Tex. App. 1988).
141. *Id.* at 652. *But see* Block v. Alpharma, Inc., No. Civ. A. 302-CV-1077, 2004 WL 555480 (N.D. Tex. 2004) (predicting that the Texas Supreme Court will extend *Copperweld* principles to intracorporate civil conspiracy claims).
142. 875 F.2d 1271 (7th Cir. 1989); *see also* U.A.W. v. Cardwell Mfg. Co., 416 F. Supp. 1267 (D. Kan. 1976).
143. *Ashland Oil*, 875 F.2d at 1281; *see also* Haroco, Inc. v. Am. Nat'l Bank & Trust Co. of Chicago, 747 F.2d 384 (7th Cir. 1984), *aff'd*, 473 U.S. 606 (1985).

Other courts have similarly limited the *Copperweld* rule to the antitrust context.[144]

Some courts, however, have applied the *Copperweld* rationale to bar non-antitrust claims.[145] For example, in *Pizza Management, Inc. v. Pizza Hut, Inc.*,[146] a federal district court declined to follow *Metropolitan Life*

---

144. *See* Borden, Inc. v. Spoor Behrins Campbell & Young, Inc., 828 F. Supp. 216, 223 (S.D.N.Y. 1993) (refusing to extend *Copperweld* to securities fraud, RICO and common law conspiracies); Stamp v. Inamed Corp., 777 F. Supp. 623, 628-29 (N.D. Ill. 1991) (declining to follow the line of cases that have applied *Copperweld* to civil conspiracies); Ashlar Fin. Servs. Corp. v. Sterling Finance Co., No. 3:00cv2814-AH, 2002 U.S. Dist. LEXIS 2086, *19-*20 (N.D. Tex. 2002) (refusing to apply *Copperweld* beyond the antitrust context); Ashlar Fin. Servs. Corp. v. Sterling Fin. Co., No. 3:00CV2814-AH, 2002 U.S. Dist. LEXIS 2086, *19-*20 (N.D. Tex. 2002) (same); Ne. Solite Corp. v. Unicon Concrete, LLC, No. 1:98CV00872, 1999 U.S. Dist. LEXIS 9762, *7-*9 (M.D.N.C. 1999) (same); Shared Commc'ns Servs. of 1800-80 JFK Boulevard Inc. v. Bell Atl. Props. Inc., 692 A.2d 570, 572-73 (Pa. App. 1997) (same); Seeco, Inc. v. Hales, 22 Sw.3d 157, 169-70 (Ark. 2000) (same); Outdoor Techs. Inc. v. Allfirst Fin. Inc., No. 99C-09-151-WTQ, 2000 Del. Super. LEXIS 16, *17-*18 (Del. App. 2000) (same); Grizzle v. Tex. Commerce Bank, N.A., 38 Sw.3d 265 (Tex. App. 2001) (same); Nilavar v. Mercy Health Sys., 142 F. Supp. 2d 859, 888-89 (S.D. Ohio 2000) (refusing to apply *Copperweld* beyond the antitrust context because it "finds no indication that Ohio courts would adopt the holding in *Copperweld* for purposes of a civil conspiracy claim").

145. *See, e.g.*, SI Handling Sys., Inc. v. Heisley, 658 F. Supp. 362 (E.D. Pa. 1986) (parent owns trade secret acquired by subsidiary); Laxalt v. McClatchy, 622 F. Supp. 737 (D. Nev. 1985) (wholly owned subsidiaries have no separate legal existence for civil conspiracy claims); *In re* Ray Dobbins Lincoln-Mercury, Inc., 604 F. Supp. 203 (W.D. Va. 1984) (*Copperweld* logic controls conspiracy claim under Virginia statute despite any distinction between Sherman Act and state statute), *aff'd*, 813 F.2d 402 (4th Cir. 1986); Ford Motor Co. v. Lyons, 405 Nw.2d 354 (Wis. App. 1987) (*Copperweld* rule applies to state statutory action for conspiracy to injure another's reputation, trade, business or profession, because the economic policy underlying this action is similar to the Sherman Act); *In re* Asbestos Litig., 509 A.2d 1116 (Del. Super. Ct. 1986) (parent corporation incapable of conspiring with its subsidiary for purposes of civil conspiracy), *aff'd*, 525 A.2d 146 (Del. 1987).

146. 737 F. Supp. 1154, 1165-66 (D. Kan. 1990).

and *Ashland*, concluding that *Copperweld* should be extended to preclude a finding of a civil conspiracy between a parent and its subsidiary to breach a contract. A similar result was reached in *American Medical International, Inc. v. Guirintano*,[147] in which a Texas appellate court concluded that *Copperweld* bars not only claims of intracorporate civil conspiracy, but also claims of tortious interference by a parent corporation with the contracts of its subsidiary.[148]

The theory of these cases is that parent and subsidiary corporations are so closely aligned that the plurality of actors necessary to a claim of conspiracy or interference is not present.[149] Several courts have employed similar reasoning to conclude that the *Copperweld* rule may shield business tort defendants.[150]

E. Discovery Issues

Business tort plaintiffs also have invoked the aid of antitrust principles in seeking broad discovery. Because the focus of the antitrust laws is on the effect of challenged conduct on competition, rather than on

---

147. 821 S.W.2d 331 (Tex. App. 1991).
148. *Id.* at 335-37.
149. *See, e.g.*, *Pizza Management*, 737 F. Supp. at 1165-66; *Am. Med.*, 821 S.W.2d at 336-37.
150. *See* Davidson & Schaaff, Inc. v. Liberty Nat'l Fire Ins. Co., 69 F.3d 868, 871 (8th Cir. 1995) (applying *Copperweld* outside of the antitrust context); Government Guarantee Fund of the Republic of Finland v. Hyatt Corp., 955 F. Supp. 441, 456-58 (V.I. 1997) (extending *Copperweld* to protect common law intracorporate civil conspiracy defendants); Trau-Med of Am., Inc. v. Allstate Ins. Co., 71 S.W.3d 691, 702-04 (Tenn. 2002) (same); Atl. Richfield Co. v. Misty Prods., Inc., 820 S.W.2d 414, 420-21 (Tex. App. 1991) (same); Siegel Transfer, Inc. v. Carrier Express, Inc., 856 F. Supp. 990, 1009 (E.D. Pa. 1994) ("It is well-settled that a corporation cannot conspire with its subsidiaries, its agents or its employees for the same reason the *Copperweld* Court found such a conspiracy to be legally impossible in the antitrust context."); First Nat'l Bank of Louisville v. Lustig, 809 F. Supp. 444, 448 (E.D. La. 1992) (following *Pizza Management*); *see also In re* ContiCommodity Servs., Inc., Securities Litig., 733 F. Supp. 1555, 1568 (N.D. Ill. 1990) (acknowledging the possibility that *Copperweld* may extend to common law conspiracy claims).

the individual plaintiff,[151] the scope of discovery in antitrust cases can be quite broad.[152] For example, the courts have held that a plaintiff alleging an anticompetitive course of conduct by the defendant may be entitled to discovery antedating the plaintiff's damages period,[153] and even the plaintiff's entry into the market.[154] By the same token, allegations of a scheme or conspiracy to fix prices or monopolize a market may afford broader discovery than would be available under state tort law.[155] Of

---

151. *See infra* text accompanying notes 165-70.
152. *See, e.g.*, United States v. Dentsply Int'l , Inc., No. 99-5MMS, 2000 U.S. Dist. LEXIS 6925, at *17 (D. Del. 2000) (agreeing with *Kellam Energy*, that broad discovery should be allowed in antitrust cases); Callahan v. A.E.V., 947 F. Supp. 175, 179 (W.D. Pa. 1996) (noting that discovery in antitrust cases is necessarily broad because the allegations involve improper business conduct); Columbia Steel Casting Co. v. Portland Gen. Elec. Co., No. 90-52Y-FR, 1992 U.S. Dist. LEXIS 3036, at *4 (D. Or. 1992) (agreeing with *Reidel* that discovery in antitrust cases is liberally granted); Riedel Int'l , Inc. v. St. Helens Inv., Inc., 633 F. Supp. 117, 119 (D. Or. 1985); Kellam Energy, Inc. v. Duncan, 616 F. Supp. 215, 217 (D. Del. 1985); United States v. IBM, 83 F.R.D. 97 (S.D.N.Y. 1979). *Cf.* Concord Boat Corp. v. Brunswick Corp., 169 F.R.D. 44, 50-51 (S.D.N.Y. 1996) (dealing with a non-party's motion for an order to quash a subpoena, and holding that certain discovery requests in an antitrust context can be too broad and thus not allowable).
153. *See, e.g.*, Quadrozzi v. City of N.Y., 127 F.R.D. 63, 75 (S.D.N.Y. 1989); Mar. Cinema Serv. Corp. v. Movies En Route, Inc., 60 F.R.D. 587, 591 (S.D.N.Y. 1973).
154. *See, e.g.*, Cont'l Ore Co. v. Union Carbide & Carbon Corp., 370 U.S. 690, 699 (1962); FTC v. Cement Inst., 333 U.S. 683, 703-05 (1948); Whittaker Corp. v. Execuair Corp., 736 F.2d 1341, 1347 (9th Cir. 1984); Reid Bros. Logging Co. v. Ketchikan Pulp Co., 699 F.2d 1292, 1305 (9th Cir. 1983); *Kellam Energy*, 616 F. Supp. at 217-18; Am. Tobacco Co. v. United States, 147 F.2d 93, 106 (6th Cir. 1944), *aff'd*, 328 U.S. 781 (1946).
155. *See, e.g.*, Estate of Le Baron v. Rohm & Haas Co., 441 F.2d 575, 577-78 (9th Cir. 1971) (documents revealing profit margins of conspirators discoverable); *Dentsply Int'l*, 2000 U.S. Dist. LEXIS 6925, at *17 (explaining that geography does not limit discovery); *In re* Market-Makers Antitrust Litig., 169 F.R.D. 493, 530 (S.D.N.Y. 1996) (explaining that because the motion to certify a class was granted, the motion to compel discovery also was granted, and that discovery could include civil investigative demands because they might lead to admissible evidence); *Kellam Energy*, 616 F. Supp. 219 (discovery not limited to local market in

course, before asserting an antitrust claim, a potential plaintiff should consider the burdens associated with such discovery, and should be prepared to respond in kind to discovery requests propounded by the defendant.

Although the scope of discovery related to antitrust claims may be broad, it should be noted that some state unfair competition statutes also may support broad discovery. This is generally due to the breadth of activities that the underlying statutes seek to prohibit. A good example are cases brought under section 17200 of the California Business and Professions Code. That statute generally prohibits "any unlawful, unfair or fraudulent business act or practice."[156] Although there is only scant case law discussing discovery under section 17200, as one author put it, "by claiming that [a] defendant has engaged in wrongful business 'practices,' plaintiffs raise issues in which a defendant's dealing with others may become discoverable."[157]

F.   Evidentiary Issues

1.   *Co-conspirator Hearsay*

A plaintiff with a viable antitrust claim may be able to introduce evidence that might be inadmissible in a suit alleging only business torts. Under the "co-conspirator hearsay rule," a plaintiff may offer into evidence statements by alleged co-conspirators of the defendant that were made during the course and in furtherance of the conspiracy.[158] In the federal courts, the judge decides whether such evidence falls within this exception, and in making that determination is not bound by the

---

which parties competed); *In re* Shopping Carts Antitrust Litig., 95 F.R.D. 299, 308-09 (S.D.N.Y. 1982) (revenue, profit and loss information discoverable); *In re* Folding Carton Antitrust Litig., 76 F.R.D. 420, 426-27 (N.D. Ill. 1977) (copies of defendants' annual reports, balance sheets, profit and loss statements, intra-company financial reports and other documents showing annual pre-tax revenue and profits discoverable).

156. CAL. BUS. & PROF. CODE § 17200.

157. WILLIAM L. STERN, BUS. & PROF. C. § 17200 PRACTICE ¶ 7:177 (2004); *see also* Cisneros v. U.D. Registry, Inc., 39 Cal. App. 4th 548, 564 (Cal. Ct. App., 1995)

158. FED. R. EVID. 801(d)(2)(E); *see also* Bourjaily v. United States, 483 U.S. 171, 183 (1987); United States v. Alameh, 341 F.3d 167, 176-177 (2d Cir. 2003); United States v. Tom, 330 F.3d 83, 94 (1st Cir. 2003).

rules of evidence, except the rules governing privileges.[159] This exception to the hearsay rule has been invoked in a variety of situations involving the joinder of antitrust and business tort claims.[160]

2. *Subjective Intent Evidence*

Conversely, the joinder of business tort claims with claims under the antitrust laws may enable a plaintiff to introduce evidence regarding the defendant's subjective intent that otherwise might be deemed inadmissible or insufficient to sustain the antitrust claims.

This issue frequently arises in predatory pricing cases, which commonly are brought under section 2 of the Sherman Act[161] and comparable provisions of state antitrust law.[162] When determining whether a defendant's low prices constitute an unlawful attempt to monopolize, the courts generally refuse to consider evidence of the defendant's subjective intent to injure its competitors through price-cutting, on the theory that the antitrust laws are concerned with injury to competition, not individual competitors,[163] and encourage vigorous

---

159. *Bourjaily*, 483 U.S. at 176-81.

160. *See, e.g.*, Rossi v. Standard Roofing, 156 F.3d 452, 457, 468 n.11 (3d Cir. 1998) (antitrust and tortious interference claims); Alvord-Polk v. F. Schumacher & Co., 37 F.3d 996, 999, 1005 n.6 (3d Cir. 1994) (antitrust and tortious interference claims); Big Apple BMW, Inc. v. BMW of No. Am., Inc., 974 F.2d 1358, 1373-74, 1382 (3d Cir. 1992) (antitrust and tortious interference claims),; E.W. French & Sons, Inc. v. Gen. Portland, Inc., 885 F.2d 1392, 1394 (9th Cir. 1989) (antitrust, unfair competition and tortious interference claims); *In re* Dual-Deck Video Cassette Recorder Antitrust Litig., 1990-2 Trade Cas. ¶ 69,141, at 64,250, 64,252-54 (D. Ariz. 1990) (antitrust and tortious interference claims); Rockwell Graphic Sys., Inc. v. DEV Indus., Inc., No. 84 C 6746, 1993 U.S. Dist. LEXIS 12709 (N.D. Ill. Sept. 10, 1993) (RICO, trade secret and unfair competition claims).

161. 15 U.S.C. § 2.

162. *See generally* ABA SECTION OF ANTITRUST LAW, STATE ANTITRUST PRACTICE AND STATUTES (3d ed. 2004).

163. *See, e.g.*, Spectrum Sports, Inc. v. McQuillan, 506 U.S. 447, 458 (1993) (explaining that "the purpose of the [Sherman Act] is not to protect businesses from the working of the market"); Conwood Co., L.P. v. U.S. Tobacco Co., 290 F.3d 768, 789 (6th Cir. 2002); Clorox Co. v. Sterling Winthrop, Inc., 117 F.3d 50, 57 (2d Cir. 1997); Int'l Travel Arrangers v.

competition and low prices for consumers.[164]   The Seventh Circuit
recently summarized the rationale underlying the exclusion of subjective
intent evidence from predatory pricing analysis as follows:

> Firms "intend" to do all the business they can, to crush their rivals if
> they can.   "'[I]ntent to harm' without more offers too vague a
> standard in a world where executives may think no further than 'Let's
> get more business.'"   Rivalry is harsh, and consumers gain the most
> when firms slash costs to the bone and pare price down to cost, all in
> pursuit of more business.   Few firms cut price unaware of what they
> are doing; price reductions are carried out in pursuit of sales, at
> others' expense.   Entrepreneurs who work hardest to cut their prices
> will do the most damage to their rivals, and they will see good in it.
> You cannot be a sensible business executive without understanding
> the link among prices, your firm's success, and other firms' distress.
> If courts use the vigorous, nasty pursuit of sales as evidence of a
> forbidden "intent," they run the risk of penalizing the motive forces
> of competition.[165]

NWA, Inc., 991 F.2d 1389, 1394-96 (8th Cir. 1993); Morgan v. Ponder,
892 F.2d 1355, 1359-68 (8th Cir. 1989); A.A. Poultry Farms, Inc. v. Rose
Acre Farms, Inc., 881 F.2d 1396, 1401-02 (7th Cir. 1989); Adjusters
Replace-A-Car, Inc. v. Agency Rent-A-Car, Inc., 735 F.2d 884, 890 (5th
Cir. 1984); Barry Wright Corp. v. ITT Grinnell Corp., 724 F.2d 227, 232
(1st Cir. 1983); Ne. Tel. Co. v. Am. Tel. & Tel. Co., 651 F.2d 76, 88 (2d
Cir. 1981); Spectators' Commc'n Network, Inc. v. Anheuser-Busch Inc.,
No. 3:95-CV-2390-P, 1998 U.S. Dist. LEXIS 19868, at *47-*48 (N.D.
Tex. 1998); Caller-Times Pbl'g Co. v. Triad Commc'ns, Inc., 826 S.W.2d
576, 587 (Tex. 1992); Ashkanazy v. I. Rokeach & Sons, Inc., 757 F. Supp.
1527, 1538 (N.D. Ill. 1991) (echoing *A.A. Poultry Farms* that with regard
to antitrust claims the concern is injury to competition). *But see* Anchor
Mfg. v. Rule Indus., 7 F.3d 986, 993-96 (11th Cir. 1993); McGahee v. N.
Propane Gas Co., 858 F.2d 1487, 1503-04 (11th Cir. 1989).

164. *See, e.g.*, Ball Mem'l Hosp., Inc. v. Mut. Hosp. Ins., Inc., 784 F.2d 1325,
1338 (7th Cir. 1986) ("[T]he deeper the injury to rivals, the greater
potential benefit.   These injuries to rivals are byproducts of vigorous
competition, and the antitrust laws are not balm for rivals' wounds.   The
antitrust laws are for the benefit of competition, not competitors.").

165. *A.A. Poultry Farms*, 881 F.2d at 1401-02 (citations omitted; quoting Barry
Wright Corp. v. ITT Grinnell Corp., 724 F.2d 227, 232 (1st Cir. 1983));
accord Caller-Times, 826 S.W.2d at 587 ("The danger of evidence of
subjective intent is that '[p]redatory pricing is difficult to distinguish from

Business tort law, on the other hand, is designed to redress injuries suffered by individual competitors.[166] Whereas for antitrust purposes "[u]nfair competition is still competition,"[167] business tort law is very much concerned with the fairness of competitive conduct. As the Fifth Circuit explained in *C.E. Services, Inc. v. Control Data Corp.*:[168]

> Competitive motive, while perhaps the start of the inquiry, is not of itself sufficient privilege or justification for interference with prospective business relations in Texas. Only "fair" competition will do, for "if there is sharp dealing or overreaching or other conduct below the behavior of fair men similarly situated, the ensuing loss should be redressed."[169]

A good illustration of the differing purposes of business tort law and antitrust law is provided in *Deauville Corp. v. Federated Department Stores.*[170] In that case, the plaintiff and the defendant were both developing competing shopping malls. Around the same time, a major retailer was seeking to become a tenant in a mall in the area. The retailer had discussions with both developers and entered into a joint venture agreement with the plaintiff (which the court found to be terminable at will) whereby it would become a tenant in the plaintiff's mall upon its completion. The defendant, aware of this agreement, convinced the retailer to become a tenant in defendant's mall. The plaintiff sued the defendant alleging monopolization and restraint of trade as well as tortious interference.

The Fifth Circuit affirmed the district court's rejection of the plaintiff's antitrust claims as a matter of law but remanded the tort claim for trial. The court found the tortious interference claim viable based simply on evidence of the defendant's subjective intent to harm the

---

vigorous price competition' and subjective evidence blurs the distinction. This is because subjective evidence of predatory intent can be ambiguous and misleading. As a result, juries may 'erroneously condemn competitive behavior.'") (quoting *Morgan*, 892 F.2d at 1359; *Ne. Tel.*, 651 F.2d at 88).

166. *See* Nw. Power Prods., Inc. v. Omark Indus., Inc., 576 F.2d 83, 88 (5th Cir. 1978).

167. *Id.*

168. 759 F.2d 1241 (5th Cir. 1985).

169. *Id.* at 1249 (quoting Leonard Duckworth, Inc. v. Michael L. Field & Co., 516 F.2d 952, 958 (5th Cir. 1975)).

170. 756 F.2d 1183 (5th Cir. 1985).

plaintiff. The Fifth Circuit reached this conclusion even though the defendant intended to compete. In the words of the Fifth Circuit, "[w]e recognize a degree of incongruity, at least on the surface, in an opinion striking down the federal antitrust claims and yet finding evidence of malice necessary to support the state claim of unlawful interference. At least one important distinction to be made is, broadly speaking, that the federal law protects competition; the state law, requiring no finding regarding market power, protects the competitor."[171]

Attempts by business tort defendants to invoke evidentiary principles developed for the resolution of antitrust claims have met with limited success. For example, in *Fineman v. Armstrong World Industries,*[172] a case involving both antitrust and tortious interference claims, the defendant argued unsuccessfully that a plaintiff asserting a claim of tortious interference in a competitive business context must meet a heightened evidentiary standard akin to that required to prove an antitrust claim.[173] Noting that the Supreme Court in *Matsushita Electric Industrial Co. v. Zenith Radio Corp.*[174] held that "conduct as consistent with permissible competition as with illegal conspiracy does not, standing alone, support an inference of antitrust conspiracy,"[175] the defendant argued that the requirement under New Jersey law of wrongful conduct involving malice – which is defined as the intentional commission of a wrongful act without justification or excuse – required application of this heightened evidentiary standard.[176]

Rejecting this argument, the court stated that it could find no such requirement in New Jersey law, and that New Jersey's "admittedly 'amorphous' element of wrongful, unjustified conduct" adequately takes into consideration procompetitive conduct.[177] In so holding, the court also rejected the defendant's argument that it would be illogical to apply differing rules of permissible inferences in antitrust and tort claims when those claims are based upon the same conduct, noting that antitrust and tort claims not only "require widely divergent proofs" but also "vindicate

---

171. *Id.* at 1196.
172. 980 F.2d 171 (3d Cir. 1992).
173. *Id.* at 186.
174. 475 U.S. 574 (1986).
175. *Id.* at 588.
176. *Fineman*, 980 F.2d at 187.
177. *Id.*

widely differing policies."[178]   Other courts have reached similar results.[179]

---

178. *Id.*
179. *See, e.g., Deauville*, 756 F.2d at 1196 n.9.

CHAPTER III

FEDERAL LAW OF UNFAIR COMPETITION

This chapter opens the substantive discussion of business tort claims. Although business torts are popularly associated with state law causes of action such as tortious interference and disparagement, a substantial body of federal statutory law reaches competitive conduct for which there may or may not also be private civil liability under the antitrust laws. This chapter examines federal laws governing unfair competition, including section 43(a) of the Lanham Act. Common law disparagement and defamation are addressed in the following chapter. – Eds.

A. Introduction

The early common law of unfair competition was a limited concept, involving the palming off of one's goods as those of another.[1] As commercial ingenuity produced new forms of piracy, "unfair competition" expanded in the early part of this century to include not only misrepresentation of the source of goods but also "misappropriation of what equitably belongs to a competitor."[2]

In recent years the field of unfair competition has continued to evolve, embracing both "statutory and nonstatutory causes of action arising out of business conduct which is contrary to honest practice in industrial or commercial matters."[3] This evolution is reflected in the

---

1. A.L.A. Schechter Poultry Corp. v. United States, 295 U.S. 495, 531 (1935); Goodyear's Rubber Mfg. Co. v. Goodyear Rubber Co., 128 U.S. 598, 604 (1888).

2. *Schecter Poultry*, 295 U.S. at 532 (citing Int'l News Serv. v. Associated Press, 248 U.S. 215, 241, 242 (1918)); *see* Cottman Transmission Sys. v. Melody, 851 F. Supp. 660, 672 (E.D. Pa. 1994); *cf.* RESTATEMENT (THIRD) OF UNFAIR COMPETITION § 38 (1993) [hereinafter RESTATEMENT].

3. Am. Heritage Life Ins. Co. v. Heritage Life Ins. Co., 494 F.2d 3, 14 (5th Cir. 1974) (citing 3 R. CALLMANN, THE LAW OF UNFAIR COMPETITION

work of the American Law Institute. Chapters 34-36 of the original Restatement of Torts contained a comprehensive treatment of unfair competition, and a tentative draft containing an updated treatment was prepared in connection with the Restatement (Second) of Torts. Recognizing that the field of unfair competition had become a specialty in its own right, "governed extensively by legislation and largely divorced from [its] initial grounding in the principles of torts,"[4] the Council of the Institute decided to reserve the area of unfair competition for its own restatement. The new Restatement (Third) of Unfair Competition represents such an "independent restatement of the law relating to unfair trade practices,"[5] including such topics as deceptive marketing, trademark infringement and misappropriation of trade secrets and other business intangibles. Noting that "the boundaries of unfair competition are not fixed,"[6] the Restatement (Third) also includes a residual category of conduct that "substantially interferes with the ability of others to compete on the merits of their products or otherwise conflicts with accepted principles of public policy recognized by statute or common law."[7]

---

§ 4.1 at 120 (3d ed. 1969)); *cf.* Standard & Poor's Corp. v. Commodity Exch., Inc., 683 F.2d 704, 710 (2d Cir. 1982) (unfair competition "has been broadly described as encompassing 'any form of commercial immorality,' or simply as 'endeavoring to reap where [one] has not sown;' it is taking 'the skill, expenditures and labors of a competitor' and 'misappropriati[ng] for the commercial advantage of one person . . . a benefit or 'property' right belonging to another. The tort is adaptable and capacious.'") (quoting Roy Export Co. Establishment of Vaduz, Liechtenstein v. Columbia Broad. Sys., 672 F.2d 1095, 1105 (2d Cir. 1982)); Nw. Airlines v. Am. Airlines, 853 F. Supp. 1110, 1113 n.4 (D. Minn. 1994) (unfair competition is not a unique tort, but rather a group of torts).

4.   RESTATEMENT, *supra* note 2, reporter's mem. at xv (Tentative Draft. No. 1, 1988) (quoting RESTATEMENT (SECOND) OF TORTS, Vol. 4 director's introduction (1979)).

5.   *Id.*

6.   *Id.* at xvii.

7.   RESTATEMENT, *supra* note 2, § 1 cmt. g.

In popular usage, "unfair competition" has been even more expansively described as a "broad class of business torts,"[8] including not only the traditional forms of misrepresentation and misappropriation, but also commercial disparagement and defamation, fraudulent conduct in business transactions and tortious interference with commercial relationships.[9] These and other business torts are addressed in the chapters that follow.[10] The discussion below examines the federal law of unfair competition, including section 43(a) of the federal Lanham Act and section 5 of the Federal Trade Commission Act.

B.   Section 43(a) of the Lanham Act

Occasionally it is written that "[t]here is no federal law of unfair competition."[11]   Such statements are best read advisedly.   As the Supreme Court has observed, the Lanham Act "was intended to make 'actionable the deceptive and misleading use of marks,' and 'to protect persons engaged in ... commerce against unfair competition.'"[12] Although the Lanham Act is primarily associated with the federal law pertaining to the infringement of registered trademarks and service

---

8.   Union Nat'l Bank of Tex. v. Union Nat'l Bank of Tex., 909 F.2d 839, 843 n.10 (5th Cir. 1990) (quoting Keebler Co. v. Rovira Biscuit Corp., 624 F.2d 366, 372 (1st Cir. 1980)).

9.   Taylor Pub'g Co. v. Jostens, Inc., 216 F.3d 465, 486 (5th Cir. 2000); W. KEETON, PROSSER AND KEETON ON THE LAW OF TORTS § 130, at 1014 (5th ed. 1984); RESTATEMENT, *supra* note 2, § 1.

10.   *See* Chap. 4 (commercial disparagement and defamation), Chap. 5 (tortious interference), Chap. 6 (fraud and misrepresentation), Chap. 7 (misappropriation of trade secrets).

11.   Wichita Clinic, P.A. v. Columbia/HCA Healthcare Corp., No. 96-1336-JTM, 1997 WL 225966, at *7 (D. Kan. 1997); Nw. Power Prods., Inc. v. Omark Indus., 576 F.2d 83, 88 (5th Cir. 1978). It is more accurately said that the federal courts have "long resisted [the] temptation to create a federal common law of unfair competition." George R. Whitten, Jr., Inc. v. Paddock Pool Builders, Inc., 508 F.2d 547, 560 (1st Cir. 1974) (footnote omitted); *cf.* Water Techs. Corp. v. Calco, Ltd., 850 F.2d 660, 670 (Fed. Cir. 1988) ("there is no federal common law of unfair competition") (citing Erie R.R. Co. v. Tompkins, 304 U.S. 64, 78-79 (1938) ("There is no federal general common law.")).

12.   Dastar Corp. v. Twentieth Century Fox Film Corp., 539 U.S. 23, 123 S. Ct. 2041, 2045 (2003) (quoting 15 U.S.C. § 1127); Two Pesos, Inc. v. Taco Cabana, Inc., 505 U.S. 763, 768 (1992) (quoting 15 U.S.C. § 1127).

marks,[13] section 43(a) of the Act is generally recognized as constituting a "federal law of unfair competition."[14] Section 43(a) provides in pertinent part:

> (1) Any person who, on or in connection with any goods or services, or any container for goods, uses in commerce any word, term, name, symbol, or device, or any combination thereof, or any false designation of origin, false or misleading description of fact, or false or misleading representation of fact which –
>
>> (A) is likely to cause confusion, or to cause mistake, or to deceive as to the affiliation, connection or association of such person with another person, or as to the origin, sponsorship, or approval of his or her goods, services, or commercial activities by another person, or
>>
>> (B) in commercial advertising or promotion, misrepresents the nature, characteristics, qualities, or geographic origin of his or her or another person's goods, services, or commercial activities,
>
> shall be liable in a civil action by any person who believes that he or she is or is likely to be damaged by such act.[15]

As the Supreme Court explained, section 43(a) "'prohibits a broader range of practices than does § 32,' which applies to registered marks."[16] The Lanham Act is cumulative of, and does not preempt, state unfair

---

13. Section 32 of the Lanham Act applies to registered marks. *See Two Pesos*, 505 U.S. 763, 768; Inwood Labs., Inc. v. Ives Labs., Inc., 456 U.S. 844, 854 (1982).
14. Keebler Co. v. Rovira Biscuit Corp., 624 F.2d 366, 372 (1st Cir. 1980). *See Union Nat'l Bank*, 909 F.2d at 843 n.10 ("trademark law is considered part of the law of unfair competition"); Nabisco Brands, Inc. v. The Quaker Oats Co., 547 F. Supp. 692, 697 (D.N.J. 1982) ("Trademark infringement is really a subspecies of the broadly defined business tort of unfair competition.") (citing Int'l Order of Job's Daughters v. Lindeburg & Co., 633 F.2d 912, 915 (9th Cir. 1980)); *see also* Zenith Elecs. Corp. v. Exzec, Inc., 182 F.3d 1340 (Fed. Cir. 1999) (holding that a patent holder's false statements in the marketplace could violate section 43(a)).
15. 15 U.S.C. § 1125(a)(1).
16. *Two Pesos*, 505 U.S. at 768 (quoting *Inwood Labs.*, 456 U.S. at 858); Sugar Busters L.L.C. v. Brennan, 177 F.3d 258, 267 (5th Cir. 1999).

competition law,[17] including state laws protecting rights in trademarks and service marks.[18]

As the Supreme Court recently cautioned, however, section 43(a) "'does not have boundless application as a remedy for unfair competition.'"[19] Rather, "'[b]ecause of its inherently limited wording, § 43(a) can never be a federal 'codification' of the overall law of 'unfair competition.'"[20]

The reach of section 43(a) also is limited to Congress' power to legislate under the Commerce Clause.[21] Although purely intrastate disputes do not fall within the Commerce Clause and are not subject to the Lanham Act,[22] the reach of the statute "is coincident with the constitutional boundary embodied in the commerce clause"[23] and is "'at

---

17.   For a listing of states in which the Unfair Trade Practices and Consumer Protection Act or an analogous statute is in effect, *see* RESTATEMENT, *supra* note 2, § 1 statutory note. For a listing of the states in which the Uniform Deceptive Trade Practices Act is in effect, *see id.* § 2 statutory note.

18.   *Keebler*, 624 F.2d at 372 n.3. "Every state has enacted legislation providing for the registration and protection of trademarks. All but a few of these statutes are derived from the Model State Trademark Bill drafted by the United States Trademark Association in 1949, as revised in 1964 and 1992." RESTATEMENT, *supra* note 2, § 9 statutory note. For a listing of such state statutes, *see id.* For a listing of state trade name registration statutes of general applicability, *see id.* § 12 statutory note. For a listing of state antidilution statutes, *see id.* § 25 statutory note.

19.   Dastar Corp. v. Twentieth Century Fox Film Corp., 539 U.S. 23 (2003) (quoting Alfred Dunhill, Ltd. v. Interstate Cigar Co., 499 F.2d 232, 237 (2d Cir. 1974)).

20.   *Id.* (quoting 4 J. MCCARTHY TRADEMARKS AND UNFAIR COMPETITION, §27:7, p. 27-14 (4th ed. 2002)).

21.   United States v. Moghadam, 175 F.3d 1269, 1278-79 (11th Cir. 1999) (citing Jellibeans, Inc. v. Skating Club of Ga., Inc., 716 F.2d 833, 838 (11th Cir. 1983)); *see also* 15 U.S.C. § 1127 ("The word 'commerce' means all commerce which may lawfully be regulated by Congress.").

22.   *Jellibeans*, 716 F.2d at 838.

23.   *Id.*

least as broad as the definition of commerce employed in any other federal statute.'"[24]

Section 43(a) proscribes two types of unfair competition: (1) false or misleading statements likely to cause confusion as to source, sponsorship or association between the defendant's goods or services and those of another, and (2) false or misleading statements made in connection with commercial advertising or promotion, regarding the plaintiff's or defendant's goods, services or commercial activities.[25]

1. *"Passing Off" and "Reverse Passing Off"*

Section 43(a)(1)(a) addresses misrepresentations regarding the origin of goods or services. "Passing off" (sometimes called "palming off") occurs when a producer misrepresents his own goods or services as those of someone else.[26] "Reversing passing off" occurs when the producer misrepresents someone else's goods or services as his own.[27] In *Dastar Corp. v. Twentieth Century Fox Film Corp.*,[28] the Supreme Court was called upon to determine what section 43(a)(1)(A) means by the "origin" of "goods." In that case the defendant copied a television series in the public domain (the copyright having expired), edited and repackaged it, and produced a series of videotapes under its own name. No reference was made to the original television series, the videotapes of the original series or the book upon which that series was based. The owners of the rights to the book and the original series claimed, among other things, that the defendant had engaged in reverse passing off by selling the series "without proper credit" to the original series.[29] The

---

24. *Id.* (quoting Shatel Corp. v. Mao Ta Lumber & Yacht Corp., 697 F.2d 1352, 1356 n.3 (11th Cir. 1983); Bulova Watch Co. v. Steele, 194 F.2d 567, 570 n.11 (5th Cir.), *aff'd*, 344 U.S. 280 (1952)).

25. 15 U.S.C. § 1125(a)(1)(A) & (B); *see* Am. Italian Pasta Co. v. New World Pasta Co., 371 F.3d. 387 (8th Cir. 2004). As discussed in the text accompanying notes 110-11, the "false statements" prong has been held to embrace "misappropriation" claims. *See, e.g.*, Kisch v. Ammirati & Puris, Inc., 657 F. Supp. 380, 385 (S.D.N.Y. 1987) (misappropriation of photograph); R.H. Donnelley Corp. v. Ill. Bell Tel. Co., 595 F. Supp. 1202, 1206 (N.D. Ill. 1984) (substituting names).

26. *Dastar*, 539 U.S. at 28 n.1.

27. *Id.*

28. *Id.* at 23.

29. *Id.* at 2044-45.

Supreme Court disagreed, holding that "origin" in section 43(a)(1)(A) refers only to the *manufacturer* of the physical goods that are sold to the public, not to the creator of the underlying work.[30] The Court noted that reading "origin" to require attribution of uncopyrighted materials would pose serious practical problems, not the least of which is that, "[w]ithout a copyrighted work as the basepoint, the word 'origin' has no discernable limits."[31] Indeed, to read the Lanham Act as creating a cause of action for plagiarism would be "akin to finding that §43(a) created a species of perpetual patent and copyright, which Congress may not do."[32] Because – unlike the patent and copyright laws – the Lanham Act was not designed to protect originality or creativity, the Court held that the term "origin of goods" refers to the producer of the tangible goods that are offered for sale, and not the author of any idea, concept or communication embodied in those goods.[33]

2. *Infringement*

Although the Lanham Act is not limited to trademark infringement, it provides a federal cause of action for infringement of both registered and unregistered marks.[34]   Because trademark and service mark infringement is a subspecies of the unfair competition reached by section 43(a),[35] the basic principles governing claims of infringement are briefly addressed below.[36]

Section 45 of the Lanham Act defines a trademark as including "any word, name, symbol, or device, or any combination thereof" used by a person "to identify and distinguish his or her goods, including a unique

---

30. *Id.* at 2047-50.
31. *Id.* at 2049.
32. *Id.* at 2049-50 (citing Eldred v. Ashcroft, 537 U.S. 186, 208 (2003)).
33. *Id.* at 2050.
34. *Dastar*, 123 S. Ct. at 2045-46.
35. Int'l Order of Job's Daughters v. Lindeburg & Co., 633 F.3d 912 (9th Cir. 1980); Nabisco Brands, Inc. v. The Quaker Oats Co., 547 F. Supp. 692, 697 (D.N.J. 1982).
36. For a comprehensive treatment of the law of trademarks, *see* R. CALLMANN, UNFAIR COMPETITION, TRADEMARKS AND MONOPOLIES (1990); GILSON, TRADEMARK PROTECTION AND PRACTICE (Supp. ed. 2000); J. MCCARTHY, TRADEMARKS AND UNFAIR COMPETITION (4th ed. 1992); *see also* RESTATEMENT, *supra* note 2, ch. 3.

product, from those manufactured or sold by others and to indicate the source of the goods, even if that source is unknown."[37] A service mark is similarly defined as "any word, name, symbol, or device, or any combination thereof" used by a person "to identify and distinguish the services of one person, including a unique service, from the services of others and to indicate the source of the services, even if that source is unknown."[38]   Section 43(a) protects both registered and qualifying unregistered marks. As the Supreme Court has noted, "the general principles qualifying a mark for registration under § 2 of the Lanham Act are for the most part applicable in determining whether an unregistered mark is entitled to protection under § 43(a)."[39]

Section 15 of the Lanham Act sets forth the requirements for a federal registration to become "incontestable" – primarily, continuous use of the mark for five consecutive years after issuance of the registration, no successful or pending challenge to the registrant's rights under the mark, and the filing of the required affidavit.[40] Infringement of such an incontestable mark is subject to eight statutory defenses, including fraud, abandonment, use of the mark to violate the antitrust laws, and equitable principles such as laches, estoppel and acquiescence.[41]

---

37.   15 U.S.C. § 1127; *see* RESTATEMENT, *supra* note 2, § 9.
38.   15 U.S.C. § 1127.
39.   Two Pesos, Inc. v. Taco Cabana, Inc., 505 U.S. 763, 768 (1992) (citing A. J. Canfield Co. v. Honickman, 808 F.2d 291, 299 n.9 (3d Cir. 1986); Thompson Med. Co. v. Pfizer, Inc., 753 F.2d 208, 215-16 (2d Cir. 1985)).
40.   15 U.S.C. § 1065.
41.   15 U.S.C. § 1115. The eight statutory defenses are as follows:
   (1)   That the registration or the incontestable right to use the mark was obtained fraudulently; or
   (2)   That the mark has been abandoned by the registrant; or
   (3)   That the registered mark is being used, by or with the permission of the registrant or a person in privity with the registrant, so as to misrepresent the source of the goods or services on or in connection with which the mark is used; or
   (4)   That the use of the name, term, or device charged to be an infringement is a use, otherwise than as a mark, of the party's individual name in his own business, or of the individual name of anyone in privity with such party, or of a term or device which is

In addition to marks, section 43(a) protects the "trade dress" of goods and services.[42] Broadly defined, trade dress is the total image and overall appearance of a business or its products,[43] and may include features such as size, shape, color or color combinations, texture, graphics, or even particular sales techniques.[44]

Trade names, which describe the manufacturer or dealer, rather than his products, are not eligible for registration under the Lanham Act.[45] As

---

descriptive of and used fairly and in good faith only to describe the goods or services of such party, or their geographic origin; or

(5) That the mark whose use by a party is charged as an infringement was adopted without knowledge of the registrant's prior use and has been continuously used by such party or those in privity with him from a date prior to (A) the date of constructive use of the mark established pursuant to section 1057(c) of this title, (B) the registration of the mark under this chapter if the application for registration is filed before the effective date of the Trademark Law Revision Act of 1988, or (C) publication of the registered mark under subsection (c) of section 1062 of this title: Provided, however, That this defense or defect shall apply only for the area in which such continuous prior use is proved; or

(6) That the mark whose use is charged as an infringement was registered and used prior to the registration under this chapter or publication under subsection (c) of section 1062 of this title of the registered mark of the registrant, and not abandoned: Provided, however, that this defense or defect shall apply only for the area in which the mark was used prior to such registration or such publication of the registrant's mark; or

(7) That the mark has been or is being used to violate the antitrust laws of the United States; or

(8) That equitable principles, including laches, estoppel, and acquiescence, are applicable.

42. *See, e.g., Two Pesos*, 505 U.S. at 770-75; *see also* RESTATEMENT, *supra* note 2, § 16.

43. *Two Pesos*, 505 U.S. at 764 n.1.

44. *See* TrafFix Devices, Inc. v. Mktg. Displays, Inc., 532 U.S. 23, 28 (2001); RESTATEMENT, *supra* note 2, § 16.

45. "A trade name describes the manufacturer or dealer, and applies not to vendible goods but to the business and its goodwill." R.R. Salvage of Conn., Inc. v. R.R. Salvage, Inc., 561 F. Supp. 1014, 1018-19 (D.R.I.

noted above, however, section 43(a) reaches beyond infringement of marks, and has "authoritatively been interpreted as creating a right to maintain an action for trade name infringement."[46]

a.   Distinctiveness

In order to qualify for protection, a mark "must be capable of distinguishing the applicant's goods [or services] from those of others."[47] As the Supreme Court explained:

> Marks are often classified in categories of generally increasing distinctiveness; following the classic formulation set out by Judge Friendly, they may be (1) generic; (2) descriptive; (3) suggestive; (4) arbitrary; or (5) fanciful.[48]

Generic marks, i.e., those that "refe[r] to the genus of which the particular product is a species,"[49] are not registrable as trademarks.[50]   A

1983) (citing New West Corp. v. NYM Co., 595 F.2d 1194, 1201 (9th Cir. 1979)); *see* RESTATEMENT, *supra* note 2, § 12.

46.   *R.R. Salvage*, 561 F. Supp. at 1019 (citing, *inter alia*, Walt-West Enter., Inc. v. Gannett Co., 695 F.2d 1050, 1054 n.6 (7th Cir. 1982); *New West Corp.*, 595 F.2d at 1201)); *see also* Ga. Carpet Sales, Inc. v. SLS Corp., 789 F. Supp. 244, 245 (N.D. Ill. 1992). "Rights previously established in a trade name, however, can prevent registration by another of a confusingly similar trademark." RESTATEMENT, *supra* note 2, § 12 cmt. c (citing 15 U.S.C. § 1052(d)). If a trade name also is used as a trademark, it may be registrable on that basis. *Id.* Also, most states afford protection to trade names through registration statutes. For a list of state trade name registration statutes of general applicability *see id.* statutory note.

47.   *Two Pesos*, 505 U.S. at 768 (citing 15 U.S.C. § 1052).

48.   *Id.* (citing Abercrombie & Fitch Co. v. Hunting World, Inc., 537 F.2d 4, 9 (2d Cir. 1976)); *see* RESTATEMENT, *supra* note 2, § 13 cmts. a-c.

49.   Park 'N Fly, Inc. v. Dollar Park & Fly, Inc., 469 U.S. 189, 194 (1985) (citing *Abercrombie & Fitch*, 537 F.2d at 9); *see* Union Nat'l Bank of Tex. v. Union Nat'l Bank of Tex., 909 F.2d 839, 845 (5th Cir. 1990) ("An example of a generic word is 'fish.' 'Fish' is a generic term which applies with equal force to sole, haddock, perch, salmon, bass and carp."); *see also* *R.R. Salvage*, 561 F. Supp. at 1020 (citing examples such as "mart" and "cola"); RESTATEMENT, *supra* note 2, § 15(1).

50.   *Park 'N Fly*, 469 U.S. at 194. A registered mark "may be canceled at any time on the grounds that it has become generic." *Id.* (citing 15 U.S.C.

mark that is merely descriptive[51] of a product is not inherently distinctive, but may "become distinctive of the applicant's goods in commerce,"[52] i.e., it may acquire a "secondary meaning."[53] "Secondary meaning is the connection in the consumer's mind between the mark and the product's producer, whether that producer is known or unknown."[54] Marks in the latter three categories – those that are suggestive,[55] arbitrary[56] or fanciful,[57] are deemed "inherently distinctive" and qualify for protection.[58] This method of classification also has been applied to trade names.[59] A trade dress that is inherently distinctive is protectable under section 43(a) without showing that is has acquired a secondary

---

§§ 1052, 1064(c)); Sport Supply Group, Inc. v. Columbia Cas. Co., 335 F.3d 453, 461 (5th Cir. 2003); *see* RESTATEMENT, *supra* note 2, § 15(2).

51. *See R.R. Salvage*, 561 F. Supp. at 1020 (citing "EVERREADY" and "Vision Center" as examples).

52. 15 U.S.C. § 1052(f).

53. *See* Two Pesos, Inc. v. Taco Cabana, Inc., 505 U.S. 763, 769 (1992); Inwood Labs., Inc. v. Ives Labs., Inc., 456 U.S. 844, 851 n.11 (1982); *see also* RESTATEMENT, *supra* note 2, § 13(b). The Commissioner of the United States Patent and Trademark Office "may accept as prima facie evidence that [a] mark has become distinctive, as used on or in connection with the applicant's goods in commerce, proof of substantially exclusive and continuous use thereof as a mark by the applicant in commerce for the five years before the date on which the claim of distinctiveness is made." 15 U.S.C. § 1052(f).

54. AmBrit, Inc. v. Kraft, Inc., 812 F.2d 1531, 1536 n.14 (11th Cir. 1986); *see* Pride Commc'ns Ltd. P'ship v. WCKG, Inc., 851 F. Supp. 895, 901 (N.D. Ill. 1994).

55. *See, e.g.*, Am. Home Prods. Corp. v. Johnson Chem. Co., 589 F.2d 103, 106 (2d Cir. 1978) ("ROACH MOTEL"); *R.R. Salvage*, 561 F. Supp. at 1020 (citing "ULTRASUEDE" and "NATIVE TAN" as examples).

56. *See, e.g.*, WGBH Educ. Found., Inc. v. Penthouse Int'l Ltd., 453 F. Supp. 1347, 1350 (S.D.N.Y. 1978) (television program named "NOVA"), *aff'd*, 598 F.2d 610 (2d Cir. 1979).

57. *See, e.g.*, Polaroid Corp. v. Polaraid, Inc., 319 F.2d 830, 831-33 (7th Cir. 1963) ("POLAROID" cameras).

58. *Two Pesos*, 505 U.S. at 768; *see* RESTATEMENT, *supra* note 2, § 13 cmt. c.

59. *See, e.g.*, S.S. Kresge Co. v. United Factory Outlet, Inc., 598 F.2d 694, 696 (1st Cir. 1979); *R.R. Salvage*, 561 F. Supp. at 1019.

meaning,[60] but proof that a product's design is distinctive requires a showing of secondary meaning.[61]

The courts have recognized a variety of ways in which distinctiveness of a term may be established, including reference to dictionary definitions, the use of consumer surveys, resort to the so-called "imagination test"[62] and by asking whether others in the same business would ordinarily need to use the term to adequately describe their own product or service.[63]   Factors to be considered when determining whether a term has acquired secondary meaning include whether purchasers of the product associate the mark with the producer, the amount and manner of advertising, volume of sales, the length and manner of use, direct consumer testimony and surveys.[64]

b.   Functionality

In order for a product or its trade dress to be entitled to protection, it also must be "nonfunctional."[65]   The purpose of the functionality doctrine is to ensure that exclusive rights do not hinder competition or impinge upon the rights of others to compete effectively.[66]   Although

---

60.   Two Pesos, Inc. v. Taco Cabana, 505 U.S. 763, 770 (1992).
61.   Wal-Mart Stores, Inc. v. Samara Brothers, Inc., 529 U.S. 205, 216 (2000).
62.   The "imagination test" asks the trier of fact to "'measure the relationship between the actual words of the mark and the product [or service] to which they are applied.'" Union Nat'l Bank of Tex. v. Union Nat'l Bank of Tex., 909 F.2d 839, 847-48 (5th Cir. 1990) (quoting Zatarains, Inc. v. Oak Grove Smokehouse, Inc., 698 F.2d 786, 792 (5th Cir. 1983)).
63.   *See id.* at 846-48.
64.   Avery Dennison Corp. v. Sumpton, 189 F.3d 868, 876 (9th Cir. 1999); *see also* International Kennel Club v. Mighty Star, Inc., 846 F.2d 1079, 1085 (7th Cir. 1988); *see* RESTATEMENT, *supra* note 2, § 13 reporters' note.
65.   *Id.*
66.   *In re* Morton-Norwich Prods., 671 F.2d 1332, 1342 (C.C.P.A. 1982); *see* Valu Eng'g, Inc. v. Rexnord Corp., 278 F.3d 1268, 1277 (D.C. Cir. 2002); Clamp Mfg. Co. v. Enco Mfg. Co., 870 F.2d 512, 516 (9th Cir. 1989); Hartford House, Inc. v. Hallmark Cards, Inc., 846 F.2d 1268, 1274 (10th Cir. 1988); Brunswick Corp. v. Spinit Reel Co., 832 F.2d 513, 519 (10th Cir. 1987).

courts vary in their definition of "functionality,"[67] under the Restatement (Third) of Unfair Competition, a design is functional if it "affords benefits in the manufacturing, marketing, or use of the goods or services with which the design is used, apart from any benefits attributable to the design's significance as an indication of source, that are important to effective competition by others and that are not practically available through the use of alternative designs."[68]

A product or its trade dress may be functional by reason of either its utility or its aesthetics. Under the "utilitarian functionality" test, the court first inquires into the de facto functionality of a product, i.e., whether it has a functional use.[69] If it does, the analysis proceeds to an inquiry into de jure functionality, i.e., whether the product is "in a particular shape because the product works better in that shape or, put another way, is the shape of the product a utilitarian design of a utilitarian object."[70] This determination turns on how essential the design is to the product's use.[71] A design is functional if it is essential to the use or purpose of the device or when it affects the cost or quality of the device.[72] The functionality doctrine was refined by the Supreme Court's decision in *TrafFix Devices Inc. v. Marketing Displays, Inc.*,[73] in which the Court expanded on the meaning of this phrase and observed that a design is functional "when exclusive use of [it] would put

---

67. *See, e.g., Brunswick Corp.*, 832 F.2d at 517-21; Sno-Wizard Mfg., Inc. v. Eisemann Prods. Co., 791 F.2d 423, 426 n.3 (5th Cir. 1986); W.T. Rogers Co. v. Keene, 778 F.2d 334, 337-48 (7th Cir. 1985).

68. RESTATEMENT, *supra* note 2, § 17; *see Hartford House*, 846 F.2d at 1274; *Brunswick Corp.*, 832 F.2d at 517-20; AmBrit, Inc. v. Kraft, Inc., 812 F.2d 1531, 1535 (11th Cir. 1986); First Brands Corp. v. Fred Meyers, Inc., 809 F.2d 1378, 1381 (9th Cir. 1987); Stormy Clime Ltd. v. ProGroup, Inc., 809 F.2d 971, 974 (2d Cir. 1987); Am. Greetings Corp. v. Dan-Dee Imports, Inc., 807 F.2d 1136, 1141 (3d Cir. 1986); *Morton-Norwich*, 671 F.2d at 1342.

69. Dentsply Int'l v. Kerr Mfg. Co., 732 F. Supp. 482, 486 (D. Del. 1990); *see Morton-Norwich*, 671 F.2d at 1337.

70. *Dentsply*, 732 F. Supp. at 486 (citing *Morton-Norwich*, 671 F.2d at 1338-39).

71. *Id.* (citing *Morton-Norwich*, 671 F.2d at 1338-39; Inwood Labs, Inc. v. Ives Labs, Inc., 456 U.S. 844, 850 n.10 (1982)).

72. TrafFix Devices, Inc. v. Mktg. Displays, Inc., 532 U.S. 23 (2001).

73. *Id.*

competitors at a significant non-reputation-related disadvantage."[74] In light of *TrafFix*, the primary test for determining functionality is whether the feature is essential to the use or the purpose of a product, or whether it affects the cost or quality of a product.[75]

The concept of "aesthetic functionality" was introduced by the Ninth Circuit's decision in *Pagliero v. Wallace China Co.*,[76] which involved the copying of floral china patterns that the plaintiff had designed for use on its own dishes. Holding that the designs were functional and therefore open to copying, the court offered the following broad explanation of aesthetic functionality:

> "Functional" in this sense might be said to connote other than a trade-mark purpose. If the particular feature is an important ingredient in the commercial success of the product, the interest in free competition permits its imitation in the absence of a patent or copyright. On the other hand, where the feature or, more aptly, design, is a mere arbitrary embellishment, a form of dress for the goods primarily adopted for purposes of identification and individuality and, hence, unrelated to basic consumer demands in connection with the product, imitation may be forbidden where the requisite showing of secondary meaning is made. Under such circumstances, since effective competition may be undertaken without imitation, the law grants protection.[77]

Subsequent decisions have limited or rejected *Pagliero's* sweeping view of aesthetic functionality.[78] Under the Restatement (Third) of

---

74. *Id.* at 32 (quoting Qualitex Co. v. Jacobson Prods. Co., 514 U.S. 159 (1995)).
75. Eppendorf-Netheler-Hinz GmbH v. Ritter GmbH, 289 F.3d 351, 356 (5th Cir. 2002) (citing *TrafFix*, 532 U.S. at 32-33).
76. 198 F.2d 339 (9th Cir. 1952).
77. *Id.* at 343 (footnotes omitted).
78. *See, e.g.*, Ferrari S.p.A. Esercizio Fabriche Automobile e Corse v. Roberts, 944 F.2d 1235, 1247 (6th Cir. 1991); Sicilia Di R. Beibow & Co. v. Cox, 732 F.2d 417, 427-28 (5th Cir. 1984); Fabrica, Inc. v. El Dorado Corp., 697 F.2d 890, 895 (9th Cir. 1983); Vuitton et Fils, S.A. v. J. Young Enters., Inc., 644 F.2d 769, 773-74 (9th Cir. 1981); Big Island Candies, Inc. v. Cookie Corner, 244 F. Supp. 2d 1086, 1090-91 (D. Haw. 2003).

Unfair Competition, a design is functional because of its aesthetic value only if it confers a significant benefit that cannot practically be duplicated by the use of alternative designs.[79] As with utilitarian functionality, the question of aesthetic functionality depends on whether exclusive use would put competitors at a significant non-reputation-related disadvantage.[80]

The courts are in disagreement over whether functionality is an affirmative defense,[81] with the burden of proof on the defendant,[82] or whether the party asserting exclusive rights should have the burden of proving that the design is nonfunctional.[83]

c.　Likelihood of Confusion

Liability under section 43(a) for false designation of origin requires proof of a reasonable likelihood of confusion.[84] As the Fifth Circuit has explained "'the gravamen for any action of trademark infringement or common law unfair competition is whether the challenged mark is likely to cause confusion.'"[85] The Restatement (Third) of Unfair Competition sets forth three general categories of factors that may be considered when assessing the likelihood of confusion. The first of these, the so-called "market factors," include the degree of similarity between the respective

---

79. RESTATEMENT, *supra* note 2, § 17 cmt. c.
80. *TrafFix*, 532 U.S. at 33.
81. *See* John H. Harland Co. v. Clarke Checks, Inc., 711 F.2d 966, 982 n.26 (11th Cir. 1983).
82. Publications Int'l, Ltd. v. Landoll, Inc., 164 F.3d 337, 339 (7th Cir. 1998); *see, e.g.*, Hartford House, Inc. v. Hallmark Cards, Inc., 846 F.2d 1268, 1271-72 n.3 (10th Cir. 1988).
83. *See, e.g.*, Versa Prods. Co. v. Champ Frame Straightening, Inc., 87 F.3d 654, 657 n.2 (4th Cir. 1996); Clamp Mfg. Co. v. Enco Mfg. Co., 870 F.2d 512, 516 (9th Cir. 1989).
84. Two Pesos, Inc. v. Taco Cabana, Inc., 505 U.S. 763, 769 (1992) (citing *Brunswick*, 832 F.2d at 516-17; *AmBrit*, 812 F.2d at 1535; First Brands Corp. v. Fred Meyers, Inc., 809 F.2d 1378, 1381 (9th Cir. 1987); Stormy Clime Ltd. v. ProGroup, Inc., 809 F.2d 971, 974 (2d Cir. 1987); Am. Greetings Corp. v. Dan-Dee Imports, Inc., 807 F.2d 1136, 1141 (3d Cir. 1986)).
85. Union Nat'l Bank of Tex. v. Union Nat'l Bank of Tex., 909 F.2d 839, 844 (5th Cir. 1990) (quoting Marathon Mfg. Co. v. Enerlite Prod. Co., 767 F.2d 214, 217 (5th Cir. 1985)).

designations;[86] the similarity of the marketing methods and channels of distribution used for the respective goods or services;[87] the characteristics of prospective purchasers of the goods or services and the degree of care they are likely to exercise in making purchasing decisions;[88] the degree of distinctiveness of the other's designation;[89] when the goods, services or business of the defendant differ in kind from those of the plaintiff, the likelihood that the defendant's prospective purchasers would expect a party in the plaintiff's position to expand its marketing or sponsorship into the product, service or business market of the plaintiff;[90] and, when the plaintiff and defendant sell their goods or services, or carry on their businesses, in different geographic markets, the extent to which the plaintiff's designation is identified with the plaintiff in the defendant's geographic market.[91]

The second category of factors, relating to the defendant's intent, focuses on whether the defendant used a designation resembling another's mark with the intent to cause confusion or to deceive.[92]

---

86. RESTATEMENT, *supra* note 2, § 21(a). This may include a comparison of the overall impression created by the designations, the pronunciation of the designations, the translation of any foreign words used, the verbal translation of pictures, illustrations or design used and the "suggestions, connotations, or meanings of the designations." *Id. See* Oakley, Inc. v. Int'l Tropic-Cal, Inc., 923 F.2d 167, 170 (Fed. Cir. 1991); Fuddrucker's, Inc. v. Doc's B.R. Others, Inc., 826 F.2d 837, 845 (9th Cir. 1987); Carson v. Here's Johnny Portable Toilets, Inc., 698 F.2d 831, 833 (6th Cir. 1983); *see also* Smith Fiberglas Prods. v. Ameron, Inc., 7 F.3d 1327, 1329 (7th Cir. 1993); Singh v. V. Patel & Sons, Inc., 851 F. Supp. 318, 321 (N.D. Ill. 1994).
87. *See* RESTATEMENT, *supra* note 2, § 21(b); *see also Carson*, 698 F.2d at 833.
88. *See* RESTATEMENT, *supra* note 2, § 21(c); *see also Carson*, 698 F.2d at 833.
89. *See* RESTATEMENT, *supra* note 2, § 21(d); *see also Carson*, 698 F.2d at 833.
90. *See* RESTATEMENT, *supra* note 2, § 21(e).
91. *See id.* § 21(f).
92. *See id.* § 22; *see also* ConAgra, Inc. v. George A. Hormel & Co., 990 F.2d 368, 369-70 (8th Cir. 1993); *Oakley*, 923 F.2d at 170; *Fuddrucker's*, 826 F.2d at 845; *Carson*, 698 F.2d at 833; Gold Seal, Inc. v. Scent Shop, Inc., 851 F. Supp. 1284-85 (E.D. Ark. 1994).

Although good faith is not a defense to infringement,[93] the courts include intent as one of the factors to be considered when evaluating the likelihood of confusion.[94]   Accordingly, if the defendant used a designation resembling another's with the intent to deceive, likelihood of confusion may be inferred.[95]   Such a likelihood to confuse may not, however, be inferred from proof that the defendant intentionally copied the other's designation if the defendant acted in good faith and the circumstances do not otherwise indicate an intent to confuse or deceive.[96]

The third category of factors involves evidence of actual confusion.[97]   It is generally recognized that a likelihood of confusion may be inferred from proof of actual confusion.[98]   Conversely, an absence of likelihood of confusion may be inferred from an absence of proof of actual confusion where the plaintiff and defendant have made significant use of their respective designations in the same geographic market for a substantial period of time, and any resulting confusion ordinarily would be manifested by provable facts.[99]

The aforementioned factors are not exclusive of all others; nor can any single factor be applied independently: "likelihood of confusion depends on the interplay of all the factors that constitute the marketing environment in which the designation is used."[100]   Further, "[n]o

---

93. *See, e.g.*, Proctor & Gamble Co. v. Amway Corp., 280 F.3d 519, 527 (5th Cir. 2002); Pizzeria Uno Corp. v. Temple, 747 F.2d 1522, 1535 (4th Cir. 1984).

94. *See, e.g.*, CAE, Inc. v. Clean Air Eng'g, Inc., 267 F.3d 660, 678 (7th Cir. 2001); Sno-Wizard Mfg. Co. v. Eisemann Prods. Co., 791 F.2d 423, 428 (5th Cir. 1986); *Fuji Photo Film*, 754 F.2d at 596-97; *Pizzeria Uno*, 747 F.2d at 1535.

95. *See id.*; RESTATEMENT, *supra* note 2, § 22(1).

96. RESTATEMENT, *supra* note 2, § 22(2).

97. *Id.* § 23; *see Oakley*, 923 F.2d at 170; *Fuddrucker's*, 826 F.2d at 845; *Carson*, 698 F.2d at 833.

98. RESTATEMENT, *supra* note 2, § 23(1); *see also* Beacon Mut. Ins. Co. v. OneBeacon Ins. Group, 376 F.3d 9, 29 (1st Cir. 2004); Soweco, Inc. v. Shell Oil Co., 617 F.2d 1178, 1186 (5th Cir. 1980).

99. RESTATEMENT, *supra* note 2, § 23(2).

100. *Id.* § 21 cmt. a; *see Smith*, 7 F.3d at 1329; *Singh*, 851 F. Supp. at 321.

mechanistic formula or list can set forth in advance the variety of factors that may contribute to the particular market context of an actor's use."[101]

Use of another's mark or trade name to accurately identify the other or its goods, services or business is not actionable as infringement, because such use is not reasonably likely to cause confusion.[102] Accordingly, comparative advertising will not give rise to liability for infringement,[103] although a false comparison may incur liability as a false statement under subsection 43(a)(1)(B) of the Lanham Act,[104] discussed below, or under the common law of disparagement.[105]

3. *False Statements*

Prior to 1988, section 43(a) of the Lanham Act covered only false statements or descriptions concerning one's own products; it did not apply to disparagement of a competitor's product.[106] As amended in 1988, however, section 43(a) covers false statements about another person's products.[107] As a result of this amendment, section 43(a) is now said to reach "commercial defamation."[108]

To establish a claim of unfair competition under amended subsection 43(a)(1)(B), a plaintiff must show

> that the defendant has made false or misleading statements as to his own product [or another's]; 2) that there is actual deception or at least a tendency to deceive a substantial portion of the intended audience; 3) that the deception is material in that it is likely to influence purchasing decisions; 4) that the advertised goods traveled in

---

101. RESTATEMENT, *supra* note 2, § 21 cmt. a.
102. *Id.* § 20 cmt. b.
103. *Id.*
104. 15 U.S.C. § 1125(a)(1)(B).
105. *See* Chapter 4.
106. *See* U.S. Healthcare v. Blue Cross of Greater Phila., 898 F.2d 914, 921 (3d Cir. 1990); Wojnarowicz v. Am. Family Ass'n, 745 F. Supp. 130, 141 (S.D.N.Y. 1990).
107. *See U.S. Healthcare*, 898 F.2d at 921-22; *Wojnarowicz*, 745 F. Supp. at 141.
108. *See, e.g.*, Sepenuk v. Marshall, No. 98 Civ. 1569(RCC), 2000 WL 1808977 (S.D.N.Y. 2000); Musicom Int'l, Inc. v. Serubo, 1994 WL 105551 (E.D. Pa.); Monoflo Int'l, Inc. v. Sahm, 726 F. Supp. 121, 126 n.10 (E.D. Va. 1989).

interstate commerce; and 5) that there is a likelihood of injury to the plaintiff in terms of declining sales, loss of good will, etc.[109]

"Characterized as a remedial statute that should be broadly construed, section 43(a) has been successfully used to combat a wide variety of deceptive commercial practices,"[110] including "palming off," false advertising, commercial defamation and misappropriation.[111] Section 43(a) is, however, expressly limited to false or misleading statements in connection with the sale of goods or services, and does not reach criticisms by consumer advocates or others not engaged in marketing a product or service.[112]

"When analyzing a challenged advertisement, the court first determines what message is conveyed."[113] Next, the court decides

---

109. *U.S. Healthcare*, 898 F.2d at 922-23 (quoting Max Daetwyler Corp. v. Input Graphics, Inc., 545 F. Supp. 165, 171 (E.D. Pa. 1982)); *see also* Nat'l Artists Mgmt. Co. v. Weaving, 769 F. Supp. 1224, 1230 (S.D.N.Y. 1991).

110. *Wojnarowicz*, 745 F. Supp. at 141 (citing PPX Enter., Inc. v. Audiofidelity, Inc., 746 F.2d 120, 125 (2d Cir. 1984)).

111. *See, e.g.*, B. Sanfield, Inc. v. Finlay Fine Jewelry Corp., 857 F. Supp. 1241, 1245-47 (N.D. Ill. 1994) (section 43(a) covers false advertising involving pricing); Kisch v. Ammirati Puris, Inc., 657 F. Supp. 380, 385 (S.D.N.Y. 1987) (misappropriation of photograph); R.H. Donnelley Corp. v. Illinois Bell Tel. Co., 595 F. Supp. 1202, 1206 (N.D. Ill. 1984) (substituting names); *cf.* RESTATEMENT, *supra* note 2, § 38.

112. *Wojnarowicz*, 745 F. Supp. at 141-42 (citing S. 1883, 101st Cong., 1st Sess., 135 Cong. Rec. 1207, 1217 (April 13, 1989)); *cf.* Bose Corp. v. Consumers Union of United States, Inc., 466 U.S. 485 (1984); Semco, Inc. v. Amcast, Inc., 52 F.3d 108, 111-14 (6th Cir. 1995) (false statements in trade journal article about product manufactured by author's company held actionable as commercial advertising or promotion); Gordon and Breach Science Pubs. S.A. v. Am. Inst. of Physics, 859 F. Supp. 1521, 1540-45 (S.D.N.Y. 1994) (non-profit publisher's surveys rating its own scientific journals as superior to others protected by First Amendment; promotional use of such surveys at conferences and press releases is commercial speech covered by section 43(a)).

113. *U.S. Healthcare*, 898 F.2d at 922 (citing Plough, Inc. v. Johnson & Johnson Baby Prods. Co., 532 F. Supp. 714, 717 (D. Del. 1982); 2 MCCARTHY, TRADEMARKS AND UNFAIR COMPETITION ¶ 27:7B (2d ed. 1984)). Whereas "[s]ometimes this determination may be made from the

whether it is false or misleading.[114]   Section 43(a) recognizes two categories of actionable statements: (1) literally false factual commercial claims; and (2) literally true or ambiguous factual claims "which implicitly convey a false impression, are misleading in context, or are likely to deceive consumers."[115] Mere "puffing," i.e., advertising "'that is not deceptive for no one would rely on its exaggerated claims,'"[116] is not actionable. Although a failure to disclose facts, standing alone, is not actionable under section 43(a), a statement made is actionable if it is either affirmatively misleading or "'untrue as a result of failure to disclose a material fact.'"[117] It is not enough to show that the claims contained in the defendant's advertisement are unsubstantiated if there is no falsity or deception.[118]

Furthermore, to be actionable the misrepresentation must be material, i.e., "'likely to influence the purchasing decision.'"[119] There is, however, "'no requirement that the falsification occur willfully and with intent to deceive.'"[120] The type of evidence needed to prove materiality varies depending on the type of recovery sought. Plaintiffs seeking to

---

advertisement on its face," *U.S. Healthcare*, 898 F.2d at 922 (citing Stiffel Co. v. Westwood Lighting Group, 658 F. Supp. 1103, 1110 (D. N.J. 1987); Ames Pub. Co. v. Walker-Davis Pubs., Inc., 372 F. Supp. 1, 12 (E.D. Pa. 1974)), "'[c]ontent can often be important in discerning the message conveyed.'" *Id.* (quoting *Plough*, 532 F. Supp. at 717).

114. *U.S. Healthcare*, 898 F.2d at 922 (citing *Stiffel*, 658 F. Supp. at 1110; 2 J. McCARTHY, TRADEMARKS AND UNFAIR COMPETITION ¶ 27:7B (2d ed. 1984); *Plough*, 532 F. Supp. at 717.

115. Am. Italian Pasta Co. v. New World Pasta Co., 371 F.3d 387, 390 (8th Cir. 2004) (quoting United Indus. Corp. v. Clorox Co., 140 F.3d 1175, 1180 (8th Cir. 1998)); *see U.S. Healthcare*, 898 F.2d at 922.

116. Toro Co. v. Textron, Inc., 499 F. Supp. 241, 253 n.23 (D. Del. 1980) (quoting 1 R. CALLMANN, UNFAIR COMPETITION, TRADEMARKS AND MONOPOLIES § 19.2(b)(2) (3d ed. 1967 & 1979 Supp.)); *see also U.S. Healthcare*, 898 F.2d at 922; *cf.* W. KEETON, PROSSER AND KEETON ON TORTS, § 109, at 757 (5th ed. 1984).

117. *U.S Healthcare*, 898 F.2d. at 921 (quoting 2 J. McCARTHY, TRADEMARKS AND UNFAIR COMPETITION ¶ 27:7B (2d ed. 1984)).

118. *See id.* at 922.

119. *Id.* (quoting *Toro*, 499 F. Supp. at 251).

120. *Id.* (quoting Parkway Baking Co. v. Freihofer Baking Co., 255 F.2d 641, 648 (3d Cir. 1958)).

recover monetary damages for advertising that is not literally false must prove actual deception.[121] Plaintiffs attempting to prove actual deception must offer evidence of actual consumer reaction to the challenged advertising or survey evidence demonstrating that a substantial number of consumers were actually misled by the advertisement.[122]

As noted above,[123] the reach of section 43(a) is as extensive with that of the Commerce Clause. Damages are discussed in Part B6, below.

4.   *Standing*

Although section 43(a) expressly affords a private right of action to "any person who believes that he or she is or is likely to be damaged" by a violation of that section,[124] the courts have placed limitations on this broad language. In *Colligan v. Activities Club of New York, Ltd.*,[125] the Second Circuit held that consumers alleging damages resulting from the false advertising of goods or services are without standing to assert a claim under section 43(a). Notwithstanding the section's plain language, the court was persuaded that "[t]he Act's purpose, as defined in § 45, is exclusively to protect the interests of a purely commercial class against unscrupulous commercial conduct."[126]

Subsequent decisions addressing the issue have concluded that standing under section 43(a) is not limited to direct competitors of the offending party. In *Waits v. Frito-Lay, Inc.*,[127] the Ninth Circuit held that section 43(a) standing exists "where the interest asserted by the plaintiff is a commercial interest protected by the Lanham Act."[128] Noting that section 43(a) is directed toward two types of conduct, "(1) false representations concerning the origin, association, or endorsement of goods or services through the wrongful use of another's distinctive mark, name, trade dress, or other device ("false association"), and (2) false representations in advertising concerning the qualities of goods or

---

121. Pizza Hut, Inc. v. Papa John's Int'l, 227 F.3d 489, 497 (5th Cir. 2000).
122. *Id.*
123. *See supra* notes 21-24 and accompanying text.
124. 15 U.S.C. § 1125(a)(1).
125. 442 F.2d 686 (2d Cir. 1971).
126. *Id.* at 692 (footnote omitted); *see* Serbin v. Ziebart Int'l Corp., 11 F.3d 1163 (3d Cir. 1993).
127. 978 F.2d 1093 (9th Cir. 1992).
128. *Id.* at 1108.

services ("false advertising"),"[129] the court concluded that standing under the "false association" prong is not limited to competitors of the wrongdoer, as others may suffer commercial harm as a result of a false association.[130] Holding that a singer had standing to complain of the unauthorized imitation of his voice in a commercial advertising, the court reconciled prior Ninth Circuit decisions that had reached different results regarding the standing of non-competitors.[131]

Other courts have concluded that standing under section 43(a) may be afforded to persons other than competitors of the wrongdoer, so long as a "commercial" interest is involved.[132] In *Serbin v. Ziebart International Corp.*,[133] the Third Circuit held that the 1988 amendment to section 43(a) did not have the effect of extending standing to consumers; only those asserting a "commercial interest" may bring suit. The Fifth Circuit has held that the focus of the Lanham Act is on anticompetitive conduct in a commercial context.[134] Borrowing from caselaw governing antitrust standing, several courts have applied a five-part test to determine standing under 43(a), under which the court is to consider (1) the nature of the plaintiff's alleged injury, including whether the injury is of a type that Congress sought to redress in providing a private remedy for violations of the statute; (2) the directness or indirectness of the asserted injury; (3) the proximity or remoteness of the party to the

---

129. *Id.* (citations omitted).
130. *Id.* at 1109-10.
131. *Id.* at 1107-10. *Compare* Halicki v. United Artists Comm., Inc., 812 F.2d 1213 (9th Cir. 1987) (defendants breached agreement with movie producer to advertise movie as rated "PG" rather than "R"; standing denied) *with* Smith v. Montoro, 648 F.2d 602 (9th Cir. 1981) (defendants substituted the name of another actor for the plaintiff in movie screen credits; standing upheld).
132. *See, e.g.,* Thorn v. Reliance Van Co., 736 F.2d 929 (3d Cir. 1984) (major shareholder of corporation had standing to challenge false advertising by competitor controlled by certain of plaintiff's fellow directors, where bankruptcy trustee of plaintiff's company failed to assert claim); *see also* *Serbin*, 11 F.3d at 1177-78 (holding that although standing is not limited to direct competitors, consumers do not have the requisite commercial interest); *cf.* Dovenmuehle v. Gilldorn Mtg. Midwest Corp., 871 F.2d 697, 699-701 (7th Cir. 1989) (discussing without deciding the issue).
133. 11 F.3d 1163 (3d Cir. 1993).
134. Proctor & Gamble Co., 242 F.3d 539 (5th Cir. 2001).

alleged injurious conduct; (4) the speculativeness of the damages claim; and (5) the risk of duplicative damages or complexity in apportioning damages.[135]

5. *Defenses*

a. Limitations and Laches

The Lanham Act does not have its own statute of limitations, and in actions involving infringement the doctrine of laches rather than limitations typically is employed when determining the availability of monetary and injunctive relief.[136] In actions under section 43(a) for deceptive marketing, the courts often refer to state statutes of limitations as a guide for determining the timeliness of the plaintiff's suit.[137] Where there is no specific state statute applicable to such claims,[138] the courts use the most analogous statute.[139]

---

135. Logan v. Burgers Ozark County Cured Hams, Inc., 263 F.3d 447, 460 (5th Cir. 2001); Conte Bros. Auto., Inc. v. Quaker State-Slick 50, Inc., 165 F.3d 221, 229 (3d Cir. 1998).

136. *See, e.g.*, United States v. Foote, 413 F.3d 1240, 1248 (10th Cir. 2005); Santana Prods., Inc. v. Bobrick Washroom Equip., Inc., 401 F.3d 123, 135 (3d Cir. 2005); What-A-Burger of Va., Inc. v. Whataburger, Inc. of Corpus Christi, Tex., 357 F.3d 441, 449 (4th Cir. 2004); *see also* RESTATEMENT, *supra* note 2, § 31.

137. *Santana Prods.*, 401 F.3d at 135; Polar Bear Prods., Inc. v. Timex Corp., 384 F.3d 700, 720 & n.17 (9th Cir. 2004).

138. *See, e.g.*, Island Steel Sys., Inc. v. Waters, 296 F.3d 200, 207-08 (3d Cir. 2002) (finding no specific Virgin Islands statute applicable to Lanham Act claims).

139. *See, e.g.*, *Island Steel*, 296 F.3d at 208-11 ("The courts addressing the question are divided on whether common law fraud claims or claims under state unfair business practices statutes are more analogous to Lanham Act claims for trademark infringement.") (citing Lyons P'ship, L.P. v. Morris Costumes, Inc., 243 F.3d 789, 796-97 (4th Cir. 2001) (applying statute of limitations of North Carolina Unfair Trade Practices Act to plaintiffs' Lanham Act Section 43(a) claims); Kason Indus., Inc. v. Component Hardware Group, Inc., 120 F.3d 1199, 1203-04 (11th Cir. 1997) (adopting the limitations period in Georgia Uniform Deceptive Trade Practices Act as most analogous cause of action under state law); Federal Express Corp. v. United States Postal Serv., 75 F. Supp. 2d 807, 816-17 (W.D. Tenn. 1999) (applying the Tennessee Consumer Protection Act's statute of

Inexcusable delay in bringing suit, resulting in prejudice to the defendant, may support the defense.[140] Mere delay in bringing suit is insufficient to support the defense;[141] if the plaintiff is unaware of the defendant's wrongful conduct[142] or the defendant is not harmed by the delay,[143] the defense will not be sustained.

It has been held that laches will not bar issuance of an injunction,[144] but is available as a bar to other relief such as damages.[145] Laches begins

---

limitations to Section 43(a) claims); Eppendorf-Netheler-Hinz GMBH v. Enterton Co., 89 F. Supp. 2d 483, 486 (S.D.N.Y. 2000) (borrowing fraud statute of limitations to create a presumption of laches applicable to plaintiff's trademark infringement claims), Harley-Davidson, Inc. v. Estate of O'Connell, 13 F. Supp. 2d 271, 279 (N.D.N.Y. 1998) (same), Derrick Mfg. Corp. v. Southwestern Wire Cloth, Inc., 934 F.Supp. 796, 804-05 (S.D. Tex. 1996) (applying fraud statute of limitations to Section 43(a) claims), and Johannsen v. Brown, 797 F.Supp. 835, 839-40 (D. Or. 1992) (same)).

140. *See* Joint Stock Soc. v. UDV N. Am., 266 F.3d 164, 185 n.12 (3d Cir. 2001) (discussing standard for laches employed by district court); Pappan Enter. v. Hardee's Food Sys., 143 F.3d 800, 804 (3d Cir. 1998).

141. In re Beaty, 306 F.3d 914, 927 (9th Cir. 2002); Bridgestone/Firestone Research, Inc. v. Automobile Club De L'Ouest De La France, 245 F.3d 1359, 1362 (Fed. Cir. 2001) ("Mere delay in asserting a trademark-related right does not necessarily result in changed conditions sufficient to support the defense of laches."); Kellogg Co. v. Exxon Corp., 209 F.3d 562, 569 (6th Cir. 2000).

142. *See, e.g., Kellogg*, 209 F.3d at 570; *Kason Indus., Inc.*, 120 F.3d at 1206.

143. *See, e.g., In re Beaty*, 306 F.3d at 927-28; *Bridgestone*, 245 F.3d at 1362 ("There must [] have been some detriment due to the delay."); Advanced Cardiovascular Sys. v. Scimed Life Sys., 988 F.2d 1157, 1161 (Fed. Cir. 1993).

144. Intertool, Ltd. v. Texar Corp., 369 F.3d 1289, 1297-98 (Fed. Cir. 2004); Virgin Enter. Ltd. v. Nawab, 335 F.3d 141, 152 (2d Cir. 2003); ProFitness Physical Therapy Center v. Pro-Fit Orthopedic & Sports Physical Therapy P.C., 314 F.3d 62, 68 (2d Cir. 2002); Jarrow Formulas, Inc. v. Nutrition Now, Inc., 304 F.3d 829, 840 (9th Cir. 2002); Lyons Partnership, L.P. v. Morris Costumes, Inc., 243 F.3d 789, 797-800 (4th Cir. 2001); *Kason Indus., Inc.*, 120 F.3d at 1207. *But see* Imagineering, Inc. v. Van Klassens, Inc., 851 F. Supp. 532, 535 (S.D.N.Y. 1994); Kusan, Inc. v. Alpha Distribs., Inc., 693 F. Supp. 1372, 1375 (D. Conn. 1988); RESTATEMENT,

to run when the plaintiff's right to sue first ripens,[146] although a change in the character or scope of the defendant's conduct may reset the laches clock.[147] Section 33(b) of the Lanham Act was amended in 1988 to provide that even an incontestable mark is subject to equitable defenses such as laches and estoppel.[148] It has been held, however, that neither laches nor equitable estoppel is available to bar an injunction in a case of intentional infringement.[149]

b.   Fair Use

Under section 28 of the Restatement (Third) of Unfair Competition, it is a defense to an action for infringement that the defendant's use of a mark or trade name is descriptive or geographically descriptive of the defendant's goods, services or business, or is a personal name of the defendant or someone connected with the defendant, and that the defendant used the designation fairly and in good faith for that purpose.[150] Similarly, the Lanham Act[151] protects the non-trademark[152]

---

supra note 2, § 31 (laches available to bar injunctive relief, damages and recovery of profits).

145. *See, e.g.*, Nartron Corp. v. STMicroelectronics, Inc., 305 F.3d 397, 412 (6th Cir. 2002); *Kellogg*, 209 F.3d at 570; Hot Wax, Inc. v. Turtle Wax, Inc., 191 F.3d 813, 822 (7th Cir. 1999).

146. What-A-Burger Of Va., Inc. v. Whataburger, Inc. Of Corpus Christi, Tex., 357 F.3d 441, 449 (4th Cir. 2004); Nartron Corp., 305 F.3d at 408; 4 J. THOMAS MCCARTHY, MCCARTHY ON TRADEMARKS AND UNFAIR COMPETITION §§ 26:43-26:44 (4th ed. 2003).

147. *See, e.g.*, Grupo Gigante S.A. De CV v. Dallo & Co., 391 F.3d 1088, 1103 (9th Cir. 2004); Danjaq LLC v. Sony Corp., 263 F.3d 942, 955 (9th Cir. 2001).

148. 15 U.S.C. § 1115(b)(8).

149. *See, e.g.*, United States v. Milstein, 401 F.3d 53, 64 (2d Cir. 2005); Hermes Intern. v. Lederer de Paris Fifth Ave., Inc., 219 F.3d 104, 107 (2d Cir. 2000). *Cf.* Kason Industries, Inc. v. Component Hardware Group, Inc., 120 F.3d 1199, 1207 (11th Cir. 1997) ("Generally, laches will not bar an injunction against an intentional infringer . . . [however], if the likelihood of confusion is inevitable, or so strong as to outweigh the effect of the plaintiff's delay in bringing a suit, a court may in its discretion grant injunctive relief, even in cases where a suit for damages is appropriately barred.").

150. RESTATEMENT, *supra* note 2, § 28.

151. *See* 15 U.S.C. § 1115(b)(4).

use of a term "fairly and in good faith only to describe the goods or services of such party, or their geographic origin."[153] "In essence, the fair use defense prevents a trademark registrant from appropriating a descriptive term for its own use to the exclusion of others, who may be prevented thereby from accurately describing their own goods."[154]

Under this doctrine, and subject to state "anti-dilution" laws,[155] "[t]he holder of a protectable descriptive mark has no legal claim to an exclusive right in the primary, descriptive meaning of the term; consequently, anyone is free to use the term in its primary, descriptive sense so long as such use does not lead to customer confusion as to the source of the goods or services."[156] In *New Kids on the Block v. New America Publishing, Inc.*,[157] the Ninth Circuit held that a defendant is entitled to avail himself of the fair use defense if he meets the following three part test. First, the product or service in question must be one not readily identifiable without use of the trademark; second, only so much of the mark or marks may be used as is reasonably necessary to identify the product or service; and third, the user must do nothing that would, in conjunction with the mark, suggest sponsorship or endorsement by the trademark holder.[158]

---

152. "It is not a trademark infringement to use words in their ordinary, rather than in their special, trademark meaning." 15 U.S.C. § 1115(b)(4); *see also, e.g.*, Century 21 Real Estate Corp. v. Lendingtree, Inc., 425 F.3d 211, 219-20 (3d Cir. 2005); Interactive Prods. Corp. v. a2z Mobile Office Solutions, Inc., 326 F.3d 687, 695 (6th Cir. 2003) (citing New Kids on the Block v. News Am. Publ'g, Inc., 971 F.2d 302, 307 (9th Cir. 1992) (holding that infringement laws "simply do not apply" to a "non-trademark use of a mark")).

153. 15 U.S.C. § 1115(b)(4); *see also, e.g.*, KP Permanent Make-Up, Inc. v. Lasting Impression I, Inc., 408 F.3d 596, 607 (9th Cir. 2005).

154. Zatarains, Inc. v. Oak Grove Smokehouse, Inc., 698 F.2d 786, 791 (5th Cir. 1983) (citing Soweco, Inc. v. Shell Oil Co., 617 F.2d 1178, 1185 (5th Cir. 1980)).

155. *See* RESTATEMENT, *supra* note 2, § 25 statutory note.

156. *Id.* (citing 1 J. MCCARTHY, TRADEMARKS AND UNFAIR COMPETITION § 11.-17, at 379 (1973)).

157. 971 F.2d 302, 308 (9th Cir. 1992).

158. *Id.*; *see also* J.K. Harris 7 Co., L.L.C. v. Kassel, 253 F. Supp. 2d 1120, 1125 (N.D. Cal. 2003).

The fair use defense is available in actions alleging false designation of origin as well as cases of simple infringement.[159] The doctrine is not available, however, where likelihood of confusion or bad faith is shown.[160]

c.   Consent and Acquiescence

Consent is a defense to an action for infringement.[161] Consent may be either express or implied, and the defense of implied consent, or "acquiescence," is based on conduct of the plaintiff that reasonably leads the defendant to believe that it will not be sued.[162] As such, the defense of acquiescence cannot be based on the plaintiff's conduct toward third parties.[163] Also, this defense is terminable at will.[164]

d.   Unclean Hands

A plaintiff's own inequitable conduct is a defense to a claim under section 43(a).[165] For example, in *Haagen-Dazs, Inc. v. Frusen Gladje Ltd.*[166] the court denied the plaintiff's application for a preliminary injunction, which was based in part on the claim that the defendant's trade dress was intended to deceive the public into believing that its ice

---

159. *See* Horphag Research Ltd. v. Pellegrini, 337 F.3d 1036, 1041 (9th Cir. 2003), *cert. denied sub nom*, Garcia v. Horphag Research Ltd., 540 U.S. 1111 (2004).

160. *See, e.g.*, KP Permanent Make-Up, Inc. v. Lasting Impression I, Inc., 408 F.3d 596, 608-09 (9th Cir. 2005); ETW Corp. v. Jireh Pub., Inc., 332 F.3d 915, 950 (6th Cir. 2003); EMI Catalogue P'ship v. Hill, Holliday, Connors, Cosmopulos Inc., 228 F.3d 56, 66 (2d Cir. 2000).

161. RESTATEMENT, *supra* note 2, § 29.

162. *See* Pappan Enter., Inc. v. Hardee's Food Sys., Inc., 143 F.3d 800, 804 (3d Cir. 1998); TMT North Am., Inc. v. Magic Touch GmbH, 124 F.3d 876, 885 (7th Cir. 1997); SunAmerica Corp. v. Sun Life Assurance Co. of Canada, 77 F.3d 1325, 1334 (11th Cir. 1996).

163. Sweetheart Plastics, Inc. v. Detroit Forming, Inc., 743 F.2d 1039, 1046 (4th Cir. 1984).

164. Menendez v. Holt, 128 U.S. 514, 524 (1888); Conagra, Inc. v. Singleton, 743 F.2d 1508, 1516 (11th Cir. 1984). *But see* Johnny's Fine Foods, Inc. v. Johnny's Inc., 286 F. Supp. 2d 876, 882 (M.D. Tenn. 2003).

165. RESTATEMENT, *supra* note 2, § 32; Worthington v. Anderson, 386 F.3d 1314, 1320-21 (10th Cir. 2004); *see also* 15 U.S.C. § 1115(b)(8).

166. 493 F. Supp. 73 (S.D.N.Y. 1980).

cream was made in Sweden, when in fact it was produced in the United States: "[S]ince plaintiff itself has attempted to package its product in such a way as to give the impression that it is of Scandinavian origin, although it too is, in fact, of domestic origin, it is guilty of the same deceptive trade practices of which it accuses defendants."[167]

In order to support this defense the plaintiff's wrongful conduct must be related to the subject matter of the section 43(a) claim,[168] and must be more than insubstantial.[169] Courts will apply the unclean hands doctrine when the plaintiff's conduct is both inequitable and involves the subject matter of the plaintiff's claim.[170] It has been said that this defense will be sustained only in the most egregious circumstances,[171] and must be proven by "'clear, unequivocal and convincing' evidence."[172]

e. Prior Use

Prior use is a defense to a claim under section 43(a).[173] It has been held that a prior use in a geographic area not yet penetrated by the

---

167. *Id.* at 76.
168. *Worthington*, 386 F.3d 1314, 1320-21; Sugar Busters LLC v. Brennan, 177 F.3d 258, 272 (5th Cir. 1999); Levi Strauss & Co. v. Shilon, 121 F.3d 1309, 1313 (9th Cir. 1997).
169. *See, e.g.*, Japan Telecom, Inc. v. Japan Telecom Am. Inc., 287 F.3d 866, 870 (9th Cir. 2002) ("To show that a trademark plaintiff's conduct is inequitable, defendant must show that plaintiff used the trademark to deceive consumers."); Ciba-Geigy Corp. v. Bolar Pharm. Co., 747 F.2d 844, 855 (3d Cir. 1984).
170. Pharmacia Corp. v. GlaxoSmithKline Consumer Healthcare, L.P., 292 F. Supp. 2d 594, 610 (W.D.N.J. 2003) (quoting Ciba-Geigy Corp., 747 F. 2d at 855).
171. *See, e.g.*, Citizens Fin. Group, Inc. v. Citizens Nat'l Bank of Evans City, 383 F.3d 110, 129-30 (3d Cir. 2004) (citing *Ciba-Geigy*, 747 F.2d at 855)); Hot Wax, Inc. v. Turtle Wax, Inc., 191 F.3d 813, 826 (7th Cir. 1999).
172. Am. Home Prods. Corp. v. Johnson & Johnson, 654 F. Supp. 568, 590-91 (S.D.N.Y. 1987) (quoting Nike, Inc. v. Rubber Mfgrs. Ass'n, 509 F. Supp. 919, 926 (S.D.N.Y. 1981)).
173. 15 U.S.C. § 1115(b)(5). *see also, e.g.*, Team Tires Plus, Ltd. v. Tires Plus, Inc., 394 F.3d 831, 835 (10th Cir. 2005); TE-TA-MA Truth Foundation— Family of URI, Inc. v. World Church of Creator, 297 F.3d 662, 667 (7th

plaintiff will provide a basis for allowing the defendant to continue its use.[174]

f.   Abandonment

Abandonment is a defense to a claim of trademark infringement.[175] Abandonment may occur in either of two circumstances. First, a mark may be deemed abandoned when its use has been discontinued with intent not to resume such use.[176] Intent not to resume may be inferred from the circumstances, and nonuse for three consecutive years is prima facie evidence of abandonment.[177]

Second, a mark is deemed abandoned when "any course of conduct of the owner, including acts of omission as well as commission, causes the mark to become the generic name for the goods or services on or in connection with which it is used or otherwise to lose its significance as a mark."[178]   Purchaser motivation is not a test for determining abandonment under this prong.[179]

6.   *Remedies*

Relief under section 43(a) may include an injunction,[180] a destruction order,[181] recovery of the defendant's profits,[182] and any damages sustained.[183] In order to recover damages under the Lanham Act, a plaintiff is required to establish (1) injury casually linked to the

---

Cir. 2002); Maktab Tarighe Oveyssi Shah Maghsoudi, Inc. v. Kianfar, 179 F.3d 1244, 1249 (9th Cir. 1999).

174. Nissan Motor Co. v. Nissan Computer Corp., 378 F.3d 1002, 1012 (9th Cir. 2004); Nat'l Ass'n for Healthcare Comm'ns, Inc. v. Central Ark. Area Agency on Aging, Inc., 257 F.3d 732, 737 (8th Cir. 2001). *But see* Enterprise Rent-A-Car Co. v. Advantage Rent-A-Car, Inc., 330 F.3d 1333, 1341-42 (Fed. Cir. 2003).

175. 15 U.S.C. § 1115(b)(2); RESTATEMENT, *supra* note 2, § 30.

176. 15 U.S.C. § 1127.

177. *Id.* "Use" means "the bona fide use of [the] mark made in the ordinary course of trade, and not made merely to reserve a right in a mark." *Id.*

178. *Id.*

179. *Id.*

180. 15 U.S.C. § 1116(a).

181. *Id.* § 1118.

182. *Id.* § 1117(a).

183. *Id.*

alleged violation, and (2) actual damages flowing from the alleged violation.[184] In *Seven-Up Co. v. Coca-Cola Co.*,[185] the Fifth Circuit held that causation of damages is not shown by a simple chronology of events and the presentation of false or misleading materials.[186]

Proof of damages cannot be based on speculation but must be established with a reasonable degree of certainty.[187] A plaintiff must specifically show the basis for recovery: that injury or profitable infringement actually occurred.[188] The failure to demonstrate that the defendant actually benefited from the alleged false advertising forecloses a claim for lost profits.[189] When the advertising is noncomparative in nature there is no presumption of causation, even when the advertising is literally false.[190] When calculating the defendant's profits, the plaintiff is required to prove the amount of the defendant's sales attributable to the violation;[191] the burden then shifts to the defendant to prove the elements of cost or other claimed deductions.[192] However, in order to establish causation of damages, a plaintiff is required to prove more than just lost profits.[193]

When assessing damages, a court may enter judgment, "according to the circumstances of the case, for any sum above the amount found as

---

184. Xoom, Inc. v. Imageline, Inc., 323 F.3d 279, 286 (4th Cir. 2003); Cashmere & Camel Hair Mfrs. Inst. v. Saks Fifth Ave., 284 F.3d 302, 318 (1st Cir. 2002); Logan v. Burgers Ozark Country Cured Hams, Inc., 263 F.3d 447, 462-65 (5th Cir. 2001).

185. 86 F.3d 1379 (5th Cir. 1996).

186. *Id.* at 1382.

187. Dyll v. Adams, 167 F.3d 945, 947 (5th Cir. 1999).

188. *See* Mackie v. Rieser, 296 F.3d 909, 911 (9th Cir. 2002); Montgomery v. Noga, 168 F.3d 1282, 1294 (11th Cir. 1999); Rite-Hite Corp. v. Kelley Co., 56 F.3d 1538, 1582 (Fed. Cir. 1995).

189. *Logan*, 263 F.2d at 464-65.

190. Laughlin Prods., Inc. v. ETS, Inc., 257 F. Supp.2d 863, 868-70 (N.D. Tex. 2002), *aff'd*, 2003 WL 21674751 (Fed. Cir. 2003); Healthpoint v. Stratus Pharm., Inc., 273 F. Supp. 2d 871, 884-86 (W.D. Tex. 2001).

191. *Id.*; 15 U.S.C. § 1117(a).

192. *Id.*

193. *See* Lindy Pen Co. v. Bic Pen Corp., 982 F.2d 1400, 1407 (9th Cir. 1993) (calculation of lost profits containing items in which no likelihood of deception existed was irreparably flawed).

actual damages, not exceeding three times such amount."[194] If the court determines that recovery based on profits is either inadequate or excessive, it may enter judgment for such sum that, in its discretion, it finds to be just, "according to the circumstances of the case."[195] In either such case, the award "shall constitute compensation and not a penalty."[196] In addition to the recovery of costs, the court may in "exceptional cases" award reasonable attorneys' fees.[197]

The general principles that govern applications for preliminary injunctive relief apply to claims under section 43(a), and involve inquiry into whether the plaintiff is likely to succeed on the merits, whether irreparable harm will occur if relief is not granted, a balancing of the hardships to the plaintiff and defendant and consideration of the public interest.[198] It has been held that in a case of infringement proof of likelihood of confusion establishes both the likelihood of success on the merits as well as the irreparable injury necessary for preliminary injunctive relief.[199] Similarly, with respect to a claim of false advertising under section 43(a), proof of a false representation likely to deceive may warrant preliminary injunctive relief.[200]

Prior to 1988, the federal courts were in disagreement as to whether the remedy sections of the Lanham Act extended to violations of section

---

194. *Id.*
195. *Id.*; *see* Tex. Pig Stands, Inc. v. Hard Rock Cafe Int'l, 951 F.2d 684, 694-96 (5th Cir. 1992) (absent proof of attempt to "palm off" defendant's product as that of plaintiff, or any diversion of sales, infringer's retention of its profits not unjust or inequitable).
196. 15 U.S.C. § 1117(a).
197. *Id.*; Scott Fetzer Co. v. House of Vacuums Inc., 381 F.3d 477, 490 (5th Cir. 2004); Idaho Potato Comm'n v. M & M Produce Farm & Sales, 335 F.3d 130, 140 (2d Cir. 2003).
198. *See generally* 11A, C. WRIGHT, A. MILLER & M. KANE, FEDERAL PRACTICE AND PROCEDURE § 2948 (1995).
199. *See, e.g.*, GoTo.com, Inc. v. Walt Disney Co., 202 F.3d 1199, 1209 (9th Cir. 2000); S&R Corp. v. Jiffy Lube Int'l, Inc., 968 F.2d 371, 375 (3d. Cir. 1992).
200. *See, e.g.*, Pizza Hut, Inc. v. Papa John's Int'l, Inc., 227 F.3d 489, 495 (5th Cir. 2000); Valu Eng'g, Inc. v. Nolu Plastics, Inc., 732 F. Supp. 1024, 1026 (N.D. Cal. 1990).

43(a) that did not involve a registered mark.[201] In order to remove any confusion, sections 34(a), 35(a) and 36 of the Act were amended in 1988 to make it clear that the availability of injunctive relief, profits, damages, costs and attorneys' fees, as well as destruction orders, do not require ownership of a registration.[202]

C.   Section 5 of the FTC Act

In 1914 Congress enacted the Federal Trade Commission Act, section 5 of which introduced the expression "unfair methods of competition."[203]   As the Supreme Court has explained, "[d]ebate apparently convinced the sponsors of the legislation that the words 'unfair competition,' in the light of their meaning at common law, were too narrow."[204] The federal courts have confirmed that this phase has a broader meaning than "unfair competition" under the common law; "that it does not admit of precise definition; its scope being left to judicial determination as controversies arise."[205] As a consequence, "[w]hat are 'unfair methods of competition' are . . . to be determined in particular instances, upon evidence, in the light of particular competitive conditions and of what is found to be a specific and substantial public interest."[206] In response to early decisions interpreting section 5 to proscribe only conduct resulting in injury to competitors,[207] Congress enacted the 1938

---

201. *See* S. Rep. No. 515, 100th Cong., 2d Sess., *reprinted in* 1988 U.S. Code Cong. & Admin. News 5577, 5601-02.

202. *See id.*; 15 U.S.C. § 1116(a) (injunctive relief), § 1117(a) (profits, damages, costs and attorneys' fees), § 1118 (destruction orders).

203. 15 U.S.C. § 45; *see* A.L.A. Schechter Poultry Corp. v. U.S., 295 U.S. 495, 532 (1935). Regarding "unfair methods of competition" in import trade, *see* 19 U.S.C. § 1337.

204. *Schechter Poultry*, 295 U.S. at 532.

205. *Id.* (citing FTC v. Raladam Co., 283 U.S. 643, 648, 649 (1931); FTC v. R.F. Keppel & Bro., Inc., 291 U.S. 304, 310-12 (1934)).

206. *Id.* at 533 (citing FTC v. Beech-Nut Packing Co., 257 U.S. 441, 453 (1922); FTC v. Klesner, 280 U.S. 19, 27, 28 (1929); FTC v. Raladam Co., 283 U.S. 643 (1931); FTC v. R.F. Keppel & Bro., Inc., 291 U.S. 304 (1934), FTC v. Algoma Lumber Co., 291 U.S. 67, 73 (1934)).

207. *See* FTC v. Raladam Co., 283 U.S. 643, 647-54 (1931); FTC v. Gratz, 253 U.S. 421, 428-29 (1920); *cf.* FTC V. Algoma Lumber Co., 291 U.S. 67 (1934); FTC v. R.F. Keppel & Bro., Inc., 291 U.S. 304 (1934); FTC v. Winsted Hosiery Co., 258 U.S. 483 (1922).

Wheeler-Lea Amendment, which extended the reach of section 5 to "unfair or deceptive acts or practices."[208] The purpose of the 1938 amendment was to make "the consumer, who may be injured by an unfair trade practice, of equal concern, before the law, with the merchant or manufacturer injured by the unfair methods of a dishonest competitor."[209] In 1975, Congress again amended section 45 to reach not only activities "in commerce" but also those "affecting commerce."[210]

The FTC Act is administered and enforced by the Federal Trade Commission. A quasi-judicial body, the FTC issues complaints, conducts hearings before administrative law judges, and affords review by the full Commission, whose decisions then are reviewable by the federal courts.[211] The FTC Act authorizes the Commission to act only in "the interest of the public."[212] Although the Commission is not authorized to decide a solely private controversy,[213] the courts accord great deference to a "public interest" determination by the Commission,[214] which will be overturned only for an abuse of discretion.[215] Although the courts have held that there is no private right of action under the FTC Act,[216] most states have enacted some version of the Unfair Trade Practices and Consumer Protection Act, which was developed by the FTC and published by the Council of State

---

208. 15 U.S.C. § 45(a)(1).
209. FTC v. Sperry & Hutchison Co., 405 U.S. 233, 244 (1972) (quoting H.R. Rep. No. 1613, 75th Cong., 1st Sess. 3 (1937)).
210. 15 U.S.C. § 45.
211. *See* 15 U.S.C. §§ 41-56; 16 C.F.R. Parts 1-16 (1993); VI E. KINTNER & W. KRATZKE, FEDERAL ANTITRUST LAW (1986); *see also Schechter Poultry*, 295 U.S. at 533.
212. 15 U.S.C. § 45(b); *see* FTC v. Klessner, 280 U.S. 19, 30 (1929).
213. *See Klessner*, 280 U.S. at 30.
214. *See, e.g.*, Slough v. FTC, 396 F.2d 870, 872 (5th Cir. 1968).
215. *Id.*
216. Holloway v. Bristol-Myers Corp., 485 F.2d 986, 997 (D.C. Cir. 1973); *see* Amalgamated Util. Workers v. Consol. Edison Co., 309 U.S. 261, 268-69 (1940) (dictum); Moore v. NY Cotton Exch., 270 U.S. 593, 603 (1926); *see also* Jeter v. Credit Bureau, Inc., 754 F.2d 907, 912 n.5 (11th Cir.), *on reh'g*, 760 F.2d 1168, 1174 n.5 (11th Cir. 1985).

Governments in 1967.[217] Many of these so-called "little FTC Acts" afford a private right of action, adopting the language in section 5 of the FTC Act prohibiting "[u]nfair methods of competition . . . and unfair or deceptive acts or practices. . . ."[218] In addition, many of them are interpreted by reference to precedent under section 5 of the FTC Act.[219] Accordingly, familiarity with section 5 often is useful when addressing issues arising in private litigation under "little FTC Acts."

1. *Unfair Methods of Competition*

Under the "unfair methods of competition" prong of section 5, the FTC is authorized to challenge violations of the federal antitrust laws.[220] This authority reaches beyond antitrust violations, however, allowing the Commission to challenge conduct that may be characterized as an "incipient" antitrust violation[221] as well as acts contrary to the "policy" of the antitrust laws,[222] and even conduct contrary to "public policy."[223] The Commission likewise has challenged a broad range of conduct under the "unfair or deceptive acts or practices" prong of section 5, including the use of false and misleading use of descriptive words,[224] pictures,[225]

217. For a listing of such statutes, *see* RESTATEMENT, *supra* note 2, § 1 statutory note note and ABA ANTITRUST SECTION, CONSUMER PROTECTION HANDBOOK (2004).
218. 15 U.S.C. § 45(a)(1).
219. *See* ABA ANTITRUST SECTION, ANTITRUST LAW DEVELOPMENTS 723 (5th ed. 2002); *see generally* ABA ANTITRUST SECTION, CONSUMER PROTECTION HANDBOOK (2004); ABA SECTION OF ANTITRUST LAW, STATE ANTITRUST PRACTICE AND STATUTES (3d ed. 2004). Several states have also enacted some form of the Uniform Deceptive Trade Practices Act, affording a private right of action to competitors likely to be injured by deceptive advertising. For a listing of such state statutes, *see* RESTATEMENT, *supra* note 2, § 2 statutory note.
220. FTC v. Ind. Fed'n of Dentists, 476 U.S. 447, 454 (1986); United States v. Cement Inst., 333 U.S. 683, 690-92 (1948).
221. FTC v. Texaco, Inc., 393 U.S. 223, 225 (1968); FTC v. Brown Shoe Co., 384 U.S. 316, 322 (1966).
222. FTC v. Beech-Nut Packing Co., 257 U.S. 441, 453 (1922).
223. *Ind. Fed'n of Dentists*, 476 U.S. at 454-55; FTC v. Sperry & Hutchinson Co., 405 U.S. 233, 244 (1972).
224. *See, e.g.*, FTC v. Amy Travel Serv., Inc., 875 F.2d 564, 569 (7th Cir. 1989) ("full-economy" airline fares); Parker Pen Co. v. FTC, 159 F.2d 509, 510-11 (7th Cir. 1946) ("guaranteed for life").

trade names and trademarks,[226] unsubstantiated product claims,[227] endorsements and testimonials,[228] unfair sales and credit practices,[229] false and misleading comparative advertising[230] and commercial disparagement,[231] among many others.[232] As such, section 5 covers much conduct that also is the subject of section 43(a) of the Lanham Act.[233]

2. *"Little FTC Acts"*

"Little FTC Acts" and analogous consumer protection statutes typically prohibit a broad range of unfair and deceptive acts and

---

225. *See, e.g.*, FTC v. U.S. Sales Corp., 785 F. Supp. 737, 745 (N.D. Ill. 1992) (picture of showroom-quality automobiles).

226. *See, e.g.*, FTC v. Royal Milling Co., 288 U.S. 212, 214-16 (1933) (use of "manufacturer" by firm that did not manufacture product); Resort Car Rental Sys., Inc. v. FTC, 518 F.2d 962, 964 (9th Cir. 1975) ("Dollar-a-Day" car rental).

227. *See, e.g.*, Thompson Med. Co. v. FTC, 791 F.2d 189, 194 (D.C. Cir. 1986) (requiring clinical trials to support claims of comparative efficacy); Bristol-Myers Co. v. FTC, 738 F.2d 554, 557 (2d Cir. 1984) (same).

228. *See, e.g.*, County Tweeds, Inc. v. FTC, 326 F.2d 144, 146-47 (2d Cir. 1964) (misrepresenting test results); Niresk Indus., Inc. v. FTC, 278 F.2d 337, 341-42 (7th Cir. 1960) (misleading use of Good Housekeeping seal).

229. *See, e.g.*, Tashoff v. FTC, 437 F.2d 707, 709 & n.3 (D.C. Cir. 1970) (bait and switch); Portwood v. FTC, 418 F.2d 419, 420-23 (10th Cir. 1969) (shipping unordered merchandise without disclosing that recipient is under no obligation to accept it).

230. *See, e.g.*, Chrysler Corp. v. FTC, 561 F.2d 357, 360-63 (D.C. Cir. 1977) (comparative advertising of automobiles).

231. *See, e.g.*, Holland Furnace Co. v. FTC, 295 F.2d 302, 305 (7th Cir. 1961) (misrepresentations regarding competitors' products); E.B. Muller & Co. v. FTC, 142 F.2d 511, 516 (6th Cir. 1944) (disparagement of competitor's product).

232. See W.J. Dunn, Annotation, What Constitutes False, Misleading or Deceptive Advertising or Promotional Practices Subject to Action by Federal Trade Commission, 65 A.L.R.2d 225 §§ 13-27 (1959); VII E. KINTNER & W. KRATZKE, FEDERAL ANTITRUST LAW §§ 49.23-.34 (1988).

233. See Serbin v. Ziebart Int'l Corp., 11 F.3d 1163, 1178-79 (3d Cir. 1993) (discussing the similar policies of the two Acts); Sandoz Pharm. Corp. v. Richardson-Vicks, Inc., 902 F.2d 222, 226-29 (3d Cir. 1990) (comparing burdens of proof for Lanham Act plaintiffs and the FTC).

practices, and "unconscionable" conduct in trade or business.[234]   In
addition, these statutes often contain a laundry list of acts and practices
deemed to be unfair or deceptive, such as "bait and switch" tactics,
deceptive pricing, false and misleading statements regarding the origin,
sponsorship, quality, characteristics and uses of goods and services, and
disparagement.[235]

While some states have construed their consumer protection acts to
be coextensive with common law fraud,[236] many have held that a finding
of fraud or an intent to deceive is not necessary to establish a violation.[237]

3. *Applicability*

In general, the purpose of these statutes is to protect the ordinary
consumer, as evidenced by both the language of the statutes and the
construction placed upon them by the courts. Many contain language
limiting their applicability to goods, property or services sold primarily
for personal, family or household use.[238]   In such cases, recovery has
been denied where the plaintiff was not a "consumer,"[239] or where the

---

234. *See Serbin*, 11 F.3d at 1178-79.
235. *See id.*
236. *See, e.g.*, Zine v. Chrysler Corp., 600 N.W.2d 384, 398 (Mich. App. 1999)
    (citing with approval Mayhall v. A.H. Pond Co., 341 N.W.2d 268, 270
    (Mich. App. 1983)); Lesher v. Baltimore Football Club, 496 N.E.2d 785,
    790 (Ind. App. 1986), *vacated in part on other grounds*, 512 N.E.2d 156
    (1987).
237. *See, e.g.*, State ex rel. Babbitt v. Goodyear Tire & Rubber Co., 626 P.2d
    1115 (Ariz. App. 1981); Urling v. Helms Exterm., 468 So. 2d 451 (Fla.
    App. 1985); Duran v. Leslie Oldsmobile, 594 N.E.2d 1355 (Ill. App.
    1992); Duhl v. Nash Realty, 429 N.E.2d 1267 (Ill. App. 1981); Church of
    the Nativity v. WatPro, Inc., 474 N.W.2d 605 (Minn. App. 1991), *aff'd*,
    491 N.W.2d 1 (Minn. 1992); Pierce v. Am. Defender Life Ins. Co., 343
    S.E.2d 174 (N.C. 1986); Bowers v. Transamerica Title Ins. Co., 675 P.2d
    193 (Wash. 1983); Robinson v. McReynolds, 762 P.2d 1166 (Wash. App.
    1988).
238. *See, e.g.*, FLA. STAT. ANN. § 501-203(1); ILL. ANN. STAT. Ch. 121-1/2,
    261(1)(e); MICH. COMP. L. ANN. § 445.902(d).
239. LJS Co. v. Marks, 480 F. Supp. 241 (S.D. Fla. 1979) (corporation that
    hired law firm not a consumer); Feldstein v. Guinan, 499 N.E.2d 535 (Ill.
    App. 1986) (physician who contracted with county for medical residency
    not a consumer); Rodriguez v. Ed Hicks Imports, 767 S.W.2d 187 (Tex.

transaction at issue was not a "consumer transaction."[240] However, other statutes have been construed as extending a right of action to business consumers,[241] and in some instances to competitors[242] as well. As noted above,[243] these "little FTC Acts" frequently are interpreted by reference to precedent under the FTC Act.[244]

4. Damages

As noted above, courts have held that there is no private right of action under the FTC Act.[245] However, a majority of the states provide a private right of action for damages, often in excess of the plaintiff's actual damages, such as treble or other enhanced damages.[246] Such statutes also commonly authorize injunctive relief and the recovery of attorney fees.[247]

App. 1989) (automobile passenger not a consumer). *But see* Warren v. Monahan Beaches Jewelry Ctr., Inc., 548 So. 2d 870 (Fla. App. 1989) (fiancee of ring purchaser was a consumer).

240. Golden Needles Knitting & Glove Co. v. Dynamic Mktg. Enters., 766 F. Supp. 421 (W.D.N.C. 1991) (commercial transactions); Kingswharf, Ltd. v. Kranz, 545 So. 2d 276 (Fla. App. 1989) (sale of real estate); State v. DeAnza Corp., 416 So. 2d 1173 (Fla. App. 1982) (lot in mobile home park); *In re* Estate of Szorek, 551 N.E.2d 697 (Ill. App. 1990) (banking practices).

241. *See, e.g.*, Cunningham v. Healthco, Inc., 824 F.2d 1448 (5th Cir. 1987); Continental Grain Co. v. Pullman Standard, Inc., 690 F. Supp. 628 (N.D. Ill. 1988).

242. Galerie Furstenberg v. Coffaro, 697 F. Supp. 1282, 1292 (S.D.N.Y. 1988) (granting limited rights to competitors); Duran v. Clover Club Foods Co., 616 F. Supp. 790 (D. Colo. 1985).

243. *See supra* note 219 and accompanying text.

244. *See* ANTITRUST LAW DEVELOPMENTS, *supra* note 219 at 723; Russell v. Dean Witter Reynolds, 510 A.2d 972 (Conn. 1986); Eastern Star, Inc. v. Union Bldg. Mat. Corp., 712 P.2d 1148 (Haw. App. 1985); Ken-Mar Finance v. Harvey, 368 S.E.2d 646 (N.C. App. 1988).

245. *See Holloway*, 485 F.2d at 997.

246. *See* ANTITRUST LAW DEVELOPMENTS, *supra* note 219 at 724.

247. *See id.*

CHAPTER IV

COMMERCIAL DISPARAGEMENT
AND DEFAMATION

Commercial disparagement and defamation are inherently "competitive" torts, involving injury to a competitor's reputation, or the reputation of its products or services. Often, such claims involve disparaging comments by one competitor about another.[1] Frequently, acts of commercial disparagement or defamation are joined with claims under sections 1 and 2 of the Sherman Act. Such conduct also may give rise to claims under the Lanham Act,[2] state unfair competition laws,[3] and the common law of tortious interference.[4] – Eds.

A. Introduction

This chapter focuses on the common law torts of commercial disparagement and defamation. Although conceptually similar, these torts address different types of conduct, have different elements and evidentiary standards, and are subject to different defenses.[5] In addition, this chapter briefly examines First Amendment limitations on the

---

1. *See, e.g.*, U.S. Healthcare, Inc. v. Blue Cross of Greater Phila., 898 F.2d 914, 922-26 (3d Cir. 1990) (allowing plaintiff in comparative advertising campaign to join disparagement and defamation actions with Sherman Act claims); *accord* Fedders Corp. v. Elite Classics, 279 F. Supp. 2d 965, 969 (S.D. Ill. 2003). *But see* Am. Prof'l Testing Serv. v. Harcourt Brace Jovanovich Legal & Prof'l Pub., Inc., 108 F.3d 1147, 1153 (9th Cir. 1997) ("[w]hile the disparagement of a rival or compromising a rival's employee may be unethical and even impair the opportunities of a rival, its harmful effects on competitors are ordinarily not significant enough to warrant recognition under § 2 of the Sherman Act.").

2. 15 U.S.C. § 1125(a). Section 43(a) is examined in Chap. 3.

3. *See id.*

4. *See* Chap. 5.

5. *See generally* RESTATEMENT (SECOND) OF TORTS § 623A cmt. g (1977) [hereinafter RESTATEMENT]; W. KEETON, PROSSER & KEETON ON THE LAW OF TORTS § 128 (5th ed. 1984) [hereinafter PROSSER & KEETON].

regulation of commercial speech, which may be relevant to the defense of such claims.

B.   Commercial Disparagement and Defamation Distinguished

Although similarities exist between commercial disparagement and defamation, the two are distinct torts.[6] While defamation law protects the plaintiff's character and reputation, disparagement law defends the quality and reputation of the plaintiff's products, goods, or services.[7] A communication regarding the plaintiff's products that also impugns the integrity of the plaintiff's business, however, may be actionable as both defamation and disparagement.[8] The Eighth Circuit framed the following oft-cited test for determining when disparagement crosses the line into defamation:

> [W]here the publication on its face is directed against goods or product of a corporate vendor or manufacturer, it will not be held libelous per se as to the corporation, unless by fair construction and without the aid of extrinsic evidence it imputes to the corporation fraud, deceit, dishonesty, or reprehensible conduct in its business in relation to said goods or product.[9]

---

6. *Compare* RESTATEMENT, *supra* note 5, § 558 *with id.*, § 623A; *accord* Atiyeh Pub., LLC, v. Times Mirror Magazines, No. Civ.A.00-CV-1962, 2000 WL 1886574 at *4 n.2 (E.D. Pa. Dec. 7, 2000); Williams v. Burns, 540 F. Supp. 1243, 1247-48 (D. Colo. 1982); Gen. Prods. Co. v. Meredith Corp., 526 F. Supp. 546, 549-54 (E.D. Va. 1981); Crinkley v. Dow Jones & Co., 385 N.E.2d 714, 719 (Ill. App. Ct. 1978); *see also* Hamlet Dev. Co. v. Venitt, 463 N.Y.S.2d 514, 515 (App. Div. 1983) ("although defamation and disparagement in the commercial context are allied in that the gravamen of both are falsehoods published to third parties, there is a distinction.").

7. *See id.*; U.S. Healthcare v. Blue Cross of Greater Phila., 898 F.2d 914, 924 (3d Cir. 1990); Polygram Records, Inc. v. Superior Court of California, 216 Cal. Rptr. 252, 254 (Ct. App. 1985); Cuba's United Ready Mix, Inc. v. Bock Concrete Found's, Inc., 785 S.W.2d 649, 651 (Mo. Ct. App. 1990).

8. *Crinkley*, 385 N.E.2d at 720; *see also* RESTATEMENT, *supra* note 5, § 573 cmt. g; § 623A cmt. g.

9. Nat'l Ref. Co. v. Benzo Gas Motor Fuel Co., 20 F.2d 763, 771 (8th Cir. 1927); *see U.S. Healthcare*, 898 F.2d at 924.

Some jurisdictions, however, do not draw a sharp distinction between disparagement and defamation,[10] while others flatly refuse to recognize disparagement because of the potential for double recovery.[11]

C. Defamation

1. Elements

The tort of commercial defamation "stems from the law's desire to remedy damage to reputation caused by falsity."[12]   The Restatement (Second) of Torts lists the following elements of a defamation claim:

1. a false and defamatory statement concerning another;
2. an unprivileged publication to a third party;
3. fault amounting at least to negligence on the part of the publisher; and
4. either actionability of the statement irrespective of special harm, or the existence of special harm caused by the publication.[13]

Each of these elements is briefly addressed below.

a.   False and Defamatory Statement

A defamatory statement is a communication that "tends so to harm the reputation of another as to lower him in the estimation of the community or to deter third persons from associating or dealing with him."[14]   In many jurisdictions it is for the court in the first instance to

---

10. *See, e.g.*, CMI, Inc. v. Intoximeters, Inc., 918 F. Supp. 1068, 1069 (W.D. Ky. 1995) (Kentucky courts provide proper relief for commercial disparagement under defamation law).

11. *See, e.g.*, Davita Inc. v. Nephrology Assocs., P.C., 253 F. Supp. 2d 1370, 1375 (S.D. Ga. 2003) (rejecting commercial disparagement under Georgia law); Carolina Indus. Prods., Inc. v. Learjet, Inc., 189 F. Supp. 2d 1147, 1167-68 (D.Kan. 2001) ("Georgia has not recognized the tort of 'injurious falsehood'").

12. 4 MCCARTHY ON TRADEMARKS AND UNFAIR COMPETITION § 101 (4th ed. 2004); *see, e.g.*, Zerpol Corp. v. DMP Corp., 561 F. Supp. 404, 408 (E.D. Pa. 1983).

13. RESTATEMENT, *supra* note 5, § 558; *see, e.g.*, Kirby v. Wildenstein 784 F. Supp. 1112, 1115 (S.D.N.Y. 1992); Swift Bros. v. Swift & Sons, Inc., 921 F. Supp. 267, 276 (E.D. Pa. 1995).

14. RESTATEMENT, *supra* note 5, § 559; *see U.S. Healthcare*, 898 F.2d at 923.

determine whether the alleged defamatory statement is capable of a defamatory meaning: if so, it is for the jury to decide whether it was so understood by the reader or listener.[15]   A defamatory communication may consist of a statement in the form of an opinion, but is actionable only if it implies the existence of underlying defamatory facts.[16]

To support a claim for defamation, the challenged statement must be not only harmful, but also false.[17]   Under the common law, a defamatory statement was deemed false unless the defendant proved its truth.[18]   In *Gertz v. Robert Welch, Inc.,*[19] however, the U.S. Supreme Court effectively altered this standard when it held that, under the First Amendment, a private figure who brings a suit for defamation against a media defendant cannot recover without some showing that the media defendant was at fault in publishing the statements in issue.   In *Philadelphia Newspapers, Inc. v. Hepps,*[20] the Court further held that, "at least where a newspaper publishes speech of 'public concern,' a private figure plaintiff cannot recover damages without also showing that the statements at issue are false."[21]

The Restatement suggests that this constitutional rule "has, as a practical matter, made it necessary for the plaintiff to allege and prove

---

15.   *See, e.g., U.S. Healthcare,* 898 F.2d at 923 (citing Corabi v. Curtis Pub. Co., 273 A.2d 899, 907 (Pa. 1971)); Solano v. Playgirl, Inc., 292 F.3d 1078, 1083 (9th Cir. 2002); RESTATEMENT, *supra* note 5, § 614.

16.   *U.S. Healthcare,* 898 F.2d at 923; RESTATEMENT, *supra* note 5, § 566. *But see* Redco Corp. v. CBS, Inc., 758 F.2d 970, 972 (3d Cir. 1985) (defamatory opinions are not actionable if the factual basis for the opinion is disclosed because "a listener may choose to accept or reject [the opinion] on the basis of an independent evaluation of the facts."); *accord* Pennpac Int'l v. Rotonics Mfg., No. Civ.A.99-CV-2890, 2001 WL 569264, at *10 (E.D. Pa. May 25, 2001).

17.   PROSSER & KEETON, *supra* note 5, § 116; RESTATEMENT, *supra* note 5, § 581A cmt. a; *see* Dun & Bradstreet, Inc. v. Greenmoss Builders, Inc., 472 U.S. 749, 765 (1985) (White, J., concurring); *U.S. Healthcare,* 898 F.2d at 923.

18.   PROSSER & KEETON, *supra* note 5, § 116 at 839; RESTATEMENT, *supra* note 5, § 581A cmt. b.

19.   418 U.S. 323, 347 (1974).

20.   475 U.S. 767 (1986).

21.   *Id.* at 768-69.

the falsity of the communication, and from a realistic standpoint, has placed the burden of proving falsity on the plaintiff."[22]

b.   Unprivileged Publication to a Third Party

"Publication" is an intentional or negligent communication to one other than the person allegedly defamed.[23] Excepting those who merely deliver or transmit defamation published by a third person, "one who repeats or otherwise republishes defamatory matter is subject to liability as if he had originally published it."[24]

"Privilege" may be either absolute or conditional.   Absolute privileges reflect "a recognition that certain persons, because of their special position or status, should be as free as possible from fear that their actions in that position might have an adverse effect upon their own personal interests."[25] An absolute privilege thus is "not conditional upon the honest and reasonable belief that the defamatory matter is true or

---

22.   RESTATEMENT, *supra* note 5, § 613 cmt. j. *Cf.* PROSSER & KEETON, *supra* note 5, § 116, at 839-40.

23.   RESTATEMENT, *supra* note 5, § 577(1). For the principles that serve to distinguish between single and multiple publications, and liability therefor, *see id.* § 577A.

24.   *Id.* § 578. Also, according to the Restatement, "[o]ne who intentionally and unreasonably fails to remove defamatory matter that he knows to be exhibited on land . . . [or other property] in his possession or under his control is subject to liability for its continued publication." *Id.* § 577(2).

25.   *Id.* Title B, intro. note; *but see* Fridovich v. Fridovich, 598 So. 2d 65, 68 (Fla. 1992) (holding that absolute privilege would not be extended to "those who make intentionally false and malicious defamatory statements to the police"); Johnson v. Dirkswager, 315 N.W.2d 215, 220-21 (Minn. 1982); *see also* Bisaccia v. Funicello, 540 N.Y.S.2d 302, 303 (App. Div. 1989) ("The doctrine of absolute privilege is founded 'upon the personal position or status of the speaker and is limited to the speaker's official participation in the processes of government'") (quoting Park Knoll Assoc. v. Schmidt, 59 N.Y.2d 205, 209 (N.Y. 1983)); Petula v. Mellody, 631 A.2d 762, 766 (Pa. 1993) ("high public officials are exempted by the doctrine of absolute privilege from civil suits for damages arising out of false defamatory statements and even from statements motivated by malice, provided that the statements are made in the course of the official's duties or powers and within the scope of the high official's authority or within his or her jurisdiction") (citations omitted).

upon the absence of ill will on the part of the actor."[26]   Absolute privileges include (1) consent,[27] (2) publications by judicial officers, attorneys, parties and witnesses involved in judicial proceedings (provided the defamatory matter bears "some relation" to the proceeding),[28] and (3) publications required by law.[29]

In contrast, conditional or qualified privileges "arise out of the particular occasion upon which the defamation is published" and are available to those "who, for the purpose of furthering the interest in question, give information which, without their knowledge or reckless disregard as to its falsity, is in fact untrue."[30]   Conditional privileges include (1) communications necessary to advance the interests of the speaker, recipient or third persons, (2) communications between persons with a common interest and (3) communications to a public officer or private citizen in furtherance of the public interest.[31]   Conditional privileges may be lost if abused;[32] examples of such abuse include publication with knowledge of the statement's falsity or reckless disregard of its truth or falsity, publication for a wrongful purpose,

---

26. RESTATEMENT, *supra* note 5, Title B, intro. note; *see* Green Acres Trust v. London, 688 P.2d 617, 621 (Ariz. 1984) ("[t]he defense is absolute in that the speaker's motive, purpose or reasonableness in uttering a false statement do not affect the defense"); Gardner v. Hollifield, 533 P.2d 730, 733-34 (Idaho 1975) (exploring policy considerations behind absolute and conditional privileges); Vigoda v. Barton, 204 N.E.2d 441, 445 (Mass. 1985) (noting, however, that "[in Mass.] absolute privilege is limited to comparatively few cases").
27. *See* RESTATEMENT, *supra* note 5, § 583.
28. *See id.* §§ 585-89; *see also id.* §§ 590 & 590A (legislators and witnesses in legislative proceedings) § 591 (executive and administrative officers), § 592 (husband and wife).
29. *See id.* § 592A.
30. RESTATEMENT, *supra* note 5, Title B, intro. note; *see* Carroll v. Robinson, 874 P.2d 1010, 1014 (Ariz. Ct. App. 1994); Davis v. John Crane, Inc., 633 N.E.2d 929, 937 (Ill. App. Ct. 1994); Larson v. Decatur Mem'l Hosp., 602 N.E.2d 864, 867, 870 (Ill. App. Ct. 1992); Lee v. Metro. Airport Comm'n, 428 N.W.2d 815, 819-20 (Minn. Ct. App. 1988).
31. *See id.* §§ 594-96, 598; *see also infra* notes 93-96 and accompanying text.
32. *See id.* § 599.

excessive or unnecessary publication, and the combination of privileged and unprivileged defamatory matter in the same communication.[33]

c.   Fault

The degree of fault required to sustain a claim of defamation is largely determined by federal constitutional principles, and depends upon both the "public" or "private" status of the plaintiff and the nature of the defamatory comment.   In *New York Times v. Sullivan*,[34] the U.S. Supreme Court held that the Constitution imposes a high burden on public officials to maintain a defamation action based upon statements regarding their conduct, fitness or roles as public officials.   They must prove by "clear and convincing evidence" that the defendant had knowledge of the falsity of the communication or acted in reckless disregard of its truth or falsity.[35]   This rule has been applied to candidates for public office and "public figures,"[36] although the *Gertz* Court refused to extend it to any matter of public interest, irrespective of the plaintiff's status.[37]

With respect to private plaintiffs (or public officials or figures in relation to purely private matters), the standards are far less demanding. In *Gertz*, the Court held that the First Amendment forbids the imposition of "liability without fault" on a publisher or broadcaster of defamatory falsehood injurious to a private individual.[38]   Beyond this minimal requirement, however, the Court has deferred to the states to "define for themselves the appropriate standard of liability."[39]   Following this

---

33.   *See id.* §§ 600, 603-605A; Johnson v. Toys "R" US-Delaware, Inc., No. 02-1986, 2004 WL 324545, at *9 (4th Cir. Feb. 23, 2004) (defendant acted with malice); *see also infra* notes 102-07 and accompanying text.

34.   376 U.S. 254, 285 (1964).

35.   *Id.*

36.   *See, e.g.*, Kiser v. Lowe, 236 F. Supp. 2d 872, 881 (S.D. Ohio 2002) (police chief); Sculimbrene v. Reno, 158 F. Supp. 2d 8, 24 (D.D.C. 2001) (F.B.I. agent acting as public official).

37.   *See Gertz*, 418 U.S. at 351-52.

38.   *Id.* at 346-47.

39.   *Id.* at 347. "This approach recognizes the strength of the legitimate state interest in compensating private individuals for wrongful injury to reputation, yet shields the press and broadcast media from the rigors of strict liability for defamation." *Id.* at 348.

holding, the Restatement recognizes that liability in so-called "private plaintiff" defamation cases may be premised on mere negligence.[40]

d. Actionability

The actionability of a defamatory comment may turn upon whether it is classified as libel or slander, and whether the plaintiff can show "special harm." Restatement section 569 provides that one who publishes a libel[41] may be subject to liability although no special harm results from the publication. Section 573 provides that "a slander that ascribes to another conduct, characteristics or a condition that would adversely affect his fitness for the proper conduct of his lawful business, trade or profession" also is actionable without proof of special harm.[42] Similarly, statements that tend "to prejudice it in the conduct of its business or to deter others from dealing with it" may defame a

---

40. RESTATEMENT, *supra* note 5, § 580B; *see* State v. Globe Commun. Corp., 622 So. 2d 1066, 1078 (Fla. Dist. App. 1993); Duran v. Detroit News, Inc., 504 N.W.2d 715, 721 (Mich. Ct. App. 1993); Costello v. Ocean County Observer, 643 A.2d 1012, 1021 (N.J. 1994); M.N. Dannenbaum, Inc. v. Brummerhop, 840 S.W.2d 624, 633 (Tex. App. 1992); Russell v. Thompson Newspapers, Inc., 842 P.2d 896, 906 (Utah 1992); Garrison v. Herbert J. Thomas Memorial Hosp. Assoc., 438 S.E.2d 6, 7, 13 (W. Va. 1993). Relying upon the plurality opinion in Rosenbloom v. Metromedia, Inc., 403 U.S. 29 (1971), some state courts have extended the "knowledge or reckless disregard" rule to private plaintiff cases involving matters of "public or general interest." *See* RESTATEMENT, *supra* note 5, § 580B cmt. c. Although such a requirement was rejected in *Gertz* as a matter of federal constitutional law, the states are free to afford greater protection than the Constitution in such cases. *See id.*

41. A libel consists of the publication of defamatory matter "by written or printed words, by its embodiment in physical form or by any other form of communication that has the potential harmful qualities characteristic of written or printed words." RESTATEMENT, *supra* note 5, § 568(1). Slander consists of any other form of communication. *Id.* § 568(2). Although some states differ, the Restatement classifies a broadcast of defamatory matter by means of radio or television as libel, irrespective of whether it is read from a manuscript. *Id.* § 568A.

42. *See Gertz*, 418 U.S. at 349. ("[t]he common law of defamation is an oddity of tort law, for it allows recovery of purportedly compensatory damages without evidence of actual loss.").

corporation, partnership or other business association.[43]   Moreover, a slander that would otherwise not be actionable may give rise to liability if it causes special harm to the plaintiff.[44]   In this context, "special harm" is the loss of something having economic or pecuniary value.[45]

2. *Remedies*

Courts usually grant compensatory relief for defamation in the form of damages, as injunctions are presumptively unconstitutional restrictions on free speech.[46]   A plaintiff who successfully establishes a libel or slander per se is entitled to recover at least nominal damages.[47]   Further, the plaintiff in a defamation action may recover damages for the proved, actual harm caused to the plaintiff's reputation.[48]   A libel or slander per se also may give rise to liability for any special harm caused by the defamatory publication.[49]   In addition to other damages, a defendant guilty of defamation may be held liable for emotional distress and bodily harm caused by the defamatory publication.[50]

---

43. *See* RESTATEMENT, *supra* note 5, §§ 561(a), 562; *see also* Gen. Prods. Co. v. Meredith Corp., 526 F. Supp. 546, 549-50 (E.D. Va. 1981). In addition, an imputation of a crime, loathsome disease or serious sexual misconduct may be actionable per se. *See* RESTATEMENT, *supra* note 5, §§ 571, 572, 574.

44. RESTATEMENT, *supra* note 5, § 575.

45. *See id.* cmt. b; PROSSER & KEETON, *supra* note 5, § 116A, at 844.

46. *See, e.g.*, Jordan v. Metro. Life Ins. Co., 280 F. Supp. 2d 104, 111 (S.D.N.Y. 2003) (citing Metro. Opera Assoc., Inc., v. Local 100, H.E.R.E.I., 239 F.3d 172, 177 (2d Cir. 2001); Org. for a Better Austin v. Keefe, 402 U.S. 415, 418-19 (1971); New Era Publ'n Int'l v. Henry Holt & Co., 695 F. Supp. 1493, 1525 (S.D.N.Y. 1988) ("we accept as black letter [law] that an injunction is not available to suppress defamatory speech.").

47. *See* RESTATEMENT, *supra* note 5, § 620; PROSSER & KEETON, *supra* note 5, § 116A, at 845.

48. *See* RESTATEMENT, *supra* note 5, § 621; PROSSER & KEETON, *supra* note 5, § 116A, at 843.

49. *See* RESTATEMENT, *supra* note 5, § 622. Regarding the definition of "legal cause," *see id.* § 622A.

50. *See* RESTATEMENT, *supra* note 5, § 623; PROSSER & KEETON, *supra* note 5, § 116A, at 844-45; *see also Gertz*, 418 U.S. at 349-50; Time, Inc. v. Firestone, 424 U.S. 448, 460 (1976).

Finally, when the plaintiff is a private figure, but the speech involves a matter of "public concern," the Constitution forbids the assessment of presumed or punitive damages without a showing of actual malice.[51] In this context, "malice" does not require a showing of ill will.[52] Rather, it requires only that the defendant had a high degree of awareness of the communication's probable falsity, or in fact entertained serious doubts as to the truth of the publication.[53] When the plaintiff is a private figure and the speech addresses a "purely private concern," however, the plaintiff may recover presumed and punitive damages without proof of actual malice.[54]

D. Commercial Disparagement

1. *Elements*

Originally known as "slander of title," the tort of injurious falsehood expanded to include disparaging and false statements about the quality of property rather than just the title to it.[55] This tort is known by several names, such as commercial disparagement, trade libel, product disparagement, and injurious falsehood.[56] Under Restatement section 623A:

---

51. *See Dun & Bradstreet*, 472 U.S. at 756; *Gertz*, 418 U.S. at 347-49.

52. *Gertz*, 418 U.S. at 334 n.6; St. Amant v. Thompson, 390 U.S. 727, 731 (1968); *see* Lerman v. Flynt Distrib. Co., 745 F.2d 123, 139 (2d Cir. 1984); Wojnarowicz v. Am. Family Ass'n, 745 F. Supp. 130, 147 (S.D.N.Y. 1990).

53. *Id.*

54. *Dun & Bradstreet*, 472 U.S. at 761; *see U.S. Healthcare*, 898 F.2d at 930.

55. *See* RESTATEMENT, *supra* note 5, § 623A; *see also* Williams v. Burns, 540 F. Supp. 1243, 1247 (D. Colo. 1982); Comment, *The Law of Commercial Disparagement: Business Defamation's Impotent Ally*, 63 YALE L.J. 65, 74-75 (1953).

56. *See, e.g.*, Neurotron Inc. v. Med. Serv. Ass'n of Pa., 254 F.3d 444, 448 (3d Cir. 2001); Cort v. St. Paul Fire and Mar. Ins. Companies, Inc., 311 F.3d 979, 986 (9th Cir. 2002); Mayflower Transit, LLC v. Prince, Civ.A.00-5354, 2004 WL 859281, at *14 (D.N.J. Mar. 30, 2004); Daniels v. St. Luke's-Roosevelt Hosp. Ctr., No. 02 Civ. 9567 2003 WL 22410623, at *7 (S.D.N.Y. Oct. 21, 2003); *see also* RESTATEMENT, *supra* note 5, § 623A cmt. a (the specific tort of disparagement is included within the general tort of "injurious falsehood").

One who publishes a false statement harmful to the interests of another is subject to liability for pecuniary loss resulting to the other if

(a)   he intends for publication of the statement to result in harm to interests of the other having a pecuniary value, or either recognizes or should recognize that it is likely to do so, and

(b)   he knows that the statement is false or acts in reckless disregard of its truth or falsity.[57]

The principle stated in section 623A applies primarily to cases of disparagement of the title to, or quality of, real or personal property.[58] In addition, it covers "other publications of false statements that do harm to interests of another having pecuniary value and so result in pecuniary loss."[59] The plaintiff does not need to show that the defendant was "substantially certain" that the statement would influence a third person; it is only necessary for the plaintiff to prove that the defendant reasonably recognized the likelihood that a third person would act on the falsehood in a manner that would result in pecuniary loss to the plaintiff.[60]

a.   False and Disparaging Statements Regarding Goods and Services

The rule of liability set forth in section 623A of the Restatement applies to the publication of matter disparaging the quality of another's real or personal property, including intangibles, which the speaker should recognize as likely to result in pecuniary loss to the other through the conduct of a third person in respect to the other's interests in the property.[61] Similar to the law of defamation, the plaintiff must

---

57.   RESTATEMENT, *supra* note 5, § 623A; *see, e.g.*, Neshewat v. Salem, 173 F.3d 357, 364 (6th Cir. 1999) (citing the Restatement); Reliance Ins. Co. v. Shenandoah South, Inc., 81 F.3d 789, 792 (8th Cir. 1996); Klein v. Victor, 903 F. Supp. 1327, 1330 (E.D. Mo. 1995); *see also* PROSSER AND KEETON, *supra* note 5, § 128, at 971.

58.   *See* RESTATEMENT, *supra* note 5, § 623A cmt. a; §§ 624, 626. *See, e.g.*, C.P. Interests, Inc. v. Cal. Pools, Inc., 238 F.3d 690, 694 (5th Cir. 2001); Gucci Am., Inc. v. Duty Free Apparel, Ltd., 277 F. Supp. 2d 269, 276 (S.D.N.Y. 2003).

59.   RESTATEMENT, *supra* note 5, § 623A cmt. a.

60.   *See id.* cmt. b; *Zerpol*, 561 F. Supp. at 408-09.

61.   RESTATEMENT, *supra* note 5, § 626.

demonstrate that the defendant communicated a false statement.[62] The plaintiff in a disparagement action, however, bears the burden of proving that the statement is false.[63] To be actionable, the false statement must be capable of influencing a third party not to deal with the plaintiff.[64] A competitor's "puffing," or general assertion that its product is superior, is not actionable unless a third party would reasonably interpret the statement as factually based and the plaintiff can prove the assertion false.[65]

The plaintiff also must prove that the third party hearing the statement understood that the defendant was referring to the plaintiff's product and interpreted the statement as disparaging.[66] Section 629 of the Restatement provides:

> A statement is disparaging if it is understood to cast doubt upon the quality of another's land, chattels or intangible things, or upon the existence or extent of his property in them, and

---

62. *See* PROSSER AND KEETON, *supra* note 5, § 128, at 967; *see also* Imperial Developers, Inc. v. Seaboard Sur. Co., 518 N.W.2d 623 (Minn. Ct. App. 1994); Abernathy & Closther v. Buffalo Broad. Co., 574 N.Y.S.2d 568, 571 (N.Y. App. Div. 1991); Teilhaber Mfg. Co. v. Unarco Materials Storage, 791 P.2d 1164, 1166 (Colo. Ct. App. 1989).

63. *See* PROSSER AND KEETON, *supra* note 5, § 128 at 967; *see also* System Operations, Inc. v. Scientific Games Dev. Corp., 555 F.2d 1131, 1141 (3d Cir. 1977); United Wild Rice, Inc. v. Nelson, 313 N.W.2d 628, 634 (Minn. 1982). Regarding constitutional limitations upon liability for defamation, *see supra* notes 19-22 and accompanying text.

64. *See* PROSSER & KEETON, *supra* note 5, § 128, at 967; *see also* Edwin L. Wiegand Co. v. Harold E. Trent Co., 122 F.2d 920, 924 (3d Cir. 1941); All Care, Inc. v. Bork, 531 N.E.2d 1033, 1037-39 (Ill. App. Ct. 1988).

65. *See* Folkers v. Am. Massage Therapy Ass'n, Inc., No. Civ.A.03-2399-KHV, 2004 WL 306913 at *10 (D. Kan. Feb. 10, 2004) ("subjective claims about products, which cannot be proven either true or false, are not actionable; they are mere 'puffing.'") (citing Lipton v. Nature Co., 71 F.3d 464, 474 (2d Cir. 1995)); Maharishi Hardy Blechman Ltd. v. Abercrombie & Fitch, 292 F. Supp. 2d 535, 552 (S.D.N.Y. 2003); *see also* SILVERBERG, COMMERCIAL DEFAMATION AND TRADE LIBEL, 1 BUSINESS TORTS § 6.03[2][b], at 6-62 to 63 (2004); RESTATEMENT, *supra* note 5, § 649 cmt. c; *see also infra* notes 98-101 and accompanying text.

66. *See* RESTATEMENT, *supra* note 5, § 629; SILVERBERG, *supra* note 65, § 6.03[2][c] at 6-63 to 64.

(a) the publisher intends the statement to cast the doubt, or

(b) the recipient's understanding of it as casting doubt was reasonable.[67]

b. Malice

As noted above, clause (b) of Restatement section 623A contemplates that the publisher of an injurious falsehood "knows that the statement is false or acts in reckless disregard of its truth or falsity."[68] Citing First Amendment concerns, the Restatement takes no position on the question of whether, in lieu of such knowledge or reckless disregard, it is sufficient that the defendant had either a motive of ill will toward the plaintiff or an intent to interfere in an unprivileged manner with his interests.[69] Nor does the Restatement take a position as to whether either of these alternative grounds, if not alone sufficient, would be sufficient if combined with a showing of the defendant's simple negligence regarding truth or falsity.[70] Consequently, there can be no strict liability for commercial disparagement; the plaintiff must prove that the defendant made communications either intending to cause the plaintiff pecuniary harm, or in circumstances under which the defendant should have known such harm would occur.[71]

c. Special/Pecuniary Damages

A plaintiff alleging commercial disparagement must prove a direct causal connection between an identifiable pecuniary loss and the defendant's conduct.[72] This requirement is necessary to support the

---

67. *Id.;* PROSSER & KEETON, *supra* note 5, § 128 at 967; *see also Cubby*, 776 F. Supp. at 142; Gen. *Prods.*, 526 F. Supp. at 553.
68. RESTATEMENT, *supra* note 5, § 623A(b).
69. *See id.* caveats; PROSSER & KEETON, *supra* note 5, § 128, at 968-70; *see also* Gen. *Prods.*, 526 F. Supp. at 553; Ruder & Finn, Inc. v. Seaboard Sur. Co., 422 N.E.2d 518, 521-22 (N.Y. 1981); Ronald K. L. Collins, *Free Speech, Food Libel, & the First Amendment . . . in Ohio*, 26 OHIO N.U. L. REV. 1, 56 (2000).
70. *See* RESTATEMENT, *supra* note 5, § 623A(b).
71. *See id.*
72. *See* PROSSER & KEETON, *supra* note 5, § 128, at 970-73; *see also Cubby*, 776 F. Supp. at 142; Santana Prods., Inc. v. Bobrick Washroom Equip., Inc., 249 F. Supp. 2d 463, 502 (M.D. Pa. 2003); Advanced Training Sys., Inc. v. Caswell Equip. Co., 352 N.W.2d 1, 7-8 (Minn. 1984).

cause of action itself, and not solely for recovery under the cause of action.[73] Courts vary as to the degree of particularity with which special damages must be proven.[74] According to the Restatement, the pecuniary loss for which the publisher is subject to liability is limited to:

> (a) the pecuniary loss that results directly and immediately from the effect of the conduct of third persons, including impairment of vendibility or value caused by the disparagement, and

> (b) the expense of measures reasonably necessary to counteract the publication, including litigation to remove the doubt cast upon vendibility or value by disparagement.[75]

A plaintiff may establish such pecuniary loss by proof of the conduct of specific persons or that the loss resulted from the conduct of numerous persons impossible to identify.[76]

2.   *Remedies*

As noted above, a commercial disparagement plaintiff must prove special harm, i.e., a "pecuniary loss that results directly and immediately from the effect of the conduct of third persons, including impairment of vendibility or value caused by disparagement."[77] Once the plaintiff proves such a pecuniary loss, the trier of fact may award compensatory damages, and in some states punitive damages.[78] Because the general rule is that a claim of commercial disparagement cannot be sustained

---

73. *See* PROSSER & KEETON, *supra* note 5, § 128, at 976; *see also* SILVERBERG, *supra* note 65, § 6.03[2][e]; Aetna Cas. & Sur. Co. v. Centennial Ins. Co., 838 F.2d 346, 351 (9th Cir. 1985); Polygram Records, Inc. v. Superior Court of Cal., 216 Cal. Rptr. 252, 255 (Ct. App. 1985); *Advanced Training*, 352 N.W.2d at 8.

74. *See* PROSSER & KEETON, *supra* note 5, § 128, at 970-73.

75. RESTATEMENT, *supra* note 5, § 633(1). Regarding when the publication of an injurious falsehood is the legal cause of pecuniary loss, *see id.* § 632.

76. *See id.* § 633(2); *see also* PROSSER & KEETON, *supra* note 5, § 128, at 970-73.

77. *Id.* § 633(1)(a). Under the Restatement, a disparagement plaintiff also may recover the expense of measures necessary to counteract the publication, including costs of litigation. *See id.* § 633(1)(b).

78. *See* PROSSER & KEETON, *supra* note 5, § 128, at 976-77; *see also* Diapulse Corp. of Am. v. Birtcher Corp., 362 F.2d 736, 744 (1966) (applying New York and federal law, the court found that the defendant went beyond mere puffing, and made libelous statements about plaintiff's product).

absent proof of a knowing or reckless falsehood, punitive damages awards in such cases should pass muster under the First Amendment.[79] Other constitutional limitations on the award of punitive damages are examined in Chapter 8.

Under appropriate circumstances, courts also will grant injunctive relief, although they are generally reluctant to do so.[80] This hesitation may stem from the judiciary's sensitivity to inhibiting free speech.[81] Although courts are more willing to grant injunctive relief in trade libel actions than in actions for defamation,[82] the line between the two is not always clear.[83] Even in the realm of commercial speech, which is generally entitled to less protection, courts are slow to issue injunctive relief.[84]

E. Defenses to Defamation and Disparagement

Truth is an absolute defense to a claim of defamation or disparagement.[85] According to the Restatement, the defendant in a

---

79. Compare *Gertz*, 418 U.S. at 334 (when defamatory statement involves issue of public concern, First Amendment does not allow recovery of presumed or punitive damages absent a showing of "actual malice") with *Dun & Bradstreet*, 472 U.S. at 760 (when plaintiff is private figure and defamatory statement not an issue of public concern, First Amendment does not require proof of actual malice before presumed or punitive damages awarded).

80. *See* PROSSER & KEETON, *supra* note 5, § 128, at 976-77.

81. *Id.; see also* Keefe, 402 U.S. at 419 ("[a]ny prior restraint on expression [of free speech] comes to this Court with a 'heavy presumption against its constitutional validity.'").

82. See Black & Yates v. Mahogany Assn., Inc., 129 F.2d 227, 235 (3d Cir. 1941) (defamation is focused on personality while disparagement/trade libel is concerned with property interest); RESTATEMENT, *supra* note 5, § 626 cmt. b.

83. *See supra* notes 5-11 and accompanying text.

84. *See* RESTATEMENT, *supra* note 5, § 626 cmt. b, § 937; PROSSER & KEETON, *supra* note 5, § 128, at 976-77.

85. For defamation, *see* RESTATEMENT, *supra* note 5, § 581A; *see also* Garrett v. Tandy Corp., 295 F.3d 94, 106 (1st Cir. 2002); Hickson Corp. v. N. Crossarm Co., 357 F.3d 1256, 1262 (11th Cir. 2004). For disparagement, *see* RESTATEMENT, *supra* note 5, § 634; *see also* David L. Aldridge Co. v. Microsoft Corp., 995 F. Supp. 728, 740 (S.D. Tex. 1998); Horning v.

defamation or disparagement action is not liable if the communication of facts or opinion is justified in truth.[86] In addition to the defense of truth, the absolute and conditional privileges available in defense of a defamation claim also are available against a claim of disparagement.[87] The absolute privileges include consent[88] and the privileges available to participants in judicial[89] and legislative[90] proceedings, publications by executive branch officers,[91] communications between husband and wife[92] and publications required by law.[93] Conditional privileges include those designed to protect communications in furtherance of legitimate interests of the speaker, recipient or third persons,[94] communications between persons with a common interest,[95] and communications to a public officer or private citizen in furtherance of the public interest.[96]

In addition, the Restatement recognizes two conditional privileges particularly applicable to claims for disparagement. First, a rival claimant may disparage another's interest in real and personal property, including intangibles, when asserting for himself an inconsistent legally

---

Hardy, 373 A.2d 1273, 1278 (Md. Ct. Spec. App. 1977) ("policy of the courts has been to encourage the publication of the truth, regardless of motive") (citations omitted).

86. *Id.*
87. *See* RESTATEMENT, *supra* note 5, § 635 (absolute privileges), § 646A (conditional privileges); *see also Burns*, 540 F. Supp. at 1248.
88. *See* RESTATEMENT, *supra* note 5, § 583; *see also* Smith v. Holley, 827 S.W.2d 433, 438 (Tex. App. 1992) (absolute privileges may "exist only in matters involving the branches of government").
89. *See* RESTATEMENT, *supra* note 5, §§ 585-89; *see also* Gen. Elec. Co. v. Sargent & Lundy, 916 F.2d 1119, 1125-27 (6th Cir. 1990).
90. *See* RESTATEMENT, *supra* note 5, §§ 590, 590A.
91. *See id.* § 591.
92. *See id.* § 592.
93. *See id.* § 592A.
94. *See id.* §§ 594, 595.
95. *See id.* § 596.
96. *See id.* § 598; *see also id.* § 597 (communications among family members) § 598A (statements by inferior state administrative officers) § 611 (reports of official proceedings and public meetings) and § 612 (persons who provide means of publishing defamatory matter published by another).

protected interest in the same property.[97]   Second, a competitor may make a biased comparison of his own goods to those of his rivals.[98] This qualified privilege to make an unduly favorable comparison is sometimes termed "sales talk" or "puffing."[99]

As one leading treatise states: "[t]he 'puffing' rule amounts to a seller's privilege to lie his head off, so long as he says nothing specific, on the theory that no reasonable man would believe him, or that no reasonable man would be influenced by such talk."[100] A person may not, however, go beyond making the unduly favorable comparison and make specific false assertions regarding the quality of his competitor's product.[101]

Except as may be permitted by these last two privileges, "a conditional privilege to publish injurious falsehood is abused under circumstances that amount to an abuse of a conditional privilege to publish defamation."[102] These include the publication of defamatory matter with knowledge of its falsity or reckless disregard as to its truth or falsity,[103] publication for a purpose other than the protection of the interest for which the privilege is afforded,[104] excessive publication,[105] publication without a reasonable belief as to its necessity to protect the

---

97.   *See id.* § 647; *see also* Cambridge Title Co. v. Transamerica Title Ins. Co., 817 F. Supp. 1263, 1277 (D. Md. 1992); Fischer v. Bar Harbor Banking & Trust Co., 673 F. Supp. 622, 626 (D. Me. 1987) (citing RESTATEMENT, *supra* note 5, § 647).

98.   *See* RESTATEMENT, *supra* note 5, § 649.

99.   *See id.* § 649 cmt. c; *U.S. Healthcare*, 898 F.2d at 924; *see also supra* note 65 and accompanying text.

100. PROSSER & KEETON, *supra* note 5, § 109 at 757.

101. *See* Testing Sys., Inc. v. MagnaFlux Corp., 251 F. Supp. 286, 289 (E.D. Pa. 1966) (refusing to allow "puffing" privilege for statement that product was 60 percent more effective than competitor's product).

102. RESTATEMENT, *supra* note 5, § 650A; *see, e.g.* Orr v. Bank of Am., NT & SA, 285 F.3d 764, 781 (9th Cir. 2002) (defendant would "not be liable unless it made the statements with actual malice, knowledge of their falsity, or reckless disregard for their truth.").

103. *Id.* § 600. Regarding the publication of defamatory rumor, *see id.* § 602.

104. *Id.* § 603.

105. *Id.* § 604.

interest for which the privilege is afforded,[106] and the publication of privileged with unprivileged defamatory matter.[107]

F.   Commercial Speech and the First Amendment

Purely commercial advertising was once regarded as unprotected by the First Amendment.[108]   The U.S. Supreme Court rejected this broad conclusion, however, in *Virginia State Board of Pharmacy v. Virginia Citizens Consumer Council,*[109] extending First Amendment protection to speech that merely proposes commercial transactions.[110]   Nevertheless, the Court recognized a "common sense" distinction between commercial speech, which occurs in an area traditionally subject to government regulation and is thus afforded less protection, and other types of speech that carry more constitutional safeguards.[111]

In *Central Hudson Gas & Electric Corp. v. Public Service Commission of New York,*[112] the Court set forth the general principles for assessing governmental restrictions on commercial speech:

> At the outset, we must determine whether the First Amendment protects the expression. For commercial speech to come within that provision, it at least must concern lawful activity and not be misleading. Next, we ask whether the asserted governmental interest is substantial.   If both inquiries yield positive answers, we must determine whether the regulation directly advances the governmental interest asserted, and whether it is not more extensive than is necessary to serve that interest.[113]

---

106. *Id.* § 605.

107. *Id.* § 605A.

108. *See* Valentine v. Chrestensen, 316 U.S. 52, 54 (1942).

109. 425 U.S. 748, 770 (1976).

110. *See id.*; United States v. Edge Broad. Co., 509 U.S. 418, 426 (1993).

111. *See Edge*, 509 U.S. at 426; Cent. Hudson Gas & Elec. Corp. v. Pub. Serv. Comm. Co. of N.Y., 447 U.S. 557, 563 (1980).

112. 447 U.S. 557 (1980); *see also* Rubin v. Coors Brewing Co., 514 U.S. 476, 486 (1995) (statutory ban on disclosure of alcohol content on beer labels failed *Central Hudson*); Ibanez v. Fla. Dep't of Bus. & Prof. Reg., 512 U.S. 136, 145 (1994) (ban on truthful advertisement of professional designations failed *Central Hudson*).

113. 447 U.S. at 566; *see Edge*, 509 U.S. at 424.

The Third Circuit applied these factors to a comparative advertising campaign by two rival health care providers in *U.S. Healthcare, Inc. v. Blue Cross of Greater Philadelphia.*[114] It noted that "[t]he Supreme Court has cited three factors to consider in deciding whether speech is commercial: (1) is the speech an advertisement; (2) does the speech refer to a specific product or service; and (3) does the speaker have an economic motivation for the speech."[115] The court concluded that advertisements published as part of a private health insurer's advertising campaign critical of the coverage and quality of care afforded by a rival health maintenance organization were commercial speech, and thus not subject to heightened constitutional protection.[116] In support of this conclusion, the court noted that although the availability and quality of health care coverage offered by alternative delivery systems unquestionably was a matter of great public concern, the alleged defamatory statements were made in the course of an advertising campaign, tailored to promote one rival system over another and made for a commercial motive.[117] Accordingly, the court concluded, "while the speech here is protected by the First Amendment, we hold that the First Amendment requires no higher standard of liability than that mandated by the substantive law for each claim."[118]

---

114. 898 F.2d 914 (3d Cir. 1990).

115. *Id.* at 933 (citing Bolger v. Youngs Drug Prods. Corp., 463 U.S. 60, 66-67 (1983)).

116. *Id.*

117. *See id.* at 934-37.

118. *Id.* at 937. The court also rejected the argument that the parties should be deemed "public figures," noting that "most advertisers – including both claimants here – seek out the media." *See id.* at 939.

CHAPTER V

THE INTERFERENCE TORTS

Survey evidence suggests that the field of tortious interference occupies the greatest area of overlap between business torts and "traditional" antitrust claims.[1] Because the essence of tortious interference is the wrongful disruption of business relationships, such claims frequently are asserted in disputes between competitors[2] as well as between firms occupying different levels of the distribution chain.[3] Not infrequently, the same commercial conduct is challenged under both theories.[4] Although the tort has been criticized for the often confusing array of elements attributed to it and the varied interpretations given those elements by courts, it remains a popular weapon.[5] As discussed in other chapters,[6] the

---

1. Harvey I. Saferstein, *The Ascendancy of Business Tort Claims in Antitrust Practice*, 59 ANTITRUST L.J. 379, 383-85, 392, 403 (1991).
2. *See, e.g.*, Hannex Corp. v. GMI, Inc. 140 F.3d 194 (2d Cir. 1998); Stearns Airport Equip. v. FMC Corp., 170 F.3d 518 (5th Cir. 1999); ID Sec. Sys. Canada, Inc. v. Checkpoint Sys., Inc., 249 F. Supp. 2d 622 (E.D. Pa. 2003).
3. *See, e.g.*, Weicht v. Suburban Newspapers of Greater St. Louis, Inc., 32 S.W.3d 592 (Mo. Ct. App. 2000) (identifying independent contract carriers who held distribution and delivery routes for newspaper chain claims of tortuous interference against newspaper chain).
4. *See, e.g.*, *ID Security Sys. Canada, Inc.*, 249 F. Supp. 2d at 663-69; Star Tobacco Inc. v. Darilek, 298 F. Supp. 2d 436 (E.D. Tex. 2003); *see also* Logic Process Corp. v. Bell & Howell Publ'ns Sys. Co., 162 F. Supp. 2d 533 (N.D. Tex. 2001).
5. Martin W. Siener, *Tortious Interference with Contract: A Tort on the Brink of Extinction*, 85 ILL. B.J. 322 (July 1997) ("[C]onfusion relating to some of the elements of the tort have diminished its effect as an intimidating weapon [and] the very existence of the tort as a viable cause of action is threatened."); Robert L. Tucker, *"And the Truth Shall Make You Free": Truth as a First Amendment Defense in Tortious Interference with Contract Cases*, 24 HASTINGS CONST. L.Q. 709 (Spring 1997)

popularity of tortious interference claims may be attributed to
many factors, not the least of which is the potential availability
of punitive damages greatly in excess of treble damage
antitrust awards.[7] – Eds.

A. Introduction

Scholars have traced the origins of tortious interference laws to
Roman law, which allowed a man to sue for harms inflicted on members
of his household.[8] As late as the early nineteenth century, however,
traditional tort law did not yet recognize business torts.[9] When the courts
first began to allow actions for economic interference, they did so only in
situations where an intentional wrong such as physical violence, fraud, or
defamation interfered with a contractual relationship.[10] As interference
torts evolved, liability eventually was found without proof of such
wrongful or illegal conduct.[11]

("Recognition of tortious interference with contract has not won universal
acclaim" because of its undefined nature and potential effect on
"commerce and individual liberty."); George Freeman, et al., '*60 Minutes'*
and the Law: Can Journalists be Liable for Tortious Interference with
Contract?, 68 N.Y. St. B.J. 24 (July/August 1996) ("[A]t the outset it
should be noted that the tort of interference with contract has been subject
to intense criticism.").

6.   *See* Chapters 1, 2.
7.   *See* Chapter 8; Kelco Disposal, Inc. v. BFI, 845 F.2d 404, 407 (2d Cir.
     1988).
8.   *See* Wal-Mart Stores, Inc. v. Sturges, 52 S.W.3d 711, 716 (Tex. 2001)
     (discussing the history of civil liability for interference).
9.   *See generally* Note, *Tortious Interference with Contractual Relations in*
     the Nineteenth Century: The Transformation of Property, Contract and
     Tort, 93 Harv. L. Rev. 1510 (1980). *But see Sturges*, 52 S.W.3d at 716
     (noting that the common law may have recognized liability for actions
     such as driving away a business's customers as early as the fourteenth
     century).
10. *See Sturges*, 52 S.W.3d at 716 (discussing the history of civil liability for
     interference).
11. For example, in *Lumley v. Gye*, (1843) 118 Eng. Rep. 740, a theater owner
     persuaded a singer to break her contract to sing at another theater. The
     court found liability on the basis that the nontortious interference was
     intentional; *see also* Salter v. Howard, 43 Ga. 601 (Ga. 1871) (enticement
     action extended to sharecroppers); Walker v. Cronin, 107 Mass. 555

Unlike traditional intentional torts such as assault and battery, where liability is likely to result upon proof of prima facie elements, there is no "bright line" defining improper economic interference. Rather, the issue often is whether the interference is justified under the circumstances.[12] In the context of an increasingly complex economy, it often is difficult to determine the point at which a competitor violates "the rules of the game," dividing acceptable and unacceptable conduct. The nature of the interfering conduct, the interest of the party being interfered with, and the relationship of the parties are three of many factors to be considered.[13]

Today the interference torts seek to draw "a line beyond which no member of the community may go in intentionally intermeddling with the business affairs of others."[14] The case law, however, abounds with considerable differences in the elements required to be proven, the available privileges and the burdens of proof. For example, several states require a plaintiff to prove that the defendant's interference is not privileged or justified, while others require the defendant to establish privilege or justification as an affirmative defense, and still others are split on the issue depending on whether the interference is with contract or prospective business relations.[15] In short, the contours of justification

---

(1871) (enticement action extended to workers engaged in boot manufacture).

12. *See* Imperial Ice Co. v. Rossier, 112 P.2d 631 (Cal. 1941). *See generally* RESTATEMENT (SECOND) OF TORTS ch. 37 & intro. note at 4-7 (1979) [hereinafter RESTATEMENT]; W. PAGE KEETON, PROSSER AND KEETON ON THE LAW OF TORTS §§ 129-30 (1984) [hereinafter KEETON] .

13. *See, e.g.*, Carvel Corp. v. Noonan, 3 N.Y.3d 182, 196 (N.Y. 2004); *see generally* RESTATEMENT, *supra* note 12, § 767.

14. City of Rock Falls v. Chicago Title & Trust Co., 300 N.E.2d 331, 333 (Ill. App. Ct. 1973).

15. *Compare* Data Based Systems, Int'l, Inc. v. Hewlett-Packard Co., No. CIV. 00-CV-4425, 2001 WL 1251212 (E.D. Pa. Sept. 26, 2001) (explaining that plaintiff must show that defendant was not privileged or justified) *with* Mason v. Wal-Mart Stores, Inc., 969 S.W.2d 160, 165 (Ark. 1998) (explaining that plaintiff must show "improper" interference and burden is on defendant to show that the interference was privileged) *with* Wal-Mart Stores, Inc. v. Sturges, 52 S.W.3d 711, 725 (Tex. 2001). In *Sturges* the Court noted that "[a]lthough the burden of proving a justification or privilege in a tortious interference with contract case is on

and privilege are neither uniform nor precise.[16] Both within and among the states, many issues remain unsettled.[17] This chapter surveys the interference torts that cause harm to economic relationships.

B.   Intentional Interference With the Performance of a Contract By a Third Person

1.   Affirmative Case: Principles and Elements

While interference torts protect both contractual and prospective economic relationships, interference with a contract is more likely to be treated as improper, particularly when the parties to the litigation are competitors.[18] In contrast to prospective economic relationships, which generally are subject to competition, "the purpose of imposing liability in tort upon persons who interfere with the contractual relations of others is

---

the defendant, most [Texas] courts have placed that burden on the plaintiff in a tortious interference with prospective business relations case." 52 S.W.3d at 727. However, the Court found that justification and privilege in the latter situation are defenses "only to the extent that they are defenses to the independent tortiousness of the defendant's conduct." *Id.*; *see also infra* notes 41-47 and accompanying text.

16.   *See, e.g.*, Envtl. Planning & Info. Council of West El Dorado County, Inc. v. Superior Court, 680 P.2d 1086, 1089-90 (Cal. 1984). *See generally* KEETON, *supra* note 12, § 129, at 979.

17.   *See, e.g.*, Roy v. Coyne, 259 Ill.App.3d 269, (Ill. App. Ct. 1 Dist. 1994); *see also* Guard-Life Corp. v. S. Parker Hardware Mfg. Corp., 406 N.E.2d 445, 448-49; RESTATEMENT, *supra* note 12, § 767 cmt. k ("[T]here is little consensus on who has the burden of raising the issue of whether the interference was improper or not and subsequently of proving that issue; and it cannot be predicted with accuracy what rule will ultimately develop."); *cf.* RESTATEMENT (THIRD) OF UNFAIR COMPETITION § 1 (1993) (advocating a principle of non-liability); *see, e.g.*, discussion *supra* note 15.

18.   Via The Web Designs, L.L.C. v. Beauticontrol Cosmetics, Inc., 2005 WL 2173801, at *5 (6th Cir. 2005) (slip op.) ("In the context of two independent competitors, analogous actions have been found to constitute tortious interference."); *see also* RESTATEMENT, *supra* note 12, § 766 cmt. b.

to protect one's interest in his contractual relations against forms of interference, which, on balance, the law finds repugnant."[19]

The Restatement's definition and commentary has been widely adopted.[20] Section 766 of the Restatement (Second) of Torts provides:

> One who intentionally and improperly interferes with the performance of a contract (except a contract to marry) between another and a third person by inducing or otherwise causing the third person not to perform the contract, is subject to liability to the other for the pecuniary loss resulting to the other from the failure of the third person to perform the contract.[21]

While the states generally follow the Restatement, the elements of an interference cause of action vary from state to state. In most states the elements include the following: (1) a valid contract between the parties; (2) the defendant's knowledge of the contract; (3) intentional acts designed to induce a breach or disruption of the contractual relationship; (4) actual breach or disruption of the relationship; and (5) resulting damage. Each of these elements is addressed below. Of course, practitioners should consult the law of the relevant jurisdiction.[22]

19. Santucci Constr. Co. v. Baxter & Woodman, Inc., 502 N.E.2d 1134, 1139 (Ill. App. Ct. 1986), *appeal denied*, 511 N.E.2d 437 (Ill. 1987).
20. *See, e.g.*, Constr. Management & Inspection, Inc. v. Caprock Comm. Corp., 301 F.3d 939, 941 (8th Cir. 2002); McClease v. R.R. Donnelley & Sons Co., 226 F. Supp. 2d 695, 703-04 (E.D. Pa. 2002); Pac. Gas & Elec. v. Bear Stearns & Co., 791 P.2d 587, 590 n.3 (Cal. 1990); Krystkowiak v. W.O. Brisben Co., 90 P.3d 859, 873 (Colo. 2004); Irwin & Leighton v. W.M. Anderson & Co., 532 A.2d 983, 992 (Del. Ch. 1987); Martin Petroleum Corp. v. Amerada Hess Corp., 769 So. 2d 1105, 1107-08 (Fla. Dist. Ct. App. 2000); Toney v. Casey's Gen. Stores, Inc., 460 N.W.2d 849, 852 (Iowa 1990); Chemawa Country Golf, Inc. v. Winuk, 402 N.E.2d 1069, 1072 (Mass. App. Ct. 1980); *Guard-Life*, 406 N.E.2d at 448; Frankel v. Ne. Land Co., 570 A.2d 1065, 1069 (Pa. Super. Ct. 1990); Wal-Mart Stores, Inc. v. Sturges, 52 S.W.3d 711, 718-21 (Tex. 2001).
21. RESTATEMENT, *supra* note 12, § 766.
22. *See, e.g.*, Mason v. Wal-Mart Stores, Inc., 969 S.W.2d 160 (Ark. 1998) (Arkansas law); Bar J. Bar Cattle Co. v. Pace, 763 P.2d 545 (Ariz. 1988) (Arizona law); Applied Equip. Corp. v. Litton Saudi Arabia Ltd., 869 P.2d 454 (Cal. 1994) (California law); Roy v. Coyne, 630 N.E.2d 1024 (Ill. 1994) (Illinois law); Birdsong v. Bydalek, 953 S.W.2d 103 (Mo. Ct. App. 1997) (Missouri law); Williams Oil Co. v. Randy Luce E-Z Mart One,

2.   *A Valid Contract Between Plaintiff and a Third Party*

Recovery under any theory of tort, including interference with contractual relations, rests on the breach of a positive duty imposed by law.[23] In the case of interference with a contract, there must be a valid, existing contract.[24] As a general rule, one who interferes with an illegal agreement or an agreement violative of public policy is not liable for pecuniary harm resulting from the interference.[25]

Only a nonparty to an existing contract may be liable for intentionally interfering with its performance.[26] This principle is

---

LLC, 757 N.Y.S.2d 341 (N.Y. App. Div. 2003) (New York law); Pleas v. Seattle, 774 P.2d 1158 (Wash. 1989) (Washington law).

23.   *See, e.g.*, Gillum v. Republic Health Corp., 778 S.W.2d 558, 565 (Tex. App. 1989).

24.   Mest v. Cabot Corp., No. Civ. A. 01-4943, 2004 WL 1102754 (E.D. Pa. May 14, 2004) (noting that plaintiffs' "most glaring omission" was their failure to "cite to any evidence of specific contracts"); Hornstein v. Podwitz, 173 N.E. 674 (N.Y. 1930); Nix v. Temple Univ., 596 A.2d 1132, 1137 (Pa. Super. Ct. 1991); Browning-Ferris, Inc. v. Reyna, 865 S.W.2d 925, 926 (Tex. 1993); *Gillum*, 778 S.W.2d at 565.

25.   *See* RESTATEMENT, *supra* note 12, § 774; *see also infra* notes 150-51 and accompanying text.

26.   *See, e.g.*, SecureInfo Corp. v. Telos corp., 387 F. Supp. 2d 593, 618 (E.D. Va. 2005); Reginald Martin Agency, Inc. v. Conseco Medical Ins. Co., 388 F. Supp. 2d 919, 930 (S.D. Ind. 2005); Mau, Inc. v. Human Technologies, Inc., 619 S.E.2d 394, 398 (Ga. App. 2005). A party to a contract cannot be held liable for intentional interference with the performance of that contract. The proper remedy is for breach of contract. *See, e.g.*, King v. Sioux City Radiological Group, PC, 985 F. Supp. 869, 882 (N.D. Iowa 1997); *Applied Equip. Corp.*, 869 P.2d at 459-61 ("One contracting party owes no general duty to another not to interfere with the performance of the contract; its duty is simply to perform the contract according to its terms."); JRS Prods., Inc. v. Matsushita Elec. Corp. of Am., 8 Cal. Rptr. 3d 840, 850-51 (Cal. Ct. App. 2004) (citing *Applied Equip. Corp.*, 869 P.2d at 459-61); Personnel One, Inc. v. John Sommerer & Co., 564 So. 2d 1217, 1218 n.1 (Fla. Dist. Ct. App. 1990). However, regarding liability for conspiracy to interfere with one's own contract, there is a split of authority. *Compare Applied Equip. Corp.*, 869 P.2d at 462 (disapproving of prior California cases that held a party to a contract could be liable in tort based on a conspiracy to interfere with its own contract), *and* Sharma v. Skaarup Ship Mgmt. Corp. 699 F. Supp. 440, 445 (S.D.N.Y. 1988), *aff'd*, 916 F.2d

significant in the context of an alleged wrongful termination of an employment contract. The question arises whether a corporate employee may be held liable for interfering with a contract between the corporation and another of its employees. Generally, because a corporation can only act through its officers and other agents, where a corporate agent acts within the scope of his corporate authority, the agent and the corporation are deemed to be one entity.[27] In such circumstances there is no "third party" against whom a claim for interference will lie.[28]

3. *Defendant's Knowledge of the Contract*

To be held liable, the defendant must have knowledge of the contract with which he is interfering,[29] as well as the fact that his conduct is interfering with the performance of the contract. "The element of knowledge is a question of fact, and proof may be predicated on circumstantial evidence."[30] However, liability does not require that the

---

820 (2d Cir. 1990) (finding a party may not be held liable), *with* Fox v. Deese, 362 S.E.2d 699, 708 (Va. 1987) (finding a party may be held liable), *and* Boyles v. Thompson, 585 S.W.2d 821, 836 (Tex. Civ. App. 1979). *See generally* CALLMANN ON UNFAIR COMPETITION, TRADEMARKS AND MONOPOLIES § 9:7 (4th ed. 2004).

27. Barker v. Kimberly-Clark Corp., 524 S.E.2d 821 (N.C. Ct. App. 2000) (recognizing that a qualified privilege may arise when managers induced their company to breach a contract with another employee, but finding no qualified privilege because the manager's actions were unrelated to the corporation's interests).

28. *See, e.g.*, Faulkner v. Arkansas Children's Hosp., 69 S.W.3d 939, 959 (Ark. 2002); Daniel Adams Assoc. v. Rimbach, 519 A.2d 997, 1002 (Pa. Super. Ct.), *appeal denied*, 535 A.2d 1056 (Pa. 1987); Latch v. Gratty, 107 S.W.3d 543, 546 (Tex. 2003); *see also* Justin Myers, Comment, *Sneaking Around the Corporate Veil: Tattooing a Parent Corporation with Liability for Tortious Interference with its Subsidiary's Contract*, 35 TEX. TECH. L. REV. 193 (2004) (discussing the "two schools of thought" within Texas courts as to whether a parent corporation can be held liable for tortious interference with a subsidiary's contract).

29. *See, e.g.*, Birdsong v. Bydalek, 953 S.W.2d 103, 110 (Mo. Ct. App. 1997); *see also* KEETON, *supra* note 12, § 129, at 982.

30. Texaco, Inc. v. Pennzoil Co., 729 S.W.2d 768, 803 (Tex. App. 1987); *see* Maxvill-Glasco Drilling Co. v. Royal Oil & Gas Co., 800 S.W.2d 384 (Tex. App. 1990) (explaining that defendant's knowledge of option

defendant have knowledge of every detail of the contract.[31] And, a defendant with the knowledge of facts giving rise to a contractual duty may be liable for interference, even if the defendant is mistaken as to whether those facts give rise to a contract.[32] On the other hand, conduct that interferes with the performance of a contract unknown to the defendant should not result in liability, as there is no "intentional" conduct.[33]

4. *Intentional and Improper Acts Designed to Induce a Breach or Disruption of the Contractual Relationship*

The plaintiff must be able to show that the defendant took an active part in persuading the other party to the contract to breach it, or otherwise intentionally acted to disrupt it.[34] Generally, merely entering into a contract with a party with the knowledge of that party's contractual obligations to someone else is not the same as inducing a breach.[35] "There must be some act of interference or of persuading a party to breach, for example by offering better terms or other incentives, for tort

---

agreement not critical because one who tortiously interferes with contractual rights is liable for the damage proximately caused).

31. *Pennzoil*, 729 S.W.2d at 796 (citing Guard-Life Corp. v. S. Parker Hardware Mfg. Corp., 406 N.E.2d 445 (N.Y. 1980)); Gold Medal Farms, Inc. v. Rutland County Co-operative Creamery, Inc., 195 N.Y.S.2d 179, 185 (N.Y. App. Div. 1959).

32. *Pennzoil*, 729 S.W.2d at 797; *see* RESTATEMENT, *supra* note 12, § 766 cmt. i.

33. RESTATEMENT, *supra* note 12, § 766 cmt. i; *see* Herrick v. Superior Court, 233 Cal. Rptr. 675, 677-78 (Cal. Ct. App. 1987) (citing Imperial Ice Co. v. Rossier, 12 P.2d 631 (Cal. 1941)) (finding no cause of action against drunk driver for damages resulting to plaintiff's business after driver collided with plaintiff's truck). Conversely, knowledge of the contract but mistaken belief as to the legal effect of the actor's conduct is not a defense. *See* RESTATEMENT, *supra* note 12, § 766 cmt. i.

34. *See, e.g.*, Jean Paul Mitchell Systems v. Randalls Food Markets, Inc., 17 S.W.3d 721 (Tex. App. 2000); *see generally* KEETON, *supra* note 12, § 129, at 982-89; RESTATEMENT, *supra* note 12, § 766 cmt. h.

35. *See Pennzoil*, 729 S.W.2d at 803 (citing P.P.X. Enters., Inc. v. Catala, 232 N.Y.S.2d 959 (N.Y. App. Div. 1962)); *Jean Paul Mitchell Systems*, 17 S.W.3d at 730 ("[A] party must be more than a willing participant; it must knowingly induce one of the contracting parties to breach its obligations."). *See generally* KEETON, *supra* note 12, § 129, at 989-90.

liability to arise."[36] Therefore, both the defendant's method and motive are important factors in establishing this element.

The act must be "improper," although the term has been criticized for its indefiniteness.[37] Generally speaking, although the term "malice" is often used in this context, it is not necessary for a plaintiff to demonstrate "ill will," hostility or dislike, or that the defendant acted with actual malice.[38] For example, in Massachusetts, if an act is "intentional and without justification," it is "malicious in law even though it arose from good motives and without express malice."[39] Theoretically, a defendant may be liable even when he acts with no desire to harm the other.[40]

A defendant is not liable, however, for actions that are considered "justified" or "privileged."[41] For example, merely competitive conduct that results in another company breaching its contract with a third party

---

36. *Pennzoil*, 729 S.W.2d at 803 (citing State Enters. Inc. v. Southridge Coop. Section 1, Inc., 238 N.Y.S.2d 724, 726 (N.Y. App. Div. 1963)).

37. *See, e.g.*, Mason v. Wal-Mart Stores, Inc., 969 S.W.2d 160, 165-66 (Ark. 1998) (citing Dan B. Dobbs, *Tortious Interference with Contractual Relationships*, 34 ARK. L. REV. 335, 345 (1980) and finding no improper conduct in Wal-Mart using economic pressure to increase its profits by eliminating Mason as a manufacturer's representative from its purchasing process).

38. *Mason*, 969 S.W.2d at 162-66 (discussing the "impropriety" requirement and citing KEETON, *supra* note 12, § 129, at 983-84, nn. 61 & 62); *see* Scutti Enterps., LLC. V. Park Place Entm't Corp., 322 F.3d 211, 216 (2d Cir. 2003); Korea Supply Co. v. Lockheed Martin Corp., 63 P.3d 937, 953 (Cal. 2003); Birdsong v. Bydalek, 953 S.W.2d 103, 113 (Mo. Ct. App. 1997). *See generally* KEETON, *supra* note 12, § 129, at 983 ("It has long been clear, however that 'malice' in the sense of ill-will or spite is not required for liability."). *But see* Lee v. Strickland, No. 03A01-9806-CH-00195, 1999 WL 233395 (Tenn. Ct. App. April 16, 1999) (finding malice or ill will to be a necessary element of tortious interference with business relations).

39. Laurendeau v. Kewaunee Scientific Equip. Corp., 456 N.E.2d 767, 773 (Mass. App. Ct. 1983), *review denied*, 459 N.E.2d 824 (Mass. 1984).

40. RESTATEMENT, *supra* note 12, § 766 cmt. r.

41. *Mason*, 969 S.W.2d at 162-66.

generally is not considered improper conduct.[42]   Nor does the communication of truthful information provide the basis for a claim of improper interference with another's contractual relationships.[43]

Some states have incorporated the concept of justification or privilege as an element that must be pled, and proven, by the plaintiff.[44] For example, in Florida and Pennsylvania a plaintiff must affirmatively show an absence of any justification or privilege.[45]   In those states, a plaintiff must be able to establish that a defendant's acts were not justified, either because the defendant used improper means, or because the interest that the defendant sought to further or protect was subordinate to the plaintiff's contractual relationship.[46]   In contrast, Arkansas, Illinois and Texas place the burden of proof on the defendant to show that the interference was justified.[47]

---

42. *Id.*; Int'l Sales and Servs., Inc. v. Austral Insulated Prods., Inc., 267 F.3d 1152, 1158 (11th Cir. 2001).
43. *See* Tucker, *supra* note 5 (noting, however, that the truth is not an absolute defense despite the First Amendment protection provided to such communications and citing RESTATEMENT, *supra* note 12, § 772(a)).
44. *See* discussion *supra* note 15.
45. Seminole Tribe of Florida v. Times Pub. Co., 780 So. 2d 310, 315 (Fla. Dist. Ct. App. 2001); *see* Killian v. McCulloch, 850 F. Supp. 1239, 1251 (E.D. Pa. 1994); Strickland v. Univ. of Scranton, 700 A.2d 979, 975 (Pa. Super. 1997).
46. *See generally Mason*, 969 S.W.2d at 162 ("[I]t is necessary for the plaintiff in an interference-with-contract claim to demonstrate that the conduct of the defendant was at least improper."); Birdsong v. Bydalek, 953 S.W.2d 103, 113 (Mo. Ct. App. 1997) (defining "improper means"); *Strickland*, 700 A.2d at 985 (same); KEETON, *supra* note 12, § 129, at 984-89.
47. *See, e.g.*, Roy v. Coyne, 630 N.E.2d 1024, 1031-32 (Ill. 1994) (placing the burden of proof on the defendant to establish the affirmative defense of justification to a claim of tortuous intereference with contract); Holloway v. Skinner, 989 S.W.2d 793, 796 (Tex. 1995) (same); Elisa Masterson White, *Arkansas Tortious Interference Law: A Proposal for Change*, 19 U. ARK. LITTLE ROCK L. REV. 81 (Fall 1996) (explaining that the burden of proof under Arkansas law is on the defendant to show justification). *But see* Bebble v. Nat'l Air Traffic Controllers Assoc., No. 00 C 4055, 2001 WL 128241 (N.D. Ill. Feb. 9, 2001) (shifting the burden of proof to the plaintiff if the complaint shows the existence of a privilege on the part of the defendant); *see also infra* notes 179-97 and accompanying text for a further discussion of privilege and justification.

5. *Breach or Disruption of the Contractual Relationship*

In some jurisdictions, it is not necessary to prove an actual breach of the contract to establish interference. It is sufficient if the defendant's conduct makes performance of the contract more difficult or decreases the benefit of the contract.[48]

In other jurisdictions, however, breach of the underlying contract is an essential element for recovery under a theory of tortious interference with contractual relations.[49]

Where the defendant induces a direct interference, this will not be a controversial element. A more difficult question arises where the defendant's conduct causes an indirect interference. For example, a defendant may induce a party to sell the defendant goods instead of selling them to the plaintiff with whom the party is under contract. As a result, the defendant indirectly prevents the plaintiff from distributing the goods to other unrelated parties. Absent proof of unlawful or illegal conduct or motive to interfere with the plaintiff's unrelated contracts, remoteness may prevent an action for interference with contractual relations between the plaintiff and his distributees.[50]

6. *Resulting Damage*

The plaintiff must suffer damages as a result of the actor's conduct, "and those damages cannot be speculative or conjectural losses."[51] Upon

---

48. Sebastian Int'l, Inc. v. Russolillo, 162 F. Supp. 2d 1198, 1204 (C.D. Cal. 2001); Bishop v. Paine Webber, Inc., No. 331709, 1999 WL 596248, at *2 (Conn. Super. Ct. July 28, 1999). *See generally* RESTATEMENT, *supra* note 12, § 766 cmt. j.

49. Jack L. Inselman & Co. v. FNB Fin. Co., 364 N.E.2d 1119, 1120 (N.Y. 1977) ("In order for the plaintiff to have a cause of action for tortious interference of contract, it is axiomatic that there must be a breach of that contract by the other party."); Hudson v. Wesley College, Inc., No. 1211, 1998 WL 939712, at *11 (Del. Ch. Dec. 23, 1998); First Union Mortg. Corp. v. Thomas, 451 S.E.2d 907, 913 (S.C. Ct. App. 1994).

50. RESTATEMENT, *supra* note 12, § 767 cmt. h; *see also* John Paul Mitchell Systems v. Randalls Food Markets, Inc., 17 S.W.3d 721, 730-31 (Tex. App. 2000) (finding that absent proof of direct inducement, requirements of an interference cause of action are not satisfied).

51. Chemawa Country Golf, Inc. v. Winuk, 402 N.E.2d 1069, 1073 (Mass. App. Ct. 1980). *See generally* KEETON, *supra* note 12, § 129, at 989.

proof of a cause of action, a plaintiff may seek to recover pecuniary loss, including consequential damage caused by the interference, as well as punitive damages.[52] In some cases, damages may not be an adequate remedy and injunctive relief also will be available to restrain the unjustified interference.[53]

7. *At-Will Contracts*

Although early cases found no liability for interference with at-will contracts, more recent case law recognizes such liability.[54] An essential element of interference with a contractual relationship is the existence of a valid contract between the plaintiff and a third party. "For purposes of proving interference with a contractual relationship, a contract is valid if it is not illegal, opposed to public policy, or otherwise void."[55] The fact that the contract is of an at-will nature does not prevent liability from claims of tortious interference; thus, employment, partnership, and supply contracts are valid contracts subject to protection.[56] Indeed, it is

---

52. RESTATEMENT, *supra* note 12, § 774A. *See generally* 3 Robert L. Haig, et al., COMMERCIAL LITIGATION IN NEW YORK STATE COURTS § 44.37 *Damages for Tortious Interference with Contractual Relationship*, (2004) (citing Guard-Life Corp. v. S. Parker Hardware Mfg. Corp., 406 N.E.2d 445 (N.Y. 1980) and Wasserman v. NRG Realty Corp., N.Y.S.2d (N.Y. App. Div. 1986)); Brookeside Ambulance, Inc. v. Walker Ambulance Serv., 678 N.E.2d 248, 253 (Ohio Ct. App. 1996); Steven W. Feldman, *Tortious Interference with Contract in Tennessee: A Practitioner's Guide*, 31 U. MEM. L. REV. 281, 314-322 (Winter 2001).
53. *See* Pac. Gas & Elec. v. Bear Stearns & Co., 791 P.2d 587, 593 n.9 (Cal. 1990); Advantage Digital Sys., Inc. v. Digital Imaging Servs., Inc., 870 So. 2d 111, 116 (Fla. Dist. Ct. App. 2003); Paul L. Pratt, P.C. v. Blunt, 488 N.E.2d 1062, 1068 (Ill. App. Ct. 1986); *see also* Haig, *supra* note 52, at § 59.16 *Remedies for Tortious Interference* (citing Fed. Waste Paper Corp. v. Garment Ctr. Capitol, 51 N.Y.S.2d 26, 28-29 (N.Y. App. Div. 1944)); *infra* notes 210-20 and accompanying text (discussing damages).
54. *See, e.g.*, 5 J.D. LEE & BARRY LINDAHL, MODERN TORT LAW LIABILITY AND LITIGATION ch. 45 *Interference with Existing or Prospective Contractual Relations* (2002) (citing Boston Glass Mfg. Co. v. Binney, 21 Mass. (4 Pick.) 425 (1827)).
55. Shamblin v. Berge, 166 Cal. App. 3d 118, 124 (Cal. Ct. App. 1985) (citing KEETON, *supra* note 12, § 129, at 994-95).
56. Bochnowski v. Peoples Fed. Sav. & Loan, 571 N.E. 2d 282, 284-85 (Ind. 1991); Juliette Fowler Homes, Inc. v. Welch Assoc., Inc., 793 S.W.2d 660,

asserted that interference lawsuits have enjoyed a resurgence in recent years in the context of at-will employment contracts.[57]

The nature of the contract may, however, affect burdens of proof or available remedies. States disagree, for purposes of the elements of an interference cause of action, on whether a distinction exists between at-will contracts and other contractual relationships. Many states, including Florida,[58] California,[59] Tennessee[60] and Texas[61] find no distinction between an at-will contract and other contracts. Under the Restatement, there is no distinction; a stranger may not properly interfere with an at-will contract prior to the contracting party's decision to terminate it.[62]

In an illustrative case from California, a power company brought suit against a brokerage firm for encouraging a county agency to litigate with the power company to determine whether the agency could terminate its at-will contract according to the contract's terms. The power company alleged that by encouraging the suit, the defendant had interfered with the plaintiff's contractual relations and business advantage, and had attempted to induce a breach of contract. The case

---

666 (Tex. 1990) (at-will contracts generally); Sterner v. Marathon Oil, 767 S.W.2d 686, 689 (Tex. 1989) (at-will employment contracts); Charolais Breeding Ranches v. F.P.C. Secs. Corp., 279 N.W.2d 493 (Wis. Ct. App. 1979); Sean Farrell, *Applying Tortious Interference Claims to At-Will Contracts*, 39 TEX. J. BUS. L. 527 (Winter 2004).

57. Frank J. Cavico, *Tortious Interference with Contract in the At-Will Employment Context*, 79 U. DET. MERCY L. REV. 503 (Summer 2002).

58. Custom Mfg. & Eng'g, Inc. v. Midway Servs., Inc., 2005 WL 1313829, at *8 (M.D. Fla. May 31, 2005).

59. Pac. Gas & Elec. v. Bear Stearns & Co., 791 P.2d 587, 590-91 (Cal. 1990).

60. New Life Corp. of Am. v. Thomas Nelson, Inc., 932 S.W.2d 921 (Tenn. Ct. App. 1996).

61. Gillum v. Republic Health Corp., 778 S.W.2d 558, 565 (Tex. App. 1989); *see also* Farrell, *supra* note 56 ("[I]n at-will contracts, one may legitimately induce contracting parties to exercise their contractual rights and terminate the contract, but it would be tortious interference to induce them to breach any contractual obligations, such as non-competition clauses or notice requirements.").

62. *See* RESTATEMENT *supra* note 12, § 766 cmt. g ("Until [the contracting party] has so terminated it, the contract remains valid and subsisting, and [third persons] may not improperly interfere with it."); *see also* Tiernan v. Charleston Area Med. Ctr., Inc., 506 S.E.2d 578, 591 (W. Va. 1998).

raised the issue of whether inducing a party to terminate its contract, according to the contract's terms, was actionable interference.[63] The Supreme Court of California concluded that it could be actionable to induce a party to an at-will contract to terminate the contract according to its terms.[64]

In contrast, New York categorizes an at-will contract as akin to a prospective economic relationship because neither an at-will contract nor a prospective economic relationship have any legal assurances of continued performance.[65] This is an important concept. Where an at-will contract is considered to be no more than a prospective economic relationship, a broader range of privilege may exist, and proof of more culpable conduct may be required.[66] In order to establish interference with a prospective economic relationship, New York requires a plaintiff to show that "wrongful means" (such as fraud or threats) were used.[67] In sum, in New York and states that consider at-will contracts to be prospective economic relationships, interference with an at-will contract may require a greater showing than interference with a contract having a specific term.

Similarly, Iowa, while recognizing a cause of action for interference with at-will contracts, holds that "the standard of proof is more demanding when the ... contract is at-will, and our law of contract interference applies different rules."[68] "There must be substantial evidence of a predominant motive by the defendant to terminate the

63. *Pac. Gas*, 791 P.2d at 590-91.
64. *Id.* The court went on to hold, however, that a claim for interference with contract or prospective economic advantage is not stated unless the encouraged litigation was without probable cause and had concluded in the interference plaintiff's favor. *See id.* at 593.
65. *See* Flash Elecs., Inc. v. Universal Music & Video Dist. Corp., 312 F. Supp. 2d 379, 404 (E.D.N.Y. 2004); Guard-Life Corp. v. S. Parker Hardware Mfg. Corp., 406 N.E.2d 445, 449 n.4 (N.Y. 1980).
66. *See Guard-Life*, 406 N.E. 2d at 449 n.4.
67. *Id.* at 449-50; *see also* Lockheed Martin Corp. v. Aatlas Commerce, Inc., 725 N.Y.S.2d 722, 725-26 (N.Y. App. Div. 2001) (explaining that in an at-will employment context, improper means could include disclosing confidential information and inducing breach of covenant not to compete)
68. King v. Sioux City Radiological Group, PC, 985 F. Supp. 869, 882-85 (N.D. Iowa 1997).

contract for improper reasons."[69] In this context, the Iowa courts define "improper" as having the purpose to financially injure or damage the plaintiff's business.[70]

Regardless of how an at-will contract is treated for purposes of burdens of proof, the Restatement indicates the at-will nature of the contract should be taken into account in determining the amount of damages recoverable.[71]

8. *Void and Voidable Contracts*

For purposes of proving interference with a contractual relationship, it is necessary that the contract be valid. If the contract is void as illegal or unenforceable, a tortious interference claim will fail as well.[72] The same is not true for voidable contracts.[73] Because voidable contracts are

---

69. *Id.* at 883-84 (citing Toney v. Casey's Gen. Stores, Inc., 460 N.W.2d 849 (Iowa 1985)).

70. *Id.* at 884 (noting that this is the same definition used in cases involving interference with a prospective contract); *accord* Compiano v. Hawkeye Bank & Trust of Des Moines, 588 N.W.2d 462, 464 (Iowa 1999); Combs & Assoc., Inc. v. Kennedy, 555 S.E.2d 634, 641 (N.C. Ct. App. 2001) (noting that North Carolina's Supreme Court has held that the party asserting a claim of tortious interference in the at-will employment context must show that the competitor acted with malice or bad faith).

71. *See* RESTATEMENT, *supra* note 12, § 766 cmt. g; *see also* RESTATEMENT, *supra* note 12, § 774A(2). *But see* Chapman v. Crown Glass Corp., 557 N.E.2d 256, 265-66 (Ill. App. Ct. 1990) (treating at-will contract as either contract or prospective business relation so long as both parties would have been willing to continue the relationship for an indefinite period of time and allowing damages for estimated future earnings and bonuses from 1979 through 1990).

72. *See* RESTATEMENT, *supra* note 12, § 766 cmt. e; *see also* 4 Haig, *supra* note 52, at § 59.12 *Tortious Interference with Existing Contract*, (citing Allied Sheet Metal Works, Inc. v. Kerby Saunders, Inc., 619 N.Y.S.2d 260, 265 (N.Y. App. Div. 1994) (tortious interference claim fails where contract barred by Statute of Frauds); Semtek Intern. Inc. v. Lockheed Martin Corp., 2003 WL 23497537, at *2-4 (Md. Cir. Ct. 2003) (tortious intereference claim fails where contract unenforceable as mere "agreement to agree"); Scotto v. Mei, 642 N.Y.S.2d 863, 865 (N.Y. App. Div. 1996) (tortuous interference claim fails where contract was illegal)).

73. *See* RESTATEMENT, *supra* note 12, § 766 cmt. f.

"at the will of the parties and not at the will of outsiders,"[74] such contracts are valid and subject to protection from interference.[75] For example, a promise may be a valid and subsisting contract even though it is voidable. Under this theory, the wrong lies in the inducement to break the contract, not in the kind of contract or relationship disrupted.[76]

Some states, such as New York, New Jersey, and Illinois, treat a voidable contract as an at-will contract or prospective economic relationship.[77] In such cases, in order for liability to result a plaintiff must prove that "wrongful means" were used to interfere with the voidable contract.[78]

> [I]n order to succeed on their tortious interference with [voidable] contract claim, plaintiffs must show that [defendant] procured [the third party's] disaffirmance of her contract by wrongful means. "Wrongful means" are defined to include "physical violence, fraud or misrepresentation, civil suits and criminal prosecutions, and some degrees of economic pressure; they do not, however, include persuasion alone although it is knowingly directed at interference with the contract."[79]

---

74. Pac. Gas & Elec. v. Bear Stearns & Co., 791 P.2d 587, 590-91 (Cal. 1990).
75. Kerkhoff v. Kerkhoff, 1999 WL 88962, at *2 (Minn. Ct. App. Feb. 23, 1999); Zimmerman v. Bank of Am., 12 Cal. Rptr. 319, 320-21 (Cal. Ct. App. 1961); see RESTATEMENT, *supra* note 12, § 766 cmt. f.
76. *Zimmerman*, 12 Cal. Rptr. at 323 ("[W]e see no good reason why the protection against the dangers of [voidable] oral agreements, which the statute affords to parties to a transaction, should inure to a stranger who seeks the destruction of the transaction and whose status fundamentally differs from that of the party whom the statute seeks to protect."); *see* RESTATEMENT, *supra* note 12, § 766 cmt. f.
77. Fineman v. Armstrong World Ind., Inc., 980 F.2d 171, 189 (3d Cir. 1992) (applying New Jersey law); J.D. Edwards & Co. v. Podany, et al., No. 94 C 4865, 1997 WL 12792, at *5 (N.D. Ill. Jan. 10, 1997); NBT Bancorp v. Fleet/Norstar Fin. Group, 553 N.Y.S.2d 864, 868 (N.Y. App. Div.), *appeal dismissed*, 562 N.E.2d 871 (N.Y. 1990) (finding complaint of interference insufficient absent allegation that merger agreement was breached).
78. *See Fineman*, 980 F.2d at 190; *NBT Bancorp*, 553 N.Y.S.2d at 868.
79. NYC Mgmt. Group, Inc. v. Miller, No. 03 Civ. 2617(RJH), 2004 WL 1087784 (S.D.N.Y. May 14, 2004).

9. *Propriety, Privilege and Justification*

Irrevocably intertwined with the concept of improper conduct[80] are the issues of propriety, privilege, and justification. As discussed earlier, courts have blurred the lines of distinction by shifting burdens of proof for these elements,[81] and often acknowledge their "all being the same concept."[82] There is no uniform definition for these concepts. This is because, unlike intentional torts to person or property, such as battery or slander, the interference torts often do not involve what is traditionally considered to be an "intentional tort." Rather, the parties' relationship is viewed as that of conflicting economic interests. In this arena, it often is difficult to define which actions are proper or justified. "Privilege," therefore, is best understood as a determination that the economic interference is justified or "proper" under the particular circumstances.[83]

Both the Restatement and the case law echo this sentiment; there is no fixed set of rules defining what conduct is or is not privileged. Depending on the circumstances, the conduct of an actor may be proper, while identical conduct in different circumstances may be improper.[84] Because each case of intentional interference presents an issue as to whether the interference is "improper," and which party's interest is superior or equal to the other's,[85] the Restatement considers this

---

80. *See supra* footnotes 34-40 and accompanying text.
81. *See supra* footnotes 15, 44-47 and accompanying text discussing that in certain states the plaintiff must show the defendant's actions were improper while in other states the burden is on the defendant to show that its actions were proper or otherwise justified.
82. Int'l Sales & Service, Inc., v. Austral Insulated Prods., Inc., 262 F.3d 1152, 1158-59 (11th Cir. 2001).
83. *See, e.g.*, Ethyl Corp. v. Balter, 386 So. 2d 1220, 1225 (Fla. Dist. Ct. App. 1980) ("[S]o long as improper means are not employed, activities taken to safeguard or promote one's financial and contractual interest are entirely non-actionable."); *Int'l Sales & Service, Inc.*, 262 F.3d at 1152 (finding that privilege of competition protects defendant's actions in breaking promise not to sell directly to plaintiff's customers if plaintiff identified those customers to defendant).
84. *See* RESTATEMENT, *supra* note 12, § 767 cmts. b, c.
85. *See, e.g.*, Hi-Tek Consulting Servs., Inc. v. Bar-Nahum, 578 N.E.2d 993, 997 (Ill. App. Ct. 1991) ("The third party claiming the privilege of legal justification must be acting to protect a conflicting interest that is considered to be of equal value to or greater than plaintiff's contractual

determination, including the appropriate burden of proof, to cause the most frequent and difficult problems.[86]

In theory, the common law adopts the term "improper" as a part of a test combining the concepts of culpability and lack of justification.[87] "Whether an intentional interference by a third party is justifiable depends upon a balancing of the importance, social and private, of the objective advanced by the interference against the importance of the interest interfered with, considering all the circumstances."[88] The Restatement's test of whether conduct is privileged or "proper" involves a process of balancing seven factors. State law also looks to these factors,[89] which are listed in section 767 of the Restatement:

(A)   the nature of the actor's conduct;

(B)   the actor's motive;

(C)   the interest of the other with which the actor's conduct interferes;

(D)   the interest sought to be advanced by the actor;

(E)   the social interests in protecting the freedom of action and contractual interest of the actor;

(F)   the proximity or remoteness of the actor's conduct to the interference; and

(G)   the relations between the parties.

---

rights...."); Evans v. Reliant Energy Inc., 2002 WL 31838088, at *3 (Tex. App. – Houston [1st Dist.] Dec. 19, 2002) ("[O]ne is privileged to interfere with another's contract (1) if the interference is done in a bona fide exercise of one's own rights, or (2) if one has a right in the subject matter equal or superior to that of the other party.").

86.   *See* RESTATEMENT, *supra* note 12, § 767 cmt. a; *see also* Morris Commc'ns Corp. v. PGA Tour, Inc., 235 F. Supp.2d 1269, 1287 (M.D. Fla. 2002).

87.   Toney v. Casey's Gen. Stores, Inc., 460 N.W.2d 849, 852 (Iowa 1990).

88.   Envtl. Planning & Info. Council of West El Dorado County, Inc. v. Superior Court, 680 P.2d 1086, 1089-90 (Cal. 1984).

89.   *See, e.g.*, Safeway Ins. Co. v. Guerrero, 106 P.3d 1020, 1027 (Ariz. 2005); Mason v. Wal-Mart Stores, Inc., 969 S.W.2d 160, 164-65 (Ark. 1998); Thomas v. Harford Mut. Ins. Co., 2004 WL 1102362, at *5 (Del. Super. Ct. April 7, 2004); Wal-Mart Stores, Inc. v. Sturges, 52 S.W.3d 711, 719 (Tex. 2001); Fred Siegel Co., L.P.A. v. Arter & Hadden, 707 N.E.2d 853, 860 (Ohio 1999).

Only after examination of these factors can a decision be made as to whether the conduct is justified or "privileged."

While each state's case law determines the relative weight to be given these factors,[90] the Restatement suggests that some common-law patterns have developed defining conduct that is privileged or actions that are not improper.[91]

For example, New York law adopts the Restatement's three primary factors: (1) the nature of the actor's conduct, (2) the actor's motive, and (3) the interests of the other with which the actor's conduct interferes.[92] New York law also considers lesser, but also important, factors, including the "motive and interests sought to be advanced by the one who interferes, the social interests in protecting the freedom of action of that person as well as the contractual interests of the party interfered with, and the proximity or remoteness to the interference of the conduct complained of."[93]

These factors do not receive uniform treatment and pleading requirements and burdens of proof vary from state to state. "At least some of the [Restatement's] factors . . . are treated as going to the culpability of the actor's conduct in the beginning, rather than to the determination of whether the conduct was justifiable as an affirmative defense."[94] A plaintiff therefore should at least plead that the actor's

---

90. *See, e.g.*, Westfield Dev. Co. v. Rifle Invest. Assoc., 786 P.2d 1112, 1117 (Colo. 1990); *Toney*, 460 N.W.2d at 853.

91. RESTATEMENT, *supra* note 12, § 767 cmt. b. For example, some courts provide corporate officers with a qualified privilege for their acts on behalf of the corporation. *See, e.g.*, Ruffino v. State Street Bank & Trust Co., 908 F. Supp. 1019, 1050 (D. Mass. 1995) ("While...a supervisor or manager enjoys a qualified privilege from liability...the privilege does not shield an employee whose actions are intentional and improper in motive or means. . . . The plaintiff must prove that the supervisor interfered with the employee's advantageous employment relationship malevolently, i.e., for a spiteful, malignant purpose, unrelated to the legitimate corporate interest.").

92. Guard-Life Corp. v. S. Parker Hardware Mfg. Corp., 406 N.E.2d 445, 448 (N.Y. 1980).

93. *Id.*

94. RESTATEMENT, *supra* note 12, § 767 cmt. b; *see also* discussion *supra* notes 15, 44-47.

conduct was not privileged, proper or justified.[95] The following discussion analyzes the factors the courts apply when determining whether the actor's conduct is justified.

10. *Nature of the Actor's Conduct*

A balancing of the Restatement's seven factors calls for a judgment of "whether . . . the conduct should be permitted without liability, despite its effect of harm to another."[96] While there is no "technical requirement" as to the kind of conduct that may result in liability,[97] the nature of the actor's conduct is probably the chief factor when determining the propriety of the conduct. For example, physical violence or an illegal restraint of trade likely will be held improper.[98] On the other hand, it is far less likely that mere persuasion will be held actionable.[99]

---

95. RESTATEMENT, *supra* note 12, § 767 cmt. b. *See generally* Atlantic Paper Box Co. v. Whitman's Chocolates, 844 F. Supp. 1038, 1047 (E.D. Pa. 1994); Della Penna v. Toyota Motor Sales, U.S.A., Inc., 45 Cal. Rptr. 2d 436, 447 (Cal. 1995). Comment b to section 767 of the Restatement states that:Justification is generally treated as a matter of defense, but not always in the tort of interference with contractual relations. Thus a court that calls the tort "malicious interference" and defines this interference without justification often decides that it is part of the plaintiff's case to plead and prove lack of justification.
RESTATEMENT, supra note 12, § 767 cmt. b.

96. *Id.*

97. *See, e.g.,* Wells Fargo Bank v. Ariz. Laborers, Teamsters & Cement Masons Local No. 395 Pension Trust Fund, 38 P.3d 12, 32 (Ariz. 2002).

98. *See generally* Birdsong v. Bydalek, 953 S.W.2d 103, 112 (Mo. Ct. App. 1997); Lee v. Strickland, No. 03A01-9806-CH-00195, 1999 WL 233395 (Tenn. Ct. App. April 16, 1999) (finding defendant liable for interference with business relations based on its conduct in threatening to physically harm third party to force it to end its business relations with plaintiff); Wal-Mart Stores, Inc. v. Sturges, 52 S.W.3d 711, 726 (Tex. 2001) (holding that a defendant who threatens a person with physical harm for doing business with the plaintiff would be liable for intentional interference); KEETON, *supra* note 12, § 129 at 992; RESTATEMENT, *supra* note 12, § 767 cmt. c.

99. *See generally Sturges.*, 52 S.W.3d at 726 ("Conduct that is merely 'sharp' or unfair is not actionable and cannot be the basis for an action for tortious interference with prospective relations...."); RESTATEMENT, *supra* note 12, § 767 cmt. c.

The particular circumstances dictate whether the actor's conduct is improper.[100] Therefore, "the issue is not simply whether the actor is justified in causing the harm, but rather whether he is justified in causing it in the manner in which he does cause it."[101] Even though innocent means are used, the interference nevertheless may be improper under the circumstances.[102] Standards of acceptable business customs or ethics are relevant, as are recognized concepts of "fair play."[103]

False and misleading representations are actionable under the laws pertaining to other torts, such as fraud,[104] defamation, and disparagement,[105] as well as the law governing trademarks and trade dress.[106] A fraudulent representation also can support an interference tort.[107]

---

100. For example, under Texas law, a defendant who knowingly makes fraudulent statements about the plaintiff to a third person would be liable, while a person who did not intend to deceive with his statements would not be liable. *See Sturges*, 52 S.W.3d at 726. Similarly, a defendant who persuades others not to deal with the plaintiff as part of an illegal boycott would be liable, while a defendant whose persuasion of others was lawful would not be liable. *See* RESTATEMENT, *supra* note 12, § 767 cmt. c.

101. RESTATEMENT, *supra* note 12, § 767 cmt. c.

102. *Id.*; *see also* Flash Elecs., Inc. v. Universal Music & Video Dist. Corp., 312 F. Supp. 2d 379, 404 (E.D.N.Y. 2004) ("[W]here there is an existing, enforceable contract and a defendant's deliberate interference results in a breach of that contract, a plaintiff may recover damages for tortious interference with contractual relations even if the defendant was engaged in lawful behavior." (citation omitted.)). *But see Birdsong*, 953 S.W.2d at 112 ("[A]n action for interference with contract does not lie where the alleged interferer has a legitimate interest, economic or otherwise, in the contract or expectancy sought to be protected and employs no 'improper means.'").

103. RESTATEMENT, *supra* note 12, § 767 cmt. c; *see also* Toney v. Casey's Gen. Stores, Inc., 460 N.W.2d 849, 853 (Iowa 1990); Mason v. Wal-Mart Stores, Inc., 969 S.W.2d 160, 165-66 (Ark. 1998).

104. *See* Chapter 6.

105. *See* Chapter 4.

106. *See* Chapter 3.

107. *See* RESTATEMENT *supra* note 12, § 767 cmt. c; *see also* Stapleton Studios, LLC v. City of New York, 802 N.Y.S.2d 54, 54 (N.Y. App. Div. 2005) (finding that statements made by city's representatives to the press were

A truthful statement, on the other hand, often can serve as a defense to a claim of tortious interference.[108] Section 772(a) of the Restatement (Second) of Torts notes:

> One who unintentionally causes a third person not to perform a contract or not to enter into a prospective contractual relation with another does not interfere improperly with the other's contractual relations by giving to the third person ... truthful information ....

Litigation and the threat of litigation can be potent economic weapons and if used as a means of harassment.[109] As discussed above, in a California case a power company brought suit against a brokerage firm for encouraging a county agency to litigate with the power company to determine whether the county agency could terminate its contract according to the contract's terms.[110] The power company alleged that by encouraging the suit, the defendant had interfered with the plaintiff's contractual relations and business advantage, and had attempted to induce a breach of contract.

In affirming dismissal of the suit, the Supreme Court of California held that a plaintiff does not state a claim for interference with contract or prospective economic advantage in such circumstances unless the plaintiff can allege that the prior litigation was without probable cause and had concluded in its favor. Despite the fact that the power company had incurred substantial attorneys' fees, the absence of any allegation of a lack of probable cause doomed the interference claim.[111]

---

susceptible of defamatory connotation and thus would support a cause of action for tortious interference with prospective business relations).

108. *See* RESTATEMENT, *supra* note 12, at § 772(a); Tucker, *supra* note 5, at 720-21 (discussing First Amendment justification); Freeman, *supra* note 5, at 25-29 (discussing privilege in the newsgathering context); Tiernan v. Charleston Area Med. Ctr., Inc., 506 S.E.2d 578, 592-93 (W. Va. 1998) (adopting § 772 of the Restatement).

109. *See, e.g.*, Norse Sys., Inc. v. Tingley Sys., Inc., 715 A.2d 807, 818 (Conn. App. Ct. 1998) (explaining that despite being barred by res judicata, claim of abuse of process where plaintiff alleged competitor commenced action with ulterior motive to harm defendant was essentially claim of tortious interference with business or contractual relations).

110. Pac. Gas & Elec. v. Bear Stearns & Co., 791 P.2d 587 (Cal. 1990).

111. *Id.* at 593.

Litigation or threat of litigation also can, in some courts, be privileged. In a case applying New Jersey law, the United States Court of Appeals for the Third Circuit held that the *Noerr-Pennington* doctrine applied to cases involving claims of tortious interference, extending the traditional reach of the doctrine beyond the antitrust context.[112] Traditionally, the *Noerr-Pennington* doctrine gives those who petition the government for redress immunity from antitrust liability.[113] In *Cheminor*, the plaintiff brought federal and state antitrust claims, along with claims for tortious interference, malicious prosecution, abuse of process, and unfair competition, against the defendant for its actions in filing a complaint against the plaintiff before the International Trade Commission and the Department of Commerce.[114] The district court dismissed all of the claims under the *Noerr-Pennington* doctrine.[115] On appeal, the Third Circuit affirmed the dismissal of all of the claims under the *Noerr-Pennington* doctrine, reasoning that, where the state tort claims were based on the same petitioning activity as the federal antitrust claims, there was no reason that the former would not similarly be barred by the doctrine.[116]

A frequently contested issue is whether an action will lie for interference with contract after the filing of a lis pendens action. There is a split among the states. Some states deem such a filing absolutely privileged.[117] Other states and the Restatement treat the filing of a lis pendens as qualifiedly privileged.[118]

---

112. Cheminor Drugs, Ltd. v. Ethyl Corp., 168 F.3d 119, 128 (3d Cir. 1999).
113. *See* Chapter 2; *see also, e.g.*, Prof'l Real Estate Investors, Inc. v. Columbia Pictures Indus., Inc., 508 U.S. 49 (1993).
114. *Cheminor Drugs*, 168 F.3d at 120.
115. *Id.*
116. *Id.* at 128; *see also*, Igen Int'l, Inc. v. Roche Diagnostics GMBH, 335 F.3d 303, 310 (4th Cir. 2003) (recognizing the decision in *Cheminor*).
117. *See, e.g.*, Woodcourt II Ltd. v. McDonald Co., 119 Cal. App. 3d 245, 248 (1981); Procacci v. Zacco, 402 So. 2d 425, 426-27 (Fla. Dist. Ct. App. 1981); Birdsong v. Bydalek, 953 S.W.2d 103, 114 (Mo. Ct. App. 1997); Heuer & Co. v. Harry, 2005 WL 3005776, at *2 (N.J. Super. Ct. Ch. Div. Nov. 4, 2005); Lone v. Brown, 489 A.2d 1192, 1197 (N.J. App. 1985), *appeal dism'd*, 511 A.2d 657 (N.J. 1986); Chale Garza Invs., Inc. v. Madaria, 931 S.W.2d 597, 600 (Tex. App. 1996); s*ee also* Tietig v. Southeast Regional Constr. Corp., 557 So. 2d 98, 99 (Fla. Dist. Ct. App.

Illegal or unlawful conduct also can be actionable as an interference tort. The balancing of the Restatement's seven factors becomes less difficult when the plaintiff proves that the defendant's conduct is in violation of antitrust laws, is in restraint of trade, or is violative of other statutes or legal precedents.[119] Similarly, threatened or actual physical violence not only may violate criminal statutes, but may result in civil liability.[120]

Economic coercion may be used as an effective incentive or disincentive in the competitive marketplace. The question of the propriety of economic pressure, coercion, exclusion, or sanctions concerns not only interference torts, but also antitrust law and the law of unfair competition. In such a case, a plaintiff may join an interference claim with claims under these alternative theories.[121]

For purposes of the interference torts, the inquiry concerns whether the economic pressure was "proper" under the circumstances. For

---

1990) (filing of lien by attorney on settlement monies is absolutely privileged and cannot be subject of action for interference), *remanded*, 617 So. 2d 761 (1993), *review denied, motion granted*, 630 So. 2d 1101 (Fla. 1993).

118. McReynolds v. Short, 564 P.2d 389, 393-94 (Ariz. Ct. App. 1977); Palmer v. Zaklama, 1 Cal. Rptr. 3d 116, 125 (Cal. Ct. App. 2003) (noting amendment to CAL. CIV. CODE § 47); Westfield Dev. Co. v. Rifle Invest. Assoc., 786 P.2d 1112, 1117 (Colo. 1990); Epstein v. Carrier, 533 A.2d 1221, 1224-35 (Conn. App. Ct. 1987); Guerdon Indus. v. Rose, 399 N.W.2d 186, 188 (Minn. Ct. App. 1987) (qualifying it as question of justification); Vintage Homes, Inc. v. Levin, 554 A.2d 989, 994 (Pa. Super. 1989), *appeal denied*, 524 Pa. 622 (1989) (qualifying it as privilege or justification); Belliveau Bldg. Corp. v. O'Coin, 763 A.2d 622, 630 (R.I. 2000); Toltec Watershed Improv. Dist. v. Johnson, 717 P.2d 808, 814-15 (Wy. 1986); *see also* RESTATEMENT, *supra* note 12, § 773.

119. *See generally* RESTATEMENT, *supra* note 12, § 767 cmt. c.

120. *Id.*

121. *See, e.g.*, Flash Elecs., Inc. v. Universal Music & Video Dist. Corp., 312 F. Supp. 2d 379, 404 (E.D.N.Y. 2004) (alleging violations of the federal antitrust statute, the Sherman Act, and tortuous interference with existing and prospective contracts); Della Penna v. Toyota Motor Sales, USA, Inc., 45 Cal. Rptr. 2d 436 (Cal. Ct. App. 1993) (alleging violations of California's state antitrust statute, the Cartwright Act, and intentional interference with economic relations); *see also* Chapter 3.

example, a competitor may use persuasion as a means of obtaining a prospective contract. Theoretically, this conduct interferes with an advantage of his competitor, but the conduct is not actionable. Conversely, a competitor may exert a more aggressive type of economic pressure, such as a refusal to deal. In determining whether the conduct is actionable, a court may consider "the object sought to be accomplished by the actor, the degree of coercion involved, the extent of harm that it threatens, the effect upon the neutral parties drawn into the situation, the effects upon competition, and the general reasonableness and appropriateness of this pressure as a means of accomplishing the actor's objective."[122] Where the conduct merely evinces the profit motive of the competitor, the court may find the conduct to be entirely "proper."[123]

11. *The Actor's Motive*

While an interference tort requires proof of an intent or purposefulness, i.e., that a result was certain from the actor's conduct, intent alone may not be sufficient to find the interference "improper." An actor may know that interference was a necessary consequence of his conduct but may have had no desire to bring it about. It is therefore important to ascertain the actor's motive. If the actor had no desire to interfere, and his intentional conduct was carried out for an entirely different reason, the conduct may be deemed justified.[124]

Conversely, the greater the degree that interference was the motive, the more weight that motive will have in the balancing of the Restatement's seven factors.[125] While ill will toward the injured party is relevant, legal "malice" – which in many states is a necessary element of interference torts – is not used in the traditional sense indicating hostility, but as a term indicating the interference was intentional and without justification.[126]

---

122. RESTATEMENT, *supra* note 12, § 767 cmt. c. *See generally* Akron Milk Producers, Inc. v. Lawson Milk Co., 147 N.E.2d 512, 515 (Ohio Ct. Common Pleas 1958).

123. *See* Mason v. Wal-Mart Stores, Inc., 969 S.W.2d 160, 165-66 (Ark. 1998).

124. *See, e.g.,* Toney v. Casey's Gen. Stores, Inc., 460 N.W.2d 849, 853 (Iowa 1990) (citing RESTATEMENT, *supra* note 12, § 767 cmt. d).

125. RESTATEMENT, *supra* note 12, § 767 cmt. d.

126. *See, e.g.,* Roy v. Coyne, 630 N.E.2d 1024, 1033 (Ill. 1994) ("The term 'malicious'...simply means that the interference must have been

While no state treats malice and motive factors exactly alike, one might loosely generalize that a finding of "malice" implies a determination that the action was not motivated out of justifiable concerns, but rather out of a desire to accomplish an act of little or no social utility.[127] In order to make this determination, one must consider the interests sought to be advanced by the actor and the relationships between the parties.[128]

12. *The Interests of the Other*

The Restatement notes that some contractual interests are entitled to greater protection than others.[129] For example, a contract may receive more protection than a prospective economic relationship. But a contract that violates public policy or a contract in restraint of trade may permit an inducement of a breach that otherwise would be actionable.[130] Accordingly, it is necessary to examine the facts of each case to determine how large an influence this factor will demand.

13. *The Actor's Interest*

A typical conflict concerns the interest of the actor, which is to gain economic success for one's self, over the interest of the other, who has an economic interest in a contract or prospective relationship. Where the

---

intentional and without justification.") (citation omitted); Laurendeau v. Kewaunee Scientific Equip. Corp., 456 N.E.2d 767, 773 (Mass. App. Ct. 1983), *review denied*, 459 N.E.2d 824 (Mass. 1984). (an act is "malicious in law even though it arose from good motives and without express malice").

127. *Compare* RRR Frams, Ltd. V. American Horse Protection Ass'n, 957 S.W.2d 121, 131, n.6 (Tex. App. 1997) (explaining that "malice" means an unlawful act done intentionally without just cause or excuse) *with* Edwards Transp. v. Circle S. Transp., 856 S.W.2d 783, 789 (Tex. App. 1993) (on rehearing) (acknowledging that statement in original opinion that "'the jury's actual malice finding is tantamount to a no justification finding' is overly broad and in error") *and* Santa Fe Energy Operating Partners, L.P. v. Carrillo, 948 S.W.2d 780, 784, n.2 (Tex. App. 1997) (noting that proof of intentional conduct without justification is sufficient).

128. *See generally* RESTATEMENT, *supra* note 12, § 767 cmt. d.

129. *Id.* § 767 cmt. e. *See generally* Builders Square, Inc. v. Illgross Partners & Co. Ltd., No. 94-C-4632, 1995 WL 452985, at *3 (N.D. Ill. July 27, 1995).

130. RESTATEMENT, *supra* note 12, § 767 cmt. e.

interest of the other is that of a binding contract, that interest may outweigh the actor's own interest in taking that right away.[131] On the other hand, where the interest is that of a prospective relationship, liability may require more culpable conduct.[132]

The actor's financial interest in a matter may cause his conduct to be considered differently than the conduct of a stranger.[133] "One who has a financial interest in the business of another is privileged purposely to cause him not to enter into or continue a relation with a third person in that business if the actor (a) does not employ improper means, and (b) acts to protect his interest from being prejudiced by the relation."[134]

Another complicated situation arises where an actor seeks to promote not his own interest, but political interests, concern for the public good, or the interests of another. For example, a party may be conducting activity that violates criminal statutes, pollutes the environment, or constitutes discriminatory practices. An actor causing a third party not to perform a contract, not to patronize the other, or not to enter into a relation with the other because of such practices will place in issue the actor's subjective state of mind. The Restatement notes that factors to be considered include whether the actor's subjective state of mind was reasonable, whether he acted in the public interest, whether the economic relationship involved was germane to the continuation of the offensive practices, and whether the actor employed wrongful means to accomplish the result.[135]

The actor's interest becomes particularly important where constitutional issues are involved. While most claims of tortious interference arise in purely commercial settings or union-management relationships,[136] the prosecution of a political agenda has occasionally been the subject of an interference claim.[137] In a California case, the publisher of a newspaper brought an action against an environmental

---

131. *Id.* at § 767 cmt. f; *see* Guard-Life Corp. v. S. Parker Hardware Mfg. Corp., 406 N.E.2d 445, 448-49 (N.Y. 1980).

132. *Guard-Life*, 406 N.E.2d at 448-49.

133. *See, e.g.*, Shapoff v. Scull, 272 Cal Rptr. 480, 484-85 (Cal. Ct. App. 1990).

134. *Id.*

135. *See* RESTATEMENT, *supra* note 12, § 767 cmt. f.

136. Envtl. Planning & Info. Council of West El Dorado County, Inc. v. Superior Court, 680 P.2d 1086, 1089-90 (Cal. 1984).

137. *Id.*

organization that called upon its members to boycott the newspaper because of alleged poor environmental practices.[138] The Supreme Court of California concluded that the environmental group was entitled to exercise its First Amendment right to protest the policies of the newspaper in this fashion, and held that the group was entitled to summary judgment.[139]

14. *Relationship Between the Parties*

The relationship between the parties may be a significant factor when determining the propriety of the actor's conduct.[140] This is particularly true in cases involving competitors. Here the courts seek to "achieve a balance of the protection of the interest of one party in future enjoyment of the contract performance and society's interest in respect for the integrity of contractual relationships" with the interfering party's right to compete freely.[141]

"Unlike the right to receive the benefits of a contract, the right to engage in a business relationship is not absolute, and must be exercised with regard to the rights of others. The rights of others most commonly take the form of lawful competition, which constitutes a privileged interference with another's business."[142]

Under the Restatement, a defendant who intentionally causes a third person not to enter into a prospective contractual relation, or not to continue an existing contract terminable at will, with the plaintiff who is his competitor, does not interfere improperly with the plaintiff's relation if the defendant does not act maliciously or wrongfully, provided that the defendant's action does not create or continue an unlawful restraint of

---

138. *Id.*
139. *Id.* at 1091-92. *But see* Gerhs v. Planned Parenthood Golden Gate, No. A092215, 2001 WL 1589217 (Cal. Ct. App. Dec. 12, 2001) (finding actions taken in political protest were not protected by the First Amendment where the political activity was not peaceful).
140. RESTATEMENT, *supra* note 12, § 767 cmt. i.
141. Guard-Life Corp. v. S. Parker Hardware Mfg. Corp., 406 N.E.2d 445, 448 (N.Y. 1980). *See generally* RESTATEMENT (THIRD) OF UNFAIR COMPETITION § 1 (1993).
142. Galinski v. Kessler, 480 N.E.2d 1176, 1182 (Ill. App. Ct. 1985) (citation omitted).

trade. The actor's purpose must also at least in part be designed to advance his interest in competing with the other party to the contract.[143]

Here also, the Restatement differentiates between the types of contracts involved. Generally, the actions of a competitor may be subject to greater protection when the conduct concerns an at-will or terminable contract or option than a contract with more binding obligations.[144] In the case of the former, competitive conduct should be considered privileged.[145]

C. Intentional Interference with Another's Performance of His Own Contract

1. *General Principles and Elements*

The Restatement provides:

> One who intentionally and improperly interferes with the performance of a contract (except a contract to marry) between another and a third person by preventing the other from performing the contract or causing his performance to be more expensive or burdensome, is subject to liability to the other for the pecuniary loss resulting to him.[146]

---

143. RESTATEMENT, *supra* note 12, § 768(1)(d). *See generally Galinski*, 480 N.E.2d at 1182 (quoting RESTATEMENT, *supra* note 12, § 766B); Thomas v. Alloy Fasteners, Inc., 664 So.2d 59, 60-61 (Fla. Dist. Ct. App. 1995 (striking portion of injunction that prohibited former employee from utilizing customer lists as such conduct does not constitute interference); Central Bank of Lake of the Ozarks v. Shackleford, 896 S.W.2d 948, 956-57 (Mo. Ct. App. 1995) (pursuing own's own existing economic interests in another's business affairs is privileged and does not create bases for interference tort); *see also* Heavener, Ogier Servs., Inc. v. R.W. Fla. Region, 418 So. 2d 1074, 1077 (Fla. Dist. Ct. App. 1982).

144. RESTATEMENT, *supra* note 12, §§ 767 cmt. i, 768; *see* West Tex. Gas, Inc. v. 297 Gas Co., 864 S.W.2d 681, 686 (Tex. App. 1993) (a competitor has a legal right to persuade a third party to terminate an at-will contract).

145. RESTATEMENT, *supra* note 12, §§ 767 cmt. i., 768. Interference with prospective business relations is addressed *infra* notes 154-207 and accompanying text.

146. RESTATEMENT, *supra* note 12, § 766A; *see* Mercury Skyline Yacht Charters v. Dave Matthews Band, Inc., No. 05-C-1698 (N.D. Ill. Nov. 22,

The main distinction between this tort and that of interference with the performance of a contract by a third person is that here, the conduct prevents the injured party himself, rather than the third person, from performing under the contract.[147]   With both torts, however, if the plaintiff's performance is prevented, or made more expensive or burdensome, the consequences are the same, i.e., the plaintiff is unable to obtain the benefits of the contract. It is immaterial whether other parties are prevented from performing the contract.[148]   Therefore, many of the same principles of interference with a third-party contract apply to interference with another's performance of his own contract.   The principles concerning intent, the means of interference, causation, malice, and damages are essentially identical.[149]

2.   *At-Will, Void, and Voidable Contracts*

Under the Restatement, if an agreement is void or illegal or against public policy, there is no protection from interference.[150]   Voidable contracts or contracts terminable at will are treated the same way here as in third-party interference cases.[151]

3.   *Factors Determining Whether Interference is Proper*

In order for liability to result, the interference must be improper so each case presents a factual issue of the propriety of the actor's conduct. While the same factors considered for interference with the performance of a contract by a third party should be evaluated, the weighing process will not necessarily produce the same result.[152] The Restatement, considers the actor's motive and the interest advanced of primary concern.[153]

2005) (finding plaintiff's failure to allege malicious and intentional inducement by defendants directed at a third party not fatal to claim).

147. RESTATEMENT, *supra* note 12, § 766A cmt. b.
148. Nesler v. Fisher & Co., 452 N.W.2d 191, 195 (Iowa 1990).
149. *See generally* RESTATEMENT, *supra* note 12, § 766A cmts. d, e, g, h & i; § 766 cmts. o, t & u; Shafir v. Steele, 727 N.E.2d 1140 (Mass. 2000).
150. RESTATEMENT, *supra* note 12, §§ 766A cmt. d; 774.
151. *Id.* § 766 cmts. f & g.
152. RESTATEMENT, *supra* note 12, § 767 cmt. j.
153. *Id.* §§ 766A cmt. e, 767 cmt. c; *see* Westfield Dev. Co. v. Rifle Invest. Assoc., 786 P.2d 1112, 1118 (Colo. 1990).

D. Intentional Interference with Prospective Business Relations

1. *Distinguished from Interference with Performance of a Contract*

"The separate cause of action for the intentional interference with a prospective contractual or economic relationship has long been recognized as distinct from the tort of interference with the performance of a contract."[154] This theory bases recovery on interference with a "relationship" between parties, irrespective of the enforceability of any underlying agreement.[155] Indeed, the common law roots of the interference torts involved the breach of an advantageous relationship, and the presence of a contract was not conditional to the suit.[156] Like interference with contractual rights, an action for interference with prospective business relations protects the right to pursue reasonable expectations of commercial relations "free from undue influence or molestation."[157]

Because this tort protects a relationship, it is no defense that there is no valid or enforceable contract,[158] or that the relationship relates to a

---

154. Coast Cities Truck Sales, Inc. v. Navistar Int'l, 912 F. Supp. 747, 772 (D.N.J. 1995) (citing Printing Mart-Morristown v. Sharp Elecs., 563 A.2d 31 (N.J. 1989)). This tort has been traced as far back as the 14th century. *See* Buckaloo v. Johnson, 537 P.2d 865, 869 n.5 (Cal. 1975).

155. *See* Sebastian Int'l, Inc. v. Russolillo, 162 F. Supp. 2d 1198, 1208 (C.D. Cal. 2001) (noting the tort has been applied to "nonformalized or anticipated business relationships" and where the existing contacts have been found to be unenforceable); Driscoll v. MacLean, No. 044453, WL 2005 2527199, at *3 (Mass. Sup. Ct. Sept. 13, 2005) ("the existence of a prospective business relationship does not turn on the existence of a valid legal contract").

156. *See* Zimmerman v. Bank of Am., 12 Cal. Rptr. 319, 321 (Cal. Ct. App. 1961).

157. Ideal Dairy Farms, Inc. v. Farmland Dairy Farms Inc., 659 A.2d 904, 932 (N.J. Super. Ct. App. Div. 1995) (citing Printing Mart-Morristown, 563 A.2d at 36; *see also* Chapman v. Crown Glass Corp., 557 N.E.2d 256, 262 (Ill. App. Ct. 1990).

158. *Sebastian Int'l, Inc.*, 162 F. Supp. 2d at 1208; *Driscoll*, WL 2005 2527199, at *3. *See generally Buckaloo*, 537 P.2d at 868-69.

contract not written.[159] An interest in an existing contract, however, may be entitled to greater protection than the more speculative interest in a prospective relationship.[160] "The chief practical distinction between interference with contract and interference with prospective economic advantage is that a broader range of privilege to interfere is recognized when the relationship or economic advantage interfered with is only prospective."[161]

Following the lead of the Restatement, case law recognizes a distinction in the propriety of the actor's conduct between interference with a contractual relationship and interference with a prospective economic advantage.[162] In the latter case, the burden on the plaintiff is higher: where the actor's conduct is intended at least in part to advance competition, no unlawful restraint of trade results, and there are no wrongful means such as violence or fraud, the plaintiff may not be able to meet its burden.[163]

---

159. Trent Partners & Assocs., Inc. v. Digital Equip. Corp., 120 F. Supp. 2d 84, 112 (D. Mass. 1999).

160. NBT Bancorp v. Fleet/Norstar Fin. Group, 553 N.Y.S.2d 864, 867 (N.Y. App. Div.), *appeal dismissed*, 562 N.E.2d 871 (N.Y. 1990).

161. Pac. Gas & Elec. v. Bear Stearns & Co., 791 P.2d 587, 590 (Cal. 1990); *see also* Flash Elecs., Inc. v. Universal Music & Video Dist. Corp., 312 F. Supp. 2d 379, 404 (E.D.N.Y. 2004) (noting that there are "more demanding requirements" for proving interference with prospective contractual relations).

162. *See, e.g.*, Guard-Life Corp. v. S. Parker Hardware Mfg. Corp., 406 N.E.2d 445, 448-49 (N.Y. 1980).

163. *Id.*; *see* PPM Am., Inc. v. Marriott Corp., 853 F. Supp. 860, 880 (D. Md. 1994) (noting that unlawful actions include violence, intimidation, defamation, injurious falsehood or fraud, institution or threat of groundless civil suits or criminal prosecution in bad faith); *see also* Adell Broad. Corp. v. Cablevision Indus., 854 F. Supp. 1280, 1293-94 (E.D. Mich. 1994) (explaining that Michigan law requires proof of a "per se" wrongful act); *NBT Bancorp*, 664 N.E.2d at 496 (holding that New York law affords greater protection to enforceable contract rights and greater deference to "free competition where the contract rights are only prospective").

2. *General Principles and Elements*

While the Restatement's analysis has been widely adopted,[164] the basic elements, as well as the available defenses, vary from state to state.[165] For example, some states require an existing relationship with the prospect of economic benefit while in other states a prospective relationship is sufficient. In some states, the interference must be independently wrongful while in other states the plaintiff need only prove intentional interference. The range of variations is exemplified by four states: California, Texas, Illinois, and New York. Under California law, the prima facie elements of the tort of interference with prospective economic advantage are:

    (1)   an economic relationship between the plaintiff and some third party, with the probability of future economic benefit to the plaintiff;

---

164. *See, e.g.*, Nesler v. Fisher & Co., 452 N.W.2d 191, 195 (Iowa 1990). The RESTATEMENT (SECOND) OF TORTS § 766B states:

    One who intentionally and improperly interferes with another's prospective contractual relation (except a contract to marry) is subject to liability to the other for the pecuniary harm resulting from loss of benefits of the relation, whether the interference consists of

    (a)   inducing or otherwise causing a third person not to enter into or continue the prospective relation or

    (b)   preventing the other from acquiring or continuing the prospective relation.

165. *See, e.g.*, Data Based Sys., Int'l, Inc. v. Hewlett-Packard Co., No. CIV. 00-CV-4425, 2001 WL 1251212, at *11 (E.D. Pa. Sept. 26, 2001) (Pennsylvania law); Smith v. St. Regis Corp., 850 F. Supp. 1296, 1323 (S.D. Miss. 1994), *aff'd*, 48 F.3d 531 (5th Cir. 1995) (Mississippi law); Sgro v. Getty Petroleum Corp., 854 F. Supp. 1164, 1183 (D.N.J. 1994), *aff'd*, 96 F.3d 1434 (3d Cir. 1996) (New Jersey law); Collins v. Nat'l Basketball Players Ass'n, 850 F. Supp. 1468, 1481 (D. Colo. 1991), *aff'd*, 976 F.2d 740 (10th Cir. 1992) (Colorado law); Hirsch v. Cooper, 737 P.2d 1092, 1097 (Ariz. App. 1986) (Arizona law); Lake Panorama Servicing Corp. v. Central Iowa Energy Coop., 636 N.W.2d 747 (Iowa 2001) (opinion text at 2001 WL 1014805) (Iowa law); Turner v. Halliburton Co., 240 Kan. 1, 722 P.2d 1106 (Kan. 1986); Powers v. Leno, 509 N.E.2d 46, 49 (Mass. App. Ct. 1987) (Massachusetts law); *Flash Elecs., Inc.*, 312 F. Supp. 2d at 404-06 (New York law).

(2)   the defendant's knowledge of the relationship;

(3)   intentional acts on the part of the defendant, which are wrongful apart from the interference itself and designed to disrupt the relationship;

(4)   actual disruption of the relationship; and

(5)   economic harm to the plaintiff proximately caused by the acts of the defendant.[166]

The elements of interference under Texas law are:

(1)   a "reasonable probability" that the plaintiff would have entered into a contractual relationship;

(2)   an "independently tortious or unlawful" act by the defendant that prevented the relationship from occurring;

(3)   the defendant did such act with a conscious desire to prevent the relationship from occurring or knew that the interference was certain to occur as a result of his conduct; and

(4)   the plaintiff suffered actual harm or damage as a result of the defendant's interference.[167]

Under Illinois law, the elements are:

(1)   the existence of a valid business expectancy by plaintiff;

(2)   the defendant's knowledge of the expectancy;

---

166. JRS Prods., Inc. v. Matsushita Elec. Corp. of Am., 8 Cal. Rptr. 3d 840, 849-50 (Cal. Ct. App. 2004); Korea Supply Co. v. Lockheed Martin Corp., 63 P.3d 937, 1153 (Cal. 2003) (citing the elements listed in Buckaloo v. Johnson, 537 P.2d 865, 871-72 (Cal. 1975), and adding the requirement that the acts be wrongful and designed to disrupt the plaintiff's relationship); *see also* Shamblin v. Berge, 166 Cal. App. 3d 118, 123 (Cal. Ct. App. 1985) ("This theory protects against acts designed to harm an economic relationship which is '*likely*' to produce economic benefit.").

167. Allied Capital Corp. v. Cravens, 67 S.W.3d 486, 491 (Tex. App. 2002); Wal-Mart Stores, Inc. v. Sturges, 52 S.W.3d 711, 726 (Tex. 2001) (holding that the defendant's conduct must be independently tortious or wrongful for a plaintiff to recover for tortious interference with prospective business relation and finding that justification and privilege are defenses "only to the extent that they are defenses to the independent tortiousness of the defendant's conduct").

(3)   the defendant's intentional and unjustified interference which prevents the realization of the business expectancy; and

(4)   damages.[168]

Under New York law, meanwhile, where the defendant is a competitor, the court looks to whether the "interference is intended at least in part to advance the competing interest of the interferer, no unlawful restraint of trade is effected, and the means employed are not wrongful."[169]

Texas and California, which rejected the "overlapping and confusing" concepts of malice, justification, and privilege to some extent by requiring that the defendant's act be independently tortious or unlawful, may have started a trend towards more clearly defining culpable conduct under this tort. Idaho, Massachusetts, and Georgia, for example, agree that the defendant's acts must be wrongful outside of the interference itself.[170]   Whether changes such as these resolve the confusion surrounding the application of privilege and justification to the tort remains to be seen.[171]

Courts also continue to differ on the extent to which the plaintiff must prove the first element, i.e., the business expectancy or prospective relationship.[172]   The tort "protects nonformalized or anticipated business

---

168. Chapman v. Crown Glass Corp., 557 N.E.2d 256, 262 (Ill. App. Ct. 1990).

169. *Flash Elecs., Inc.*, 312 F. Supp. 2d at 404 (*citing Guard-Life*, 406 N.E.2d at 445); *see also* 2 W. Michael Garner, FRANCHISE & DISTR. LAW & PRAC. § 9:38 *Tortious Interference with Prospective Contractual Relations* (2003) (providing overview of state laws on tortious interference with prospective contractual relations). *But see* State Street Bank & Trust Co. v. Inversiones Errazuriz Limitada, 374 F.3d 158, 171 (2d Cir. 2004) (listing the elements as whether: (1) the plaintiff "had a business relationship with a third party; (2) the defendant knew of that relationship and intentionally interfered with it; (3) the defendant acted solely out of malice, or used dishonest, unfair, or improper means; and (4) the defendant's interference caused injury to the relationship.")

170. Wade Holt, Wal-Mart v. Sturges, *Tortious Interference with Prospective Contractual Relations: Texas Officially Adopts the Modern Rule*, 54 BAYLOR L. REV. 537, 550-51 (Spring 2002).

171. *See id.* at 551 (noting that "all is not entirely clear" under the so-called "modern rule").

172. *See supra* notes 167 & 168; *see also* Garner, *supra* note 169, at § 9:38 and notes 16-18 (noting that Florida does not allow recovery where the

relationships which are reasonably certain to occur, but which are nonetheless prospective."[173] The relationship between a plaintiff and a third party cannot simply be characterized as an economic relationship, nor can the relationship simply be to a class of as yet unknown people.[174] This tort protects expectancies involved in ordinary commercial dealings, not "expectancies" involved, for example, in governmental licensing processes.[175] In addition to proving the existence of the relationship, a party must be able to establish that "it is reasonably probable that the lost economic advantage would have been realized but for the defendant's interference."[176]

It is not, however, always necessary for the plaintiff prove that the defendant was aware of the exact prospective relationship. In an Iowa case,[177] for example, a plaintiff developer alleged that the defendant, a competitor for lessees, had interfered with the timely completion of an office building by the filing of meritless lawsuits and pressuring building inspectors and other public officials. This conduct undermined confidence in the plaintiff's project and led to the plaintiff's failure to finance the project through a bank loan or syndication. Following a jury award of compensatory and punitive damages, the trial court entered a judgment notwithstanding the verdict, holding that there was no evidence

---

relations merely were based upon the expectation that a past customer would return or that a new customer would continue to do business with the plaintiff; while New York requires that the customers be specifically identified; and New Jersey allows a plaintiff to show that a particular category of contractual relations were at issue).

173. Sebastian Int'l, Inc. v. Russolillo, 162 F. Supp. 2d 1198, 1208 (C.D. Cal. 2001) (citing PMC, Inc. v. Saban Entm't, Inc., 52 Cal. Rptr. 2d 877 (Cal. Ct. App. 1996)).

174. Westside Center Assocs. v. Safeway Stores 23, Inc., , 49 Cal. Rptr. 2d 793, 803-804 (Cal. Ct. App. 1996) (citing Blank v. Kirwan, 703 P.2d 58, 70 (Cal. 1985)); Daimler Chrysler Corp. v. Kirkhart, 561 S.E.2d 276, 286 (N.C. Ct. App. 2002) (cause of action fails where plaintiff "failed to identify any particular contract that a third party has been induced to refrain from entering into with Plaintiff").

175. *Blank*, 703 P.2d at 70.

176. Lake Panorama Servicing Corp. v. Cent. Iowa Energy Co-op., 636 N.W.2d 747 (Iowa 2001) (opinion text at 2001 WL 1014805). *See generally* KEETON, *supra* note 12, § 130, at 1006-07.

177. Nesler v. Fisher & Co., 452 N.W.2d 191 (Iowa 1990).

that the plaintiff had a binding contract with the financing bank, that the plaintiff had not commenced his syndication efforts until after the defendants' actions, or that the defendants knew of the plaintiff's relationship with the bank at the time of their activities. The Iowa Supreme Court reversed, noting that the plaintiff did not need to prove specific knowledge of the plaintiff's relationship with the financing bank. The prospective business advantage was the completion of the project and sale of the building. The defendant's awareness that some financing would be necessary was sufficient to uphold a verdict of interference with a prospective economic advantage.[178]

3. Defenses and Privileges

The privilege issue is particularly significant in controversies involving competitors for a prospective advantage. "Unlike the right to receive the benefits of a contract, the right to engage in a business relationship is not absolute, and must be exercised with regard to the rights of others."[179] In the broadest sense, each time parties compete, they interfere with the prospective business advantage of each other.[180] Recognizing that "interference" cannot be so broadly construed, the Eleventh Circuit has held that there is no liability for merely giving truthful information, even if the facts are presented in such a way as to leave no doubt that they are being presented as a reason for refusing to deal with another.[181] Leading commentators similarly note:

> [W]here the plaintiff's contractual relations are merely contemplated or potential it is considered to be in the interest of the public that any competitor should be free to divert them to himself by all fair and reasonable means . . . .[182]

---

178. *Id.* at 196.
179. Galinski v. Kessler, 480 N.E.2d 1176, 1182 (Ill. App. Ct. 1985).
180. *See* Los Angeles Land Co. v. Brunswick Corp., 6 F.3d 1422, 1430 (9th Cir. 1993) ("'Perhaps the most significant privilege or justification for interference with a prospective business advantage is free competition.'") (quoting Buckaloo v. Johnson, 537 P.2d 865, 872 (Cal. 1975)).
181. Worldwide Primates, Inc. v. McGreal, 26 F.3d 1089, 1092 (11th Cir. 1994).
182. KEETON, *supra* note 12, § 130, at 1012; *see* Morris Commc'ns Corp. v. PGA Tour, Inc., 235 F. Supp. 2d 1269, 1287 (M.D. Fla. 2002); *see also* Dawson v. W. & H. Voortman, Ltd., 853 F. Supp. 1038, 1044 (N.D. Ill.

This qualified "competitive privilege" to interfere with prospective business relationships is widely recognized,[183] although its permutations are not always thoroughly understood.[184] This privilege is reflected in section 768 of the Restatement (Second) of Torts, which provides:

> (1) One who intentionally causes a third person not to enter into a prospective contractual relation with another who is his competitor or not to continue an existing contract terminable at will does not interfere improperly with the other's relation if
>
> 1. the relation concerns a matter involved in the competition between the actor and the other and
>
> 2. the actor does not employ wrongful means and

1994) (noting that if the interference involves only the defendant's exercise of rights that it already possesses to protect its financial interest, a claim for tortious interference with prospective business relationships will not stand), *clarified, amended*, No. 92-C-8088, 1994 U.S. Dist. LEXIS 4661 (N.D. Ill. Apr. 8, 1994).

183. RESTATEMENT, *supra* note 12, § 768; *see* Int'l Sales & Servs., Inc. v. Austral Insulated Prods., Inc., 267 F.3d 1152, 1159 (11th Cir. 2001) (adopting the Restatement's competition privilege and noting "[w]hether interference with a business relationship is privileged 'depends upon a balancing of the importance . . . of the objective advanced by the interference against the importance of the interference interfered with, considering all circumstances among which the methods and means used and the relation of the parties are important'"); Wiggins v. Hitchens, 853 F. Supp. 505, 512 (D.D.C. 1994); Wal-Mart Stores, Inc. v. Sturges, 52 S.W.3d 711, 728 (Tex. 2001) (O'Neill, J., concurring) ("Texas law encourages economic competition and does not generally subject businesses to tort liability for tough but honest practices."); *see also* Haig, *supra* note 52, § 59.15 *Defenses to Tortious Interference Claims* (citing Foster v. Churchill, 665 N.E.2d 153, 156 (N.Y. 1996) for the proposition that economic self-interest is a defense to tortious interference with prospective business advantage unless there is a showing of malice or illegality).

184. *See* Carvel Corp. v. Noonan, 350 F.3d 6, 23 (2d Cir. 2003) (certifying question to the New York Court of Appeals as to the standard for proving a cause of action against competitors versus non-competitors, i.e., "whether a plaintiff must show that a competitor-defendant acted 'wrongfully' but show that a non-competitor defendant acted only 'improperly'"), certifying question to 818 N.E.2d 1100 (N.Y. 2004) (answering question without reference to whether the parties were competitors).

3. his action does not create or continue an unlawful restraint of trade and

4. his purpose is at least in part to advance his interest in competing with the other.

(2) The fact that one is a competitor of another for the business of a third person does not prevent his causing a breach of an existing contract with the other from being an improper interference if the contract is not terminable at will.185

This rule is a special application of the principle that actionable interference must be "improper,"[186] and recognizes that one's privilege to engage in business and to compete with others implies a privilege to induce third persons to do business with him rather than with his competitors.[187] Accordingly, it is generally accepted that a competitor who causes a third person not to enter into a prospective contractual relation, or not to continue in existing contracts terminable at will, is not liable for interference so long as the competitor does not employ improper means and his purpose is at least in part to advance his interest in competing with the other.[188] Under the Restatement, however, this rule does not apply in cases of interference with an existing contract not terminable at will.[189]

The Restatement (Third) of Unfair Competition rejects the notion that competition is a defense, justification or privilege, in favor of "a

---

185. RESTATEMENT, *supra* note 12, § 768.

186. *Id.* at § 768(1) cmt. b.

187. Rice v. Hulsey, 829 N.E.2d 87, 91-91 (Ind. Ct. App. 2005).

188. *See id.*; Waldrep Bros. Beauty Supply v. Wynn Beauty Supply Co., 992 F.2d 59, 63 (4th Cir. 1993); Data Based Sys., Int'l, Inc. v. Hewlett-Packard Co., No. CIV. 00-CV-4425, 2001 WL 1251212, at *13 (E.D. Pa. Sept. 26, 2001) (citing RESTATEMENT, *supra* note 12, § 767); W. Oliver Tripp Co. v. Am. Hoechst Corp., 616 N.E.2d 118, 125 (Mass. App. Ct. 1993); Killian Constr. Co. v. Jack D. Ball & Assoc., 865 S.W.2d 889 (Mo. Ct. App. 1993); *Sturges*, 52 S.W.3d at 728 (O'Neill, J., concurring); Allied Capital Corp. v. Cravens, 67 S.W.3d 486, 491 (Tex. App. 2002) (recognizing that plaintiff cannot recover against a defendant whose persuasion of others not to deal with them is lawful; "sharp or unfair" conduct not enough).

189. RESTATEMENT, *supra* note 12, § 768(2) cmt. h. For a detailed discussion of the competitive privilege, see Chapter 2.

general principle of non-liability."[190] This view is consonant with the recognition underlying the Restatement (Third) that there is a "freedom to compete" in the marketplace that should be upheld absent the use of unfair means.[191]

Another frequently asserted privilege involves the exercise of ownership rights or a superior financial interest in the subject matter of the alleged interference. The theory behind this privilege is that in some instances an actor's conduct may protect an interest that the law deems of greater importance than the plaintiff's rights.[192]

The duty of corporate officers and directors to corporate shareholders under state law may outweigh any duty owed to other contractual parties, and the conduct of those officers may be privileged under state law.[193] This privilege often is closely intertwined with the malice concept, however, and one acting maliciously may as a result lose the protection of the privilege.[194] For example, in *Chapman v. Crown Glass Corp.*,[195] the defendant claimed that it was improper to instruct the jury that he could be found liable for tortiously interfering with the corporation's contractual or prospective economic relationships only "if he acted for his own personal interest and contrary to the best interest of the corporation." The defendant argued that a proper instruction required the jury to find liability only if the defendant had actual malice.[196] The Illinois appellate court upheld the jury instruction as being consistent with a finding of actual malice, however, noting that the decision to terminate the plaintiff was not justified because the defendant's scheme

---

190. RESTATEMENT (THIRD) OF UNFAIR COMPETITION § 1 cmt. a (1993).

191. *See id.*

192. Chapman v. Crown Glass Corp., 557 N.E.2d 256, 262 (Ill. App. Ct. 1990).

193. *Id.* at 263.

194. *See, e.g.,* Arlington Heights Nat'l Bank v. Arlington Heights Fed. Sav. & Loan Ass'n, 229 N.E.2d 514, 518 (Ill. 1967) ("Most courts have held . . . that in a tort action for interference with contract wherein the alleged wrongful conduct is conditionally privileged, the plaintiff must show actual malice on the part of the defendant in order to sustain such a cause of action."); *see also* Los Angeles Land Co. v. Brunswick Corp., 6 F.3d 1422, 1430-31 (9th Cir. 1993) (finding that interference is privileged even if done at least in part to advance an interest in competing with the other).

195. 557 N.E.2d 256 (Ill. App. Ct. 1990).

196. *Id.* at 263.

to isolate the plaintiff and force him to sell his interest in the corporation was for the personal gain of the defendant and contrary to the best interests of the company.[197]

4. *Burdens and Types of Proof*

While the prima facie elements of this tort often are quite similar, the burden of proof can vary greatly from state to state. Courts vary over whether, and under what circumstances, the plaintiff or defendant bears the burden of proof with respect to an asserted privilege or justification.[198] In some jurisdictions, the plaintiff bears the burden of proving that the interference was "improper," or that the defendant's conduct exceeded the scope of the privilege.[199] In other jurisdictions, the privilege is a defense to be proven by the defendant.[200] Some courts have held that the burden shifts depending on whether or not a qualified privilege exists.[201]

---

197. *Id.* at 263-64; *see* MidAmerican Energy Co. v. Utility Res. Corp., No. 03-C-2313, 2003 WL 22359526, at *2-3 (N.D. Ill. Oct. 15, 2003) (quoting HPI Health Care Servs. Inc. v. Mt. Vernon Hosp., Inc., 545 N.E.2d 672, 678 (Ill. 1989)).

198. *See* RESTATEMENT (THIRD) OF UNFAIR COMPETITION § 1 cmt. a (1993) (citing RESTATEMENT, *supra* note 12, § 676 cmt. k ("There is as yet no consensus with respect to the allocation of the burdens of pleading and proof under the general tort of intentional interference with prospective economic relations.")).

199. *See, e.g.*, Amerinet, Inc. v. Xerox Corp., 972 F.2d 1483, 1506-07 (8th Cir. 1992); *MidAmerican Energy Co.*, 2003 WL 22359526, at *2-3; Data Based Sys., Int'l, Inc. v. Hewlett-Packard Co., No. CIV. 00-CV-4425, 2001 WL 1251212, at *11 (E.D. Pa. Sept. 26, 2001).

200. Greenberg v. Mount Sinai Med. Ctr., 629 So. 2d 252, 255 (Fla. Dist. Ct. App. 1993); Belliveau Bldg. Corp. v. O'Coin, 763 A.2d 622, 627 (R.I. 2000); Wal-Mart Stores, Inc. v. Sturges, 52 S.W.3d 711, 725, 727 (Tex. 2001) (placing burden of proof on plaintiff in tortious interference with business relations case).

201. Bebble v. Nat'l Air Traffic Controllers Assoc., No. 00 C 4055, 2001 WL 128241 (N.D. Ill. Feb. 9, 2001) (finding existence of justification an affirmative defense unless "the complaint itself establishes the existence of a privilege, in which case the plaintiff bears the burden of pleading and proving that the defendant acted outside the privilege"); Roy v. Coyne, 630 N.E.2d 1024, 1033 (Ill. 1994); Zdeb v. Baxter Int'l, Inc., 697 N.E.2d 425, 631-32 (Ill. App. Ct. 1998).

Aside from the issue of the proper allocation of evidentiary burdens, the type of proof required to establish this tort also varies from jurisdiction to jurisdiction. In Texas, for example, the plaintiff must show that the defendant's acts would be actionable under a recognized tort.[202] Iowa, on the other hand, looks solely to the defendant's motivation in determining if the conduct was improper. The conduct is only improper if undertaken with "the sole or predominant purpose to injure or financially destroy" another entity.[203] In Connecticut, the issue is not whether the party intended to injure, but whether it interfered without justification and with knowledge of the plaintiff's contractual rights.[204] In New Jersey, a plaintiff must demonstrate "the intentional doing of a wrongful act without justification or excuse."[205] A "wrongful act" means "any act which will . . . infringe upon the rights of another to his damage, except and unless it be done in the exercise of an equal or superior right."[206]

Where allegations hinge on alleged interference by conversations rather than deeds, proof that the defendant had discussions with third parties may not be enough; the plaintiff may have to prove the specific words or information communicated by the defendant and show that those specific words chilled or terminated a prospective relationship.[207]

---

202. *See Sturges*, 52 S.W.3d at 726 (rejecting the concepts of malice, justification and privilege as "overlapping and confusing"); Allied Capital Corp. v. Cravens, 67 S.W.3d 486, 491 (Tex. App. 2002) (rejecting claim because plaintiff could show no independently tortious act; "sharp or unfair" conduct not enough).

203. *Lake Panorama Servicing*, 636 N.W.2d 747, 2001 WL 1014805, at *4 (quoting Compiano v. Hawkeye Bank & Trust, 588 N.W.2d 462, 464 (Iowa 1999)). Iowa does not require such a showing for interference with contract actions. *See* King v. Sioux City Radiological Group, PC, 985 F. Supp. 869, 882 (N.D. Iowa 1997).

204. Boulevard Assoc. v. Sovereign Hotels, 72 F.3d 1029, 1035 (2d Cir. 1995).

205. Sgro v. Getty Petroleum Corp., 854 F. Supp. 1164, 1183 (D.N.J. 1994), *aff'd*, 96 F.3d 1434 (3d Cir. 1996).

206. *Id.*

207. *See generally* Nadel v. Play-by-Play Toys & Novelties, Inc., 208 F.3d 368, 382 (2d Cir. 2000); Adolph Coors Co. v. Rodriguez, 780 S.W.2d 477, 486 (Tex. App. 1989) (finding proof of conversations not enough; specific evidence of wrongful information required).

E. Negligent Interference with Contract or Prospective Contractual Relations

The common law generally does not recognize a cause of action for negligent interference with contract or prospective economic relations.[208] Policy reasons for the reluctance to provide relief under this theory include concerns about imposing liability in the absence of the actor's awareness of a contractual or prospective economic relationship, the potential chilling effect on a defendant's actions, and the threat of disproportionate awards of damages relative to the negligent conduct.[209]

F. Damages

1. *Compensatory Damages*

Actual damage is a necessary element of a claim of intentional interference both with the performance of a contract and with an advantageous relationship.[210] "Whether the interference is with an existing contract or a prospective contractual relation, one who becomes liable for it is liable for damages for the pecuniary loss of the benefits of the contract or the relation."[211] Damages may flow from the tort that

---

208. *See, e.g.*, Mest v. Cabot Corp., No. Civ. A. 01-4943, 2004 WL 1102754, at *5 (E.D. Pa. May 14, 2004) ("There is no cause of action for negligent interference with business under Pennsylvania law."); Wauseon Plaza Ltd. P'ship v. Wauseon Hardware Co., 807 N.E.2d 953, 962 (Ohio Ct. App. 2004) ("Ohio law does not recognize negligent interference with a business relationship."); *cf.* Ragsdale v. Mount Sinai Med. Ctr. of Miami, 770 So. 2d 167 (Fla. Dist. Ct. App. 2000) (negligent interference allowed where duty of care owed); *see also* Lee & Lindahl, *supra* note 54, at 45-5 ("There is little support for the tort of negligent interference with contract.").

209. *See* KEETON, *supra* note 12, § 129 at 982, 997; *see also* Herrick v. Superior Court, 233 Cal. Rptr. 675, 676 (Cal. Ct. App. 1987); Ragsdale v. Mt. Sinai Med. Center of Miami, 770 So. 2d 167, 169 n.2 (Fla. Dist. Ct. App. 2000) (citing Florida Power & Light v. Fleitas, 488 So. 2d 148 (Fla. Dist. Ct. App. 1986)).

210. Worldwide Primates, Inc. v. McGreal, 26 F.3d 1089, 1091-92 (11th Cir. 1994); *see also* Mass Cash Register, Inc. v. Comtrex Sys. Corp., 901 F. Supp. 404, 422 (D. Mass. 1995) (finding no intentional interference with an advantageous business relationship where no actual damages resulted).

211. RESTATEMENT, *supra* note 12, § 774A cmt. b; *see* Getschow v. Commonwealth Edison Co., 444 N.E.2d 579, 586 (Ill. App. Ct. 1982),

otherwise would not be recoverable in a breach of contract action.[212] Damages may include the pecuniary loss of the benefits of the contract; where there is a prospective relation, any consequential losses for which interference is a legal cause; and damages for emotional distress if such damages are reasonably expected from the interference.[213]

If the case involves interference with a contract by inducement or by causing a third party to breach the contract with the other, the fact that the third person is liable for the breach does not affect the amount of damages awardable against the actor; but any damages in fact paid by the third person will reduce the damages actually recoverable on the judgment.[214] "And when the defendant interferes with prospective contractual relations, the plaintiff may recover the lost profits that would have been made from the prospective contracts."[215]

2. *Punitive Damages*

Generally, punitive damages are allowable in actions for interference with a contract or business relationship.[216] As with other intentional torts, the circumstances determine whether punitive damages are appropriate.

---

aff'd in part and rev'd in part, 459 N.E.2d 1332 (Ill. 1984) (awarding four and a half years of projected lost profits for tortious interference with at-will contract); Maxvill-Glasco Drilling Co. v. Royal Oil & Gas Co., 800 S.W.2d 384, 386-87 (Tex. App. 1990).

212. RESTATEMENT, *supra* note 12, § 774A.
213. *Id.*
214. *Id.*
215. *Id.* at § 774A cmt. b.
216. *See* Miteva v. Third Point Mgmt. Co., 323 F. Supp. 2d 573, 587 (S.D.N.Y. 2004) (citing Carvel Corp. v. Noonan, 350 F.3d 6, 24 (2d Cir. 2003); Fieldturf Int'l. Inc. v. Triexe Mgmt. Group, No. 03 C 3512, 2004 WL 866494 (N.D. Ill. Apr. 16, 2004); Finney v. Lockheart, 217 P.2d 19 (Cal. 1950); Rueben H. Donnelley Corp. v. Brauer, 655 N.E.2d 1162, 1172 (Ill. App. Ct. 1995); Alexander & Alexander Inc. v. B. Dixon Evander & Assocs., Inc. 336 A.2d 260, 269 (Md. 1994); Navistar intern. Transp. Corp. v. Vernon Klein Truck & Equip., 919 P.2d 443, 446 (Okl. Civ. App. 1994); *see also* RESTATEMENT, *supra* note 12, § 774A cmt. a.

For example, punitive damages have been awarded in cases of interference with an attorney-client contract or relationship,[217] where the defendant has induced a breach of a contract not to compete,[218] where the defendant has interfered with a broker's commission contract on the sale of real property,[219] and where the defendant has induced persons not to purchase goods from the plaintiff.[220] Limitations upon punitive damages awards are examined in Chapter 8.

---

217. Farish v. Bankers' Multiple Life Ins. Co., 425 So. 2d 12 (Fla. Dist. Ct. App. 1982), *quashed in part, approved in part*, 464 So. 2d 530 (Fla. 1985) (upholding trial judge's grant of new trial to adequately instruct the jury that punitive damages were discretionary in nature).
218. Cherne Indus., Inc. v. Grounds & Assoc., Inc., 278 N.W.2d 81 (Minn. 1979) (finding evidence of malice and support for punitive damages award where despite two former employees' knowledge of the obligations to remain with their employer, the defendant nonetheless encouraged them to breach the contract by coming to work for defendant in competition with the plaintiff's business and bringing along with them confidential information).
219. Duff v. Engleberg, 47 Cal. Rptr. 114 (Cal. Ct. App. 1965).
220. Finney v. Lockheart, 217 P.2d 19 (Cal. 1950). *But see* Getschow v. Commonwealth Edison Co., 459 N.E.2d 1332 (Ill. 1984) (overturning award of punitive damages).

CHAPTER VI

FRAUD AND MISREPRESENTATION

Although not inherently "competitive" torts, fraud and misrepresentation potentially apply to a broad range of commercial conduct. It is not uncommon for competitors to bolster antitrust claims with claims of fraudulent conduct;[1] more frequently, distributors or retailers join antitrust claims against their suppliers with allegations of fraud or misrepresentation.[2] Not unlike the Federal Trade Commission (FTC) Act and Lanham Act,[3] which seek to prohibit misrepresentations in markets for goods and services, the antifraud provisions of the securities laws seek to promote truthful disclosure in the capital markets. And RICO claims – which often are predicated on allegations of fraud – frequently are brought in the competitive context.[4] This chapter addresses each of these varieties of the business torts of fraud and misrepresentation. – Eds.

---

1.   *See, e.g.*, Int'l Travel Arrangers v. NWA, Inc., 991 F.2d 1389 (8th Cir. 1993) (antitrust and fraud claims by wholesale tour operator against airline, affiliated air carrier and tour operator); DeLong Equip. Co. v. Washington Mills Electro Minerals Corp., 990 F.2d 1186 (11th Cir. 1993) (antitrust and fraud claims by distributor against manufacturer and another distributor), *amended*, 997 F.2d 1340 (11th Cir. 1993).

2.   *See supra* note 1; Tel-Phonic Servs., Inc. v. TBS Int'l Inc., 975 F.2d 1134 (5th Cir. 1992) (antitrust, RICO and fraud claims by purchasers and marketers of computer equipment and telephone calling software against seller and its parent corporation); Tunis Bros. Co. v. Ford Motor Co., 952 F.2d 715 (3d Cir. 1991) (antitrust and fraud claims by tractor dealer against manufacturer and employees).

3.   15 U.S.C. §§ 45, 1125; *see supra* Chapter 3.

4.   *Tel-Phonic Servs., Inc.*, 975 F.2d at 1137-41; Cayman Explor. Corp. v. United Gas Pipe Line Co., 873 F.2d 1357 (10th Cir. 1989) (antitrust and RICO claims by natural gas producer against pipeline company).

A.　Introduction

Although fraud is a frequently-asserted business tort, the necessity of proving intent and the "clear and convincing" evidentiary standard imposed by many jurisdictions make it difficult to prove.　Plaintiffs seeking to avoid these hurdles have increasingly relied upon the related tort of negligent misrepresentation, which has been applied by courts in a variety of circumstances to impose liability upon those, such as attorneys, accountants, and bankers, who are in the business of supplying information.　In addition, statutory causes of action sounding in tort may be available in addition to, or in lieu of, common law claims.[5]　This chapter surveys causes of action frequently asserted in business tort litigation to redress fraudulent and misleading conduct.

B.　Common Law Fraud

1.　*Nature of the Action*

The fraud claim owes its existence to a perceived need to redress invasions of financial and commercial interests.[6]　Also known as "misrepresentation," "fraudulent misrepresentation" and "deceit," fraud actions are available to protect intangible economic interests of persons induced to enter into transactions as a consequence of the fraudulent misrepresentations of others.[7]　Fraud is distinguishable from breach of warranty, which also is based upon commercial representations, in that fraud generally encompasses proof of fault (an intent to deceive),

---

5.　Every state has enacted a "little FTC" act, prohibiting, in one form or another, deceptive, and sometimes unfair, trade practices. *See* Chapter 3; *see generally* ABA ANTITRUST SECTION, CONSUMER PROTECTION HANDBOOK (2004).　While these statutes vary widely in their exact wording, most either prohibit a detailed list of specified practices and then contain a catch-all provision, or simply omit the detailed listing and contain only a broadly-worded prohibition.　In addition to these little FTC acts, some states, including Texas, have enacted industry specific fraud statutes. *See, e.g.*, TEX. BUS. & COM. CODE ANN. § 27.01, Fraud in Real Estate and Stock Transactions, and § 27.02, Certain Insurance Claims for Excessive Charges.

6.　*See* W. PAGE KEETON, PROSSER AND KEETON ON THE LAW OF TORTS § 105, at 726 (5th ed. 1984) [hereinafter KEETON].

7.　*See id.*

whereas warranty liability is based upon an implied obligation to guarantee the truth of the warrantor's statements.[8]

2. *Elements*

The courts are in general agreement regarding the essential elements of fraud. They are commonly stated to be:

(1) A material misrepresentation made by the defendant;

(2) The defendant's knowledge of the falsity of the representation, sometimes referred to as "scienter;"

(3) The defendant's intent to induce the plaintiff to rely upon the representation;

(4) The plaintiff's justifiable reliance upon the representation; and

(5) Damage resulting from the plaintiff's reliance upon the representation.[9]

3. *Material Misrepresentation*

Ordinarily, a fraud action must be supported by a representation by the defendant to the plaintiff that is definite and certain,[10] although some courts have held that a representation susceptible of two interpretations,

---

8.   *Id.* at 728-29.

9.   Andersons, Inc. v. Consol, Inc., 348 F.3d 496, 505 (6th Cir. 2003) (Ohio law); Clardy Mfg. Co. v. Marine Midland Bus. Loans, Inc., 88 F.3d 347, 359 (5th Cir. 1996) (Texas law); Booze v. Allstate Ins. Co., 750 A.2d 877, 880 (Pa. Super. Ct. 2000); Hammer v. Nikol, 659 A.2d 617, 619-20 (Pa. Commw. Ct. 1995); Gennari v. Weichert Co. Realtors, 691 A.2d 350, 367 (N.J. 1997).

10.   Glen Holly Entm't, Inc. v. Tektronix, Inc. 352 F.3d 367, 379 (9th Cir. 2003) (California law); Cook, Perkiss & Liehe, Inc. v. N. Cal. Collection Serv., Inc., 911 F.2d 242, 246 (9th Cir. 1990) (California law); *In re* Advanta Corp. Sec. Litig., 180 F.3d 525, 538 (3d Cir. 1999) ("[V]ague and general statements of optimism 'constitute no more than puffery and are understood by reasonable investors as such.'") (quoting *In re* Burlington Coat Factory Secs. Litig., 114 F.3d 1410 (3d Cir. 1997); *In re* Lernout & Hauspie Sec. Litig., 286 B.R. 33, 42-43 (Bankr. D. Mass. 2002); Rich Food Servs., Inc. v. Rich Plan Corp., No. 03-1198, 2004 WL 937260, at *4 (4th Cir. May 3, 2004).

154   *Business Tort Law*

one of which is false, may support an action for fraud.[11]   Conduct, as well as words, may constitute a fraudulent representation.[12]

The majority of courts have held that an actionable representation must be a statement of fact;[13] under this view, statements of opinion are not actionable as fraud.[14] This "opinion privilege" is commonly applied to "sales talk" and "puffing," which are thus shielded from liability.[15] Misrepresentations of law also are generally held to be expressions of opinion and thus not actionable.[16]   However, some courts have held that statements of opinion not honestly held may constitute actionable fraud.[17]

---

11. *In re* Lafratte, 281 B.R. 575, 579 (M.D. Pa. 2002).
12. Olney Sav. & Loan Ass'n v. Trinity Banc Sav. Ass'n, 885 F.2d 266, 272 (5th Cir. 1989); T.A. Pelsue Co. v. Grand Enters., Inc., 782 F. Supp. 1476, 1488 (D. Colo. 1991); *see* Chase Manhattan Bank, N.A. v. Fidata Corp., 700 F. Supp. 1252 (S.D.N.Y. 1988).
13. *See, e.g.*, Next Century Commc'ns Corp. v. Ellis, 318 F.3d 1023, 1027-28 (11th Cir. 2003) (Georgia law); Rodowicz v. Mass. Mut. Life Ins. Co., 192 F.3d 162, 175 (1st Cir. 1999) (Mass. law); Wheatcraft v. Wheatcraft, 825 N.E.2d 23, 31 (Ind. Ct. App. 2005); Thompson v. Bank of N.Y., 862 So.2d 768, 769 (Fla. Dist. Ct. App. 2003).
14. *Clardy Mfg.*, 88 F.3d at 359-60; Circle Group Internet, Inc. v. Fleishman-Hillard, Inc., 231 F. Supp. 2d 801, 803-04 (N.D. Ill. 2002).
15. *Glen Holly Entm't*, 352 F.3d at 379; Speakers of Sport, Inc. v. Proserv, Inc., 178 F.3d 862, 866-67 (7th Cir. 1999); Greenberg v. Chrust, 282 F. Supp. 2d 112, 120-21 (S.D.N.Y. 2003); Sheth v. N.Y. Life Ins. Co., 709 N.Y.S.2d 74, 75 (N.Y. 2000).
16. *See* Compressed Gas Corp., Inc. v. U.S. Steel Corp., 857 F.2d 346, 351 (6th Cir. 1988); Amoco Oil Co. v. Ashcraft, 791 F.2d 519, 521 (7th Cir. 1986) (misrepresentation of meaning of guaranty); Macon-Bibb County Hosp. Auth. v. Georgia Kaolin Co., 646 F. Supp. 90 (M.D. Ga. 1986) (insurance coverage as opinion of law non-actionable), *aff'd*, 817 F.2d 98 (11th Cir. 1987).
17. *Clardy Mfg.*, 88 F.3d at 359-60 (quoting Transp. Ins. Co. v. Faircloth, 898 S.W.2d 269 (Tex. 1995) ("An expression of an opinion as to the happening of a future event may also constitute fraud where the speaker purports to have special knowledge of facts that will occur or exist in the future.")); Georgen-Saad v. Tex. Mut. Ins. Co., 195 F. Supp. 2d 853, 860-61 (W.D. Tex. 2002); Fed. Reserve Bank of S.F. v. HK Systems, No. C-95-1190 MHP, 1997 WL 227955, at *5 (N.D. Cal. 1997) (quoting Cooper v. Jevne, 128 Cal. Rptr. 724 (1976)) ("[I]f a person advances an opinion in which he

Generally, an action for fraud may not be based upon the nonperformance of a promise relating to future acts, unless it can be shown that there was no intent to honor the promise at the time that it was made.[18]

It should be noted that the Restatement (Second) of Torts, rejects several of the limitations noted above. Specifically, section 525 (Liability for Fraudulent Misrepresentation) states:

> One who fraudulently makes a misrepresentation of fact, opinion, intention or law for the purpose of inducing another to act or refrain from action in reliance upon it, is subject to liability to the other in deceit for pecuniary loss caused to him by his justifiable reliance upon the misrepresentation.[19]

Although it sometimes has been said that mere silence will not constitute actionable fraud,[20] it is now settled in many jurisdictions that fraud may arise through the concealment of a material fact, as well as through an affirmative misrepresentation.[21] The failure to disclose a material fact amounts to misrepresentation where the disclosure would

---

does not honestly or cannot reasonably believe, then an action for affirmative fraud will lie if the remaining elements of the tort are present."); Arkoma Basin Exploration Co. v. FMF Assoc. 1990-A, Ltd., 118 S.W.3d 445, 453 (Tex. App. 2003) (applying Virginia law).

18. Coleman v. Sears, Roebuck & Co., 319 F. Supp. 2d 544 (W.D. Pa. 2003); Gouge v. BAX Global, Inc., 252 F. Supp. 2d 509 (N.D. Ohio 2003); Martens v. Minn. Mining & Mfg. Co., 616 N.W.2d 732 (Minn. 2000).

19. RESTATEMENT (SECOND) OF TORTS § 525 (1977); *see also* Nelson v. Taff, 499 N.W.2d 685, 687-88 (Wis. App. 1993) (collecting cases).

20. KEETON, *supra* note 6, § 106, at 737.

21. Bank of Montreal v. Signet Bank, 193 F.3d 818, 827 (4th Cir. 1999); Hitachi Credit Am. Corp. v. Signet Bank, 166 F.3d 614, 629 (4th Cir. 1999) ("[C]oncealment, whether by word or conduct, may be the equivalent of a false representation because it always involves deliberate non-disclosure designed to prevent another from learning the truth. Moreover, a party's willful nondisclosure of a material fact that he knows is unknown to the other party may evince an intent to practice actual fraud.") (internal quotations and citations omitted); Banque Arabe et Internationale D'Investissement v. Md. Nat'l Bank, 57 F.3d 146, 153 (2d Cir. 1995) (New York law).

correct a mistake as to an assumption basic to the plaintiff's understanding of the transaction.[22]

Some courts have held that the concealment of a material fact is not actionable absent a duty to disclose.[23] Such a duty may arise from inequality of position, a fiduciary relationship between the parties, or the demonstration of superior knowledge on the part of the defendant that is not within the fair and reasonable reach of the plaintiff.[24]

In order to support an action for fraud, the defendant's misrepresentation must have been material. A representation is material if a reasonable person would attach importance to the representation in determining his or her course of action.[25] A *false* representation is another essential element of an action for fraud – no fraud exists where the defendant's representations are true.[26]

4. *Scienter*

Because fraud is an intentional tort, it is not established absent proof of "scienter," or an intent to deceive.[27] This element is present when the

22. Highlands Ins. Co. v. Hobbs Group, LLC, 373 F.3d 347, 355 (3d Cir. 2004); Rachman Bag Co. v. Liberty Mut. Ins. Co., 46 F.3d 230, 235-37 (2d Cir. 1994); *see also* RESTATEMENT (SECOND) OF CONTRACTS § 160 (1979) ("Action intended or known to be likely to prevent another from learning a fact is equivalent to an assertion that the fact does not exist.").
23. Flouring on Call, Ltd. v. Fluorogas Ltd., 380 F.3d 849, 859 (5th Cir. 2004); *Bank of Montreal*, 193 F.3d at 827; *Rachman Bag Co.*, 46 F.3d at 235-37.
24. Coburn Supply Co. v. Kohler Co., 342 F.3d 372, 378 (5th Cir. 2003); *Andersons*, 348 F.3d at 505-09; Mathias v. Accor Econ. Lodging, Inc., 347 F.3d 672, 675 (7th Cir. 2003); Travelers Indem. Co. of Ill. v. CDL Hotels USA, Inc., 322 F. Supp. 2d 482, 499 (S.D.N.Y. 2004); Lesavoy v. Lane, 304 F. Supp. 2d 520, 526 (S.D.N.Y. 2004); Frye v. Am. Gen. Fin., Inc., 307 F. Supp. 2d 836, 842-43 (S.D. Miss. 2004).
25. United States v. Hasson, 333 F.3d 1264, 1270-71 (11th Cir. 2003); *Andersons*, 348 F.3d at 505-09; Moore v. Painewebber, Inc., 189 F.3d 165, 170 (2d Cir. 1999); *In re* Immobilaire, IV, Ltd., 314 B.R. 139, 159 (Bankr. S.D. Ohio 2004).
26. Hannoon v. Fawn Eng'g Corp., 324 F.3d 1041, 1048 (8th Cir. 2003); Kennedy Ship & Repair, L.P. v. Loc Tran, 256 F. Supp. 2d 678, 686 (S.D. Tex. 2003).
27. KEETON, *supra* note 6, § 107, at 741.

defendant's representation was made with knowledge of its falsity or with reckless disregard of (or conscious indifference to) its truth or falsity.[28] The fact that the defendant's representations ultimately were determined to be false, standing alone, however, is insufficient to establish the element of intent.[29] Where the defendant's error is honest and innocent, intentional fraud is not established.[30]

5. *Intent to Induce Reliance*

More than mere participation is necessary to give rise to liability for fraud; the participation must be knowing, with the intent to induce the other party's action.[31] It has been held that "the intent element in fraud, consisting of the intent to induce reliance, constitutes a subjective intent to injure."[32] It also has been held that the intent element requires a great degree of purposeful conduct; that is, the mere fact that it should be known to the defendant that another will rely upon his or her representation is insufficient to give rise to liability.[33]

6. *Reliance*

Actionable fraud also must "induce reliance," that is, it must "be both believed . . . and acted upon."[34] Absent reliance, the plaintiff cannot show that he or she was injured by the fraud.[35]

---

28. Club Car, Inc. v. Club Car (Quebec) Import, Inc., 362 F.3d 775, 783 (11th Cir. 2004); Hoseman v. Weinschneider, 322 F.3d 468, 476-77 (7th Cir. 2003); Ellipsis, Inc. v. Colorworks, Inc., 329 F. Supp. 2d 962, 968 (W.D. Tenn. 2004).

29. Taylor Inv. Corp. v. Weil, 169 F. Supp. 2d 1046, 1063 (D. Minn. 2001); Dahlmann v. Sulcus Hospitality Techs. Corp., 63 F. Supp. 2d 772, 777 (E.D. Mich. 1999).

30. Real Estate Fin. v. Resolution Trust Corp., 950 F.2d 1540, 1544 (11th Cir. 1992).

31. Doe v. Sw. Grain, 309 F. Supp. 2d 1119, 1124 (D.N.D. 2004); *In re* Santos, 304 B.R. 639, 664 (D.N.J. 2004); Indy Lube Invs., L.L.C. v. Wal-Mart Stores, Inc., 199 F. Supp. 2d 1114, 1120 (D. Kan. 2002).

32. SL Indus., Inc. v. Am. Motorists Ins. Co., 607 A.2d 1266, 1277 (N.J. 1992); *see also* Morton Int'l, Inc. v. Gen. Accident Ins. Co. of Am., 629 A.2d 831, 879 (N.J. 1993).

33. *In re* Miller, 282 B.R. 569, 575 (D. Conn. 2002).

34. AMPAT/Midwest, Inc. v. Ill. Tool Works, Inc., 896 F.2d 1035, 1041 (7th Cir. 1990).

The plaintiff must also demonstrate that his or her reliance on the defendant's misrepresentation was reasonable and justified under the circumstances.[36] Some courts have held that reliance on a misrepresentation is not reasonable where the plaintiff could have discovered the truth through the exercise of reasonable diligence,[37] although the contrary has been held by other courts.[38] However, a plaintiff who assumes a risk of which he is aware cannot establish the element of reliance.[39] Similarly, reliance is not established if the plaintiff did not believe the defendant's representations.[40]

Reliance upon mere predictions has been held to be unreasonable.[41] Similarly, courts frequently have held that vague, general statements are insufficient to induce reasonable reliance.[42] Continued reliance upon oral representations after entry into a written agreement also has been held to be unreasonable.[43]

Some courts have applied a subjective standard to the determination of reasonable reliance; under this standard, the "capacity and experience" of the plaintiff are relevant to the question of reasonableness.[44]

---

35. Kennedy v. Venrock Assocs., 348 F.3d 584, 592 (7th Cir. 2003).
36. Am. Trim, L.L.C. v. Oracle Corp., 383 F.3d 462, 473 (6th Cir. 2004); Bank of China, N.Y. Branch v. NBM LLC, 359 F.3d 171, 178 (2d Cir. 2004).
37. Lewis v. Bank of Am. NA, 343 F.3d 540, 546-47 (5th Cir. 2003); Soliman v. Philip Morris Inc., 311 F.3d 966, 975-76 (9th Cir. 2002).
38. S.C. Johnson & Son, Inc. v. Dowbrands, Inc., 294 F. Supp. 2d 568, 593 (D. Del. 2003).
39. Dexter Corp. v. Whittaker Corp., 926 F.2d 617, 620 (7th Cir. 1991); *AMPAT/Midwest, Inc.*, 896 F.2d at 1042; Fashion House, Inc. v. K Mart Corp., 892 F.2d 1076, 1093 (1st Cir. 1989).
40. Apex Oil Co. v. Belcher Co. of N.Y., 855 F.2d 997, 1008 (2d Cir. 1988).
41. *Gouge*, 252 F. Supp. 2d at 515; *Martens*, 616 N.W.2d at 747.
42. Hinchey v. NYNEX Corp., 979 F. Supp. 40, 44 (D. Mass. 1997); Boyle v. Douglas Dynamics, LLC, No. 03-2430, 2004 WL 1171370, at *4 (1st Cir. May 25, 2004).
43. Dallas Aerospace, Inc. v. CIS Air Corp., 352 F.3d 775, 785 (2d Cir. 2003); Cook v. Little Caesar Enters., Inc., 210 F.3d 653, 658 (6th Cir. 2000).
44. Wittekamp v. Gulf & Western, Inc., 991 F.2d 1137, 1144 (3d Cir. 1993).

7. *Damages*

The courts are divided on the question of the proper measure of compensatory damages for fraud, with most courts applying one of two standards to determine the plaintiff's loss.[45]

The majority view allows "benefit of the bargain" damages, which may include lost profits.[46] The appropriate measure of lost profits recoverable under the benefit-of-the-bargain rule is net profits, not gross profits.[47] Consequential damages, if proven with reasonable certainty, also are recoverable under this rule.[48]

The minority view permits the plaintiff to recover "out of pocket" losses, defined as the difference between what the plaintiff lost and what was obtained in the transaction.[49] Lost profits or wages generally are considered to be consequential or indirect damages, which are not recoverable under the out-of-pocket rule.[50]

In addition to compensatory damages, courts have permitted the award of punitive damages in fraud actions, and have applied various standards when determining whether punitive damages may be awarded. Many jurisdictions do not permit punitive damages on proof of fraud alone, but require accompanying aggravating circumstances.[51] In such cases, punitive damages have been permitted where the evidence would support a finding that the defendant's conduct was "willful and

45. *See* KEETON, *supra* note 6, § 110, at 767.
46. *In re* Lauer, 371 F.3d 406, 411 (8th Cir. 2004) (Missouri law); Coffel v. Stryker Corp., 284 F.3d 625, 637 (5th Cir. 2002) (Texas law).
47. *Tunis Bros.*, 952 F.2d at 735.
48. *In re Lauer*, 371 F.3d at 412; *Coffel*, 284 F.3d at 639-40; Bird v. Chezik Homerun, Inc., 152 F.3d 1014, 1017 (8th Cir. 1998); *Usery*, 123 F.3d at 1096.
49. Dresser-Rand Co. v. Virtual Automation, Inc., 361 F.3d 831, 843 (5th Cir. 2004) (Texas law); Whitney Holdings, Ltd. v. Givotovsky, 988 F. Supp. 732, 736 (S.D.N.Y. 1997); Twenty First Century L.P. v. LaBianca, No. 92 CV 2913(ILG), 2001 WL 761163, at *2 (E.D.N.Y. May 2, 2001).
50. *Dresser-Rand*, 361 F.3d at 843; *Whitney Holdings*, 988 F. Supp. at 736; *Twenty First Century*, 2001 WL 761163, at *2.
51. *Coffel*, 284 F.3d at 639-40 (Texas law requires proof of conscious indifference); *Gennari*, 691 A.2d at 368.

wanton,"[52] or "outrageous."[53]   Others permit an award of punitive damages upon proof of an intent to deceive or reckless disregard of the truth (sometimes referred to as "actual malice").[54] A minority permit the imposition of punitive damages on a finding of fraud alone.[55]

Punitive damages awards have frequently survived state and federal constitutional challenges on grounds of excessiveness.[56] Limitations upon punitive damages awards are addressed in Chapter 8.

8.   *Burden of Proof*

In order to recover for fraud, a plaintiff bears the burden of establishing the existence of each of the essential elements of the tort.[57] It often has been said that fraud is "never presumed,"[58] and that a plaintiff alleging fraud bears the burden of establishing the elements of the tort by clear and convincing evidence.[59]

---

52.   Todd Shipyards Corp. v. Cunard Line, Ltd., 943 F.2d 1056, 1063 (9th Cir. 1991) (New York law) (quoting Faller Group, Inc. v. Jaffe, 564 F. Supp. 1177, 1185 (S.D.N.Y. 1983)); Pazdziora by Pazdziora v. Syntex Labs., Inc., 774 F. Supp. 1100, 1103-04 (N.D. Ill. 1991).
53.   Hughes v. Consol-Pa. Coal Co., 945 F.2d 594, 616 (3d Cir. 1991) (Pennsylvania law).
54.   *Gennari*, 691 A.2d at 368.
55.   *See, e.g.*, Hunt v. Miller, 908 F.2d 1210, 1216 n.15 (4th Cir. 1990).
56.   Rhone-Poulenc Agro, S.A. v. DeKalb Genetics Corp., 345 F.3d 1366, 1371-72 (Fed. Cir. 2003); United Int'l Holdings, Inc. v. Wharf (Holdings) Ltd., 210 F.3d 1207, 1231-33 (10th Cir. 2000); Gibson v. Total Car Franchising Corp., 223 F.R.D. 265, 275-76 (M.D.N.C. 2004).
57.   St. Paul Fire and Marine Ins. Co. v. Ellis & Ellis, 262 F.3d 53, 63 (1st Cir. 2001); *In re* e.Spire Commc'ns, Inc., 293 B.R. 639, 647-48 (D. Del. 2003).
58.   *Sw. Grain*, 309 F. Supp. 2d at 1124; Osborn v. Univ. Med. Assocs. of the Med. Univ. of S. Carolina, 278 F. Supp. 2d 720, 733 (D.S.C. 2003).
59.   *Dallas Aerospace, Inc.*, 352 F.3d at 784-85; *Hoseman*, 322 F.3d at 476; *In re* McGinnis, 306 B.R. 279, 285-86 (W.D. Mo. 2004); Law v. Camp, 116 F. Supp. 2d 295, 308 (D. Conn. 2000). *But see* Liodas v. Sahadi, 562 P.2d 316, 320-324 (Cal. 1977) (fraud need be proved only by a preponderance of the evidence); Holliday v. Rain and Hail L.L.C., 690 N.W.2d 59, 64 (Iowa 2004) (fraud must be established by a preponderance of evidence that of a character or nature that is "clear, satisfactory, and convincing"); Caputo v. Prof'l Recovery Servs., Inc., 261 F. Supp. 2d 1249, 1264-65 (D. Kan. 2003) ("The burden of proving fraud is by a preponderance of the evidence, which must be clear, convincing, and satisfactory.").

C. Negligent Misrepresentation

1. *Nature of the Action*

A growing number of jurisdictions now recognize the tort of "negligent misrepresentation," which permits recovery under varying circumstances for misrepresentations that were negligently, but not intentionally, made. This trend is reflected in the Restatement (Second) of Torts § 552(1) ("section 552"), which provides:

> One who, in the course of his business, profession or employment, or in any other transaction in which he has a pecuniary interest, supplies false information for the guidance of others in their business transactions, is subject to liability for pecuniary loss caused to them by their justifiable reliance upon the information, if he fails to exercise reasonable care or competence in obtaining or communicating the information.

The tort of negligent misrepresentation has been broadly applied by some courts to permit plaintiffs who are not parties to contracts for professional services to recover for the negligent dissemination of false or misleading information.

2. *Elements*

In order to state a claim for negligent misrepresentation, the plaintiff must generally prove the following elements:

(a) That the defendant, in the course of its business or profession, supplied information for the guidance of others in their business transactions;

(b) That the information supplied by the defendant was false or materially inaccurate;

(c) That the defendant failed to exercise due care to ensure the truth and accuracy of the information;

(d) That the plaintiff justifiably relied upon the information in its business transactions; and

(e) That the plaintiff suffered resulting pecuniary damages.[60]

---

60. H.C. Smith Invs., L.L.C. v. Outboard Marine Co., 377 F.3d 645, 651-52 (6th Cir. 2004); Burlington Ins. Co. v. Okie Dokie, Inc., No. 03-2002,

A number of states that recognize this tort have expressly adopted section 552.[61] Federal maritime law also recognizes negligent misrepresentation and has adopted section 552.[62]

3. *"Business of Supplying Information"*

Following the Restatement definition, most courts have limited the applicability of this tort to professionals in the business of supplying information. Application of this standard has resulted in fact-intensive inquiries into the meaning of the phrase "business of supplying information."[63] Liability has been imposed under this rule upon accountants,[64] attorneys,[65] banks and financial services institutions,[66]

2004 WL 1749170, at *2-4 (D.D.C. Aug. 2, 2004); Prather v. Utiliquest, L.L.C., 313 F. Supp. 2d 666, 671 (S.D. Tex. 2004); Jackson v. Drake Univ., 778 F. Supp. 1490, 1494 (S.D. Iowa 1991); Craig v. First Am. Capital Res., Inc., 740 F. Supp. 530, 540 (N.D. Ill. 1990); Somarelf v. Am. Bureau of Shipping, 704 F. Supp. 59, 64 (D.N.J. 1988).

61. *See, e.g.*, St. Joseph's Hosp. & Med. Ctr. v. Reserve Life Ins. Co., 742 P.2d 808, 813 (Ariz. 1987); First Nat'l Bank in Lamar v. Collins, 616 P.2d 154, 155 (Colo. Ct. App. 1980); D'Ulisse-Cupo v. Bd. of Dirs. of Notre Dame High Sch., 520 A.2d 217, 223 (Conn. 1987); Presnell Constr, Managers, Inc. v. Eh Constr., L.L.C., 134 S.W.3d 575, 582 (Ky. 2004); Marram v. Kobrick Offshore Fund, Ltd., 809 N.E.2d 1017, 1031 (Mass. 2004); Chapman v. Rideout, 568 A.2d 829, 830 (Me. 1990); Bonhiver v. Graff, 248 N.W.2d 291, 298-99 (Minn. 1976); First Money, Inc. v. Frisby, 369 So.2d 746, 750 (Miss. 1979); State Bank of Townsend v. Maryann's, Inc., 664 P.2d 295, 301 (Mont. 1983); Amato v. Rathbun Realty, Inc., 647 P.2d 433, 434 (N.M. 1982).

62. Otto Candies, L.L.C. v. Nippon Kaiji Kyokai Corp., 346 F.3d 530, 534-35 (5th Cir. 2003), *cert. denied*, 124 S. Ct. 2067 (2004).

63. *See, e.g.*, Rankow v. First Chicago Corp., 870 F.2d 356, 361-66 (7th Cir. 1989) (holding that a precise, case-specific inquiry is required to determine whether a particular enterprise is in the business of supplying information for the guidance of others in their business transactions); Sain v. Cedar Rapids Cmty. Sch. Dist., 626 N.W.2d 115, 125-27 (Iowa 2001); *In re* Estate of Madigan, No. 03-0048, 2004 WL 1159659, at *1-2 (Iowa Ct. App. May 26, 2004).

64. *Sain*, 626 N.W.2d at 123, 126; Duke v. Touche Ross & Co., 765 F. Supp. 69, 77 (S.D.N.Y. 1991); Guenther v. Cooper Life Scis., Inc., 759 F. Supp. 1437, 1442-43 (N.D. Cal. 1990); Dalton v. Alston & Bird, 741 F. Supp. 1322, 1334-35 (S.D. Ill. 1990).

independent auditors,[67] investment brokers,[68] and high school guidance counselors,[69] among others.

Conversely, it has been held that the tort of negligent misrepresentation is not available to permit recovery by one corporation against another as a result of a failed merger,[70] by a purchaser against a retailer in the business of selling and servicing merchandise,[71] by employees against a polygraph technician retained by their employer,[72] by a corporation against the designer of promotional products,[73] or by a purchaser of a farm from an estate against the estate's executor.[74]

Courts that have not relied upon the Restatement definition of negligent misrepresentation have refused to impose liability in the absence of privity or a special relationship.[75] Other courts have indicated that a relationship approaching that of privity is sufficient to support a claim.[76]

---

65. *Sain*, 626 N.W.2d at 123, 126; Home Budget Loans v. Jacoby & Meyers Law Offices, 255 Cal. Rptr. 483, 486-87 (Cal. Ct. App. 1989).
66. DuQuoin State Bank v. Norris City State Bank, 595 N.E.2d 678, 681-83 (Ill. App. Ct. 1992); Bottrell v. Am. Bank, 773 P.2d 694, 706 (Mont. 1989).
67. Shamrock Assocs. v. Sloane, 738 F. Supp. 109, 118 (S.D.N.Y. 1990).
68. McCracken v. Edward D. Jones & Co., 445 N.W.2d 375, 381-82 (Iowa Ct. App. 1989).
69. *Sain*, 626 N.W.2d at 126-27.
70. Budget Mktg., Inc. v. Centronics Corp., 927 F.2d 421, 428 (8th Cir. 1991).
71. G & H Soybean Oil v. Diamond Crystal Specialty Foods, Inc., 796 F. Supp. 1214, 1218 (S.D. Iowa 1992); Meier v. Alfa-Laval, Inc., 454 N.W.2d 576, 581 (Iowa 1990).
72. Hall v. United Parcel Serv. of Am., Inc., 555 N.E.2d 273, 277-78 (N.Y. 1990).
73. August, Bishop & Meier, Inc. v. Premium Link, Ltd., 738 F. Supp. 1166, 1169 (N.D. Ill. 1990).
74. *In re Estate of Madigan*, 2004 WL 1159659, at *1-2.
75. *See, e.g.*, Superior Bank, F.S.B. v. Tandem Nat'l Mortgage, Inc., 197 F. Supp. 2d 298, 319-21 (D. Md. 2000); Flow Indus., Inc. v. Fields Constr. Co., 683 F. Supp. 527, 529 (D. Md. 1988).
76. *See, e.g.*, Citytrust v. Atlas Capital Corp., 570 N.Y.S.2d 275, 277-78 (N.Y. App. Div. 1991) (holding that absent either actual privity of contract, or an underlying relationship between the parties so close as to be the functional

4. *Falsity*

Some courts have required that a negligent misrepresentation claim be supported by a false statement or assertion, thus rejecting the notion that failure to disclose information may be actionable as negligent misrepresentation.[77] Others have held that the "false information" essential to the maintenance of this claim may be communicated indirectly, by nondisclosure of known material facts.[78]

Expressions of opinion have been held insufficient to support a negligent misrepresentation action, unless "parties are on unequal footing and do not have equal knowledge or means of knowledge."[79] Additionally, alleged misrepresentations must be factual and not "promissory or related to future events."[80]

5. *Due Care*

Negligent misrepresentation involves a breach of a duty to exercise "reasonable care or competence"[81] in obtaining and communicating information upon which others may reasonably be expected to rely in the conduct of their economic affairs.[82] A misrepresentation will be considered negligent if the misrepresenter "'has not discovered or communicated certain information the ordinary person in his or her

---

equivalent of contractual privity, the defendant will not be found liable for negligence).

77. *See, e.g.,* Brug v. Enstar Group, Inc., 755 F. Supp. 1247, 1253 (D. Del. 1991); *In re* Convergent Techs. Sec. Litig., 721 F. Supp. 1133, 1139 n.4 (N.D. Cal. 1988), *aff'd*, 948 F.2d 507 (9th Cir. 1991); Byrum v. Brand, 268 Cal. Rptr. 609, 621 (Cal. Ct. App. 1990); Twelve Knotts Ltd. P'ship v. Fireman's Ins. Co., 589 A.2d 105, 112 (Md. App. 1991).

78. *See, e.g., Highland Ins.*, 373 F.3d at 355; Temp-Way Corp. v. Cont'l Bank, 139 B.R. 299, 325 (Bankr. E.D. Pa. 1992), *aff'd*, 981 F.2d 1248 (3d Cir. 1992); Smith v. Frandsen, 94 P.3d 919, 923 (Utah 2004) (holding that an omission may be actionable as a negligent misrepresentation where the defendant has a duty to disclose); Amtruck Factors, a Div. of Truck Sales v. Int'l Forest Prods., 795 P.2d 742, 748 (Wash. Ct. App. 1990).

79. Frank v. Fitz Enters., Inc., 806 P.2d 720, 721 (Or. Ct. App. 1991).

80. Eternity Global Master Fund Ltd. v. Morgan Guar. Trust Co. of N.Y., 375 F.3d 168, 187-88 (2d Cir. 2004).

81. Wash. Mut. Bank, FA v. Advanced Clearing, Inc., 679 N.W.2d 207, 210 (Neb. 2004).

82. *See, e.g.,* RESTATEMENT (SECOND) OF TORTS § 552 cmt. e (1977).

position would have discovered or communicated.'"[83] Where the misrepresenter is a licensed professional, such as an accountant, attorney, or broker,[84] a malpractice standard is imposed, even though the liability may extend to parties other than the professional's clients where an intent to induce the third party's reliance is shown.[85]

6. *Justifiable Reliance*

In order to state a claim for negligent misrepresentation, the plaintiff must show that she used the information supplied by the defendant in a business transaction with a third party,[86] and that the reliance on any alleged misrepresentations was justified[87] and not unreasonable as a matter of law.[88] At least one court has held that an action for negligent misrepresentation can be maintained only by persons for whom the representations were intended, thus striking down the claim of an insurance agent who was the subject of false published reports that his license had been revoked or suspended.[89]

7. *Damages*

The majority of courts that have considered the question of damages limit compensatory damages for negligent misrepresentation to the

---

83. Davis v. U.S. Bancorp, No. 03-3153, 2004 WL 2008656, at *6 (8th Cir. Sep. 10, 2004) (quoting Florenzano v. Olson, 387 N.W.2d 168, 174 (Minn. 1986)).
84. *See supra* notes 65, 66 & 69.
85. *See, e.g.,* First Fla. Bank v. Max Mitchell & Co., 558 So.2d 9, 16 (Fla. 1990) (holding that an accountant is liable for negligence to a third party when the accountant fails to exercise reasonable and ordinary care in preparing a client's financial statements and then attempts to induce the third party to loan or invest with the client by personally delivering and presenting those statements to the third party).
86. *Craig,* 740 F. Supp. at 540.
87. *Eternity Global Master Fund,* 375 F.3d at 187, 189-90; *Washington Mut. Bank,* 679 N.W.2d at 213.
88. *Marram,* 809 N.E.2d at 1031; Williams v. Berube & Assocs. 26 S.W.3d 640, 645 (Tenn. Ct. App. 2000) (holding that plaintiff in a negligent misrepresentation case must prove that it justifiably relied on the defendant's statements).
89. Pannell v. Associated Press, 690 F. Supp. 546, 551 (N.D. Miss. 1988).

plaintiff's out-of-pocket losses,[90] but this most likely does not include the legal costs and fees associated with filing a negligent misrepresentation complaint.[91] Some courts applying this rule have allowed consequential damages,[92] while others have not.[93] A few courts have allowed benefit-of-the-bargain damages,[94] or have applied a flexible rule permitting whichever of these measures of damages can be proven with sufficient certainty.[95] Regardless of which approach the court utilizes to measure damages, the plaintiff must be able to show a causal nexus between its alleged reliance on the negligent misrepresentations and any damages.[96]

Most courts have not permitted the recovery of punitive damages for negligent misrepresentation.[97]

---

90. *See* Mammas v. Oro Valley Townhouses, Inc., 638 P.2d 1367, 1368-69 (Ariz. Ct. App. 1981); Danca v. Taunton Sav. Bank, 429 N.E.2d 1129, 1134 (Mass. 1982); First Interstate Bank of Gallup v. Foutz, 764 P.2d 1307, 1309-10 (N.M. 1988); Costa v. Niemon, 366 N.W.2d 896, 900-01 (Wis. 1985).

91. Gagnon Welding & Contracting Corp. v. Town of Lynnfield, No. 00-P-1562, 2002 WL 31698148, at *2-3 (Mass. App. Ct. Dec. 3, 2002).

92. Gyldenvand v. Schroeder, 280 N.W.2d 235, 238-40 (Wis. 1979) (holding that damages are recoverable if proven with reasonable certainty); *Costa*, 366 N.W.2d at 901.

93. Frame v. Boatmen's Bank of Concord Vill., 824 S.W.2d 491, 496-97 (Mo. Ct. App. 1992).

94. Kramer v. Chabot, 564 A.2d 292, 294-95 (Vt. 1989).

95. Ward Dev. Co. v. Ingrao, 493 A.2d 421, 428-29 (Md. Ct. Spec. App. 1985) (applying a flexible approach).

96. Goering v. Chapman Univ., 17 Cal. Rptr. 3d 39, 47-49 (Cal. Ct. App. 2004).

97. Reid v. Moskovitz, 208 Cal. App. 3d 29, 32 (Cal. Ct. App. 1989); Rogers v. Mitzi, 584 So. 2d 1092, 1094 (Fla. Dist. Ct. App. 1991); Crowley v. Global Realty, Inc., 474 A.2d 1056, 1058 (N.H. 1984); *cf.* Indosuez v. Barclays Bank PLC, 580 N.Y.S.2d 765, 767 (N.Y. App. Div. 1992) (holding that punitive damages are only available in actions where there has been a public wrong, or where the parties are in a fiduciary or confidential relationship). *But see* Browne v. Maxfield, 663 F. Supp. 1193, 1206-07 (E.D. Pa. 1987) (holding that punitive damages are not unavailable as a matter of law, but rather are an extreme remedy only available when the actor appreciates that his or her conduct creates a high degree of risk).

8. *Burden of Proof*

The majority of jurisdictions to consider the question have held that the plaintiff must prove the negligent misrepresentation claim by a preponderance of the evidence.[98] Under New York law, however, the clear and convincing evidentiary standard applicable to fraud is also applied to negligent misrepresentation claims.[99]

D. Federal Statutory Causes of Action

Numerous federal statutory causes of action are available to redress fraud and misrepresentation, generally in connection with the offer, purchase, and sale of securities. Of these, section 12(a)(2) (formerly 12(2)) of the Securities Act of 1933, as amended ("Securities Act"),[100] and section 10(b) of the Securities Exchange Act of 1934, as amended ("Exchange Act")[101] are among the most commonly asserted private rights of action. The following overview of these statutory claims is not intended to be exhaustive,[102] but to present in broad outline the essential elements of these claims.

1. *Section 12(a)(2) of the Securities Act*

Section 12(a)(2) of the Securities Act imposes civil liability for the offer or sale of a security, in interstate commerce or through the mails, by means of a prospectus or oral communication, which either (1) contains an untrue statement of a material fact, or (2) omits a material fact that was necessary under the circumstances in order to make the statements made not misleading.[103] In *Gustafson v. Alloyd Co.*,[104] the

---

98. Birt v. Wells Fargo Home Mortg., Inc., 75 P.3d 640, 656 (Wyo. 2003); Spragins v. Sunburst Bank, 605 So. 2d 777, 780 (Miss. 1992); Golden Cone Concepts, Inc. v. Villa Linda Mall, Ltd., 820 P.2d 1323, 1327 (N.M. 1991); Weisman v. Connors, 540 A.2d 783, 798 n.5 (Md. 1988); DiPerri v. Tothill, 531 A.2d 342, 344 (N.H. 1987); Atkins v. Kirkpatrick, 823 S.W.2d 547, 552 (Tenn. App. 1991);
99. Fromer v. Yogel, 50 F. Supp. 2d 227, 243 (S.D.N.Y. 1999).
100. 15 U.S.C. § 77l(a)(2).
101. 15 U.S.C. § 78j(b).
102. For a general discussion of civil liability for fraud and misrepresentation under the federal securities laws, *see* IX LOUIS LOSS & JOEL SELIGMAN, SECURITIES REGULATION Ch. 11 (3d ed. 1998).
103. 15 U.S.C. § 77l(a)(2). Section 12(a)(2) provides:

Supreme Court held that section 12(a)(2) applies only to registered public offerings of securities, and does not reach so-called "secondary market" transactions.

In order to recover under section 12(a)(2), the plaintiff must show that (1) the defendant made a false or misleading statement of material fact or omitted to state a material fact, (2) the plaintiff was not aware of the untruth or omission, and (3) the defendant knew, or in the exercise of reasonable care could have known, of the untruth or omission.[105] Liability under section 12(a)(2) is very nearly strict liability, and no showing of scienter is required.[106] Thus, liability extends to negligent misrepresentations.[107]

Any person who – . . .

(2) offers or sells a security (whether or not exempted by the provisions of section 3, other than paragraphs (2) and (14) of subsection (a) thereof), by the use of any means or instruments of transportation or communication in interstate commerce or of the mails, by means of a prospectus or oral communication, which includes an untrue statement of a material fact or omits to state a material fact necessary in order to make the statements, in the light of the circumstances under which they were made, not misleading (the purchaser not knowing of such untruth or omission), and who shall not sustain the burden of proof that he did not know, and in the exercise of reasonable care could not have known, of such untruth or omission, shall be liable subject to subsection (b) to the person purchasing such security from him, who may sue either at law or in equity in any court of competent jurisdiction, to recover the consideration paid for such security with interest thereon, less the amount of any income received thereon, upon the tender of such security, or for damages if he no longer owns the security. *Id.*

104. 513 U.S. 561, 580 (1995).
105. Cook v. Avien, Inc., 573 F.2d 685, 693 (1st Cir. 1978); Alton Box Bd. Co. v. Goldman, Sachs & Co., 560 F.2d 916, 918 (8th Cir. 1977).
106. Wertheim & Co. v. Codding Embryol. Scis., Inc., 620 F.2d 764, 766 (10th Cir. 1980); Gridley v. Sayre & Fisher Co., 409 F. Supp. 1266, 1272 (D.S.D. 1975), *aff'd*, 550 F.2d 551 (8th Cir. 1977); Odette v. Shearson, Hammill & Co., 394 F. Supp. 946, 956 (S.D.N.Y. 1975).
107. Stewart v. Bennett, 359 F. Supp. 878, 884 n.16 (D. Mass. 1973).

The test of materiality under section 12(a)(2) is the same as the test under other federal securities statutes, that is, whether there is a substantial likelihood that a reasonable person would consider the fact important in determining a course of action.[108] In other words, a fact is material if there is a substantial likelihood that the fact would have been viewed by the reasonable investor as having significantly altered the "total mix" of information.

The plaintiff in a section 12(a)(2) action is not required to prove due diligence; all that is required is ignorance of the alleged untruth or omission.[109] Similarly, reliance is not a precondition to recovery.[110] However, the defense of in pari delicto is available in actions under this section when the plaintiff bears sufficient responsibility for the violations he seeks to redress.[111]

To avoid liability under section 12(a)(2), the defendant must prove that he "did not know, and in the exercise of reasonable care could not have known, of the claimed misrepresentation or omission."[112]

Liability under section 12(a)(2) extends not only to the actual "seller" of the security but also to controlling persons (under § 15 of the Securities Act),[113] "sellers" who are agents rather than principals, and others who successfully solicit the purchase of securities and are motivated at least in part by the desire to serve their own financial interests or the interests of the securities owner.[114]

Section 12(a)(2) claims may be filed in either state or federal court. If filed in state court such a claim may not be removed to federal court.[115] A successful plaintiff may tender the security and recover the

108. *See* TSC Indus. v. Northway, Inc., 426 U.S. 438, 449 (1976); *Alton Box Board*, 560 F.2d at 919-20; Anixter v. Home-Stake Prod. Co. (*In re* Home-Stake Prod. Co. Sec. Litig.), 76 F.R.D. 351, 372 (N.D. Okla. 1977).
109. Sanders v. John Nuveen & Co., 619 F.2d 1222, 1229 (7th Cir. 1980); Gilbert v. Nixon, 429 F.2d 348, 356 (10th Cir. 1970).
110. Smolen v. Deloitte, Haskins, & Sells, 921 F.2d 959, 963 (9th Cir. 1990). *But see* Haralson v. E.F. Hutton Group, Inc., 919 F.2d 1014 (5th Cir. 1990) (must have reasonable and justifiable reliance); *Gilbert*, 429 F.2d at 356.
111. *See* Pinter v. Dahl, 486 U.S. 622, 632-41 (1988) (involving § 12(1)).
112. Heffernan v. Pac. Dunlop GNB Corp., 965 F.2d 369, 373 (7th Cir. 1992).
113. *See* 15 U.S.C. § 77o.
114. *Pinter*, 486 U.S. at 647 (construing § 12(1)).
115. 15 U.S.C. § 77v(a).

consideration paid, with interest, less the amount of any income received, or may recover damages if the plaintiff no longer owns the security.[116] A defendant may prove that all or part of the loss otherwise recoverable was due to causes other than the alleged misrepresentation or omission, in which case that portion of the loss is not recoverable.[117] The courts are divided over whether punitive damages may be recovered.[118] A section 12(a)(2) claim must be filed within one year after the plaintiff discovered, or in the exercise of reasonable diligence should have discovered, the untrue statement or omission, or within three years after the sale.[119]

2. *Section 10(b) of the Exchange Act*

Section 10(b) of the Exchange Act, also known as the "catch-all" antifraud provision of the Exchange Act,[120] makes it "unlawful for any person . . . to use or employ . . . any manipulative or deceptive device or contrivance in contravention of" rules promulgated by the Securities and Exchange Commission ("SEC").[121] Rule 10b-5, promulgated by the SEC under section 10(b), prohibits, in addition to material misrepresentations and omissions, any "artifice to defraud" or any act "which operates or would operate as a fraud or deceit" in connection with the purchase or sale of securities.[122] Although neither section 10(b) nor Rule 10b-5 expressly provides for a private right of action, the federal courts have long recognized an implied right of action under these provisions.[123]

Liability under Rule 10b-5 is not limited to common law fraud, but extends to misleading and deceptive acts and practices within the

---

116. 15 U.S.C. § 77l.
117. 15 U.S.C. § 77l(c).
118. *See, e.g.*, Hill York Corp. v. Am. Int'l Franchises, Inc. 448 F.2d 680, 697 (5th Cir. 1971) (no); Nagel v. Prescott & Co., 36 F.R.D. 445, 449 (N.D. Ohio 1964) (yes).
119. 15 U.S.C. § 77m.
120. *See* Bochicchio v. Smith Barney, Harris Upham & Co., 647 F. Supp. 1426, 1429-30 (S.D.N.Y. 1986).
121. 15 U.S.C. § 78j(b).
122. 17 C.F.R. § 240.10b-5 (2004); *see* Santa Fe Indus. v. Green, 430 U.S. 462, 471 (1977).
123. *See* Superintendent of Ins. of N.Y. v. Bankers Life & Cas. Co., 404 U.S. 6, 13 n.9 (1971).

meaning of the rule.[124] Thus, for example, a false promise to perform an act in the future can constitute a misleading and deceptive practice under Rule 10b-5, even though it will not support a fraud action under state law, if the promise is a part of the consideration given for the purchase or sale of securities.[125] Neither mere negligence[126] nor a breach of fiduciary duty unaccompanied by manipulation or deception,[127] however, will support a claim under Rule 10b-5.

The essential elements of a claim under Rule 10b-5 are (1) the existence of a fraudulent scheme or a misrepresentation or omission of a material fact in connection with the purchase or sale of a security, (2) in the case of misrepresentation, detrimental reliance, (3) scienter and (4) the use of any instrumentality of interstate commerce or the mails or of any facility of any national securities exchange.[128]

A fact is considered to be material, "if its existence or nonexistence is a matter to which a reasonable person would attach importance in determining his choice of action in a transaction."[129] Stated otherwise, a fact is material if there is a substantial likelihood that the fact would have been viewed by the reasonable investor as having significantly altered the "total mix" of information.[130]

To prove scienter in a Rule 10b-5 case, the plaintiff must show that the defendant engaged in "knowing or intentional misconduct,"[131] or acted with "an intent to deceive."[132] Although mere negligence is not "a

---

124. Messer v. E.F. Hutton & Co., 833 F.2d 909, 914 (11th Cir. 1987), *modified on other grounds*, 847 F.2d 673 (11th Cir. 1988).
125. *Id.* at 914.
126. Ernst & Ernst v. Hochfelder, 425 U.S. 185, 199 (1976).
127. *Santa Fe Indus.*, 430 U.S. at 474-77.
128. Cahill v. Arthur Anderson & Co., 659 F. Supp. 1115, 1124 (S.D.N.Y. 1986), *aff'd*, 822 F.2d 14 (2d Cir. 1987); *Bochicchio*, 647 F. Supp. at 1429.
129. Toombs v. Leone, 777 F.2d 465, 469 (9th Cir. 1985) (citing TSC Indus. v. Northway, Inc., 426 U.S. 438, 449, (1976)).
130. Paul v. Berkman, 620 F. Supp. 638, 641 (W.D. Pa. 1985).
131. Mayer v. Oil Field Sys. Corp., 803 F.2d 749, 756 (2d Cir. 1986); Wechsler v. Steinberg, 733 F.2d 1054, 1058 (2d Cir. 1984) (quoting Ernst & Ernst. v. Hochfelder, 425 U.S. 185, 197 (1976)).
132. *Wechsler*, 733 F.2d at 1058; *see also Ernst & Ernst*, 425 U.S. at 193; Gert v. Elgin Nat'l Indus., 773 F.2d 154, 157 (7th Cir. 1985).

substitute for scienter" for the purposes of the rule,[133] reckless conduct may be sufficient to constitute the requisite scienter.[134]

Reliance is a "necessary element" of a misrepresentation claim under Rule 10b-5, and usually "requires proof that the misrepresentation actually induced the plaintiff to act differently than he [otherwise] would have acted in his investment decision."[135] Reliance, to support a claim, must be reasonable under the circumstances.[136]

In *Basic, Inc. v. Levinson*,[137] however, the Supreme Court held in a plurality opinion that reliance may be presumed in so-called "fraud on the market" cases. Under this theory of reliance, when material misrepresentations are disseminated into an "open and developed market," an investor who buys or sells stock at the market price may be presumed to have done so in reliance on the integrity of that price; "[b]ecause most publicly available information is reflected in market price, an investor's reliance on any public material misrepresentations, therefore, may be presumed for purposes of a Rule 10b-5 action."[138] This presumption may be overcome: "Any showing that severs the link between the alleged misrepresentation and either the price received (or paid) by the plaintiff, or his decision to trade at a fair market price, will be sufficient to rebut the presumption of reliance."[139]

Positive proof of reliance is not necessary where a duty to disclose material information has been breached.[140] In a case involving an omission, however, the plaintiff must establish a duty to disclose the

---

133. *Ernst & Ernst*, 425 U.S. at 201; Wise v. Kidder Peabody & Co., 596 F. Supp. 1391, 1395 (D. Del. 1984); Crook v. Shearson Loeb Rhoades, 591 F. Supp. 40, 47 (N.D. Ind. 1983).
134. Hollinger v. Titan Capital Corp., 914 F.2d 1564, 1568-69 (9th Cir. 1990); Kehr v. Smith Barney, Harris Upham & Co., 736 F.2d 1283, 1286 (9th Cir. 1984); Nelson v. Serwold, 576 F.2d 1332, 1337 (9th Cir. 1978).
135. Schick v. Steiger, 583 F. Supp. 841, 848 (E.D. Mich. 1984).
136. *See* Nick v. Shearson/Am. Express, Inc., 612 F. Supp. 15, 18 (D. Minn. 1984).
137. 485 U.S. 224 (1988).
138. *Id.* at 247.
139. *Id.* at 248.
140. Affiliated Ute Citizens of Utah v. United States, 406 U.S. 128, 153-54 (1972).

information in issue.[141] The defense of *in pari delicto* is available in actions under Rule 10b-5.[142]

Liability under Rule 10b-5 extends not only to principals but to agents and controlling persons.[143] In *Central Bank of Denver, N.A. v. First Interstate Bank of Denver, N.A.*,[144] however, the Supreme Court held that a private plaintiff cannot maintain a private right of action under Rule 10b-5 based upon a theory of "aiding and abetting" liability.[145] As a matter of federal law, defendants in Rule 10b-5 actions have a right to seek contribution from others having joint responsibility for the violation.[146]

Unlike section 12(a)(2), which provides for concurrent state and federal jurisdiction, jurisdiction over claims under Rule 10b-5 lies exclusively in the federal courts.[147] Another difference is that section 12(a)(2) extends relief only to buyers, while Rule 10b-5 affords a remedy to buyers and sellers alike.[148]

Because section 10(b) and Rule 10b-5 contain no damages provisions, the courts have drawn upon common law principles when assessing damages.[149] Punitive damages, however, are not recoverable.[150]

---

141. *See, e.g.,* Dirks v. SEC, 463 U.S. 646 (1983); Chiarella v. U.S., 445 U.S. 222, 228 (1980).
142. See Bateman Eichler, Hill Richards, Inc. v. Berner, 472 U.S. 299, 306-15 (1985).
143. *See* 15 U.S.C. § 78t; *Hollinger*, 914 F.2d at 1576-78 (section 20(a) of the 1934 Act supplements, rather than supplants, the common law theory of respondent superior as a basis for vicarious liability).
144. 511 U.S. 164 (1994).
145. *Id.* at 183.
146. Musick, Peeler & Garrett v. Employers Ins. of Wasau, 508 U.S. 286 (1993).
147. 15 U.S.C. § 78aa.
148. *See* Herman & MacLean v. Huddleston, 459 U.S. 375, 382 (1983) (purchasers as well as sellers may sue); Blue Chip Stamps v. Manor Drug Stores, 421 U.S. 723, 731-32 (1975).
149. *See, e.g.,* Randall v. Loftsgaarden, 478 U.S. 647, 661-64 (1986); *Affiliated Ute Citizens*, 406 U.S. at 154-55.
150. *See* 15 U.S.C. § 78bb(a); Osofsky v. Zipf, 645 F.2d 107, 111 (2d Cir. 1981); Myzel v. Fields, 386 F.2d 718, 748 (8th Cir. 1967).

The Supreme Court has adopted a uniform statute of limitations for private actions under Rule 10b-5, requiring that they be filed within one year after the plaintiff discovered the facts constituting the violation, and in no event more than three years after the violation, and holding that equitable tolling is not applicable to such actions.[151] Under section 804 of the Sarbanes-Oxley Act of 2002 ("SOX"),[152] Congress extended the statute of limitations for private rights of action that involve a claim of fraud, deceit, manipulation, or contrivance in contravention of a regulatory requirement concerning the securities laws. Section 804 of SOX added 28 U.S.C. § 1658(b), providing that such claims may be brought not later than the earlier of two years after discovery of the facts constituting the violation or, in no event more than five years after the violation.[153] This new limitations period applies to all proceedings commenced on or after July 30, 2002.[154]

3. *Section 18(a) of the Exchange Act*

Section 18(a) of the Exchange Act provides a private right of action to any person who purchases or sells a security at a price that was affected by a material misstatement or omission made in an application, report or document filed with the Securities and Exchange Commission.[155] Under section 18(a), a plaintiff may bring an action against any person who made, or caused to be made, such misstatement

---

151. Lampf, Pleva, Lipkind, Prupis & Petigrow v. Gilberton, 501 U.S. 350 (1991). Regarding when limitations begins to run under *Lampf's* one-year/three-year rule, *compare* Tregenza v. Great Am. Commc'ns Co., 12 F.3d 717 (7th Cir. 1993) (inquiry notice versus actual knowledge) *with* Dodds v. Signa Sec., Inc., 12 F.3d 346 (2d Cir. 1993) (one-year rule starts from inquiry or constructive notice). In response to *Lampf*, Congress enacted section 27A of the Securities Exchange Act, 15 U.S.C. § 78aa-1, which specifies limitations for actions filed on or before June 19, 1991. In Plaut v. Spendthrift Farm, Inc., 514 U.S. 211 (1995), the Supreme Court held that section 27A is unconstitutional to the extent it requires federal courts to reopen final judgments entered before its enactment. *Id.* at 225-26.
152. 15 U.S.C. § 7201, *et seq.*
153. Section 804(a)(2) of SOX, amending 28 U.S.C. § 1658.
154. Section 804(b) of SOX.
155. 15 U.S.C. § 78r; *see In re* Caesars Palace Sec. Litig., 360 F. Supp. 366 (S.D.N.Y. 1973) (omissions also state a claim under Section 18(a)).

or omission.[156] The plaintiff must establish both the materiality of the misstatement or omission and actual reliance on the filed document.[157] It is not enough to show that the misstatement or omission affected the market price of the security.[158] A plaintiff is not required to establish the defendant's scienter;[159] however, a statutory defense is available if the defendant can prove "that he acted in good faith and had no knowledge that such statement was false or misleading."[160] A private right of action under section 18 must be brought within one year after the plaintiff discovers the facts constituting the violation and, in no event more than three years after the violation.[161]

4. *RICO*

The Racketeer Influenced and Corrupt Organizations Act ("RICO")[162] was enacted as part of the Organized Crime Control Act of 1970.[163] Although RICO was designed primarily as a criminal statute, it also contains a private right of action,[164] which affords treble damages and attorneys' fees to any "person" (including a business entity) who suffers an injury to its business or property as a result of a violation of

---

156. 15 U.S.C. § 78r.
157. *Id; see* Ross v. A.H. Robbins Co., 607 F.2d 545, 552-53 (2d Cir. 1979); Heit v. Wietzen, 402 F.2d 909, 916 (2d Cir. 1968).
158. 15 U.S.C. § 78r.
159. *Id.*
160. 15 U.S.C. § 78r(a); *see Ross*, 607 F.2d at 556.
161. 15 U.S.C. § 78r(c).
162. 18 U.S.C. §§ 1961-1968.
163. Pub. L. No. 91-452, 84 Stat. 922. This discussion of RICO is not intended to be exhaustive. For general treatises on this topic, see DAVID R. MCCORMACK, RACKETEER INFLUENCED CORRUPT ORGANIZATIONS: CIVIL AND CRIMINAL (1988 & Supp. 2004); DAVID B. SMITH & TERRANCE G. REED, CIVIL RICO (2004).
164. 18 U.S.C. § 1964; *see* DAVID B. SMITH & TERRANCE G. REED, CIVIL RICO (2004); J. RAKOFF & H. GOLDSTEIN, RICO: CIVIL AND CRIMINAL, LAW AND STRATEGY (1989).

section 1962 of the statute.[165] Federal and state courts have concurrent jurisdiction over civil RICO claims.[166]

Section 1962 specifies four types of conduct that violate the statute. Subsection (a) declares it unlawful for a person who has received income from a "pattern of racketeering activity" or from the collection of an unlawful debt (*e.g.*, loan sharking) to use or invest that income in the acquisition, establishment or operation of an "enterprise." [167]

Subsection (b) makes it unlawful for a person to acquire or maintain an interest in, or control of, an enterprise through a pattern of racketeering activity or the collection of an unlawful debt.[168]

Subsection (c), which is the most frequently invoked provision, declares it unlawful for a person employed by or associated with an enterprise to conduct or participate in the conduct of the enterprise's affairs through a pattern of racketeering activity or the collection of an unlawful debt.[169]

Subsection (d) makes it unlawful for a person to conspire to violate subsections (a)-(c).[170]

Because the terms "enterprise" and "pattern of racketeering activity" have specific statutory meanings, they are briefly discussed below.

a.   "Enterprise"

Section 1961(4) defines an "enterprise" to include "any individual, partnership, corporation, association, or other legal entity, and any union or group of individuals associated in fact although not a legal entity."[171] In *United States v. Turkette*,[172] the Supreme Court held that a RICO enterprise can be either a legitimate or illegitimate entity or association, and that an enterprise is separate and distinct from the "pattern of

---

165. 18 U.S.C. § 1964(c); *see* 18 U.S.C. § 1961(3) (defining "person" as including "any individual or entity capable of holding a legal or beneficial interest in property").
166. Tafflin v. Levitt, 493 U.S. 455, 467 (1990).
167. 18 U.S.C. § 1962(a).
168. 18 U.S.C. § 1962(b).
169. 18 U.S.C. § 1962(c).
170. 18 U.S.C. § 1962(d).
171. *Id.* § 1961(4).
172. 452 U.S. 576 (1981).

racketeering activity."[173] There exists a split of authority in the federal circuit courts as to whether *Turkette* requires proof that a RICO enterprise have an "ascertainable structure" distinct from the associations necessary to conduct the pattern of racketeering activity.[174]

The existence of an enterprise may be proven "by evidence of an ongoing organization, formal or informal, and by evidence that the various associates function as a continuing unit."[175] Entities and groups considered "enterprises" for RICO purposes include such varied units as brokerage houses,[176] the office of the governor of a state,[177] a sheriff's department,[178] a corporation,[179] a group of corporations,[180] and a limited partnership,[181] among many others. It is generally recognized that the "culpable person" and "enterprise" cannot be the same for purposes of subsection 1962(c),[182] but may be the same for purposes of subsection 1962(a).[183]

b.   "Pattern of Racketeering"

---

173. *Id.* at 580-83.
174. *Compare, e.g.*, United States v. Bledsoe, 674 F.2d 647, 663-64 (8th Cir. 1982) (yes), *with* United States v. Patrick, 248 F.3d 11, 17-19 (1st Cir. 2001) (no).
175. *Turkette*, 452 U.S. at 583.
176. Muro v. E.F. Hutton, 643 F. Supp. 53, 63-66 (S.D.N.Y. 1986).
177. United States v. Thompson, 685 F.2d 993, 994 (6th Cir. 1982); *see also* United States v. Freeman, 6 F.3d 586, 596-97 (9th Cir. 1993) (offices of state assembly district constituted enterprise).
178. United States v. Thomas, 749 F. Supp. 847, 848-49 (M.D. Tenn. 1990).
179. 18 U.S.C. § 1961(4); Cedric Kushner Promotions, Ltd. v. King, 533 U.S. 158, 163-66 (2001); United States v. Feldman, 853 F.2d 648, 655-56 (9th Cir. 1988).
180. United States v. Huber, 603 F.2d 387, 393-94 (2d Cir. 1979); *see also* *Feldman*, 853 F.2d at 655-56; United States v. Thevis, 665 F.2d 616, 625 (5th Cir. 1982) (group of individuals associated with various corporations).
181. Eisenberg v. Gagnon, 564 F. Supp. 1347, 1353 (E.D. Pa. 1983).
182. *See, e.g.*, United States v. Goldin Indus., Inc., 219 F.3d 1268, 1270-71 (11th Cir. 2000); United States v. Computer Sciences Corp., 689 F.2d 1181, 1190 (4th Cir. 1982), *overruled en banc on other grounds by* Busby v. Crown Supply, Inc., 896 F.2d 833 (4th Cir. 1990).
183. *See, e.g.*, Busby v. Crown Supply, Inc., 896 F.2d 833, 840-42 (4th Cir. 1990); Haroco, Inc. v. Am. Nat'l Bank & Trust Co. of Chicago, 747 F.2d 384, 401-02 (7th Cir. 1984), *aff'd on other grounds*, 473 U.S. 606 (1985).

Section 1961 defines a "pattern of racketeering activity" as two or more acts of racketeering, one of which occurred after the passage of RICO and within ten years of the date of the other act of racketeering.[184] It is not necessary that the defendant have been convicted of the underlying predicate offenses.[185] The shorthand test for establishing a pattern of racketeering activity is described as "continuity plus relationship."[186] "Continuity" refers either to a closed period of repeated conduct, or to past conduct that by its nature projects into the future with a threat of repetition.[187] The term "relationship" refers to similarity of acts, victims, methods, or results, and is used to determine whether the conduct in question forms a criminal pattern.[188] Although the longer the scheme lasts, the greater the likelihood continuity will be found, schemes of short duration may qualify if the threat of continuing activity exists.[189]

Prior to 1993, the courts were divided over the issue of whether civil liability under section 1962(c) required proof of the defendant's "participation" in the operation or management of an enterprise.[190] In *Reves v. Ernst & Young*[191] the Supreme Court resolved this issue, holding that liability under section 1962(c) cannot be imposed absent proof that the defendant participated in the operation or management of the enterprise itself.[192]

As noted above, "racketeering activity," within the meaning of RICO, includes a host of statutory violations, including mail and wire

---

184. 18 U.S.C. § 1961(5).
185. Sedima, S.P.R.L. v. Imrex Co., 473 U.S. 479, 491-93 (1985).
186. *See* H.J. Inc. v. N.W. Bell Tel. Co., 492 U. S. 229, 239 (1989); *Sedima*, 473 U.S. at 496 n.14.
187. *H.J.*, 492 U.S. at 241.
188. *Id.* at 240-42.
189. *Id.* at 241-42.
190. *See, e.g.*, Bank of Am. Nat'l Trust & Sav. Ass'n v. Touche Ross & Co., 782 F.2d 966, 970 (11th Cir. 1986) (rejecting requirement); Bennett v. Berg, 710 F.2d 1361, 1364 (8th Cir. 1983) (en banc) (requiring participation).
191. 507 U.S. 170 (1993).
192. *Id.* at 183-84.

fraud.[193]   Although, prior to 1995 securities fraud also qualified as a predicate offense under RICO, the Private Securities Litigation Reform Act of 1995 amended section 1964(c) to provide that RICO is no longer available to redress conduct that is actionable under the federal securities laws, unless the defendant has been criminally convicted in connection with the fraud.[194]

A fraud claim under RICO differs from a state common law fraud claim. To prove fraud amounting to a RICO violation, there must be an enterprise, an effect upon interstate commerce, and two predicate offenses.[195]   When predicate acts such as mail or wire fraud are relied upon to establish the requisite pattern of racketeering activity, the elements of those offenses must be shown in addition to the other elements of a RICO claim.[196]

Generally, a RICO violation alleging one of these types of fraud as a predicate act requires proof that the claimed misrepresentation was false,[197] that the target of the fraud did in fact rely upon the misrepresentation,[198] and that the plaintiff sustained an injury.[199]   An intent to defraud also is a necessary element of this claim.[200] RICO does not require proof that either the enterprise or the predicate acts of racketeering were motivated by an economic purpose.[201]

---

193. 18 U.S.C. § 1961(1); *see* Lum v. Bank of Am., 361 F.3d 217, 223-27 (3d Cir. 2004).

194. 18 U.S.C. § 1964(c); *see* Bald Eagle Area Sch. Dist. v. Keystone Fin., Inc., 189 F.3d 321, 322-28 (3d Cir. 1999).

195. Zurkowsky v. Gov't Dev. Bank, 52 B.R. 1007, 1012 (D.P.R. 1985).

196. *See, e.g.*, Corcoran v. Am. Plan Corp., 886 F.2d 16, 19 (2d Cir. 1989); Ruffu v. Johnson & Johnson, Inc., 181 F.R.D. 341, 343 (E.D. Tex. 1998).

197. Penry v. Hartford Fire Ins. Co., 662 F. Supp. 792, 794 (E.D. Tex. 1987).

198. Summit Props. Inc. v. Hoechst Celanese Corp., 214 F.3d 556, 562 (5th Cir. 2000).

199. *Sedima*, 473 U.S. at 496; Kaiser Cement Corp. v. Fischbach & Moore, Inc., 793 F.2d 1100, 1104 (9th Cir. 1986).

200. St. Paul Mercury Ins. Co. v. Williamson, 224 F.3d 425, 441 (5th Cir. 2000).

201. National Org. for Women, Inc. v. Scheidler, 510 U.S. 249, 256-62 (1994).

c.   Remedies

As noted above, RICO provides that any person injured in his "business or property" by reason of a violation of section 1962 shall recover treble the damages he sustains and the cost of suit, including a reasonable attorneys' fee.[202] In interpreting this provision the Supreme Court has rejected the argument that recovery under RICO is limited to damages for "racketeering injury" akin to the "antitrust injury" required for recovery under the federal antitrust laws.[203] In *Sedima, S.P.R.L. v. Imrex Co.*,[204] the Court held that a RICO plaintiff has standing if he has been injured in his business or property by the predicate offenses that comprise the RICO violation.[205] In cases brought under section 1962(c), "the compensable injury necessarily is the harm caused by predicate acts sufficiently related to constitute a pattern, for the essence of the violation is the commission of those acts in connection with the conduct of the enterprise."[206] Accordingly, "[a]ny recoverable damages occurring by reason of a violation of § 1962(c) will flow from the commission of the predicate acts."[207]

Only those damages proximately caused by a violation of section 1962 may be recovered under RICO.[208] The "injury" for which a RICO plaintiff may recover is statutorily limited to an injury to his business or property;[209] thus, personal injury claims are excluded under the statute.[210] However, nothing in the statute requires that the protected property

---

202. 18 U.S.C. § 1964(c).
203. *Sedima*, 473 U.S. at 494-99; *cf.* Brunswick Corp. v. Pueblo Bowl-O-Mat, Inc., 429 U.S. 477, 489 (1977) (explaining "antitrust injury").
204. 473 U.S. 479.
205. *Id.* at 496-97.
206. *Id.* at 497.
207. Id.
208. Holmes v. Secs. Investor Prot. Corp., 503 U.S. 258, 265-68 (1992).
209. 18 U.S.C. § 1964(c); Bast v. Cohen, Dunn & Sinclair, PC, 59 F.3d 492, 495 (4th Cir. 1995).
210. *Bast*, 59 F.3d at 495; Doe v. Roe, 958 F.2d 763 (7th Cir. 1992); Gentry v. Resolution Trust Corp., 937 F.2d 899 (3d Cir. 1991).

interest be commercial,[211] although it does require that the property injury result in tangible financial loss to the plaintiff.[212]

RICO does not expressly afford a right to injunctive relief, and the courts are divided over whether such relief is available in the absence of such a statutory grant.[213]

The statute of limitations for civil RICO claims is four years from the accrual of the plaintiff's cause of action.[214] In *Rotella v. Wood*,[215] the Supreme Court held that the limitation period begins to run when the RICO plaintiff discovers or should have discovered the injury.[216] In a RICO case based on securities fraud with respect to which the defendant has been criminally convicted, limitations runs from the date on which the conviction becomes final.[217]

---

211. Oscar v. Univ. Students Co-op Ass'n, 939 F.2d 808, 811 (9th Cir. 1991), *rev'd en banc on other grounds*, 965 F.2d 783 (9th Cir. 1992).

212. Oscar v. Univ. Students Co-op Ass'n, 965 F.2d 783, 785 (9th Cir. 1992).

213. *Compare, e.g.*, National Org. of Women, Inc. v. Scheidler, 267 F.3d 687, 695-700 (7th Cir. 2001), *rev'd on other grounds*, 537 U.S. 393 (2003) (yes), *with* Religious Tech. Ctr. v. Wollersheim, 796 F.2d 1076, 1082-89 (9th Cir. 1986) (no).

214. Agency Holding Corp. v. Malley-Duff & Assocs., Inc., 483 U.S. 143, 146-57 (1987).

215. 528 U.S. 549, 558-60 (2000).

216. *See, e.g.*, Granite Falls Bank v. Henrickson, 924 F.2d 150, 151-52 (8th Cir. 1991); Bath v. Bushkin, Gaims, Gaines & Jonas, 913 F.2d 817, 820-21 (10th Cir. 1990); Bivens Gardens Office Bldg., Inc. v. Barnett Bank of Fla., 906 F.2d 1546, 1554-55 (11th Cir. 1990) (1991).

217. 18 U.S.C. § 1964(c).

CHAPTER VII

MISAPPROPRIATION OF TRADE SECRETS

*The alleged misappropriation by one competitor of the
trade secrets of another frequently gives rise to combined
antitrust/business tort litigation. As demonstrated in Chapter
1, although antitrust claims may arise out of predatory or
exclusionary conduct, mere proof of tortious conduct, standing
alone, is insufficient to establish an antitrust claim.
Nonetheless, proof of such conduct may be strong evidence of
predatory intent, and may support punitive damages awards
greatly in excess of the statutory treble damages allowed under
the antitrust laws. This chapter addresses the
misappropriation of confidential business information, or trade
secrets, by one competitor from another. – Eds.*

A. Introduction

State trade secret law is invoked to redress the misappropriation of
confidential business information that, although not patentable,
nonetheless qualifies for trade secret protection. The discussion that
follows examines the principles generally applicable to claims of trade
secret misappropriation as reflected in the Restatement (Third) of Unfair
Competition, the Uniform Trade Secrets Act and similar state statutes.[1]

B. Purposes of Trade Secret Protection

As the Supreme Court has acknowledged, "[t]he maintenance of
standards of commercial ethics and the encouragement of invention are

---

1. For a list of states that have adopted the Uniform Trade Secrets Act or a
    similar statute, *see* RESTATEMENT (THIRD) OF UNFAIR COMPETITION § 39,
    statutory note (1993) [hereinafter RESTATEMENT]; *see also* MILGRAM ON
    TRADE SECRETS (1991). Misappropriation of trade secrets also may give
    rise to criminal liability under state and federal statutes; *see, e.g.*, TEX.
    PENAL CODE ANN. § 31.05(b) (Vernon 1994); 18 U.S.C. §§ 1341, 1343
    (mail and wire fraud); National Stolen Property Act, 18 U.S.C. § 2314.

the broadly stated policies behind trade secret law."[2] The Court also recognized that, "[a] most human fundamental right, that of privacy, is threatened when industrial espionage is condoned or is made profitable."[3] Courts also emphasize that misappropriation is a violation of property rights,[4] and the Supreme Court has held that trade secrets recognized as property rights under state law are protected by the Taking Clause of the Fifth Amendment.[5] As one court has stated, "the theoretical basis for recovery on a trade secret claim is not merely the breach of a confidential relationship, but also the adverse use of the plaintiffs intellectual property."[6]

C. No Federal Preemption

Because the element of secrecy in trade secret law avoids concerns over state interference with the federal policy of free access to information in the public domain, neither the Patent Clause of the United States Constitution[7] nor the federal patent laws[8] preempts the state law of

2. Kewanee Oil Co. v. Bicron Corp., 416 U.S. 470, 481 (1974) (involving manufacturer of synthetic crystals seeking permanent injunction against company composed of former employees); *see also* Rockwell Graphic Sys., Inc. v. DEV Indus., Inc., 925 F.2d 174, 178 (7th Cir. 1991) (describing one concept of protection as "encouraging inventive activity by protecting [the owner's] fruits from efforts at appropriation that are . . . sterile wealth-distributive-not productive-activities."); CVD, Inc. v. Raytheon Co., 769 F.2d 842, 850 (1st Cir. 1985); Am. Can Co. v. Mansukhani, 742 F.2d 314, 329 (7th Cir. 1984); PepsiCo, Inc. v. Redmond, 54 F.3d 1262, 1268 (7th Cir. 1995) (quoting 2 Melvin F. Jager, TRADE SECRETS LAW § IL.01 [7], at IL-12 (1994)); A. F. Stoddard & Co., Ltd. v. Dann, 564 F.2d 556, 563, (D.C.Cir. 1977).

3. *Kewanee Oil*, 416 U.S. at 487 (citing Note, *Patent Preemption of Trade Secret Protection of Inventions Meeting Judicial Standards of Patentability*, 87 HARV. L. REV. 807, 828 (1974)).

4. Carpenter v. United States, 484 U.S. 19, 26 (1987); *see also* Ruckelshaus v. Monsanto Co., 467 U.S. 986, 1001-04 (1984); Chicago Lock Co. v. Fanberg, 676 F.2d 400, 404 (9th Cir. 1982); Scharmer v. Carrollton Mfg. Co., 525 F.2d 95, 99 (6th Cir. 1975).

5. *Ruckelshaus*, 467 U.S. at 1003-04.

6. Anaconda Co. v. Metric Tool & Die Co., 485 F. Supp. 410, 426 (E.D. Pa. 1980) (involving alleged misappropriation of profile and winding machine used in producing telephone cord armor).

7. U.S. CONST. art. I, § 8, cl. 8.

trade secrets.[9] Federal patent law may, however, preempt state laws that significantly interfere with the use of information that has been publicly disclosed or is readily ascertainable from public sources.[10]

When determining whether a trade secret claim is preempted, federal copyright law[11] requires careful examination of the facts of the particular case. The courts have employed two approaches when analyzing the preemption issue. The "extra element" test focuses on whether the trade secret claim simply is equivalent to a copyright claim, and therefore preempted.[12] Other courts emphasize the scope of protection under the copyright and trade secret laws to determine if a claim is preempted.[13]

D. "Trade Secret" Defined

Section 39 of the Restatement (Third) of Unfair Competition defines a trade secret as follows:

> A trade secret is any information that can be used in the operation of a business or other enterprise and that is sufficiently valuable and

---

8. 35 U.S.C. §§ 1-376.
9. Kewanee Oil Co. v. Bicron Corp., 416 U.S. 470, 493 (1974).
10. *See* Bonito Boats v. Thunder Craft Boats, Inc., 489 U.S. 141, 156-57 (1989); Vornado Air Circulation Sys., Inc. v. Duracraft Corp., 58 F.3d 1498, 1503 (10th Cir. 1995).
11. 17 U.S.C. §§ 101-1101.
12. *See, e.g.*, Trandes Corp. v. Guy F. Atkinson Co., 996 F.2d 655, 660 (4th Cir. 1993) (applying the "extra element" test to find that the breach of confidentiality qualitatively distinguishes trade secret misappropriation from copyright claims based solely on copying); Computer Assocs. Int'l v. Altai, Inc., 982 F.2d 693, 716-17 (2d Cir. 1992); Data Gen. Corp. v. Grumman Sys. Support Corp., 36 F.3d 1147, 1164 (1st Cir. 1994) (citing Gates Rubber Co. v. Bando Chem. Indus. Ltd., 9 F.3d 823, 846-47 (10th Cir. 1993).
13. *See, e.g.*, Warrington Assocs., Inc. v. Real-Time Eng. Sys., Inc., 522 F. Supp. 367, 368 (N.D. Ill. 1981) (holding claims for misappropriation of computer software were not preempted since copyright protection extends only to expression while trade secret protection extends to ideas); S. Mississippi Planning & Dev. Dist., Inc. v. Robertson, 660 F.Supp. 1057, 1061, (S.D.Miss. 1986).

secret to afford an actual or potential economic advantage over others.[14]

This definition appears to be somewhat broader than that set forth in the original Restatement of Torts, which described a trade secret as:

> any formula, pattern, device or compilation of information which is used in one's business, and which gives him an opportunity to obtain an advantage over competitors who do not know or use it. It may be a formula for a chemical compound, a process of manufacturing, treating or preserving materials, a pattern for a machine or other device, or a list of customers . . . .[15]

The new Restatement definition dispenses with a prior requirement (found in the comments to the Restatement entry) that the information be capable of "continuous use in the operation of a business";[16] accordingly, a trade secret may relate to transitory events such as "secret bids and impending business announcements or information whose secrecy is quickly destroyed by commercial exploitation."[17] Trade secret law has been applied to protect a wide variety of technology and business information, including products and processes,[18] computer programs,[19]

---

14. RESTATEMENT, *supra* note 1, § 39; *see also* Cook, Inc. v. Boston Scientific Corp., 206 F.R.D. 244, 248 (2001).

15. RESTATEMENT OF TORTS § 757 cmt. b (1939). This definition has been cited by the Supreme Court. Ruckelshaus v. Monsanto Co., 467 U.S. 986, 1001 (1984). It has also been formally embraced by other courts. See, e.g., Religious Tech. Ctr. v. Wollersheim, 796 F.2d 1076, 1089-90 (9th Cir. 1986); Apollo Techs. Corp. v. Centrosphere Indus. Corp., 805 F. Supp. 1157, 1197 (D.N.J. 1992); Plastic & Metal Fabricators v. Roy, 303 A.2d 725, 729 n.2 (Conn. 1972).

16. RESTATEMENT OF TORTS § 757 cmt. b (1939).

17. RESTATEMENT, *supra* note 1, § 39 cmt. d. The prior Restatement extended protection against the improper acquisition of such information "under rules virtually identical to those applicable to trade secrets." RESTATEMENT OF TORTS § 759 cmt. c (1939).

18. Salsbury Labs. v. Merieux Labs., 908 F.2d 706 (11th Cir. 1990) (poultry vaccine); Shamrock Techs., Inc. v. Med. Sterilization, Inc., 808 F. Supp. 932 (E.D.N.Y. 1992) (processing polytetrafluoroethylene), *aff'd*, 6 F.3d 788 (2d Cir. 1993); Union Carbide Corp. v. Tarancon Corp., 742 F. Supp. 1565 (N.D. Ga. 1990) (fluorination); Biodynamic Techs. v. Chattanooga Corp., 644 F. Supp. 607 (S.D. Fla. 1986) (orthopedic device); Dutch Cookie Mach. Co. v. Vande Vrede, 286 N.W. 612 (Mich. 1939).

customer and supplier lists,[20] financial information,[21] and business methods.[22] The existence of a trade secret is a question of fact.[23] As discussed below, it is not enough for a trade secret plaintiff to prove the existence of a trade secret and its possession by another; rather, a claim of misappropriation also requires proof of wrongful conduct.[24]

E. Elements of the Claim

The elements of a claim for misappropriation of trade secrets are:

(1) the defendant's wrongful acquisition of the plaintiff's trade secret, or

(2) the defendant's use or disclosure of the secret without the owner's consent, under circumstances placing the defendant on notice that the defendant acquired the secret (a) under a duty of confidence or through improper means, or (b) from or through a person who acquired it by improper means, or disclosed it in breach of a duty of confidence, or (c) through an accident or mistake, unless the acquisition was the result of the owner's failure to take reasonable precautions to protect the secret.[25]

---

19. MAI Sys. Corp. v. Peak Computer, Inc., 991 F.2d 511 (9th Cir. 1993); Integrated Cash Mgmt Servs., Inc. v. Digital Trans., Inc., 920 F.2d 171 (2d Cir. 1990); CMAX/Cleveland, Inc. v. UCR, Inc., 804 F. Supp. 337 (M.D. Ga. 1992); Gates Rubber Co. v. Bando Am., Inc., 798 F. Supp. 1499 (D. Colo. 1992), *modified*, 9 F.3d 823 (10th Cir. 1993); ISC-Bunker Ramo Corp. v. Altech, Inc., 765 F. Supp. 1310 (N.D. Ill. 1990).

20. Morton v. Rank Am., Inc., 812 F. Supp. 1062 (C.D. Cal. 1993); *In re* Alert Holdings, Inc., 148 B.R. 194 (Bankr. S.D.N.Y. 1992).

21. Sw. Whey, Inc. v. Nutrition 101, Inc., 117 F. Supp. 2d 770 (C.D. Ill. 2000); Revere Transducers, Inc. v. Deere & Co., 595 N.W.2d 751 (Iowa 1999); *In re* Urgent Med. Care, Inc., 153 B.R. 784 (Bankr. S.D. Ohio 1993).

22. Tan-Line Studios, Inc. v. Bradley, 1 U.S.P.Q.2d 2032 (E.D. Pa. 1986).

23. Chevron U.S.A., Inc. v. Roxen Serv., Inc., 813 F.2d 26, 29 (2d Cir. 1987) (New York law); Lear Siegler, Inc. v. Ark-Ell Springs, Inc., 569 F.2d 286, 288-89 (5th Cir. 1978) (Mississippi law). *Contra Rockwell*, 925 F.2d at 180 (Illinois law); Secure Servs. Tech., Inc. v. Time and Space Processing, Inc., 722 F. Supp. 1354, 1359 (E.D. Va. 1989) (California law).

24. *See generally* RESTATEMENT, *supra* note 1, § 39 cmt. b, § 40.

25. *See* RESTATEMENT, *supra* note 1, § 40; *see also* Hurst v. Hughes Tool Co., 634 F.2d 895, 896 (5th Cir. 1981) (no misappropriation of boron coatings

In order to support a claim for misappropriation, a trade secret plaintiff must sufficiently define the information allegedly deserving trade secret protection to enable the court to apply the foregoing criteria.[26] The purported trade secret must have some value and give the holder some advantage over those who do not possess it.[27] Further, the information sought to be protected must in fact be a secret,[28] and the defendant must know, or have reason to know, that it is a trade secret.[29]

It is not necessary that the information be wholly unknowable to others; it is sufficient that it is not readily ascertainable from other sources.[30]

---

in drill bits and wear surfaces when defendant asked plaintiff questions and plaintiff did not suggest that the information was confidential); RESTATEMENT OF TORTS § 757 (1939).

26. Trandes Corp. v. Guy F. Atkinson Co., 996 F.2d 655, 661-62 (4th Cir. 1993) (holding that plaintiff must allege more than that it has a secret, and must rely on more than conclusional allegations); *see* MAI Sys. Corp. v. Peak Computer, Inc., 991 F.2d 511, 522 (9th Cir. 1993) (vacating permanent injunction relating to computer software). CAL. CIV. PROC. CODE § 2019 ("The party alleging the misappropriation shall identify the trade secret with reasonable particularity.").

27. Ruckelshaus v. Monsanto Co., 467 U.S. 986, 1012 n.15 (1984) (holding that if the public disclosure of information reveals the harmful side effects of a product and profits subsequently decline, the information does not provide an advantage and there is no misappropriation of a trade secret); Phillips v. Frey, 20 F.3d 623, 628 (5th Cir. 1994); FMC Corp. v. Spurlin, 596 F. Supp. 609, 613 (W.D. Pa. 1984); Olson v. Nieman's Ltd., 579 N.W.2d 299, 314 (Iowa, 1998).

28. Kewanee Oil Co. v. Bicron Corp., 416 U.S. 470, 475 (1974); Picker Int'l v. Parten, 935 F.2d 257, 264 (11th Cir. 1991) (holding that information not secret when technical manuals were left with customers and training classes were attended by non-employees); Self Directed Placement Corp. v. Control Data Corp., 908 F.2d 462, 465 (9th Cir. 1990); Allied Supply Co. v. Brown, 585 So. 2d 33, 36 (Ala. 1991).

29. RESTATEMENT, *supra* note 1, § 40; Conmar Prods. Corp. v. Universal Slide Fastener Co., 172 F.2d 150 (2nd Cir. 1949).

30. Consol. Brands v. Mondi, 638 F. Supp. 152, 156 (E.D.N.Y. 1986) (holding that customer lists of fountain syrups manufacturer are not trade secrets because every soft drink seller is a potential customer); Barr-Mullin, Inc. v. Browning, 424 S.E.2d 226, 230 (N.C. App. 1993); Boeing Co. v. Sierracin

"Secrecy" in the context of trade secrets usually implies at least minimal novelty if only because, ordinarily, that which is not novel already is known.[31] Similarly, information, techniques or technologies that are generally known, in common use, or readily ascertainable by common means do not qualify as trade secrets.[32] Thus, if the "secret" information could be compiled from public sources, it will not be afforded protection.[33] However, a trade secret can exist in a combination of characteristics and components each of which, by itself, is in the public domain, if the unique combination of these elements provides a competitive advantage to the holder.[34] For example, in *BIEC International, Inc. v. Global Steel Services, Inc.*,[35] the plaintiff alleged misappropriation of its aluminum-zinc technology, along with its manuals, mailing lists, terms of licenses agreements, and marketing information. Rejecting the defendant's contention that the information was public knowledge, the court found that although the plaintiff's

---

Corp., 738 P.2d 665, 674 (Wash. 1987); ILG Indus., Inc. v. Scott, 273 N.E.2d 393, 396 (Ill. 1971).

31. *Kewanee Oil*, 416 U.S. at 476 (citing Comment, *The Stiffel Doctrine and the Law of Trade Secrets*, 62 Nw. U.L. Rev 956, 969 (1968)); Mitchell Novelty Co. v. United Mfg. Co., 199 F.2d 462, 465 (7th Cir. 1952); Dionne v. Se. Form Converting & Packaging, Inc., 397 S.E.2d 110, 113 (Va. 1990).

32. Computer Care v. Service Sys. Enters., 982 F.2d 1063, 1072 (7th Cir. 1992) (finding, *inter alia*, that use of a follow-up letter to a customer who does not respond to a repair shop's service reminder letter and automatically removing non-responding customers from a database are not novel ideas, and thus do not warrant trade secret protection); Coenco, Inc. v. Coenco Sale Inc., 940 F.2d 1176, 1179 (8th Cir. 1991) (plaintiff offered no evidence that elements of chicken coop are not readily ascertainable by proper means); Pub. Sys., Inc. v. Towry, 587 So.2d 969, 971-72 (Ala. 1991).

33. *See* Union Sav. Am. Life Ins. Co. v. North Cent. Life Ins. Co., 813 F. Supp. 481, 494 (S.D. Miss. 1993); Nat'l Instrument Labs., Inc. v. Hycel, Inc., 478 F. Supp. 1179, 1183 (D. Del. 1979); Picker Int'l Inc. v. Parten, 935 F.2d 257, 264 (11th Cir. 1991).

34. Apollo Techs. Corp. v. Centrosphere Indus. Corp., 805 F. Supp. 1157, 1197 (D.N.J. 1992); Computer Assocs. Int'l v. Bryan, 784 F. Supp. 982, 988 (E.D.N.Y. 1992); Integrated Cash Mgmt. Servs., Inc. v. Digital Transactions, Inc., 920 F.2d 171, 174 (2nd Cir. 1990).

35. 791 F. Supp. 489 (E.D. Pa. 1992).

parameters and procedures were in the public domain,[36] the precise "configuration, juxtaposition, and assemblage" of the information was entitled to trade secret protection.[37]

The relevant factors in determining whether information qualifies as a trade secret include the extent to which the information is known outside of the plaintiff's business, the extent to which it is known by employees and others involved in the business, the extent of the measures taken to guard the secrecy of the information, the value of the information to the plaintiff and his competitors, the amount of money and effort expended to develop the information, and the ease or difficulty with which the information could be duplicated or acquired by proper means.[38] The existence of an agreement between a plaintiff and defendant characterizing the information as a trade secret is an important factor in analyzing whether a trade secret exists, but is not determinative.[39]

Although a trade secret holder has a duty to take reasonable steps to ensure the secrecy of the trade secret,[40] absolute secrecy is not required to obtain protection.[41] The holder of a trade secret may divulge his information to a limited extent without destroying its status as a trade secret, such as disclosure to others in furtherance of the holder's economic interests.[42] Thus, the necessary element of secrecy is not lost

---

36. *Id.* at 540-41.
37. *Id.* at 543.
38. Baxter Int'l v. Morris, 976 F.2d 1189, 1193 (8th Cir. 1992) (quoting Nat'l Rejectors, Inc. v. Trieman, 409 S.W.2d 1, 19 (Mo. 1966) (en banc)); Wilson v. Electro Marine Sys., Inc., 915 F.2d 1110, 1115 (7th Cir. 1990); Licata & Co. v. Goldberg, 812 F. Supp. 403, 410 (S.D.N.Y. 1993); *BIEC Int'l*, 791 F. Supp. at 539.
39. *See* Gary Van Zeeland Talent, Inc. v. Sandas, 267 N.W.2d 242, 250 (Wis. 1978) ("While a declaration that the [information] is of value may have some persuasiveness in showing that the employer attempted to keep the [information] a secret, it is the public's right to have reasonable competition . . . .").
40. E.I. duPont deNemours & Co. v. Christopher, 431 F.2d 1012, 1015-16 (5th Cir. 1970).
41. When in litigation, a trade secret holder should obtain a protective order to restrict access to the secret. *See* Seattle Times Co. v. Rhinehart, 467 U.S. 20, 34 (1984).
42. Metallurgical Indus. v. Fourtek, Inc., 790 F.2d 1195, 1200 (5th Cir. 1986).

if the holder of the trade secret reveals it to another in confidence. A duty of confidence arises if (1) an express promise of confidentiality was made prior to the disclosure of the trade secret; or (2) disclosure occurred under circumstances in which the relationship between the parties justified the conclusion that at the time the disclosure was made, the recipient knew or had reason to know the disclosure was intended to be in confidence, and the disclosing party reasonably implied an agreement to an obligation of confidentiality.[43] The element of secrecy is not lost by sharing the trade secret with employees in whom it is necessary to confide the secret in order to apply it to the uses for which it is intended.[44] Employees or former employees who use or disclose the trade secrets of their employers or former employers in violation of their duties of confidence are subject to liability under section 40 of the Restatement.[45]

Some jurisdictions hold that if the information is acquired and used in a manner that breaches a confidential relationship, liability will attach irrespective of whether the information could have been acquired lawfully.[46] A third party who knowingly benefits from a trade secret obtained by a person in a confidential relationship with the plaintiff is liable to the plaintiff for misappropriation.[47]

The "improper means" of trade secret acquisition prohibited by section 40 of the Restatement include:

> theft, fraud, unauthorized interception of communications, inducement of or knowing participation in a breach of confidence, and other means either wrongful in themselves or wrongful under the circumstances of the case. Independent discovery and analysis of

---

43. RESTATEMENT, *supra* note 1, § 41.
44. Kewanee Oil Co. v. Bicron Corp., 416 U.S. 470, 475 (1974) (citing Cincinnati Bell Foundry Co. v. Dodds, 10 Ohio Dec. Reprint 154, 156 (Super. Ct. 1887)); *see also* Phillips v. Frey, 20 F.3d 623, 629 (5th Cir. 1994).
45. RESTATEMENT, *supra* note 1, § 42.
46. *See* Jeter v. Associated Rack Corp., 607 S.W.2d 272, 276 (Tex. App. 1980).
47. Baystate Techs., Inc. v. Bentley Sys., Inc., 946 F.Supp. 1079, 1091 (D.Mass. Dec 06, 1996) (citing Data Gen. Corp. v. Grumman Sys. Support Corp., 795 F. Supp. 501, 507 (D. Mass. 1992), *aff'd* 36 F.3d 1147 (1st Cir. 1994).

publicly available products or information are not improper means of acquisition.[48]

Unlike patents, trade secrets are not protected from use by others absent breach of confidence or knowing reliance on the breach of confidence of another.[49] Thus, trade secret law does not offer protection against discovery by fair and honest means, such as independent investigation, accidental disclosure or reverse engineering.[50]

Section 40 of the Restatement does not limit improper "use" of trade secrets to the sale of goods. Therefore, "any exploitation of the trade secret that is likely to result in injury to the trade secret owner or enrichment to the defendant is a 'use' under [section 40]."[51] A defendant need not improperly use all of the trade secret in order to be found liable; rather, use of "any substantial portion," or even a modified version, is sufficient.[52] Evidence of improper use arises from likeness among products and a disclosure to the defendant.[53] However, the composition

---

48.   RESTATEMENT, *supra* note 1, § 43.
49.   Servo Corp. of Am. v. Gen. Elec. Co., 393 F.2d 551, 555 (4th Cir. 1968); Licata & Co. v. Goldberg, 812 F. Supp. 403, 409 (S.D.N.Y. 1993).
50.   Kewanee Oil Co. v. Bicron Corp., 416 U.S. 470, 489-90 (1974); Bonito Boats v. Thunder Craft Boats, Inc., 489 U.S. 141, 160 (1989); Apollo Techs. Corp. v. Centrosphere Indus. Corp., 805 F. Supp. 1157, 1197-98 n. 53 (D.N.J. 1992); Merchant & Evans, Inc. v. Roosevelt Bldg. Prods. Co., 963 F.2d 628, 638 (3d Cir. 1992); Radioptics, Inc. v. U.S., 621 F.2d 1113, 1129 (Ct. Cl. 1980).
51.   RESTATEMENT, *supra* note 1, § 40 cmt. c; *see also* Metallurgical Indus. Inc. v. Fourtek, Inc., 790 F.2d 1195, 1205 (5th Cir. 1986); Johnson v. Benjamin Moore & Co., 788 A.2d 906, 914 (N.J. App. Div. 2002).
52.   *Id. See In re* Innovative Constr. Sys., Inc., 793 F.2d 875, 886-87 (7th Cir. 1986) (finding misappropriation of brick paneling although the original concept had been modified due to climate and availability of raw materials); Sikes v. McGraw-Edison Co., 665 F.2d 731, 734-35 (5th Cir. 1982) (holding defendant liable despite the use of a different method of attaching nylon to the end of the wand of a power lawn trimmer); Reingold v. Swiftships, Inc., 126 F.3d 645, 651 (5th Cir. 1997); Mangren Research and Dev. Corp. v. Nat'l Chem. Co., 87 F.3d 937 (7th Cir. 1996).
53.   Phillips v. Frey, 20 F.3d 623, 628 (5th Cir. 1994) (finding evidence of misappropriation of a manufacturing process from defendant's testimony that he did not know how to mass produce deer stands prior to touring plaintiff's business and reviewing a videotape sent to defendant by

of the public domain must be examined when comparing the similarity of products.[54]

F. Defenses

Several defenses are available in trade secret litigation. The most commonly invoked are that (1) the "trade secret" was readily ascertainable from information in the public domain;[55] (2) the defendant independently developed the information claimed to be a trade secret;[56] (3) the plaintiff did not take adequate steps to ensure the confidentiality of the secret;[57] and (4) the secret was abandoned.[58] The existence of a privilege to disclose trade secrets has been asserted as a defense,[59] as has

---

plaintiff); Smith v. Dravo Corp., 203 F.2d 369, 377 (7th Cir. 1953) (finding evidence of misappropriation from showing that defendant did not begin design of a freight container until after it had access to plaintiff's plans during purchase negotiations).

54. *See, e.g.*, Am. Can Co. v. Mansukhani, 742 F.2d 314, 329-30 (7th Cir. 1984); Berry v. Glidden Co., 92 F. Supp. 909, 914 (S.D. N.Y. 1950) (finding no liability because most of the ingredients in a wood finishing formula were common knowledge in the trade, and the only unique feature was known to the defendant prior to disclosure).

55. Boeing Co. v. Sierracin Corp., 738 P.2d 665, 674 (Wash. 1987); Data Gen. Corp. v. Digital Computer Controls, 297 A.2d 437, 438 (Del. 1972); *see also* Machen, Inc. v. Aircraft Design, Inc., 828 P.2d 73, 77 (Wash. Ct. App. 1992).

56. RTE Corp. v. Coatings, Inc., 267 N.W.2d 226, 232 (Wis. 1978).

57. Rockwell Graphic Sys., Inc. v. DEV Indus., Inc., 925 F.2d 174, 180 (7th Cir. 1991); Defiance Button Mach. Co. v. C & C Metal Prods., 759 F.2d 1053, 1063 (2d Cir. 1985); Learning Curve Toys, Inc., v. Playwood Toys, Inc., 342 F.3d 714 (7th Cir. 2003); Pioneer Hi-Bred Int'l v. Holden Found. Seeds, Inc., 35 F.3d 1226, 1236 (8th Cir. 1994); United States v. Lange, 312 F.3d 263, 266 (7th Cir. 2002).

58. Drill Parts & Serv. Co. v. Joy Mfg. Co., 439 So.2d 43, 49 (Ala. 1983), *superseded by statute*, Allied Supply Co. v. Brown, 585 So. 2d 33, 36 n. 3 (Ala. 1991).

59. *See, e.g.*, Sys. Operations, Inc. v. Scientific Games Dev. Corp., 425 F. Supp. 130 (D.N.J. 1977) (state lottery official could disclose trade secrets relating to security of lottery tickets).

the absence of actual or constructive knowledge that the disclosure or use was wrongful.[60]

Information is readily ascertainable if it is available in trade journals, reference books or other published materials.[61] A defendant claiming independent development bears the burden of proving that fact.[62] Trade secret protection terminates upon disclosure of the protected information in a patent.[63] Related information that is not disclosed, however, remains protectable.[64]

G. Remedies

In most business tort litigation, the principal relief sought is monetary damages. Not so in trade secret litigation. Particularly in cases where the defendant is accused of spiriting away the plaintiff's employees and stealing its technology, the preferred remedy is to seek an

---

60. *See, e.g.*, Amberley Co. v. Brown Co., 408 F.2d 1358, 1361-62 (6th Cir. 1969) (finding no liability when defendant was assured that the third party disclosing the process was not in a confidential relationship with the plaintiff and that the prowess was already in the public domain); Constr. Tech. v. Lockformer Co., 704 F. Supp. 1212, 1226 (S.D.N.Y. 1989) (finding no misappropriation where plaintiff failed to allege defendant had notice that information it received from a third party was confidential).

61. T.P. Labs. v. Huge, 261 F. Supp. 349, 358-59 (E.D. Wis. 1965), *aff'd*, 371 F.2d 231 (7th Cir. 1966); Pezrow Corp. v. Seifert, 602 N.Y.S.2d 468, 469 (N.Y. App. 1993); Pub. Sys., Inc. v. Towry, 587 So.2d 969 (Ala.1991); Dynamics Research Corp. v. Analytic Sci. Corp., 400 N.E.2d 1274 (Mass. Ap. Ct. 1980); Van Prods. Co. v. Gen. Welding and Fabricating Co., 213 A.2d 769 (Pa. 1965); Microbiological Research Corp. v. Muna, 625 P.2d 690 (Utah 1981).

62. Integrated Cash Mgmt Servs., Inc. v. Digital Trans., Inc., 732 F.Supp 370, 377-78 (S.D.N.Y. 1989); Henry Hope X-Ray Prods., Inc. v. Marron Carrel, Inc., 674 F.2d 1336, 1341 (9th Cir. 1982); Norbrook Labs. Ltd. v. G.C. Hanford Mfg. Co., 297 F. Supp. 2d 463 (N.D. N.Y. 2003).

63. Midland-Ross Corp. v. Sunbeam Equip. Corp., 316 F. Supp. 171, 177 (W.D. Pa. 1970), *aff'd*, 435 F.2d 159 (3d Cir. 1970); Arco Indus. Corp. v. Chemcast Corp. 633 F.2d 435; 443 (6th Cir. 1980); *see* Shamrock Techs., Inc. v. Med. Sterilization, Inc., 808 F. Supp. 932, 938 (E.D.N.Y. 1992).

64. Henry Hope X-Ray Prods., Inc. v. Marron Carrel, Inc., 674 F.2d 1336, 1342 (9th Cir. 1982); *see* Christianson v. Colt Indus. Operating Corp., 870 F.2d 1292, 1303 (7th Cir. 1989).

injunction prohibiting further use or disclosure.[65] Courts also have issued injunctions to prevent threatened use or disclosure of trade secrets.[66] Generally, a substantial threat of injury must exist before the remedy of injunction will issue-mere suspicion or apprehension of injury is not sufficient.[67] However, under certain circumstances a court may find that future disclosure of trade secrets simply is inevitable, and grant an injunction. In *FMC Corporation v. Varco International, Inc.*,[68] the plaintiff filed suit to prevent its former engineering manager from disclosing trade secrets regarding an "increased-radius swivel joint" to his new employer, one of the plaintiff's competitors. The former employee was hired by the defendant as vice-president of manufacturing, and would be directly involved in the development of a swivel joint. In reversing the trial court and granting an injunction, the Fifth Circuit concluded that, "[e]ven assuming the best of good faith," the former employee would have difficulty separating his knowledge gained while employed by the plaintiff from his work for the defendant.[69]

A defendant may be enjoined from using a trade secret and anything that is substantially derived from the secret.[70] An injunction should not unnecessarily enjoin the use of information that is beyond the scope of

---

65. *See generally* MILGRAM ON TRADE SECRETS § 7.08[1] (1991).
66. Baxter Int'l v. Morris, 976 F.2d 1189, 1194 (8th Cir. 1992); Allis-Chalmers Mfg. Co. v. Cont'l Aviation & Eng'g. Corp., 255 F. Supp. 645, 654 (E.D. Mich. 1966); Den-Tal-Ez, Inc. v. Siemens Capital Corp., 9 U.S.P.Q.2d 1932, 1944 (Pa. Super. 1988).
67. *Allis-Chalmers*, 255 F. Supp. at 654, *see also* Pepsico, Inc. v. Redmond, 54 F.3d 1262 (7th Cir. 1995); Campbell Soup Co. v. ConAgra, Inc., 977 F.2d 86, 93 (3d Cir. 1992).
68. 677 F.2d 500 (5th Cir. 1982).
69. *Id.* at 504-05; *accord Allis-Chalmers*, 255 F. Supp. at 654; *see also* Weed Eater, Inc. v. Dowling, 562 S.W.2d 898, 902 (Tex. App. 1978) ("[t]he only effective relief for [plaintiff] is to restrain [the former employee] from working for [defendant] in any capacity relating to the manufacture [by defendant of the product in question].").
70. Motorola, Inc. v. Computer Displays Int'l, 739 F.2d 1149, 1156 (7th Cir. 1984) (enjoining defendant from selling display monitors substantially like a model manufactured by plaintiff).

the trade secret.[71] Therefore, an injunction should not continue beyond the time the defendant could have acquired the information through appropriate means.[72] Moreover, an injunction protecting trade secret information must be sufficiently definite to give fair notice to the defendant of the conduct that is prohibited.[73] In *E. W. Bliss Company v. Struthers-Dunn, Inc.*,[74] the Eighth Circuit set aside a temporary injunction prohibiting disclosure of trade secrets involving solid-state control systems. The district court's injunction stated in part, "[a]ll defendants separately and jointly are restrained from using or disclosing trade secrets and confidential information of plaintiff to any person, firm or corporation."[75] The court of appeals found the injunction overly vague, placing the burden of reaching an erroneous legal conclusion as to whether a design concept was a trade secret on the defendants.[76] The court noted that according to the injunction as written, one defendant would be presumed to know all of the plaintiff's confidential technical information.[77]

As noted above, an injunction is not available once the trade secret has been disclosed by way of a patent.[78] However, where the public disclosure of a trade secret results from the actions of the defendant, rather than the plaintiff, several courts have held that the defendant should not be permitted to rely upon the loss of secrecy to avoid an

---

71. Sigma Chem. Co. v. Harris, 794 F.2d 371, 375 (8th Cir. 1986), *aff'd without opinion*, 855 F.2d 856 (8th Cir. 1988); Am. Can Co. v. Mansukhani, 742 F.2d 314, 333 (7th Cir. 1984).

72. Lamb-Weston, Inc. v. McCain Foods, Ltd., 941 F.2d 970, 974 (9th Cir. 1991) (holding that eight month injunction regarding the manufacture of curlicue french fries was proper); *Sigma Chemical*, 794 F.2d at 375 (holding that injunction unlimited as to time enjoining employee from disclosing trade secrets was improper); *see also* SI Handling Sys., Inc. v. Heisley, 753 F.2d 1244, (3d Cir. 1985).

73. *Am. Can*, 742 F.2d at 332.

74. 408 F.2d 1108 (8th Cir. 1969).

75. *Id.* at 1113.

76. *Id.* at 1114; *accord* 3M v. Pribyl, 259 F.3d 587, 597-98 (7th Cir. 2001).

77. *Id.* The court further found that the injunction prohibited lawful competition by the defendant. *Id.* at 1115.

78. *See supra* text accompanying note 63; Conmar Prods. Corp. v. Universal Slide Fastener Co., 172 F.2d 150, 155 (2d Cir. 1949); Midland-Ross Corp. v. Sunbeam Equip. Corp., 316 F. Supp. 171, 177-78 (W.D. Pa. 1970).

injunction for the period of time it would have taken the defendant to acquire the information by proper means.[79]

The courts have exercised considerable flexibility in determining appropriate formulae for awarding monetary relief in trade secret actions.[80] The proper measure of money damages for misappropriation of trade secrets has been variously held to be the plaintiff's lost profits;[81] the defendant's profits gained from the misappropriation;[82] the greater of the plaintiff's lost profits or the defendant's gain;[83] or the fair market value of the use of the information at the time of the misappropriation.[84] At least one court has held that recovery of damages for both lost profits and unjust enrichment does not constitute an impermissible double recovery.[85] In an appropriate case, both actual and punitive damages are commonly available.[86]

---

79. Lamb-Weston, Inc. v. McCain Foods, Ltd., 941 F.2d 970, 975 (9th Cir. 1991); Aerosonic Corp. v. Trodyne Corp., 402 F.2d 223, 227 (5th Cir. 1968).

80. Univ. Computing Co. v. Lykes-Youngstown Corp., 504 F.2d 518, 538 (5th Cir. 1974).

81. Hayes-Alhion v. Kuberski, 311 N.W.2d 122, 127-29 (Mich. Ct. App. 1981), *modified*, 364 N.W.2d 609 (Mich. 1984).

82. Reinforced Molding Corp. v. Gen. Elec. Co., 592 F. Supp. 1083, 1088 (W.D. Pa. 1984).

83. Clark v. Bunker, 453 F.2d 1006, 1011 (9th Cir. 1972).

84. *University Computing*, 504 F.2d at 539.

85. Telex Corp. v. IBM Corp., 510 F.2d 894, 931-32 (10th Cir. 1975).

86. Elec. Data Sys. Corp. v. Sigma Sys. Corp., 500 F.2d 241, 245-46 (5th Cir); Mason v. Jack Daniel Distillery, 518 So.2d 130, 135 (Ala. Civ. App. 1987); Centrol, Inc. v. Morrow, 489 N.W.2d 890, 896 (S.D. 1992).

CHAPTER VIII

LIMITATIONS ON PUNITIVE DAMAGES

Among all of the reasons offered for the popularity of business torts over time, perhaps none has been more often cited than the availability of punitive damages. With the increased frequency and magnitude of punitive damages claims, however, have come increased limitations upon punitive awards, most notably by the U.S. Supreme Court, including its most recent decision in State Farm Mutual Automobile Insurance Co. v. Campbell. Legislative efforts at tort reform both pre- and post-Campbell impose additional limitations on punitive damages. This chapter examines the important Supreme Court decisions on the issue of punitive damages, as well as efforts by the lower federal courts, state courts, and legislatures to define the standards under which punitive damages may be imposed. – Eds.

A. Introduction

This Chapter reviews the historical forces that have influenced this area of law and analyzes the various Supreme Court decisions and significant state rulings and statutory responses that define the law of punitive damages as it exists today.

B. The Nature and Purpose of Punitive Damages

The Supreme Court's jurisprudence in this area is driven by the fundamental difference between compensatory and punitive damages. Whether cast as general or special, compensatory damages "are intended to redress the concrete loss that the plaintiff has suffered by reason of the defendant's wrongful conduct."[1] Punitive damages, by contrast, are designed for deterrence and punishment.[2]

---

1. State Farm Mut. Auto. Ins. Co. v. Campbell, 538 U.S. 408, 416 (2003) (internal quotations marks omitted), on remand at Campbell v. State Farm

As the concept of compensatory damages has evolved over the years to include compensation for intangible injuries, the concept of punitive damages has evolved as well. The English Courts of the 18th Century resorted to the doctrine of exemplary (or punitive) damages to authorize monetary awards exceeding a party's tangible harm, explaining that such awards were justified as compensation for mental suffering, wounded dignity, and injured feelings.[3] As late as the middle of the 20th Century, several American states still viewed punitive damages as a means of compensating a party for intangible injury not accounted for in the legal measure of compensatory damages.[4]

Today, punitive damages are not required to compensate a litigant. Because compensatory damages now redress intangible harms such as pain and suffering, and intentional, or even negligent, infliction of emotional distress,[5] "it should be presumed a plaintiff has been made whole for his injuries by compensatory damages."[6] "As the types of compensatory damages available to plaintiffs have broadened, . . . the theory behind punitive damages has shifted toward a more purely punitive (and therefore less factual) understanding."[7] Consequently, it is now well-established that compensatory and punitive damages serve distinct purposes.[8] Rather than serving as a determination of intangible harm suffered by a party, "[p]unitive damages serve a broader function; they are aimed at deterrence and retribution."[9]

Mut. Auto. Ins. Co., 98 P.3d 409 (Utah 2004); Cooper Indus., Inc. v. Leatherman Tool Group, Inc., 532 U.S. 424, 432 (2001).

2. *Campbell*, 538 U.S. at 416.
3. Note, *Exemplary Damages in the Law of Torts*, 70 HARV. L. REV. 517, 519 (1957).
4. *Id.* at 520 and n.32.
5. *Cf.* Bogle v. McClure, 332 F.3d 1347, 1358-59 (11th Cir. 2003), *cert. dismissed*, 124 S. Ct. 1168 (2004).
6. *Campbell*, 538 U.S. at 419.
7. *Cooper Indus., Inc.*, 532 U.S. at 437 n.11.
8. *Id.* at 432.
9. *Campbell*, 538 U.S. at 416; Pac. Mut. Life Ins. Co. v. Haslip, 499 U.S. 1, 19 (1991); *Cooper Indus., Inc.*, 532 U.S. at 432.

C.   Supreme Court Jurisprudence Before Campbell

1.   *Eighth Amendment*

The Eighth Amendment provides that "[e]xcessive bail shall not be required, nor excessive fines imposed, nor cruel and unusual punishments inflicted."[10]   However, while punitive damages are imposed through the authority of courts, serve to advance governmental interests in punishment and deterrence,[11] and have been described as a quasi-criminal punishment[12] and a type of "private fine,"[13] the Excessive Fines Clause of the Eighth Amendment is not a meaningful restraint on either the availability or amount of punitive damages.

The Supreme Court addressed this issue in *Browning-Ferris Industries of Vermont, Inc. v. Kelco Disposal, Inc.*[14]   In *Kelco*, a Vermont waste-disposal company sued a national waste-disposal giant in federal district court, alleging attempted monopolization in violation of the Sherman Act and interference with contract under Vermont common law. The jury found in favor of the plaintiff on both claims and awarded $51,146 in compensatory damages and $6 million in punitive damages. On appeal, the defendant challenged the punitive award as violative of the Excessive Fines Clause. The Second Circuit rejected this argument, and the Supreme Court agreed.

The Court unanimously held that the Excessive Fines Clause does not apply to awards of punitive damages in cases between private parties where the government has neither prosecuted the action nor has any right to receive a share of the award.[15]   The Court explained that the primary purpose of the Eighth Amendment is to prevent the government from abusing its prosecutorial power, rather than to limit the amount of civil damages or to prescribe the purposes for which they may be awarded.[16] Noting that the history of the Eighth Amendment provides convincing evidence that the Excessive Fines Clause was intended to limit only

---

10.   U.S. CONST. amend. VIII.
11.   *Cooper Indus., Inc.*, 532 U.S. at 432; Browning-Ferris Indus. of Vt., Inc. v. Kelco Disposal, Inc., 492 U.S. 257, 268, 275 (1989).
12.   *Haslip*, 499 U.S. at 19.
13.   *Cooper Indus., Inc.*, 532 U.S. at 432.
14.   492 U.S. 257 (1989).
15.   *Id.* at 266.
16.   *Id.*

those fines directly imposed by, and payable to, the government, the Court concluded that the fact that punitive damages are imposed through the authority of courts and serve to advance governmental interests in punishment and deterrence is insufficient to support the application of the Excessive Fines Clause to a case involving private parties.[17]

Notwithstanding *Kelco*, however, there may be circumstances under which the Excessive Fines Clause will limit punitive damages awards. As discussed later in this chapter, several states now require by statute that portions of certain punitive damages awards be remitted to the state – and there are cases in which the government, as a plaintiff, seeks the recovery of punitive damages. The Supreme Court has left open the question of whether punitive damages awards in these types of cases must comply with the Eighth Amendment.[18]

2. *Due Process Jurisprudence, Circa 1991-1994*

Under the Due Process Clause of the Fourteenth Amendment, no state shall "deprive any person of life, liberty, or property, without due process of law."[19] Because the imposition of punitive damages "is an exercise of state power,"[20] an award of punitive damages must comply with both the procedural and substantive protections of the Due Process Clause.[21] In three cases decided in 1991, 1993, and 1994, the Supreme Court analyzed the common law approach to the assessment of punitive

---

17. *Id.* at 268, 275.
18. *See, e.g., id. at* 263-64 ("Whatever the outer confines of the Clause's reach may be, we now decide only that it does not constrain an award of money damages in a civil suit when the government neither has prosecuted the action nor has any right to receive a share of the damages awarded."); *Cooper Indus., Inc.*, 532 U.S. at 424-25; *see also* Watson v. Johnson Mobile Homes, 284 F.3d 568, 572 (5th Cir. 2002) ("The imposition of punitive damages under state law is constrained by the Eighth and Fourteenth Amendments, the first proscribing excessive fines and cruel and unusual punishment, the second making grossly excessive punishments unlawful under its Due Process Clause.").
19. U.S. CONST. amend. XIV, § 1.
20. Honda Motor Co. v. Oberg, 512 U.S. 415, 434-35 (1994); BMW of N. Am., Inc. v. Gore, 517 U.S. 559, 572 n.17 (1996).
21. *Oberg*, 512 U.S. at 434-45.

damages and held that, if followed, the common law approach comports with the requirements of procedural due process.[22]

3.   *Haslip*

The *Kelco* court declined to address the defendant's argument that the punitive award in that case was excessive under the Due Process Clause of the Fourteenth Amendment, finding that the defendant had waived that argument by failing to raise it in the courts below.[23]   The Supreme Court addressed this issue two years later in *Haslip*.

Pacific Mutual Life Insurance Co. v. Haslip[24] arose out of the misappropriation of insurance premiums by an individual insurance agent, resulting in the lapse of health insurance policies issued to a group of Alabama municipal employees.   The employees sued the agent for fraud and sought to hold Pacific Mutual liable under the theory of respondeat superior.[25]   A jury found both the agent and Pacific Mutual liable to the employees and awarded to Haslip compensatory damages in the amount of $200,000 (including out-of-pocket expenditures of less than $4,000) and punitive damages in the amount of $840,000.[26]   Pacific Mutual appealed, and the verdict was upheld by the Supreme Court of Alabama.   Pacific Mutual then appealed to the U.S. Supreme Court, arguing that the punitive damages award violated the Fourteenth Amendment's Due Process Clause.[27]

The Supreme Court held the amount of punitive damages did not violate the Due Process Clause.   The Court recognized that the punitive award was more than four times the total amount of compensatory damages, more than 200 times the out-of-pocket expenses of the employee who had received the largest award, and greatly in excess of the permissible state statutory fine for insurance fraud.[28]   However, the Court found that the record amply supported the jury's finding that the agent was acting on behalf of Pacific Mutual when he defrauded the

---

22.   *Haslip*, 499 U.S. at 17; TXO Prod. Corp. v. Alliance Res. Corp., 509 U.S. 443, 455-57 (1993); *Oberg*, 512 U.S. at 430.
23.   *Kelco Disposal, Inc.*, 492 U.S.
24.   499 U.S. 1 (1991).
25.   *Id.* at 6.
26.   *Id.* at 6 n.2.
27.   *Id.* at 6-8.
28.   *Id.* at 23-24.

plaintiffs, and that the imposition of punitive damages against Pacific Mutual under the principle of respondeat superior did not violate the company's due process rights.[29]

The Court then reviewed the traditional common law criteria for awarding punitive damages, which require a jury to consider the gravity of the defendant's conduct and the need to deter similar wrongful conduct, and noted that under the common law approach the jury's determination in this regard is reviewable by both the trial and appellate courts to ensure that it is reasonable.[30] The Court also noted that every state and federal court, including the Supreme Court, that has considered the issue has ruled that the common law method of assessing punitive damages does not itself violate due process. In light of this history, the Court concluded that the common law method is not "so inherently unfair as to deny due process and be *per se* unconstitutional."[31]

The Court then considered the question of whether the particular punitive damages award before it violated due process, noting that "general concerns of reasonableness and adequate guidance from the court when the case is tried to a jury properly enter into the constitutional calculus."[32] While declining to fashion a bright-line rule, the Court approved the criteria developed by the Alabama Supreme Court for scrutinizing juries' punitive awards. Those criteria included: the reasonableness of the relationship between the punitive award and the harm resulting from the defendant's conduct; factors relating to the culpability of the defendant's conduct; the extent to which the defendant profited from its wrongdoing and the desirability of eliminating that profit; the defendant's financial position; the cost of the litigation; and the mitigating effect of criminal sanctions and/or other civil awards against the defendant for the same conduct.[33] After considering these criteria, the Court determined that the jury's award did not "cross the line into the area of constitutional impropriety."[34]

---

29. *Id.* at 12-14.
30. *Id.* at 15-16.
31. *Id.* at 17.
32. *Id.* at 18.
33. *Id.* at 21-22.
34. *Id.* at 24 (footnote omitted).

a. *Production Corp.*

In *TXO Production Corp. v. Alliance Resources Corp.*,[35] TXO was found to have deliberately embarked on a malicious, fraudulent scheme to lower the oil and gas royalties owed certain landowners by raising a frivolous claim that a third party actually owned the oil and gas mining rights.[36] On the landowners' slander of title counterclaim, a jury awarded $19,000 in actual damages and $10 million in punitive damages (a 526:1 ratio).[37]

The West Virginia Supreme Court of Appeals affirmed the judgment.[38] The U.S. Supreme Court affirmed. In a plurality opinion,[39]

---

35. 509 U.S. 443 (1993).

36. *Id.* at 447-51.

37. *Id.* at 446.

38. TXO Prod. Corp. v. Alliance Res. Corp., 419 S.E.2d 870, 887 (W. Va. 1992), *aff'd*, 509 U.S. 443 (1993). The West Virginia Supreme Court of Appeals, using unusually colorful language, noted that, while punitive damages originally were imposed only to deter malicious conduct, the definition of malice had been expanded to include not only "mean-spirited" conduct, but also "extremely negligent conduct that is likely to cause serious harm." The court labeled defendants falling into these two categories "really mean defendants" and "really stupid defendants." 419 S.E.2d at 888. In cases involving "really stupid defendants" and compensatory damages that "are neither negligible nor very large," the court held that the outer limit of punitive damages is roughly 5 to 1. *Id.* at 889. When compensatory damages are minimal, however, that is not necessarily the case, and a much greater ratio may be appropriate. Where the defendant is "really mean," the court held that the limits must be higher in order to "deter future evil acts by the defendant." *Id.*

39. Three justices concurred in the result but wrote separately to express their opinion that there is no substantive due process limit on the quantum of punitive damages. 509 U.S. at 466-69 (Kennedy, J., concurring in part and concurring in the judgment); *id.* at 470-72 (Scalia, J., with whom Thomas, J., joined, concurring in the judgment). Justice Kennedy found this case to be "close and difficult" but voted to affirm the award because of the factual findings that TXO had acted "through a 'pattern and practice of fraud, trickery and deceit' and employed 'unsavory and malicious practices' in the course of its business dealings" with the landowners. *Id.* at 468-699 (Kennedy, J., concurring). Three justices dissented, arguing that this punitive damages award violated due process and was likely the

the Court held that a "dramatic disparity" between compensatory and punitive damages is not controlling "in a case of this character."[40] Dismissing its own statements in *Haslip*, the Court expressly rejected an approach that focuses entirely on the relationship between actual and punitive damages. Rather, the Court found it appropriate to consider both the magnitude of the potential harm that the defendant could have caused had its plan succeeded (had the scheme succeeded, the landowners would have been deprived of $1 million to $8.3 million in royalty payments), and the possible harm to other victims if the defendant continued its conduct in the future.[41]

The Court also rejected TXO's argument that punitive damages awards should be subject to "heightened scrutiny" to determine whether they violate notions of fundamental fairness.[42] The Court noted the presence of the following "safeguards" of fundamental fairness in the judicial process: the requirement that jurors be determined to be impartial; the fact that the jury's assessment of damages is the product of collective deliberation based upon the evidence and the arguments of the parties; and the availability of post-trial review by both the judge who presided over the case and by appellate courts.[43] The Court then stated: "Assuming that fair procedures were followed, a judgment that is a product of that process is entitled to a strong presumption of validity. Indeed, there are persuasive reasons for suggesting that the presumption should be irrebuttable . . . or virtually so."[44]

b.   *Oberg*

In *Oberg v. Honda Motor Co.*,[45] a products liability case alleging the negligent design of an all-terrain vehicle, the Oregon Supreme Court was called upon to apply *Haslip* to an award of $5 million in punitive

---

result of a jury seeking to punish a large, wealthy, and unpopular out-of-state corporation. *Id.* at 472-500 (O'Connor, J., along with Justices White and Souter, dissenting).

40.   509 U.S. at 462.
41.   *Id.* at 460-61.
42.   *Id.* at 456.
43.   *Id.* at 456-58.
44.   *Id.* at 457 (citations omitted).
45.   851 P.2d 1084 (Or. 1993).

damages on an actual damages award of $919,390.[46] The defendant argued on appeal that *Haslip* requires post-trial appellate review of the reasonableness of punitive damages awards, and that a 1910 amendment to the Oregon Constitution prohibiting judicial review of a punitive damages award "unless the court can affirmatively say there is no evidence to support the verdict" violated defendants' due process rights under the U.S. Constitution.[47] The Oregon Supreme Court rejected this argument.[48]

The U.S. Supreme Court reversed, holding that Oregon's denial of judicial review of the amount of punitive damages violated due process, because Oregon had removed one of the common law procedural safeguards for ensuring against the excessiveness of such awards, without providing any substitute safeguard or first establishing that the danger of arbitrary awards had subsided so as to eliminate the need for such safeguards.[49]

Noting that its opinions in both *Haslip* and *TXO* had strongly emphasized the importance of the procedural component of the Due Process Clause, the Court focused its analysis on Oregon's departure from traditional procedures, which it described as reducing the judge "to the status of a mere monitor."[50]

The Court noted that judicial review of the size of punitive awards had been a safeguard against excessive awards "for as long as punitive damages have been awarded."[51] The Court found that there was "a dramatic difference" between the review of punitive damages under the common law and the scope of review available in Oregon, inasmuch as Oregon provided no procedure for obtaining relief where the only error claimed was the amount of punitive damages awarded.[52]

---

46. Based on a jury finding allocating 20 percent of the fault to the plaintiff, the trial court reduced the compensatory award by 20 percent. *Id.* at 1086 n.1.
47. *Id.* at 1091. The Oregon Supreme Court decided *Oberg* before the Supreme Court decided *TXO*. *See id.* at 1091 n.8.
48. *Id.* at 1094 (citing *Haslip*, 499 U.S. at 17-19).
49. Honda Motor Co. v. Oberg, 512 U.S. 415, 429-30 (1994).
50. *Id.* at 421.
51. *Id.*
52. *Id.* at 426.

After finding that Oregon's abrogation of well-established common law procedural protections "raises a presumption that its procedures violate the Due Process Clause,"[53] the Court considered and rejected the plaintiff's argument that Oregon's existing safeguards against arbitrary awards were adequate. These safeguards included limiting punitive awards to the amount specified by the plaintiff, requiring a clear and convincing standard of proof, determining pre-verdict the maximum allowable punitive damages, and providing detailed jury instructions.[54] The Court also rejected the plaintiff's argument that there is a historical basis for making the jury the final arbiter of the amount of punitive damage awards.[55]

4.   Gore: *The Birth of Substantive Due Process "Guidepost Analysis"*

"The Due Process Clause guarantees more than fair process."[56] It also "provides heightened protection against government interference with certain fundamental rights and liberty interest."[57] "Grossly excessive" punitive damages awards are prohibited by the Due Process Clause because they "further[] no legitimate purpose and constitute[] an arbitrary deprivation of property."[58]

In *BMW of North America, Inc. v. Gore* [cite], a case decided in 1996, the Supreme Court, for the first time, vacated a punitive damages award on the ground that it was unconstitutionally excessive. The issue at trial was BMW's nationwide policy of not informing its dealers (or the dealers' customers) of pre-delivery damage to new cars, when the cost of the repair did not exceed three percent of the car's suggested retail price. Gore purchased a BMW that fell into that category and sued BMW, alleging that its failure to disclose the fact that the car had been repainted amounted to the suppression of a material fact.[59] The jury returned a

---

53.   *Id.* at 430.
54.   *Id.* at 432-34.
55.   *Id.* at 434-35.
56.   Washington v. Glucksberg, 521 U.S. 702, 719 (1997).
57.   *Id.* at 720.
58.   *Campbell*, 538 U.S. at 417; BMW of N. Am., Inc. v. Gore, 517 U.S. 559, 562 (1996).
59.   *Gore*, 517 U.S. at 563.

verdict finding BMW liable for compensatory damages of $4,000, and assessing $4 million in punitive damages.[60]

The trial judge denied BMW's post-trial motion to set aside the punitive damages award, holding, among other things, that the award was not "grossly excessive" and thus did not violate the Due Process Clause. The Alabama Supreme Court agreed but reduced the award to $2 million on the ground that, in computing the amount, the jury had improperly multiplied Gore's compensatory damages by the number of similar sales in all states, not just those in Alabama. The U.S. Supreme Court reversed, holding that the $2 million punitive damages award was grossly excessive and exceeded the constitutional limit of due process.

Noting that a punitive damages award violates due process only when it fairly can be categorized as "grossly excessive" in relation to a state's legitimate interests in punishing unlawful conduct and deterring its repetition, the Court "focus[ed] [its] attention first on the scope of Alabama's legitimate interests in punishing BMW and deterring it from future misconduct."[61]

The Court stated that, under principles of state sovereignty and comity, one state is prohibited from enacting policies for the entire nation or otherwise imposing its policy choices on other states. Accordingly, any economic penalty inflicted by a state "must be supported by the State's interest in protecting its own consumers and its own economy."[62] Alabama cannot "punish BMW for conduct that was lawful where it occurred" or that "had no impact on Alabama or its residents," and Alabama certainly cannot sanction BMW "to deter conduct that is lawful in other jurisdictions."[63] Therefore, Gore's award had to be analyzed based only on the conduct that occurred in Alabama, "with consideration given only to the interests of Alabama consumers."[64]

The Court held that, under "[e]lementary notions of fairness enshrined in our constitutional jurisprudence," a person must not only receive fair notice of "the conduct that will subject him to punishment,

---

60. *Id.* at 565.
61. *Id.* at 568.
62. *Id.* at 572.
63. *Id.* at 572-73.
64. *Id.* at 573-74.

but also of the severity of the penalty that a State may impose."[65] Whether a person has received proper notice can be determined by considering "[t]hree guideposts": (1) reprehensibility (the degree of reprehensibility of the defendant's conduct); (2) ratio (the disparity between actual and punitive damages); and (3) disparity (the difference between the award at issue and civil penalties authorized or imposed in comparable cases).[66] Evaluating these guideposts, the Court held that the $2 million award against BMW was "grossly excessive."[67]

Reviewing the evidence, the Court held that none of the aggravating factors associated with the first guidepost (reprehensibility) was present. The harm inflicted on Gore "was purely economic in nature," given that the presale repainting "had no effect on [the car's] performance or safety features, or even its appearance for at least nine months after his purchase"; BMW's conduct thus "evinced no indifference to or reckless disregard for the health and safety of others."[68] While Gore argued that BMW's nondisclosure formed a part of a nationwide pattern of unlawful conduct, the Court disagreed, noting that several states had adopted statutory disclosure requirements that a corporate executive could reasonably have interpreted as establishing safe harbors.[69] Finally, there was no evidence that BMW engaged in "deliberate false statements, acts of affirmative misconduct, or concealment of evidence of improper motive."[70]

As for the second guidepost (ratio), Gore's $2 million award was 500 times the amount of the actual harm determined by the jury, and there was "no suggestion that Dr. Gore or any other BMW purchaser was threatened with any additional potential harm by BMW's nondisclosure policy."[71] Quoting *Haslip*, the Court emphasized that "'[w]e need not, and indeed we cannot, draw a mathematical bright line between the constitutionally acceptable and the constitutionally unacceptable that would fit every case.'"[72] "When the ratio is a breathtaking 500 to 1,

---

65. *Id.* at 574.
66. *Id.* at 574-75.
67. *Id.* at 575.
68. *Id.* at 576.
69. *Id.* at 577-78.
70. *Id.* at 579.
71. *Id.* at 582.
72. *Id.* at 582-83 (quoting *Haslip*, 499 U.S. at 18).

however, the award must surely 'raise a suspicious judicial eyebrow.'"[73] The ratio, the Court concluded, was clearly outside the acceptable range.[74]

As for the third guidepost (disparity), the $2 million award was substantially greater than Alabama's applicable $2,000 statutory fine and similar penalties imposed by other states. The Court further noted that none of the pertinent statutes or interpretive decisions would have put an out-of-state distributor on notice that it might be subject to a multimillion dollar sanction.[75]   Moreover, in the absence of a history of noncompliance with known statutory requirements, there was no basis for assuming that a more modest sanction would not have been sufficient.[76]

The Court concluded: "we are fully convinced that the grossly excessive award imposed in this case transcends the constitutional limit."[77] As for "[w]hether the appropriate remedy require[d] a new trial or merely an independent determination by the Alabama Supreme Court of the award necessary to vindicate [Alabama consumers'] economic interests," this was a matter for that court to address in the first instance.[78]

5. Cooper Industries: *Appellate Review of Punitive Damages Awards*

While *Gore* made it clear that there are due process limitations on the size of punitive damages awards, its three-part guidepost analysis did little to inspire uniform decision-making in the lower courts. In cases decided after *Gore*, courts were willing to find a wide variety of ratios constitutionally acceptable. In *Cooper Industries, Inc. v. Leatherman Tool Group, Inc.*,[79] the Supreme Court revisited the issue of punitive damages, focusing again on procedural due process.

---

73. *Id.* at 583 (quoting *TXO Prod. Corp.*, 509 U.S. at 481 (O'Connor, J., dissenting)).
74. *Id.*
75. *Id.* at 584.
76. *Id.* at 584-85.
77. *Id.* at 585-86.
78. *Id.* at 586.
79. 532 U.S. 424 (2001).

Cooper Industries involved a compensatory award of $50,000 and a punitive damages award of $4.5 million for trademark infringement and related claims.[80] The district court rejected Cooper Industries' argument that the punitive damages award was grossly excessive under *Gore* and entered judgment on the jury's verdict.[81] The Ninth Circuit affirmed, concluding that the district court did not abuse its discretion in declining to reduce that award.[82]

The Supreme Court reversed, holding that appellate courts should apply a de novo standard when reviewing district court determinations of the constitutionality of punitive damages awards, and further ruling that the Ninth Circuit had erred in applying the less demanding abuse-of-discretion standard.[83] The Court reasoned that while a jury's assessment of compensatory damages is essentially a factual determination, "its imposition of punitive damages is an expression of its moral condemnation."[84] States have broad authority in both authorizing and limiting punitive damages awards; therefore, a federal appellate court must review a trial court's punitive damages ruling under an abuse-of-discretion standard *when no constitutional issue is raised.*[85]

Constitutional challenges, the Court explained, present a different issue. The Due Process Clause imposes substantive limits on state discretion, makes the Eighth Amendment's Excessive Fines clause applicable to the states, and (as demonstrated in *Gore*) prohibits states from imposing "grossly excessive" punishments.[86] While recognizing that the constitutional line is "inherently imprecise," courts must nevertheless focus on the three guideposts (reprehensibility, ratio, and disparity) to determine if that line has been crossed.[87] The Court concluded that appellate review of this criteria should be "an independent examination" rather than the more deferential abuse of discretion review.[88]

---

80. *Id.* at 426.
81. *Id.* at 429.
82. *Id.* at 430-31.
83. *Id.* at 431.
84. *Id.* at 432.
85. *Id.* at 433.
86. *Id.* at 433-34.
87. *Id.* at 434-35.
88. *Id.* at 435-36.

The Court gave several reasons for this ruling. First, because the meaning of a concept such as "gross excessiveness" "cannot be articulated with precision" and is a "fluid concept" that "'calls for the application of a constitutional standard to the facts of a particular case,'" de novo review is appropriate.[89] Second, "'the legal rules for probable cause and reasonable suspicion acquire content only through application. Independent review is therefore necessary if appellate courts are to maintain control of, and to clarify, the legal principles.'"[90] Lastly, de novo review "'tends to unify precedent'" and "'stabilize the law.'"[91]

The Court further explained that any procedural shift would not implicate a plaintiff's Seventh Amendment right to a jury trial "[b]ecause the jury's award of punitive damages does not constitute a finding of 'fact.'"[92]

D. *Campbell*: The Supreme Court Readdresses Substantive Due Process Limitations on Punitive Damages Awards

Two years after deciding *Cooper Industries*, the Supreme Court in *State Farm Mutual Automobile Insurance Co. v. Campbell*,[93] reexamined substantive due process limitations on punitive damages awards. *Campbell* amplified the *Gore* standards and set out additional limits on punitive damages awards by: (1) limiting the power of a state to punish a defendant for illegal conduct committed in another state; (2) clarifying what evidence may be considered in assessing punitive damages; and (3) establishing a presumption that the ratio between punitive and compensatory damages should not exceed a single digit.[94]

In *Campbell*, Curtis Campbell caused an automobile accident in which one person was killed and another permanently disabled.[95] Campbell's insurer, State Farm Mutual Automobile Insurance Company ("State Farm"), contested liability and declined to settle the claims

---

89. *Id.* (quoting United States v. Bajakajian, 524 U.S. 321, 336-37 & n.10 (1998)).
90. *Id.* at 436 (quoting Ornelas v. United States, 517 U.S. 690, 697 (1996)).
91. *Id.* (quoting *Ornelas*, 517 U.S. at 697-98).
92. *Id.* at 437.
93. 538 U.S. 408 (2003).
94. *Id.* at 419-29.
95. *Id.* at 412-13.

against him for the $50,000 policy limit.[96] Ignoring the advice of its own
investigators, State Farm took the case to trial, assuring Campbell and his
wife that "'their assets were safe, that they had no liability for the
accident, that [State Farm] would represent their interests, and that they
did not need to procure separate counsel.'"[97]   A Utah jury found
otherwise, determining that Campbell was completely at fault and
returning a judgment against him for $185,849, well over three times the
policy limit.[98]

State Farm initially refused to cover the $135,849 in excess liability,
even telling Campbell (through its counsel) that "[y]ou may want to put
for sale signs on your property to get things moving."[99]   State Farm later
reconsidered, however, and paid the entire judgment after Campbell's
appeal was unsuccessful.[100]   Nevertheless, Mr. and Mrs. Campbell sued
State Farm for bad faith, fraud, and intentional infliction of emotional
distress.[101]

The trial court initially granted summary judgment to State Farm, on
the ground that it had already paid the excess verdict, but that ruling was
reversed on appeal.[102]   On remand, the trial court denied State Farm's
motion to exclude evidence of "dissimilar out-of-state conduct."[103]   In
the first (liability) phase of a bifurcated trial, the jury found that State
Farm's decision not to settle was unreasonable.[104]   Before the second
phase on damages, the Supreme Court decided *Gore*.[105]   As it had done
in the first phase, the *Campbell* trial court again denied State Farm's
motion to exclude evidence of dissimilar out-of-state conduct, and
admitted evidence of State Farm's business practices in numerous states
– evidence that did not relate to the type of bad faith claim underlying the

---

96. *Id.* at 413.
97. *Id.* at 413 (quoting State Farm Mut. Auto Ins. Co. v. Campbell, 65 P.3d
     1134, 1142 (Utah 2001)).
98. *Id.* at 413.
99. *Id.*
100. *Id.*
101. *Id.* at 414.
102. *Id.*
103. *Id.*
104. *Id.*
105. *Id.*

Campbells' complaint.[106] The jury awarded the Campbells $2.6 million in compensatory damages and $145 million in punitive damages.[107] The trial court reduced the compensatory damages award to $1 million and the punitive damages award to $25 million, but the Utah Supreme Court, applying *Gore*, reversed and reinstated the $145 million punitive damages award.[108]

The Supreme Court granted certiorari and reversed. Applying the *Gore* guideposts and reviewing the judgment de novo, the Court stated that "this case is neither close nor difficult," and held that a punitive damages award of $145 million, supported by a compensatory damages award of only $1 million, is excessive and violates the Due Process Clause.[109]

Building on its analysis in *Gore* and *Cooper Industries*, the Court expressed concern "over the imprecise manner in which punitive damages systems are administered."[110] Jury instructions leave juries with wide discretion, and vague instructions to avoid "passion or prejudice" provide little guidance.[111] Quoting *Oberg*, the Court stated that "'the presentation of evidence of a defendant's net worth creates the potential that juries will use their verdicts to express biases against big businesses, particularly those without strong local presences.'"[112] These concerns are heightened, the Court explained, "when the decisionmaker is presented . . . with evidence that has little bearing as to the amount of punitive damages that should be awarded."[113]

Addressing the reprehensibility guidepost – "'[t]he most important indicium of the reasonableness of a punitive damages award'"[114] – the Court stated that a court must consider whether:

> the harm caused was physical as opposed to economic; the tortious conduct evinced an indifference to or a reckless disregard of the

---

106. *Id.*
107. *Id.* at 415.
108. *Id.* at 415-16.
109. *Id.* at 418, 429.
110. *Id.* at 417.
111. *Id.*
112. *Id.* (quoting *Oberg*, 512 U.S. at 432).
113. *Id.* at 418.
114. *Id.* at 419 (quoting *Gore*, 517 U.S. at 575).

health or safety of others; the target of the conduct had financial vulnerability; the conduct involved repeated actions or was an isolated incident; and the harm was the result of intentional malice, trickery, or deceit, or mere accident.[115]

The Court stated that the presence of any one of these factors may not in itself be sufficient to sustain an award, and that the absence of all of them "renders any award suspect."[116] Because a plaintiff presumably has been made whole by compensatory damages, "punitive damages should only be awarded if the defendant's culpability, after having paid compensatory damages, is so reprehensible as to warrant the imposition of further sanctions to achieve punishment or deterrence."[117]

Acknowledging that State Farm's claims handling "merits no praise," the Court ruled that "a more modest punishment for this reprehensible conduct could have satisfied the State's legitimate objectives, and the Utah courts should have gone no further."[118] *Gore* made it clear that a state cannot punish a defendant for conduct that may have been lawful where it occurred.[119] Taking this concept further, the Court stated: "Nor, as a general rule, does a State have a legitimate concern in imposing punitive damages to punish a defendant for unlawful acts committed outside of the State's jurisdiction."[120] The problem in *Campbell*, the Court observed, was that the case "was used as a platform to expose, and punish, the perceived deficiencies of State Farm's operations throughout the country."[121]

Commenting on the evidence relevant to reprehensibility, the Court stated: "Lawful out-of-state conduct may be probative when it demonstrates the deliberateness and culpability of the defendant's action in the State where it is tortious, but that conduct must have a nexus to the specific harm suffered by the plaintiff."[122] The problem was that the courts below "awarded punitive damages to punish and deter conduct

---

115. *Id.* (citing *Gore*, 517 U.S. at 576-77).
116. *Id.*
117. *Id.*
118. *Id.* at 419-20.
119. *Id.* at 421 (citing *Gore*, 517 U.S. at 572).
120. *Id.*
121. *Id.* at 420.
122. *Id.* at 422.

that bore no relation to the Campbells' harm."[123] "Due process does not permit courts . . . to adjudicate the merits of other parties' hypothetical claims against a defendant under the guise of the reprehensibility analysis . . . ."[124] Such a punishment "creates the possibility of multiple punitive damages awards for the same conduct."[125]

The award could not be sustained on a "recidivist" theory either, because "courts must ensure the conduct in question replicates the prior transgressions" (the Utah court did not do so) and there was "scant evidence of repeated misconduct of the sort that injured [the Campbells]."[126] Concluding, the Court held that "because the Campbells have shown no conduct by State Farm similar to that which harmed them, the conduct that harmed them is the only conduct relevant to the reprehensibility analysis."[127]

Regarding the second *Gore* guidepost (ratio), the Court reiterated its reluctance to fashion a bright-line rule.[128] The Court stated, however, that "in practice, few awards exceeding a single-digit ratio between punitive and compensatory damages, to a significant degree, will satisfy due process."[129] The *Campbell* Court further noted that in *Haslip* it had "concluded that an award of more than four times the amount of compensatory damages might be close to the line of constitutional impropriety,"[130] and in *Gore* it again cited that 4-to-1 ratio and further referenced a history spanning centuries of "providing for sanctions of double, treble, or quadruple damages to deter and punish,"[131] ratios that are "not binding" but are instead "instructive."[132]

The Court in *Campbell* further concluded that higher ratios may be appropriate, for example, "where 'a particularly egregious act has resulted in only a small amount of economic damages,'" or "where 'the injury is hard to detect or the monetary value of noneconomic harm

123. *Id.*
124. *Id.* at 423.
125. *Id.*
126. *Id.*
127. *Id.* at 424.
128. *Id.* at 424-25.
129. *Id.* at 425.
130. *Id.* (citing *Haslip*, 499 U.S. at 23-24).
131. *Id.* (citing *Gore*, 517 U.S. at 581 & n.33).
132. *Id.*

might have been difficult to determine.'"[133]   Where "compensatory damages are substantial," however, "then a lesser ratio, perhaps only equal to compensatory damages, can reach the outermost limit of the due process guarantee."[134]

The 145-to-1 ratio awarded the Campbells was excessive for several reasons.   The Campbells had already been awarded $1 million in compensatory damages for a year and a half of emotional distress; the distress they suffered was likely a component of both the compensatory and punitive damages awards; and the size of the award was grossly disproportionate to the harm suffered by the Campbells.[135]   Commenting again on "wealth evidence," the Court stated that "[t]he wealth of a defendant cannot justify an otherwise unconstitutional punitive damages award."[136]

The Court spent little time addressing the third guidepost, disparity. Noting that the most relevant civil sanction under Utah state law for the wrong done to the Campbells, "grand fraud," appeared to be a $10,000 fine, the award was clearly unjustified.[137]   While the Utah Supreme Court sought to justify the award based on the existence of a "broad fraudulent scheme," such a scheme was only substantiated through "out-of-state and dissimilar conduct."[138]   The evidence, therefore, was insufficient to justify the award.

The Court concluded that "[t]he punitive award of $145 million, therefore, was neither reasonable nor proportionate to the wrong committed, and it was an irrational and arbitrary deprivation of the property of [State Farm]."[139]   The Court remanded the case to the Utah courts to determine the "proper calculation of punitive damages under the principles [the Court] discussed."[140]

---

133. *Id.* (quoting *Gore*, 517 U.S. at 582).
134. *Id.*
135. *Id.* at 426-28.
136. *Id.* at 427.
137. *Id.* at 428.
138. *Id.*
139. *Id.* at 429.
140. *Id.*

E. Lower Court Application of the *Gore* Guideposts

1. *Reprehensibility*

The Supreme Court's decisions have now been applied in the lower courts, which have reached varying results. We examine the application of each of the Supreme Court's three guideposts below.

The first *Gore* guidepost is reprehensibility. In considering this guidepost, the role of the court is to determine where, on the scale of outrageousness, the defendant's conduct fits. As the Supreme Court has exaplained, the amount of punitive damages awarded should not exceed that required to serve a state's interests in deterrence and retribution.[141]

For example, in *Watson v. Johnson Mobile Homes*,[142] a mobile home purchaser provided a $4,000 downpayment that was to be refunded if the financing company denied her credit application, but forfeited if she was approved for credit but did not complete the purchase.[143] When the purchaser's credit application was rejected, the seller suggested that increasing the downpayment an additional $3,000, increasing the frequency of payments at an increased interest rate, and including an arbitration provision in the transaction, would secure the creditline.[144] The buyer declined these terms, and the seller refused to refund the initial deposit.

A jury found the seller liable for intentional breach of contract, fraud, and conversion. The purchaser's deposit was substantially higher than the seller's other customers who forfeited their deposit. The jury awarded $4,000 in actual damages and $700,000 in punitive damages.

The Fifth Circuit reduced the punitive damages award to $150,000 because the court did not find substantial reprehensibility. The court found that although the seller clearly acted wrongly, there was no pattern of malfeasance, and the buyer's health and safety were not placed at risk.[145] Further mitigating the seller's blameworthiness, the court noted that requiring a reasonable, non-refundable loan application fee to process such an application was acceptable, that the high amount of the

---

141. *Gore*, 517 U.S. at 575.
142. 284 F.3d 568 (5th Cir. 2002).
143. *Id.* at 570.
144. *Id.* at 572.
145. *Id.* at 574.

buyer's deposit appeared to be an isolated case, that the vast majority of credit applicants either completed the purchase or had their deposit returned, and that there was no evidence of physical abuse or emotional suffering. Hence, the buyer's damages were the result of economic injury.[146]

On the other hand, in *Stogsdill v. Healthmark Partners, LLC*,[147] a nursing home was held vicariously liable for the conduct of its nurse employees that resulted in the death of a resident. A jury awarded the decedent's estate $500,000 in compensatory damages and $5 million in punitive damages.

On appeal, the Eighth Circuit agreed that "the degree of reprehensibility is substantial":

> The trial evidence established that [the nursing home's] nurses failed to treat Stogsdill's lengthy constipation and ignored their duty to contact her treating physician despite numerous requests that they do so. In addition, there was evidence of a practice of careless and at times fraudulent charting of residents' condition. The result was not merely economic injury. Because of [the nursing home] staff's conscious indifference to her life-threatening change in condition, Stogsdill suffered a perforated bowel, the worst case of abdominal contamination her surgeon had ever seen, and death.[148]

Nevertheless, the court ordered that the punitive damages award be reduced to $2 million.[149] Despite the finding of "substantial" reprehensibility, the court held that there was "no evidence" that the nurses' conduct "was the result of intentional malice, trickery or deceit."[150] In addition, the jury was allowed to consider evidence of the general condition of the nursing home – evidence irrelevant to the conduct that caused Stogsdill's injuries.[151] Finally, the court was concerned that the closing argument of the plaintiff's counsel, which blamed not the nurses but the "people at the top," was a blatant appeal to anti-business bias and led to an award that exceeded that state's interest

---

146. *Id.* at 572-73.
147. 377 F.3d 827 (8th Cir. 2004).
148. *Id.* at 832.
149. *Id.* at 834.
150. *Id.* at 832 (quoting *Campbell*, 538 U.S. at 419).
151. *Id.*

in deterrence and retribution by punishing the nursing home for separate conduct that did not cause Stogsdill's injury.[152]

2. *Ratio*

The Supreme Court's second guidepost, ratio, requires a court "to police a range, not a point."[153] While the "single-digit multiplier range" presumably passes constitutional muster, lower courts have not hesitated to approve much higher ranges in cases where only nominal damages are awarded or when the application of a single digit multiplier will not adequately punish egregious conduct.

In *Asa-Brandt, Inc. v. ADM Investor Services, Inc.*,[154] the Eighth Circuit affirmed a substantial award of punitive damages, $1.25 million, for breach of fiduciary duty in a case where only nominal damages had been awarded. Because the evidence presented to the jury showed that the defendant would have gained $3.9 million as a result of the breach, the ratio of the punitive damages to the potential harm was well within constitutional limits.[155]

Similarly, a jury's decision that a hotel pay two bedbug bitten plaintiffs $5,000 each in compensatory damages and $186,000 each in punitive damages – a 37:1 ratio – was affirmed precisely because a lower ratio would not adequately punish the hotel for its deliberate misconduct.[156] In affirming the award, the Seventh Circuit focused on the ability of punitive damages to provide deterrence and retribution. Compensatory damages alone do not adequately punish tortfeasors if: (1) "they are difficult to determine in the case of acts that inflict largely dignitary harms"; (2) they are "too slight to give the victim an incentive to sue"; and (3) a defendant willing to pay compensatory damages could "commit the offensive act with impunity."[157] In light of the hotel's outrageous behavior (repeatedly renting rooms known to be infested with bedbugs and that had been placed on a "do not rent" list), coupled with the fact that the compensable harm was slight and difficult to determine, the larger ratio of punitive damages served the salutary purpose of

---

152. *Id.* at 832-33.
153. Mathias v. Accor Econ. Lodging, Inc., 347 F.3d 672, 678 (7th Cir. 2003).
154. 344 F.3d 738 (8th Cir. 2003).
155. *Id.* at 747.
156. *Mathias*, 347 F.3d at 678.
157. *Id.* at 677.

limiting the hotel's ability to profit from its fraud and reducing the incentive to escape detection and private prosecution.[158]

Conversely, in an invasion of privacy case, the South Dakota Supreme Court reversed a punitive damages award that was 20 times the $25,000 awarded in compensatory damages.[159] In that case, an attorney who had been asked to consider the merits of a discrimination claim returned material to a former employee by mailing the documents to the employee's former work address. Acting in the ordinary course of business, a supervisor opened the package. But after he ascertained its contents, he distributed photocopies of the materials and then tried to cover up his opening of the package.[160]

In reviewing the punitive damages award, the court found that the reprehensibility analysis weighed against a finding of reasonableness – the harm was purely economic, the information gathered was already available to the employer or was otherwise subject to discovery in the event of litigation. It was an isolated event – not the result of a policy or practice but conduct by one supervisor in one situation – and no one else's privacy was put at risk. Because, in the court's view, the plaintiff had already been highly compensated by the $25,000 compensatory damage award, proportionality weighed in favor of reducing the punitive award to around the size of the compensatory award.[161]

In *Campbell*, the Supreme Court indicated that the $1 million compensatory award was substantial and stated that a substantial compensatory award "likely would justify a punitive damages award at or near the amount of compensatory damages."[162] On remand, however, the Utah Supreme Court reasoned that State Farm's misconduct warranted an award of over $9 million in punitive damages, slightly in

---

158. *Id.*
159. Roth v. Farner-Bocken Co., 667 N.W.2d 651 (S.D. 2003).
160. *Id.* at 658.
161. *Id.* at 661-64.
162. *Campbell*, 538 U.S. at 429; *see also, e.g.*, Boerner v. Brown & Williamson Tobacco Co., 394 F.3d 594, 603 (8th Cir. 2005) (remitting punitive damages award from $15 million to $5 million where compensatory damages were some $4 million, a ratio of approximately 1-to-1; although finding conduct reprehensible, because "the punitive damages award is excessive when measured against the substantial compensatory damages award," "a low ratio is called for here").

excess of a 9-to-1 ratio, a decision the U.S. Supreme Court thereafter decided not to address.[163]

One author surveying post-*Campbell* decisions notes that, in the first year since *Campbell* was handed down, a greater percentage of federal decisions have exceed a 9-to-1 ratio than have state decisions.[164]

3. *Disparity*

The Supreme Court's third guidepost, disparity, requires a comparison between the punitive damages award and the civil or criminal penalties imposed in other cases for comparable conduct.[165] In *Campbell*, the Court cautioned that "[p]unitive damages are not a substitute for the criminal process, and the remote possibility of a criminal sanction does not automatically sustain a punitive damages award."[166]

Nevertheless, such comparisons can serve to put a defendant on notice of the potential liability for egregious conduct. In ordering remittitur in *Stogsdill*, the Eighth Circuit found that the civil and criminal penalties available against the nursing home were disproportionate to and could not justify the initial punitive damage award of $5 million.[167] Yet, in *Stamathis v. Flying J, Inc.*,[168] the court held that a $350,000 punitive damage award on claims of defamation and malicious prosecution "was not grossly disproportionate to any comparable civil and criminal penalties that [the defendants] might face."[169] In reaching this conclusion, the court noted that, although there were no civil penalties imposed by state law for the defendants' conduct (having the plaintiff

---

163. Campbell v. State Farm Mut. Auto. Ins. Co., 98 P.3d 409, 420 (Utah), *cert. denied*, 125 S. Ct. 114 (2004).
164. Samuel A. Thumma, *Punitive Damages: Post-"Campbell" Cases*, NAT'L L.J., June 7, 2004, at 13 ("[T]he federal cases applying *Campbell* in the first year after that decision allowed higher ratios than did the state cases. Including nominal-damages cases, more than 25% of the federal cases applying *Campbell* allowed a ratio exceeding 9-to-1, while fewer than 15% of the state cases allowed such ratios to stand.").
165. *Gore*, 517 U.S. at 582; *Campbell*, 538 U.S. at 428.
166. *Campbell*, 538 U.S. at 428.
167. 377 F.3d at 834.
168. 389 F.3d 429 (4th Cir. 2004).
169. *Id.* at 444.

arrested without probable cause), the defendants did have notice of the potential for a lawsuit and the state's cap on punitive damages awards. Further, making a false report to the police could be punished by up to a year in jail.[170]

In a police brutality case, the Second Circuit evaluated the amount of punitive damages awarded in similar cases.[171] Noting that only nominal damages had been awarded on the victim's abuse of process claim, the court concluded that a multiplier was not a good tool to assess the constitutionality of the punitive damages award.[172] Therefore, the court surveyed the conduct in similar cases and reduced the punitive damages from $1.275 million to $75,000.[173]

F. State Law Limitations on Punitive Damages

In addition to the decisions of the Supreme Court discussed above, within the last twenty years, many states have been proactive in limiting the availability of punitive damages. "As in the criminal sentencing context, legislatures enjoy broad discretion in authorizing and limiting permissible punitive damages awards."[174] Their actions have resulted in procedural and substantive limitations on punitive damages awards.[175]

1. *State Procedural Limitations on Punitive Damages*

Procedurally, several states have passed legislation designed to ensure that only more egregious conduct is punished by an award of punitive damages. At least three states have enacted general prohibitions on punitive damages awards.[176]

Less drastically, several states restrict the availability of punitive damages to those cases where the tortfeasor acted with malice,

---

170. *Id.*
171. DiSorbo v. Hoy, 343 F.3d 172 (2d Cir. 2003).
172. *Id.* at 187.
173. *Id.* at 188-89.
174. *Cooper Indus., Inc.*, 532 U.S. at 433.
175. *See* James F. Williams and Justin L. Moon, *Punitive Damages after* State Farm: *Jurisprudential Developments and Legislative Trends*, ABA SECTION OF LITIG. AND ABA CTR. FOR CONTINUING L. EDUC., 2004, at 18-27 & App. A.
176. LA. CIV. CODE ANN. art. 3546 (2004); N.H. REV. STAT. ANN. § 507:16 (2003); S.D. CODIFIED LAWS § 21-1-4 (2004).

deliberately intended to harm the victim, or otherwise breached a heightened duty of care, at least with respect to certain types of claims. In these states, punitive damages may not be awarded against a defendant whose conduct is merely negligent.[177]

---

177. *See, e.g.*, Homewood Fishing Club v. Archer Daniels Midland Co., 605 N.E.2d 1140, 1148 (Ill. App. Ct. 1992) (Illinois requires fraud, actual malice, deliberate violence or oppression, or willful or grossly negligent conduct involving some element of outrage); First Nat'l Bank of Fort Smith v. Kan. City S. Ry. Co., 865 S.W.2d 719, 726-27 (Mo. Ct. App. 1993) (Missouri requires complete indifference or conscious disregard for safety of others); Coakley v. Daniels, 840 S.W.2d 367, 372 (Tenn. Ct. App. 1992) (requiring fraudulent, malicious, oppressive, or grossly negligent conduct); *see also* ALA. CODE § 6-11-20(a) (2003) (defendant must consciously or deliberately engaged in oppression, fraud, wantonness, or malice with regard to plaintiff); ALASKA STAT. § 09.17.020(b) (2003) (defendant's conduct must be outrageous, including acts done with malice or bad motives or evidenced reckless indifference to interest of another person); ARK. CODE ANN. § 16-55-206 (2004) (defendant must or should know conduct would result in injury and continued conduct with malice or in reckless disregard of consequences, or defendant intentionally pursued course of conduct for purpose of causing injury or damage); CAL. CIV. CODE § 3294 (2004) (requiring proof defendant is guilty of oppression, fraud, or malice); COLO. REV. STAT. § 13-21-102(1)(a) (2004) (injury must be attended by circumstances of fraud, malice, or willful and wanton conduct); FLA. STAT. ANN. § 768.72(2) (2004) (requiring intentional misconduct or gross negligence); GA. CODE ANN. § 51-12-5.1(b) (2003) (plaintiff must prove defendant's actions showed willful misconduct, malice, fraud, wantonness, oppression, or conscious indifference to consequences); IDAHO CODE § 6-1604(1) (2004) (claimant must prove oppressive, fraudulent, malicious, or outrageous conduct); IOWA CODE ANN. § 668A.1(1a) (2003) (defendant must act with willful and wanton disregard for rights or safety of another); KAN. STAT. ANN. § 60-3701(c) (2003) (plaintiff must prove defendant acted with willful or wanton conduct, fraud, or malice); MINN. STAT. ANN. § 549.20(1)(a) (2004) (acts of defendant must show deliberate disregard for rights or safety of others); MISS. CODE ANN. § 11-1-65(1)(a) (2003) (requiring actual malice, gross negligence evincing a willful, wanton, or reckless disregard for safety of others, or actual fraud); MONT. CODE ANN. § 27-1-221(1) (2003) (requiring actual fraud or actual malice); NEV. REV. STAT. ANN. § 42.005(1) (2003) (oppression, fraud or malice, express or implied); N.J. STAT. ANN. § 2A15-5.12 (2004) (actual malice or willful

In conjunction with limiting the type of conduct for which punitive damages may be awarded, it is not uncommon to impose upon plaintiffs a heightened burden of proving the defendant's conduct. Whereas liability for compensatory damages may be established by a preponderance of the evidence, clear and convincing evidence of conduct meeting the requisite standard is required in many jurisdictions before punitive damages may be awarded.[178]

Several states have also instituted "gatekeeping" measures. The form varies, but the overall effect is that liability for punitive damages must be established before the factfinder is permitted to determine the sum of the punitive damages to be awarded. In some states, the trial

---

and wanton disregard); N.C. GEN. STAT. § 1D-15(a) (2004) (fraud, malice, or willful or wanton conduct must be present and relate to injury for which compensatory damages are awarded); OHIO REV. CODE ANN. § 2315.21(B) (2004) (malice, aggravated or egregious fraud, oppression, or insult); S.D. CODIFIED LAWS §§ 21-1-4.1, 21-3-2 (2004) (trial court must first find willful, wanton, or malicious conduct on part of defendant; jury must then find defendant guilty of oppression, fraud, or malice); TEX CIV. PRAC. & REM. CODE ANN. § 41.003(a) (2004) (fraud, malice, or gross negligence); UTAH CODE ANN. § 78-18-1(1)(a) (2003) (acts or omissions of tortfeasor must be result of willful and malicious or intentionally fraudulent conduct, or conduct that manifests a knowing and reckless indifference toward, and disregard of, rights of others).

178. *See, e.g.*, ALA. CODE § 6-11-20(a) (2003); ALASKA STAT. § 09.17.020 (2003); ARK. CODE ANN. § 16-55-207 (2004); CAL. CIV. CODE § 3294(a) (2004); FLA STAT. ANN. § 768.725 (2004); GA. CODE ANN. § 51-12-5.1(b) (2003); IDAHO CODE § 6-1604 (2004); IND. CODE ANN. § 34-51-3-2 (2004); KAN. STAT. ANN. § 60-3701(c) (2003); MINN. STAT. ANN. § 549.20(1)(a) (2004); MISS. CODE ANN. § 11-1-65(a) (2003); MONT. CODE ANN. § 27-1-221(5) (2003); NEV. REV. STAT. ANN. § 42.005 (2003); N.D. CENT. CODE § 32-03.2-11 (2003); N.J. STAT. ANN. § 2A:15-5.12(a) (2004); OHIO REV. CODE ANN. § 2315.21(B) (2004); OKLA. STAT. ANN. Tit. 23, § 9.1(B)-(D) (2004); OR. REV. STAT. § 31.730 (2003); S.C. CODE ANN. § 15-33-135 (2003); S.D. CODIFIED LAWS § 21-1-4.1 (2004); TEX. CIV. PRAC. & REM. CODE ANN. § 41.003(b) (2004); UTAH CODE ANN. § 78-18-1(1)(a) (2003); *see also* Peters v. Boulder Ins. Agency, Inc., 829 P.2d 429, 434 (Colo. Ct. App. 1991) (Colorado requires proof beyond a reasonable doubt that defendant acted with wanton and reckless disregard or evil intent).

judge acts as gatekeeper.[179]   In others, the trial is bifurcated so that punitive damages may be awarded only if the defendant has been found to have engaged in conduct that merits monetary punishment.[180]

---

179. COLO. REV. STAT. § 13-21-102(1.5)(a) (2004) (claims for punitive damages to be by amendment to pleadings after initial disclosures and plaintiff establishes prima facie proof of triable issue); FLA. STAT. ANN. § 768.72(1) (2004) (claims for punitive damages to be by amendment to complaint after reasonable showing by evidence in record or proffered by claimant of reasonable basis for recovery); IDAHO CODE § 6-1604(2) (2004) (pleading may be amended pursuant to pretrial motion and after hearing if, after weighing evidence presented, court concludes that moving party has established reasonable likelihood of proving facts at trial sufficient to support award of punitive damages); KAN. STAT. ANN. § 60-3703 (2003) (court to allow amendment to pleading to seek punitive damages on motion and on basis of supporting and opposing affidavits presented that plaintiff has established probability of prevailing on claim); MINN. STAT. ANN. § 549.191 (2004) (punitive damages to be claimed by motion to amend pleadings, supported by affidavits showing factual basis for claim, and after hearing in which court finds prima facie evidence in support of motion); S.D. CODIFIED LAWS § 21-1-4.1 (2004) (no discovery concerning punitive damages before court finds, after hearing and based upon clear and convincing evidence, reasonable basis to find willful, wanton, or malicious conduct on part of party claimed against).

180. CAL. CIV. CODE § 3295(d) (2004) (at request of defendant, liability and damage phases of trial are bifurcated); GA. CODE ANN. § 51-12-5.1(d)(1) (2003) (factfinder to first determine whether to award punitive damages and then trial to be recommenced to receive evidence as to amount); KAN. STAT. ANN. § 60-3701(a) (2003) (liability for and amount of punitive damages to be determined in bifurcated proceedings before same factfinder); MD. CODE ANN., CTS. & JUD. PROC. § 10-913(a) (2004) (evidence of defendant's financial means not admissible until finding of liability and punitive damages supportable under facts); MINN. STAT. ANN. § 549.20(4) (2004) (upon request of any party, whether and in what amount punitive damages to be awarded is bifurcated from issue of compensatory damages); MISS. CODE ANN. § 11-1-65(1) (2003) (issue of punitive damages bifurcated from issue of compensatory damages); MO. ANN. STAT. § 510.263(1) (2004) (upon request of any party, issue of amount of punitive damages bifurcated from whether they may be awarded); MONT. CODE ANN. § 27-1-221(7)(a) (2003) (issue of amount of punitive damages award bifurcated from issue of whether to allow punitive damages award); NEV. REV. STAT. ANN. § 42.005(3) (2003) (same); N.J.

Other efforts to limit the availability of punitive damages also exist. One state expressly requires unanimity among jurors in both the granting of punitive damages and the amount of such an award.[181] At least two states permit a reduction in the punitive damages awarded if punitive damages have already been assessed against the tortfeasor for the same conduct.[182]   Vicarious or joint and several liability, including an employer's liability through the doctrine of respondeat superior, may be an insufficient basis for the imposition of punitive damages.[183]

STAT. ANN. § 2A:15-5.13 (2004) (bifurcated); N.D. CENT. CODE § 32-03.2-11(2) (2003) (at request of either party, factfinder to determine liability for compensatory damages before considering liability for punitive damages); OKLA STAT. ANN., Tit. 23, §§ 9.1(B)-(D) (2004) (separate jury proceeding for punitive damages); UTAH CODE ANN. § 78-18-1(2) (2003) (evidence of party's wealth or financial condition admissible only after finding of liability for punitive damages made).

181. TEX. CIV. PRAC. & REM. CODE § 41.003(d) (2004).

182. FLA. STAT. ANN. § 768.72(1) (2004); MO. ANN. STAT. § 510.263(4) (2004).

183. *See, e.g.,* Coty v. Ramsey Assocs., Inc., 546 A.2d 196, 206 (Vt. 1988) (holding under Vermont law that "joint and several liability does not attach in the context of punitive damages"); Embrey v. Holly, 442 A.2d 966, 974 (Md. 1982) (apportionment among defendants proper); ALASKA STAT. § 09.17.020(k) (2003) (punitive damages may not be awarded against employer under principles of vicarious liability unless (1) employer or employer's managerial agent (a) authorized act or omission and manner in which act was performed or omission occurred; or (b) ratified or approved act or omission after act or omission occurred; or (2) employee (a) was unfit to perform act or avoid omission and employer or employer's managerial agent acted recklessly in employing or retaining employee; or (b) was employed in managerial capacity and was acting within scope of employment); CAL. CIVIL CODE § 3294(b) (2004) (no employer liability for acts of employees unless employer had advance knowledge of unfitness of employee and employed him with conscious disregard of rights or safety of others or authorized or ratified wrongful conduct for which damages are awarded or was personally guilty of oppression, fraud, or malice); FLA. STAT. ANN. §§ 768.72(2), (3) (2004) (liability for punitive damages only if defendant is personally guilty of intentional misconduct or gross negligence; employers liable for punitive damages based on acts of employees only if employee's conduct is otherwise subject to punitive damages and employer actively and knowingly participated in such

2. *Other State Limitations on Punitive Damages*

Nearly half of the states have imposed a statutory cap on punitive damages. Typically, these caps take the form of some multiple of the damages awarded or a statutory maximum, whichever is greater.[184]

---

conduct; knowingly condoned, ratified, or consented to such conduct; or employer's gross negligence contributed to loss, damages, or injury suffered by claimant); KAN. STAT. ANN. § 60-3701(d) (2003) (employer not liable for punitive damages unless employee's conduct was authorized or ratified by person expressly empowered to do so on behalf of principal or employer); MINN. STAT. ANN. § 549.20(2) (2004) (punitive damages may be assessed against employer for acts of employee only if employer authorized doing and manner of employee's act, or employee agent was unfit and employer deliberately disregarded high probability that agent was unfit, or employee was employed in managerial capacity with authority to establish policy and make planning level decisions for principal and was acting in scope of employment, or managerial agent of employer ratified or approved act while knowing of its character and probable consequences); NEV. REV. STAT. ANN. § 42.007(1) (2003) (employer not liable for punitive damages as result of wrongful act of employee unless employer had advance knowledge that employee was unfit for purposes of employment and employed him with conscious disregard of rights or safety of others; employer expressly authorized or ratified wrongful act of employee for which damages are awarded; or employer is personally guilty of oppression, fraud, or malice); N.C. GEN. STAT. § 1D-15(c) (2004) (vicarious liability not basis for punitive damages; rather, one must participate in conduct that qualifies for punitive damages).

184. *See, e.g.*, ALA. CODE § 6-11-21(a) (2003) (providing for cap on punitive damages at greater of three times compensatory damages or $500,000); ALASKA STAT. § 09.17.020(f) (2003) (same); FLA. STAT. ANN. § 768.73(1)(a) (2004) (same); ARK. CODE ANN. § 16-55-208(a) (2004) (three times amount of compensatory damages awarded, not to exceed $1 million, or $250,000, whichever is greater); IDAHO CODE § 6-1604(3) (2004) (three times compensatory damages awarded, or $250,000, whichever is greater); IND. CODE ANN. § 34-51-3-4 (2004) (three times amount of compensatory damages awarded, or $50,000, whichever is greater); NEV. REV. STAT. ANN. § 42.005 (2003) (with some exceptions, limit of punitive damages is three times amount of compensatory damages if compensatory damages exceed $100,000 or more, or $300,000 if compensatory damages award is less than $100,000); N.J. STAT. ANN. § 2A:15-5.14(b) (2004) (punitive damages award limited to five times

Depending on the jurisdiction, the comparison may be to compensatory damages, or even actual damages.[185] One state has limited the amount of punitive damages that may be assessed to the amount of compensatory damages that are awarded.[186] A few states have imposed flat numerical caps on punitive damages,[187] while a few other states base the quantum of punitive damages on a defendant's net worth.[188] Another state limits punitive damages to the gross annual income of the tortfeasor.[189] And one state limits punitive damages to the greater of $200,000 or two times economic damages, plus the lesser of non-economic damages or $750,000.[190]

Many of the states with caps on punitive damages have, like the courts that review punitive damages awards for compliance with due process, struggled to maintain the balance between deterrence and retribution on the one hand, and the individualized assessment of the defendant's conduct on the other. The statutory caps on punitive damages are replete with exceptions based on the conduct of the defendant. Implicitly, this is accomplished by tying the quantum of punitive damages available to some multiple of the non-punitive

---

compensatory damages award or $350,000, whichever is greater); N.C. GEN. STAT. § 1D-25(b) (2004) (three times compensatory damages award or $250,000, whichever is greater); N.D. CENT. CODE § 32-03.2-11 (2003) (two times amount of compensatory damages or $250,000, whichever is greater).

185. OKLA. STAT. ANN., Tit. 23, § 9.1 (2004) (depending on intent and malice of defendant, punitive damages award limited to greater of $100,000 or actual damages awarded or greater of $500,000 or two times actual damages awarded).

186. *See, e.g.*, COLO. REV. STAT. § 13-21-102(1)(a) (2004) (exemplary damages may not exceed actual damages awarded).

187. GA. CODE ANN. § 51-12-5.1(g) (2003) (punitive damages award may not exceed $250,000 except in products liability cases); VA. CODE ANN. § 8.01-38.1 (2004) (punitive damages limited to $350,000).

188. MISS. CODE ANN. § 11-1-65(3)(a) (2003) (providing for sliding scale of caps based on net worth of defendant); MONT. CODE ANN. § 21-1-220(3) (2003) (punitive damages award may not exceed $10 million or 3 percent of defendant's net worth, whichever is less).

189. KAN. STAT. ANN. § 60-3701(e) (2003) (punitive damages to be lesser of $5 million or gross annual income earned by defendant).

190. TEX. CIV. PRAC. & REM. CODE § 41.008(b) (2004).

damages that are awarded to the complaining party. Explicitly, the statutory caps may raise, or even eliminate, the limits on punitive damages if the defendant's injury-causing conduct is found to be especially blameworthy and thus more reprehensible.[191]

Some states have imposed limits on non-economic damages, and this, too, can limit punitive damages.[192] Where such limits have been upheld,[193] a state statute that ties the amount of punitive damages to the other damages that have been awarded will further decrease the quantum of punitive damages that may be assessed. Limitations on non-economic damages may, however, be a double-edged sword. States that limit non-economic damages but do not also limit punitive damages present plaintiffs with a potentially persuasive argument that the Due Process Clause will permit a larger ratio of punitive to compensatory damages than the 4:1 ratio the *Gore* Court found "close to the line." After all, one of the primary assumptions underlying the Court's due process analysis – that the injured party has been fully compensated for her injuries by the non-punitive damages award – no longer would be accurate in this circumstance.

---

191. *See, e.g.*, OKLA. STAT. ANN., Tit. 23, § 9.1 D (no limitation on punitive damages that may be awarded when defendant acts intentionally and with malice toward others and court finds beyond reasonable doubt that defendant engaged in life-threatening conduct); MISS. CODE ANN. § 11-1-65(3)(d) (2003) (cap on punitive damages does not apply if, inter alia, injury-causing conduct of defendant leads to felony conviction or occurred while defendant was under influence of alcohol or illegal drugs); ARK. CODE ANN. § 8.01-38.1(b) (2004) (cap on punitive damages does not apply if jury finds defendant intentionally pursued course of conduct for purpose of causing injury or damage and conduct did, in fact, harm plaintiff).
192. *See, e.g.*, COLO. REV. STAT. § 13-21-102.5 (2004); IDAHO CODE § 6-1603 (2003); MD. CODE ANN., CTS. & JUD. PROC. § 11-108 (2004); MISS. CODE ANN. § 11-1-60 (2003); MO. ANN. STAT. § 538.210 (2004) (relating to actions against health care providers); OR. REV. STAT. § 31-710 (2003).
193. Some states have enacted limits on non-economic damages only to have these statutes declared unconstitutional. *See, e.g.*, Best v. Taylor Mach. Works, 689 N.E.2d 1057, 1077-78 (Ill. 1997) (declaring unconstitutional 735 ILL. STAT. ANN. §§ 5/2-1115.05 et. seq.).

Some states, by statute, have asserted a claim to some portion of the punitive damages that are awarded to a plaintiff.[194] These statutes, however, may resurrect the issue in *Kelco* – whether the Eighth Amendment's Excessive Fines Clause limits an award of punitive damages. In deciding *Kelco*, the Supreme Court expressly limited its holding: "Whatever the outer confines of the Clause's reach may be, we now decide only that it does not constrain an award of money damages in a civil suit when the government neither has prosecuted the action nor has any right to receive a share of the damages awarded."[195] At least one federal district court has held that a Georgia statute entitling the state to 75 percent of a punitive damages award converts a civil action into one "where fines are being made for the benefit of the State, contrary to the constitutional prohibitions as to excessive fines and contrary to the double jeopardy clause of the Fifth Amendment to the Constitution of the United States."[196] However, Georgia's high court subsequently has

---

194. ALASKA STAT. ANN. § 09.17.020(j) (2003) (50 percent of punitive damages awarded are to be deposited in state's general fund); GA. CODE ANN. § 51-12-5.1(e)(2) (2003) (no limit to punitive damages for product liability actions, but 75 percent of punitive damages award, less proportionate part of costs and attorney's fees, are to be deposited with state); IND. CODE ANN. § 34-51-3-6 (2004) (75 percent of punitive damages awarded to be retained by state); IOWA CODE ANN. § 668A1 (2003) (if injury causing conduct of defendant was not directed specifically at claimant, claimant receives 25 percent of award and remaining 75 percent of punitive damages award is to be paid to civil reparations trust fund); MO. ANN. STAT. § 537.675 (2004) (50 percent of all punitive damages awards, less attorney's fees and costs, to be deposited in state's Tort Victims' Compensation Fund); OR. REV. STAT. § 31.735 (2003) (60 percent of punitive damages awarded to be paid to Criminal Injuries Compensation Account of the Department of Justice Crime Victims' Assistance Section); UTAH CODE ANN. § 78-18-1 (2003) (50 percent of punitive damages award, after first $20,000, to be paid to state's general fund).

195. *Browning-Ferris Indus. of Vt., Inc.*, 492 U.S. at 263-64.

196. McBride v. Gen. Motors Corp., 737 F. Supp. 1563, 1578 (M.D. Ga. 1990) (construing GA. CODE ANN. § 51-12-5.1(e)(2)).

upheld the statute's constitutionality, though it did not address any Eighth Amendment concerns.[197]

---

197. Mack Trucks, Inc. v. Conkle, 436 S.E.2d 635, 639-40 (Ga. 1993) (upholding constitutionality of GA. CODE ANN. § 51-12-5.1(e)(2) as not violating equal protection principles and not constituting a taking under Fifth and Fourteenth Amendments; jury award of $2 million in punitive damages against manufacturer for failure to recall or to warn of inadequacy of frame rail on truck was not so excessive as to violate due process clauses of Georgia Constitution and U.S. Constitution, Eighth Amendment of U.S. Constitution, or excessive fines clause of Georgia Constitution).

PART II

BUSINESS TORT LITIGATION

**Subject Matter Jurisdiction in
Antitrust and Business Tort Litigation**

**Personal Jurisdiction, Process, and
Venue in Antitrust and Business Tort Litigation**

Forum Selection in Antitrust and Business Tort Litigation

Removal and Remand

Issues Relating to Parallel Litigation

Preemption and Commerce Clause Issues

CHAPTER IX

SUBJECT MATTER JURISDICTION IN ANTITRUST AND BUSINESS TORT LITIGATION

This chapter opens the discussion of procedural issues commonly encountered in antitrust and business tort litigation. When evaluating choices among federal and state statutory and common law claims potentially available to address marketplace conduct, subject matter jurisdiction often becomes a threshold issue. Personal jurisdiction, process, and venue are treated in the next chapter. – Eds.

A. Introduction

This chapter examines issues that typically arise in assessing subject matter jurisdiction of the state and federal courts in antitrust and business tort litigation. While relatively straightforward, the authorities governing subject matter jurisdiction and the strategy involved in determining when to pursue the subject matter jurisdiction of a particular court often determine the outcome of a variety of procedural issues related to the initial stages of business litigation, such as removal and remand, transfer of venue, and preemption, which are treated in subsequent chapters.

B. Types of Federal Subject Matter Jurisdiction

Subject matter jurisdiction is literally the power of a court to entertain and adjudicate certain types of disputes.[1] A judgment rendered in a court without subject matter jurisdiction is invalid.[2] While most state courts generally possess subject matter jurisdiction over actions brought under federal or state law unless a statute excludes it, a federal

---

1. 1 ROBERT L. HAIG, BUSINESS AND COMMERCIAL LITIGATION IN FEDERAL COURTS § 1.1, at 3 (1998).

2. Caterpillar Inc. v. Lewis, 519 U.S. 61, 77 (1996) (district court must possess federal court subject matter jurisdiction when judgment is rendered for it to be valid); Gen. Star Nat'l Ins. Co. v. Administratia Asiguararilor de Stat, 289 F.3d 434, 437 (6th Cir. 2002) (judgment is void if rendered by court lacking subject matter jurisdiction); Antoine v. Atlas Turner, Inc., 66 F.3d 105, 108 (6th Cir. 1995) (same).

court may exercise subject matter jurisdiction only when it is specifically authorized to do so. Federal courts are thus commonly referred to as courts of "limited," rather than "general," jurisdiction.[3] A party intending to litigate in federal court, either by initiating the lawsuit or seeking removal, bears the burden of establishing the court's jurisdictional authority over the case.[4]

Federal subject matter jurisdiction over a particular controversy must derive from an act of Congress.[5] Even a contractual agreement between parties is incapable of conferring subject matter jurisdiction on a federal court.[6] The principal federal statutes relating to business tort litigation and conferring subject matter jurisdiction on federal courts are set out in Chapter 85 of the Judicial Code (codified at Title 28 of the United States Code), and deal with the three main types of federal subject matter jurisdiction: federal question,[7] diversity,[8] and supplemental jurisdiction.[9]

---

3. Bender v. Williamsport Area Sch. Dist., 475 U.S. 534, 541 (1986); Empagran S.A. v. F. Hoffman-LaRoche Ltd., 388 F.3d 337, 346 (D.C. Cir. 2004); Tsegay v. Ashcroft, 386 F.3d 1347, 1353 (10th Cir. 2004); De Asencio v. Tyson Foods, Inc., 343 F.3d 301, 310 n.14 (3d Cir. 2003); Marine Equip. Mgmt. Co. v. United States, 4 F.3d 643, 646 (8th Cir. 1993); United States v. Chambers, 944 F.2d 1253, 1258 (6th Cir. 1991); *see generally* 13 CHARLES ALAN WRIGHT ET AL., FEDERAL PRACTICE AND PROCEDURE § 3522 (2d ed. 1997).
4. *See, e.g.*, McNutt v. Gen. Motors Acceptance Corp., 298 U.S. 178, 189 (1936) (party seeking to litigate in federal court bears burden of establishing jurisdictional basis for doing so); Herrick Co. v. SCS Commc'ns, Inc., 251 F.3d 315, 323 (2d Cir. 2001) (burden lies with party attempting to bring action to federal court).
5. *See McNutt*, 298 U.S. at 189.
6. Sosna v. Iowa, 419 U.S. 393, 398 (1975); *see also* Binder v. Price Waterhouse & Co., LLP (*In re* Resorts Int'l, Inc.), 372 F.3d 154, 161 (3d Cir. 2004) (parties cannot create subject matter jurisdiction by their own agreement).
7. *See* 28 U.S.C. § 1331.
8. *See id.* § 1332.
9. *See id.* § 1367.

1. *Federal Question Jurisdiction*

Federal question jurisdiction derives from the nature of the asserted claim. The general federal question statute provides that federal district courts shall have original jurisdiction of all civil actions arising under the Constitution, laws, or treaties of the United States, without regard to the amount in controversy between the parties.[10]

A cause of action is generally deemed to "arise under" federal law either when the cause of action is created by federal law or is grounded in state law but requires the resolution of a substantial question of federal law involving a significant federal interest.[11] "Federal law" includes federal statutes, federal administrative agency regulations,[12] as well as

---

10. *Id.* § 1331. The elimination of the amount-in-controversy requirement has rendered statutes, such as those that confer federal subject matter jurisdiction over claims arising under federal antitrust laws, largely redundant. *See* 13B WRIGHT ET AL., *supra* note 3, § 3574.

11. *See* Franchise Tax Bd. of Cal. v. Constr. Laborers Vacation Trust for S. Cal., 463 U.S. 1, 9-10 (1983) (case "arises under" federal law when substantial disputed issue of federal law is necessary element of state law claim); Ayres v. GM, 234 F.3d 514, 518 (11th Cir. 2000) (litigation of claim depends on resolution of substantial, disputed question of federal law); Pacheco de Perez v. AT&T Co., 139 F.3d 1368, 1373 (11th Cir. 1998) (case "arises under federal law if federal law creates cause of action or if substantial disputed issue of federal law is necessary element of state law claim); Ormet Corp. v. Ohio Power Co., 98 F.3d 799, 806 (4th Cir. 1996) (even though claim is created by state law, it may involve resolution of federal question sufficient to give rise to jurisdiction under § 1331); *see also* Carpenter v. Wichita Falls Indep. Sch. Dist., 44 F.3d 362, 371 (5th Cir. 1995) (federal question jurisdiction may exist over state law claim when prior judgment on federal question completely precluded state claim). *But see* Rivet v. Regions Bank of La., 522 U.S. 470, 478 (1998) (rejecting Fifth Circuit approach and holding that "claim preclusion by reason of a prior federal judgment is a defensive plea that provides no basis for removal under § 1441(b)").

12. Reno v. Catholic Soc. Servs., Inc., 509 U.S. 43, 56 (1993); Dixie Fuel Co. v. Comm'r of Soc. Sec., 171 F.3d 1052, 1057 (6th Cir. 1999) (finding jurisdiction of federal district courts over reviews of federal agency actions under § 1331), *overruled on other grounds*, Barnhart v. Peabody Coal Co., 537 U.S. 149 (2003).

federal common law.[13]   Courts have also recognized that international law may be considered as part of the laws of the United States for purposes of federal question jurisdiction.[14]

As noted above, certain federal statutes confer subject matter jurisdiction upon the district courts relating to particular subject matters. To invoke federal subject matter jurisdiction on the basis of a federal statute, a party must show that the cause of action pled arises under the statutory jurisdictional grant.   These statutes include those related to admiralty and maritime law,[15] bankruptcy,[16] statutory interpleader,[17] commerce and antitrust,[18] patents and other intellectual property rights,[19] civil rights,[20] the Federal Deposit Insurance Corporation,[21] and the Racketeer Influenced and Corrupt Organizations ("RICO") Act.[22]

There is federal question jurisdiction only over *claims* arising under federal law. Conversely, the existence of a federal *defense* to a state law

---

13.   Illinois v. City of Milwaukee, 406 U.S. 91, 100 (1972) (claims grounded in federal common law may give rise to federal court jurisdiction), *vacated on other grounds*, 451 U.S. 304 (1981); Frank v. Bear Stearns & Co., 128 F.3d 919, 922 (5th Cir. 1997) (federal question jurisdiction may exist in actions arising under federal common law); Bollman Hat Co. v. Root, 112 F.3d 113, 115 (3d Cir. 1997) (federal question jurisdiction will support claims arising under federal statute as well as federal common law).

14.   Torres v. S. Peru Copper Corp., 113 F.3d 540, 542 n.7 (5th Cir. 1997) (recognizing creation of federal common law in area of foreign relations in determining subject matter jurisdiction); *see also* Tex. Indus., Inc. v. Radcliff Materials, Inc., 451 U.S. 630, 641 (1981) (allowing federal common law in area of foreign relations as means of conferring federal question jurisdiction); Republic of Philippines v. Marcos, 806 F.2d 344, 352 (2d Cir. 1986) (even though action was based on state law theory, "an examination shows that the plaintiff's claims necessarily require determinations that will directly and significantly affect American foreign relations").

15.   28 U.S.C. § 1333.

16.   *Id.* § 1334.

17.   *Id.* § 1335.

18.   *Id.* § 1337.

19.   *Id.* § 1338.

20.   *Id.* § 1343.

21.   12 U.S.C. §§ 1441a, 1819.

22.   18 U.S.C. §§ 1961 *et seq.*

claim will not support federal question jurisdiction, even when the defense is specifically asserted in the defendant's answer or anticipated in the plaintiff's pleadings.[23] This principle applies even when parties agree that the only disputed issue in the case is the availability of a federal defense.[24]

The federal issue also must be "substantial" to sustain federal question jurisdiction. Historically, federal courts have been prohibited from exercising jurisdiction over issues when the federal claims are "so attenuated and unsubstantial as to be absolutely devoid of merit."[25] Substantiality, however, does not refer to the value of the claim at issue. In *Hagans v. Lavine*,[26] the Supreme Court stated that "substantial" means that a claim is not "essentially fictitious," "implausible," or "patently without merit."[27] A party need not prove in advance that it will ultimately or even likely succeed on the merits of a federal cause of action; federal question jurisdiction remains even if a court eventually determines that the federal cause of action lacks merit.[28]

2. *Diversity Jurisdiction*

Article III of the U.S. Constitution authorizes federal courts to entertain suits between citizens of different states, as well as for cases or controversies between "a State, or the Citizens thereof, and foreign States, Citizens, or Subjects."[29] Section 1332 of Title 28, which provides

---

23. Caterpillar Inc. v. Williams, 482 U.S. 386, 392 (1987); Franchise Tax Bd. of Cal. v. Constr. Laborers Vacation Trust for S. Cal., 463 U.S. 1, 9-12 (1983).

24. *Williams*, 482 U.S. at 393.

25. Newburyport Water Co. v. Newburyport, 193 U.S. 561, 579 (1904); *see also* EEOC v. Chicago Club, 86 F.3d 1423, 1428 (7th Cir. 1996); Wiley v. NCAA, 612 F.2d 473, 477 (10th Cir. 1979).

26. 415 U.S. 528 (1974).

27. *Id.* at 537, 542-43; *see also* Zheng v. Reno, 166 F. Supp. 2d 875, 880 (S.D.N.Y. 2001); Bartolini v. Ashcroft, 226 F. Supp. 2d 350, 354 (D. Conn. 2002).

28. Bell v. Hood, 327 U.S. 678, 682 (1946) (allegation of substantial federal claim is sufficient to invoke subject matter jurisdiction even if ultimately dismissed on merits for failure to state cause of action); *see also* Steel Co. v. Citizens for a Better Env't, 523 U.S. 83, 89 (1998) ("the absence of a valid . . . cause of action does not implicate subject-matter jurisdiction").

29. U.S. CONST. art. III, § 2.

the statutory authority for diversity jurisdiction, provides that "[t]he district courts shall have original jurisdiction of all civil actions where the matter in controversy exceeds the sum or value of $75,000, exclusive of interest and costs, and is between

(1)   citizens of different States;

(2)   citizens of a State and citizens or subjects of a foreign state;

(3)   citizens of different States and in which citizens or subjects of a foreign state are additional parties; and

(4)   a foreign state . . . as plaintiff and citizens of a State or of different States.[30]

The grounds for diversity jurisdiction must be set forth either in the initial complaint or in the defendant's removal papers.[31]   Courts generally determine diversity jurisdiction soon after a case is filed in federal court.[32]   Once a federal court has determined that diversity jurisdiction is present, subsequent events typically will not oust such jurisdiction.[33]   Defects in jurisdictional allegations, including diversity jurisdiction, may be amended and cured, by leave of court, in both the trial and appellate courts.[34]

Determining proper citizenship is the primary inquiry in assessing diversity jurisdiction. The citizenship of an individual party is based upon his or her domicile, which is defined as the "place where [a party]

30.   28 U.S.C. § 1332(a).

31.   McNutt v. Gen. Motors Acceptance Corp., 298 U.S. 178, 189 (1936) (burden of establishing grounds for diversity jurisdiction lies with party invoking such jurisdiction); Herrick Co. v. SCS Commc'ns, Inc., 251 F.3d 315, 322-23 (2d Cir. 2001) (same); Coyne v. Am. Tobacco Co., 183 F.3d 488, 492-93 (6th Cir. 1998) (same); Advani Enters., Inc. v. Underwriters at Lloyds, 140 F.3d 157, 160 (2d Cir. 1998) (same).

32.   Newman-Green, Inc. v. Alfonzo-Larrain, 490 U.S. 826, 830 (1989).

33.   *See, e.g.*, Allen v. R&H Oil & Gas Co., 63 F.3d 1326, 1336 (5th Cir. 1995) (amendment to plaintiff's complaint limiting damages to amounts below jurisdictional threshold will not divest jurisdiction); Freeport-McMoRan, Inc. v. K N Energy, Inc., 498 U.S. 426, 428 (1991) (addition of nondiverse, nonessential party cannot destroy jurisdiction).

34.   28 U.S.C. § 1653; *see also* Whitmire v. Victus Ltd., 212 F.3d 885, 890 (5th Cir. 2000) (trial court abused its discretion in refusing to permit party to amend jurisdictional allegations to assert diversity jurisdiction and allowing party to amend on appeal).

has his true, fixed and permanent home and principal establishment, and to which he has the intention of returning whenever he is absent therefrom."[35] Courts have historically held that, because an individual has only one domicile, an individual may be the citizen of only one state for diversity jurisdiction purposes.[36]

A corporation, however, may maintain "dual citizenship," because it is deemed to be a citizen of both the state of incorporation and the state of its principal place of business.[37] For businesses that conduct critical corporate functions in multiple locations, determining "principal place of business" citizenship can be complicated. Some courts have adopted a "nerve center" approach whereby the focus is on where corporate policies are primarily formulated.[38] Other approaches focus on the locations of the corporate assets, facilities, and employees.[39] The more modern approach – referred to at times as the "total activity" test[40] – is to evaluate where most of the corporate activity occurs by examining both the location of a corporation's "nerve center" and its primary place of corporate activity.[41]

---

35. CHARLES ALAN WRIGHT, LAWS OF FEDERAL COURT § 26, at 161 (5th ed. 1994).
36. Williamson v. Osenton, 232 U.S. 619, 625 (1914) (individual party can only be citizen of one state at a time); Keys Youth Servs., Inc. v. City of Olathe, 248 F.3d 1267, 1272 (10th Cir. 2001) (party has one domicile at a time); Bank One v. Montle, 964 F.2d 48, 49 (1st Cir. 1992) (for diversity purposes, person is citizen of state of domicile); Lundquist v. Precision Valley Aviation, Inc., 946 F.2d 8, 10 (1st Cir. 1991) (same); Avins v. Hannum, 497 F. Supp. 930, 942 (E.D. Pa. 1980) (party may only be citizen of one state at a time).
37. 28 U.S.C. § 1332(c)(1); *see also* Dimmitt & Owens Fin., Inc. v. United States, 787 F.2d 1186, 1190 (7th Cir. 1986).
38. Topp v. CompAir, Inc., 814 F.2d 830, 834-35 (1st Cir. 1987).
39. *See, e.g.*, Grand Union Supermarkets of the V.I., Inc. v. H.E. Lockhart Mgmt., Inc., 316 F.3d 408, 411 (3d Cir. 2003); Kelly v. U.S. Steel Corp., 284 F.2d 850, 854 (3d Cir. 1960); Anniston Soil Pipe Co. v. Cent. Foundry Co., 216 F. Supp. 473, 475-76 (N.D. Ala. 1963), *aff'd*, 329 F.2d 313, 313 (5th Cir. 1964).
40. J.A. Olson Co. v. City of Winona, 818 F.2d 401, 404 (5th Cir. 1987) (applying the "total activity" test).
41. Toms v. Country Quality Meats, Inc., 610 F.2d 313, 315 (5th Cir. 1980); Lugo-Vina v. Pueblo Int'l, Inc., 574 F.2d 41, 44 (1st Cir. 1978); Daris *ex*

A domestic corporation having its principal place of business abroad seemingly provides an exception to the "dual citizenship" rule. In *Torres v. Southern Peru Copper Corp.*,[42] the Fifth Circuit held that a domestic corporation with its principal place of business in a foreign state is considered to be a citizen only of its state of incorporation.[43] In contrast, a foreign corporation incorporated abroad may be found to be a citizen of the state where it has its principal place of business.[44] A federal corporation established under a congressional act, however, cannot be sued in a federal diversity case because, as a general matter, such a corporation is not considered to be a citizen of any particular state.[45]

An unincorporated association, such as a general or limited partnership, is deemed to be a citizen of *every* state in which its partners are citizens.[46] In a shareholder derivative action, only the named shareholders of a corporation are considered for purposes of determining diversity jurisdiction.[47] Section 1332 also provides special rules for determining the citizenship of resident aliens[48] and legal

---

rel. Estate of Hart v. Trumbo, Inc., No. 102-CV-183, 2002 WL 31992187, at *2 (N.D. Miss. Dec. 2, 2002).

42. 113 F.3d 540 (5th Cir. 1997).
43. *Id.* at 543. The Fifth Circuit further stated that it was aware of no other authority for determining the citizenship of a domestic corporation with its principal place of business in a foreign state. *Id.*
44. Danjaq, S.A. v. Pathe Commc'ns Corp., 979 F.2d 772, 776 (9th Cir. 1992) (foreign corporation maintained citizenship in state of principal place of business); Panalpina Welttransport GmBh v. Geosource, Inc., 764 F.2d 352, 354 (5th Cir. 1985).
45. Bankers' Trust Co. v. Tex. & Pac. Ry. Co., 241 U.S. 295, 310 (1916); *see also* Weathermon v. Disabled Am. Veterans, 15 F. Supp. 2d 940, 941 (D. Neb. 1998) (no diversity jurisdiction because DAV is national citizen). *But see* Patterson v. Am. Nat'l Red Cross, 101 F. Supp. 655, 657 (S.D. Fla. 1951) (finding diversity jurisdiction because corporation created by congressional act granting its corporate existence was citizen of District of Columbia).
46. Carden v. Arkoma Assocs., 494 U.S. 185, 189 (1990).
47. Weinstock v. Kallet, 11 F.R.D. 270, 272 (S.D.N.Y. 1951); *see generally* 7C WRIGHT ET AL., *supra* note 3, § 1822.
48. 28 U.S.C. § 1332(a); *see* JPMorgan Chase Bank v. Traffic Stream (BVI) Infrastructure Ltd., 536 U.S. 88, 99-100 (2002) (corporation organized

representatives.[49] In class actions, the citizenship of the named class representatives controls the diversity analysis.[50] Diversity, therefore, is required only between the named plaintiffs and named defendants to a class action; the citizenship of the absent class members is not considered.[51]

Section 1332 requires complete diversity of citizenship, meaning that diversity is destroyed when a single plaintiff shares citizenship with a single defendant.[52] Because the statute requires both complete diversity of citizenship and at least $75,000 in controversy, a plaintiff seeking to avoid removal based on diversity jurisdiction may either join a non-diverse defendant or specifically plead for an amount damages less than $75,000.[53] Additionally, and as discussed more fully in Chapter 12, even when the parties are diverse the plaintiff may avoid removal by filing suit in a state court of the defendant's home state.[54]

---

under laws of British Virgin Islands is deemed citizen of foreign state for purposes of alienage jurisdiction under § 1332(a)(2)).

49. 28 U.S.C. § 1332(c)(2).
50. Supreme Tribe of Ben Hur v. Cauble, 255 U.S. 356, 365-66 (1921), *overruled on other grounds*, Toucey v. N.Y. Life Ins. Co., 314 U.S. 118, 138 (1941); Kerney v. Fort Griffin Fandangle Ass'n, 624 F.2d 717, 719 (5th Cir. 1980); *see also* Rosmer v. Pfizer, 263 F.3d 110, 112 (4th Cir. 2001).
51. *Cauble*, 255 U.S. at 365-66.
52. *See* Romero v. Int'l Terminal Operating Co., 358 U.S. 354, 361-62 (1959), *superceded by rule on other grounds*, U.S. Express Lines, Ltd. v. Higgins, 281 F.3d 383, 390 (3d Cir. 2002); *see also, e.g.*, Lee v. Am. Nat'l Ins. Co., 260 F.3d 997, 1005 (9th Cir. 2001) ("The parties in this case remain citizens of different states, over whom the federal court may exercise jurisdiction . . . . [Plaintiff's] lack of standing [as to one defendant] only renders his claims against [the non-diverse defendant] nonjusticiable in federal court, but does not alter the presence of complete diversity."); Krueger v. Cartwright, 996 F.2d 928, 931 (7th Cir. 1993); Jernigan v. Ashland Oil, Inc., 989 F.2d 812, 814 (5th Cir. 1993); Sweeney v. Westvaco Co., 926 F.2d 29, 41 (1st Cir. 1991).
53. *See* Shaw v. Dow Brands, Inc., 994 F.2d 364, 366 (7th Cir. 1993); 14A WRIGHT ET AL., *supra* note 3, § 3725.
54. 28 U.S.C. § 1441(b); *see also* Hurt v. Dow Chem. Co., 963 F.2d 1142, 1145 (8th Cir. 1992); Hartford Accident & Indem. Co. v. Costa Lines Cargo Servs., Inc., 903 F.2d 352, 358 (5th Cir. 1990).

The presence of a "stateless citizen" (a United States citizen domiciled abroad[55]) precludes federal diversity jurisdiction.[56] Finally, for diversity purposes, federal courts do not recognize dual citizenship with respect to persons who are citizens of both the United States and a foreign country; instead, federal courts recognize only the American nationality of the dual citizen in determining diversity jurisdiction.[57]

With respect to determining the amount in controversy, federal law determines the value of a claim, even a claim asserted under state law.[58] Where a statute provides for treble damages, such damages can be considered in determining the amount in controversy.[59] Likewise, claims for punitive damages may be included in calculating the amount in controversy[60] unless such damages are "patently frivolous and without foundation" or otherwise unavailable as a matter of state substantive law.[61] As a general matter, attorneys' fees are excluded in determining

---

55. 1 HAIG, *supra* note 1, § 1.7, at 29.
56. Sadat v. Mertes, 615 F.2d 1176, 1180 (7th Cir. 1980); Smith v. Carter, 545 F.2d 909, 911 (5th Cir. 1977).
57. Mutuelles Unies v. Kroll & Linstrom, 957 F.2d 707, 711 (9th Cir. 1992); Action S.A. v. Marc Rich & Co., 951 F.2d 504, 507 (2d Cir. 1991) (only American nationality of dual citizen should be recognized under § 1332(a)(2)); *Sadat*, 615 F.2d at 1187 (same).
58. Horton v. Liberty Mut. Ins. Co., 367 U.S. 348, 352-53 (1961); *see also* Hart v. Schering-Plough Corp., 253 F.3d 272, 274 (7th Cir. 2001) (damages and costs used in calculating jurisdictional amount in controversy is governed by federal law).
59. *In re* High Fructose Corn Syrup Antitrust Litig., 936 F. Supp. 530, 533 (C.D. Ill. 1996); Kenebrew v. Conn. Gen. Life Ins. Co., 882 F. Supp. 749, 751 (N.D. Ill. 1995).
60. Golden v. Golden, 382 F.3d 348, 355 (3d Cir. 2004) (valid requests for punitive damages will generally satisfy amount in controversy requirement); Dow Agrosciences LLC v. Bates, 332 F.3d 323, 326 (5th Cir. 2003) (same)); Hartford Ins. Group v. Lou-Con Inc., 293 F.3d 908, 910 (5th Cir. 2002) (including punitive damages in amount in controversy calculation); Crawford v. F. Hoffman-LaRoche Ltd., 267 F.3d 760, 766 (8th Cir. 2001) (punitive damages may be used to establish diversity jurisdiction); Allison v. Sec. Benefit Life Ins. Co., 980 F.2d 1213, 1215 (8th Cir. 1992) (same).
61. *Golden*, 382 F.3d at 355; Byrd v. Corestates Bank, N.A. (*In re* Corestates Trust Fee Litig.), 39 F.3d 61, 64 (3d Cir. 1994) (same); *see also* Hayes v. Equitable Energy Res. Co., 266 F.3d 560, 572 (6th Cir. 2001) (punitive

the amount in controversy.[62] Nonetheless, where a statute mandates or allows for the recovery of attorneys' fees or where such fees are provided for by contract, attorneys' fees may be included with the amount in controversy.[63]

When a claim is one for declaratory or injunctive relief, the amount in controversy is measured by the value of the object of the litigation. This may include the value of the right to be protected or the value of the extent of the injury to be prevented.[64]

---

damages must be considered in jurisdictional amount in controversy unless apparent to "legal certainty" that such amounts cannot be recovered); Holley Equip. Co. v. Credit Alliance Corp., 821 F.2d 1531, 1535 (11th Cir. 1987) (same).

62. Mo. State Life Ins. Co. v. Jones, 290 U.S. 199, 200 (1933); Spielman v. Genzyme Corp., 251 F.3d 1, 7 (1st Cir. 2001).

63. *Jones*, 290 U.S. at 200; *Spielman*, 251 F.3d at 7 (noting exceptions to general rule); Velez v. Crown Life Ins. Co., 599 F.2d 471, 474 (1st Cir. 1979) (recognizing two logical exceptions to general rule that attorneys' fees are excluded in determining amount in controversy); Cordero, Miranda & Pinto v. Winn, 721 F. Supp. 1496, 1497 (D.P.R. 1989) (attorneys' fees not included in calculating jurisdictional amount unless authorized by statute, contract, or other legal authority); *see also* Johnson v. Am. Online, Inc., 280 F. Supp. 2d 1018, 1025-26 (N.D. Cal. 2003) (attorneys' fees may be included in calculating jurisdictional amount in controversy where underlying statute allows recovery of such fees).

64. *See, e.g.*, Hunt v. Wash. State Apple Adver. Comm'n, 432 U.S. 333, 347 (1977) (in actions seeking declaratory or injunctive relief, it is well established that amount in controversy is measured by value of object of litigation); Young v. Leventhal, 389 F.3d 1, 3 (1st Cir. 2004) (same, citing *Hunt*); America's Moneyline Inc. v. Coleman, 360 F.3d 782, 786 (7th Cir. 2004) (value of object of litigation is pecuniary result that would flow to plaintiff or defendant from court's granting injunction or declaratory judgment); Bates, 332 F.3d at 326 (when claim is one for declaratory relief, amount in controversy is determined by value of right to be protected or extent of injury to be prevented); Cincinnati Ins. Co. v. Zen Design Group, Ltd., 329 F.3d 546, 548 (6th Cir. 2003) (same); Federated Mut. Ins. Co. v. McKinnon Motors, LLC, 329 F.3d 805, 807 (11th Cir. 2003) (same); Cohn v. Petsmart, Inc., 281 F.3d 837, 840 (9th Cir. 2002) (same); Dixon v. Edwards, 290 F.3d 699, 711 (4th Cir. 2002) (determining amount in controversy satisfied on grounds that, if contract were declared null and injunction entered, one defendant would lose compensation of

With respect to class actions, the Supreme Court previously in *Zahn v. International Paper Co.*,[65] required each plaintiff in the class to satisfy the jurisdictional amount in controversy requirement.[66] Thereafter, however, there remained a split among the federal circuits as to whether the passage of the Judicial Improvements Act in 1990,[67] which clarified the supplemental jurisdiction of the federal courts, overruled *Zahn*.[68] In 2000, the Supreme Court addressed this issue but split 4-4 in its decision.[69]

This year, however, the Court with a clear majority held that the supplemental jurisdiction statute gives a district court that has diversity jurisdiction over one plaintiff's claim, including the amount in controversy, jurisdiction over other plaintiffs' (including unnamed class members') similar claims, without regard to the amount in controversy for each of their individual claims.[70] For that reason, the supplemental

---

over $75,000 and another defendant would be deprived of services valued at more than $75,000).

65. 414 U.S. 291 (1973).

66. *Id.* at 301.

67. *See* 28 U.S.C. § 1367.

68. *See* Trimble v. Asarco, Inc., 232 F.3d 946, 961 (8th Cir. 2000) (*Zahn* remains controlling law); Leonhardt v. W. Sugar Co., 160 F.3d 631, 641 (10th Cir. 1998) (same); Meritcare Inc. v. St. Paul Mercury Ins. Co, 166 F.3d 214, 218 (3d Cir. 1999) (same). *But see* Free v. Abbott Labs., Inc. (*In re* Abbott Labs.), 51 F.3d 524, 529 (5th Cir. 1995) (holding that Judicial Improvements Act of 1998 overruled *Zahn*), *aff'd*, 529 U.S. 333 (2000) (per curiam; judgment affirmed by equally divided Court); Olden v. LaFarge Corp., 383 F.3d 495, 502 (6th Cir 2004) (same); Rosmer v. Pfizer Inc., 263 F.3d 110, 114 (4th Cir. 2001) (same); Stromberg Metal Works, Inc. v. Press Mech., Inc., 77 F.3d 928, 930 (7th Cir. 1996) (same); *see also* del Rosario Ortega v. Star-Kist Foods, Inc., 370 F.3d 124, 143 (1st Cir. 2004) (expressing no view on issue whether § 1367 overturns Supreme Court's holding in *Zahn* that each member in diversity-only class action must meet jurisdictional amount in controversy), *cert. granted*, 125 S. Ct. 314 (2004).

69. In 2000, the Court affirmed by an equally divided court a Fifth Circuit decision which had overruled *Zahn*. *Free (In re Abbott Labs.)*, 529 U.S. at 333; *see also* Del Vecchio v. Conseco, Inc., 230 F.3d 974, 977 (7th Cir. 2000) (discussing *Free*).

70. Exxon Mobil Corp. v. Allapattah Servs., Inc., 125 S. Ct. 2611, 2625 (2005) (appeal combined with *del Rosario Ortega*).

jurisdiction statute overturns the Court's decision to the contrary in *Zahn*.[71]

The punitive damages claims of individual class action members may not ordinarily be aggregated for jurisdictional purposes.[72] Although some federal circuits as recently as the mid-1990s permitted aggregation of punitive damages across a class of plaintiffs, those courts have retreated from these decisions and now generally prohibit aggregation.[73]

An exception to the "complete diversity" and "amount-in-controversy" requirements in diversity cases warrants special mention. The federal district courts have original jurisdiction over interpleader actions when the amount in controversy is $500 or more[74] and there is "minimal diversity" between the parties.[75] Minimum diversity requires that at least one plaintiff and one defendant be citizens of different states.[76] Once diversity jurisdiction has been established, diversity is not destroyed even if a stakeholder is discharged, leaving only non-diverse parties.[77]

---

71. *See id.*
72. *Crawford*, 267 F.3d at 765; *see also* Gibson v. Chrysler Corp., 262 F.3d 927, 945-47 (9th Cir. 2001); Martin v. Franklin Capital Corp., 251 F.3d 1284, 1292-93 (10th Cir. 2001); Morrison v. Allstate Indem. Co., 228 F.3d 1255, 1264-65 (11th Cir. 2000); Ard v. Transcon. Pipe Line Corp., 138 F.3d 596, 601-02 (5th Cir. 1998); Anthony v. Sec. Pac. Fin. Servs., Inc., 75 F.3d 311, 315 (7th Cir. 1996). *But see* Snyder v. Harris, 394 U.S. 332, 335 (1969) (distinct claims of two or more plaintiffs cannot be aggregated except when plaintiffs "write to enforce a single title or right in which they have a common and undivided interest").
73. *See* Cohen v. Office Depot, Inc., 204 F.3d 1069, 1073-77 (11th Cir. 2000), *overruling* Tapscott v. MS Dealer Serv. Corp., 77 F.3d 1353 (11th Cir. 1996); *Ard*, 138 F.3d at 601-02 (refusing to follow cases aggregating punitive damages across class plaintiffs, outside of context of Mississippi law).
74. 28 U.S.C. § 1335(a); CNA Ins. Cos. v. Waters, 926 F.3d 247, 250 n.5 (3d Cir. 1991).
75. State Farm Fire & Cas. Co. v. Tashire, 386 U.S. 523, 530 (1967); *Waters*, 926 F.2d at 250 n.5; Metro. Life Ins. Co. v. Capozzoli, 9 F. Supp. 2d 645, 646 (W.D. Va. 1998).
76. *Tashire*, 386 U.S. at 530.
77. Leimbach v. Allen, 976 F.2d 912, 917 (4th Cir. 1992).

**3.   *Federal Jurisdiction for Certain Class Actions Under
       The Class Action Fairness Act of 2005***

On February 18, 2005, President Bush signed the Class Action
Fairness Act of 2005 (the "Act").[78] Among other things, the Act creates
federal jurisdiction for certain class actions. It also provides for removal
of certain class actions to federal court.[79] The Act is applicable to class
actions commenced after enactment.[80]

Under the Act, a federal court "shall have original jurisdiction" over
any non-securities[81] civil action: (1) in which the matter in controversy
exceeds $5 million[82] (the claims of the class members "shall be"
aggregated to make this determination[83]); (2) brought as a class action
with more than 100 plaintiffs[84]; and (3) where one of the following is
present: (i) a class member is a citizen of a state different from any
defendant; (ii) a class member is a foreign state (or a citizen of a foreign
state) and any defendant is a citizen of a state; or (iii) a class member is a
citizen of a state and any defendant is a foreign state (or a citizen of a

---

78.   S. 5, 109th Cong. (2005). The full title of the Act is "A BILL To amend
      the procedures that apply to consideration of interstate class actions to
      assure fairer outcomes for class members and defendants, and for other
      purposes." *Id.*
79.   *See infra* Chapter 12.
80.   Exxon Mobil Corp. v. Allapattah Servs., Inc., 125 S. Ct. 2611, 2628 (2005)
      (Act "is not retroactive"). The Act is a short, nine-section bill. Sections 3-
      5 are the Act's substantive provisions – respectively the consumer class
      action bill of rights, the provision for federal district court jurisdiction, and
      the provision for removal. Sections 1 and 2 are prefatory in nature, listing
      the short title, table of contents, and statement of Congressional findings
      and purposes. Section 6 requires preparation of a report on class action
      settlements. Section 7 requires enactment of already-enacted changes to
      the federal rule of civil procedure governing class actions. Section 8
      subordinates the Act to statutory rulemaking authority given to the
      Supreme Court and federal Judicial Conference. Section 9 lists the Act's
      effective date. All subsequent references are to the Act as codified.
81.   28 U.S.C. § 1332(d)(9).
82.   *Id.* § 1332(d)(2).
83.   *Id.* § 1332(d)(6).
84.   *Id.* § 1332(d)(5)(B).

foreign state).[85] Hence, the requirement of "complete diversity" no longer applies to certain class actions.

A court can decline to exercise jurisdiction over a class in which greater than one-third but less than two-thirds of the class members and the primary defendants are citizens of the state in which the action was originally filed.[86] The law provides a list of 6 factors for the court to consider: (1) whether the claims asserted involve matters of national or interstate interest; (2) whether the claims are governed by the law of the state in which the action was filed; (3) whether the action was pleaded in a way to avoid federal jurisdiction; (4) whether the action was brought in a forum with a nexus to the class members, the alleged harm, or the defendants; (5) whether the number of class members resident in the state in which the action was filed is substantially larger than the number from any other state and the citizenship of the other members is dispersed among a substantial number of states; and (6) whether, during the prior three years, one or more class actions asserting similar claims has been filed.[87]

A court must decline to exercise jurisdiction over a class action if the following factors exist: (1) more than two-thirds of the class members are citizens of the state in which the action was originally filed; (2) at least one defendant against whom significant relief is sought and whose alleged conduct forms a significant basis for the claims is a citizen of the state in which the action was originally filed; (3) the principal injuries occurred in the state in which the action was originally filed; *and* (4) during the prior 3 years, no other class actions have been filed asserting similar factual allegations against any of the defendants.[88] In addition, a court must decline to exercise jurisdiction over a class if more than two-thirds of the class members and the primary defendants are citizens of the state in which the action was originally filed.[89]

For jurisdiction purposes, the term "class action" includes *any* litigation in which "monetary relief claims of 100 or more persons are

---

85. *Id.* § 1332(d)(2)(A)-(C).
86. *Id.* § 1332(d)(3).
87. *Id.* § 1332(d)(3)(A)-(F).
88. *Id.* § 1332(d)(4).
89. *Id.* § 1332(d)(4)(B).

proposed to be tried jointly."[90] This new federal diversity jurisdiction
does not apply if the primary defendants are states, state officials, or
governmental entities against whom the district court may be foreclosed
from ordering relief.[91] There are further exclusions based upon certain
limited types of cases and claims.

4. *Pendent and Supplemental Jurisdiction*

    a. Pendent Jurisdiction

Especially in complex commercial disputes, it is common for the
same conduct to give rise to claims under both federal and state law.
Courts have long recognized under the doctrine of "pendent" (now
"supplemental") jurisdiction that where a federal court has obtained
jurisdiction over a federal claim, related claims arising under state law
may be asserted in the same action.[92] A federal district court's authority
to adjudicate pendent state law claims is not limitless, however,
particularly when a court dismisses the federal claims during the course
of the litigation.

The modern rules concerning pendent jurisdiction were established
in the Supreme Court's 1966 decision in *United Mine Workers v.
Gibbs*.[93] There, the Supreme Court held that pendent jurisdiction over
state law claims is appropriate when (1) the federal claim has sufficient
substance to confer subject matter jurisdiction on the federal court; (2)
the state and federal claims derive from a "common nucleus of operative
fact"; and (3) those claims are such that one would ordinarily expect to
try them all in one judicial proceeding.[94]

The Supreme Court noted, however, that pendent jurisdiction is not
a plaintiff's right, but rather a judicial power to be exercised by the court,

---

90. *Id.* § 1332(d)(11)(B). This provision gives jurisdiction to mass asbestos
    and other environmental bodily injury actions. Exempted is any lawsuit
    (a) in which all of the claims concern injuries and events occurring in the
    forum (or in adjoining states), (b) where the claims were aggregated by
    defense motion, or (c) brought pursuant to state statute authorizing claims
    on behalf of the general public. *Id.*
91. *Id.* § 1332(d)(5)(A).
92. *See Hagans*, 415 U.S. at 554; 28 U.S.C. § 1367.
93. 383 U.S. 715 (1966).
94. *Id.* at 725.

in its discretion, and further stated that a district court should reexamine pendent jurisdiction at each stage of the litigation, by weighing policy considerations such as judicial economy, convenience and fairness to the litigants, and comity.[95] If these factors do not weigh in favor of maintaining pendent jurisdiction, as when a federal claim is dismissed and only state law claims remain, the district court may dismiss the state law claims without prejudice.[96] Even where the federal claims are not dismissed, if the state issues substantially predominate in terms of proof, the scope of the issues raised, or the comprehensiveness of the remedies sought, the state claims may be dismissed without prejudice, for resolution in state court.[97]

Soon after *Gibbs* was decided, the Supreme Court in *Rosado v. Wyman*[98] held that a trial court's discretion over the administration of pendent claims is broad enough to allow the court to retain such claims, even after the federal claim has been rendered moot.[99] The Court concluded that, because mootness usually is beyond the control of the parties and often occurs at the last stages of trial, dismissal of a pendent claim in such circumstances would frustrate judicial economy.[100]

In the wake of *Rosado*, it has been widely recognized that federal courts possess considerable discretion when determining whether to dismiss or retain pendent state law claims after the federal claims have been dismissed or rendered moot. For example, in *Union City Barge Line, Inc. v. Union Carbide Corp.*,[101] the Fifth Circuit held that a district court had discretion to exercise pendent jurisdiction over state law business tort claims, even though it had entered summary judgment on the federal antitrust claims.[102]

Federal courts' discretionary authority over pendent state law claims was further analyzed by the Supreme Court in 1988 in *Carnegie-Mellon*

---

95. *Id.* at 726-27.
96. *Id.*
97. *Id.* at 727.
98. 397 U.S. 397 (1970).
99. *Id.* at 404.
100. *Id.* at 404-05.
101. 823 F.2d 129 (5th Cir. 1987).
102. *Id.* at 142; *see also, e.g.,* Gem Corrugated Box Corp. v. Nat'l Kraft Container Corp., 427 F.2d 499, 501 n.1 (2d Cir. 1970).

University v. Cohill.[103] The *Cohill* court held that when a case is removed from state court to federal court, the federal court may, after dismissal of the federal claims, exercise its discretion to remand the state law claims to state court rather than either retaining or dismissing them.[104]

b.   Supplemental Jurisdiction

In 1990, Congress codified the doctrines of pendent and ancillary jurisdiction under the rubric of "supplemental jurisdiction." Section 310 of the Judicial Improvement Act of 1990[105] expressly authorizes district courts to assume supplemental jurisdiction over claims that are "so related" to claims within the original jurisdiction of the court "that they form part of the same case or controversy under Article III" of the Constitution.[106] The statute effectively overruled the Supreme Court's 1989 decision in *Finley v. United States*,[107] which had placed severe limitations on the joinder of additional defendants on grounds of "pendent party jurisdiction."[108]

For a federal court to exercise supplemental jurisdiction, the three criteria set forth by the Supreme Court in *Gibbs* must be satisfied.[109] The primary requirement is federal jurisdiction over the original controversy. If original federal jurisdiction is lacking, supplemental jurisdiction becomes a moot issue.[110] The supplemental jurisdiction statute codifies

---

103. 484 U.S. 343 (1988).
104. *Id.* at 357.
105. 28 U.S.C. § 1367 (applying to civil actions filed on or after December 1, 1990).
106. *Id.* § 1367(a).
107. 490 U.S. 545 (1989).
108. *Id.* at 556.
109. *E.g.*, MCI Telecomms. Corp. v. Teleconcepts, Inc., 71 F.3d 1086, 1102 (3d Cir. 1995) (citing *Gibbs*, 383 U.S. at 725).
110. *See id.* at 1093-96, 1102 (federal court should undertake threshold analysis of determining whether original federal jurisdiction is present before determining whether to apply supplemental jurisdiction over related state claims); Gill v. Upson Reg'l Med. Ctr., 1 F. Supp. 2d 1480, 1481 (M.D. Ga. 1998) (unless there exists initial basis for federal jurisdiction in first instance, there can be no supplemental jurisdiction over state claims); *see also* Sarmiento v. Tex. Bd. of Veterinarian Med. Exam'rs, 939 F.2d 1242, 1245 (5th Cir. 1991) (federal court may retain supplemental jurisdiction

the federal common law precedent requiring that the state law issue be so effectively intertwined with the federal claim on which jurisdiction is based that the two form the same case or controversy.[111] A good example of such an intertwined set of claims is a cross-claim for contribution or indemnity, which necessarily arises from the same operative facts as the primary claim on which it is based.[112]

The statute also sets forth the circumstances under which a federal district court may decline to exercise supplemental jurisdiction over state law claims, which include:

> "(1) the claim raises a novel or complex issue of State law, (2) the claim substantially predominates over the claim or claims over which the district court has original jurisdiction, (3) the district court has dismissed all claims over which it has original jurisdiction, or (4) in exceptional circumstances, there are other compelling reasons for declining jurisdiction."[113]

Once a federal court decides it has supplemental jurisdiction over a state law claim, it is not obligated to reconsider the issue unless requested by one of the parties.[114] If the court decides not to entertain the non-federal

---

even when federal claim alleged is deemed "frivolous or a mere matter of form").

111. Krell v. Prudential Ins. Co. of Am. (*In re* Prudential Ins. Co. of Am. Sales Practices Litig.), 148 F.3d 283, 301 (3d Cir. 1998) (any exercise of supplemental jurisdiction must meet Article III case or controversy requirement).

112. Allen v. City of Los Angeles, 92 F.3d 842, 846 (9th Cir. 1996) (affirming supplemental jurisdiction over state law cross-claims for attorneys' fees in civil rights action because defendant's entitlement to reimbursement formed part of same case or controversy as plaintiff's claims); Acri v. Varian Assocs., Inc., 114 F.3d 999, 1001 (9th Cir. 1997) (*Allen* does not impose obligation on federal courts to conduct § 1367(c) analysis sua sponte whenever any of its factors is implicated).

113. 28 U.S.C. § 1367(c); *see also Allen*, 92 F.3d at 846; Shanaghan v. Cahill, 58 F.3d 106, 110 (4th Cir. 1995); McLaurin v. Prater, 30 F.3d 982, 985 (8th Cir. 1994); Exec. Software N. Am., Inc. v. U.S. Dist. Court, 24 F.3d 1545, 1555-56 (9th Cir. 1994); Tinius v. Carroll Co. Sheriff Dep't, 255 F. Supp. 2d 971, 977-78 (N.D. Iowa 2003).

114. *Acri*, 114 F.3d at 1001; *see also* Myers v. County of Lake, 30 F.3d 847, 848-50 (7th Cir. 1994) (finding jurisdiction over state law claims and noting that no party had requested the district court to exercise

claim, it can dismiss the claim without prejudice or, if removed to federal court, remand the claim back to state court.[115]

The four circumstances under which a federal court may decline supplemental jurisdiction are a codification of the factors set forth in *Gibbs* and its progeny, as well as a recognition that federal courts may abstain from determining complex or novel issues of state law.[116] Since the supplemental jurisdiction statute's enactment in 1990, courts have warned that supplemental jurisdiction should not be used as a device to expand federal jurisdiction over disputes that state courts are better suited to decide.[117] While federal courts often decline to retain jurisdiction over state law claims after dismissing the federal claims on which federal jurisdiction was originally based,[118] a federal court has discretion to retain supplemental jurisdiction if justified under considerations of

---

discretionary authority to decline supplemental jurisdiction under § 1367(c)); Doe by Fein v. District of Columbia, 93 F.3d 861, 871 (D.C. Cir. 1996) (challenge to court's exercise of supplemental jurisdiction, when one of discretionary factors weighs against federal jurisdiction, is waivable).

115. *Cohill*, 484 U.S. at 351; Hinson v. Norwest Fin. S.C., Inc., 239 F.3d 611, 619 (4th Cir. 2001).

116. *Gibbs*, 383 U.S. at 725.

117. *See, e.g.*, Valencia ex rel. Franco v. Lee, 316 F.3d 299, 306 (2d Cir. 2003) (exercise of supplemental jurisdiction is abuse of discretion when federal claim is dismissed at early stage and state claims turn on unresolved questions of state law that "dictate that these questions be left for decision by the state courts"); Rounsevill v. Zahl, 13 F.3d 625, 631 (2d Cir. 1994) (novel state law claim is best left for state court after dismissal of federal claim); Williams v. Van Buren Township, 925 F. Supp. 1231, 1237-38 (E.D. Mich. 1996) (refusing to invoke supplemental jurisdiction over claims for violation of Michigan law, even though claims arose out of same set of facts as federal claim, because state law claims raised novel and complex issues of state law best left to the Michigan state courts); *see also* Int'l Ass'n of Firefighters of St. Louis v. City of Ferguson, 283 F.3d 969, 975-76 (9th Cir. 2002).

118. Batiste v. Island Records, Inc., 179 F.3d 217, 227-28 (5th Cir. 1999) (reversing district court's decision to decline jurisdiction over state law claims, after dismissal of federal claims, because state law issues were not difficult to adjudicate, case had been pending for several years, and court was "intimately familiar" with remaining state law claims).

judicial economy, convenience, fairness, and comity.[119]   Finally, the "exceptional circumstances" provision of the statute grants discretion to decline supplemental jurisdiction over state law claims, even in the absence of the statutory factors set forth in the supplemental jurisdiction statute, when "compelling reasons" exist for declining jurisdiction.[120]

C. Tolling

The Judicial Improvement Act also provides that the limitations period for any state law claim asserted under the supplemental jurisdiction statute is tolled while the case is pending in federal court, and for a period of thirty days thereafter (unless state law provides for a longer tolling period).[121]   Therefore, if a federal district court dismisses supplemental state law claims without prejudice, a plaintiff will have to make sure that state law provides for a longer tolling period or otherwise re-file the claims in state court within thirty days of dismissal.[122]

D. Exclusive versus Concurrent Jurisdiction

Another issue in forum selection is whether subject matter jurisdiction over a particular claim lies exclusively in the federal or state courts, or whether those courts have concurrent jurisdiction over the claim.   Congress has specifically provided for exclusive federal court jurisdiction over a wide variety of civil claims, including those arising under the federal antitrust laws,[123] the Securities Exchange Act,[124] and

---

119. *Cohill*, 484 U.S. at 357; *see also* Che v. Mass. Bay Transp. Auth., 342 F.3d 31, 37 (1st Cir. 2003); Correspondent Servs. Corp. v. First Equities Corp., 338 F.3d 119, 126-27 (2d Cir. 2003); Pickern v. Best W. Timber Cove Lodge, 194 F. Supp. 2d 1128, 1133 (E.D. Cal. 2002).
120. 28 U.S.C. § 1367(c)(4).
121. 28 U.S.C. § 1367(d); *see* Jinks v. Richland County, 538 U.S. 456, 464-67 (2003) (Section 1367(d) is not unconstitutional and applies to claims brought against a state's political subdivisions). *But see* Raygor v. Regents of The Univ. of Minn., 534 U.S. 533, 542-48 (2002) (no tolling of statute of limitations for claims against nonconsenting states filed in federal court but subsequently dismissed on sovereign immunity grounds).
122. *See, e.g.*, GA. CODE ANN. § 9-2-61 (2004) (six-month tolling period); N.Y. C.P.L.R. § 205(a) (McKinney 2004) (same).
123. 15 U.S.C. § 15; *see* Freeman v. Bee Mach. Co., 319 U.S. 448, 451 n.6 (1943); Blumenstock Bros. Adver. Agency v. Curtis Pub. Co., 252 U.S.

the federal patent and copyright laws.[125] In other instances, the federal
and state courts share concurrent jurisdiction over federal claims,
including civil claims under the RICO statute,[126] section 12(2) of the
Securities Act of 1933,[127] and the federal trademark laws, including
section 43(a) of the Lanham Act.[128]

Where federal courts maintain exclusive jurisdiction, the state courts
are without subject matter jurisdiction to decide the exclusively-federal
claim, whether asserted in the plaintiff's complaint or the defendant's
counterclaim.[129] The state courts may, however, entertain the validity of
federal defenses, even when the state court would otherwise lack
jurisdiction to adjudicate an affirmative claim under the same statute.[130]
The Third Circuit has held that a state court which does not have
jurisdiction to hear an exclusively-federal claim may nonetheless
approve a state class action settlement releasing such a claim, stating
further that the state court's approval order was entitled to full faith and

---

436, 441 (1920); State v. Am. League of Prof'l Baseball Clubs, 460 F.2d
654, 658 (9th Cir. 1972).

124. 15 U.S.C. § 78aa; *see* Ceres Partners v. GEL Assocs., 918 F.2d 349, 352
(2d Cir. 1990), *superseded by statute on other grounds as stated in* Lavian
v. Haghnazari, 884 F. Supp. 670, 677 n.4 (E.D.N.Y. 1995).

125. 28 U.S.C. § 1338(a); *see* Bonito Boats, Inc. v. Thunder Craft Boats, Inc.,
489 U.S. 141, 162 (1989) (patent laws); Sears, Roebuck & Co. v. Stiffel
Co., 376 U.S. 225, 231 (1964) (copyright laws).

126. Tafflin v. Levitt, 493 U.S. 455, 458 (1990) (resolving prior conflict among
federal appellate courts and certain state supreme courts).

127. 15 U.S.C. § 77(v); *see* Emrich v. Touche Ross & Co., 846 F.2d 1190, 1197
(9th Cir. 1988) (while Congress has provided for concurrent jurisdiction in
cases arising under the 1933 Act, if such a case is filed in state court, it
may not be removed pursuant to § 77(v)(a)).

128. 28 U.S.C. § 1338(a); *see* Stanford Telecomms. Inc. v. U.S. Dist. Ct. for N.
Dist. of Cal., No. 88-7425, 1989 WL 418538, at *1 (9th Cir. Feb. 24,
1989); Bear Creek Prods., Inc. v. Saleh, 643 F. Supp. 489, 491 (S.D.N.Y.
1986).

129. *See, e.g.*, Jack's Cookie Co. v. Du-Bro Foods, Inc., 546 N.Y.S.2d 809, 812
(1989) (state court lacked jurisdiction over federal antitrust counterclaim).

130. *See, e.g.*, Franchise Tax Bd. of Cal. v. Constr. Laborers Vacation Trust for
S. Cal., 463 U.S. 1, 12 n.12 (1983); Hernandez-Agosto v. Romero-Barcelo,
748 F.2d 1, 2-4 (1st Cir. 1984).

credit and that the preclusive effect of the state court judgment barred subsequent litigation of the federal claims in federal court.[131]

Even if a federal claim is available, a litigant is not obligated to assert it. The fact that the same conduct may give rise to both federal and state law claims does not prevent a plaintiff from foregoing the federal claim and pursuing its remedies in state court, or vice versa. This principle has been applied in circumstances where a plaintiff has declined to assert a claim under federal antitrust law and has proceeded solely under state antitrust law, thereby risking a later res judicata bar to the federal claim.[132]

When the requirements for diversity jurisdiction are present, the federal and state courts generally have concurrent jurisdiction over the state law claims. As discussed in Chapter 13, however, the federal courts may choose to abstain from deciding novel issues of state law or other matters traditionally left to the determination of state courts.

E.   Challenges to Subject Matter Jurisdiction

As a general matter, federal courts are obligated – before resolving a case on the merits – to determine whether federal subject matter jurisdiction exists. The procedural rules are designed to foster such an early determination,[133] which is necessary to prevent the district court and the parties from expending significant time and expense in litigating a claim the court does not have the power to decide.[134]   Any party may

---

131. Grimes v. Vitalink Commc'ns Corp., 17 F.3d 1553, 1556, 1561-64 (3d Cir. 1994).
132. *See, e.g.*, *Williams*, 482 U.S. at 392; Ashley v. Sw. Bell Tel. Co., 410 F. Supp. 1389, 1393 (W.D. Tex. 1976); City of Galveston v. Int'l Org. of Masters, 338 F. Supp. 907, 909 (S.D. Tex 1972); *see generally* ABA SECTION OF ANTITRUST LAW, STATE ANTITRUST PRACTICE AND STATUTES (3d ed. 2004).
133. FED. R. CIV. P. 12(b).
134. Elliott v. Tilton, 62 F.3d 725, 729 (5th Cir. 1995) (parties and district court should address subject matter jurisdiction at outset of case rather than on appeal and "prior to a substantial investment in case preparation"), *vacated on other grounds*, 69 F.3d 35, 36 (5th Cir.), *vacated on other grounds*, 89 F.3d 260, 262 (5th Cir. 1996).

challenge federal jurisdiction, even the party that originally invoked it.[135] A party can even admit the existence of federal court jurisdiction and later challenge its existence during the same proceeding.[136]

Even when the parties fail to raise the issue, the federal district courts are required to examine the basis of their jurisdiction.[137] Subject matter jurisdiction may be challenged at any time, including when a case is on appeal.[138] Both trial and appellate courts must dismiss a case sua sponte if federal jurisdiction is found to be lacking.[139] Parties cannot, by stipulation, consent, waiver or otherwise, confer federal jurisdiction on a district court.[140] Otherwise, subject matter jurisdiction could be broadened through the conduct or consent of the parties, in violation of the fundamental rule that federal courts are courts of limited jurisdiction, and possess only that jurisdiction specifically authorized by the Constitution or Congress.[141]

A federal judgment rendered without subject matter jurisdiction may not, however, be collaterally attacked in another proceeding.[142]

---

135. Am. Fire & Cas. Co. v. Finn, 341 U.S. 6, 16-17 (1951) (party which originally brought case to federal court may challenge it during same proceeding), *superseded by statute on other grounds as stated in* D'Ambrosio v. Chicago Truck Drivers, No. 89 C 6666, 1991 WL 96445, at *2 (N.D. Ill. May 31, 1991).
136. Eisler v. Stritzler, 535 F.2d 148, 151 (1st Cir. 1976).
137. Louisville & Nashville R.R. Co. v. Mottley, 211 U.S. 149, 152 (1908); Bracken v. Matgouranis, 296 F.3d 160, 162 (3d Cir. 2002) (recognizing court's duty to examine basis of jurisdiction).
138. Chicot County Drainage Dist. v. Baxter State Bank, 308 U.S. 371, 376-77 (1940); *see also* FED. R. CIV. P. 12(h)(3).
139. *Louisville & Nashville R.R. Co.*, 211 U.S. at 152; Crosby by Crosby v. Holsinger, 816 F.2d 162, 163 (4th Cir. 1987).
140. *Sosna*, 419 U.S. at 398 (agreement of parties insufficient to cure jurisdictional defects); Giannakos v. M/V Bravo Trader, 762 F.2d 1295, 1297 (5th Cir. 1985) (parties' conduct, even amounting to waiver or estoppel, cannot create federal jurisdiction).
141. *Giannakos*, 762 F.2d at 1297.
142. *See Chicot County Drainage Dist.*, 308 U.S. at 376-77. Although the holding in *Chicot County Drainage* appears to conflict with the principle that subject matter jurisdiction may not be waived, "the principle of finality of judgments in this context overrides competing factors of federal jurisdiction." 1 HAIG, *supra* note 1, § 1.5, at 8.

CHAPTER X

PERSONAL JURISDICTION, PROCESS, AND VENUE IN ANTITRUST AND BUSINESS TORT LITIGATION

Like subject matter jurisdiction, personal jurisdiction often is an issue at the inception of antitrust and business tort litigation – which now includes Internet cases. So, too, are the issues of process and venue. Some federal statutes – such as the antitrust and securities laws – provide for nationwide service of process; in cases involving parties from different states, the ability to effect extraterritorial service may weigh in favor of asserting such federal claims. In contrast, venue choices in state court often are as rich or richer than those available in the federal courts. This chapter surveys how personal jurisdiction, process, and venue may vary in antitrust and business tort litigation; how these and other factors impact on choice of forum is addressed in Chapter 11. – Eds.

A. Introduction

Assuming a court has subject matter jurisdiction, its power over a defendant is a function of three related concepts: personal jurisdiction, service of process, and venue. The rules governing these concepts may vary depending upon the forum chosen and the substantive claims asserted.

In particular, the assertion of federal antitrust or other statutory claims may significantly impact the plaintiff's venue choices, as well as the defendant's transfer opportunities. This chapter addresses the interplay of the constitutional and procedural rules determining a court's ability to assert and retain personal jurisdiction in antitrust and business tort litigation.

B. Personal Jurisdiction and Service of Process

1. *General Federal Due Process Constraints*

The requirement that a court have personal jurisdiction over the defendant in a federal question case stems from the Due Process Clause of the Fifth Amendment.[1] The test for personal jurisdiction requires that the defendant have "minimum contacts" with the forum and that maintenance of the suit "not offend 'traditional notions of fair play and substantial justice.'"[2]

When a federal court adjudicates state-created rights under diversity jurisdiction, the constitutional inquiry is guided by the same Fourteenth Amendment standards applicable to state long-arm jurisdiction. The critical question is whether the defendant has sufficient minimum contacts with the forum state to permit the exercise of jurisdiction over it.[3] A plaintiff may seek to establish "general jurisdiction" over a defendant by showing that the defendant maintained "continuous and systematic" contacts with the forum state.[4] Or a plaintiff may seek to establish "specific jurisdiction" by showing that the defendant purposely directed his activities at residents of the forum and that the plaintiff's claims arise out of or relate to those activities.[5]

In federal question cases, there has been disagreement over whether the federal courts are constrained by Fourteenth Amendment standards or by the broader standards emanating from the Fifth Amendment, which focus on the defendant's aggregate contacts with the United States.[6]

---

1. Ins. Corp. of Ireland v. Compagnie des Bauxites de Guinee, 456 U.S. 694, 702 (1982).
2. Int'l Shoe Co. v. Washington, 326 U.S. 310, 316 (1945); *see* Asahi Metal Indus. Co. v. Superior Court of Cal., 480 U.S. 102, 105, 108-09 (1987).
3. Burger King Corp. v. Rudzewicz, 471 U.S. 462, 474 (1985).
4. *See* Helicopteros Nacionales de Colombia, S.A. v. Hall, 466 U.S. 408, 414 n.9 (1984). Additionally, the Supreme Court has held that transient jurisdiction, acquired by personally serving a nonresident defendant while physically present in the forum state, is a constitutionally valid method of asserting general jurisdiction. Burnham v. Superior Court of Cal., 495 U.S. 604, 628 (1990) (the Due Process Clause of the Fourteenth Amendment does not prohibit California courts from exercising jurisdiction over nonresident based on fact of in-state service of process).
5. *See Burger King Corp.*, 471 U.S. at 472-73; *Hall*, 466 U.S. at 414 n.8.
6. *See, e.g.*, Cargill Inc. v. M/V Paschalis, No. 86 Civ. 0805, 1997 WL 17950, at *1-2 (S.D.N.Y. Sept. 30, 1987) (noting disagreement over use of nationwide contacts in consideration of personal jurisdiction); Superior Coal Co. v. Ruhrkohle, A.G., 83 F.R.D. 414, 418 (E.D. Pa. 1979) (although Fifth Amendment Due Process Clause permits aggregation of defendant's contacts across the nation, no federal statute authorizes district

Strict application of the minimum contacts doctrine in the federal courts cannot always be reconciled with various federal statutes authorizing nationwide service of process, such as Section 12 of the Clayton Act.[7] The Supreme Court has not considered the constitutionality of this national or aggregate contacts theory,[8] and federal circuit courts are split over whether only a national contacts analysis is required when process is served under a federal statute's nationwide service of process provision.[9]

Until 1993, in the absence of a federal statutory provision for service, a federal court's jurisdiction in federal question cases could be limited by the forum state's long-arm statute, not because of the Due

---

courts to take nationwide contacts into consideration; no personal jurisdiction where defendant lacked adequate minimum contacts with forum state); *see also* Herbert Hovenkamp, *Personal Jurisdiction and Venue in Private Antitrust Actions in Federal Court: A Policy Analysis*, 67 IOWA L. REV. 485, 500-01 (1982); *see generally* 4 CHARLES ALAN WRIGHT & ARTHUR R. MILLER, FEDERAL PRACTICE AND PROCEDURE § 1067.1 (3d ed. 2002) (discussing development of minimum contacts doctrine).

7. 15 U.S.C. § 22; *see also* 15 U.S.C. § 77(v) (the Securities Act), 15 U.S.C. § 78aa (the Securities Exchange Act), 15 U.S.C. § 49 (the Federal Trade Commission Act); 18 U.S.C. § 1965 (the Racketeer Influenced and Corrupt Organizations Act).

8. Omni Capital Int'l, Ltd. v. Randolph Wolff & Co., 484 U.S. 97, 102 n.5 (1987) (citing Asahi Metal Indus. Co., 480 U.S. at 113 n.*).

9. *Compare* Autoscribe Corp. v. Goldman & Steinberg, No. 94-1749, 1995 U.S. App. LEXIS 2848, at *7 (4th Cir. Feb. 3, 1995), Busch v. Buchman, Buchman & O'Brien Law Firm, 11 F.3d 1255, 1258 (5th Cir. 1994), United Liberty Life Ins. Co. v. Ryan, 985 F.2d 1320, 1330 (6th Cir. 1993), United Elec., Radio & Mach. Workers v. 163 Pleasant St. Corp., 960 F.2d 1080, 1085 (1st Cir. 1992), Go-Video, Inc. v. Akai Elec. Co., 885 F.2d 1406, 1414-16 (9th Cir. 1989), Lisak v. Mercantile Bancorp, Inc., 834 F.2d 668, 671-72 (7th Cir. 1987), Hogue v. Milodon Eng'g, Inc., 736 F.2d 989, 991 (4th Cir. 1984), FTC v. Jim Walter Corp., 651 F.2d 251, 256 (5th Cir. 1981), *and* Tex. Trading & Milling Corp. v. Fed. Republic of Nigeria, 647 F.2d 300, 314-15 (2d Cir. 1981), *with In re* Vitamins Antitrust Litig., 94 F. Supp. 2d 26, 38-39 (D.D.C. 2000), *and* GTE New Media Servs. Inc. v. BellSouth Corp., 199 F.3d 1343, 1350 (D.C. Cir. 2000) (*citing* Goldlawr, Inc. v. Heiman, 288 F.2d 579, 581 (2d Cir. 1961), *rev'd on other grounds*, 369 U.S. 463 (1962)); *see* discussion *infra* Parts E.1, E.2.

Process Clause of the Fifth Amendment, but rather by the incorporation of state law governing service under Rule 4(e) of the Federal Rules of Civil Procedure.[10] In 1993, the Supreme Court amended Rule 4 to close this gap by providing that, "[i]f the exercise of jurisdiction is consistent with the Constitution and laws of the United States, serving a summons or filing a waiver of service is also effective, with respect to claims arising under federal law, to establish personal jurisdiction over the person of any defendant who is not subject to the jurisdiction of the courts of general jurisdiction of any state."[11] As a result, personal jurisdiction in federal question cases is no longer subject to the peculiarities of individual state long-arm statutes.

2. *State Long-Arm Statutes*

State long-arm statutes generally predicate personal jurisdiction over nonresidents upon doing business in the state, the commission of a specified act within the jurisdiction, or the commission of an act outside the jurisdiction that has consequences within it. Usually, courts must apply the long-arm statute of the state in which they sit when determining whether they may exercise personal jurisdiction over a defendant.[12]

Illinois enacted the first comprehensive long-arm statute,[13] which has served as a model for several other states, including Florida,[14] Washington,[15] Idaho,[16] and Hawaii.[17] Some statutes purport to assert

---

10. FED. R. CIV. P. 4(e). Prior to the 1993 amendments, Rule 4(e) required that extraterritorial service not authorized by federal statute be made "under the circumstances and in the manner prescribed" by state law. *See Omni Capital Int'l, Ltd.*, 484 U.S. at 104-08 (because Louisiana's long-arm statute was more restrictive than Due Process Clause and defendants had insufficient contacts with Louisiana to satisfy long-arm statute, court did not have jurisdiction).

11. FED. R. CIV. P. 4(k)(2) ("Territorial Limits of Effective Service"). This amendment became effective December 1, 1993; *see* 61 U.S.L.W. 4365, 4368 (Apr. 27, 1993).

12. *See* Graphic Controls Corp. v. Utah Med. Prods., 149 F.3d 1382, 1385-86 (Fed. Cir. 1998); Delgado v. Reef Resort Ltd., 364 F.3d 642, 644 (5th Cir. 2004)

13. 735 ILL. COMP. STAT. 5/2-209 (2005).

14. FLA. STAT. ANN. § 48.193(1) (2005).

15. WASH. REV. CODE § 4.28.185 (2005).

jurisdiction to the fullest permissible constitutional limits.[18]   Other "enumerated act" long-arm statutes provide that a defendant is amenable to the jurisdiction of the state's courts if it transacts any business within the state; commits a tort within the state; owns, uses, or possesses real property within the state; or contracts to insure any person, property, or risk located within the state.[19] Some states have amended their "doing business" statutes to broaden the meaning of that term as an alternative way of giving their courts long-arm jurisdiction.[20] In states that have an enumerated act statute, a court must determine both: (1) whether the requirements of that statute are satisfied; and (2) whether the exercise of jurisdiction would violate the Due Process Clause. For "constitutional limits" long-arm statutes, these two steps collapse into one.[21]

States have employed a variety of methods to limit the availability of their long-arm statutes. For example, some long-arm statutes apply only to corporate defendants,[22] while others are available only to resident plaintiffs.[23]   Other states restrict the reach of their statutes to jurisdictional acts occurring within the state. Such statutes predicate jurisdiction on a forum-based act ("specific jurisdiction" or "limited personal jurisdiction"), as opposed to "continuous and systematic" or "substantial" activities in the state ("general personal jurisdiction"), and require that the cause of action "aris[e] from" the particular act on which jurisdiction is based.[24]

---

16. IDAHO CODE §§ 5-514, 5-515 (Michie 2004).
17. HAW. REV. STAT. § 634-35 (2004).
18. TEX. CIV. PRAC. & REM. CODE ANN. §§ 17.041-.045 (Vernon 2004); WIS. STAT. ANN. § 801.05 (2005).
19. *E.g.*, CAL. CIV. PROC. CODE § 410.10 (West 2005); MICH. COMP. LAWS ANN. § 600.705 *et seq.* (West 2005); R.I. GEN. LAWS § 9-5-33 (2004).
20. *See* 16 JAMES WM. MOORE ET AL., MOORE'S FEDERAL PRACTICE § 106.60[1] (3d ed. 1999).
21. *See* Imo Indus., Inc. v. Kiekert A.G., 155 F.3d 254, 258 (3d Cir. 1998).
22. *E.g.*, TENN. CODE ANN. § 20-2-201 (2005); VT. STAT. ANN. tit. 12, § 855 (2004) (Annot. at 1).
23. *E.g.*, VT. STAT. ANN. tit. 12, § 855 (2004) (Annot. at 1).
24. *E.g.*, MASS. GEN. LAWS ANN. ch. 223A, § 3 (West 2005) (prohibiting its application when claim arose in another state and plaintiff was nonresident); N.Y. C.P.L.R. § 302 (McKinney 2004) (requiring doing of business or act or omission within state).

Under all state statutes, however, personal jurisdiction and service of process must be consistent with the Due Process Clause of the Fourteenth Amendment. Any statutory method of service is deemed valid if it is reasonably calculated to convey notice to the defendant. Although the statutes vary, most states provide for personal service upon the defendant wherever he can be found, within or outside of the state.[25]

3. *Federal Rules for Service of Process*

Several federal statutory schemes contain special provisions authorizing nationwide service of process. These include the Clayton Act,[26] the Securities Act of 1933,[27] the Securities Exchange Act of 1934,[28] the Racketeer Influenced and Corrupt Organizations ("RICO") Act,[29] and the Federal Trade Commission Act.[30]

If no special federal statute applies, Rule 4(e), as amended in 1993, allows service of process upon individuals within a judicial district of the United States: "pursuant to the law of the state in which the district court is located, or in which service is effected"; or (2) "by delivering a copy of the summons and of the complaint" personally to the defendant or "to an agent authorized by appointment or by law to receive service of process"; or by leaving copies thereof at the individual's home "with some person of suitable age and discretion then residing therein."[31]

---

25. *E.g.*, 735 ILL. COMP. STAT. 5/2-208, 2-209 (2005).
26. 15 U.S.C. § 22.
27. *Id.* § 77v(a).
28. *Id.* § 78aa; *see* Busch v. Buchman, Buchman & O'Brien, Law Firm, 11 F.3d 1255, 1257 (5th Cir. 1994).
29. 18 U.S.C. § 1965; *see* ESAB Group, Inc. v. Centricut, Inc., 126 F.3d 617, 626 (4th Cir. 1997); Am. Trade Partners v. A-1 Int'l Importing Enters., 755 F. Supp. 1292, 1302 (E.D. Pa. 1990); Soltex Polymer Corp. v. Fortex Indus., 590 F. Supp. 1453, 1458 (E.D.N.Y. 1984), *aff'd*, 832 F.2d 1325, 1330 (2d Cir. 1987).
30. 15 U.S.C. § 49; *see* Williams v. Mercer (*In re* Certain Complaints Under Investigation by an Investigatory Comm. of the Judicial Council of the Eleventh Circuit), 783 F.2d 1488, 1516 (11th Cir. 1986) (noting FTC's authority to issue nationwide subpoenas); FTC v. Jim Walter Corp., 651 F.2d 251, 256 (5th Cir. 1981) (permitting nationwide enforcement of administrative subpoena).
31. FED. R. CIV. P. 4(e).

Rule 4(f) allows service to be made upon a party in a foreign country in the following ways:

(1) by any internationally agreed means reasonably calculated to give notice, such as those means authorized by the Hague Convention . . . ; or

(2) if there is no internationally agreed means of service or the applicable international agreement allows other means of service, provided that service is reasonably calculated to give notice:

    (A) in the manner prescribed by the law of the foreign country . . . ; or

    (B) as directed by the foreign authority in response to a letter rogatory or letter of request; or

    (C) unless prohibited by the law of the foreign country, by

        (i) delivery to the individual personally . . . ; or

        (ii) any form of mail requiring a signed receipt, [if addressed and mailed] by the clerk of the court . . . ; or

(3) by any other means not prohibited by international agreement as may be directed by the court.[32]

Accomplishing service of process can sometimes be quite challenging in countries that have no international treaty with the U.S., especially if the non-signatory country has passed legislation restricting service of process by outsiders.[33]

Rule 4(k) authorizes extraterritorial service to the extent permitted by the law of the state in which the district court sits. With respect to claims arising under federal law, however, Rule 4(k) allows extraterritorial service consistent with the Constitution and the laws of

---

32. FED. R. CIV. P. 4(f).

33. *See, e.g.*, Prewitt Enters., Inc. v. Org. of Petroleum Exporting Countries, 353 F.3d 916, 922-23 (11th Cir. 2003) (American plaintiff's service of process on the Organization of the Petroleum Exporting Countries (OPEC) at its residence in Austria was invalid because: (1) Austria is not a signatory to the Hague Service Convention; (2) applicable Austrian law prohibits service of process without OPEC's consent; and (3) there are no means for service upon OPEC available under the Federal Rules of Civil Procedure.

the United States, even as to defendants not subject to the jurisdiction of the state courts.[34]

C. Venue in Federal and State Court

The question of personal jurisdiction is distinct from the question of proper venue.[35] That a defendant may be subject to the personal jurisdiction of a particular court does not answer the question of whether venue is proper in that court; if it is not and a proper objection is made, the court will be powerless to entertain the plaintiff's claims.[36] In the federal courts, venue is prescribed by statute,[37] and, with the possible exception of so-called "local" actions (such as those involving real property),[38] is governed exclusively by federal law.[39]

1. Federal Venue Statutes

The general federal venue statute prescribes venue depending upon whether jurisdiction is based on diversity or the existence of a federal question. Private civil actions based solely upon diversity of citizenship may be brought in:

> (1) a judicial district where any defendant resides, if all defendants reside in the same State, (2) a judicial district in which a substantial

---

34. FED. R. CIV. P. 4(k). Rule 4(k) also authorizes extraterritorial service on parties joined under Rules 14 and 19, if served within a judicial district of the United States not more than one hundred miles from the place from which the summon issued, as well as service on persons subject to the federal interpleader jurisdiction. *Id.*

35. Action Embroidery Corp. v. Atl. Embroidery Inc., 368 F.3d 1174, 1178-79 (9th Cir. 2004) (personal jurisdiction distinct from question of venue); Leroy v. Great W. United Corp., 443 U.S. 173, 180 (1979) (venue and personal jurisdiction are entirely different questions for court to resolve); Neirbo Co. v. Bethlehem Shipbuilding Corp., 308 U.S. 165, 167-68 (1939) (differentiating between court's power of jurisdiction and litigant's convenience of venue).

36. *See, e.g.,* Brown v. Pyle, 310 F.2d 95, 96-97 (5th Cir. 1962).

37. *See* FED. R. CIV. P. 82 (venue not affected by Federal Rules of Civil Procedure).

38. *See generally* 15 CHARLES ALAN WRIGHT & ARTHUR R. MILLER, FEDERAL PRACTICE AND PROCEDURE § 3822 (2d ed. 1986).

39. *Leroy,* 443 U.S. at 183 n.15; *see* 15 WRIGHT & MILLER, *supra* note 38, § 3803.

part of the events or omissions giving rise to the claim occurred, or a substantial part of property that is the subject of the action is situated, or (3) a judicial district in which the defendants are subject to personal jurisdiction at the time the action is commenced, if there is no district in which the action may otherwise be brought.[40]

Private civil actions including a federal question may be brought in:

(1) a judicial district where any defendant resides, if all defendants reside in the same State, (2) a judicial district in which a substantial part of the events or omissions giving rise to the claim occurred, or a substantial part of property that is the subject of the action is situated, or (3) a judicial district in which any defendant may be found, if there is no district in which the action may otherwise be brought.[41]

Several special statutes prescribe venue in particular types of cases. In addition to those applicable to federal antitrust claims,[42] special venue statutes of potential applicability to business tort litigation include those for claims under the federal securities laws,[43] federal patent and copyright laws,[44] and RICO actions,[45] among others.[46] Although a special venue statute will be deemed to control over the general venue statute,[47] absent evidence of a contrary intent, the general venue statute, Section 1391, is read as supplementing the special venue statutes.[48]

In a case involving defendants residing in, or various property located in, different districts in the same state, venue is proper in any of those districts.[49] In 1988, Congress repealed a provision requiring suit to

---

40. 28 U.S.C. § 1391(a).
41. *Id.* § 1391(b).
42. *See* 15 U.S.C. §§ 15, 22.
43. *Id.* §§ 77v(a) (1933 Act), 78aa (1934 Act).
44. 28 U.S.C. § 1400(a), (b).
45. 18 U.S.C. § 1965.
46. *See generally* 15 WRIGHT & MILLER, *supra* note 38, § 3825.
47. Fourco Glass Co. v. Transmirra Prods. Corp., 353 U.S. 222, 225 (1957).
48. *See* 15 WRIGHT & MILLER, *supra* note 38, § 3803; *see also* Go-Video, Inc. v. Akai Elec. Co., 885 F.2d 1406, 1409-13 (9th Cir. 1989) (antitrust laws); Miller Brewing Co. v. Landau, 616 F. Supp. 1285, 1291 (E.D. Wis. 1985) (RICO); VE Holding Corp. v. Johnson Gas Appliance Co., 917 F.2d 1574, 1583-84 (Fed. Cir. 1990) (patent laws).
49. 28 U.S.C. § 1392(a).

be brought in a particular division within a district.[50]   As discussed below, this change had the effect of expanding parties' venue options when choosing between federal and state courts.

2.   *State Venue Statutes*

Under early common law, venue was limited to the county in which the cause of action arose.[51]   As times and circumstances changed, the courts allowed plaintiffs to employ a fictitious averment that the cause of action arose in a county (such as that of the defendant's residence) other than the one in which it in fact arose.   The system of rules for determining whether this fiction would be upheld or disregarded in individual cases gave rise to the modern distinction between local and transitory actions.[52]

Although statutory venue provisions have replaced the common law in many jurisdictions, the central features of the common law system are found in the venue statutes of most states, as well as in the general federal venue statute.[53] Differences abound, however, as special statutes that prescribe venue for particular types of disputes are common. Moreover, a major structural distinction between federal and state venue, the geographical basis upon which venue is prescribed, may produce major differences in venue as between federal and state courts.

The federal venue statutes delineate venue on the basis of federal judicial districts, which may encompass numerous counties, and even entire states.[54]   Depending upon the number and location of divisions located within a particular federal judicial district, federal and state court venue for the same action may lie in different cities, or even counties.

---

50. The former statute, 28 U.S.C. § 1393, was repealed by Act of Nov. 19, 1988, Pub. L. No. 100-702, 102 Stat. 4664.

51. *See, e.g.*, Crawford v. Carson, 78 S.E.2d 268, 272-73 (W. Va. 1953); Coleman v. Lucksinger, 123 S.W. 441, 442 (Mo. 1909); Hunt v. Pownal, 9 Vt. 411, 1837 WL 2009, at *4 (1837); Little v. Chicago, St. Paul, Minneapolis & Omaha Ry. Co., 67 N.W. 846, 847-48 (Minn. 1896).

52. *See generally* 92A C.J.S. *Venue* §§ 2-4 (2000); 77 AM. JUR. 2D *Venue* § 2 (2004) ("A cause of action was transitory if the transaction on which it was founded might have taken place anywhere; an action was local if the transaction could have happened only in a particular place.").

53. *See* 28 U.S.C. § 1391.

54. *See id.* §§ 81-131.

Although Congress has enacted various special venue statutes, in most instances they are supplemented by Section 1391(b). In contrast, state law may provide for exclusive venue over not only local actions, such as those involving real property, but in other cases as well.[55] Furthermore, whether or not deemed "exclusive," special state venue statutes, such as those that prescribe venue under so-called "little FTC" acts,[56] also supplement venue options. Because venue over transitory actions in federal court is determined exclusively by federal law, such special state venue provisions will have no effect in federal court.

3. *Contractual Forum Selection*

Federal and state courts respond in differing ways to contractual provisions undertaking to provide where suit may be brought. In the past, such forum selection clauses were disfavored by American courts.[57] Judicial reluctance to enforce such clauses was typically based on the theory that they were "contrary to public policy" or attempted to "oust the jurisdiction" of the court.[58] Although some jurisdictions continue to invalidate or limit the enforceability of such clauses,[59] the federal courts and many states have adopted a generally hospitable attitude toward them.[60] In diversity cases, federal, rather than state, law controls whether and to what extent such clauses will be enforced.[61]

---

55. *See* 92A C.J.S. *Venue* § 23 (2002).
56. *See, e.g.*, TEX. BUS. & COM. CODE ANN. § 17.56 (Vernon 2004).
57. M/S Bremen v. Zapata Off-Shore Co., 407 U.S. 1, 9 n.10 (1972).
58. *See id.*
59. *E.g.*, Rutter v. BX of Tri-Cities, Inc., 806 P.2d 1266, 1268 (Wash. Ct. App. 1991); White-Spunner Constr., Inc. v. Cliff, 588 So. 2d 865, 866 (Ala. 1991); Prof'l Ins. Corp. v. Sutherland, 700 So. 2d 347, 349-50 (Ala. 1997) (harshly criticizing *White-Spunner* as incongruous with modern law favoring forum selection clauses unless they violate public policy or are untenable); Fid. & Deposit Co. v. Gainesville Iron Works, Inc., 189 S.E.2d 130, 131 (Ga. Ct. App. 1972); Smith v. Watson, 44 S.W.2d 815, 817 (Tex. Civ. App. 1931).
60. Burger King Corp. v. Rudzewicz, 471 U.S. 462, 481 (1985) (allowing Florida franchisor to sue Michigan franchisee in Florida based on contractual forum selection clause); Detroit Coke Corp. v. NKK Chem. U.S.A., Inc., 794 F. Supp. 214, 217 (E.D. Mich. 1992); *see also* U.S. Trust Co. v. Bohart, 495 A.2d 1034, 1040 (Conn. 1985). For a federal and state-by-state analysis, *see* Francis M. Dougherty, Annotation, *Validity of*

4. *Transfer and Forum Non Conveniens*

Another way courts may differ over venue involves the issue of transfer. In multistate cases, federal courts enjoy the advantages of a unitary judicial system and a statutory transfer mechanism; in single state cases, federal and state court transfer rules may vary greatly.

a. Federal Court

In federal court, transfer between judicial districts is governed by Section 1404(a) of Title 28 of the U.S. Code, which gives the federal courts broad discretion to transfer a civil action to any other district or division where it might have been brought for "the convenience of parties and witnesses, in the interest of justice."[62] If the district court determines that venue is improper, the court is authorized either to dismiss the action for improper venue or, "in the interest of justice," to transfer the case to any district court or division in which it could have originally and properly been brought.[63] Before the enactment of § 1404(a) in 1948, a district court could dismiss an action on the grounds of forum non conveniens but did not have the authority to transfer the action to another district court.[64]

Under Section 1404(a), the "interest of justice" is a separate factor to be considered when determining whether a case should be transferred, and it may outweigh factors of convenience to the parties and witnesses.[65] Although Section 1404(a) does not specifically address the issue of duplicative litigation, courts frequently transfer cases under this section to another court where a related case is pending, finding it in the

---

Contractual Provision Limiting Place or Court in Which Action May Be Brought, 31 A.L.R. 4TH 404 (1984).

61. Stewart Org., Inc. v. Ricoh Corp., 487 U.S. 22, 32 (1988) (28 U.S.C. § 1404(a) governs district court's decision whether to give effect to forum selection clause).

62. 28 U.S.C. § 1404(a).

63. *Id.* § 1406(a).

64. *See* 15 WRIGHT & MILLER, *supra* note 38, § 3841; *see also* Piper Aircraft Co. v. Reyno, 454 U.S. 235, 265-66 (1981).

65. Van Dusen v. Barrack, 376 U.S. 612, 625 (1964); 15 WRIGHT & MILLER, *supra* note 38, § 3854.

"interests of justice" to do so.[66] The Supreme Court has stressed that permitting two cases that are pending simultaneously in different district courts and involving the same issues is wasteful of time, energy, and money and is what Section 1404(a) was designed to prevent.[67] The Court also noted that such concurrent litigation leads to a race to the courthouse among litigants for a trial in the district court each prefers.[68]

When determining which of two possible federal district courts should hear a case, a principal concern is the convenience of litigants and witnesses.[69] Courts consider a variety of factors when deciding whether to transfer under Section 1404(a), including which forum is most convenient to the parties and witnesses; which state's substantive laws will apply; where the conduct giving rise to the claim occurred; where documents and other evidence concerning the matter are located; in which court the case will proceed to trial most quickly; and which case was filed first.[70] The court also may transfer a case, in the interest of justice, if it would allow the joinder of other necessary defendants, or where it would allow the joinder of a third-party defendant who is not subject to process in the original forum.[71] The courts weigh these factors on a case-by-case basis.[72]

There is only one significant limitation on a federal court's ability to transfer an action to another district court. Section 1404(a) permits the transfer only to district courts in which the case originally could have been brought. Thus, Section 1404(a) prohibits transfer to a court where

66. 15 WRIGHT & MILLER, *supra* note 38, § 3854, at 442-49; *see also* Animal Sci. v. Chinook Group, Ltd. (*In re* Vitamins Antitrust Litig.), 263 F. Supp. 2d 67, 71 (D.D.C. 2003) (denying transfer as not serving "interests of justice").
67. Cont'l Grain Co. v. Barge FBL-585, 364 U.S. 19, 26 (1960).
68. *Id.*
69. Denver & Rio Grande & W.R. Co. v. Bd. of R.R. Trainmen, 387 U.S. 556, 560 (1967).
70. *See* KENT SINCLAIR, SINCLAIR ON FEDERAL CIVIL PROCEDURE 148-57 (1992).
71. *See id.*
72. Van Dusen v. Barrack, 376 U.S. 612, 643 (1964); *see generally* 15 WRIGHT & MILLER, *supra* note 38, §§ 3847-54.

subject matter jurisdiction is lacking, where personal jurisdiction over the defendants does not exist, or where venue is improper.[73]

When a diversity case is transferred under Section 1404(a), the court to which the case is transferred must apply the state law that would have been applied had there been no change of venue.[74] In *Van Dusen v. Barrack*,[75] the Supreme Court held that the law applicable to diversity cases does not change upon a transfer initiated by a defendant because Section 1404(a) should not deprive the parties of state law advantages that exist absent diversity. Section 1404(a) should not promote, create, or multiply opportunities for forum shopping; rather, the decision to transfer venue should turn on considerations of convenience and the interests of justice rather than on possible prejudice resulting from a change of law.[76]

In *Ferens v. John Deere Co.*,[77] the Supreme Court extended *Van Dusen* to embrace instances in which the plaintiff initiates the transfer. In *Ferens*, the plaintiff was injured by a machine the defendant manufactured in Pennsylvania.[78] After the Pennsylvania two-year statute of limitations for tort actions had expired, the plaintiff filed a diversity suit in federal district court in Pennsylvania raising contract and warranty claims, as to which the applicable Pennsylvania statute of limitations had not run. The plaintiff also filed an action in the federal district court in Mississippi, where the defendant did business, alleging tort causes of action, which were governed by Mississippi's six-year tort statute of limitations.[79] The plaintiff then moved under Section 1404(a) to transfer the action from Mississippi to Pennsylvania, which motion was granted.[80] On appeal, the Supreme Court held that the federal court in Pennsylvania was required to apply Mississippi's six-year statute of

---

73. *See, e.g.*, Abdulghani v. V.I. Sea Plane Shuttle, Inc., 749 F. Supp. 113, 114 (D.V.I. 1990) (case could not be transferred under § 1404(a) because of lack of subject matter jurisdiction and improper venue).

74. *Van Dusen*, 376 U.S. at 637-39 (§ 1404 transfer accomplishes "but a change of courtrooms").

75. 376 U.S. 612.

76. *Id.* at 635-37.

77. 494 U.S. 516 (1990).

78. *Id.* at 519.

79. *Id.* at 519-20.

80. *Id.* at 520.

limitations.[81] The Court further observed that prospective certainty and judicial economy both favor a simple rule that the choice of law rules of the transferor forum apply independent of which party makes the Section 1404(a) motion.[82]

The *Van Dusen-Ferens* choice-of-law rule does not apply when venue is improper or personal jurisdiction is lacking in the tranferor court. In those cases, the transferee court is free to apply the state law that would have been applied had the suit originally been filed there.[83] Nor does the *Van Dusen-Ferens* rule apply when federal law supplies the rule of decision; in such cases, the transferee court applies the law of the circuit in which it sits.[84]

---

81. *Id.* at 526.
82. *Id.* at 530-31.
83. Phillips v. Ill. Cent. Gulf R.R., 874 F.2d 984, 988 (5th Cir. 1989); Manley v. Engram, 755 F.2d 1463, 1467 n.10 (11th Cir. 1985); Nelson v. Int'l Paint Co., 716 F.2d 640, 643 (9th Cir. 1983); *see* 15 WRIGHT & MILLER, *supra* note 38, § 3846, at 365-66; *see also* 28 U.S.C. § 1631 (when an action is transferred to cure want of jurisdiction, it "shall proceed as if it had been filed in . . . the court to which it is transferred on the date upon which it was actually filed in . . . the court from which it is transferred"); Ross v. Colo. Outward Bound Sch., Inc., 822 F.2d 1524, 1527 (10th Cir. 1987) (interpreting § 1631 as prescribing law of transferee court).
84. *In re* Korean Air Lines Disaster, 829 F.2d 1171, 1173-76 (D.C. Cir. 1987) (involving § 1407 transfer), *aff'd sub nom on other grounds*, 490 U.S. 122 (1989); *see also* Menowitz v. Brown, 991 F.2d 36, 40-41 (2d Cir. 1993) (same); Ctr. Cadillac, Inc. v. Bank Leumi Trust Co., 808 F. Supp. 213, 222-24 (S.D.N.Y. 1992) (involving § 1404(a) transfer), *aff'd*, 99 F.3d 401, 401 (2d Cir. 1995); TBG, Inc. v. Bendis, No. 89-2423-0, 1992 U.S. Dist. LEXIS 5940, at *14-15 (D. Kan. Mar. 5, 1992) (same); Isaac v. Life Investors' Ins. Co. of Am., 749 F. Supp. 855, 863 (E.D. Tenn. 1990) (same); *cf.* Eckstein v. Balcor Film Investors, 8 F.3d 1121, 1126-27 (7th Cir. 1993) (agreeing in general with *Korean Air Lines*, but interpreting § 27A of Securities Exchange Act to require different result with respect to Rule 10b-5 claims filed on or before June 19, 1994 and criticizing *Menowitz* with respect to whether tranferor's or transferee's choice of law should apply in case transferred between courts, where issue arises under federal rather than state law).

b.   Forum Non Conveniens

Because there is no general procedure for transferring cases from a
federal court to the courts of another nation, federal courts employ the
common law doctrine of forum non conveniens. This doctrine permits
courts to decline jurisdiction when trial elsewhere would be more
appropriate. A trial court has wide discretion to determine the most
appropriate forum by balancing public and private interest factors, such
as the convenience of witnesses and litigants and the local interest in
having controversies decided at home, while still giving substantial
deference to a plaintiff's choice of forum.[85]

Common law forum non conveniens remains a significant
consideration in transnational cases.[86] Historically, courts have refused
to apply forum non conveniens to dismiss federal antitrust claims,
holding that sufficiently similar causes of action were unavailable in
other countries and thus no adequate alternative forum existed.[87]
However, at least two courts have recently held that antitrust claims are
dismissible under forum non conveniens.[88]

---

85.   Gulf Oil Corp. v. Gilbert, 330 U.S. 501, 504-09 (1947).
86.   *See, e.g.*, Piper Aircraft v. Reyno, 454 U.S. 235, 255-56 (1981) (endorsing
dismissal for transnational forum non conveniens); *see also* William L.
Reynolds, *The Proper Forum for a Suit: Transnational Forum Non
Conveniens and Counter-Suit Injunctions in the Federal Courts*, 70 TEX.
L. REV. 1663, 1693-94 (1992) (although courts seldom explicitly rely upon
citizenship as ground for dismissal, courts are loathe to use scarce judicial
resources on foreigners); *see also* Sheila L. Birnbaum & Douglas Dunham,
Foreign Plaintiffs and Forum Non Conveniens, 16 BROOK. J. INT'L L. 241,
265 (1990) (when evidence on causation, liability, and damages is located
in foreign forum, courts tend to dismiss claim).
87.   *See, e.g.*, Indus. Inv. Dev. Corp. v. Mitsui & Co., 671 F.2d 876, 890 (5th
Cir. 1982), *vacated on othergrounds and remanded*, 460 U.S. 1007,
reaff'd, 704 F.2d 785 (5th Cir. 1983).
88.   *See* Capital Currency Exch. v. Nat'l Westminster Bank PLC, 155 F.3d
603, 609 (2d Cir. 1998) (dismissing Sherman Act claims brought against
British bank under forum non conveniens doctrine); CSR Ltd. v. Fed. Ins.
Co., 146 F. Supp. 2d 556, 565 (D.N.J. 2001) (because "U.S. antitrust law is
not categorically distinct from the antitrust laws that are enforceable in
certain other nations," "the doctrine of forum non conveniens is
appropriately applied in antitrust cases"). Chapter 11 examines the impact
that forum non conveniens and transfer may have upon choice of forum.

c.   State Court

While there is no procedure generally available for transferring cases between the state courts of different states, a state court may exercise its discretion to stay its proceedings in deference to a concurrent action in another state court, in federal court, or in another country.[89]   In addition, the doctrine of forum non conveniens may be available to secure dismissal of the state court proceeding.   The Supreme Court's opinion in *Gulf Oil Corp. v. Gilbert*[90] is the leading expression of the doctrine.   Under the *Gilbert* analysis, a court should first determine whether there exists an alternative forum in which the defendant is amenable to process.   If such a forum exists, the court then weighs the interests of the parties along with the interests of the original forum; unless the balance is strongly in favor of the defendant, the plaintiff's choice of forum will be upheld.[91]   As the Supreme Court explained in *Gilbert*'s companion case of *Koster v. Lumbermans Mutual Casualty Co.*,[92] "the ultimate inquiry is where trial will best serve the convenience of the parties and the ends of justice."[93]

Whether a defendant may utilize the forum non conveniens doctrine to avoid jurisdiction in a particular state depends upon that state's statutory and common law treatment of the doctrine.   While most states

---

89.   *See* Chapter 13.
90.   330 U.S. 501 (1947).
91.   *Id.* at 508.   The interests that the *Gilbert* Court catalogued include the relative ease of access to sources of proof; availability of compulsory process for attendance of unwilling witnesses; the local interest in having localized controversies decided at home; and the appropriateness in having the trial of a diversity case in a forum where the court that is at home with the state law that must govern the case. *Id.* at 508-09.
92.   330 U.S. 518 (1947).
93.   *Id.* at 527.

utilize a test similar to the federal standard, at least two, Louisiana[94] and California,[95] do not recognize the forum non conveniens doctrine.

D. Class Actions

1. *Bases for Filing Class Actions in Federal and State Court*

Rule 23 of the Federal Rules of Civil Procedure does not expand or limit federal jurisdiction or venue but merely sets the requirements for a class action. To bring a class action in federal court, a plaintiff must show that:

> (1) the class is so numerous that joinder of all members is impracticable, (2) there are questions of law or fact common to the class, (3) the claims or defenses of the representative parties are typical of the claims or defenses of the class, and (4) the representative parties will fairly and adequately protect the interests of the class.[96]

In addition to these statutory requirements, courts have held that there must be "some evidence that a class exists and that the class can be defined with reasonable specificity" for a class action to stand.[97] Further, the plaintiffs must establish diversity jurisdiction if the claim is under state law.[98]

In addition to satisfying the requirements under Rule 23(a) and related case law, the class must fall within one of the subsets of Rule 23(b). Most antitrust class actions are filed under Rule 23(b)(3), which requires "that the questions of law or fact common to the members of the class predominate over any questions affecting only individual members,

---

94.   Kassapas v. Arkon Shipping Agency, Inc., 485 So. 2d 565, 566 (La Ct. App. 1986) (Louisiana does not recognize the forum non conveniens doctrine); *see also* Fox v. Bd. of Supervisors of La. State Univ. & Agric. & Mech. Coll., 576 So. 2d 978, 990 (La. 1991) ("Louisiana courts may not dismiss cases for forum non conveniens" except where allowed by statute).

95.   *See* Stangvik v. Shiley, Inc., 54 Cal. 3d 744, 751-52 (1991) (California does not employ forum non conveniens unless court decides that suitable, alternative forum exists).

96.   FED. R. CIV. P. 23(a).

97.   ABA ANTITRUST SECTION, ANTITRUST LAW DEVELOPMENTS 940 (5th ed. 2002) (footnote omitted).

98.   *Id.* at 941.

and that a class action is superior to other available methods for the fair and efficient adjudication of the controversy."[99]

Antitrust cases that may be appropriate for class action treatment under Rule 23(b)(3) include actions asserting a conspiracy in restraint of trade, especially cases of price-fixing. A determination that a conspiracy exists usually is common to all class members and may predominate over any individual issues in the case, thereby satisfying the first requirement of Rule 23(b)(3).[100]

Rule 23(b)(3) class actions are useful where numerous persons have suffered small monetary damages from violations of federal regulatory statutes that require no jurisdictional amount. However, courts are split as to whether the claim of each class member must exceed the required jurisdictional amount, exclusive of interest and costs, in cases where a jurisdictional amount is required.[101]

The development of state rules for class action litigation has been heavily influenced by Rule 23.[102] As a result, the prerequisites for maintaining a class action in state courts are similar to those of Rule 23. However, many states that have modeled their class action statutes on Rule 23 nonetheless have created bodies of case law that are more restrictive than Rule 23.[103] Counsel for a putative class therefore should

---

99. FED. R. CIV. P. 23(b); *see, e.g.*, Rosario v. Livaditis, 963 F.2d 1013, 1015-18 (7th Cir. 1992).
100. *See, e.g.*, Eisen v. Carlisle & Jacquelin, 391 F.2d 555, 565-66 (2d Cir. 1968) (despite differences between buyers and sellers of odd-lots on New York Stock Exchange, conspiracy claim against two brokerage firms for conspiring to monopolize odd-lot trading had common nucleus of operative facts).
101. This split among circuits involves the question of whether recent amendments to 28 U.S.C. § 1367 have superseded *Zahn v. International Paper Co.*, 414 U.S. 291 (1973), which held that each class member must meet the jurisdictional amount in diversity actions brought under state antitrust laws). *Zahn*, 414 U.S. at 301. *Compare* Gibson v. Chrysler, 261 F.3d 927 (9th Cir. 2001) (amendments superseded *Zahn*), *with* Trimble v. Asarco, 232 F.3d 946 (8th Cir. 2000) (because *Zahn* had not been superseded, each class member must still meet jurisdictional amount).
102. *See, e.g.*, 735 ILL. COMP. STAT. 5/2-801 (2005).
103. For example, New York's class action statute, N.Y. C.P.L.R. § 901(b) (McKinney 2004), does not permit class action suits for recovery of

be cognizant of any variance in a state class action statute that might impact upon plaintiffs' choice of forum.[104]

2. *Prefiling Jurisdictional Considerations*

Before filing a class complaint, counsel for the named plaintiffs must make sure it will be possible to comply with the requirements for jurisdiction, service of process, and venue. Because a class action is a representative action on behalf of absent class members, personal jurisdiction over all class members is not required to reach a binding judgment as to the common issues decided in the class action.[105] It is unnecessary for every class member to have minimum contacts with the federal or state forum involved for that forum to have jurisdiction over absent class members sufficient to issue a final judgment binding on all members of the class.[106]

Similarly, when a plaintiff sues a class of defendants, personal jurisdiction over, and service of process on, the representative defendants is all that is required.[107] Diversity jurisdiction need only exist as between the named parties, without regard to the citizenship of absent defendant class members.[108] Due process jurisdictional considerations in defendant class actions are lessened because such actions commonly involve claims under antitrust or securities statutes authorizing nationwide service of process. Such circumstances are deemed to satisfy jurisdictional notions of minimum contacts.[109]

---

penalties or minimum statutory amounts; a class plaintiff in state court therefore would need to find a federal statute (e.g., the Truth in Lending Act) and seek class certification on the ground that the federal statute authorized a class remedy. *See* Note, *Finding a Forum For The Class Action: Issues of Federalism Posed by Recent Limitations On Use of Federal Courts*, 28 SYRACUSE L. REV. 1009, 1036 (1977).

104. *See, e.g.*, 4 ALBA CONTE & HERBERT B. NEWBERG, NEWBERG ON CLASS ACTIONS § 13.13 (4th ed. 2002).

105. Am. Pipe & Constr. Co. v. Utah, 414 U.S. 538, 550-52 (1974).

106. Phillips Petroleum Co. v. Shutts, 472 U.S. 797, 806-14 (1985).

107. FED. R. CIV. P. 23(a).

108. *See* Snyder v. Harris, 394 U.S. 332, 340 (1969).

109. CONTE & NEWBERG, *supra* note 104, § 4.52; Spencer Williams, *Some Defendants Have Class: Some Reflections on the GAP Securities Litigation*, 89 F.R.D. 287, 292 (1980).

Proper venue, like diversity of citizenship, need only exist as to the named parties.[110] It is not necessary that all class members reside in the same district. When a class of defendants is involved, plaintiff's counsel should take venue requirements into consideration in selecting representatives of the defendants' class. If venue is improper regarding a representative defendant, that party may be dismissed and the action may continue if the remaining defendants adequately represent the class.[111]

3. Jurisdiction and Choice of Law in Multistate Class Actions

Courts are divided over the issue whether multistate class suits are limited by state court territorial limitations for exercising personal jurisdiction. Prevailing federal and state precedents support a federal or state court's power to certify and bind a multistate or national class.[112] The majority of courts have deemed adequate representation a sufficient ground for authorizing multistate class suits and appear to have concluded that personal jurisdiction over absent class members is not necessary to maintain a class action commenced in federal court.[113] Some states, however, have determined that their courts may not exercise jurisdiction over nonresidents in a multistate class action.[114]

Class members who are not personally subject to a state court's jurisdiction must satisfy several requirements before the court may assert jurisdiction over their claims. Where absent class action plaintiffs lack the minimum contacts with the forum that would support personal jurisdiction over a defendant, the forum state must provide minimal

---

110. Appleton Elec. Co. v. Advance-United Expressways, 494 F.2d 126, 140 (7th Cir. 1974).

111. CONTE & NEWBERG, *supra* note 105, § 6.12; Carolina Cas. Ins. Co. v. Local No. 612 Int'l Bhd. of Teamsters, 136 F. Supp. 941, 943 (N.D. Ala. 1956).

112. *See, e.g.*, CONTE & NEWBERG, *supra* note 105, § 13.36; Miner v. Gillette Co., 428 N.E.2d 478, 482 (Ill. 1981).

113. *See Shutts*, 472 U.S. at 814. Whether the same rule applies to class actions filed in federal court is less clear. *See* Integra v. Fid. Capital Appreciation Fund (*In re* Integra Resources, Inc.), 354 F.3d 1246, 1264-65 (10th Cir. 2004) (discussing U.S. Supreme Court's decision not to address this issue in *Ticor Title Ins. Co. v. Brown*, 511 U.S. 117, 121 (1994)).

114. *See, e.g.*, Feldman v. Bates Mfg. Co., 362 A.2d 1177, 1180 (N.J. Super. Ct. App. Div. 1976).

procedural due process protections. These protections include the following:

(1) nonresident plaintiffs must "receive notice" and must be provided the "opportunity to be heard and participate in the litigation";

(2) the notice must be "the best practicable, 'reasonably calculated, under all the circumstances,' to apprise interested parties of the pendency of the action'";

(3) the notice should "describe the action and the plaintiffs' rights in it";

(4) absent plaintiffs must be provided with an "opt-out" form by which they may make a "request for exclusion"; and

(5) nominal parties must "adequately represent the interests of the absent class members."[115]

Due process does not require nonresident claimants to "opt in" to the class.[116] A plaintiff may consent to jurisdiction in any forum, and silence after notice has been deemed is adequate evidence of that consent.[117]

In determining choice of law in multistate class actions, if the laws of the various states involved are in conflict, the forum court must consider whether the exercise of personal jurisdiction over the foreign parties is appropriate. The substantive law of the forum state may be applied where that state has "'significant contact or significant aggregation of contacts' to the claims asserted by each member of the plaintiff class, contacts 'creating State interests' ... ensur[ing] that the choice of [its] law is not arbitrary or unfair."[118]

---

115. *Shutts*, 472 U.S. at 812.

116. *Id.* at 812-13 (requiring all plaintiffs to affirmatively request inclusion in class would impede prosecution of actions which involve large number of claims).

117. *Id.* at 812-14.

118. *Id.* at 821-22; Martin v. Heinold Commodities, Inc., 510 N.E.2d 840, 846 (Ill. 1987) (quoting *Shutts*).

E. Federal Antitrust Claims: Jurisdiction, Service of Process, and Venue

As noted above, when federal claims are involved, jurisdiction, service of process, and venue often are complicated by special statutes that supplement the general provisions. Private claims under the antitrust laws are illustrative of these additional complexities.

1. *Section 12 of the Clayton Act*

Personal jurisdiction over a corporate defendant in an antitrust action is governed by Section 12 of the Clayton Act.[119] Although section 12 does not specifically mention the exercise of personal jurisdiction, some courts have interpreted the statute's authorization of service outside the state to permit federal courts to exercise nationwide personal jurisdiction over corporate antitrust defendants on the basis of the defendant's "national contacts."[120]

Whether a court holds that the national contacts test is applicable in an antitrust case often depends on how that court interprets the service of process provision in section 12. Federal courts are divided on whether section 12 authorizes worldwide service of process on defendants failing to satisfy the section 12 venue provision. Section 12 is divisible into two provisions. The first provision sets forth criteria for proper venue in antitrust cases. The second provision authorizes service of process upon an antitrust defendant "wherever" that defendant "may be found." Section 12 provides:

---

119. 15 U.S.C. § 22.
120. *See, e.g.*, Kingsepp v. Wesleyan Univ., 763 F. Supp. 22, 24 (S.D.N.Y. 1991); Grosser v. Commodity Exch., Inc., 639 F. Supp. 1293, 1312 (S.D.N.Y. 1986) (requiring plaintiff to establish that venue as to its antitrust claim lies in district where suit is brought), *aff'd without opinion*, 859 F.2d 148 (2d Cir. 1988); Dunham's, Inc. v. Nat'l Buying Syndicate of Tex., 614 F. Supp. 616, 623 (E.D. Mich. 1985) (pertinent inquiry is whether defendant was "transacting business" within district); Stabilisierungsfonds Fur Wein v. Kaiser Stuhl Wine Distribs. Pty. Ltd., 647 F.2d 200, 204 n.6 (D.C. Cir. 1981) (service of process provisions of antitrust statutes serve more importantly to define competence of federal courts in particular classes of cases to proceed against nonresident defendants).

Any suit, action, or proceeding under the antitrust laws against a corporation may be brought not only in the judicial district whereof it is an inhabitant, but also in any district wherein it may be found or transacts business; and all process *in such cases* may be served in the district of which it is an inhabitant, or wherever it may be found.[121]

Courts have interpreted the phrase "in such cases" in section 12 in two different ways. The Third and Ninth Circuits have held that "in such cases" refers to any case brought against a corporation under the antitrust laws.[122] Under this broad interpretation, section 12 authorizes worldwide service of process: a defendant who neither "inhabit[s]" nor "transacts business" within a given forum can nonetheless be served there.

In contrast, the D.C. Circuit recently held that the service of process provision in the second half of section 12 only applies when a defendant meets the venue requirements in the first half of section 12.[123] Under this narrower interpretation that originated in the Second Circuit,[124] worldwide service of process is only available if the defendant has already satisfied the requirements of the section 12 venue provision.

Under Rule 4(k)(1)(D) of the Federal Rules of Civil Procedure, "service of a summons . . . is effective to establish jurisdiction over the person of a defendant . . . when authorized by a statute of the United States."[125] Courts that hold that section 12 provides for nationwide service of process often also conclude that the combination of section 12 and Rule 4(k)(1)(D) authorizes courts to apply a national contacts test in

---

121. 15 U.S.C. § 22 (emphasis added). To be "found" within a district, a corporation typically must be doing business in such a manner and to such an extent that actual presence is established. *See* Eastman Kodak Co. v. S. Photo Co., 273 U.S. 359, 371 (1927) (corporation transacts business in district if, in ordinary and usual sense, it transacts business therein of any substantial character).

122. *See In re* Auto. Refinishing Paint Antitrust Litig., 358 F.3d 288, 294-97 (3d Cir. 2004); Go-Video, Inc. v. Akai Elec. Co., 885 F.2d 1406, 1413 (9th Cir. 1989); *In re* New Motor Vehicles Canadian Exp. Antitrust Litig., 307 F. Supp. 2d 145, 149 (D. Me. 2004).

123. *See In re* Vitamins Antitrust Litig., 94 F. Supp. 2d 26, 38-39 (D.D.C. 2000); GTE New Media Servs. Inc. v. BellSouth Corp., 199 F.3d 1343, 1350 (D.C. Cir. 2000) (citing *Heiman*, 288 F.2d at 581).

124. *See Heiman*, 288 F.2d at 581.

125. FED. R. CIV. P. 4(k)(1)(D).

antitrust cases.[126] Those courts interpreting section 12 as not authorizing worldwide service of process are less likely to recognize a national contacts test in the antitrust context.[127]

The federal long-arm provision also provides for a modified national contacts test for certain types of federal question claims.[128] Under Rule 4(k)(2), service of process can be used to obtain personal jurisdiction over a defendant if: (1) the claim arises under federal law; (2) the defendant is beyond the reach of any state court of general jurisdiction; and (3) the federal court's exercise of personal jurisdiction over the defendant does not offend the Constitution or other federal law.[129] Thus, for Rule 4(k)(2) to be beneficial, the foreign defendant usually must be: (a) unreachable under the long-arm statutes of any single forum; but (b) reachable under the national contacts test.[130]

The inquiry whether a defendant is "transacting business" in the forum state or district can be particularly important in those jurisdictions where the venue provision of section 12 must be satisfied for nationwide jurisdiction to be available. Fewer local contacts are needed to establish that a defendant is "transacting business" under section 12 than are needed to establish that the defendant is "doing business" for general jurisdictional purposes.[131] In determining whether a corporation is

---

126. *See In re Auto. Refinishing Paint Antitrust Litig.*, 358 F.3d at 298-99; *Go-Video, Inc.*, 885 F.2d 1406; *In re New Motor Vehicles Canadian Export Antitrust Litig.*, 307 F. Supp. 2d at 149.

127. *See, e.g.*, *In re Vitamins Antitrust Litig.*, 94 F. Supp. 2d at 31; *GTE New Media Servs. Inc.*, 199 F.3d at 1351.

128. FED. R. CIV. P. 4(k)(2).

129. United States v. Swiss Am. Bank, 191 F.3d 30, 38 (1st Cir. 1999); *see also* World Tanker Carriers Corp. v. M/V Ya Mawlaya, 99 F.3d 717, 720 (5th Cir. 1996) (under Rule 4(k)(2), foreign defendant's contacts with nation as whole are enough to justify personal jurisdiction over defendant on federal claim, even though defendant had not had sufficient minimum contacts to satisfy long-arm statute of any particular state).

130. *See, e.g.*, Sea-Roy Corp. v. Parts R Parts, No. 1:94CV59, 1995 U.S. Dist. LEXIS 21859, at *37-*41 (M.D.N.C. Aug. 15, 1995) (Rule 4(k)(2) did not apply because German corporation was amenable to personal jurisdiction in another state).

131. *See* Noise Reduction, Inc. v. Nordam Corp., No. 90C6497, 1991 U.S. Dist. LEXIS 17830, at *13-*16 & n.7 (N.D. Ill. Dec. 6, 1991) (rejecting contention that term "reside" as applied to venue for corporate defendants

"transacting business" for venue purposes, courts have considered the following:

(1)   continuity of the defendant's activities in the district;[132]

(2)   the volume of the defendant's business in the district;[133]

(3)   the relationship between the defendant's activities in the district and the nature of the cause of action;[134]

(4)   activities in the district by a subsidiary controlled by the defendant;[135]

---

is equivalent of "doing business"); GE v. Bucyrus-Erie Co., 550 F. Supp. 1037, 1041 n.5 (S.D.N.Y. 1982) (availability of service and personal jurisdiction under Clayton Act does not depend upon meeting its venue requirements); Dunlop Tire & Rubber Corp. v. Pepsico, Inc., 591 F. Supp. 88, 90 (N.D. Ill. 1984) ("transacts business" under Section 12 of the Clayton Act should be interpreted more broadly than concept of "carrying on business" under Section 7 of the Sherman Act); Hitt v. Nissan Motor Co., 399 F. Supp. 838, 840 (S.D. Fla. 1975) (fewer local contacts are necessary to find corporation is "transacting business" under Section 12 of the Clayton Act than Section 7 of the Sherman Act). *But see* Stewart Org., Inc. v. Ricoh Corp., 810 F.2d 1066, 1073 n.5 (11th Cir.), *aff'd*, 487 U.S. 22, 30-31 (1988) (claims could be filed in both Alabama and New York under *Erie* doctrine); 15 WRIGHT & MILLER, *supra* note 38, § 3818, at 179-80 ("On the better view, 'transacts business' in § 12 of the Clayton Act means the same thing as 'doing business' in the general venue statute, 28 U.S.C. § 1391(c).").

132. *Compare* Keeton v. Hustler Magazine, Inc., 465 U.S. 770, 781 (1984) (out-of-state publisher's continuous and deliberate exploitation of forum state market sufficient to support assertion of jurisdiction in libel action arising out of activity in forum state), *with* Amateur-Wholesale Elecs. v. R.L. Drake Co., 515 F. Supp. 580, 584-85 (S.D. Fla. 1981) (use of two trade shows by defendant to display products in Florida over 2-3 year period insufficient to give requisite degree of continuous local contact to constitute "transacting business").

133. *See* Int'l Shoe Co. v. Washington, 326 U.S. 310, 320 (1945); Expoconsul Int'l Inc. v. A/E Systems, Inc., 711 F. Supp. 730, 733 (S.D.N.Y. 1989).

134. *See* Burger King Corp. v. Rudzewicz, 471 U.S. 462, 472-73 (1985).

135. *Compare* Chrysler Corp. v. GM, 589 F. Supp. 1182, 1200 (D.D.C. 1984) (where parent corporation exercises continuing supervision and intervention in subsidiary's affairs, subsidiary's activities are attributable to parent for venue purposes under section 12), *with* Omega Homes, Inc. v. Citicorp Acceptance Co., 656 F. Supp. 393, 400 (W.D. Va. 1987) (while

(5) local telephone or other listings of the defendant within the district;136

(6) the existence of directors' meetings, business correspondence, payment of salaries, or purchase of machinery within the district;137

(7) the defendant's subjection to state regulation;138

(8) the amount of the defendant's goodwill activities within the district;139 and

(9) attendance at alleged conspiratorial meetings within the district.140

Despite a trend toward reading the "transacting business" language expansively, courts have interpreted the statute to require some amount of business continuity and more than a few isolated and peripheral contacts with the particular judicial district.[141]

---

parent corporation provided huge amounts of capital, contributed management advice, and was largely responsible for dictating dimension and scope of subsidiaries, jurisdiction and venue under section 12 was not proper with respect to parent, based upon subsidiary's activities within district, absent proof of parent's role subsequent to creation and launching of subsidiary).

136. Caribe Trailers Sys., Inc. v. P.R. Mar. Shipping Auth., 475 F. Supp. 711, 716 (D.D.C. 1979) (no venue over corporate defendant in antitrust action where no defendant was incorporated or licensed to do business in district, none directly conducted business or had principal place of business there, and none maintained corporate records, telephones, telephone listings, or bank accounts there).

137. Perkins v. Benguet Consol. Mining Co., 342 U.S. 437, 448 (1952) (based on personal affairs conducted in state, state court could either take or decline jurisdiction); *cf. Hall*, 466 U.S. at 416 (neither purchases nor acceptance of checks drawn on bank in forum state sufficient to establish in personam jurisdiction).

138. Agra Chem. Distrib. Co. v. Marion Labs., Inc., 523 F. Supp. 699, 702 (W.D.N.Y. 1981).

139. *Id.*

140. Ohio-Sealy Mattress Mfg. Co. v. Kaplan, 429 F. Supp. 139, 141 (N.D. Ill. 1977) (conspiratorial meetings may be sufficient to establish venue under § 1391 as to each defendant present there).

141. *See, e.g.*, O.S.C. Corp. v. Toshiba Am., Inc., 491 F.2d 1064, 1067-68 (9th Cir. 1974) (refusing section 12 venue over Japanese parent corporation

Where a foreign corporation has a wholly-owned U.S. subsidiary through which it conducts any considerable amount of business, the foreign parent corporation may be amenable to the jurisdiction of a U.S. court on the ground it is "transacting business" through its subsidiary.[142] The mere existence of a parent-subsidiary relationship between two entities does not permit a court automatically to impute the subsidiary's contacts to the parent.[143] Generally, a subsidiary's contacts are attributable to the parent company only if the court concludes that the subsidiary is acting as the parent's "general agent" or "alter ego."[144]

The factors to be considered in this analysis include, for example, the parent's actual control over the subsidiary; the existence of common offices, common officers, or an agency agreement; and the subsidiary's sale of the parent corporation's products.[145] Where the activities of a

---

which did not make deliveries directly to forum district); Fox-Keller v. Toyota Motor Sales, USA, Inc., 338 F. Supp. 812, 815 (E.D. Pa. 1972) (Pennsylvania venue over California corporation improper under section 12 because defendant made no sales to distributors in Pennsylvania and maintained no office or agent in Pennsylvania).

142. Sumitomo Shoji Am., Inc. v. Avagliano, 457 U.S. 176, 182-89 (1982); *see also In re* Tamoxifen Citrate Antitrust Litig., 262 F. Supp. 2d 17, 23 (E.D.N.Y. 2003) (British parent company had sufficient minimum contacts with United States, where parent company was actively participating in subsidiaries' U.S. marketing efforts and transacting business in U.S. through those subsidiaries); *In re* Cardizem CD Antitrust Litig., 105 F. Supp. 2d 618, 672 (E.D. Mich. 2000) (German pharmaceutical holding company purposely availed itself of privilege of conducting business in all U.S. states through actions of its wholly owned subsidiary, despite two layers of subsidiaries between holding company and U.S. subsidiary and total separation of operations and management between entities).

143. Modesto City Sch. v. Riso Kagaku Corp., 157 F. Supp. 2d 1128, 1132 (E.D. Cal. 2001).

144. Atlantigas Corp. v. Nisource, Inc., 290 F. Supp. 2d 34, 48 (D.D.C. 2003) ("exception exists . . . when the party contesting jurisdiction is found to be nothing more than the alter ego of an affiliated corporation over which the court does have jurisdiction"); *Modesto City Sch.*, 157 F. Supp. 2d at 1132 (discussing Ninth Circuit's "agency test" for determining whether domestic subsidiary is "general agent" of foreign parent company such that parent is amenable to jurisdiction because of subsidiary's contacts).

145. *See, e.g.*, Phone Directories Co. v. Contel Corp., 786 F. Supp. 930, 940-42 (D. Utah 1992) (Delaware holding company had sufficient control over

domestic subsidiary of a foreign parent support a conclusion that the parent is "found" within that district, or that the subsidiary is acting as the parent's general agent, service of process on the parent at the subsidiary's offices may constitute effective service upon the parent.[146]

Section 12 has been held to permit service of process upon an alien corporation found outside the United States by personal service on the corporation's general manager at its headquarters abroad.[147] Worldwide service of process has been held to be available under section 12, even in cases where venue is not established under that section but lies instead under Section 1391(b).[148]

Prior to the 1993 amendment to Rule 4 of the Federal Rules of Civil Procedure, courts had held that, while the Clayton Act may provide jurisdiction over a corporate defendant, the court must look to the long-arm statute of the state in which it sits to reach the corporation's officers.[149] Rule 4(k) now authorizes extraterritorial service on corporate officers with respect to claims arising under federal law, irrespective of state law.

---

wholly-owned subsidiary's directory advertising activities to make venue in subsidiary's state appropriate); Hoffman Motors Corp. v. Alfa Romeo S.p.A., 244 F. Supp. 70, 75-77 (S.D.N.Y. 1965) (venue appropriate in forum of subsidiary where foreign parent completely controlled and supervised 95%-owned subsidiary).

146. Lamb v. Volkswagenwerk Aktiengesellschaft, 104 F.R.D. 95, 101 (S.D. Fla. 1985) (control exercised by West German parent corporation over wholly-owned American subsidiary was sufficient basis for finding that parent transacted business in Florida or that subsidiary acted as parent's agent); Zisman v. Sieger, 106 F.R.D. 194, 200-01 (N.D. Ill. 1985) (considering service on local agent of foreign defendant).

147. *Hoffman Motors Corp.*, 244 F. Supp. at 79-80 (no reason to limit service to within United States); *see also Go-Video, Inc.*, 885 F.2d at 1417 (involving service of process on Japanese corporation in its home jurisdiction).

148. *Go-Video, Inc.*, 885 F.2d at 1413. *But see* Michelson v. Merrill Lynch, Pierce, Fenner & Smith, Inc., 709 F. Supp. 1279, 1287 (S.D.N.Y. 1989) (extraterritorial service of process provision of section 12 applicable only to cases satisfying its specific venue provision).

149. Daniel v. Am. Bd. of Emergency Med., 802 F. Supp. 912, 919 (W.D.N.Y. 1992) (jurisdiction over individual corporate officers and directors cannot be predicated merely upon jurisdiction over corporation).

2. *Section 4 of the Clayton Act*

Section 4 of the Clayton Act establishes venue in antitrust actions against either individuals or corporations.[150] It provides that a private antitrust claim may be brought against individuals or corporations "in the district in which the defendant resides or is found or has an agent."[151]

Section 4 contains no provision for extraterritorial service of process on non-corporate defendants and does not authorize service upon non-corporate defendants in any district other than that in which the suit is brought.[152] The 1993 amendment to Rule 4, however, authorizes such extraterritorial service with respect to federal claims.

F.   Personal Jurisdiction and the Internet

In recent years, federal courts have sought to fashion guidelines for determining when personal jurisdiction may be predicated upon a defendant's Internet activity, including operation of a website.[153] Not surprisingly, these guidelines remain a work in progress.[154] Courts are split in their reliance upon two distinct tests for determining when a defendant's maintenance of a website can justify the exercise of personal jurisdiction in particular cases.

1. *The* Zippo *Test*

The *Zippo* test, as set forth in *Zippo Manufacturing Co. v. Zippo Dot Com, Inc.,*[155] is applied by the majority of federal courts. The test focuses on the volume and quality of the website interaction between the nonresident defendant and the forum to determine in a particular case whether a court's exercise of personal jurisdiction is proper. The court in *Zippo* held that "the likelihood that personal jurisdiction can be constitutionally exercised" on the basis of a defendant's website

---

150. 15 U.S.C. § 15.
151. *Id.*
152. *Daniel*, 802 F. Supp. at 919; Pocahontas Supreme Coal Co. v. Nat'l Mines Corp., 90 F.R.D. 67, 69-70 (S.D.N.Y. 1981).
153. *See* Toys "R" Us, Inc. v. Step Two, S.A., 318 F.3d 446, 451 (3d Cir. 2003).
154. *Id.*
155. 952 F. Supp. 1119 (W.D. Pa. 1997).

operations is "directly proportionate to the nature and quality of commercial activity that [the] entity conducts over the Internet."[156]

The *Zippo* test classifies websites into three categories: "passive," "mildly interactive," and "fully interactive" websites.[157] Courts applying *Zippo* have consistently held that a defendant's operation of a passive website that does "little more than make information available to those who are interested" is insufficient to establish personal jurisdiction.[158] In contrast, the operation of a fully interactive website often is enough to establish personal jurisdiction over a website owner.[159]

The most disputed cases often involve mildly interactive websites. Under the *Zippo* test, without proof of a defendant doing "something more" than operating a passive website, courts have been reluctant to confer jurisdiction.[160] To satisfy *Zippo*'s "something more" requirement, courts have examined such things as website traffic, online sales, or "other evidence that Internet activity was directed at, or bore fruit in, the

---

156. *Id.* at 1124 (upholding exercise of personal jurisdiction because defendant actively targeted forum's residents through his website).
157. *Id.*
158. GTE New Media Servs. Inc. v. BellSouth Corp., 199 F.3d 1343, 1350 (D.C. Cir. 2000) (rejecting plaintiff's argument that defendant corporation's websites alone were sufficient to establish general jurisdiction over corporation in antitrust action); *see also* Cybersell, Inc. v. Cybersell, Inc., 130 F.3d 414, 419-20 (9th Cir. 1997); Carefirst of Md., Inc. v. Carefirst Pregnancy Ctrs., Inc., 334 F.3d 390, 400-01 (4th Cir. 2003); Mink v. AAAA Dev. LLC, 190 F.3d 333, 336-37 (5th Cir. 1999); Roche v. Worldwide Media, Inc., 90 F. Supp. 2d 714, 718-19 (E.D. Va. 2000); Bensusan Rest. Corp. v. King, 937 F. Supp. 295, 301 (S.D.N.Y. 1996), *aff'd*, 126 F.3d 25, 29 (2d Cir. 1997).
159. *See generally* CompuServe, Inc. v. Patterson, 89 F.3d 1257, 1264-66 (6th Cir. 1996); Sports Auth. Mich., Inc. v. Justballs, Inc., 97 F. Supp. 2d 806, 813-15 (E.D. Mich. 2000); Bridgeport Music v. Agarita Music, 182 F. Supp. 2d 653, 661 (M.D. Tenn. 2002); *see also Zippo Mfg. Co.*, 952 F. Supp. at 1124 (if "the defendant enters into contracts with residents of a foreign jurisdiction that involve the knowing and repeated transmission of computer files over the Internet, personal jurisdiction is proper").
160. *Cybersell, Inc.*, 130 F.3d at 419; *GTE New Media Servs. Inc.*, 199 F.3d at 1350; Millennium Enters., Inc. v. Millennium Music, LP, 33 F. Supp. 2d 907, 921 (D. Or. 1999).

forum state" when determining whether the exercise of personal
jurisdiction is proper.[161]

2.   *The Effects Doctrine*

The "effects doctrine" flows from *Calder v. Jones*[162] and generally
applies only to intentional tort claims.[163] In *Calder*, a California resident
filed a libel action against Florida-based National Enquirer magazine and
two of its employees for printing harmful allegations about the resident's
personal life.[164] The National Enquirer and the two employees moved to
quash the service of process for lack of personal jurisdiction. The
Supreme Court held that, because "[t]he article was drawn from
California sources, and the brunt of the harm, in terms both of
respondent's emotional distress and the injury to her professional
reputation, was suffered in California," "[j]urisdiction over petitioners is
therefore proper in California based on the 'effects' of their Florida
conduct in California."[165] The Enquirer's "intentional, and allegedly
tortious, actions were expressly aimed at California" and "impugned" a
California resident.[166]

To satisfy the purposeful availment requirement under the effects
doctrine, the plaintiff must show that the defendant has committed: "(1)
intentional actions (2) expressly aimed at the forum state (3) causing
harm, the brunt of which is suffered – and which the defendant knows is
likely to be suffered – in the forum state."[167]

---

161. iAccess, Inc. v. WEBcard Techs., Inc., 182 F. Supp. 2d 1183, 1188 (D.
     Utah 2002) (although defendant operated interactive website, because it
     did not specifically direct any activities at forum state, personal
     jurisdiction could not be exercised).
162. 465 U.S. 783.
163. *Id.* at 789-91.
164. *Id.* at 789 (printing allegation, among others, that entertainer Shirley Jones
     "drank so heavily as to prevent her from fulfilling her professional
     obligations").
165. *Id.* (citing World-Wide Volkswagen Corp. v. Woodson, 444 U.S. 286,
     297-98 (1980)).
166. *Id.*
167. Panavision Int'l, L.P. v. Toeppen, 141 F.3d 1316, 1322 (9th Cir. 1998)
     (citing Core-Vent Corp. v. Nobel Indus. AB, 11 F.3d 1482, 1486 (9th Cir.
     1993)).

The seminal case applying the effects doctrine to Internet activity is *Panavision International, L.P. v. Toeppen.*[168] The Ninth Circuit decided *Toeppen* approximately one year after applying the *Zippo* test in a different Internet case.[169] The nonresident defendant in *Toeppen* was a cyber-squatter who had registered domain names using trademarks of California-based companies. The court held that, because this defendant knew his conduct would injure companies in California, he had purposefully availed himself of California's jurisdiction through his tortious website-related activities.[170] Other courts have employed the effects doctrine in general settings to determine whether a defendant's website operations were sufficient to justify the exercise of personal jurisdiction.[171]

G. Practical Considerations: Selection of a Forum

1. *Jurisdiction, Service of Process, Venue, and Transferability*

In sum, there are several advantages to suing in a federal forum, including broader jurisdiction and venue provisions as well as broader service of process in cases brought under certain federal statutory provisions. However, when a federal court adjudicates state-created rights under diversity jurisdiction, a federal court's jurisdiction over nonresident defendants may be limited by the forum state's long-arm statute. States that restrict the reach of their long-arm statutes, *e.g.*, by requiring that the jurisdictional act occur in the state and that the cause of action arise from the particular act on which jurisdiction is based – to the extent those requirements are not met in a specific case – should be

---

168. 141 F.3d 1316.
169. *Cybersell, Inc.*, 130 F.3d at 419-20.
170. *Toeppen*, 141 F.3d at 1322.
171. *See, e.g., Patterson*, 89 F.3d at 1266 (nonresident defendant's repeated online threats to file suit against Ohio-based corporation sufficient for Ohio to assert personal jurisdiction); Rio Props., Inc. v. Rio Int'l Interlink, 284 F.3d 1007, 1020-21 (9th Cir. 2002) (Costa Rican company purposefully availed itself to Nevada under effects doctrine); Am. Info. Corp. v. Am. Infometrics, Inc., 139 F. Supp. 2d 696, 699-701 (D. Md. 2001) (applying effects doctrine but not finding purposeful availment by defendant operating passive website).

avoided in favor of states with more comprehensive long-arm statutes that extend jurisdiction to the full extent allowed by due process.

Venue is one of the most important and least considered factors in determining whether to file in federal or state court. Because federal judicial districts are not coterminous with the geographical units (usually counties) into which the states are divided for venue purposes, venue may lie in different cities or even different counties, depending upon whether suit is filed in federal or state court. The choice between federal and state court likewise may bear heavily on whether special venue statutes, or contractual choice-of-forum clauses, are enforced.

Transferability also may bear upon a plaintiff's choice of forum. If a defendant can be found within the state, a state court will generally have less flexibility in transferring the case at the defendant's request to another state than would a federal court, which can accomplish such a transfer under § 1404(a). The defendant, of course, may be able to nullify a plaintiff's choice of a state court forum through removal. However, under § 1441(b), removal rights can be waived, and removal based on diversity is not available to a defendant corporation or individual that is a citizen of the forum state.

2.   *Whether to Assert Federal Claims*

Where a plaintiff has a viable federal claim against one or more corporate defendants, it may be advantageous to file an action in federal court asserting both federal claims and any pendent state statutory or common law claims the plaintiff may have. Section 12 of the Clayton Act permits federal courts to exercise nationwide personal jurisdiction over corporate antitrust defendants and authorizes service of process upon a defendant corporation wherever it may be found. Likewise, the recent amendments to Rule 4 expand a plaintiff's options regarding extraterritorial service.

3.   *Multi-State Considerations*

When personal jurisdiction and service of process considerations afford a plaintiff more than one state from which to choose, choice of venue becomes increasingly complex because the plaintiff must make a federal vs. state court comparison in each jurisdiction. Further, because under the federal removal statute a defendant who is a citizen of the state in which suit is brought may not remove on grounds of diversity of citizenship, a plaintiff desiring to avoid removal and remain in state court against a diverse defendant therefore may find it advantageous to file suit in the defendant's home state.[172]

---

172. *See* Chapter 12.

CHAPTER XI

FORUM SELECTION IN ANTITRUST AND BUSINESS TORT LITIGATION

The factors that may affect a party's choice of forum may be broadly divided into three categories: (1) those that influence the plaintiff's choice among available causes of action and determine the substantive law that will govern those claims; (2) those that involve a court's power to assume jurisdiction over particular claims and parties; and (3) those that relate to differences in the way courts conduct their proceedings and adjudicate the claims before them. Chapters 1 and 2 address the substantive interplay of antitrust and business tort law, whereas Chapters 9 and 10 examine the threshold of procedural issues of jurisdiction, process, and venue. This chapter explores the interplay of these and other factors. – Eds.

A. Introduction

There are a variety of factors that may impact a plaintiff's choice of forum, including jurisdiction and the selection of the causes of action to be brought. Factors that upon first inspection might seem to limit a plaintiff's choice of forum frequently combine to present a rich array of options to both plaintiffs and defendants. Many commercial injuries may be cast in a variety of state and federal common law and statutory claims, and although the federal and state courts have enclaves of exclusive jurisdiction, they share extensive concurrent jurisdiction, especially in multistate cases. Similarly, liberal rules governing the permissible joinder of parties and claims often present plaintiffs with much flexibility in framing pleadings that accord with the rules governing jurisdiction, venue, and process, while enabling the plaintiff to assert its most promising claims in the forum perceived as most advantageous.

Beyond the factors that inform a plaintiff's ability to assert particular claims against particular defendants in a particular court lies the question whether that court offers the best forum for the plaintiff's claims. This inquiry runs deeper than speculation into whether particular judges or juries might be more hospitable to a plaintiff's case than others; rather, the application of choice-of-law rules may imply significant advantages in terms of both procedural and substantive law, depending upon the forum in which suit is brought. Indeed, because of the variety of causes of action based in state law, where an action is filed and which state's law applies often determines the available viable causes of action. The introduction of such considerations further complicates the overall "mix" of factors that bear upon the task of choosing the optimal forum in which to assert – and defend – antitrust and business tort claims.

B. Choice-of-Law

Considerations relating to choice-of-law often are among the most important – and neglected – factors in the forum selection calculus. Under the Restatement (Second) of Conflicts of Laws, the courts generally apply the "most significant relationship" test when selecting the substantive law that will govern disputes involving contractual and tort claims.[1] Procedural issues, on the other hand, are governed by the law of the forum.[2] Although contracting parties are generally free to choose the law that will govern their relationship,[3] a court will not enforce such a provision when the chosen state has no substantial relationship to the parties or the transaction and there is no other

---

1.   *See, e.g.*, SIL-FLO, Inc. v. SFHC, Inc., 917 F.2d 1507, 1512 (10th Cir. 1990); FMC Corp. v. Capital Cities/ABC, Inc., 915 F.2d 300, 302 (7th Cir. 1990); Fashion House, Inc. v. K Mart Corp., 892 F.2d 1076, 1092 (1st Cir. 1989); *see generally* RESTATEMENT (SECOND) OF CONFLICTS OF LAWS §§ 145, 188 (1969) [hereinafter RESTATEMENT]. Where the parties do not raise a question as to choice of law in a diversity case, the law of the forum state presumptively governs. *See* Kritikos v. Palmer Johnson, Inc., 821 F.2d 418, 421 (7th Cir. 1987).

2.   *See, e.g.*, Keeton v. Hustler Magazine, Inc., 465 U.S. 770, 778 n.10 (1984); Equitable Life Assurance Soc'y of the United States v. McKay, 861 F.2d 221, 222 (9th Cir. 1988); *see generally* RESTATEMENT, *supra* note 1, § 122.

3.   RESTATEMENT, *supra* note 1, § 187(2); *see, e.g.*, Wallace Hardware Co. v. Abrams, 223 F.3d 382, 399-400 (6th Cir. 2000) (upholding Tennessee choice of law provision in contract where parties were represented by counsel and application of Tennessee law did not violate public policy of forum state).

reasonable basis for the parties' choice,[4] or when application of the law of the chosen state would violate a "fundamental policy" of the forum state.[5]

To determine which state law supplies the substantive rule of decision, a federal court will apply the choice-of-law rules of the forum state.[6] Once a federal court determines which state's law governs, it is bound to follow the decisions of that state's highest court on the issue in question; if there are no such decisions, the federal court must make an educated guess as to how the state's highest court would rule.[7] With respect to federal claims, federal courts are free to apply federal common law,[8] but may choose to apply the choice-of-law rules of the forum state.[9]

---

4. *See, e.g.,* Wright-Moore Corp. v. Ricoh Corp., 908 F.2d 128, 132 (7th Cir. 1990); *see generally* RESTATEMENT, *supra* note 1, § 187(a).

5. *See, e.g., Wright-Moore Corp.,* 908 F.2d at 132; *see generally* RESTATEMENT, *supra* note 1, § 187(2)(b).

6. Klaxon Co. v. Stentor Elec. Mfg. Co., 313 U.S. 487 (1941); Griffin v. McCoach, 313 U.S. 498 (1941); *see also* Day & Zimmermann, Inc. v. Challoner, 423 U.S. 3 (1975); 28 U.S.C. § 1652.

7. *See, e.g.,* Nobs Chem., USA, Inc. v. Koppers Co., 616 F.2d 212, 214 (5th Cir. 1980). In making such an educated guess, it is unlikely that a federal court will be as receptive as a state court in addressing a claim requiring a stretch – or a novel interpretation – of state law. To quote the Seventh Circuit:

> The plaintiffs are asking us to innovate boldly in the name of the Illinois courts, and such a request is better addressed to those courts than to a federal court. If the plaintiffs had filed this case in an Illinois state court and it had been removed to a federal district court, they would have had no choice, and then we would have been duty-bound to be as innovative as we thought it plausible to suppose the Illinois courts would be.

   Haynes v. Alfred A. Knopf, Inc., 8 F.3d 1222, 1234 (7th Cir. 1993); *see also* Todd v. Societe BIC, S.A., 21 F.3d 1402, 1412 (7th Cir. 1994) ("When given a choice between an interpretation of Illinois law which reasonably restricts liability, and one which greatly expands liability, we should choose the narrower and more reasonable path (at least until the Illinois Supreme Court tells us differently).").

8. *See, e.g.,* Wells Fargo Asia Ltd. v. Citibank, N.A., 936 F.2d 723, 726 (2d Cir. 1991); Harris v. Polskie Linie Lotnicze, 820 F.2d 1000, 1003-04 (9th Cir. 1987); *cf.* Penwest Dev. Corp. v. Dow Chem. Co., 667 F. Supp. 436,

Special choice-of-law rules apply when a suit is transferred from one federal district court to another. In *Van Dusen v. Barrack*,[10] the Supreme Court held that when a diversity case is transferred at the defendant's request pursuant to Section 1404(a) of Title 28 of the U.S. Code, the transferee court is "obligated to apply the state law that would have been applied if there had been no change of venue."[11] The Supreme Court extended this rule in *Ferens v. John Deere Co.*,[12] holding that the transferor court's law controls irrespective of whether the plaintiff or defendant seeks the transfer. This rule applies, however, only if suit was properly filed in the transferor court; if venue was improper or personal jurisdiction was lacking in that court, the transferee court is free to apply the law that would have been applied had the action originally been filed there.[13] When federal law supplies the rule of decision, the *Van Dusen-Ferens* rule does not apply, and the transferee court applies the law of the circuit in which it sits.[14]

---

441 (E.D. Mich. 1987) (applying *Klaxon* where jurisdiction is based upon both federal question and diversity of citizenship).

9. *See, e.g.*, Barkanic v. Gen. Admin. of Civil Aviation of People's Republic of China, 923 F.2d 957, 960-61 (2d Cir. 1991); *cf. Penwest Dev. Corp.*, 667 F. Supp. at 441.

10. 376 U.S. 612 (1964).

11. *Id.* at 639.

12. 494 U.S. 516 (1990).

13. Phillips v. Ill. Cent. Gulf R.R., 874 F.2d 984, 988 (5th Cir. 1989); Manley v. Engram, 755 F.2d 1463, 1467 n.10 (11th Cir. 1985); Nelson v. Int'l Paint Co., 716 F.2d 640, 643 (9th Cir. 1983); *see* 15 CHARLES ALAN WRIGHT ET AL., FEDERAL PRACTICE AND PROCEDURE § 3846, at 364-66 (1986); *see also* 28 U.S.C. § 1631 (providing that when an action is transferred to cure a want of jurisdiction, it "shall proceed as if it had been filed in . . . the court to which it is transferred on the date upon which it was actually filed in . . . the court from which it is transferred"); Ross v. Colo. Outward Bound Sch., Inc., 822 F.2d 1524, 1527 (10th Cir. 1987) (interpreting § 1631 as prescribing law of transferee court).

14. *In re* Korean Air Lines Disaster, 829 F.2d 1171, 1173-76 (D.C. Cir. 1987) (28 U.S.C. § 1407 transfer), *aff'd sub nom on other grounds*, 490 U.S. 122 (1989); *accord* Menowitz v. Brown, 991 F.2d 36, 40-41 (2d Cir. 1993) (28 U.S.C. § 1407 transfer); Ctr. Cadillac, Inc. v. Bank Leumi Trust Co., 808 F. Supp. 213, 222-24 (S.D.N.Y. 1992) (28 U.S.C. § 1404(a) transfer), *aff'd*, 99 F.3d 401 (2d Cir. 1995); TBG, Inc. v. Bendis, No. 89-2423-0, 1992 U.S. Dist. LEXIS 5940, at *14-15 (D. Kan., Mar. 5, 1992) (28 U.S.C.

C. Forum Non Conveniens/Transfer

While a plaintiff has control over the initial choice of forum, doctrines of transfer and forum non conveniens provide defendants with the ability to upset a plaintiff's litigation strategy and assert control over where the litigation is situated. Transfer and forum non conveniens principles provide a defendant the ability to force a plaintiff to litigate in a different federal district, a different county, or even a different country than originally selected by the plaintiff.[15]

D. Pleading Requirements

Differences in pleading requirements may impact a party's choice of forum, particularly when a claim is founded upon suspicion or incomplete information. A key distinction often found between the federal standard and that of a particular state is the degree of factual specificity required.

Federal Rule of Civil Procedure 8(a)(2) requires a party to plead "a short and plain statement of the claim showing that the pleader is entitled to relief." This federal standard, called "notice pleading," avoids distinctions between conclusions of law, ultimate facts, and evidentiary facts.[16] To quote one commentator:

> First, the rule eliminates the seemingly endless controversies concerning what constitutes a "cause of action" and what is a "fact" as opposed to mere evidence or a conclusion of law. Second, the rule . . . abolishes the requirement that a cause of action be stated . . . . [A] party is permitted to recover whenever she has a valid claim, even

---

§ 1404(a) transfer); Issac v. Life Investors Ins. Co. of Am., 749 F. Supp. 855, 863 (E.D. Tenn. 1990) (28 U.S.C. § 1404(a) transfer); *cf.* Eckstein v. Balcor Film Investors, 8 F.3d 1121, 1126-27 (7th Cir. 1993) (generally agreeing with *Korean Air Lines*, but interpreting Section 27A of the Securities Exchange Act to require a different result with respect to Rule 10b-5 claims filed on or before June 19, 1991).

15. *See supra* Chapter 10.
16. 2A JAMES WM. MOORE ET AL., MOORE'S FEDERAL PRACTICE ¶ 8.13, at 8-61 (2d ed. 1995); *see, e.g.*, United States v. Employing Plasterers Ass'n of Chicago, 347 U.S. 186, 188-89 (1954); Littleton v. Berbling, 468 F.2d 389, 394 (7th Cir. 1972), *vacated and remanded on other grounds*, 414 U.S. 514 (1974); Oil, Chem. & Atomic Workers Int'l Union, AFL-CIO v. Delta Ref. Co., 277 F.2d 694, 697 (6th Cir. 1960).

though her attorney fails to perceive the proper basis of the claim at the pleading stage.[17]

In *Leatherman v. Tarrant County Narcotics Intelligence and Coordination Unit*,[18] the U.S. Supreme Court confirmed that the Federal Rules mandate a liberal standard of pleading. There, the Court struck down the Fifth Circuit's heightened pleading standard in Section 1983 cases, declaring:

> We think that it is impossible to square the "heightened pleading standard" applied by the Fifth Circuit in this case with the liberal system of "notice pleading" set up by the Federal Rules. Rule 8(a)(2) requires that a complaint include only "a short and plain statement of the claim showing that the pleader is entitled to relief." In *Conley v. Gibson*, we said in effect that the Rule meant what it said. . . .[19]

This liberal standard is tempered by Rule 9(b), which requires factual specificity when pleading fraud, and by Rule 11, which requires that a pleading both "have evidentiary support" and be "warranted by existing law."[20] In addition, notwithstanding this "liberal" standard of pleading, Rule 12(b)(6) authorizes the dismissal of pleadings that fail to state a claim upon which relief can be granted; survey evidence suggests that the federal courts' increased willingness to "weed out" insufficient complaints may account in part for the increased resort by business tort plaintiffs to state courts.[21]

Most states' pleading requirements were derived from the more rigid "Field Code," a code of procedure formulated by David Field for New York in 1848 that is still applied in some form in several states. The Field Code required a "statement of the facts constituting a cause of

---

17. JACK H. FRIEDENTHAL ET AL., CIVIL PROCEDURE 253 (1985).

18. 507 U.S. 163 (1993).

19. *Id.* at 168 (citation omitted).

20. However, to quote Judge Easterbrook, "Rule 11 requires not that counsel plead facts but that counsel know facts after conducting a reasonable investigation – and then only enough to make it reasonable to press litigation to the point of seeking discovery." *Frantz v. U.S. Powerlifting Fed'n*, 836 F.2d 1063, 1068 (7th Cir. 1987).

21. *See generally* Harvey I. Saferstein, *The Ascendancy of Business Tort Claims in Antitrust Practice*, 59 ANTITRUST L.J. 379, 383-84, 398-402 (1991).

action, in ordinary and concise language, without repetition, and in such a manner as to enable a person of common understanding to know what was intended."[22] Since the adoption of the Federal Rules in 1938, however, many states have shifted to the federal standard.

In 1986, two commentators published a comprehensive survey of the civil procedures of the 50 states and the District of Columbia.[23] They found that 23 of the 51 state jurisdictions had systematically replicated the Federal Rules,[24] and another eleven jurisdictions had adopted their own notice pleading standard.[25] The remaining seventeen jurisdictions fell into the fact pleading category, although some of those jurisdictions follow the Federal Rules in other respects.[26] In 1989, using the incorporation of the 1983 amendments to the Federal Rules 11 and 26 as a metric, another commentator found that only eight jurisdictions continued to systematically replicate the Federal Rules.[27] In an update of the 1986 survey discussed above, one commentator found that only two state systems, Wyoming and Utah, remained virtual replicas of the

---

22. Richard L. Marcus, *The Revival of Fact Pleading Under the Federal Rules of Civil Procedure*, 86 COLUM. L. REV. 433, 438 (1986).
23. John B. Oakley & Arthur F. Coon, *The Federal Rules in State Courts: A Survey of State Court Systems of Civil Procedure*, 61 WASH. L. REV. 1367 (1986).
24. These jurisdictions were: Alabama, Alaska, Arizona, Colorado, District of Columbia, Hawaii, Indiana, Kentucky, Maine, Mass., Minnesota, Montana, New Mexico, North Dakota, Ohio, Rhode Island, South Dakota, Tennessee, Utah, Vermont, Washington, West Virginia, and Wyoming. *See* Oakley & Coon, *supra* note 23, at 1377-78.
25. These jurisdictions were: Georgia, Idaho, Iowa, Kansas, Michigan, Mississippi, Nevada, New Hampshire, North Carolina, Oklahoma, and Wisconsin. *See id.*
26. These jurisdictions were: Arkansas, California, Connecticut, Delaware, Florida, Illinois, Louisiana, Maryland, Missouri, Nebraska, New Jersey, New York, Oregon, Pennsylvania, South Carolina, Texas, and Virginia. *See id.*
27. Stephen N. Subrin, *Federal Rules, Local Rules, and State Rules: Uniformity, Divergence, and Emerging Procedural Patterns*, 137 U. PA. L. REV. 1999, 2037 (1989). Those jurisdictions were Minnesota, Montana, North Dakota, Tennessee, Utah, Vermont, Washington, and West Virginia. *Id.*

federal system by adopting the majority of the 1980 to 2000 amendments to the Federal Rules.[28]

Interestingly, a code-based, fact pleading system is still followed in some of the most populated jurisdictions. For example, New York requires that a complaint contain a statement of facts "sufficiently particular to give the court and parties notice of the transactions, occurrences, or series of transactions or occurrences intended to be proved and the material elements of each cause of action."[29] California requires a "statement of facts constituting the cause of action, in ordinary and concise language."[30] While the Illinois Code mandates "a plain and concise statement of the pleader's cause of action,"[31] there is no question that Illinois is a fact pleading jurisdiction; Illinois courts require that a complaint "contain facts and not merely conclusions."[32]

Another potential difference between federal and state pleading practice involves dismissal. Rule 12(b)(6) of the Federal Rules of Civil Procedure provides a procedure by which a defendant may challenge the legal sufficiency of the plaintiff's allegations; in the words of the Rule, a complaint may be dismissed for "failure to state a claim upon which relief can be granted." Many states have comparable, although not necessarily identical, provisions.[33] As noted above,[34] the increased willingness of federal courts to enforce Rule 12(b)(6) may account in part for the increased popularity of state courts in business tort litigation. Although several states have adopted rules similar to Federal Rule of Civil Procedure 11, there may be significant differences in the form and content of Federal Rule 11 and the corresponding analogue of a particular state.

---

28. John B. Oakley, *A Fresh Look at the Federal Rules in State Courts*, 3 NEV. L.J. 354, 383 (2003).

29. *See* N.Y. C.P.L.R. 3013 (Consol. 2005).

30. CAL. CIV. PROC. CODE § 425.10(a); *see* Oakley & Coon, *supra* note 23, at 1383.

31. 735 ILL. COMP. STAT. ANN. 5/2-603(a) (West 2005).

32. Harris v. Johnson, 578 N.E.2d 1326, 1328 (Ill. App. Ct. 1991).

33. *Cf.* ARK. R. CIV. P. 12(b)(6) ("failure to state facts upon which relief can be granted"); TEX. R. CIV. P. 91 (use of special exceptions to "point out intelligibly and with particularity the defect, omission, obscurity, duplicity or other insufficiency in the allegations in the pleading excepted to").

34. *See supra* note 21 and accompanying text.

E. Discovery Differences

Differences in available discovery procedures also may influence the choice of forum. In many states whose rules of procedure do not track the federal rules, the federal discovery rules may afford more liberal discovery. One example is Rule 30(b)(6), which compels a party to designate for deposition a person qualified to testify about the "matters on which examination is requested." This rule increasingly is employed at the outset of litigation as a shortcut to meaningful discovery.[35]

Another feature of the Federal Rules not found in the discovery rules of many states is Rule 32(a)(2), which allows the use of a deposition of a party (including a party's officer, director, managing agent or Rule 30(b)(6) designee) at trial "for any purpose." The Federal Rules also do not brook the more cumbersome distinctions between "discovery" and "evidence" depositions to which some states still cling.[36]

Dramatic distinctions in discovery practice between the federal system and state courts took effect in 1993, when the U.S. Supreme Court approved extensive amendments to the Federal Rules of Civil Procedure.[37] The key feature – an automatic duty of disclosure – marked a radical departure from traditional discovery practice in the federal courts. This duty of disclosure relates to information such as both initial disclosures and the disclosure of expert testimony.[38] The 2000 Amendment to Rule 26 established a nationally uniform practice for these initial disclosure provisions.

Amended Rule 26 was complemented by changes to Rule 37 sanctioning the nondisclosure of required information by barring the introduction of such evidence and informing the jury of the nondisclosure; other possible sanctions include the payment of attorneys' fees and the preclusion of the noncomplying party from conducting discovery.[39] Other changes include (1) an amendment to Rule 30 that

---

35. *See generally* Mark A. Cymrot, *The Forgotten Rule*, LITIGATION, Spring 1992, at 6.
36. *See, e.g.*, ILL. SUP. CT. R. 202, 212 (West 2005).
37. *See* Proposed Amendments to the Federal Rules of Civil Procedure, 61 U.S.L.W. 4365 (U.S. Apr. 27, 1993).
38. FED. R. CIV. P. 26(a)(1), (2).
39. FED. R. CIV. P. 37(c).

sets a presumptive limit of ten depositions per side,[40] as well as a new limit to each deposition of "one day of seven hours,"[41] (2) an amendment to Rule 33 that sets a presumptive limit of twenty-five interrogatories per side;[42] and (3) changes to Rules 33, 34 and 36 that precluded requests under such rules until the Rule 26 disclosures are made.[43]

Quoting from the Notes of the Advisory Committee on Civil Rules, "[t]he purpose of the revision [to Rule 26] is to accelerate the exchange of basic information about the case and to eliminate the paper work involved in requesting such information."[44] Coupled with presumptive limits on depositions and interrogatories, the automatic duty of disclosure necessitates in-depth analysis of the legal and factual basis for the parties' claims at the outset of litigation.

F. Summary Judgment

The U.S. Supreme court issued three opinions in 1986 that expanded the federal law of summary judgment: *Matsushita Electrical Industrial Co. v. Zenith Radio Corp.*;[45] *Anderson v. Liberty Lobby, Inc.*;[46] and *Celotex Corp. v. Catrett.*[47] Although all three of the cases have expanded the federal law of summary judgment, *Matsushita* is unique in that it was based on antitrust law. That being said, a later Supreme Court

---

40. FED. R. CIV. P. 30(a)(2).
41. FED. R. CIV. P. 30(d)(2).
42. FED. R. CIV. P. 33(a).
43. FED. R. CIV. P. 33(a), 34(b), 36(a).
44. Committee on Rules of Practice and Procedure of the Judicial Conference of the U.S., *Preliminary Draft of Proposed Amendments to the Federal Rules of Civil Procedure and the Federal Rules of Evidence* (Aug. 1991), *reprinted in* 137 F.R.D. 53, 99 (Sept. 1991) [hereinafter Preliminary Draft]. The Notes also cite two law review articles which discuss the concepts underlying the duty of disclosure: Wayne Brazil, *The Adversary Character of Civil Discovery: A Critique and Proposals for Change*, 31 VAND. L. REV. 1348 (1978); and William W. Schwarzer, *The Federal Rules, the Adversary Process, and Discovery Reform*, 50 U. PITT. L. REV. 703, 721-23 (1989). *See* Preliminary Draft, 137 F.R.D. at 99-100.
45. 475 U.S. 574 (1986).
46. 477 U.S. 242 (1986).
47. 477 U.S. 317 (1986).

case, *Eastman Kodak Co. v. Image Technical Services, Inc.*,[48] appears to have limited the impact of *Matsushita* in antitrust cases.

In *Matsushita*, American manufacturers of television sets brought an antitrust suit against Japanese manufacturers alleging that they had conspired to drive the American manufactures from the market by engaging in a scheme to fix and maintain artificially low prices in the American market by fixing and maintaining artificially high prices in the Japanese market.[49] The court of appeals had held that summary judgment was not appropriate, and the Supreme Court reversed and remanded. The Supreme Court ruled that on a motion for summary judgment:

> If the factual context renders respondents' claim implausible – if the claim is one that simply makes no economic sense – respondents must come forward with more persuasive evidence to support their claim than would otherwise be necessary.[50]

According to the court, in the above circumstance, the nonmovant must proffer evidence that "tend[s] to exclude the possibility" of independent action by the alleged conspirators.[51]

Anderson involved a libel action brought against a magazine, its publisher, and its chief executive officer. The district court granted summary judgment in favor of plaintiffs and the court of appeals affirmed in part and reversed in part.[52] The Supreme Court reversed and held that a ruling on a motion for summary judgment or directed verdict "necessarily implicates the substantive evidentiary standard of proof that would apply at the trial on the merits."[53] Thus in ruling on a motion for summary judgment, a court "must view the evidence presented through the prism of the substantive evidentiary burden."[54]

In *Celotex*, the Supreme Court held that Federal Rule of Civil Procedure 56(c) mandated the entry of summary judgment after adequate time for discovery against a party who fails to make a showing sufficient

---

48. 504 U.S. 451 (1992).
49. *Matsushita Elec. Indus. Co.*, 475 U.S. at 577.
50. *Id.* at 587.
51. *Id.* at 597 (internal quotations omitted).
52. *Anderson*, 477 U.S. at 242.
53. *Id.* at 252.
54. *Id.* at 254.

to establish the existence of an essential element to that party's case and on which that party will bear the burden of proof at trial.[55] If that showing is made, the burden then shifts to the opponent to produce evidence establishing a genuine issue of material fact. The opponent may not rely on the allegation in the pleading but must set forth "specific facts showing that there is a genuine issue for trial."[56]

Later, in *Kodak*, the Supreme court stated that "[t]he Court's requirement in *Matsushita*[,] that the plaintiffs' claims make economic sense, did not introduce a special burden on plaintiffs facing summary judgment in antitrust cases."[57] The Court in *Kodak* also stated that "*Matsushita* . . . did not hold that if the moving party enunciates *any* economic theory supporting its behavior, regardless of its accuracy in reflecting the actual market, it is entitled to summary judgment."[58] Rather, "*Matsushita* demands only that the nonmoving party's inferences be reasonable in order to reach the jury, a requirement that was not invented, but merely articulated, in that decision."[59] The Court in *Kodak* also made a distinction on the facts of *Matsushita* noting:

> [T]he facts in this case are just the opposite. The alleged conduct – higher service prices and market foreclosure – is facially anticompetitive and exactly the harm that antitrust laws aim to prevent. In this situation, *Matsushita* does not create any presumption in favor of summary judgment for the defendant.[60]

Although nothing in *Kodak* appears to impair the authority of *Anderson* and *Celotex*, as noted above it does raise questions about the application of *Matsushita* in the antitrust context.

G.   Trial Subpoena Practice

In 1991, a significant amendment to Rule 45 of the Federal Rules of Civil Procedure took effect, which can allow a party to compel the attendance at trial of a nonparty witness residing in another part of the

---

55.   *Celotex Corp.*, 477 U.S. at 317.
56.   *Id.* at 322.
57.   Eastman *Kodak*, 504 U.S. at 468.
58.   *Id.*
59.   *Id.*
60.   *Id.* at 478.

country. Under certain circumstances this procedural tool could render a federal forum more advantageous.

This provision in Rule 45 provides that if a subpoena

> requires a person who is not a party or an officer of a party to incur substantial expense to travel more than 100 miles to attend trial, the court may, to protect a person subject to or affected by the subpoena, quash or modify the subpoena or, if the party in whose behalf the subpoena is issued shows a substantial need for the testimony or material that cannot be otherwise met without undue hardship and assures that the person to whom the subpoena is addressed will be reasonably compensated, the court may order appearance or production only upon specified conditions.[61]

The Rule recognizes, albeit implicitly, that depositions are a poor substitute for live testimony. Nonetheless, given the increasing acceptance of videotaped depositions, it should be an extraordinary situation that would merit the compulsion of a cross-country trip to testify in somebody else's fight.[62] While the Rule lifts the "substantial need" test from Rule 26(b)(3), the Advisory Committee offered no examples of what this means in the context of trial testimony. One possibility could be the case of a party's former executive who played a key role in the events leading up to the lawsuit.

Although this amendment to Rule 45 is addressed to nonparties, it also should affect a party's ability to compel current employees of an adverse party to attend trial. While, in the past, parties themselves could be counted upon to appear at trial, nothing in the Rules guaranteed that any particular officer or employee would testify; counsel had to hope for a cooperative opponent or a court that would strongly suggest that particular party-related witnesses attend. Amended Rule 45 thus was intended to bring greater certainty to this aspect of trial preparation.[63]

---

61. FED. R. CIV. P. 45(c)(3)(B)(iii).
62. *See* Michael P. Kenny & William H. Jordan, *Trial Presentation Technology: A Practical Perspective*, 67 TENN. L. REV. 587, 587, 591 (2000); David B. Hennes, Comment, *Manufacturing Evidence for Trial: The Prejudicial Implications of Videotaped Crime Scene Reenactments*, 142 U. PA. L. REV. 2125, 2133 (1994).
63. Other changes to the Rule include the abandonment of the requirement that a subpoena duces tecum seeking documents be part of a deposition

H. Jury Practice

Two principal distinctions between federal and state court jury practice are the size of the jury and the unanimity requirement. An amendment to Rule 48 of the Federal Rules of Civil Procedure, effective December 1, 1991, reduced the numerical disparity between state and federal court juries; that amendment requires that alternate jurors participate in the verdict.[64] Hence, assuming that no jurors drop out in the course of a trial, a typical federal jury should consist of eight members, as opposed to the twelve person jury prevalent in state court practice. Still, the disparity in the size of the jury and the unanimity requirement (or lack thereof) could play a significant role in the outcome of a case. While the nature of the inquiry renders empirical conclusions difficult, studies have confirmed what common sense would dictate: larger juries tend to include a greater diversity of viewpoints, and there is less compromising on damages in majority verdicts.

A larger jury is statistically more likely to be representative of a community and include a minority viewpoint.[65] Where unanimity is required, this feature should result in more hung juries. One commentator, in explaining data reflecting that twelve-member juries were twice as likely to "hang" as six-member juries, stated:

> Hung juries almost always arise from situations in which there were originally several dissenters. Even if only one holds out, his having once been a member of a group is essential in sustaining him against the majority's efforts to make the verdict unanimous. Fewer hung

---

subpoena. *See generally* David D. Siegel, *Federal Subpoena Practice Under the New Rule 45 of the Federal Rules of Civil Procedure*, 139 F.R.D. 197 (Jan. 1992).

64. Revised Rule 48 reads:

> The court shall seat a jury of not fewer than six and not more than twelve members and all jurors shall participate in the verdict unless excused from service by the court pursuant to Rule 47(c). Unless the parties otherwise stipulate, (1) the verdict shall be unanimous and (2) no verdict shall be taken from a jury reduced in size to fewer than six members.

FED. R. CIV. P. 48.

65. JOHN GUINTHER, THE JURY IN AMERICA 77 (1988).

juries can be expected in six-member juries for two reasons: first,
. . . , there will be fewer holders of minority positions . . . ; second, if
a dissenter appears, he is more likely to be the only one on the jury.
Lacking any . . . support for his position, he is more likely to abandon
it.[66]

Hung juries in civil cases are rare.[67]   The dynamic of the holdout
juror may, however, have a dramatic effect on a damage award, because
the damage amount may be the trade-off to reach a unanimous verdict.
To quote one commentator:

> [W]hen the proplaintiff faction is in the majority, it may obtain the
> concessions from the defense minority . . . by lowering the amount it
> wishes to award in damages. When the opposite situation arises, the
> prodefense forces may eventually allow a plaintiff's verdict, but only
> if the plaintiff-minority agrees to a reduced damages award.[68]

Such a trade-off is less likely to occur in cases decided by a majority
verdict. Indeed, one study found that in over half of the plaintiff verdicts
studied where unanimity was required, the majority traded a higher
reward to achieve unanimity, and that such a compromise occurred only
a third of the time in majority verdict jurisdictions (although the number
of compromises increased in suburban, majority verdict courts).[69]

These tendencies should play a role in a choice-of-forum analysis.
All other factors being equal, a plaintiff with a strong case on liability
could achieve a higher award in a jurisdiction allowing a majority
verdict. Likewise, in a situation where there are holdouts on the issue of
liability, an award could be lower in federal courts and other jurisdictions
where unanimity is required.[70]

---

66. Hans Zeisel, . . . *And Then There Were None: The Diminution of the
     Federal Jury*, 38 U. CHI. L. REV. 710, 719 (1971).
67. One study concluded that hung juries occur in civil cases less than one
     percent of the time. GUINTHER, *supra* note 65, at 82 n.73.
68. Edith Greene, *On Juries and Damage Awards: The Process of
     Decisionmaking*, 52 LAW & CONTEMP. PROBS. 225, 240 (1989).
69. GUINTHER, *supra* note 65, at 82 n.73.
70. Amended Rule 48, like its predecessor, allows a majority verdict by
     stipulation of the parties. FED. R. CIV. P. 48.

I.   Other Factors

Other factors may impact a choice-of-forum analysis. For example, there could be differences in evidentiary rules. Even when state law supplies the applicable substantive rule of decision, evidentiary questions in federal court are governed by the Federal Rules of Evidence.[71] Where there are marked differences in the relevant federal and state evidentiary rules, this factor may alter the choice-of-forum calculus.

One evidentiary distinction that could impact this analysis arises from the Supreme Court's ruling in *Daubert v. Merrell Dow Pharmaceuticals, Inc.*[72] In *Daubert*, the Supreme Court announced a departure from the standard for admitting expert testimony initially staked out in *Frye v. United States*,[73] which required that a foundation for scientific evidence include proof that the "principle" upon which it is based "must be sufficiently established to have gained general acceptance in the particular field to which it belongs."[74]

In *Daubert*, the plaintiffs claimed that certain birth defects were caused by the mother's ingestion of Bendectin during pregnancy. The defendants moved for summary judgment, arguing that since no study revealed a statistically significant relationship between the incidence of birth defects and Bendectin, the plaintiffs' expert's causation theory lacked general acceptance in scientific circles.[75]

The district court granted the motion, relying on Federal Rule of Evidence 703 which states:

> The facts or data in the particular case upon which an expert bases an opinion or inference may be those perceived by or made known to the expert at or before the hearing. If of a type reasonably relied upon by experts in the particular field in forming opinions or inferences upon the subject, the facts or data need not be admissible in evidence.[76]

---

71.   *See* FED. R. EVID. 101.
72.   509 U.S. 579 (1993).
73.   293 F. 1013 (D.C. Cir. 1923)
74.   *Id.* at 1014.
75.   *Daubert*, 509 U.S. at 582.
76.   FED. R. EVID. 703.

On appeal, the Ninth Circuit affirmed, expressly relying on *Frye*'s "general acceptance" standard.[77]

The Supreme Court reversed, holding that the common law rule of *Frye* did not survive the enactment of the Federal Rules of Evidence. While finding no "general acceptance" requirement in the Federal Rules, the court emphasized that trial courts have a gatekeeping function to perform in deciding to admit expert testimony under Rule 702.[78] According to the court, "[t]he focus ... must be solely on [underlying] principles and methodology, not on the conclusions that they generate."[79] The court also directed trial courts to consider the following criteria in determining whether to admit expert testimony: whether the hypothesis has been tested, whether the technique has been subjected to peer review and publication, whether the technique has an ascertainable error rate, and whether the methodology used to generate the conclusion is generally accepted.[80]

Based upon *Daubert* and its progeny, Rule 702 was amended in 2000 and now provides:

> If scientific, technical, or other specialized knowledge will assist the trier of fact to understand the evidence or to determine a fact in issue, a witness qualified as an expert by knowledge, skill, experience, training, or education, may testify thereto in the form of an opinion or otherwise, if (1) the testimony is based upon sufficient facts or data, (2) the testimony is the product of reliable principles and methods, and (3) the witness has applied the principles and methods reliably to the facts of the case.[81]

These principles under *Daubert* and Rule 702 have been applied to business torts cases, including in areas such as damages.[82]

---

77. 951 F.2d 1128, 1129-30 (9th Cir. 1991).
78. *Daubert*, 509 U.S. at 589-90 ("The primary locus of this obligation is Rule 702, which clearly contemplates some degree of regulation of the subjects and theories about which an expert may testify. 'If scientific, technical, or other specialized knowledge will assist the trier of fact to understand the evidence or to determine a fact in issue,' an expert 'may testify thereto.'").
79. *Id.* at 595.
80. *Id.* at 593-94.
81. FED. R. EVID. 702.
82. *See, e.g.*, El Aguila Food Prods., Inc. v. Gruma Corp., No. 04-20125, 2005 WL 1156090 (5th Cir. May 17, 2005) (affirming trial court's grant of

In addition to evidentiary issues, courts vary greatly in the amount of time to trial. This, too, can be a factor in selecting among state fora.[83]

Case management procedures, which can vary dramatically from forum to forum – even within the federal system – also play a role in choice-of-forum analysis. For example, some state court systems in urban areas use "motion judges" for all pretrial motions, and do not assign a trial judge until the case is scheduled for trial. Such a system may be unpalatable to a party expecting numerous pleading and discovery disputes, or hoping for a preliminary reading of how the trial judge perceives the merits of the case. A similar system may exist at the federal level under a different name. In congested federal districts, magistrate judges increasingly are assuming the role of state court motion judges.

---

summary judgment upon excluding antitrust plaintiffs' damages and causation experts' testimony in suit where competitors claimed that tortilla manufacturer violated antitrust laws by agreeing to pay retailers in return for preferential shelf placement of its products); City of Tuscaloosa v. Harcros Chems., Inc., 158 F.3d 548, 565 (11th Cir. 1998) (scrutinizing antitrust plaintiffs' experts under *Daubert*) (D. Kan. 1995); Frymire-Brinati v. KPMG Peat Marwick, 2 F.3d 183, 186-87 (7th Cir. 1993) (trial court ran afoul of *Daubert* by failing to conduct preliminary assessment of accounting expert's methodology before allowing him to testify); *In re* Aluminum Phosphide Antitrust Litig., 893 F. Supp. 1497, 1507 (D. Kan. 1995) (excluding testimony of antitrust plaintiffs' damages expert under *Daubert* upon concluding that expert's underlying methodology was unsound as based on "unjustified assumptions [that did] not account for changes in other relevant market conditions").

83.   JOHN GOERDT ET AL., EXAMINING COURT DELAY: THE PACE OF LITIGATION IN 26 URBAN TRIAL COURTS, 1987 23 (1989).

CHAPTER XII

REMOVAL AND REMAND

Removal and remand often are among the most hotly-contested aspects of litigation involving antitrust and business tort claims. A plaintiff who perceives as more advantageous state court rules governing such factors as pleading requirements, summary judgment, discovery, jury selection and numerosity and time-to-trial, will seek to ensure that the litigation proceeds in state court. Conversely, a defendant who sees advantage in having these or other matters governed by federal rules will search for a way to remove the case to federal court. Because this contest usually comes at the inception of the litigation, its outcome affects much that follows. – Eds.

A. Introduction

In federal court, the general removal statute is Section 1441 of Title 28 of the U.S. Code, which provides in pertinent part:

(a) Except as otherwise expressly provided by Act of Congress, any civil action brought in a State court of which the district courts of the United States have original jurisdiction, may be removed by the defendant or the defendants, to the district court of the United States for the district and division embracing the place where such action is pending. For purposes of removal under this chapter, the citizenship of defendants sued under fictitious names shall be disregarded.

(b) Any civil action of which the district courts have original jurisdiction founded on a claim or right arising under the Constitution, treaties or laws of the United States shall be removable without regard to the citizenship or residence of the parties. Any other such action shall be removable only if none of the parties in interest properly joined and served as defendants is a citizen of the State in which such action is brought.[1]

This statute is strictly construed against removal.[2]

B.   Pleading to Avoid Removal

Because removal jurisdiction may be predicated upon the existence of a federal claim or the diverse citizenship of the parties, a case cannot be removed to federal court if the case (1) contains no federal claims (such as those under the federal antitrust or securities laws[3]); (2) is brought in the defendant's home state; or (3) includes at least one nondiverse party as a defendant.

1.   The Well-Pleaded Complaint Rule

Under the so-called "well-pleaded complaint rule," a case arises under federal law only if a federal question appears on the face of the plaintiff's well-pleaded complaint; federal jurisdiction is lacking even if a defense is alleged to be based exclusively on federal law.[4] The well-pleaded complaint rule reflects the long-held policy that "the party who brings a suit is master to decide what law he will rely upon."[5] As applied to the removal context, the well-pleaded complaint rule means

---

1.   28 U.S.C. § 1441(a)-(b). In addition to section 1441, Congress has provided for removal of specific civil actions not discussed in this chapter. *See, e.g.*, 28 U.S.C. § 1442 (suits against federal officers); 28 U.S.C. § 1443 (suits in which civil rights are denied). Congress has also guaranteed certain plaintiffs their choice of forum by prohibiting removal in specific instances. *See, e.g.*, 28 U.S.C. § 1445(a) (Federal Employers' Liability Act suits).

2.   *See, e.g.*, Syngenta Crop Prot., Inc. v. Henson, 537 U.S. 28, 32 (2002) (citing Shamrock Oil & Gas Corp. v. Sheets, 313 U.S. 100, 108-09 (1941)); Samuel-Bassett v. KIA Motors Am., Inc., 357 F.3d 392, 396 (3d Cir. 2004) (removal statute is strictly construed against removal to honor Congressional intent to restrict federal diversity jurisdiction).

3.   A notable exception is a claim under the Securities Act of 1933, which by statute is nonremovable. *See* 15 U.S.C. § 77v(a).

4.   Aetna Health Inc. v. Davila, 542 U.S. 200, 124 S. Ct. 2488, 2494 (2004); Franchise Tax Bd. v. Constr. Laborers Vacation Trust, 463 U.S. 1, 9 (1983).

5.   Castro v. United States, 540 U.S. 375, 386 (2003) (quoting The Fair v. Kohler Die & Specialty Co., 228 U.S. 22, 25 (1913)).

that "a defendant may not [generally] remove a case to federal court unless the *plaintiff's* complaint establishes that the case 'arises under' federal law."[6]

Applying this principle, the assertion of federal defenses cannot create grounds for removal. Since it is the plaintiff's complaint that determines the removability of the action, the nature of the defense is irrelevant for purposes of removal. As the Supreme Court explained in *Rivet v. Regions Bank of Louisiana*:[7]

> [A] case may not be removed to federal court on the basis of a federal defense, . . . even if the defense is anticipated in the plaintiff's complaint, and even if both parties admit that the defense is the only question truly at issue in the case.[8]

Even a counterclaim asserting a federal antitrust claim,[9] a third-party claim asserting federal RICO violations,[10] or other federal question counterclaims or third-party claims cannot support removal to federal court.[11] As the Supreme Court has stated, whether "a case is one arising under [federal law], in the sense of the jurisdictional statute, . . . must be determined from what necessarily appears in the plaintiff's statement of his own claim in the bill or declaration, unaided by anything

---

6. *Aetna Health*, 124 S. Ct. at 2494 (quoting *Franchise Tax Board*, 463 U.S. at 10 (brackets in *Aetna Heath*; emphasis in *Franchise Tax Board*)).
7. 522 U.S. 470 (1998).
8. *Id.* at 475; *see also* Caterpillar Inc. v. Williams, 482 U.S. 386, 393 (1987); *Franchise Tax Board*, 463 U.S. at 14 (federal defense not a basis for removal); Loftis v. United Parcel Serv., Inc., 342 F.3d 509, 515 (6th Cir. 2003).
9. *See In re* Adams, 809 F.2d 1187, 1188 (5th Cir. 1987) ("Appellant strenuously argues that he pleaded counterclaims based on federal antitrust law. The district court aptly noted that these are unavailing to compel federal court jurisdiction, based on the well-pleaded complaint rule.").
10. Metro Ford Truck Sales, Inc. v. Ford Motor Co., 145 F.3d 320, 327 (5th Cir. 1998).
11. *See, e.g.*, Ballard's Serv. Ctr., Inc. v. Transue, 865 F.2d 447, 449 (1st Cir. 1989); Brae Asset Fund, L.P. v. Dion, 929 F. Supp. 29, 30 (D. Mass. 1996) ("[I]f the plaintiff's well-pleaded complaint discloses no basis for federal jurisdiction, the defendant must litigate the claims – even any affirmative federal defenses, or counterclaims, it may assert – in state court." (internal citations omitted)).

alleged in anticipation of avoidance of defenses which it is thought the defendant may interpose."[12]

However, cases that are simply "artful pleading" to avoid removal to federal court will not defeat a removal motion. As leading commentators in this area explain:

> A corollary of the well-pleaded complaint rule is the artful-pleading doctrine. Stated in the most general terms, the doctrine provides that a plaintiff cannot frustrate a defendant's right of removal by carefully pleading the case without reference to any federal law. Although it is true that the plaintiff is considered master of his complaint and may choose not to assert a federal right that is available and thus rely only on rights created under state law, when the causes of action in the plaintiff's complaint, if properly pled, would make the case removable, the plaintiff cannot disguise inherently federal causes of action.[13]

Two scenarios give rise to application of the artful pleading doctrine.[14] The doctrine applies "where federal law completely preempts an asserted state-law claim, for a claim of that preempted character is, from its inception, a claim that can arise only under federal, not state, law."[15] The artful pleading doctrine also applies when "(1) 'a substantial, disputed question of federal law is a *necessary* element of . . .

---

12. Okla. Tax Comm'n v. Graham, 489 U.S. 838, 841 (1989) (quoting Taylor v. Anderson, 234 U.S. 74, 75-76 (1914) (brackets and ellipsis in *Oklahoma Tax Commission*)).

13. 14B Charles Alan Wright & Arthur R. Miller, Federal Practice and Procedure § 3722, at 436 (3d ed. 1998 & Supp. 2004) (footnote omitted).

14. A third scenario – that "a defense of federal claim preclusion against a state law claim created removal jurisdiction," *id.* at 437 – previously had some currency under prior Supreme Court decisions. *See* Federated Dept. Stores, Inc. v. Moitie, 452 U.S. 394 (1981). The Court in *Rivet*, however, rejected this application of the artful pleading doctrine. 522 U.S. at 478 ("*Moitie* did not create a preclusion exception to the rule, fundamental under currently governing legislation, that a defendant cannot remove on the basis of a federal defense").

15. *Rivet*, 522 U.S. at 471 (citing Metro. Life Ins. Co. v. Taylor, 481 U.S., at 65-66 (1987)); Lippitt v. Raymond James Fin. Servs., Inc., 340 F.3d 1033, 1041 (9th Cir. 2003); MSOF Corp. v. Exxon Corp., 295 F.3d 485, 490 (5th Cir. 2002).

the well-pleaded state claim,' or the claim is an 'inherently federal claim' articulated in state-law terms; or (2) 'the right to relief depends on the resolution of a substantial, disputed federal question.'"[16]

2. *Bringing Suit in the Defendant's Home State*

When removal is sought to be based solely on diversity jurisdiction, Section 1441(b) expressly requires that none of the defendants be a citizen of the forum state.[17]

Although a plaintiff may be tempted to prevent removal by suing in a defendant's home state, other factors may militate against doing so. If the defendant's home state is far away from the plaintiff's, for example, factors such as cost, inconvenience and loss of "home court advantage" may discourage a plaintiff from filing in a defendant's home state. Similarly, the impact of any choice-of-law or conflict-of-law provisions of the forum state should be analyzed to determine whether they will impact on the plaintiff's substantive claims.

3. *Fraudulent Joinder*

Inclusion of a nondiverse plaintiff or an employee or subsidiary of a corporate defendant as an additional defendant may prevent removal on diversity grounds. However, unjustified manipulation of parties in order to defeat removal may be prevented under the doctrine of fraudulent joinder.

Joinder is considered fraudulent when there are false allegations of jurisdictional fact.[18] More commonly, fraudulent joinder is invoked

---

16. *Lippitt*, at 1042 (emphasis & ellipsis in original; citations & internal quotation marks omitted); Int'l Armor & Limousine Co. v. Moloney Coachbuilders, Inc., 272 F.3d 912, 915 (7th Cir. 2001) ("In our notice-pleading regime . . . the district court looks past the surface allegations to make its own assessment of what law the claim arises under.").

17. *See, e.g.*, Spencer v. United States Dist. Court, 393 F.3d 867, 870 (9th 2004) (explaining that the forum defendant rule reflects the belief that there is less reason to fear state court prejudice against defendants if one or more is from the forum state); Hurley v. Motor Coach Indus., Inc., 222 F.3d 377, 378 (7th Cir. 2000). As discussed below, fraudulently-joined defendants are not counted for purposes of removal and remand.

when the claim against the nondiverse defendant has no possible chance of success in state court,[19] when the cause of action against a resident defendant is defective as a matter of law,[20] or when there is no good faith intention to prosecute the action against the resident defendant or to seek a joint judgment.[21]

In order to determine whether a party has been fraudulently joined "the court may 'pierce the pleadings' and consider summary judgment-type evidence to determine whether the plaintiff truly has a reasonable possibility of recovery in state court."[22] All parties may submit affidavits and deposition transcripts.[23] The proceeding is similar to that used when ruling on a motion for summary judgment,[24] and generally an evidentiary hearing is not required.[25]

Some courts hold that a federal court may disregard nominal resident defendants if complete relief may be afforded against nonresident defendants.[26] This rule usually has been limited to cases where injunctive relief is the sole relief requested.[27] As a general rule,

---

18. Gray ex rel. Rudd v. Beverly Enters.-Miss., Inc., 390 F.3d 400, 405 (5th Cir. 2004); Mayes v. Rapoport, 198 F.3d 457, 464 (4th Cir. 1999); Triggs v. John Crump Toyota, Inc., 154 F.3d 1284, 1287 (11th Cir. 1998).
19. Lerma v. Univision Commc'ns, Inc., 52 F. Supp. 2d 1011, 1014 (E.D. Wis. 1999); *Gray*, 390 F.3d at 408.
20. Burchett v. Cargill, Inc., 48 F.3d 173, 176 (5th Cir. 1995).
21. Mersmann v. Cont'l Airlines, 335 F. Supp. 2d 544, 548 (D.N.J. 2004) (quoting Batoff v. State Farm Ins. Co., 977 F.2d 848, 851 (3d Cir. 1992)); *see also* Williams v. Motel 6 Multipurpose, Inc., 120 F. Supp. 2d 776, 779 (E.D. Ark. 1998).
22. *Gray*, 390 F.3d at 405 (quoting Travis v. Irby, 326 F.3d 644, 648-49 (5th Cir. 2003)); *see also* Morris v. Princess Cruises, Inc., 236 F.3d 1061, 1068 (9th Cir. 2001).
23. *Morris*, 236 F.3d at 1068; *see also* Hart v. Bayer Corp., 199 F.3d 239, 247 (5th Cir. 2000).
24. McKee v. Kansas City S. Ry. Co., 358 F.3d 329, 334 (5th Cir. 2004); Crowe v. Coleman, 113 F.3d 1536, 1538 (11th Cir. 1997).
25. Sid Richardson Carbon & Gasoline Co. v. Interenergy Res., Ltd., 99 F.3d 746, 751 (5th Cir. 1996).
26. *See* Rose v. Giamatti, 721 F. Supp. 906, 922 (S.D. Ohio 1989) (nominal party against whom no relief is requested may be disregarded for purposes of determining diversity of citizenship).
27. 758 F. Supp. 1399, 1404 (D. Colo. 1989).

"[w]here a plaintiff seeks monetary damages against defendants alleged to be jointly and severally liable the court may not disregard properly joined defendants simply because a non-resident defendant has the capital reserves to satisfy an entire judgment."[28]

A typical antitrust case involving fraudulent joinder of a local defendant is *Frontier Airlines, Inc. v. United Air Lines, Inc.*[29] In that case, Frontier filed an action in Colorado state court against United alleging violations of Colorado's antitrust and unfair competition statutes, tortious interference with contract and prospective contractual relations, and breach of contract. Several weeks later, Frontier joined United's resident sales manager, a Colorado resident, in an attempt to prevent removal. United nevertheless removed the case to federal court, alleging that the sales manager had been fraudulently joined for the sole purpose of preventing removal. The court denied Frontier's motion to remand and held that "if the plaintiff fails to state a cause of action against the resident defendant who defeats diversity, and the failure is obvious according to the settled rules of the state, the joinder of the resident is fraudulent" and removal is appropriate.[30]

The court in *Lerma v. Univision Communications, Inc.*[31] considered the question of the legitimacy of a nondiverse plaintiff. In that case, a Milwaukee television station and five individuals filed an antitrust action in Wisconsin state court, seeking to prevent defendant Univision from terminating the station's over-the-air broadcast of Univision's Spanish-language network programming. Two of the individual plaintiffs – Lerma and Omar – were California residents, as was Univision. Univision removed the case to federal court, asserting that Lerma's and Omar's claims were joined for the sole purpose of preventing removal. The court upheld removal, finding that "Lerma and Omar cannot possibly state a claim upon which a state court would find in their favor against Univision. As a result, they are both disregarded for diversity jurisdiction purposes, removal was proper, and the claims of these two plaintiffs will be dismissed."[32]

---

28. *Id.*
29. *Id.*
30. *Id.* at 1403.
31. 52 F. Supp. 2d 1011 (E.D. Wis. 1999).
32. *Id.* at 1027.

Although *Lerma* and *Frontier Airlines* demonstrate the successful invocation of the fraudulent joinder doctrine, there is a heavy burden on a defendant wishing to prove fraudulent joinder.[33] The court must evaluate the record in the light most favorable to the plaintiff, resolving all issues of fact as well as all questions of controlling substantive law against removal.[34] However, "if there is a colorable basis for predicting that a plaintiff may recover against non-diverse defendants, [the court] must remand the action to state court."[35]

Just as there is a heavy burden on defendants attempting to demonstrate fraudulent joinder, there also are heavy penalties on defendants whose attempts to remove based on fraudulent joinder are unsuccessful. Section 1447(c) provides that an "order remanding the case may require payment of just costs and any actual expenses, including attorney fees, incurred as a result of the removal." Most courts hold that the plaintiff is presumptively entitled to such an award and that bad faith removal need not be shown.[36]

---

33.   *See, e.g.*, Whitaker v. Am. Telecasting, Inc., 261 F.3d 196, 207 (2d Cir. 2001) (clear and convincing evidence required); Hart v. Bayer Corp., 199 F.3d 239, 246 (5th Cir. 2000); Hartley v. CSX Transp., Inc., 187 F.3d 422, 424 (4th Cir. 1999).

34.   Ross v. Citifinancial, Inc., 344 F.3d 458, 463 (5th Cir. 2003); Pampillonia v. RJR Nabisco, Inc., 138 F.3d 459, 461 (2d Cir. 1998).

35.   Coyne v. Am. Tobacco Co., 183 F.3d 488, 493 (6th Cir. 1999); *see also* Greene v. Wyeth, 344 F. Supp. 2d 674, 682 (D. Nev. 2004) (holding that a court must remand if there is a "non-fanciful possibility" that the plaintiff can state a claim against the nondiverse defendant).

36.   Tenner v. Zurek, 168 F.3d 328, 329-30 (7th Cir. 1999) (collecting cases); *see also* Lyons v. Lutheran Hosp., No. 104CV0728DFHVSS, 2004 WL 2272203, at *6 (S.D. Ind. Sept. 15, 2004) ("[T]he issue of fraudulent joinder in this case is not close. . . . The applicable standard requires [the removing defendant] to show that plaintiff has no viable claim against the [allegedly fraudulently joined defendant] even if all debatable questions of fact and law are resolved in plaintiff's favor. [The removing defendant] cannot meet this standard. Accordingly, the general presumption in favor of a fee award applies."); Ampere Auto. Corp. v. Fullen, No. 01 C 6818, 2001 WL 1268554, at *5 (N.D. Ill. Oct. 17, 2001) ("Complete diversity was plainly absent on the face of the state court complaint. Despite defendants' insistence on the application of the fraudulent joinder rule to a non-diverse plaintiff, defendants fail to satisfy their heavy burden under

C. Procedural Requirements for Removal

The procedural requirements for removal are relatively straightforward:

(a) A defendant or defendants desiring to remove any civil action or criminal prosecution from a State court shall file in the district court of the United States for the district and division within which such action is pending a notice of removal signed pursuant to Rule 11 of the Federal Rules of Civil Procedure and containing a short and plain statement of the grounds for removal, together with a copy of all process, pleadings, and orders served upon such defendant or defendants in such action.

(b) The notice of removal of a civil action or proceeding shall be filed within thirty days after the receipt by the defendant, through service or otherwise, of a copy of the initial pleading setting forth the claim for relief upon which such action or proceeding is based, or within thirty days after the service of summons upon the defendant if such initial pleading has then been filed in court and is not required to be served on the defendant, whichever period is shorter.[37]

1. *Receipt of the "Initial Pleading" and the Thirty-Day Rule*

The determination of what constituted the "initial pleading" or receipt other than through service for removal purposes used to be an unclear and sometimes chancy proposition. In 1999, however, the Court held in *Murphy Brothers, Inc. v. Michetti Pipe Stringing, Inc.* that a pleading received prior to service of summons did not constitute an initial pleading under section 1446(b).[38] The Court also spelled out how

---

that doctrine. 'Improper removal prolongs litigation (and jacks up fees).' Accordingly, an award of attorneys' fees and costs under § 1447(c) is warranted." (quoting Wisconsin v. Hotline Indus., 236 F.3d 363, 367 (7th Cir. 2000))).

37. 28 U.S.C. § 1446(a)-(b).

38. 526 U.S. at 356; *see also* Whitaker v. Am. Telecasting, Inc., 261 F.3d 196, 202 (2d Cir. 2001) ("[C]ommencement of the removal period could only be triggered by formal service of process, regardless of whether the

its focus on service of summons fit into the four main categories state provisions for service of summons:

> In each of the four categories, the defendant's period for removal will be no less than 30 days from service, and in some categories, it will be more than 30 days from service, depending on when the complaint is received. . . .

> First, if the summons and complaint are served together, the 30-day period for removal runs at once. Second, if the defendant is served with the summons but the complaint is furnished to the defendant sometime after, the period for removal runs from the defendant's receipt of the complaint. Third, if the defendant is served with the summons and the complaint is filed in court, but under local rules, service of the complaint is not required, the removal period runs from the date the complaint is made available through filing. Finally, if the complaint is filed in court prior to any service, the removal period runs from the service of the summons.[39]

Because the removal statutes are to be strictly construed against removal and in favor of remand, the thirty-day limit must be strictly adhered to. The courts are unanimous in holding that the period may not be extended.[40]

Moreover, in a case involving multiple defendants, all defendants must join in and consent to the removal. Therefore, if one defendant desires to remove, that defendant must not only obtain the consent of all

---

statutory phrase 'or otherwise' hints at some other proper means of receipt of the initial pleading.").

39.   526 U.S. at 354.
40.   *See, e.g.*, Seaton v. Jabe, 992 F.2d 79, 81 (6th Cir. 1993) ("[The] strict time requirement for removal in civil cases is not jurisdictional; rather, 'it is a strictly applied rule of procedure and untimeliness is a ground for remand so long as the timeliness defect has not been waived.'" (footnote omitted) (quoting Northern Illinois Gas Co. v. Airco Indus. Gases, 676 F.2d 270, 273 (7th Cir. 1982))); Total Energy Corp. v. Stolt, 334 F. Supp. 2d 413, 414 (S.D.N.Y. 2004) ("[T]his Court cannot extend the Defendants' time to file the Notice of Removal past the thirty-day period."); Stone Street Capital, Inc. v. McDonald's Corp., 300 F. Supp. 2d 345, 350 (D. Md. 2003) ("[T]he court cannot extend the time for filing removal because it simply does not have the authority to extend the removal period.").

the defendants, but must do so in a timely fashion.[41] Prior to *Murphy Brothers* this unanimity requirement lead courts to hold that if an earlier-served defendant failed to file a notice of removal within thirty days, then no other defendant – not even a defendant who was served after expiration of the initial thirty-day period – could obtain removal.[42] Since the *Murphy Brothers* decision, courts have taken the position that the removal statute allows "each defendant thirty days after receiving service within which to file a notice of removal, regardless of when – or if – previously served defendants had filed such notices."[43]

2. *Amount in Controversy and Citizenship Requirements*

Similarly, in cases involving diversity jurisdiction, defendants should be prompt in ascertaining the citizenship of all parties, as well as the amount in controversy.

> A case is removable when the initial pleading enables the defendant to intelligently ascertain removability from the face of such pleading, so that in its petition for removal[, the] defendant can make a short and plain statement of the grounds for removal as required [by] 28 U.S.C. § 1446(a). A pleading enables a defendant to intelligently ascertain removability when it provides the necessary facts to support [the] removal petition.   In cases where removal is based upon diversity, the facts required to support the removal petition include the amount in controversy and the address of each party.[44]

If the "initial pleading" provides a sufficient basis upon which to ascertain the amount in controversy and the address of each party, the

---

41. *See, e.g.*, Harper v. AutoAlliance Int'l, Inc., 392 F.3d 195, 201 (6th Cir. 2004) ("The rule of unanimity requires that in order for a notice of removal to be properly before the court, all defendants who have been served or otherwise properly joined in the action must either join in the removal, or file a written consent to the removal." (quoting Brierly v. Alusuisse Flexible Packaging, Inc., 184 F.3d 527, 533 n.3 (6th Cir. 1999))).

42. *See, e.g.*, Getty Oil Corp., a Div. of Texaco, Inc. v. Ins. Co. of North Am., 841 F.2d 1254, 1263 (5th Cir. 1988).

43. Marano Enters. of Kan. v. Z-Teca Restaurants, L.P., 254 F.3d 753, 756 (8th Cir. 2001) (citing *Murphy Brothers*); *see also* Loftis v. United Parcel Serv., Inc., 342 F.3d 509, 516 (6th Cir. 2003).

44. Whitaker v. Am. Telecasting, Inc., 261 F.3d 196, 206 (2d Cir. 2001) (brackets in original; citations & internal quotation marks omitted).

defendants must remove within thirty days after receipt of the pleading.[45] This burden to ascertain the removability of a case is so heavy that some courts have held that even if the initial pleading fails to state a specific amount in controversy, but alleges severe damages (such as permanent physical injuries), the defendant is deemed to be on notice of the removability of the case.[46] Similarly, if a defendant subsequently obtains knowledge of the plaintiff's citizenship or the amount in controversy independently of the plaintiff, at least one court has held that the defendant may not sit on its right to remove.[47]

3. Subsequent Removability

In certain circumstances, a case that is not removable initially may be subsequently removed. Section 1446 of Title 28 of the U.S. Code provides:

> If the case stated by the initial pleading is not removable, a notice of removal may be filed within thirty days after receipt by the defendant, through service or otherwise, of a copy of an amended pleading, motion, order or other paper from which it may first be ascertained that the case is one which is or has become removable.[48]

---

45. *See, e.g.*, Net 2 Press, Inc. v. Nat'l Graphic Supply Corp., 324 F. Supp. 2d 15, 18 (D. Me. 2004).

46. *See, e.g.*, Turner v. Wilson Foods Corp., 711 F. Supp. 624, 626 (N.D. Ga. 1989) (holding that a complaint alleging severe burns, permanent injuries, and lifelong medical expenses is sufficient to put a defendant on notice of removability even though the complaint did not allege a specific damage amount). *But see Whitaker*, 261 F.3d at 206 (holding that the appropriate "standard requires a defendant to apply a reasonable amount of intelligence in ascertaining removability, [but] does not require a defendant to look beyond the initial pleading for facts giving rise to removability").

47. Weaver v. Miller Elec. Mfg. Co., 616 F. Supp. 683, 686 (S.D. Ala. 1985). *But see* Nasso v. Seagal, 263 F. Supp. 2d 596, 605 (E.D.N.Y. 2003) (because the "initial and amended complaints alleged that Films and Steamroller were citizens of the same state, the case stated by the initial [and amended] pleadings was not removable for the purposes of § 1446(b) even if defendants knew that Films and LLC were not licensed to conduct business in New York" (brackets in original; citation & internal quotation marks omitted)).

48. 28 U.S.C. § 1446(b).

Defendants thus have thirty days within which to remove after the case "has become removable." This thirty-day period begins to run from the moment the defendant receives some "other paper" that indicates a basis for removal with sufficient clarity that the defendant is able "to intelligently ascertain removability so that" the defendant in the notice of removal "can make a simple and short statement of the facts."[49] Examples of documents constituting "other paper" include deposition transcripts,[50] interrogatory answers,[51] demand letters,[52] and third-party documents.[53] In addition, some courts have even held that oral notice of the removability of a case constitutes "receipt" of an "other paper."[54] To ensure not running afoul of these strict removal time limits, defendants should seek removal immediately upon notice or discovery, in any form, and from any source, of any facts that appear to allow for removal.

4. One-Year Time Limit for Removability

Section 1446 limits the removal period in a diversity case that was initially not removable to one year. "If the case stated by the initial pleading is not removable, . . . [it] may not be removed on the basis of jurisdiction conferred by section 1332 of this title more than 1 year after commencement of the action."[55] The one-year period runs from the time the action is "commenced," and not from the receipt of the initial

---

49. *See, e.g.*, Huffman v. Saul Holdings L.P., 194 F.3d 1072, 1078 (10th Cir. 1999); *see also* Bosky v. Kroger Tex., LP, 288 F.3d 208, 211 (5th Cir. 2002).

50. *See, e.g., Huffman*, 194 F.3d at 1078 ("[T]he removal period commences with the giving of the testimony, not the receipt of the transcript.").

51. Akin v. Ashland Chem. Co., 156 F.3d 1030, 1035 (10th Cir. 1998).

52. Addo v. Globe Life & Acc. Ins. Co., 230 F.3d 759, 761 (5th Cir. 2000) ("[T]he majority of lower courts to have considered this issue hold that a post-complaint demand letter is 'other paper' under § 1446(b).").

53. Lovern v. Gen. Motors Corp., 121 F.3d 160, 161 (4th Cir. 1997) (police report).

54. *See, e.g.*, Hillard v. Kaiser Found. Health Plan of Mid-Atl. States, Inc., 169 F. Supp. 2d 416, 417 (D. Md. 2001) ("counsel's representations"); *Huffman*, 194 F.3d at 1078 (holding that thirty-day period commences "with the giving of the testimony, not the receipt of the transcript").

55. 28 U.S.C. § 1446(b).

pleading triggering the initial thirty-day time period for removal, or from the service of an "other paper" showing the case to be removable.

If a plaintiff voluntarily[56] settles with or dismisses a diversity-destroying defendant within one year after the commencement of the action, the remaining defendants may remove; however, if such settlement or dismissal occurs more than one year after the action's commencement, the remaining defendants cannot remove.

5. *Waiver*

Additionally, defendants must not to take any action that could be deemed a waiver of their right to remove. Waiver occurs when a defendant clearly and unequivocally evidences an intent to so waive.[57] As the majority of courts have held, "preliminary conduct by a defendant short of his actual litigation of the merits or his voluntary invocation of state court jurisdiction for his own purposes does not constitute a waiver of his right to remove."[58] Thus, the filing of answers and compulsory counterclaims, service of interrogatories, responses to temporary restraining orders, and even the filing of a pleading raising a defense that might be conclusive of the merits does not constitute a waiver of a right to remove.[59] In contrast, the filing of a motion for directed verdict and

---

56. In diversity cases, dismissal of all non-diverse defendants that results from something other than the voluntary action of the plaintiff does not give rise to removability. Poulos v. Naas Foods, Inc., 959 F.2d 69, 71 (7th Cir. 1992); Dowd v. Alliance Mortg. Co., 339 F. Supp. 2d 452, 454 -455 (E.D.N.Y. 2004); Bejcek v. Allied Life Fin. Corp., 131 F. Supp. 2d 1109, 1113 (S.D. Iowa 2001) ("A defendant cannot create diversity-of-citizenship jurisdiction by its own actions when jurisdiction did not exist at the time of the filing of the state-court action."); *see also* Insinga v. LaBella, 845 F.2d 249, 254 (11th Cir. 1988) (recognizing certain exceptions to rule).

57. *See, e.g.,* Rabbi Jacob Joseph School v. Province of Mendoza, 342 F. Supp. 2d 124, 128 (E.D.N.Y. 2004).

58. Haun v. Retail Credit Co., 420 F. Supp. 859, 863 (W.D. Pa. 1976); *see also* Tex. First Nat'l Bank v. Wu, 347 F. Supp. 2d 389, 397 (S.D. Tex. 2004) ("If a defendant acts merely to preserve the status quo and not to resolve the merits, no waiver occurs.").

59. *See, e.g.,* Tedford v. Warner-Lambert Co., 327 F.3d 423, 428 (5th Cir. 2003) ("Nothing Warner-Lambert did, including agreeing to a trial date in Eastland County before it learned of the DeLuca nonsuit, submitted the

for mistrial before removal has been held to constitute a waiver of a right to remove, as may the filing of a permissive counterclaim or a cross-claim.[60]

D. Procedures Subsequent to Removal

1. *Answer and Jury Demand*

The timing of the answer to a removed complaint is governed not by statue or Rule 12 of the Federal Rules of Civil Procedure, but rather by Rule 81 of the Federal Rules of Civil Procedure. The rule provides that if the case was removed prior to the defendant filing an answer in state court, the defendant:

> shall answer or present the other defenses or objections available under these rules within 20 days after the receipt through service or otherwise of a copy of the initial pleading setting forth the claim for relief upon which the action or proceeding is based, or within 20 days after the service of summons upon such initial pleading, then filed, or within 5 days after the filing of the petition for removal, whichever period is longest.[61]

The same rule addresses invocation of the right to trial by jury in removed actions. If the party desiring a jury did not perfect a demand for a jury in state court prior to removal, a removing party must serve a jury demand within ten days after the party served the notice of removal and any other party must serve a jury demand within ten days after service upon that party of the notice of removal.[62]

2. *Disavowing a Federal Claim*

When faced with removal, some plaintiffs will disavow a federal claim in order to facilitate remand. This issue commonly arises when a plaintiff originally asserts a federal claim and, subsequent to removal,

---

cause to adjudication on the merits. . . . Accordingly, we find that Warner-Lambert did not waive its right to remove.").

60. *See, e.g.*, Foley v. Allied Interstate, Inc., 312 F. Supp. 2d 1279, 1282 (C.D. Cal. 2004) ("[A] defendant may inadvertently waive its right of removal when, after it is apparent that the case is removable, the defendant litigates on the merits in state court.").

61. FED. R. CIV. P. 81(c).

62. *Id.*

seeks to dismiss that claim. The leading case in this area is the Supreme Court's 1988 decision in *Carnegie-Mellon University v. Cohill.*[63] In that case, plaintiffs brought suit in state court asserting both federal and state law claims. Defendants then removed the case to federal court. Although plaintiffs did not initially contest removal, six months later they amended their complaint to drop the federal claim and concurrently moved to remand the case to state court. The district court remanded the case, and the court of appeals affirmed.

Invoking *United Mine Workers of America v. Gibbs,*[64] the Supreme Court likewise affirmed, holding that principles of judicial economy, fairness and comity require federal courts to flexibly examine motions to remand on a case-by-case basis. In rejecting the defendants' argument that giving district courts discretion to remand cases in these circumstances would reward manipulative tactics, the Court concluded that such manipulation may be taken into account by the district court when determining whether a balancing of the *Gibbs* factors supports a remand in the particular case.[65]

Following this lead, several courts have denied remand in cases where the facts suggested manipulation. For example, in *Harper v. AutoAlliance International, Inc.,*[66] the Sixth Circuit Court of Appeals affirmed the trial court's decision to not remand after dismissal of the plaintiff's federal claims, in part because of apparent forum manipulation:

> It was only after the district court had denied his first motion to remand that Harper dropped his Title VII claim. Then, Harper did not immediately move for remand, but instead proceeded with his remaining claims in federal court for almost six months more. Only after discovery had been completed, the dispositive motion deadline had passed, and Harper was faced with dismissal of all of his claims on summary judgment, did he again seek remand to the state court. We agree with the district court that "[s]uch timing appears suspicious and raises questions about Plaintiff's motives in seeking remand." Accordingly, we hold that the district court did not abuse

---

63. 484 U.S. 343 (1988).
64. 383 U.S. 715 (1966).
65. Carnegie-Mellon Univ. v. Cohill, 484 U.S. 343, 357 (1988).
66. 392 F.3d 195 (6th Cir. 2004).

its discretion in retaining supplemental jurisdiction over Harper's state law claims.[67]

One court has even gone so far as to dismiss with prejudice federal claims brought by a plaintiff who tried to forum shop by amending its complaint to drop federal claims in order to achieve remand.[68] Other courts have noted that they have the power to remand the case, and yet assess monetary sanctions on plaintiffs who engage in such manipulative forum shopping.[69]

E. Removal of Certain Class Actions to Federal Court Under The Class Action Fairness Act of 2005

On February 18, 2005, President Bush signed the Class Action Fairness Act of 2005 (the "Act").[70] Among other things, the Act creates federal jurisdiction for certain class actions and removal of certain class actions to federal court.   The Act is applicable to class actions commenced *after* enactment.[71]

---

67.   *Id.* at 211-12; *see also* Naragon v. Dayton Power & Light Co., 934 F. Supp. 899, 902 (S.D. Ohio 1996) (denying remand because "Plaintiff is plainly, almost confessedly, engaged in forum manipulation"); Guillot v. Bellsouth Telecomms., Inc., 923 F. Supp. 112, 114 (W.D. La. 1996) (denying remand on the ground that a "naked attempt at forum manipulation should not be allowed"), *aff'd*, 100 F.3d 953 (5th Cir. 1996) (Table).

68.   Austwick v. Board of Educ. of Township High School Dist. #113, Lake County, 555 F. Supp. 840, 843 (N.D. Ill. 1983) (dismissing with prejudice claims of plaintiff who amended complaint to drop federal claims in the hopes of obtaining remand to state court).

69.   *See id.* at 843 n.2; Brandenburg v. City of Chicago, 129 F.R.D. 159, 161 (N.D. Ill. 1989).

70.   S. 5, 109th Cong. (2005). The full title of the Act is "A BILL To amend the procedures that apply to consideration of interstate class actions to assure fairer outcomes for class members and defendants, and for other purposes." *Id.*

71.   The Act is a short, nine-section bill. Sections 3-5 are the Act's substantive provisions – respectively the consumer class action bill of rights, the provision for federal district court jurisdiction, and the provision for removal. Sections 1 and 2 are prefatory in nature, listing the short title, table of contents, and statement of Congressional findings and purposes. Section 6 requires preparation of a report on class action settlements.

1. *Federal Jurisdiction for Certain Class Actions*

The Act provides for federal jurisdiction in non-securities[72] class actions (1) where the aggregate[73] amount in controversy exceeds $5 million,[74] (2) with more than 100 plaintiffs,[75] (3) where the primary defendants are not governmental entities,[76] and (4) in which any plaintiff is citizen of a state different from any defendant.[77] Courts are to decline jurisdiction, however, in most cases where two-thirds of the plaintiffs are citizens of the forum state,[78] and have limited authority to decline jurisdiction when one-third of the plaintiffs are citizens of the forum.[79] For jurisdiction purposes, the term "class action" includes any litigation in which "monetary relief claims of 100 or more persons are proposed to be tried jointly."[80]

2. *Removal of Certain Class Actions to Federal Court*

The Class Action Fairness Act, also discussed in Chapter 9, authorizes removal of any class action over which the federal courts have federal jurisdiction[81] without regard to otherwise-applicable prohibitions

---

Section 7 requires enactment of already-enacted changes to the federal rule of civil procedure governing class actions. Section 8 subordinates the Act to statutory rulemaking authority given to the Supreme Court and federal Judicial Conference. Section 9 lists the Act's effective date. All subsequent references are to the Act [as] [as it will be] codified.

72. *Id.* § 1332(d)(9).
73. *Id.* § 1332(d)(6).
74. *Id.* § 1332(d)(2).
75. *Id.* § 1332(d)(5)(B).
76. *Id.* § 1332(d)(5)(A).
77. *Id.* § 1332(d)(2)(A)-(C) (overriding the ban on jurisdiction unless every plaintiff is citizen of a state different from every defendant).
78. *Id.* § 1332(d)(4).
79. *Id.* § 1332(d)(3).
80. *Id.* § 1332(d)(11)(B). This provision gives jurisdiction to mass asbestos and other environmental bodily injury actions. Exempted is any lawsuit (a) in which all of the claims concern injuries and events occurring in the forum (or in adjoining states), (b) where the claims were aggregated by defense motion, or (c) brought pursuant to state statute authorizing claims on behalf of the general public. *Id.*
81. 28 U.S.C. § 1453(a), (d).

on removal of cases (a) more than one year old,[82] (b) where a defendant is a citizen of the forum,[83] or (c) in which all of the defendants do not consent to removal.[84]

The Act also provides for discretionary federal appellate review of remand orders,[85] provided "application is made to the court of appeals" within seven days of entry of the order.[86]   The court of appeals is to dispose of the appeal within 60 days,[87] although that period can be extended indefinitely by agreement of the parties,[88] or for 10 days for good cause shown.[89]   If disposition of the appeal does not occur within the statutorily-prescribed time period (including extensions), the appeal is denied.[90]

---

82. *Id.* § 1453(b).
83. *Id.*
84. *Id.*
85. *Id.* § 1453(c)(1).
86. *Id.*
87. *Id.* § 1453(c)(2).
88. *Id.* § 1453(c)(3)(A).
89. *Id.* § 1453(c)(3)(B).
90. *Id.* § 1453(c)(4).

CHAPTER XIII

ISSUES RELATING TO PARALLEL LITIGATION

The potential for multiple proceedings often arises in antitrust and business tort litigation. This chapter addresses the procedural issues that frequently arise in disputes involving multiple proceedings. – Eds.

A. Introduction

Parties in antitrust and business tort litigation commonly disagree on the "proper" forum for a dispute. Factors including jury pool demographics, local publicity, docket speed, perceived judicial expertise, evidentiary restrictions on expert testimony, and counsels' familiarity with local procedures may affect parties' preference for one court over another. Because these cases frequently involve numerous parties with different interests and the ability to bring separate actions in the forums of their choice, such disputes frequently trigger multiple proceedings in different courts. In addition, business tort cases often run in tandem with administrative and criminal proceedings, raising an array of complex issues in concurrent private civil litigation (such as adverse civil inferences from Fifth Amendment invocations, waivers of attorney-client privilege, preclusive effects from criminal or administrative findings, and alternative discovery opportunities from the government's investigation). These factors frequently cause one party to attempt to stay private proceedings until the government actions have been resolved. In all these situations, parties commonly employ an array of litigation strategies designed to promote the action in their chosen forum but to dismiss, stay, or otherwise impede concurrent litigation elsewhere.

The more common of these strategies include motions for stays under a court's inherent powers, invocation of abstention doctrines, requests for anti-suit injunctions, and attempts to transfer claims. The following discussion addresses each of these strategies as well as the role of claim and issue preclusion in disputes involving multiple proceedings.

B.   Stay or Abatement of State Court Proceedings

State courts generally have the discretion, but usually not the obligation, to stay or dismiss proceedings before them when there is a concurrent related action in another state court, in a federal court, or in another country.[1] When both actions involve the same or similar parties and issues, state courts frequently stay their own proceedings to await the outcome of the foreign action.[2] The reasons most frequently cited by courts for granting such stays include: (1) preventing a multiplicity of actions,[3] (2) promoting principles of comity,[4] and (3) protecting the defendant from harassment or unnecessary inconvenience.[5]

State courts typically rely on the following factors in deciding whether to impose a stay in favor of another action: (1) which action was filed first;[6] (2) the comparative progress of both proceedings;[7] (3) the potential res judicata effect of the action pending in the foreign jurisdiction;[8] (4) the interest of the forum state in the action;[9] and

---

1.   *See, e.g.*, Howerton v. Grace Hosp., Inc., 476 S.E.2d 440 (N.C. Ct. App. 1996); Tonnemacher v. Touche Ross & Co., 920 P.2d 5 (Ariz. Ct. App. 1996); City of Miami Beach v. Miami Beach Fraternal Order of Police, 619 So. 2d 447 (Fla. Dist. Ct. App. 1993); Baisley v. Vielle (*In re* Marriage of Baisley), 749 P.2d 446 (Colo. Ct. App. 1987).

2.   *See, e.g.*, El Paso Natural Gas Co. v. TransAm. Natural Gas Corp., 669 A.2d 36 (Del. 1995); Donnkenny, Inc. v. Nadler, 544 F. Supp. 166 (S.D.N.Y. 1982).

3.   *See, e.g.*, Zurich Ins. Co. v. Baxter Int'l, Inc., 670 N.E.2d 664 (Ill. 1996).

4.   *See, e.g.*, Fried v. Bergman, 736 So. 2d 1281 (Fla. Dist. Ct. App. 1999); Commercial Union Ins. Co. v. Wheeling Pittsburgh Corp., 666 N.E.2d 571 (Ohio. Ct. App. 1995); Brooks Erection Co. v. William R. Montgomery & Assocs., Inc., 576 S.W.2d 273 (Ky. Ct. App. 1979); Simmons v. Sup. Ct. of Los Angeles County, 214 P.2d 844 (Cal. Ct. App. 1950).

5.   *See, e.g.*, HFTP Invs., LLC v. ARIAD Pharms., Inc., 752 A.2d 115 (Del. Ch. 1999) (comparing expense and speed of resolving dispute in either forum).

6.   *See, e.g.*, Acierno v. New Castle County, 679 A.2d 455 (Del. 1996); Am. Home Prods. Corp. v. Adriatic Ins. Co., 668 A.2d 67 (N.J. Super. Ct. App. Div. 1995).

7.   *See, e.g.*, First Midwest Corp. v. Corporate Fin. Assocs., 663 N.W.2d 888 (Iowa 2003).

8.   *See, e.g.*, Wiseman v. Law Research Serv., Inc., 270 N.E.2d 77 (Ill. App. Ct. 1971).

(5) whether the foreign proceeding provides the parties the ability to obtain complete relief.[10]

Conversely, motions for stays are more likely to be denied if (1) there are material differences between the named parties in both cases,[11] (2) if the actions involve different facts,[12] (3) if different legal claims are asserted or different remedies are pursued in either court,[13] and (4) if a judgment in the foreign jurisdiction will not fully resolve the disputes asserted in the forum state.[14] While many states hold that the power to stay or dismiss duplicative actions is inherent in the court,[15] a number of jurisdictions have enacted statutes expressly providing such authority.[16] Moreover, a state court may stay an action as to one or more of the parties, while allowing it to proceed as to other parties.[17]

State business tort cases are most likely to be stayed or abated when there are pending federal actions based on specialized federal laws (e.g.,

---

9. *See, e.g.*, Biondi v. Scrushy, 820 A.2d 1148 (Del. Ch. 2003).

10. *See, e.g.*, First Midwest Corp. v. Corporate Fin. Assocs., 663 N.W.2d 888 (Iowa 2003); *El Paso Natural Gas Co.*, 669 A.2d at 38 n.1. *But cf.* Derdiger v. Tallman, 773 A.2d 1005 (Del. Ch. 2000) (allowing stay even though cases involved different named representatives in separate putative class actions).

11. *See, e.g.*, Del-Val Fin. Corp. v. FDIC, 598 N.Y.S.2d 197, 198 (N.Y. App. Div. 1993) (citing "no identity of parties" as one factor in denying motion to stay action); Argonaut Ins. Co. v. Occidental Petroleum Corp., 430 N.Y.S.2d 982 (N.Y. Sup. Ct. 1980).

12. *See, e.g.*, Cong. Factors Corp. v Meinhard Commercial Corp., 493 N.Y.S.2d 917 (N.Y. Sup. Ct. 1985).

13. *See, e.g.*, Keene Corp. v R.W. Taylor Steel Co., 594 P.2d 889 (Utah 1979); Coaxial Commc'ns, Inc. v. CNA Fin. Corp., 367 A.2d 994 (Del. 1976).

14. *See, e.g.*, May v. Smithkline Beecham Clinical Lab., Inc., 710 N.E.2d 460 (Ill. App. Ct. 1999).

15. *See, e.g.*, Myshko v. Galanti, 309 A.2d 729 (Pa. 1973) (involving dismissal of action in equity when similar action was pending at law).

16. *See, e.g.*, GA. CODE ANN. § 9-2-44; N.Y. C.P.L.R. 3211(a), ¶ 4 (permitting New York courts to dismiss action on grounds that there is "another action pending between the same parties for the same cause of action in a court of any state or the United States"); 735 ILL. COMP. STAT. ANN. 5/2-619(a)(3) (West 2005) (providing Illinois courts discretion to dismiss action if "there is another action pending between the same parties for the same cause").

17. *See, e.g.*, Sparrow v. Nerzig, 89 S.E.2d 718 (S.C. 1955).

securities fraud, misappropriation of trademarks, or patent infringement) and the federal litigation could potentially resolve some or all of the state court claims.[18] In such cases, state courts frequently defer to federal courts perceived to have greater expertise with, or exclusive jurisdiction over, the subject matter.[19]

C. Federal Court Abstention

In several distinct circumstances, the federal courts may abstain from exercising their jurisdiction over cases in an effort to avoid needless conflicts with litigation proceeding in the state courts. Such abstention is a "judge-made doctrine" that was first fashioned in 1941 in *Railroad Commission v. Pullman Co.*[20] Through five[21] distinguishable lines of

---

18. *See, e.g.*, Gunn v. Palmieri, 552 N.Y.S.2d 129 (N.Y. App. Div. 1990) (involving state claims for fraud and unjust enrichment and federal RICO claims based on same facts); Bank of N.Y. v. Levy, 506 N.Y.S.2d 767 (App. Div. 1986) (involving concurrent federal action for alleging massive securities fraud and racketeering); Reliance Ins. Co. v. Tiger Int'l, Inc., 457 N.Y.S.2d 813 (App. Div. 1983) (involving pending securities litigation in federal court); Lanova Corp. v Atlas Imperial Diesel Engine Co., 64 A.2d 419 (Del. 1949) (involving state claim for fraudulently withheld royalties and concurrent federal action addressing whether patent was procured by fraud).
19. *See, e.g.*, Barron v. Bluhdorn, 414 N.Y.S.2d 15, 16 (App. Div. 1979) ("there is no question that [the federal court] possesses greater familiarity with violations of securities laws . . . and exclusive jurisdiction with respect to those arising under the Securities Exchange Act of 1934").
20. Zwickler v. Koota, 389 U.S. 241, 248 (1967); R.R. Comm'n of Tex. v. Pullman Co., 312 U.S. 496 (1941).
21. Given the slight distinctions between some of the federal abstention doctrines, courts and commentators are not in full agreement concerning how many separate categories actually exist. *See, e.g.*, Colo. River Water Conserv. Dist. v. United States, 424 U.S. 800 (1976) (recognizing three previously identified categories of abstention and creating a fourth); Vulcan Materials Co. v. City of Tehuacana, 238 F.3d 382, 390 (5th Cir. 2001) ("There are four general categories of abstention."); In re Burns & Wilcox, Ltd., 54 F.3d 475, 478 n.8 (8th Cir. 1995) (identifying at least three distinct categories); Bickham v. Lashof, 620 F.2d 1238, 1242 (7th Cir. 1980) (identifying three categories); Empire Distribs. of N.C., Inc. v. Schieffelin & Co., 677 F. Supp. 847, 854 (W.D.N.C. 1988) ("Yet, there are

cases, the federal courts have crafted separate doctrines under which they will defer to state court adjudication. Named for the Supreme Court cases first espousing these doctrines, the five categories of abstention include: (1) *Pullman* abstention, under which federal courts stay cases to avoid unnecessarily deciding constitutional issues and provide state courts the opportunity to decide underlying state law questions;[22] (2) *Burford* abstention, which allows federal courts to dismiss actions that bear on questions of important state policy usually involving comprehensive state regulatory schemes;[23] (3) *Thibodaux* abstention, requiring the federal courts to yield jurisdiction in diversity cases involving important questions of undetermined state law bearing on vital state interests;[24] (4) *Younger* abstention, prohibiting federal courts from enjoining certain state actions (primarily criminal proceedings);[25] and (5) *Colorado River* abstention, which allows federal courts to dismiss or stay federal cases to avoid duplication of concurrent state adjudication in exceptional circumstances.[26] Importantly, these doctrines can be raised sua sponte,[27] and they can even be invoked at the appellate level.[28]

1.   *Pullman Abstention*

In 1941, the Supreme Court crafted the first abstention doctrine in *Railroad Commission of Texas v. Pullman Co.*[29] In an effort to avoid premature constitutional decisions on matters involving uncertain state laws, *Pullman* abstention allows federal courts to stay a federal case pending state court determination of those state law issues. This doctrine is commonly justified as a method of promoting judicial efficiency,

---

five categories of cases in which abstention, either by dismissal or stay, is the appropriate course of action."), *aff'd*, 859 F.2d 1200 (4th Cir. 1988).

22.   *Pullman Co.*, 312 U.S. at 498-500.
23.   Burford v. Sun Oil Co., 319 U.S. 315, 317-18 (1943).
24.   La. Power & Light Co. v. Thibodaux, 360 U.S. 25, 27-28 (1959).
25.   Younger v. Harris, 401 U.S. 37, 52 (1971).
26.   Colo. River Water Conserv. Dist. v. United States, 424 U.S. 800, 813 (1976).
27.   *See, e.g.*, Bellotti v. Baird, 428 U.S. 132 (1976); Cruz v. Melecio, 204 F.3d 14, 22 n.7 (1st Cir. 2000); Murphy v. Uncle Ben's, Inc., 168 F.3d 734, 737 (5th Cir. 1999).
28.   *See, e.g.*, H.C. ex rel. Gordon v. Koppel, 203 F.3d 610, 613-14 (9th Cir. 2000).
29.   312 U.S. 496 (1941).

avoiding unnecessary friction between federal and state courts, and reducing the likelihood of erroneous interpretations of state law.[30] The two necessary elements of *Pullman* abstention are: (1) an uncertain question of state law, and (2) a possible resolution of the state law question that would obviate the need to resolve, or substantially narrow, a constitutional question.[31] Thus, *Pullman* abstention is not available when a state statute plainly violates the federal constitution.[32]

Like the four other abstention doctrines, courts have the discretion to abstain under *Pullman*, and their decisions will only be reviewed for abuse of discretion.[33] When *Pullman* is invoked, federal courts usually stay actions, and thereby maintain jurisdiction, to provide the state courts the opportunity to decide the issues of state law before the litigants return to federal court for adjudication of remaining federal issues.[34] Sometimes, however, a federal court will dismiss an action and direct the parties to litigate all remaining state and federal issues in the state

---

30. *See, e.g.*, Rivera-Puig v. Garcia-Rosario, 983 F.2d 311, 321 (1st Cir. 1992); Rivera Vazquez v. Asociacion de Residentes de Univ. Gardens, Inc., 220 F. Supp. 2d 95 (D.P.R. 2002).

31. *See, e.g.*, Harrison v. NAACP, 360 U.S. 167 (1959); Biegenwald v. Fauver, 882 F.2d 748 (3d Cir. 1989). Notably, a third element, that the case concern a sensitive matter of state policy, is also referenced by numerous cases. *See, e.g.*, Porter v. Jones, 319 F.3d 483 (9th Cir. 2003); Chamber of Commerce of U.S. v. Lockyer, 225 F. Supp. 2d 1199 (C.D. Cal. 2002), *aff'd*, 364 F.3d 1154 (9th Cir. 2004); Meadow Valley Contractors, Inc. v. Johnson, 89 F. Supp. 1180 (D. Nev. 2000).

32. *See, e.g.*, Haw. Hous. Auth. v. Midkiff, 467 U.S. 229, 237 (1984); Lind v. Grimmer, 859 F. Supp. 1317 (D. Haw. 1993), *aff'd*, 30 F.3d 1115 (9th Cir. 1994).

33. *See, e.g.*, Bethlehem Contracting Co. v. Lehrer/McGovern, Inc., 800 F.2d 325 (2d Cir. 1986); Bascom v. Perry, 357 F. Supp. 431, 432 (N.D. Iowa 1973) ("The doctrine of abstention gives a federal district court the discretion to decline or to postpone the exercise of its jurisdiction in deference to state court resolution of underlying issues of state law.").

34. *See, e.g.*, Allen v. McCurry, 449 U.S. 90, 101 n.17 (1980); Harrison v. NAACP, 360 U.S. 167, 177 (1959) (*Pullman* abstention "does not, of course, involve the abdication of federal jurisdiction, but only the postponement of its exercise"); Cranley v. Nat'l Life Ins. Co., 144 F. Supp. 2d 291 (D. Vt. 2001) (usual course under *Pullman* is for district court to stay, rather than dismiss, action), *aff'd*, 318 F.3d 105 (2d Cir. 2003); Getty Petroleum Corp. v. Harshbarger, 807 F. Supp. 855 (D. Mass. 1992).

court.[35] While, as noted above, *Pullman* abstention is justified in part on grounds of judicial efficiency, commentators have argued that abstention promotes piecemeal litigation, protracting the case, and increasing the expense to all parties.[36] Indeed, invoking *Pullman* abstention is a litigation strategy frequently favored by defendants who wish to delay the progress of litigation or otherwise increase a plaintiff's expense and inconvenience in pursuing a claim.

In the business tort context, *Pullman* abstention is commonly addressed when federal courts are faced with constitutional challenges to broadly written state unfair trade practice laws.[37] For instance, in *Word of Faith Outreach Center Church, Inc. v. Morales*,[38] the Fifth Circuit relied on *Pullman* to reverse the district court's finding that the application of Texas' "little FTC Act" violated the defendant's First Amendment rights of free association, noting that "unsettled questions regarding the application of state law in this case, depending upon how a state court would resolve them, could have mooted the federal constitutional issue."[39]

2. *Burford Abstention*

Two years after the Supreme Court established the *Pullman* doctrine, it decided *Burford v. Sun Oil Co.*,[40] holding that federal courts could, and sometimes must, dismiss certain actions involving complicated issues that are typically managed by comprehensive state regulatory schemes. In *Burford*, the Court held that a federal district

---

35. *See, e.g.*, England v. La. State Bd. of Med. Exam'rs, 375 U.S. 411 (1964).
36. *See generally* Martha A. Field, *Abstention In Constitutional Cases: The Scope Of The Pullman Abstention Doctrine*, 122 U. PA. L. REV. 1071, 1090 (1974) (criticizing doctrine in light of significant transaction costs and inefficiencies it creates).
37. *See, e.g.*, Am. Charities for Reasonable Fundraising Regulation, Inc. v. Shiffrin, 46 F. Supp. 2d 143 (D. Conn. 1999) (involving challenge to Connecticut Unfair Trade Practices Act), *aff'd*, 205 F.3d 1321 (2d Cir. 2000); Globe Glass & Mirror Co. v. Brown, 888 F. Supp. 768 (E.D. La. 1995) (involving Louisiana unfair trade practices statute); Tex. v. Synchronal Corp., 800 F. Supp. 1456 (W.D. Tex. 1992) (involving Texas Deceptive Trade Practices-Consumer Protection Act).
38. 986 F.2d 962 (5th Cir. 1993).
39. *Id.* at 968.
40. 319 U.S. 315 (1943).

court should have dismissed a challenge to an order by the Texas Railroad Commission allowing new wells in East Texas because the case involved complex and specialized issues of parochial state interests. Citing Texas' complex administrative oversight of oil drilling, the need to maintain centralized decision-making over all drilling decisions, the state's system of consolidated adjudication in one court, available state appellate review, and the importance of petroleum resources to the Texas economy, the Court held that abstention was justified.[41] Accordingly, *Burford* abstention has been found appropriate when: (1) there are "difficult questions of state law bearing on policy problems of substantial public import whose importance transcends the result in the case then at bar," or (2) if the "exercise of federal review . . . would be disruptive of state efforts to establish a coherent policy with respect to a matter of substantial public concern."[42]

Over the past fifteen years, the Supreme Court has curtailed the range of cases in which *Burford* abstention can be applied. In *New Orleans Public Service, Inc. v. Council of City of New Orleans*,[43] the Supreme Court limited the doctrine to cases in which the exercise of federal jurisdiction threatens to "disrupt the State's attempt to ensure uniformity in the treatment of an essentially local problem."[44] Thus, the Court held that the mere existence of a complex state administrative process does not necessitate *Burford* abstention.   Thereafter, in *Quackenbush v. Allstate Insurance Co.*,[45] the Court held that *Burford* abstention only applies to claims for declaratory or injunctive relief because "the power to dismiss under the *Burford* doctrine, as with other abstention doctrines, derives from the discretion historically enjoyed by courts of equity" and could not normally be applied to suits for monetary damages.[46] This limitation on *Burford* abstention reduces its application

---

41. *Id.* at 319-20.
42. New Orleans Pub. Serv., Inc. v. Council of New Orleans, 491 U.S. 350, 361 (1989); *see also* Time Warner Cable v. Doyle, 66 F.3d 867 (7th Cir. 1995); Nelson v. Murphy, 44 F.3d 497, 500-01 (7th Cir. 1995).
43. 491 U.S. 350 (1989).
44. *Id.* at 362.
45. 517 U.S. 706 (1996).
46. *Id.* at 727-28 (citation omitted). While the *Quackenbush* Court appeared to state that all federal abstention doctrines are limited to equity cases, the

in private tort actions, which usually involve damage claims, making it relevant only to a small number of federal business tort or unfair competition cases seeking injunctive or declaratory relief and involving concurrent regulatory proceedings by private parties or state officials (e.g., insurance commissioners, securities regulators, or state attorneys general) against one of the parties in the federal equity action.[47]

Unlike *Pullman* abstention, courts deferring to state administrative procedures under the *Burford* doctrine normally dismiss the action and completely relinquish jurisdiction over the case,[48] thereby closing the door to the federal courts barring possible, though rare, Supreme Court appellate review. In situations in which an action is originally filed in state court and later removed to federal court, the federal court may abstain under the *Burford* doctrine by merely remanding the case to the state court, rather than dismissing it.[49]

Court has previously approved abstention in cases involving actions at law. *See, e.g.*, La. Power & Light Co. v Thibodaux, 360 U.S. 25 (1959).

47. *See, e.g.*, First Penn-Pac. Life Ins. Co v. Evans, 304 F.3d 345, 348-51 (4th Cir. 2002) (involving *Burford* abstention of fraud claims brought by insurance company that was subject of highly regulated state receivership proceedings brought about to enforce state securities and insurance laws and involving liquidation of company assets), *cert. denied*, 538 U.S. 944 (2003); *cf.* Holden v. Connex-Metalna Mgmt. Consulting GmbH, 302 F.3d 358, 363-64 (5th Cir. 2002) (*Burford* abstention was not warranted for declaratory judgment action between insurance companies pursuing declaration of rights under policies, even after Pennsylvania state insurance commissioner ordered one of insurers into rehabilitation and stayed all actions against it, on grounds that state proceeding did not involve decisive issue of state law); Feige v. Sechrest, 90 F.3d 846 (3d Cir. 1996) (stay, rather than dismissal, was permitted under *Burford*, in action seeking damages against insolvent insurer for fraud, misrepresentation, and tortious interference with contract because state liquidation proceeding was pending and federal fraud claims were bound up in liquidation process).

48. *See* Field, *supra* note 36, at 1153; Constr. Aggregates Corp. v. Rivera de Vicenty, 573 F.2d 86, 89 (1st Cir. 1978); United States v. Riverside Labs., Inc., 678 F. Supp. 1352, 1360-61 & nn.14, 15 (N.D. Ill. 1988); Oler v. Trustees of Cal. State Univ. & Colls., 80 F.R.D. 319, 320 (N.D. Cal. 1978).

49. *See, e.g.*, Corcoran v. Ardra Ins. Co., 842 F.2d 31, 36 (2d Cir. 1988).

3.   *Thibodaux Abstention*

In 1959, the Supreme Court recognized a third basis for abstention in *Louisiana Power & Light Co. v. Thibodaux*,[50] in which the Court created an exception to its previously-announced rule that federal courts should not abstain in diversity cases merely because state law is unclear.[51] Considered by many commentators to be a mere extension of the *Burford* doctrine,[52] *Thibodaux* involved a federal district court's abstention from a case involving a Florida corporation's state law challenge to a city's attempt to condemn its property under its eminent domain powers.   Upholding the propriety of the district court's abstention, the Supreme Court held that the "special and peculiar nature" of eminent domain proceedings and their intimate involvement with the state government's "sovereign prerogative" justified abstention when important issues of state law remained unclear.[53]

However, in *Allegheny County v. Frank Mashuda Co.*,[54] a decision released on the same day as *Thibodaux*, the Court emphasized the limited scope of the *Thiboduax* holding.   In *Mashuda*, the district court dismissed a challenge to Pittsburgh's use of its eminent domain powers to take the plaintiff's land and subsequently lease it to private businesses. Because Pennsylvania law clearly prohibited a city from using its eminent domain powers to take property for private commercial use, the Court held that abstention was not justified.   Thus, the Court held that

---

50.   360 U.S. 25 (1959).
51.   *See* Meredith v. Winter Haven, 320 U.S. 228, 236 (1943) (founding anti-abstention position in diversity cases as upholding Congress' "policy of opening the federal courts to suitors in all diversity cases involving the jurisdictional amount").
52.   Notably, some courts consider *Thibodaux* abstention simply to be an expansion or subset of the *Burford* abstention doctrine rather than an entirely new and distinct category of abstention. *See, e.g.*, Grode v. Mut. Fire, Marine & Inland Ins. Co., 8 F.3d 953, 957 (3d Cir. 1993) ("*Thibodaux* is really a variant of the *Burford* abstention doctrine and has not evolved as a separate doctrine of its own."); Canaday v. Koch, 608 F. Supp. 1460, 1468 n.10 (S.D.N.Y. 1985), *aff'd*, 768 F.2d 501 (2d Cir 1985).
53.   *Thibodaux*, 360 U.S. at 27-28.
54.   360 U.S. 185 (1959).

important issues of state concern, like eminent domain, were not enough to justify abstention if there was no ambiguity in state law on the issue.[55]

Read together, *Thibodaux* and *Mashuda* establish the principle that abstention could be appropriate in a federal diversity case, if the action concerns: (1) unclear questions of state law, and (2) significant state policy interests that are closely involved with the state's sovereign powers.[56] Like the *Pullman* doctrine, *Thibodaux* abstention requires a stay of federal proceedings until the meaning of a disputed state statute is resolved by the state courts.[57]

Since 1959, the Supreme Court has only decided one case in this area. In *Kaiser Steel Corp. v. W.S. Ranch Co.*,[58] the Court further defined the type of state interests that will justify abstention under *Thibodaux*. *Kaiser Steel* involved a plaintiff's challenge under the New Mexico Constitution to that state's grant of water rights on the plaintiff's land to a neighboring steel company. Because the state constitutional question raised was "a truly novel one," the Court held that "[s]ound judicial administration require[d]" abstention, and the federal district court sitting in diversity should not have decided the case.[59] Thus, the *Kaiser Steel* Court held that state policy interests other than eminent domain could necessitate *Thibodaux* abstention if state law issues raised in the federal court were sufficiently unclear. Moreover, in the last four decades, the lower federal courts have applied the *Thibodaux* doctrine to additional state interests as varied as state taxation,[60] legal services in

---

55. *Id.* at 192 ("eminent domain is no more mystically involved with 'sovereign prerogative'" than other interests commonly dealt with by federal courts).

56. *See, e.g.*, Polygon Ins. Co. v. Honeywell Int'l, Inc., 143 F. Supp. 2d 211 (D. Conn. 2001) (uncertain state law is not enough to warrant *Thibodaux* abstention if case does not involve peculiarly important state policy interest); Epps v. Lauderdale County, 139 F. Supp. 2d 859 (W.D. Tenn. 2000) (*Thibodaux* abstention was not justified if state law was settled).

57. *See, e.g.*, Starzenski v. City of Elkhart, 842 F. Supp. 1132, 1139 (N.D. Ind. 1994) ("*Thibodaux* abstention is a stay of federal proceedings until the meaning of a disputed state statute is resolved by state court.")

58. 391 U.S. 593 (1968).

59. *Id.* at 594.

60. *See* Keleher v. New England Tel. & Tel. Co., 947 F.2d 547 (2d Cir. 1991).

divorce actions,[61] construction of trusts,[62] child support,[63] and policy exceptions to recoveries of life insurance.[64]

Like the *Burford* doctrine, *Thibodaux* abstention is rarely invoked by the federal courts and is unlikely to be available in business tort litigation outside of federal equity cases in which a plaintiff is seeking injunctive or declaratory relief affecting areas of peculiarly local interest (e.g., land or natural resources) when state courts are available and better situated to adjudicate the dispute.

4. *Younger Abstention*

In 1971, the Supreme Court defined a fourth abstention doctrine in *Younger v. Harris*.[65] Founded on the notion of comity and "proper respect for state functions,"[66] *Younger* holds that federal courts should not enjoin pending state criminal proceedings unless the federal plaintiff can show that: (1) the state prosecution was brought in bad faith; (2) the criminal law at issue is patently unconstitutional; or (3) the federal petitioner lacks any adequate state forum to raise federal statutory or constitutional defenses.[67] As originally articulated, these exceptions are rarely satisfied.[68]

---

61. *See* Phillips, Nizer, Benjamin, Krim & Ballon v. Rosenstiel, 490 F.2d 509, 516 (2d Cir. 1973) (abstention would have been justified had issue been raised appropriately).

62. *See* Reichman v. Pittsburgh Nat'l Bank, 465 F.2d 16, 18 (3d Cir. 1972) (deferring to Pennsylvania Orphans' Court).

63. *See* Magaziner v. Montemuro, 468 F.2d 782, 787 (3d Cir. 1972) (deferring to Family Division of Pennsylvania Court of Common Pleas).

64. *See* Morgan v. Equitable Life Assurance Soc'y, 446 F.2d 929, 932 (10th Cir. 1971).

65. 401 U.S. 37 (1971).

66. *Id.* at 44.

67. *Id.* at 52; *see also Colo. River Water Conserv. Dist.*, 424 U.S. at 816 (defining *Younger* abstention).

68. *But cf.* Gibson v. Berryhill, 411 U.S. 564 (1973) (federal plaintiff lacked any legitimate remedy before Alabama State Court of Optometry on licensing dispute because court was biased against optometrists, like petitioner, who were not self-employed).

The reasoning of *Younger*, however, has been expanded to cover requests for federal declaratory relief concerning state prosecutions,[69] as well as state civil and administrative enforcement proceedings, "if the State's interests in the proceeding are so important that exercise of the federal judicial power would disregard the comity between the States and the National Government."[70] As such, the Supreme Court has relied upon the *Younger* doctrine for refusing to disrupt state proceedings as diverse as state bar attorney disciplinary actions,[71] state public nuisance proceedings,[72] sex discrimination investigations by state civil rights commissions,[73] state actions to recover welfare payments,[74] contempt proceedings against judgment debtors,[75] and child custody hearings.[76] Moreover, the lower federal courts have applied *Younger* to an even broader category of state civil actions that involve important state interests.[77]

Importantly, *Younger* has been cited by the federal courts as a basis for refusing to enjoin state actions brought by state agencies under deceptive business practice laws,[78] and thus business tort litigators

---

69. *See, e.g.*, Samuels v. Mackell, 401 U.S. 66 (1971); Redner v. Citrus County, 919 F.2d 646 (11th Cir. 1990).
70. Pennzoil Co. v. Texaco, Inc., 481 U.S. 1, 11 (1987).
71. *See* Middlesex County Ethics Comm. v. Garden State Bar Ass'n, 457 U.S. 423 (1982).
72. *See* Huffman v. Pursue, Ltd., 420 U.S. 592 (1975).
73. *See* Ohio Civil Rights Comm'n v. Dayton Christian Sch., Inc., 477 U.S. 619 (1986).
74. *See* Trainor v. Hernandez, 431 U.S. 434 (1977).
75. *See* Juidice v. Vail, 430 U.S. 327 (1977).
76. *See* Moore v. Sims, 442 U.S. 415 (1979).
77. *See, e.g.*, Family Found. Inc. v. Brown, 9 F.3d 1075, 1078 (4th Cir. 1993) (finding substantial state interest in regulating state election process); Alleghany Corp. v. Pomeroy, 898 F.2d 1314 (8th Cir. 1990) (finding important state interest in state's regulation of its insurance companies); Goleta Nat'l Bank v. Lingerfelt, 211 F. Supp. 2d 711 (E.D.N.C. 2002) (state enforcement of predatory lending and consumer protection laws involved important state interest); Metro. Hosp. v. Thornburgh, 667 F. Supp. 208 (E.D. Pa. 1987) (state regulation of in-state hospitals involved important state interest).
78. *See, e.g.*, Williams v. Washington, 554 F.2d 369 (9th Cir. 1977) (concerning Washington state's allegations that federal plaintiff had

defending similar state criminal and civil actions are unlikely to convince a federal court to disrupt the state case, even if the state forum is likely to ignore meritorious federal statutory or constitutional defenses. Rather, these defenses should be raised at the state level and preserved for potential appeal to the state appellate courts and, potentially, discretionary appellate review by the U.S. Supreme Court.

5. Colorado River Abstention

In business tort litigation, it is not uncommon for: (1) state court defendants to file reactive suits against state court plaintiffs or codefendants in federal court, seeking a more favorable forum for counterclaims or crossclaims[79] and (2) state court plaintiffs to file materially identical actions in federal court, attempting to avoid an unfavorable ruling in the state action or impose additional burdens on defendants.[80]

The Supreme Court addressed such duplicative litigation in *Colorado River Water Conservation District v. United States*,[81] in which it crafted an additional ground for federal deference to ongoing state court proceedings. Under the *Colorado River* doctrine, the Court held that federal courts may abstain from exercising jurisdiction when there is identical, concurrent state litigation, but only in exceptional circumstances.[82] While recognizing that the federal courts have a "virtually unflagging obligation . . . to exercise the jurisdiction given them" and a pending state case does not necessarily bar a federal suit

engaged in unfair and deceptive business practices); *Lingerfelt*, 211 F. Supp. 2d 711; State Farm Mut. Auto. Ins. Co. v. Metcalf, 902 F. Supp. 1216 (D. Haw. 1995).

79. *See, e.g.*, N. Am. Boxing Org. Intercont'l, Inc. v. N. Am. Boxing Org., Inc., 40 F. Supp. 2d 55 (D.P.R. 1999) (involving federal suit alleging unfair competition and trademark infringement brought by defendant in state court action involving same parties and facts).
80. *See, e.g.*, Weinstock v. Cleary, Gottlieb, Steen & Hamilton, 815 F. Supp. 127 (S.D.N.Y. 1993) (involving federal RICO action brought against law firm and other defendants in federal court after plaintiffs received unfavorable ruling in previously filed and almost identical state court case), *aff'd*, 16 F.3d 501 (2d Cir. 1994).
81. 424 U.S. 800 (1976).
82. *Id.* at 813.

concerning the same subject matter,[83] the Court held that "'wise judicial administration'" provides a basis for staying or dismissing federal actions in truly "exceptional" circumstances.[84]

In *Colorado River* and a subsequent case, *Moses H. Cone Memorial Hospital v. Mercury Construction Corp.*,[85] the Court articulated the following six factors that should be considered in determining whether wise judicial administration outweighs a court's duty to adjudicate controversies properly before it: (1) the relative costs and inconvenience of piecemeal litigation; (2) whether the state court has assumed jurisdiction over property involved in the suit; (3) which suit was filed first; (4) the relative inconvenience of either forum to the parties; (5) whether the case concerns federal claims or defenses; and (6) whether the state court proceedings will protect the rights of all parties.[86]   In *Moses H. Cone*, however, the Court cautioned that a court's "decision whether to dismiss a federal action because of parallel state-court litigation does not rest on a mechanical checklist, but on a careful balancing of the important factors as they apply in a given case, with the balance heavily weighted in favor of the exercise of jurisdiction."[87]

Consistent with this strong presumption in favor of the exercise of federal jurisdiction, the federal courts often reject *Colorado River* motions to stay or dismiss federal business tort cases.[88]   Where (by

---

83.   *Id.* at 817.
84.   *Id.* (quoting Kerotest Mfg. Co. v. C-O-Two Fire Equip. Co., 342 U.S. 180 (1952)).
85.   460 U.S. 1 (1983).
86.   *Colorado River, Moses H. Cone*, 424 U.S. at 818-19; 460 U.S. at 23-24.
87.   *Moses H. Cone*, 460 U.S. at 16. Notably, the Court has held that its exceptional circumstances test does not apply to federal declaratory judgment actions brought by state court defendants. Wilton v. Seven Falls Co., 515 U.S. 277 (1995) (district courts have greater degree of discretion to stay or dismiss declaratory judgment actions in federal courts in light of pending related state court litigation).
88.   *See, e.g.*, Life-Link Int'l, Inc. v. Lalla, 902 F.2d 1493 (10th Cir. 1990) (finding no exceptional circumstances supporting *Colorado River* deference in federal trademark infringement and unfair competition action); Ramirez Commercial Arts, Inc. v. Flexcon Co., 242 F. Supp. 2d 113 (D.P.R. 2002) (finding abstention unwarranted in federal unfair trade practices action); Ambrose v. New England Ass'n of Sch. & Colls., Inc., 100 F. Supp. 2d 48 (D. Me. 2000) (finding no exceptional circumstances

application of the Supreme Court's six factor analysis) "exceptional circumstances" exist, however, federal district courts will stay or dismiss and thereby defer to the pending state court litigation.[89]

D. Anti-Suit Injunctions

Just as parties litigating in multiple forums may request that courts stay or dismiss cases filed against them, they may also request injunctions to interrupt other parallel proceedings. The following discussion addresses five such scenarios: (1) federal court injunctions against proceedings in other federal courts; (2) federal court injunctions against state court proceedings; (3) state court injunctions against federal court proceedings; (4) state court injunctions against proceedings in the courts of other states; and (5) attempts by foreign courts to enjoin proceedings in courts of the United States. Each variety is briefly addressed below.

---

supported abstention in federal action asserting unfair trade practice claims), *aff'd on other grounds*, 252 F.3d 488 (1st Cir. 2001).

89. *See, e.g.*, MicroSource, Inc. v. Superior Signs, Inc., No. Civ. A. 3:97-CV-2733, 1998 WL 119537 (N.D. Tex. Mar. 9, 1998) (abstaining in case involving duplicative federal claims for unfair competition and theft of trade secrets); Silvaco Data Sys., Inc. v. Technology Modeling Assocs., Inc., 896 F. Supp. 973 (N.D. Cal. 1995) (involving federal claims of false advertising and unfair competition); Ruth's Chris Steak House Franchise, Inc. v. Wamstad, No. 94-2612, 1994 WL 660508 (E.D. La. Nov. 22, 1994) (federal case involving claims for false advertising and unfair competition was materially same as state court action, and circumstances were exceptional and warranted abstention); Thompson v. Ashner, 601 F. Supp. 471 (N.D. Ill. 1985) (abstaining in case involving federal claims of trademark infringement and unfair competition under Lanham Act where plaintiff had previously filed identical state court trademark infringement suit); Entex Indus., Inc. v. Warner Commc'ns, 487 F. Supp. 46 (C.D. Cal. 1980) (mere fact that federal trademark infringement and unfair competition claims were filed before similar state suit was initiated by federal defendant did not immunize suit from *Colorado River* abstention because federal plaintiff had been warned in advance of upcoming state filing).

1. *Multiple Federal Proceedings*

Because parties in business tort litigation are often sophisticated and well-funded litigants, it is not uncommon for such parties to seek tactical advantages by filing duplicative actions (seeking traditional or declaratory relief) in more than one federal court.[90] In such cases, federal courts have discretion to enjoin the filing of related lawsuits in other federal district courts,[91] and a court's decision to enjoin, or not to enjoin, a concurrent federal action will only be reversed for an abuse of discretion.[92]

As a general matter, district courts give preference to whichever federal action is filed first. Under the first filed rule, the district court which first has proper jurisdiction over a dispute should adjudicate the

---

90. *See, e.g.*, 3M v. Rynne, 661 F.2d 722 (8th Cir. 1981) (involving initial action for misappropriation of trade secrets and reactive suit in separate federal court for antitrust violations); Worldwide Sport Nutritional Supplements, Inc. v. Five Star Brands, LLC, 80 F. Supp. 2d 25 (N.D.N.Y. 1999) (involving initial suit for theft of trade secrets followed by reactive declaratory judgment action requesting ruling that no trade secrets existed in separate federal court); N.W. Airlines, Inc. v. Am. Airlines, Inc., 792 F. Supp. 655 (D. Minn. 1992) (involving initial action by Northwest Airlines for declaratory judgment that hiring at-will employees was protected commercial competition and subsequent action by American Airlines alleging tortious interference with contract and unfair competition for hiring such employees), *aff'd*, 989 F.2d 1002 (8th Cir. 1993); United Fruit Co. v. Standard Fruit & S.S. Co., 282 F. Supp. 338 (D. Mass. 1968) (enjoining later-filed declaratory judgment action concerning allegations of trademark infringement and asserting claims of unfair competition, because issues raised in second action were more properly presented as defenses and counterclaims in initial action).

91. *See, e.g.*, Kerotest Mfg. Co., 342 U.S. 180 (acknowledging propriety of injunction preventing progress of subsequently filed patent infringement case); N.W. Airlines, Inc. v. Am. Airlines, Inc., 989 F.2d 1002 (8th Cir. 1993); EEOC v. Univ. of Pa., 850 F.2d 969, 971 (3d Cir. 1988) (first filed rule "gives a court 'the power' to enjoin the subsequent prosecution of proceedings involving the same parties and the same issues already before another district court"), *aff'd*, 493 U.S. 182 (1990).

92. *See, e.g.*, Mun. Energy Agency v. Big Rivers Elec. Corp., 804 F.2d 338, 343 (5th Cir. 1986) ("But we will reverse a district court's decision not to enjoin another proceeding only if the district court abused its discretion.").

case, and it has the power to enjoin any subsequently-initiated proceedings involving the same parties and issues.[93] This rule advances "the inherently fair concept that the party who commenced the first suit should generally be the party to attain its choice of venue."[94] However, the courts have repeatedly recognized that "the first-filed rule is not intended to be rigid, mechanical or inflexible, but is to be applied in a manner best serving the interests of justice."[95] Thus, while priority to the first-filed suit is given great weight, courts may also consider a wide variety of equitable factors such as convenience to the parties and

---

93. *See, e.g., Univ. of Pa.*, 850 F.2d at 971; Warshawsky & Co. v. Arcata Nat'l Corp., 552 F.2d 1257, 1260 (7th Cir. 1977); Am. Soc'y for Testing & Materials v. Corrpro Cos., 254 F. Supp. 2d 578 (E.D. Pa. 2003).

94. Ontel Prods., Inc. v. Project Strategies Corp., 899 F. Supp. 1144, 1150, 1153 n.13 (S.D.N.Y. 1995).

95. Boatmen's First Nat'l Bank v. Kan. Pub. Employees Ret. Sys., 57 F.3d 638, 641 (8th Cir. 1995); *see also* 800-Flowers, Inc. v. Intercont'l Florist, Inc., 860 F. Supp. 128, 133 (S.D.N.Y. 1994) (it is "well established that district courts need not slavishly adhere to the first filed rule").

witnesses,[96] the temporal proximity of the successive federal filings,[97] and whether the first suit was filed in anticipation of a later filed action.[98]

2.   *Federal Court Injunctions of State Court Proceedings*

When parallel, duplicative business tort or unfair competition cases are pending in both state and federal courts, parties seeking to limit the litigation to a single forum may either move the federal court to abstain from hearing the federal case (as previously described) or seek a federal court injunction of the concurrent state action.[99] However, with a few

---

96.   *See, e.g.*, William Gluckin & Co. v. Int'l Playtex Corp., 407 F.2d 177, 179-80 (2d Cir. 1969); Remington Prods. Corp. v. Am. Aerovap, Inc., 192 F.2d 872 (2d Cir. 1951); Mode Art Jewelers Co. v. Expansion Jewelry, Ltd., 409 F. Supp. 921, 923 (S.D.N.Y. 1976); Polaroid Corp. v. Casselman, 213 F. Supp. 379 (S.D.N.Y. 1962); Turbo Mach. Co. v. Proctor & Schwartz, Inc., 204 F. Supp. 39 (E.D. Pa. 1962). Notably, the courts' convenience analysis can consider many of the factors relevant to a request for transfer under 28 U.S.C. § 1404(a) such as the availability of documentary evidence, the nexus between the forum and the events giving rise to suit, and the fact that the movant already has retained counsel in the first action. *See, e.g.*, Columbia Plaza Corp. v. Sec. Nat'l Bank, 525 F.2d 620 (D.C. Cir. 1975); Telephonics Corp. v. Lindly & Co., 291 F.2d 445 (2d Cir. 1961); Helene Curtis Indus., Inc. v. Sales Affiliates, Inc., 199 F.2d 732 (2d Cir. 1952).

97.   *See, e.g.*, Affinity Memory & Micro v. K&Q Enters., 20 F. Supp. 2d 948, 954-55 (E.D. Va. 1998) (recognizing closeness of both filings as factor weighing against strict application of first filed rule); Ontel Prods., Inc. v. Project Strategies Corp., 899 F. Supp. 1144, 1153 (S.D.N.Y. 1995) (priority rule can be "disregarded where the competing suits were filed merely days apart").

98.   *See, e.g.*, Boatmen's First Nat'l Bank of Kan. City v. Kan. Pub. Employees Ret. Sys., 57 F.3d 638, 641 (8th Cir. 1995); Mission Ins. Co v. Puritan Fashions Corp., 706 F.2d 599, 602 n.3 (5th Cir. 1983) ("[a]nticipatory suits are disfavored because they are an aspect of forum-shopping").

99.   *See, e.g.*, Foster v. Hallco Mfg. Co., 897 F. Supp. 477 (D. Or. 1995) (involving related state tortious interference with business, trade defamation, and RICO claims and related linked federal action); Next Level Commc'ns L.P. v. DSC Commc'ns Corp., 179 F.3d 244 (5th Cir. 1999) (involving federal and state actions addressing same claims of trade secret theft); W.W. Enter., Inc. v. Charlotte Motor Speedway, Inc., 753 F.

limited exceptions, federal courts are prohibited under the Anti-Injunction Act from enjoining state court proceedings.[100] The act provides that:

> A court of the United States may not grant an injunction to stay proceedings in a State court except as expressly authorized by Act of Congress, or where necessary in aid of its jurisdiction, or to protect or effectuate its judgments.

Thus, while the Anti-Injunction Act "generally bars federal courts from granting injunctions to stay proceedings in state courts,"[101] the statute provides three specific exceptions, allowing injunctions if they are: (1) expressly authorized by an Act of Congress; (2) necessary in aid of the federal court's jurisdiction; or (3) necessary to protect or effectuate the federal court's judgment.[102] In addition, the Supreme Court has recognized a fourth exception to the act's prohibition, allowing federal injunctions if they are sought by the United States to protect important national interests.[103]

With respect to the first exception, the Anti-Injunction Act does not apply in circumstances where Congress has expressly authorized federal court injunctions of state court proceedings. While this exception does not require that a federal statute specifically reference the Anti-Injunction Act,[104] the federal statute must establish an identifiable and enforceable federal right or remedy that a state proceeding could impair if not enjoined.[105] The test "is whether an Act of Congress, clearly creating a federal right or remedy enforceable in a federal court of equity, could be given its intended scope only by the stay of a state court

---

Supp. 1326 (W.D.N.C. 1990) (involving state trademark infringement action arising from same dispute as federal antitrust action).
100. Act of March 2, 1793, c. 22, § 5, 1, 28 U.S.C. § 2283.
101. Choo v. Exxon Corp., 486 U.S. 140, 142 (1988).
102. 28 U.S.C. § 2283.
103. *See* Leiter Minerals, Inc. v. United States, 352 U.S. 220 (1957).
104. Amalgamated Clothing Workers of Am. v. Richman Bros. Co., 348 U.S. 511, 516 (1955); Desmond v. McColl (*In re* BankAmerica Corp. Sec. Litig.), 263 F.3d 795 (8th Cir. 2001).
105. *See, e.g.*, Mitchum v. Foster, 407 U.S. 225, 237-38 (1972); *Desmond*, 263 F.3d at 801 (Private Securities Litigation Reform Act created numerous procedural protections against strike suits that required enforcement via federal court injunctions halting state court proceedings).

proceeding."[106]   Although the lower federal courts are split on whether
certain federal statutes satisfy this test,[107] the Supreme Court has
definitively held that the following statutes authorize federal injunctions
of state court proceedings: (1) the Bankruptcy Act,[108] (2) the removal
statute,[109] (3) the shipowner's liability statute,[110] (4) farm mortgage
statutes,[111] (5) the Interpleader Act,[112] (6) the Civil Rights Act,[113] (7) the
Anti-Drug Abuse Act of 1988,[114] and (8) the Agricultural Credit Act.[115]

   Notably for antitrust litigators, in *Vendo Co. v. Lektro-Vend
Corp.*,[116] the Supreme Court held that the Clayton Act's civil remedies
provision (Section 26 of Title 15 of the U.S. Code), which authorizes
private federal suits to enjoin violations of the federal antitrust laws, does
not satisfy the Anti-Injunction Act's "expressly authorized" exception.[117]
Noting the strong presumption against finding that a congressional
statute provides for federal injunctions of state court proceedings and the
lack of any indication in the Clayton Act or its legislative history that its
provisions "contemplate[d] or envision[ed] any necessary interaction
with state judicial proceedings," the *Vendo* Court held that Section 26 did
not authorize injunctions of state court proceedings.[118]   As such, the
antitrust laws are of little use in enjoining a state court proceeding, even

106. *Mitchum*, 407 U.S. at 238.
107. *Compare* Stockslager v. Carroll Elec. Coop. Corp., 528 F.2d 949, 951-52
     (8th Cir. 1976) (National Environmental Policy Act qualifies for the
     "express[] authorization" exception to § 2283), *with* Bd. of Supervisors v.
     Cir. Ct. of Dickenson County, 500 F. Supp. 212, 213-14 (W.D. Va. 1980)
     (National Environmental Policy Act does not qualify for "expressly
     authorized" exception).
108. *See* Vendo Co. v. Lektro-Vend Corp., 433 U.S. 623 (1977).
109. *See* Dietzsch v. Huidekoper, 103 U.S. 494 (1881).
110. *See* Providence & N.Y.S.S. Co. v. Hill Mfg. Co., 109 U.S. 578 (1883).
111. *See* Kalb v. Feuerstein, 308 U.S. 433 (1940).
112. *See* Dugas v. Am. Sur. Co., 300 U.S. 414 (1936).
113. *See* Mitchum v. Foster, 407 U.S. 225 (1972).
114. *See* McFarland v. Scott, 512 U.S. 849 (1994).
115. *See* Zajac v. Fed. Land Bank, 909 F.2d 1181 (8th Cir. 1990).
116. 433 U.S. 623 (1977).
117. *Id.* at 631-33.
118. *Id.* at 640-41.

though a pending federal antitrust action may involve the same parties and issues as a duplicative state case.[119]

The second exception to the Anti-Injunction Act allows a federal court to enjoin state court proceedings when necessary "in aid of its jurisdiction." For example, a federal court may enjoin a state court proceeding to protect its in rem jurisdiction over property, if the federal court exercised such jurisdiction before the state court.[120]

However, aside from so-called "real" actions involving a federal court's in rem jurisdiction, the Anti-Injunction Act's "in aid of its jurisdiction" exception has been narrowly construed. In *Atlantic Coast Line Railroad v. Brotherhood of Locomotive Engineers*,[121] the Supreme Court held that this exception does not empower district courts to enjoin simultaneous duplicative litigation in the state courts because pursuing identical claims in separate courts is an inherent byproduct of the dual federal system of concurrent jurisdiction. Thus, parallel state litigation does not constitute the level of interference necessary to permit injunctive relief under the Anti-Injunction Act's second exception.[122] Rather, the *Atlantic Coast* Court held that an injunction may issue in aid of a federal court's jurisdiction only when the state court proceeding is "so interfering with a federal court's consideration or disposition of a case as to seriously impair the federal court's flexibility and authority to decide that case."[123] Moreover, the Supreme Court has determined that the "in aid of its jurisdiction" exception does not authorize injunctions of state court proceedings on the basis that the state court has invaded a field that Congress has intentionally preempted with federal

---

119. *See, e.g.*, W.W. Enter., Inc. v. Charlotte Motor Speedway, Inc., 753 F. Supp. 1326 (W.D.N.C. 1990) (refusing to enjoin state trademark infringement action in light of state defendant's pursuit of antitrust claims in federal court because § 26 does not expressly provide exception to Anti-Injunction Act).

120. *See* Donovan v. City of Dallas, 377 U.S. 408 (1964).

121. 398 U.S. 281 (1970).

122. *Id.* at 294-95.

123. *Id.* at 295; *see also* Bennett v. Medtronic, Inc., 285 F.3d 801, 805-07 (9th Cir. 2002); Winkler v. Eli Lilly & Co., 101 F.3d 1196, 1201 (7th Cir. 1996) ("in aid of its jurisdiction" exception is very limited and only applies when state court proceedings threaten to render exercise of federal jurisdiction nugatory).

legislation.[124]   Rather, litigants are directed to raise the preemption argument in the state proceeding and seek an appeal if necessary through the state appellate courts and subsequently to the U.S. Supreme Court.[125]

The Anti-Injunction Act's third exception is frequently referred to as the "relitigation" exception.[126]   "[F]ounded in the well-recognized concepts of res judicata and collateral estoppel," this exception was designed "to permit a federal court to prevent state litigation of an issue that previously was ... decided by the federal court."[127]   Under this exception, federal courts may enjoin any further state proceedings that threaten either to relitigate matters previously adjudicated by the federal court or to impair the effect of a prior federal judgment.[128]   Notably, the relitigation exception only applies to claims or issues that have been actually decided by a federal court,[129] and federal courts demand "a strong and unequivocal showing" that a conclusively-determined federal issue is at stake in the state proceeding "because res judicata and collateral estoppel may be raised as defenses in the state court proceeding."[130]   Hence, a federal injunction is prohibited if there is no clear final federal court decision in jeopardy of being relitigated, even if

---

124. Amalgamated Clothing Workers of Am. v. Richman Bros., 348 U.S. 511, 516 (1955).
125. *See Atl. Coast Line R.R.*, 398 U.S. at 294 (federal courts may not "enjoin state court proceedings merely because those proceedings ... invade an area preempted by federal law, even when the interference is unmistakably clear").
126. *See Choo*, 486 U.S. at 147.
127. *Id.*
128. *See, e.g.*, G.C. & K.B. Invs., Inc. v. Wilson, 326 F.3d 1096, 1106-07 (9th Cir. 2003).
129. *See, e.g., Atl. Coast Line R.R.*, 398 U.S. 281; Henry v. Farmer City State Bank, 630 F. Supp. 844 (C.D. Ill. 1986) (approving federal court injunction of state court common-law fraud claim against bank by bankrupt merchant in mortgage foreclosure where federal court had previously dismissed claims from same transaction for lack of injury), *aff'd in part, rev'd in part*, 808 F.2d 1228 (7th Cir. 1986).
130. Foster v. Hallco Mfg. Co., 897 F. Supp. 477, 479 (D. Or. 1995) (third exception not met in state court action for tortious interference with business, trade defamation, and state RICO violations because issues litigated and finally determined in federal case were not being litigated again in state court).

a state action threatens a protected federal right or invades an area preempted by federal law.[131]

Finally, the Supreme Court has held that the Anti-Injunction Act does not prohibit the United States from obtaining an injunction of state court proceedings to prevent threatened irreparable injury to an important national interest,[132] and this exception to the Act's reach applies to federal agencies.[133] Nevertheless, federal courts have no obligation to enjoin state court proceedings merely because the United States has moved for an injunction,[134] and the government must still prove that the threatened injury could not otherwise be protected.[135]

3. *Federal Injunctions of International Proceedings*

As international commerce has increased, parallel litigation in the courts of foreign nations has become more commonplace. In these cases, parties may seek to have a United States federal court enjoin an adversary from pursuing foreign litigation.

While federal courts have discretion to enjoin parties before them from commencing or proceeding with litigation in foreign countries,[136] there is a split among the federal circuits concerning the circumstances under which such injunctions can be granted.[137] While at least one

---

131. *See Choo*, 486 U.S. at 149-50.
132. Leiter Minerals, Inc. v. United States, 352 U.S. 220 (1957); Ark. v. Farm Credit Servs., 520 U.S. 821 (1997); *see also* United States v. Wood, 295 F.2d 772 (5th Cir. 1961) (United States could obtain injunction enjoining state criminal prosecution).
133. *See* NLRB v. Nash-Finch Co., 404 U.S. 138 (1971).
134. *See* United States v. Certified Indus., Inc., 361 F.2d 857, 859 (2d Cir. 1966).
135. *See* United States v. Dewar, 18 F. Supp. 981 (D. Nev. 1937).
136. *See, e.g.*, Kaepa, Inc. v. Achilles Corp., 76 F.3d 624, 627-28 (5th Cir. 1996) (upholding decision to grant anti-suit injunction); Allendale Mut. Ins. Co. v. Bull Data Sys., Inc., 10 F.3d 425, 431-33 (7th Cir. 1993) (advocating relaxed approach to foreign antisuit injunctions); Seattle Totems Hockey Club, Inc. v. NHL, 652 F.2d 852, 856 (9th Cir. 1981).
137. See generally Laura M. Salava, *Legislative Reform: Balancing Comity With Antisuit Injunctions: Considerations Beyond Jurisdiction*, 20 J. LEGIS. 267 (1994) (highlighting circuit split).

circuit court has held that such injunctions are generally inappropriate,[138] numerous federal district courts have enjoined foreign litigation if a foreign case involves the same issues and parties as the federal action and the federal action would be dispositive of the foreign case.[139] However, because courts grant these injunctions pursuant to their equitable powers, they frequently consider a broad array of equitable considerations (e.g., the convenience of the parties[140] and whether the foreign litigation is vexatious or oppressive[141]) when weighing whether to issue a foreign antisuit injunction.[142]   Notably, this prerogative is available to state, as well as federal, courts.[143]

4. State Court Injunctions of Federal Court Proceedings

Here the rule is clear: a state court is powerless to enjoin parties from prosecuting federal court proceedings.[144]   This rule applies regardless whether the state court injunction purports to enjoin the

---

138. *See* Laker Airways, Ltd. v. Sabena, Belgian World Airlines, 731 F.2d 909 (D.C. Cir. 1984) (allowing American courts to enjoin pursuit of any subsequently-filed actions in foreign countries would destroy principle of concurrent American-foreign jurisdiction over parallel in personam claims); *see also* Gau Shan Co. v. Bankers Trust Co., 956 F.2d 1349, 1354-55 (6th Cir. 1992) (advocating stricter approach to granting such injunctions); China Trade & Dev. Corp. v. M.V. Choong Yong, 837 F.2d 33, 36-37 (2d Cir. 1987) (same).

139. *See, e.g.*, Canadian Filters (Harwich) Ltd. v. Lear-Siegler, Inc., 412 F.2d 577 (1st Cir. 1969); *Allendale Mut. Ins.*, 10 F.3d 425; *Seattle Totems Hockey Club, Inc.*, 652 F.2d at 855-56.

140. *Seattle Totems Hockey Club, Inc.*, 652 F.2d at 855-56.

141. Cargill, Inc. v. Hartford Accident & Indem. Co., 531 F. Supp. 710 (D. Minn. 1982).

142. George A. Bermann, *The Use of Anti-Suit Injunctions in International Litigation*, 28 COLUM. J. TRANSNAT'L L. 589, 630-31 (1990).

143. *See, e.g.*, Gannon v. Payne, 706 S.W.2d 304, 306-07 (Tex. 1986); Owens-Illinois v. Webb, 809 S.W.2d 899 (Tex. App. 1991).

144. *See, e.g.*, Gen. Atomic Co. v. Felter, 434 U.S. 12, 12 (1977) ("it is not within the power of state courts to bar litigants from filing and prosecuting in personam actions in the federal courts"); Donovan v. City of Dallas, 377 U.S. 408, 413 (1964) (stating that "state courts are completely without power to restrain federal-court proceedings in in personam actions").

prosecution of pending federal court proceedings or the filing of future proceedings.[145]

5. *State Court Injunctions Against Proceedings in Different Courts Within a State and in the Courts of Another State*

Because the substantive laws and evidentiary standards in different states can dramatically affect the success of numerous categories of claims or defenses in many business tort and unfair competition cases,[146] litigants commonly file duplicative actions in different states, attempting to have more favorable law applied to the case.[147] Moreover, parties will sometimes file dual actions in different courts within one state to take advantage of perceived jury bias or to avoid an unfavorable ruling by the first court to exercise jurisdiction.[148]

In response to such forum shopping between and within states, courts have long recognized the equitable authority of state courts to enjoin parties over which they have jurisdiction from filing or

---

145. *Felter*, 434 U.S. at 17 ("the rights conferred by Congress to bring in personam actions in federal courts are not subject to abridgment by state-court injunctions, regardless of whether the federal litigation is pending or prospective"); Fragoso v. Lopez, 991 F.2d 878, 881 (1st Cir. 1993).

146. *See generally* Antony L. Ryan, *Principles of Forum Selection*, 103 W. VA. L. REV. 167 (2000). For instance, while many states will not recognize a claim for tortious interference with contract if the underlying contract is invalid, *see, e.g.*, Tom's Amusement Co. v. Total Vending Servs., 533 S.E.2d 413 (Ga. Ct. App. 2000), other jurisdictions "recognize[] a tort action for interference with a contract even if the contract is unenforceable," Saunders v. Superior Court, 33 Cal. Rptr. 2d 438, 444 (Ct. App. 1994), and such claims arise from interstate transactions.

147. *See, e.g.*, Pfaff v. Chrysler Corp., 567 N.E.2d 52 (Ill. App. 1991) (involving initial tort action in Illinois, a state that does not recognize certain indemnity actions, and defendant's attempt to file subsequent action in Michigan, a state that does allow indemnity claims, to bring an indemnity action against third-party defendant).

148. This is not a recent phenomenon but a centuries-old tactic. *See, e.g.*, Conover v. City of N.Y., 14 How. Pr. 550 (N.Y. Sup. Ct. 1857) (courts should not "permit a transition from it to another court by such a party, after an adverse decision on his claim in the court to which resort is first had by him").

prosecuting actions in foreign states or other courts of the same state.[149] Because this authority emanates from the state courts' equitable powers and jurisdiction over parties before the court,[150] these injunctions limit the conduct of those parties, rather than foreign courts.[151]

However, principles of comity "require[] that courts exercise this equitable power sparingly, and only in very special circumstances."[152] Thus, state courts are reluctant to enjoin parties from pursuing litigation in foreign states, and interstate anti-suit injunctions should only be granted in extraordinary cases where they are necessary to prevent manifest injustice.[153]

Generally, mere parallel litigation in a foreign state will not warrant an injunction: "concerns such as duplication of parties and issues, the expense and effort of simultaneous litigation in two courts, and the danger of a race to judgment and inconsistent adjudications, ordinarily will not be grounds to restrain a party from proceeding with a suit in a court having jurisdiction of the matter."[154] Rather, the general rule is that two courts having concurrent prescriptive jurisdiction over the same controversy should be allowed to proceed separately to judgment, and

---

149. *See, e.g.*, Cole v. Cunningham, 133 U.S. 107 (1890); Christensen v. Integrity Ins. Co., 719 S.W.2d 161 (Tex. 1986); Pauley Petroleum, Inc. v. Cont'l Oil Co., 231 A.2d 450 (Del. Ch. 1967), *aff'd*, 239 A.2d 629 (Del. 1968); Sanders v. Yates, 109 S.E.2d 739 (Ga. 1959); James v. Grand Trunk W. R.R., 152 N.E.2d 858 (Ill. 1958); O'Loughlin v. O'Loughlin, 78 A.2d 64 (N.J. 1951); Mason v. Harlow, 114 P. 218 (Kan. 1911); Hawkins v. Ireland, 67 N.W. 73 (Minn. 1896).

150. *See* State v. 91st Street Joint Venture, 625 A.2d 953 (Md. 1993).

151. *See, e.g.*, Pfaff v. Chrysler Corp., 610 N.E.2d 51 (Ill. 1992).

152. Christensen v. Integrity Ins. Co., 719 S.W.2d 161, 163 (Tex. 1986); *see also O'Loughlin*, 78 A.2d 64; Childress v. Johnson Motor Lines, Inc., 70 S.E.2d 558 (N.C. 1952).

153. Auerbach v. Frank, 685 A.2d 404 (D.C. 1996); Total Minatome Corp. v. Santa Fe Minerals, Inc., 851 S.W.2d 336, 339 (Tex. App. 1993) (interstate anti-suit injunctions are only acceptable "to prevent manifest wrong and injustice").

154. *Auerbach*, 685 A.2d at 409; *see also* Laker Airways, Ltd. v. Sabena, Belgian World Airlines, 731 F.2d 909, 928 (D.C. Cir. 1984); Compagnie des Bauxites de Guinea v. Ins. Co. of N. Am., 651 F.2d 877, 887 (3d Cir. 1981), *aff'd*, 456 U.S. 694 (1982); Gannon v. Payne, 706 S.W.2d 304, 307 (Tex. 1986).

judgment once obtained in one proceeding may be offered as res judicata in the other.[155]

Conversely, interstate anti-suit injunctions may be justified in circumstances in which prosecution of the foreign proceedings will result in: (1) vexatious or harassing litigation,[156] (2) "fraud, gross wrong or oppression,"[157] or (3) "the taking of unconscionable advantage" by one party over another.[158]

As a general matter, "[t]he rules against anti-suit injunctions are more relaxed when the injunction runs against concurrent litigation within a single forum."[159] In such circumstances, "respect for a co-equal sovereign's jurisdiction is not implicated and is more easily out-weighed by the economies achieved through avoidance of duplicative actions."[160] Thus, the power of a state court to enjoin parties from proceeding in another court of the same state is generally recognized.[161] Indeed, this power approximates the power of a federal district court to enjoin parties from proceeding before another federal district court.[162]

E.　Multidistrict Federal Litigation

Increasingly, multiple cases involving related parties and events are brought in numerous different federal district courts across the country. Following a nationwide waive of antitrust claims against electrical equipment manufacturers in the early 1960s, Congress enacted legislation that created the Judicial Panel on Multidistrict Litigation ("JPML") to establish Multidistrict Litigation ("MDL") procedures in

---

155. *Laker Airways Ltd.*, 731 F.2d at 929; *Gannon*, 706 S.W.2d at 306-07; *see Pfaff*, 610 N.E.2d 51.

156. N.Y., C. & S.L.R. Co. v. Matzinger, 25 N.E.2d 349, 350 (Ohio 1940); *Christensen*, 719 S.W.2d at 163.

157. *Pfaff*, 610 N.E.2d at 55; *see also* Buckley v. Buckley, 350 P.2d 44 (Kan. 1960).

158. *Buckley*, 350 P.2d at 48.

159. *Laker Airways Ltd.*, 731 F.2d at 927 n.49.

160. *Id.* (citing *Colo. River Water Conserv. Dist.*, 424 U.S. at 817; Roth v. Bank of the Commonwealth, 583 F.2d 527, 538 (6th Cir. 1978)).

161. *See, e.g.*, State ex rel. Bardacke v. Welsh, 698 P.2d 462, 467 (N.M. Ct. App. 1985); *Gannon*, 706 S.W.2d at 305.

162. *See* discussion *supra* Part C.4.

future mass litigation.[163] MDL proceedings were created to assemble related cases before one federal judge to efficiently oversee and coordinate all pretrial discovery and motion practice.[164]

Consisting of seven circuit and district court judges, the JPML has the authority to transfer civil actions involving one or more common questions of fact that are pending in different districts to a single district court for consolidated discovery and pretrial motions if the JPML determines that the transfer promotes the "just and efficient conduct" of the actions and is "for the convenience of parties and witnesses."[165] Either party in any case potentially qualifying for MDL treatment may move the JPML to consolidate the case with other related cases for MDL proceedings, and the JPML may act sua sponte to do the same.[166] Notably, if related "tag-along action[s]" are filed after other similar cases have been transferred and assembled in one court for MDL treatment, those later cases can be transferred to the MDL court after parties to the "tag-along action" have had notice and an opportunity to oppose the transfer.[167] Moreover, the JPML may separate any unrelated claim, cross-claim, counter-claim, or third-party claim from an action transferred to the MDL court and remand that claim to the original transferor court.[168]

Generally, MDL proceedings conform to the following pattern: (1) the JPML selects a single federal district judge to serve as the MDL

---

163. 28 U.S.C. § 1407; *see* H.R. Rep. No. 90-1130, at 3 (1968), reprinted in 1968 U.S.C.C.A.N. 1898, 1899; S. Rep. No. 90-454, at 3-5 (1967) (noting federal courts' creative management of enormous wave of civil antitrust litigation following criminal convictions of several manufacturers of electrical equipment and stating that future nationwide litigation was likely to emanate in antitrust, securities, mass disaster, mass tort, patent, and trademark contexts). Notably, 28 U.S.C. § 1407 grants the JPML authority to promulgate rules of procedure for MDL practice.

164. *Id.*

165. *See* 28 U.S.C. § 1407(a).

166. *See id.* § 1407(c).

167. *See id.*

168. *See id.* § 1407(a); *see also In re* 1980 Decennial Census Adjustment Litig., 506 F. Supp. 648, 650 (J.P.M.L. 1981) ("The Panel is empowered by statute to couple its order of transfer with a simultaneous separation and remand of any claims in an action.").

court; (2) all related cases are transferred to that federal judge for pretrial procedures; (3) the MDL judge presides over and manages nationwide, coordinated discovery and pretrial motions practice; (4) if the cases are not disposed of during pretrial stages, they are each remanded to their original districts for trial.[169] Once the cases are initially consolidated with the MDL court, the transferor courts lose all power and the transferee court assumes full responsibility.[170] Similarly, if the cases are remanded, the original transferor courts once again resume full authority.[171]

During pretrial discovery, documents are normally produced only once, materials are made available at a centralized document depository, interrogatories are usually served on behalf of an entire series of related cases, and witnesses are rarely deposed more than once by a group of lead counsel.[172] Notably, most MDL cases are either settled or dismissed in the MDL court and, thus, few are actually remanded for trial.[173]

---

169. *See generally* MANUAL FOR COMPLEX LITIGATION (FOURTH) § 2.13 (2004).

170. Notably, the MDL court may overrule orders previously issued by the transferor courts, *see, e.g.*, Stavro v. Upjohn Co. (*In re* Upjohn Co. Antibiotic Cleocin Prods. Liab. Litig.), 664 F.2d 114 (6th Cir. 1981); *In re* Multi-Piece Rim Prods. Liab. Litig., 653 F.2d 671, 676-77 (D.C. Cir. 1981), permit amendments to the pleadings, *see, e.g.*, *In re* Equity Funding Corp. of Am. Sec. Litig., 416 F. Supp. 161, 177 (C.D. Cal. 1976), and decide dispositive motions, *see, e.g.*, Kaufman v. Trump's Castle Funding (*In re* Donald J. Trump Casino Sec. Litig.–Taj Mahal Litig.), 7 F.3d 357, 367-68 (3d Cir. 1993).

171. *See, e.g.*, *In re* Upjohn Co. Antibiotic Cleocin Prods. Liab. Litig., 508 F. Supp. 1020 (E.D. Mich. 1981).

172. *See, e.g.*, Drelles v. Metro. Life Ins. Co., 90 Fed. Appx. 587, 588 (3d Cir. 2004) (involving case management order by MDL court that established centralized document depository), *cert. denied*, 125 S. Ct. 56 (2004); *In re* Multidistrict Litig. Involving Butterfield Patent Infringement, 328 F. Supp. 513, 514 (J.P.M.L. 1970) (discussing advantages of consolidated depositions in MDL proceedings).

173. *See* MANUAL FOR COMPLEX LITIGATION (FOURTH) § 20.132 (2004) ("Few cases are remanded for trial; most multidistrict litigation is settled in the transferee court."). From 1968 until September 30, 2004, the JPML has transferred 176,163 cases pursuant to 28 U.S.C. § 1407. Only 10,899 of those cases have been remanded by the panel. Judicial Panel on

In determining whether MDL treatment is appropriate for a group of cases, the JPML usually considers what efficiencies would be achieved via consolidation, the nature of the cases, JPML precedent in similar cases, the number of cases and parties, and the relative progress of the separate cases. In deciding what district court should oversee MDL proceedings, the JPML usually considers the locations of parties, witnesses, and documents to find the "center of gravity of the litigation" and then considers other factors like where the first case was filed, the relative interest of potential transferee courts, and the relative speed of potential transferee courts' dockets.[174]

In the business tort context, MDL cases frequently involve antitrust[175] and securities fraud.[176] However, both antitrust actions brought by the United States[177] and actions brought by the Securities and Exchange Commission for injunctive relief[178] are expressly exempted from MDL treatment. Moreover, while it is not uncommon for business tort cases to involve related federal criminal prosecutions, the JPML has no authority under Section 1407 to transfer criminal cases. The Panel

---

Multidistrict Litigation, Statistical Analysis of Multidistrict Litigation 2004, at 4.1 (http://www.jpml.uscourts.gov/StatisticalAnalysis2004.pdf).

174. *See* Gregory Hansel, *Extreme Litigation: An Interview with Judge Wm. Terrell Hodges, Chairman of the Judicial Panel on MultiDistrict Litigation*, 19 MAINE BAR J. 16 (2004); Earle F. Kyle, IV, *The Mechanics of Motion Practice Before the Judicial Panel on Multidistrict Litigation*, 175 F.R.D. 589 (1997).

175. *See, e.g.*, Baum Res. & Dev. Co. v. Hillerich & Bradsby Co. (*In re* Baseball Bat Antitrust Litig.), 112 F. Supp. 2d 1175 (J.P.M.L. 2000); *In re* Amino Acid Lysine Antitrust Litig., 910 F. Supp. 696 (J.P.M.L. 1995); *In re* Cuisinart Food Processor Antitrust Litig., 506 F. Supp. 651 (J.P.M.L. 1981); *In re* Cal. Armored Car Antitrust Litig., 476 F. Supp. 452 (J.P.M.L. 1979); *In re* Wheat Farmers Antitrust Class Action Litig., 366 F. Supp. 1087 (J.P.M.L. 1973).

176. *See, e.g.*, Hart v. GM (*In re* GM Class E Stock Buyout Sec. Litig.), 696 F. Supp. 1546 (J.P.M.L. 1988); Abernathy v. Great Sw. Corp. (*In re* Penn Cent. Sec. Litig.), 62 F.R.D. 181, 187 (E.D. Pa. 1974).

177. 28 U.S.C. § 1407(g) (exempting antitrust actions brought by United States).

178. 15 U.S.C. § 78u(g) (exempting injunctive actions instituted by Securities and Exchange Commission unless Commission consents to consolidation).

has frequently addressed this problem by transferring civil actions to a court presiding over related criminal prosecutions.[179]

Finally, while there are currently no statutes or rules authorizing transfer, consolidation, and management of most related cases filed in separate states, Congress has recently enlarged federal diversity jurisdiction to cover additional classes of related state litigation.[180] In addition to numerous informal judicial practices developed to manage such cases,[181] the Class Action Fairness Act of 2005 broadens federal jurisdiction over such cases.[182]

F. Transfer and Forum Non Conveniens

In addition to (or in lieu of) seeking an anti-suit injunction to prevent the prosecution of parallel proceedings in another court, a party may ask the other court for relief, such as to transfer venue or dismiss under the doctrine of forum non conveniens. Chapter 10 discusses the standards applied to these motions.

G. Claim and Issue Preclusion

Business tort litigators involved in parallel litigation must be attentive to the potential res judicata effects of any findings or judgments in all related cases. Res judicata is a broad term comprising two related doctrines, both of which concern the preclusive effect of prior adjudications: (1) claim preclusion, referring to the use of a judgment to foreclose (by bar or merger) any future litigation on that claim; and (2) issue preclusion or collateral estoppel, referring to the use of a judgment to estop relitigation of individual facts or questions that were actually litigated and decided in a prior action.[183] Both doctrines have

---

179. *See* MANUAL FOR COMPLEX LITIGATION (FOURTH) § 20.2 (2004).
180. *See* 28 U.S.C. § 1369 (providing that federal district courts shall have original jurisdiction of any civil action involving minimal diversity between adverse parties that arises from single accident, where at least 75 natural persons have died in accident at discrete location under specified circumstances as part of 2002 Multiparty Multiforum Jurisdiction Act).
181. *See* MANUAL FOR COMPLEX LITIGATION (FOURTH) § 20.3 (2004).
182. *See* Chapters 9 and 12.
183. *See* Migra v. Warren City Sch. Dist. Bd. of Educ., 465 U.S. 75 (1984). Notably, the term res judicata is sometimes used by courts as interchangeable with claim preclusion, rather than a broad umbrella term

"the dual purpose of protecting litigants from the burden of relitigating an identical issue with the same party or his privy and of promoting judicial economy by preventing needless litigation,"[184] and both doctrines apply in the state and federal courts.[185]

Claim preclusion takes effect when a final judgment on the merits is rendered by a court of competent jurisdiction, and the doctrine bars a plaintiff and his privies from bringing a subsequent lawsuit for the same claim against the defendant or his privies.[186] When a plaintiff obtains a judgment in an action, any later claim is considered merged into the judgment. Conversely, when a judgment is rendered for a defendant, that judgment will bar any future claim. Importantly, claim preclusion applies even though the judgment may have been wrong or rests on a legal principle that is subsequently overruled in a later case.[187]

In contrast, issue preclusion bars a party and his privies from relitigating any discrete issue that was litigated and decided in a prior action.[188] For issue preclusion to take effect, the issues must: (1) be the same, (2) actually litigated, (3) actually decided, and (4) necessary to the prior judgment.[189] Unlike claim preclusion, issue preclusion may be invoked by a party who was a stranger to the prior litigation.[190] Such nonmutual issue preclusion can be used both defensively and, in more limited circumstances, offensively.[191] Importantly, trial courts are provided significant discretion to consider all circumstances surrounding

---

for both claim and issue preclusion. *See, e.g., Allen,* 449 U.S. at 94 (distinguishing between collateral estoppel, or issue preclusion, and res judicata).

184. Parklane Hosiery Co. v. Shore, 439 U.S. 322, 325 (1979).

185. *See, e.g.,* DaCruz v. State Farm Fire & Cas. Co., 846 A.2d 849 (Conn. 2004); Stevedoring Servs. of Am., Inc. v. Eggert, 914 P.2d 737 (Wash. 1996); Riley v. Maloney, 499 Nw.2d 18 (Iowa 1993).

186. *See, e.g.,* Kremer v. Chem. Constr. Corp., 456 U.S. 461 (1982); Pelletier v. Zweifel, 921 F.2d 1465 (11th Cir. 1991).

187. *See, e.g.,* Federated Dep't Stores, Inc. v. Moitie, 452 U.S. 394, 398 (1981).

188. *See, e.g., Kremer,* 456 U.S. at 466 n.6.

189. *See, e.g.,* Hirschfeld v. Spanakos, 104 F.3d 16, 19 (2d Cir. 1997).

190. *See, e.g.,* Blonder-Tongue Labs., Inc. v. Univ. of Ill. Found., 402 U.S. 313 (1971) (abandoning collateral estoppel's prior mutuality requirement).

191. *See Parklane Hosiery Co.,* 439 U.S. at 324-31 (establishing doctrine of offensive nonmutual collateral estoppel and enumerating several factors that weigh against invoking the doctrine).

both the prior and pending litigation and exercise their discretion to determine whether nonmutual issue preclusion should be permitted in any particular case.[192]

When the state courts are confronted with judgments from a foreign state, they are obliged under the Full Faith and Credit Clause of the Constitution[193] to give the foreign judgment the same preclusive effect as would be given that judgment under the law of the State in which the judgment was rendered.[194] "For claim and issue preclusion (res judicata) purposes, in other words, the judgment of the rendering State gains nationwide force."[195]

While the Constitution does not mandate that state court judgments be honored by the federal courts, "[a]s one of its first acts, Congress directed that all United States courts afford the same full faith and credit to state court judgments that would apply in the State's own courts."[196] Currently codified at Section 1738 of Title 28 of the U.S. Code, the Full Faith and Credit statute requires that properly-authenticated state court judgments "shall have the same full faith and credit in every court within the United States and its Territories and Possessions as they have by law or usage in the courts of such State, Territory or Possession from which they are taken."[197] Under this statute, federal courts must give the same preclusive effect to state court judgments as the issuing courts of that state.[198] Where concurrent actions have been filed, whether involving two state courts or a state and federal court, the first judgment to be entered will have claim or issue preclusive effect without regard to the order in which the two cases were commenced.[199]

---

192. *See, e.g., id.* at 330-31; *Blonder-Tongue Labs, Inc.*, 402 U.S. at 333-34.

193. U.S. CONST. art. IV, § 1.

194. Nevada v. Hall, 440 U.S. 410, 422 (1979).

195. Baker by Thomas v. GM, 522 U.S. 222, 233 (1998).

196. *Kremer*, 456 U.S. at 462-63.

197. 28 U.S.C. § 1738.

198. *Migra*, 465 U.S. 75; *Allen*, 449 U.S. at 96.

199. *See, e.g.,* Lesher v. Lavrich, 784 F.2d 193, 195 (6th Cir. 1986); Sidag A.G. v. Smoked Food Prods. Co., 776 F.2d 1270, 1274 (5th Cir. 1985); Unger v. Consol. Foods Corp., 693 F.2d 703, 705 (7th Cir. 1982); *see also* 18 CHARLES A. WRIGHT & ARTHUR R. MILLER, FEDERAL PRACTICE AND PROCEDURE § 4404 (2d ed. 1981).

CHAPTER XIV

PREEMPTION AND COMMERCE CLAUSE ISSUES

As demonstrated in the preceding chapters, much commercial conduct is subject to overlapping federal and state regulatory schemes. In many instances, such as the case of the federal and state antitrust laws, those schemes are largely complimentary. In other cases, however, federal and state law may serve different policy goals, if not actually conflict. Relatedly, state laws may impact interstate commerce in a way that raises constitutional concerns. This chapter addresses issues that commonly arise in antitrust and business tort litigation under the Supremacy and Commerce Clauses of the U.S. Constitution. – Eds.

A. Introduction

For constitutional purposes, the business activities that give rise to antitrust and business tort disputes commonly involve interstate commerce. Examining the scope of Congress' power under the Commerce Clause, which provides that "[t]he Congress shall have Power . . . [t]o regulate Commerce . . . among the several States,"[1] the Supreme Court has held that Congress may regulate not only activities "in" interstate commerce – i.e., those that take place across state boundaries – but also activities "affecting" commerce. Thus, even commercial transactions of a purely intrastate character may be regulated under the Commerce Clause if they substantially affect interstate commerce.[2]

The intersection of state business tort law[3] and interstate commerce raises two distinct, but related, constitutional issues. First, to what extent does federal antitrust law, which regulates interstate and foreign

---

1.   U.S. CONST. art. I, § 8, cl. 3.
2.   Hodel v. Va. Surface Mining & Reclamation Ass'n, 452 U.S. 264, 276-77 (1981); Wickard v. Filburn, 317 U.S. 111, 127-28 (1942).
3.   *See generally* ABA SECTION OF ANTITRUST LAW, STATE ANTITRUST PRACTICE AND STATUTES (3d ed. 2004).

commerce,[4] preempt state tort law in restraint of trade and unfair competition cases?   Second, under what circumstances does the application of state tort law to activities affecting interstate commerce exceed the states' powers of regulation under the "dormant" aspect of the Commerce Clause, which, under longstanding Supreme Court precedent, impliedly limits the permissible scope of state regulation affecting interstate commerce?

Preemption and the Commerce Clause are often analyzed together, but courts and commentators struggle to articulate the link between the two doctrines. The Court has distinguished between these clauses in the Constitution, noting that while the dormant Commerce Clause creates a right "to engage in interstate trade free from restrictive state regulation," the Supremacy Clause[5] does not create any rights; instead, it secures the existence of federal rights by ensuring that they take priority over conflicting state law.[6] Some commentators analyze both doctrines as virtually interchangeable tools that Congress and the courts can use to allocate responsibilities among Congress and the states to regulate interstate commerce.[7]

B.   Preemption

The Supremacy Clause provides for the supremacy of federal law over the law of the individual states:

> This Constitution, and the Laws of the United States which shall be made in Pursuance thereof . . . shall be the supreme Law of the Land;

---

4.   *See, e.g.*, Sherman Act, §§ 1, 2, 15 U.S.C. §§ 1, 2; Clayton Act, § 7, 15 U.S.C. § 18.

5.   U.S. CONST. art. VI, cl. 2.

6.   Dennis v. Higgins, 498 U.S. 439, 447-50 (1991).

7.   *See* Jim Chen, *A Vision Softly Creeping: Congressional Acquiescence and the Dormant Commerce Clause*, 88 MINN. L. REV. 1764, 1782 (2004) ("Congress enjoys virtually unfettered discretion to reassign responsibility over an aspect of interstate commerce. As a general rule, Congress may choose to delegate regulatory responsibility over interstate commerce to the states. Complete delegation negates any judicial role under the dormant Commerce Clause. Congress may also elect to craft a more nuanced approach to 'cooperative federalism' by adopting a careful mix of expressly preemptive statutory provisions and savings clauses.").

and the Judges in every State shall be bound thereby, any Thing in the Constitution or Laws of any State to the Contrary notwithstanding.[8]

The Supreme Court has established three circumstances under which it will consider state law to have been preempted by federal law. First, Congress may preempt state authority by so stating in explicit terms.[9] Second, in the absence of explicit preemptive language, state law is preempted where it regulates conduct in a field that Congress intended the federal government to occupy exclusively.[10] A court may infer such intent from a "scheme of federal regulations . . . so pervasive as to make reasonable the inference that Congress left no room for the States to supplement it," or where an Act of Congress "touch[es] a field in which the federal interest is so dominant that the federal system will be assumed to preclude enforcement of state laws on the same subject."[11] When issues of "field" preemption are raised and the field Congress is said to have preempted falls into an area traditionally occupied by the states, congressional intent to supersede state law must be clear and manifest.[12] Third, state law also is preempted to the extent it actually conflicts with federal law.[13] Such a conflict arises when "compliance with both federal and state regulations is a physical impossibility,"[14] or when state law "stands as an obstacle to the accomplishment and execution of the full purposes and objectives of Congress."[15] Although these categories of express, field, and conflict preemption are now well established, the Court itself has acknowledged that the categories are not "rigidly distinct."[16]

The Supreme Court has applied these general principles in the antitrust context on several occasions, most frequently when a party

---

8.   U.S. CONST. art. VI, cl. 2.
9.   Jones v. Rath Packing Co., 430 U.S. 519, 525 (1977); *see* Barnett Bank, N.A. v. Nelson, 517 U.S. 25, 31 (1996); Am. Airlines v. Wolens, 513 U.S. 219, 222 (1995).
10. English v. GE, 496 U.S. 72, 78-79 (1990).
11. Rice v. Santa Fe Elevator Corp., 331 U.S. 218, 230 (1947).
12. *English*, 496 U.S. at 79; *Jones*, 430 U.S. at 525; *Rice*, 331 U.S. at 230.
13. Hillsborough County, Fla. v. Automated Med. Labs., Inc., 471 U.S. 707, 713 (1985).
14. Fla. Lime & Avocado Growers, Inc. v. Paul, 373 U.S. 132, 142-43 (1963).
15. Hines v. Davidowitz, 312 U.S. 52, 67 (1941).
16. *English*, 496 U.S. at 79 n.5.

contends that state law either permits or requires conduct in restraint of trade and thus conflicts with the Sherman Act. In light of the states' traditional role in the regulation of trade and commerce, the Court has been loathe to find preemption in these cases absent a clear and direct conflict between state law and the Sherman Act. For instance, in *Exxon Corp. v. Governor of Maryland*,[17] the Court rejected a preemption challenge to a Maryland petroleum distribution statute that, according to the plaintiff, undermined the competitive balance that Congress had struck between the Sherman Act and the Robinson-Patman Act:

> This is merely another way of stating that the Maryland statute will have an anticompetitive effect. In this sense, there is a conflict between the statute and the central policy of the Sherman Act – our "charter of economic liberty." Nevertheless, this sort of conflict cannot itself constitute a sufficient reason for invalidating the Maryland statute. For if an adverse effect on competition were, in and of itself, enough to render a state statute invalid, the States' power to engage in economic regulation would be effectively destroyed.[18]

Only when a state law that restricts or regulates competition irreconcilably conflicts with federal antitrust policy by mandating or authorizing conduct constituting a violation of federal law, or by placing irresistible pressure on a private party to engage in such conduct, will that law be deemed preempted by federal antitrust laws.[19]

The inclusion of state law tort claims in restraint of trade litigation raises the opposite problem from that addressed in *Exxon* – whether state law theories of recovery that go beyond the Sherman Act, either by penalizing conduct that does not violate the Sherman Act, by providing remedies in addition to those provided by the Sherman Act, or by providing the plaintiffs with procedural advantages not available to them under the Sherman Act, are preempted. The Supreme Court spoke to this issue in its 1989 decision in *California v. ARC America Corp.*[20]

---

17. 437 U.S. 117 (1978).

18. *Id.* at 133 (citation omitted); *see also* New Motor Vehicle Bd. v. Orrin W. Fox Co., 439 U.S. 96, 110-11 (1978).

19. Rice v. Norman Williams Co., 458 U.S. 654, 661 (1982).

20. 490 U.S. 93 (1989). *ARC America* remains a leading case addressing preemption doctrine. Several years after the decision, in *Crosby v. National Foreign Trade Council*, 530 U.S. 363 (2000), the Court relied

In *ARC America*, the Court unanimously rejected the proposition that state laws governing trade and business practices can be preempted on the theory they impose liability beyond that authorized by federal law. At issue were state statutes that allowed indirect purchasers to recover damages for violations of state antitrust law notwithstanding the fact that, under *Illinois Brick Co. v. Illinois*,[21] those same indirect purchasers were not entitled to recover under federal antitrust law. The Court emphasized that there is a presumption against preemption in the antitrust context "[g]iven the long history of state common-law and statutory remedies against monopolies and unfair business practices."[22]   There being no express preemption by Congress nor any contention that Congress had preempted the field, the defendants asserted that state laws permitting indirect purchaser recoveries in the antitrust context posed an obstacle to the accomplishment of the purposes and objectives of Congress as reflected in the Sherman Act.[23]   The Court rejected this contention, noting that the state laws at issue were "consistent with the broad purposes of the federal antitrust laws: deterring anticompetitive conduct and ensuring the compensation of victims of that conduct."[24] Finally, the justices commented that the Supremacy Clause does not bar state law

---

upon *ARC America* in holding that a federal act impliedly preempted a Massachusetts state law that threatened to "frustrat[e] federal statutory objectives." *Id.* at 366.

21.   431 U.S. 720 (1977).

22.   *ARC Am. Corp.*, 490 U.S. at 101.   This once-dominating presumption against preemption has been called into question in some contexts.   In *Crosby*, the Court left "for another day a consideration in this context [involving a preempted state statute regulating trade with Burma] of a presumption against preemption." 530 U.S. at 374 n.8. The presumption appears to remain strong in some contexts, such as areas "traditionally regulated by the [s]tates." *See* Cal. v. FERC, 495 U.S. 490, 497 (1990). The presumption also retains vitality regarding matters implicating public health concerns. *See* Pharm. Research & Mfrs. of Am. v. Walsh, 538 U.S. 644, 666 (2003) ("The presumption against federal pre-emption of a state statute designed to foster public health has special force when it appears . . . that the two governments are pursuing 'common purposes.'") (internal citation omitted) (quoting New York State Dep't of Soc. Servs. v. Dublino, 413 U.S. 405, 421 (1973)).

23.   *See Davidowitz*, 312 U.S. at 67.

24.   *ARC Am. Corp.*, 490 U.S. at 102.

causes of action "solely because they impose liability over and above that authorized by federal law, and no clear purpose of Congress indicates that we should decide otherwise in this case."[25]

In light of *ARC America* and its progeny, it will be a rare case in which claims under state law for restraint of trade or unfair competition, or common law torts such as interference with contract, will be deemed preempted by federal law. The reported cases from the lower courts since *ARC America* confirm that the case stands as a formidable obstacle to preemption defenses to business tort claims.[26] Absent a direct and

---

25. *Id.* at 105 (citation omitted).
26. *E.g.*, Mack v. Bristol-Myers Squibb Co., 673 So. 2d 100, 107 (Fla. Dist. Ct. App. 1996) (relying in part on *ARC America* to hold no federal preemption of state deceptive trade practices act claim); *see also* Kellogg Co. v. F. Hoffman La Roche Ltd. (*In re* Vitamins Antitrust Litig.), 259 F. Supp. 2d 1, 2 (D.D.C. 2003) (although no pass through defense exists under federal law, defendants in state antitrust claim could put on evidence of downstream pass through of overcharges; applying holding of *ARC America* that Congress did not preempt state statutes allowing indirect purchaser actions); Postema v. Nat'l League of Prof'l Baseball Clubs, 799 F. Supp. 1475, 1487-89 (S.D.N.Y. 1992) (baseball antitrust exemption does not preclude assertion by umpire of restraint of trade claims arising under state common law), *rev'd on other grounds*, 998 F.2d 60 (2d Cir. 1993); *In re* Lower Lake Erie Iron Ore Antitrust Litig., 759 F. Supp. 219, 231 (E.D. Pa. 1991) (refusing to apply preemption to bar application of Ohio antitrust law for which there is no statute of limitation), *aff'd in part and rev'd in part on other grounds*, 998 F.2d 1144 (3d Cir. 1993); Mech. Rubber & Supply Co. v. Am. Saw & Mfg. Co., 747 F. Supp. 1292, 1296 (C.D. Ill.) (it is "clear" after *ARC America* "that federal antitrust law is not intended in any direct way to preempt state antitrust law except where there might be a direct conflict between the two laws"), *vacated in part on other grounds*, 810 F. Supp. 986 (C.D. Ill. 1990); Elkins v. Microsoft Corp., 817 A.2d 9, 15 (Vt. 2002) ("under *ARC America* states are free to determine how best to protect consumers against antitrust violations"); McShares, Inc. v. Barry, 970 P.2d 1005, 1012 (Kan. 1998) (no federal field preemption of antitrust and restraint of trade). *But see In re* Initial Pub. Offering Antitrust Litig., Nos. 01 Civ.2014 (WHP), 01 Civ.11420 (WHP), 2004 WL 789770, at *3 (S.D.N.Y. Apr. 13, 2004) (federal securities regulatory regime preempted state antitrust claims even under *ARC America* analysis); Owens v. Pepsi Cola Bottling Co., 412 S.E.2d 636, 641-42 (N.C. 1992) (North Carolina unfair trade practices law preempted

irreconcilable conflict between state business tort law and federal antitrust law, defendants in business tort cases may find it difficult to invoke federal preemption.

C. The Commerce Clause

1. *General Principles*

By its terms, the Commerce Clause affirmatively grants to Congress the power to regulate interstate commerce but says nothing about the states' regulatory powers in the commercial field. Nonetheless, beginning in the Nineteenth Century with decisions such as *Cooley v. Board of Wardens of the Port of Philadelphia*,[27] the Supreme Court has recognized that "this affirmative grant of authority to Congress also encompasses an implicit or 'dormant' limitation on the authority of the States to enact legislation affecting interstate commerce."[28] The dormant aspect of the Commerce Clause has been described by the Court as a necessary tool to preserve the national common market envisaged by the framers of the Constitution. For instance, in *Hughes v. Oklahoma*,[29] the Court explained:

> The few simple words of the Commerce Clause . . . reflected a central concern of the Framers that was an immediate reason for calling the Constitutional Convention: the conviction that in order to succeed, the new Union would have to avoid the tendencies toward economic Balkanization that had plagued relations among the Colonies and later among the States under the Articles of Confederation.[30]

Similarly, in an often-quoted passage from *H.P. Hood & Sons, Inc. v. Du Mond*,[31] the Court stated:

> Our system, fostered by the Commerce Clause, is that every farmer and every craftsman shall be encouraged to produce by the certainty that he will have free access to every market in the Nation, that no

---

by federal Soft Drink Interbrand Competition Act of 1980 to extent that state law proscribed wholesaling restrictions specifically exempted from federal antitrust law).

27. 53 U.S. (12 How.) 299 (1851).
28. Healy v. Beer Inst., 491 U.S. 324, 326 n.1 (1989).
29. 441 U.S. 322 (1979).
30. *Id.* at 325; *accord* Dennis v. Higgins, 498 U.S. 439, 447 (1991).
31. 336 U.S. 525 (1949).

home embargoes will withhold his export, and no foreign state will by customs duties or regulations exclude them. Likewise, every consumer may look to the free competition from every producing area in the Nation to protect him from exploitation by any. Such was the vision of the Founders; such has been the doctrine of this Court which has given it reality.[32]

The Commerce Clause thus prohibits the individual states from acting as separate economic units to the detriment of the nation as a whole.[33]

Of course, not every exercise of state power with some impact on interstate commerce is invalid. As a general proposition (and absent conflicting federal legislation), the states retain authority under their general police powers to regulate matters of "legitimate local concern," even though interstate commerce may be affected.[34] Where such legitimate local interests are implicated, the task of defining the appropriate scope of state regulation consistent with the Commerce Clause often is a matter of "delicate adjustment."[35]

---

32. *Id.* at 539.
33. Fulton Corp. v. Faulkner, 516 U.S. 325, 330-31 (1996) (dormant Commerce Clause "effectuates the Framers' purpose to 'preven[t] a State from retreating into economic isolation or jeopardizing the welfare of the Nation as a whole, as it would do if it were free to place burdens on the flow of commerce across its borders that commerce wholly within those borders would not bear'") (citation omitted); *see also* West Lynn Creamery, Inc. v. Healy, 512 U.S. 186, 204-06 (1994); Wardair Canada, Inc. v. Fla. Dep't of Revenue, 477 U.S. 1, 7-8 (1986); City of Philadelphia v. N.J., 437 U.S. 617, 623 (1978).
34. Lewis v. BT Inv. Managers, Inc., 447 U.S. 27, 36 (1980) (internal quotations omitted); *see also* S. Pac. Co. v. Ariz., 325 U.S. 761, 767 (1945) ("[T]here is a residuum of power in the state to make laws governing matters of local concern which nevertheless in some measure affect interstate commerce or even, to some extent, regulate it.").
35. *Lewis*, 447 U.S. at 36 (internal quotations omitted). The Supreme Court has concluded that there are limits on Congress' Commerce Clause powers, about which limits the Court, including with recent changes in its members, assuredly will continue to speak. *See* U.S. v. Lopez, 514 U.S. 549, 549-65 (1995) (Gun-Free School Zones Act, making it federal offense for any individual knowingly to possess firearm at place that individual knows or has reasonable cause to believe is school zone, exceeded Congress' Commerce Clause authority, because possession of gun in local

Commerce Clause controversies typically arise when a state official seeks injunctive relief to enforce a state law or regulation that allegedly burdens interstate commerce impermissibly. However, a damage award under such state law in civil litigation likewise is subject to constitutional challenge under the Commerce Clause.[36] Moreover, common law and statutory claims also should be subject to scrutiny under the dormant Commerce Clause. As the Supreme Court stated in *BMW of North America, Inc. v. Gore*,[37] "[s]tate power may be exercised as much by a jury's application of a state rule of law in a civil lawsuit as by a statute."[38]

---

school zone was not economic activity that "substantially affect[ed] interstate commerce"); Gonzalez v. Raich, 125 S. Ct. 2195, 2201-15 (2005) (application of Controlled Substances Act provisions criminalizing manufacture, distribution, or possession of marijuana to intrastate growers and users of marijuana for medical purposes did not violate Commerce Clause; as compared to *Lopez*, "[t]he statutory scheme that the Government is defending in this litigation is at the opposite end of the regulatory spectrum").

36. *See* Cent. GMC, Inc. v. GM, 946 F.2d 327, 334 (4th Cir. 1991); *see also* San Diego Bldg. Trades Council v. Garmon, 359 U.S. 236, 247 (1959) ("[R]egulation can be as effectively exerted through an award of damages as through some form of preventive relief."); Lett v. Paymentech, Inc., 81 F. Supp. 2d 992 (N.D. Cal. 1999) (dismissing claim in private damages action because statute on which claim was based discriminated against out-of-state businesses in violation of dormant Commerce Clause); Palmer-Lucas, Inc. v. Martin's Herend Imports, Inc., 827 F. Supp. 345 (W.D. Pa. 1993) (same); John Havlir & Assocs., Inc. v. Tacoa, Inc., 810 F. Supp. 752 (N.D. Tex. 1993) (same).

37. 517 U.S. 559 (1996).

38. *Id.* at 572 n.17. Despite the Court's statement in *Gore*, some lower courts have expressed doubt about applying the Commerce Clause to state common law causes of action. *See* City of N.Y. v. Beretta USA Corp., 315 F. Supp. 2d 256, 285 (E.D.N.Y. 2004) ("The applicability of the Commerce Clause to state common law actions is unsettled."); Crowley v. Cybersource Corp., 166 F. Supp. 2d 1263, 1272 (N.D. Cal. 2001) ("Indeed, the Third Circuit has expressed doubt as to whether state common law claims could violate the dormant commerce clause."). *But see* Stone ex rel. Estate of Stone v. Frontier Airlines, Inc., 256 F. Supp. 2d 28, 45 (D. Mass. 2002) ("The same balancing test is used regardless of

Courts typically apply a two-stage inquiry in evaluating a dormant Commerce Clause challenge to state regulation. "[T]he first step . . . is to determine whether [the challenged measure] 'regulates evenhandedly with only "incidental" effects on interstate commerce, or discriminates against interstate commerce.'"[39] A state regulation found to be discriminatory is virtually per se invalid,[40] and the measure will be struck down unless it "advances a legitimate local purpose that cannot be adequately served by reasonable nondiscriminatory alternatives."[41] By contrast, under the test first announced in *Pike v. Bruce Church, Inc.*,[42]

> Where the statute regulates even-handedly to effectuate a legitimate local public interest, and its effects on interstate commerce are only incidental, it will be upheld unless the burden imposed on such commerce is clearly excessive in relation to the putative local benefits . . . . If a legitimate local purpose is found, then the question becomes one of degree. And the extent of the burden that will be tolerated will of course depend on the nature of the local interest involved, and on

---

whether the state law in question emerges from common law or directly from a statute or regulation.").

39. *Faulkner*, 516 U.S. at 331 (citation omitted). In Gen. *Motors Corp. v. Tracy*, 519 U.S. 278 (1997), the Court clarified that "[c]onceptually . . . any notion of discrimination assumes a comparison of substantially similar entities." *Id.* at 298 (footnote omitted). If the out-of-state entity challenging an allegedly discriminatory regulation does not actually compete with allegedly favored in-state entities, "there can be no local preference . . . to which the dormant Commerce Clause may apply." *Id.* at 300.

40. Camps Newfound/Owatonna, Inc. v. Town of Harrison, Me., 520 U.S. 564, 574 (1997); *see also* C&A Carbone, Inc. v. Town of Clarkstown, 511 U.S. 383, 393 (1994) ("By itself, . . . revenue generation is not a local interest that can justify discrimination against interstate commerce."); City of Philadelphia v. N.J., 437 U.S. 617, 624 (1978) ("[W]here simple economic protectionism is effected by state legislation, a virtually per se rule of invalidity has been erected.").

41. *Camps Newfound/Owatonna, Inc.*, 520 U.S. at 581 (citation and internal quotation marks omitted); *see also C&A Carbone, Inc.*, 511 U.S. at 392-93; Me. v. Taylor, 477 U.S. 131, 138 (1986).

42. 397 U.S. 137 142 (1970).

whether it could be promoted as well with a lesser impact on interstate activities.[43]

There is no clear line separating state regulation that is subject to heightened scrutiny from that subject to the more lenient balancing approach.[44] "In either situation the critical consideration is the overall effect of the statute on both local and interstate activity."[45] A state statute that directly regulates or discriminates against interstate commerce, or one that favors in-state over out-of-state economic interests, will be subjected to strict scrutiny.[46] Efforts by a state to expand the reach of its laws to commerce beyond its boundaries also may constitute "economic protectionism" sufficient to warrant strict judicial scrutiny.[47]

Classification of the state law at issue often is determinative of the outcome. State laws examined under the stringent standard of review reserved for cases of economic protectionism are likely to be found invalid under the Commerce Clause.[48] Laws examined under the *Pike*

---

43. *Id.* at 142.
44. *Tracy*, 519 U.S. at 299 n.12 ("There is, however, no clear line between these two strands of analysis . . . .").
45. *C&A Carbone, Inc.*, 511 U.S. at 402 (quoting Brown-Forman Distillers Corp. v. N.Y. State Liquor Auth., 476 U.S. 573, 579 (1986)).
46. *Brown-Forman Distillers Corp.*, 476 U.S. at 579; *see also* Wyo. v. Okla., 502 U.S. 437 (1992) (Commerce Clause directly limits power of states to discriminate against interstate commerce).
47. *Brown-Forman Distillers Corp.*, 476 U.S. at 579-80 (Commerce Clause forbids state from regulating out-of-state transaction).
48. *See, e.g., Camps Newfound/Owatonna, Inc.*, 520 U.S. at 595 (invalidating Maine statute providing tax exemption to in-state charities but limiting exemption to charities primarily serving Maine residents); New Energy Co. v. Limbach, 486 U.S. 269, 278-79 (1988) (standards for justifying discriminatory provision are high); *Lewis*, 447 U.S. at 36 (virtual per se rule of invalidity for protectionist legislation); City of Philadelphia v. N.J., 437 U.S. 617, 624 (1978) (same); Cooper v. McBeath, 11 F.3d 547, 552-54 (5th Cir. 1994) (Texas alcoholic beverage permitting statute requiring applicant to demonstrate sustained Texas citizenship or residency held invalid); Lett v. Paymentech, Inc., 81 F. Supp. 2d 992, 998-1000 (N.D. Cal. 1999) (California statute subjecting employers without permanent and fixed place of business in state to treble damages for employing California employee on commission basis without providing employee with written

balancing test generally fare better if they promote some legitimate local interest.[49]

---

contract was discriminatory on its face and violative of dormant Commerce Clause); Pete's Brewing Co. v. Whitehead, 19 F. Supp. 2d 1004, 1010-17 (W.D. Mo. 1998) (Missouri statute regulating content of beer labels invalidated under dormant Commerce Clause because it had discriminatory purpose and effect of protecting market share of in-state brewers who were legislation's chief proponents); State ex rel. Brady v. Preferred Network, Inc., 791 A.2d 8, 17-20 (Del. Ch. 2001) (provision of Delaware Consumer Fraud Act making it unlawful for florists located outside of local calling area to list local telephone number in local directory without disclosing florist's location discriminated against interstate commerce and could not survive heightened scrutiny); *cf. Taylor*, 477 U.S. at 151-52 (upholding discriminatory statute because of lack of nondiscriminatory alternative to serve legitimate local purpose).

49. *Compare* Nw. Cent. Pipeline Corp. v. State Corp. Comm'n of Kan., 489 U.S. 493, 525-26 (1989) (upholding evenhanded gas proration order as exercise of state's traditional power over natural gas production), *and* Minn. v. Clover Leaf Creamery Co., 449 U.S. 456, 471-74 (1981) (milk packaging statute that did not discriminate between interstate and intrastate commerce was valid, notwithstanding burden on out-of-state plastics industry, in light of state's interest in energy conservation and solid waste disposal), *and* Eby-Brown Co. v. Wis. Dep't of Agric., 295 F.3d 749, 756-57 (7th Cir. 2002) (non-discriminatory price requirements imposed on tobacco wholesalers under Wisconsin Unfair Sales Act did not unduly burden interstate commerce in violation of the dormant Commerce Clause), *with* Edgar v. MITE Corp., 457 U.S. 624, 643-46 (1982) (facially neutral state takeover law held invalid under Commerce Clause because state had no interest in protecting nonresident shareholders or regulating internal affairs of foreign corporations), *and* Raymond Motor Transp., Inc. v. Rice, 434 U.S. 429, 444-45 (1978) (facially neutral truck length limitation invalidated because "[s]tate . . .virtually defaulted in its defense of the regulations as a safety measure"), *and* Pioneer Military Lending, Inc. v. Manning, 2 F.3d 280, 283-85 (8th Cir. 1993) (imposition of Missouri's small loan regulatory scheme on Nebraska lender offering loans to nonresident military personnel in Missouri held invalid under Commerce Clause in light of "relatively slight local interests served"). *Edgar* was a plurality decision, but that portion of the plurality opinion addressing the *Pike* issue garnered a fifth vote. *See Edgar*, 457 U.S. at 646 (Powell, J., concurring in part).

Private restraint of trade or unfair competition lawsuits in which state business tort claims are asserted typically do not implicate the Commerce Clause's proscription against economic discrimination, as the legal rules on which such claims are based generally do not distinguish between interstate and intrastate commerce.[50] The geographic scope of such state law theories of recovery often will be considerably less certain, however, and may raise significant concerns of improper "extraterritorial effects" under the dormant Commerce Clause.

2. *Action Despite Congressional Silence: Extraterritorial Effects Under the Commerce Clause*

In some sense every claim that a state law is invalid under the Commerce Clause raises the specter of extraterritorial effects, for all so-called "dormant" Commerce Clause cases concern the impact of state law on events outside of the state.[51] During the 1930's and 1940's, however, the Supreme Court expressed special concern in dicta about one particular type of extraterritorial effect, namely, the projection of one state's laws beyond its own borders to govern events occurring outside in other states.[52] In three opinions rendered during the 1980's, the Court

---

50. A statutory cause of action explicitly favoring in-state economic interests over those from outside the state likely will be deemed unconstitutional on the grounds that it is difficult to conceive of a legitimate justification for such a distinction. *See Hughes*, 441 U.S. at 336-38; *cf. Lett*, 81 F. Supp. 2d at 998-1000; Palmer-Lucas, Inc. v. Martin's Herend Imps., Inc., 827 F. Supp. 345, 347-48 (W.D. Pa. 1993); John Havlir & Assocs., Inc. v. Tacoa, Inc., 810 F. Supp. 752, 757-59 (N.D. Tex. 1993).

51. *See Brown-Forman Distillers Corp.*, 476 U.S. at 579 (critical consideration in Commerce Clause cases is effect of state statute on both local and interstate activity).

52. *See, e.g.*, S. Pac. Co. v. Ariz., 325 U.S. 761, 770-71 (1945); Baldwin v. G.A.F. Seelig, Inc., 294 U.S. 511, 521 (1935). In *Southern Pac.*, the Court held that in light of the national concern with uniformity of railroad regulations and the dubious safety justification proffered by the state for its law, Arizona's train length limitation unduly burdened interstate commerce. *See S. Pac. Co*, 325 U.S. at 770-71. At issue in *Baldwin* was a New York milk price law that prevented a New York milk dealer from reselling milk in New York that it had purchased outside the state at prices lower than permitted by the New York statute for in-state purchases. The Court found the application of New York's law in that setting equivalent to

addressed the issue of "extraterritorial effects" more directly than in its prior jurisprudence. Those decisions provide the framework for evaluating the contention that a state's laws are being applied to regulate the commerce of other states in violation of the Commerce Clause.

The first of these decisions, *Edgar v. MITE Corp.*,[53] involved a challenge to the Illinois Business Takeover Act. That act required that any takeover offer for the shares of a "target company" be registered with the Illinois Secretary of State, who had the authority to call a hearing concerning the offer and, under certain circumstances, deny registration to the offer altogether. The term "target company" included any corporation or other issuer of securities of which shareholders located in Illinois owned ten percent of the class of equity securities subject to the offer, or which had other significant local contacts.[54] In a plurality opinion, four justices found the statute invalid, notwithstanding its facial neutrality, because it directly regulated interstate commerce.[55] First, the plurality observed that the statute regulated transactions occurring wholly outside Illinois, namely those between the offeror and non-Illinois shareholders, and could apply to a tender offer even if not a single shareholder was from Illinois.[56] Without referring specifically to either of the two tiers of review ordinarily employed in dormant Commerce Clause cases, the plurality commented:

> It is therefore apparent that the Illinois statute is a direct restraint on interstate commerce and that it has a sweeping extraterritorial effect.... The Commerce Clause ... precludes the application of a state statute to commerce that takes place wholly outside of the

---

an unconstitutional tariff on interstate commerce. *See Baldwin*, 294 U.S. at 521.

53.   457 U.S. 624 (1982).

54.   The statute also applied when any two of the following three conditions were met: "the corporation has its principal executive office in Illinois, is organized under the laws of Illinois, or has at least 10% of its stated capital and paid-in surplus represented within the State." *See id.* at 627.

55.   The four justice plurality, joined by Justice Powell, also found the impact of the Illinois act on interstate commerce unjustified by any legitimate state interest, thus rendering the act invalid under the *Pike* balancing test. *See id.* at 643-46.

56.   *Id.* at 641-42.

State's borders, whether or not the commerce has effects within the State.[57]

These four justices found support for this conclusion in the jurisdictional limitations placed on state courts, for "[i]n either case, 'any attempt "directly" to assert extraterritorial jurisdiction over persons or property would offend sister States and exceed the inherent limits of the State's power.'"[58]

Four years later, in *Brown-Forman Distillers Corp. v. New York State Liquor Authority*,[59] the Court explicitly adopted "extraterritorial effects" as the basis for invalidating a state law, finding the law at issue to be a direct regulation of interstate commerce that, like discrimination against interstate commerce, resulted in a rule of virtual per se illegality. The state of New York required every liquor distiller or producer selling liquor to wholesalers within the state to do so at a price no higher than the lowest price it charged wholesalers anywhere else in the country. The Court commented critically on the effect of this statute on the internal affairs of other states:

> Once a distiller has posted prices in New York, it is not free to change its prices elsewhere in the United States during the relevant month. Forcing a merchant to seek regulatory approval in one State before undertaking a transaction in another directly regulates interstate commerce. While New York may regulate the sale of liquor within its borders, and may seek low prices for its residents, it may not "project its legislation into [other States] by regulating the price to be paid" for liquor in those States.[60]

The Court in *Brown-Forman* expressed special concern that this outward projection of state regulation could subject businesses to inconsistent obligations in different states.[61] Finding New York's effort to promote the interests of its consumers at the expense of those in other states to be a form of economic protectionism, akin to discrimination

---

57. *Id.* at 642-43.
58. *Id.* at 643 (quoting Shaffer v. Heitner, 433 U.S. 186, 197 (1977)).
59. 476 U.S. 573 (1986).
60. *Id.* at 582-83 (citations and footnote omitted) (quoting *Baldwin*, 294 U.S. at 522).
61. *Id.* at 583-84.

against interstate commerce, it invalidated the statute as inconsistent with the Commerce Clause.[62]

The third decision in this line, *Healy v. Beer Institute*,[63] involved a Connecticut liquor price affirmation statute that differed only slightly in its relevant particulars from the New York statute at issue in *Brown-Forman*.[64] Relying upon *Edgar* and *Brown-Forman*, the Supreme Court found Connecticut's law to be unconstitutional, in the process explaining why a statute with an overbroad extraterritorial reach cannot stand under the Commerce Clause:

> The principles guiding this assessment, principles made clear in *Brown-Forman* and in the cases upon which it relied, reflect the Constitution's special concern both with the maintenance of a national economic union unfettered by state-imposed limitations on interstate commerce and with the autonomy of the individual [s]tates within their respective spheres.[65]

The Court then identified three propositions that its jurisprudence concerning the extraterritorial effects of state economic regulation may be said to represent:

> First, the "Commerce Clause . . . precludes the application of a state statute to commerce that takes place wholly outside of the State's border, whether or not the commerce has effects within the State," and, specifically, a State may not adopt legislation that has the practical effect of establishing "a scale of prices for use in other states." Second, a statute that directly controls commerce occurring wholly outside the boundaries of a State exceeds the inherent limits of the enacting State's authority and is invalid regardless of whether the statute's extraterritorial reach was intended by the legislature. The critical inquiry is whether the practical effect of the regulation is to

---

62. *Id.* at 579-80.
63. 491 U.S. 324 (1989).
64. The New York statute required every liquor distiller or producer to affirm that the prices charged to New York wholesalers were no higher than the lowest price at which the same product would be sold in any other state during the entire month covered by the particular affirmation. The Connecticut statute required out-of-state shippers to affirm that their posted Connecticut prices, as of the date of affirmation, were no higher than prices in bordering states. *Id.* at 331-35.
65. *Id.* at 335-36.

control conduct beyond the boundaries of the State. Third, the practical effect of the statute must be evaluated not only by considering the consequences of the statute itself, but also by considering how the challenged statute may interact with the legitimate regulatory regimes of other States and what effect would arise if not one, but many or every, State adopted similar legislation.[66]

Applying these principles, the Court found that the Connecticut statute carried with it the "kind of potential regional and even national regulation of the pricing mechanism for goods [that] is reserved by the Commerce Clause to the Federal Government."[67]

Edgar, Brown-Forman, and *Healy,* considered together, establish that certain extraterritorial applications of state law are invalid. Yet these cases fail to establish any bright line rule to distinguish permissible from impermissible extraterritorial effects. Indeed, the *Healy* majority noted that the issue was one of degree, "the critical consideration in determining whether the extraterritorial reach of a statute violates the Commerce Clause [being] the overall effect of the statute on both local and interstate commerce."[68]

Exxon Corp. v. Governor of Maryland[69] provides some guidance, although limited, on the sort of extraterritorial effect that will be considered permissible. At issue in *Exxon* was a Maryland statute that prohibited petroleum producers and refiners from operating any retail service stations within the state and required that any temporary price reductions granted by a producer or refiner to any service station in Maryland be extended uniformly to all service stations supplied within the state. The plaintiffs, a group of non-Maryland producers and refiners, argued that since there were no producers or refiners located within Maryland, the statute either discriminated against or at least impermissibly burdened interstate commerce. The Supreme Court rejected these claims, finding that "interstate commerce is not subjected

---

66. *Id.* at 336 (citation and footnote omitted).
67. *Id.* at 340. The Connecticut statute regulated only interstate shippers, not those based in the State. Hence, the Supreme Court held, as an alternative ground, that the law unconstitutionally discriminated against interstate commerce. *Id.* at 340-41.
68. *Id.* at 337 & n.14.
69. 437 U.S. 117 (1978).

to an impermissible burden simply because an otherwise valid regulation causes some business to shift from one interstate supplier to another."[70]

Perhaps anticipating this response, the *Exxon* plaintiffs, in an argument evocative of those later adopted by the Court in *Edgar, Brown-Forman,* and *Healy,* further asserted that by forcing them to alter their national distribution systems, the Maryland statute impermissibly interfered with the natural functioning of the interstate market for petroleum products. In a similar fashion, they also argued that the state could not constitutionally regulate the retail marketing of gasoline because the market for petroleum products was a national one that only Congress could regulate. In short, they asserted that Maryland's statute required that they alter product distribution decisions made outside of Maryland affecting the entire nation, not just Maryland.[71]

Rejecting these contentions, the Court first observed that the Commerce Clause does not protect "the particular structure or methods of operation in a retail market."[72] Second, the Court held that the Commerce Clause rarely preempts an entire field from state regulation:[73] "In the absence of a relevant congressional declaration of policy, or a showing of a specific discrimination against, or burdening of, interstate commerce, we cannot conclude that the States are without power to regulate in this area."[74] *Exxon* thus demonstrates that the states retain authority to regulate commercial activity within their borders, even if that regulation disrupts a national pattern of business activity by a company headquartered outside the state.

In *CTS Corp. v. Dynamics Corp. of America,*[75] the Supreme Court expanded upon *Exxon* to suggest that when a state law regulates subject matter traditionally considered within the state's province and does so

70. *Id.* at 127.
71. *Id.*
72. *Id.* at 127; *see also* Valley Bank of Nev. v. Plus Sys., Inc., 914 F.2d 1186, 1190-93 (9th Cir. 1990) (recognizing ability of states to enact "legislation that affects the interdependent relationships constituting commercial activity").
73. The Court appeared to recognize an exception in certain transportation cases in which a lack of national uniformity would impede the flow of interstate goods. *See Exxon Corp.,* 437 U.S. at 128.
74. *Id.* at 128-29.
75. 481 U.S. 69 (1987).

without subjecting interstate actors to a significant danger of inconsistent requirements, the Commerce Clause will tolerate extensive governance of out-of-state activities. *CTS* involved the constitutionality of a state takeover statute that applied only to businesses incorporated in, and with other substantial connections to, Indiana. The Court upheld the Indiana law, rejecting a proffered analogy to *Brown-Forman* and *Edgar*, which it interpreted as "cases . . . invalidat[ing] statutes that may adversely affect interstate commerce by subjecting activities to inconsistent regulations."[76]

The *CTS* Court first noted that, as was true in *Exxon, Brown-Forman*, and *Edgar*, the statute did not discriminate in favor of in-state interests. The Court further found it significant that there was no danger of inconsistent multi-state regulation, for "[s]o long as each State regulates voting rights only in the corporations it has created, each corporation will be subject to the law of only one State."[77] It failed to attribute constitutional significance to the tendency of the Indiana act to hinder interstate tender offers: "It . . . is an accepted part of the business landscape in this country for States to create corporations, to prescribe their powers, and to define the rights that are acquired by purchasing their shares."[78] Moreover, because the Indiana act applied only to corporations incorporated, and with a substantial number of shareholders located, in Indiana, the act promoted substantial state interests, unlike the Illinois law at issue in *Edgar*, which applied even to transactions in which Illinois had virtually no interest.[79]

More recently, the Supreme Court discussed the application of its extraterritoriality jurisprudence to state law tort claims in *BMW of North America, Inc. v. Gore*,[80] which principally involved a challenge under the Due Process Clause to a punitive damages award on a fraud claim under Alabama law.[81] The plaintiff in *Gore* alleged that he was defrauded because BMW of North America, Inc. ("BMW"), failed to disclose that the vehicle the plaintiff had purchased had been repainted.[82] The jury

---

76.   *Id.* at 88.
77.   *Id.* at 89.
78.   *Id.* at 91.
79.   *Id.* at 93-94.
80.   517 U.S. 559 (1996).
81.   *Gore* is also discussed in Chapter 8 ("Limitations on Punitive Damages").
82.   *Id.* at 564.

awarded the plaintiff $4 million in punitive damages, basing the award, in part, on evidence of similar sales in other states.[83] BMW's policy concerning when presale repairs must be disclosed, however, was consistent with the laws of roughly 25 states.[84] The Alabama Supreme Court subsequently ordered a remittitur of $2 million, holding that the jury should not have considered BMW's acts in other jurisdictions.[85]

In addressing the "scope of Alabama's legitimate interests in punishing BMW and deterring it from future misconduct,"[86] the Court noted that states do not uniformly regulate disclosure of presale automobile repairs.[87] Rather, there exists "a patchwork of rules representing the diverse policy judgments" of the states.[88] Even if the rule of full disclosure advocated by the plaintiff in *Gore* was wisest, the Court observed that no single state could impose its policy choice on other states.[89] Invoking *Healy*, the Court further stated: "Similarly, one State's power to impose burdens on the interstate market for automobiles is not only subordinate to the federal power over interstate commerce, but is also constrained by the need to respect the interests of other States."[90] The Court concluded that "a State may not impose economic sanctions on violators of its laws with the intent of changing the tortfeasors' lawful conduct in other States."[91] Thus, Alabama was without power "to punish BMW for conduct that was lawful where it occurred and that had no impact on Alabama or its residents."[92]

---

83. *Id.* at 564-65.
84. *Id.* at 565.
85. *Id.* at 567.
86. *Id.* at 568.
87. *Id.* at 569.
88. *Id.* at 570.
89. *Id.* at 571.
90. *Id.*
91. *Id.* at 572.
92. *Id.* at 572-73.   More recently, in *Pharmaceutical Research and Manufacturers of America v. Walsh*, 538 U.S. 644 (2003), the Supreme Court rejected an extraterritoriality challenge to a Maine statute requiring drug manufacturers to enter a rebate agreement with the state or face certain consequences under the state's Medicaid program. The Court, like the court of appeals below, quickly dismissed this argument because "the Maine Act does not regulate the price of any out-of-state transaction, either by its express terms or by its inevitable effect." 538 U.S. at 669.

The pronouncement in *Gore* leaves room for litigants to argue that a state is permitted to regulate out-of-state conduct with a deleterious impact on the state or its residents, contrary to a literal reading of the Court's prior statements that the dormant Commerce Clause precludes states from regulating commerce wholly outside their borders "whether or not the commerce has effects within the State."[93]

Despite their sometimes contradictory directions, these cases, together with lower court cases applying their holdings, provide some general guidelines concerning Commerce Clause treatment of state laws and regulations with "extraterritorial effects." First, any state statute or rule that regulates transactions occurring entirely outside of the state's boundaries is problematic.[94] In contrast, if a state statute offers

---

93. *Healy*, 491 U.S. at 336; *see also* Jack L. Goldsmith, *The Internet and the Dormant Commerce Clause*, 110 YALE L.J. 785, 790 (2001) (arguing that formulation in *Healy* is "clearly too broad" and that "[s]cores of state laws validly apply to and regulate extrastate commercial conduct that produces harmful local effects").

94. *See* C&A Carbone, Inc. v. Town of Clarkstown, 511 U.S. 383, 392-93 (1994) (states and localities may not attach restrictions to exports or imports to control commerce in other states); *Healy*, 512 U.S. at 192-96 (invalidating Massachusetts assessment on milk sold by in-state dealers because it operated as tax on out-of-state products); *In re* Brand Name Prescription Drugs Antitrust Litig., 123 F.3d 599, 613 (7th Cir. 1997) (noting, in antitrust context, that "'[a] state's power to regulate interstate commerce is limited, however, by the provisions of the federal Constitution that limit the extraterritorial powers of state government. A state cannot regulate sales that take place wholly outside it."); Pac. Nw. Venison Producers v. Smitch, 20 F.3d 1008, 1015 (9th Cir. 1994) (finding impact of state law on commerce beyond state's borders of special importance in balancing burden on interstate commerce with state's putative interest); NCAA v. Miller, 10 F.3d 633, 639 (9th Cir. 1993) (invalidating Nevada statute purporting to govern NCAA enforcement proceedings because, inter alia, it could regulate "a product in interstate commerce that occurs wholly outside Nevada's borders"); Wright-Moore Corp. v. Ricoh Corp., 908 F.2d 128, 134 & n.2 (7th Cir. 1990) (application of Indiana franchise law to control who sells copiers in other states may present difficulties under Commerce Clause); Am. Meat Inst. v. Barnett, 64 F. Supp. 2d 906, 919 (D.S.D. 1999) (South Dakota statute prohibiting price discrimination in sale of livestock held to violate dormant Commerce Clause because it regulated prices that must be paid by South Dakota

protection to parties located within or with some substantial nexus to the state, a Commerce Clause challenge is less likely to succeed.[95] Second, a

---

packers to producers in other states); Marigold Foods, Inc. v. Redalen, 834 F. Supp. 1163, 1168-70 (D. Minn. 1993) (Minnesota milk assessment law invalid for regulating activities of out-of-state producers); Motor Vehicle Mfrs. Ass'n of U.S., Inc. v. Abrams, 720 F. Supp. 284, 288 (S.D.N.Y. 1989) (invalidating provision of New York's "lemon law" that required out-of-state agents to provide notice to out-of-state manufacturers); MaryCLE, LLC v. First Choice Internet, Inc., No. 248514, 2004 WL 2895955, at *5-*6 (Md. Cir. Ct. Dec. 9, 2004) (Maryland's Commercial Electronic Mail Act violated dormant Commerce Clause because "the statute, as applied in this case, seeks to regulate the transmission of commercial email between persons in states outside of Maryland, even when the email never enters Maryland, as long as the recipient is a Maryland resident").

95. *See* Gravquick A/S v. Trimble Navigation Int'l Ltd., 323 F.3d 1219, 1223-25 (9th Cir. 2003) (application of California Equip. Dealer Act to contract between supplier located in California and dealer located in Denmark did not violate Commerce Clause); Pharm. Care Mgmt. Ass'n v. Rowe, 307 F. Supp. 2d 164, 174-76 (D. Me. 2004) (holding, on motion for preliminary injunction, that disclosure provisions of Maine unfair prescriptive drug practices statute did not have impermissible extraterritorial effect because disclosure was required only to "covered entity" with significant ties to Maine or with respect to contract for pharmacy benefits management entered into in Maine); Health Care Serv. Corp. v. Mylan Labs., Inc. (*In re* Lorazepam & Clorazepate Antitrust Litig.), 295 F. Supp. 2d 30, 47-50 (D.D.C. 2003) (holding, on motion to dismiss, that dormant Commerce Clause did not bar Illinois-based health services organization from pursuing monopolization and price fixing claims against pharmaceutical company under Illinois Antitrust Act for drug sales in Texas and New Mexico); Synergy Mktg., Inc. v. Home Prods. Int'l, No. CIV. 00-796 (JRT/FLN), 2001 WL 1628691, at *5 (D. Minn. Sept. 6, 2001) (application of Minnesota statute regulating termination of sales representative's contract between Delaware manufacturer and Minnesota corporation acting as manufacturer's representative in Wisconsin did not violate Commerce Clause); Stone ex rel. Estate of Stone v. Frontier Airlines, Inc., 256 F. Supp. 2d 28, 45-47 (D. Mass. 2002) (state law tort claims based on airline's failure to carry defibrillators did not violate dormant Commerce Clause under *Healy*; airline flew in and out of state and served plaintiff and her husband, both residents of state); New England Dragway, Inc. v. M-O-H Enters., Inc., 817 A.2d 288 (N.H. 2003) (upholding constitutionality of

state statute that governs the activities of a corporation organized under the laws of that state likely will be deemed valid, even if applied to corporate affairs occurring outside the state.[96]

Third, state regulation of subject matter traditionally deemed of special local concern will be viewed deferentially.[97] Fourth, and perhaps most importantly, any state law that threatens to subject an interstate actor to inconsistent requirements is suspect.[98] This principle is

---

New Hampshire's Security Takeover Distribution Act, which applied when target company had substantial nexus with state).

96. *See, e.g.*, A.S. Goldmen & Co. v. N.J. Bureau of Sec., 163 F.3d 780, 784-89 (3d Cir. 1999) (New Jersey Securities Act did not have impermissible extraterritorial effect insofar as it allowed New Jersey Bureau of Securities to block in-state broker dealer from extending offers to sell securities that were not registered in New Jersey to residents of other states where securities were qualified for sale); Hoylake Invs., Ltd. v. Bell, 723 F. Supp. 576, 579-80 (D. Kan. 1989) (application of Kansas Insurance Holding Companies Act to tender offer made by British company was valid because offer, if successful, would result in change of control of Kansas insurer); *In re* Air Crash Disaster at Stapleton Int'l Airport, Denver, Colo., 720 F. Supp. 1505, 1517-18 (D. Colo. 1989) (Commerce Clause permits application of Texas Deceptive Trade Practices Act in litigation against Texas corporation arising out of air crash in Colorado), *rev'd in part on other grounds sub nom.*, Johnson v. Cont'l Airlines Corp., 964 F.2d 1059 (10th Cir. 1992).

97. *See, e.g.*, Sears, Roebuck & Co. v. Brown, 806 F.2d 399, 409 (2d Cir. 1986) (banking); Tousley v. N. Am. Van Lines, Inc., 752 F.2d 96, 103 (4th Cir. 1985) (protection of in-state investors); S. Union Co. v. Mo. Pub. Serv. Comm'n, 138 F. Supp. 2d 1201, 1209 (W.D. Mo. 2001) (natural gas utility), *aff'd*, 289 F.3d 503 (8th Cir. 2002).

98. *See, e.g.*, *Miller*, 10 F.3d at 639-40 (invalidating Nevada statute purporting to govern NCAA enforcement proceedings because, inter alia, of strong possibility of inconsistent legislation in other states); Country Classic Dairies, Inc. v. Mont. Dep't of Commerce Milk Control Bureau, 847 F.2d 593, 594-96 (9th Cir. 1988) (case remanded to consider whether Montana's attempts to regulate transactions taking place in Wyoming create "impermissible risk of inconsistent regulation by different States"); Bruce Church, Inc. v. United Farm Workers of Am., AFL-CIO, 816 P.2d 919, 925-27 (Ariz. Ct. App. 1991) (Arizona cannot project its law into California to penalize conduct legal under California law); *cf. New England Dragway, Inc.*, 817 A.2d at 290-91 (New Hampshire's Security

illustrated by several recent decisions in which courts have invalidated laws directly regulating commercial activities on the Internet.[99]

The foregoing considerations are relevant not only when determining the constitutionality of a state law of clear import, but also in guiding a court in its interpretation of a state law of uncertain scope. For example, in *Central GMC, Inc. v. General Motors Corp.*,[100] a Maryland truck dealer argued that his franchisor's decision to discontinue its line of heavy trucks constituted a franchise termination governed by Maryland's vehicle franchise act. In rejecting this argument, the Fourth Circuit commented that, if accepted, it would threaten national manufacturers with inconsistent and uncertain restrictions on product withdrawals in violation of the principles enunciated in *Healy* and *Edgar*. The Court's decision to interpret the

---

Takeover Distribution Act unlikely to subject interstate actors to inconsistent regulations because act provides that it will not apply to takeover bids for target company organized in another jurisdiction if compliance with New Hampshire act *and* laws of incorporating jurisdiction would be impossible or New Hampshire law is more restrictive than law of incorporating jurisdiction).

99. *See, e.g.*, PSINet, Inc. v. Chapman, 362 F.3d 227, 239-40 (4th Cir. 2004) (invalidating Virginia law criminalizing knowing distribution of pornographic materials to minors by electronic means); Am. Booksellers Found. v. Dean, 342 F.3d 96, 102-04 (2d Cir. 2003) (enjoining enforcement of similar Vermont law as to plaintiffs' Internet activity; "We think it likely that the internet will soon be seen as falling within the class of subjects that are protected from State regulation because they 'imperatively demand[ ] a single uniform rule.'"); ACLU v. Johnson, 194 F.3d 1149, 1160-63 (10th Cir. 1999) (affirming preliminary injunction against enforcement of similar New Mexico statute); Am. Libraries Ass'n v. Pataki, 969 F. Supp. 160, 168 (S.D.N.Y. 1997) ("The unique nature of the Internet highlights the likelihood that a single actor might be subject to haphazard, uncoordinated, and even outright inconsistent regulation by states that the actor never intended to reach and possibly was unaware were being accessed"). *But see* State v. Heckel, 24 P.3d 404, 408-13 (Wash. 2001) (upholding constitutionality of Washington's commercial electronic mail act because only burden act imposed on spammers was requirement of truthfulness and, while other states regulated spam, obligations they imposed were not irreconcilable with Washington's law).

100. 946 F.2d 327 (4th Cir. 1991).

Maryland statute restrictively was supported by Commerce Clause concerns.[101]

In summary, business tort claims grounded in state law, but based upon activities in or affecting interstate commerce, often raise Commerce Clause issues. The ordinary run of Commerce Clause decisions invalidating laws that discriminate against out-of-state actors will be of limited relevance in such cases. The trilogy of Supreme Court decisions from the 1980s holding unconstitutional those state laws with an excessive extraterritorial reach may be invoked in appropriate circumstances to prevent a plaintiff from using favorable law from one state to recover for activities occurring largely outside that state's borders. Just as significantly, a defendant may be able to raise the Commerce Clause's restraints upon the extraterritorial application of state law to guide a court toward a narrow interpretation of that law.

The tension between the constitutional principle that, in matters of interstate commerce "our economic unit is the Nation,"[102] and the trend in restraint of trade and unfair competition cases of plaintiffs to rely upon theories of recovery grounded in state tort law, rather than federal antitrust law, ensures that the Commerce Clause will continue to be a factor in such cases.

---

101. *Id.* at 334; *see also* Dean Foods Co. v. Brancel, 187 F.3d 609, 619 (7th Cir. 1999) (construing Wisconsin milk-pricing regulations prohibiting payment of volume premiums as inapplicable to sales between Wisconsin producers and Illinois processor that were consummated in Illinois); Morley-Murphy Co. v. Zenith Elecs. Corp., 142 F.3d 373, 378-81 (7th Cir. 1998) (narrowly construing Wisconsin Fair Dealership law as inapplicable to manufacturer's termination of Wisconsin dealer in out-of-state territories to avoid potential Commerce Clause violation); K-S Pharmacies, Inc. v. Am. Home Prods. Corp., 962 F.2d 728, 730-31 (7th Cir. 1992) (interpreting Wisconsin "most favored purchaser" statute narrowly to avoid extraterritorial application) (internal quotations omitted); N.H. Auto. Dealers Ass'n, Inc. v. GM, 801 F.2d 528, 531-32 (1st Cir. 1986) (Commerce Clause concerns support narrow interpretation of state car dealer law); *Bruce Church, Inc.*, 816 P.2d at 927-28 (duty to interpret statute so as to avoid Commerce Clause problems).

102. H.P. Hood & Sons, Inc. v. Du Mond, 336 U.S. 525, 537 (1949).

ABA SECTION OF ANTITRUST LAW
COMMITMENT TO QUALITY

The Section of Antitrust Law is committed to the highest standards of scholarship and continuing legal education. To that end, each of our books and treatises is subjected to rigorous quality control mechanisms throughout the design, drafting, editing, and peer review processes. Each Section publication is drafted and edited by leading experts on the topics covered and then rigorously peer reviewed by the Section's Books and Treatises Committee, at least two Council members, and then other officers and experts. Because the Section's quality commitment does not stop at publication, we encourage you to provide any comments or suggestions you may have for future editions of this book or other publications.

Defending Liberty
Pursuing Justice